TAKING SIDES

Clashing Views on

Political Issues

SIXTEENTH EDITION, EXPANDED

TAKING SIDES

Clashing Views on

Political Issues

SIXTEENTH EDITION, EXPANDED

Selected, Edited, and with Introductions by

George McKenna
City College, City University of New York

and

Stanley Feingold
City College, City University of New York

 **Higher Education**

Boston   Burr Ridge, IL   Dubuque, IA   New York   San Francisco   St. Louis
Bangkok   Bogotá   Caracas   Kuala Lumpur   Lisbon   London   Madrid   Mexico City
Milan   Montreal   New Delhi   Santiago   Seoul   Singapore   Sydney   Taipei   Toronto

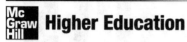

Higher Education

TAKING SIDES: CLASHING VIEWS ON POLITICAL ISSUES,
SIXTEENTH EDITION, EXPANDED

Published by McGraw-Hill, a business unit of The McGraw-Hill Companies, Inc., 1221 Avenue of the Americas, New York, NY 10020. Copyright © 2010 by The McGraw-Hill Companies, Inc. All rights reserved. Previous edition(s) 2009, 2008, 2007. No part of this publication may be reproduced or distributed in any form or by any means, or stored in a database or retrieval system, without the prior written consent of The McGraw-Hill Companies, Inc., including, but not limited to, in any network or other electronic storage or transmission, or broadcast for distance learning.

Some ancillaries, including electronic and print components, may not be available to customers outside the United States.

Taking Sides® is a registered trademark of The McGraw-Hill Companies, Inc.
Taking Sides is published by the **Contemporary Learning Series** group within the McGraw-Hill Higher Education division.

1 2 3 4 5 6 7 8 9 0 DOC/DOC 0 9

MHID: 0-07-812752-1
ISBN: 978-0-07-812752-6
ISSN: 1080-580x

Managing Editor: *Larry Loeppke*
Senior Managing Editor: *Faye Schilling*
Senior Developmental Editor: *Jill Peter*
Editorial Coordinator: *Mary Foust*
Editorial Assistant: *Nancy Meissner*
Production Service Assistant: *Rita Hingtgen*
Permissions Coordinator: *Shirley Lanners*
Senior Marketing Manager: *Julie Keck*
Marketing Communications Specialist: *Mary Klein*
Marketing Coordinator: *Alice Link*
Senior Project Manager: *Jane Mohr*
Design Specialist: *Tara McDermott*

Compositor: Macmillan Publishing Solutions
Cover Image: © Eyewire (Photodisc)/Punchstock

Library of Congress Cataloging-in-Publication Data

Main entry under title:
    Taking Sides: Clashing Views on Political Issues/Selected, Edited, and with Introductions by George McKenna and Stanley Feingold—16th edition, expanded

    Includes bibliographical references.
    1. United States—Politics and government—1945—. I. McKenna, George, *comp.* II. Feingold, Stanley, *comp.*
        320´.973

Preface

Dialogue means two people talking about the same issue. This is not as easy as it sounds. Play back the next debate between the talking heads you see on television. Listen to them trying to persuade each other—actually, the TV audience—of the truth of their own views and of the irrationality of their opponents' views.

What is likely to happen? At the outset, they will probably fail to define the issue with enough clarity and objectivity to make it clear exactly what it is that they are disputing. As the philosopher Alasdair MacIntyre has put it, the most passionate pro and con arguments are often "incommensurable"—they sail past each other because the two sides are talking about different things. As arguments proceed, both sides tend to employ vague, emotion-laden terms without spelling out the uses to which the terms are put. When the heat is on, they may resort to shouting epithets at one another, and the hoped-for meeting of minds will give way to the scoring of political points and the reinforcement of existing prejudices. For example, when the discussion of affirmative action comes down to both sides accusing the other of "racism," or when the controversy over abortion degenerates into taunts and name-calling, then no one really listens and learns from the other side.

It is our conviction that people *can* learn from the other side, no matter how sharply opposed it is to their own cherished viewpoint. Sometimes, after listening to others, we change our view entirely. But in most cases, we either incorporate some elements of the opposing view—thus making our own richer—or else learn how to answer the objections to our viewpoint. Either way, we gain from the experience. For these reasons, we believe that encouraging dialogue between opposed positions is the most certain way of enhancing public understanding.

The purpose of this 16th edition of *Taking Sides* is to continue to work toward the revival of political dialogue in America. As we have done in the past 15 editions, we examine leading issues in American politics from the perspective of sharply opposed points of view. We have tried to select authors who argue their points vigorously but in such a way as to enhance our understanding of the issue.

We hope that the reader who confronts lively and thoughtful statements on vital issues will be stimulated to ask some of the critical questions about American politics. What are the highest priority issues with which government must deal today? What positions should be taken on these issues? What should be the attitude of Americans toward their government? Our conviction is that a healthy, stable democracy requires a citizenry that considers these questions and participates, however indirectly, in answering them. The alternative is apathy, passivity, and, sooner or later, the rule of tyrants.

Plan of the book Each issue has an issue *introduction*, which sets the stage for the debate as it is argued in the YES and NO selections. Each issue concludes with a *postscript* that makes some final observations and points the way to other questions related to the issue. In reading the issue and forming your own opinions you should not feel confined to adopt one or the other of the positions presented. There are positions in between the given views or totally outside them, and the *suggestions for further reading* that appear in each issue postscript should help you find resources to continue your study of the subject. We have also provided relevant Internet site addresses (URLs) on the *Internet References* page that accompanies each part opener. At the back of the book is a listing of all the *contributors to this volume,* which will give you information on the political scientists and commentators whose views are debated here.

Changes to this edition   Over the last 30 years, *Taking Sides* has undergone extensive changes and improvements, and we have continued to keep it up with the changing times. In this edition, we present five new issues: Is Congress a "Broken Branch"? (Issue 6), Should the President Be Allowed "Executive Privilege"? (Issue 7), Is Homosexual Conduct Constitutionally Protected? (Issue 8), Should the Government Provide National Health Insurance? (Issue 11), and Is China a Military Threat to the United States? (Issue 20).

We worked hard on what we hope will be a truly memorable 16th edition, and we think you will like the result. Let us know what you think by writing to us in care of McGraw-Hill Contemporary Learning Series, 501 Bell St., 4th Floor, Dubuque, IA 52001 or e-mailing us at GMcK1320@aol.com or stanleyfeingold@ q.west.net. Suggestions for further improvements are most welcome!

A word to the instructor   An *Instructor's Resource Guide with Test Questions* (multiple-choice and essay) is available through the publisher for the instructor using *Taking Sides* in the classroom. A general guidebook, *Using Taking Sides in the Classroom,* which discusses methods and techniques for integrating the pro-con approach into any classroom setting, is also available. An online version of *Using Taking Sides in the Classroom* and a correspondence service for *Taking Sides* adopters can be found at http://www.mhcls.com/usingts/.

Taking Sides: Clashing Views on Political Issues is only one title in the *Taking Sides* series. If you are interested in seeing the table of contents for any of the other titles, please visit the *Taking Sides* Web site at http://www. mhcls.com/ takingsides/.

Acknowledgments   We are grateful to Laura McKenna for her help and suggestions in preparing this edition. Thanks also to the Morris Raphael Cohen Library of City College, the public library of Tenafly, New Jersey—especially to Agnes Kolben; and the Suzzallo & Allen Library of the University of Washington— especially to Barbara Arrowsmith.

We also appreciate the spontaneous letters from instructors and students who wrote to us with comments and observations. Many thanks to Larry Loeppke and Jill Peter for their able editorial assistance. Needless to say, the responsibility for any errors of fact or judgment rests with us.

George McKenna
Stanley Feingold

Contents In Brief

Contents

and equitable law enforcement. Frank Sharry, executive director of the National Immigration Forum, contends that the "enforcement only" approach ignores the fact that the United States has an increasingly integrated labor market with Latin America, and recommends a comprehensive approach combining border control with expanded legal channels.

United States Supreme Court Justice John Paul Stevens believes that the Constitution creates "a wall of separation" between church and state that can be rarely broached and only insofar as the state recognition of religion does not express a bias in support of particular religious doctrines. United States Supreme Court Justice Antonin Scalia believes that both the Constitution and American history support the sympathetic acknowledgement of the nearly universal American belief in mono-theistic religion as reflected in presidential proclamations, public oaths, public monuments, and other displays.

J. R. Dunn, a military editor and author, believes that the radical Islamists are losing the support of the Iraqi people, that Iraq is moving toward democracy, and that the war against terror is being won. In the same fashion, America and its allies will thwart Iran's quest for nuclear weapons. Robert Jervis, a professor of international relations, maintains that the war in Iraq distracted the United States from the war against terrorism, that preventive war risks grave errors of judgment, and that victory in Iraq will not necessarily result in more democracy or less terrorism.

Daniel Pipes, director of the Middle East Forum, argues that "heightened scrutiny" of Muslims and Middle Eastern-looking people is justified because, while not all Muslims are Islamic extremists, all Islamic extremists are

Muslims. Law professor David A. Harris opposes profiling people of Middle Eastern appearance because, like racial profiling, it compromises civil liberties and actually damages our intelligence efforts.

International relations professor Robert J. Lieber believes that the United States, as the world's sole superpower, is uniquely capable of providing leadership against the threats of terrorism and weapons of mass destruction, as well as extending the rule of law and democracy. Author Niall Ferguson maintains that, despite America's military and economic dominance, it lacks both the long-term will and the capital and human investment that would be necessary to sustain its dominance.

Aviva Aron-Dine, former policy analyst at the Center on Budget and Policy Priorities, believes that the tax cuts adopted in the George W. Bush presidency have hurt the economy, have not benefited most Americans, and have increased the national debt. Brian Riedl, budget analyst at The Heritage Foundation, concludes that the tax cuts adopted in the presidency of George W. Bush have encouraged economic growth, benefited lower-income Americans most, and have increased tax revenues.

Robert Borosage, codirector of the Campaign for America's Future, contends that conservative policies have failed because they make America weaker abroad and more unequal at home. Alfred Regnery, publisher of the *American Spectator* magazine, contends that conservative principles are powerfully resilient, have been woven into our laws and institutions, and may well be the most accepted political force in America.

Correlation Guide

The *Taking Sides* series presents current issues in a debate-style format designed to stimulate student interest and develop critical thinking skills. Each issue is thoughtfully framed with an issue summary, an issue introduction, and a postscript. The pro and con essays—selected for their liveliness and substance—represent the arguments of leading scholars and commentators in their fields.

Taking Sides: Clashing Views on Political Issues, 16/e Expanded is an easy-to-use reader that presents issues on important topics such as *global terrorism, unilateral war powers, national health insurance,* and *immigration.* For more information on *Taking Sides* and other *McGraw-Hill Contemporary Learning Series* titles, visit www.mhcls.com.

This convenient guide matches the issues in **Taking Sides: Political Issues, 16/e Expanded** with the corresponding chapters in two of our best-selling McGraw-Hill Political Science textbooks by Harrison et al. and Patterson.

Taking Sides: Political Issues, 16/e Expanded	American Democracy Now by Harrison et al.	We the People, 8/e by Patterson
Issue 1: Should Americans Believe in a Unique American "Mission"?	**Chapter 1:** American Democracy: People, Politics, and Participation **Chapter 6:** Political Socialization and Public Opinion	**Chapter 1:** American Political Culture: Seeking a More Perfect Union
Issue 2: Is Democracy the Answer to Global Terrorism?	**Chapter 17:** Foreign Policy and National Security	**Chapter 17:** Foreign and Defense Policy: Protecting the American Way
Issue 3: Should America Adopt Public Financing of Political Campaigns?	**Chapter 9:** Elections, Campaigns, and Voting	**Chapter 7:** Political Participation and Voting: Expressing the Popular Will **Chapter 8:** Political Parties, Candidates, and Campaigns: Defining the Voter's Choice
Issue 4: Does the President Have Unilateral War Powers?	**Chapter 12:** The Presidency	**Chapter 12:** The Presidency: Leading the Nation
Issue 5: Should the Courts Seek the "Original Meaning" of the Constitution?	**Chapter 2:** The Constitution **Chapter 14:** The Judiciary	**Chapter 2:** Constitutional Democracy: Promoting Liberty and Self-Government
Issue 6. Is Congress a "Broken Branch"?	**Chapter 11:** Congress	**Chapter 11:** Congress: Balancing National Goals and Local Interests
Issue 7: Should the President Be Allowed "Executive Privilege"?	**Chapter 12:** The Presidency	**Chapter 12:** The Presidency: Leading the Nation
Issue 8: Is Homosexual Conduct Constitutionally Protected?	**Chapter 2:** The Constitution **Chapter 4:** Civil Liberties **Chapter 5:** Civil Rights	**Chapter 2:** Constitutional Democracy: Promoting Liberty and Self-Government **Chapter 4:** Civil Liberties: Protecting Individual Rights **Chapter 5:** Equal Rights: Struggling Toward Fairness

continued

Taking Sides: Political Issues, 16/e Expanded	*American Democracy Now* by Harrison et al.	*We the People, 8/e* by Patterson
Issue 9: Does Affirmative Action Advance Racial Equality?	**Chapter 4:** Civil Liberties **Chapter 5:** Civil Rights	**Chapter 5:** Equal Rights: Struggling Toward Fairness **Chapter 16:** Welfare and Education Policy: Providing for Personal Security and Need
Issue 10: Should Abortion Be Restricted?	**Chapter 4:** Civil Liberties **Chapter 5:** Civil Rights	**Chapter 4:** Civil Liberties: Protecting Individual Rights
Issue 11: Should the Government Provide National Health Insurance?	**Chapter 13:** The Bureaucracy **Chapter 16:** Domestic Policy	**Chapter 13:** The Federal Bureaucracy: Administering the Government
Issue 12: Is America Becoming More Unequal?	**Chapter 4:** Civil Liberties **Chapter 5:** Civil Rights	**Chapter 5:** Equal Rights: Struggling Toward Fairness
Issue 13: Does the Patriot Act Abridge Essential Freedom?	**Chapter 4:** Civil Liberties **Chapter 5:** Civil Rights **Chapter 16:** Domestic Policy	**Chapter 4:** Civil Liberties: Protecting Individual Rights **Chapter 5:** Equal Rights: Struggling Toward Fairness **Chapter 17:** Foreign and Defense Policy: Protecting the American Way
Issue 14: Stopping Illegal Immigration: Should Border Security Come First?	**Chapter 16:** Domestic Policy	**Chapter 5:** Equal Rights: Struggling Toward Fairness
Issue 15: Should There Be a "Wall of Separation" Between Church and State?	**Chapter 6:** Political Socialization and Public Opinion	**Chapter 6:** Public Opinion and Political Socialization: Shaping the People's Voice
Issue 16: Does the War in Iraq Help the War Against Terrorism?	**Chapter 17:** Foreign Policy and National Security	**Chapter 17:** Foreign and Defense Policy: Protecting the American Way
Issue 17: Is "Middle Eastern" Profiling Ever Justified?	**Chapter 4:** Civil Liberties **Chapter 5:** Civil Rights **Chapter 16:** Domestic Policy **Chapter 17:** Foreign Policy and National Security	**Chapter 4:** Civil Liberties: Protecting Individual Rights **Chapter 17:** Foreign and Defense Policy: Protecting the American Way
Issue 18: Is the Use of Torture Against Terrorist Suspects Ever Justified?	**Chapter 4:** Civil Liberties **Chapter 5:** Civil Rights **Chapter 16:** Domestic Policy **Chapter 17:** Foreign Policy and National Security	**Chapter 4:** Civil Liberties: Protecting Individual Rights **Chapter 17:** Foreign and Defense Policy: Protecting the American Way
Issue 19: Is Warrantless Wiretapping in Some Cases Justified to Protect National Security?	**Chapter 4:** Civil Liberties **Chapter 5:** Civil Rights **Chapter 16:** Domestic Policy **Chapter 17:** Foreign Policy and National Security	**Chapter 4:** Civil Liberties: Protecting Individual Rights **Chapter 17:** Foreign and Defense Policy: Protecting the American Way
Issue 20: Is China a Military Threat to the United States?	**Chapter 17:** Foreign Policy and National Security	**Chapter 17:** Foreign and Defense Policy: Protecting the American Way
Issue 21: Must America Exercise World Leadership?		**Chapter 1:** American Political Culture: Seeking a More Perfect Union
Issue 22: Should Federal Taxes Be Increased?	**Chapter 16:** Domestic Policy	**Chapter 6:** Public Opinion and Political Socialization: Shaping the People's Voice
Issue 23: Does Conservatism Get the World Wrong?		**Chapter 6:** Public Opinion and Political Socialization: Shaping the People's Voice

Introduction

Labels and Alignments in American Politics

George McKenna
Stanley Feingold

American politics heated up quite a bit in 2008. Issues like the war in Iraq, taxes, medical costs, civil liberties, and national security kept the pot boiling as Democrats and Republicans finalized their choice of candidates for the fall election and then squared off against each other. The contests had been simmering for at least six months before the first primaries and caucuses were held in January. Columnists and pundits were reading the polls and handicapping the races like sports announcers: this one was ahead, but that one was gaining momentum, the other one was doing well at first but then stumbled. Finally with the primaries over and the horserace narrowed down to two major-party candidates, the cheering and the jeering grew louder as the race headed toward the finish.

During this long season of politiking, certain political labels kept popping up in newspaper columns, radio and TV programs, and the Internet. Rudy Giuliani was tagged as the most "liberal" of the major Republican candidates, at least on "social issues," while Mike Huckabee was thought by many to be the most "conservative" on social issues, although perhaps the most "liberal" Republican on economic issues. Hillary Clinton was said to be moving toward "moderate" positions on issues, while John Edwards was considered quite "liberal." Some Internet blogs were called "extremist" by their critics, while other critics thought that "extremist" would better describe some radio talk-show hosts. But self-described "pluralists" were among those who insisted that what counted was the variety of opinions, so that opinion groups could openly challenge the pretensions of rival groups.

Liberal, conservative, moderate, extremist, pluralist—what do these terms mean? Or do they have any meaning? Some political analysts regard them as arbitrary labels slapped on by commentators seeking quick ways to sum up candidates (or in some cases to demonize them). The reaction against the ideological labels is understandable, not only because they are often used too loosely but, as we shall see, because the terms themselves can evolve over time. Nevertheless, we think there are some core meanings left, so if they are used carefully, they can help us locate positions on the political stage and the actors who occupy them. In this Introduction we shall try to spell out the meanings of these terms, at least as they are used in American politics, and illustrate these terms by showing how they fit some of the issues presented in this book.

Liberals Versus Conservatives: An Overview

Let us examine, very briefly, the historical evolution of the terms *liberalism* and *conservatism.* By examining the roots of these terms, we can see how these philosophies have adapted themselves to changing times. In that way, we can avoid using the terms rigidly, without reference to the particular contexts in which liberalism and conservatism have operated over the past two centuries.

Classical Liberalism

The classical root of the term *liberalism* is the Latin word *libertas,* meaning "liberty" or "freedom." In the early nineteenth century, liberals dedicated themselves to freeing individuals from all unnecessary and oppressive obligations to authority—whether the authority came from the church or the state. They opposed the licensing and censorship of the press, the punishment of heresy, the establishment of religion, and any attempt to dictate orthodoxy in matters of opinion. In economics, liberals opposed state monopolies and other constraints upon competition between private businesses. At this point in its development, liberalism defined freedom primarily in terms of freedom *from.* It appropriated the French term *laissez-faire,* which literally means "leave to be." Leave people alone! That was the spirit of liberalism in its early days. It wanted government to stay out of people's lives and to play a modest role in general. Thomas Jefferson summed up this concept when he said, "I am no friend of energetic government. It is always oppressive."

Despite their suspicion of government, classical liberals invested high hopes in the political process. By and large, they were great believers in democracy. They believed in widening suffrage to include every white male, and some of them were prepared to enfranchise women and blacks as well. Although liberals occasionally worried about "the tyranny of the majority," they were more prepared to trust the masses than to trust a permanent, entrenched elite. Liberal social policy was dedicated to fulfilling human potential and was based on the assumption that this often-hidden potential is enormous. Human beings, liberals argued, were basically good and reasonable. Evil and irrationality were believed to be caused by "outside" influences; they were the result of a bad social environment. A liberal commonwealth, therefore, was one that would remove the hindrances to the full flowering of the human personality.

The basic vision of liberalism has not changed since the nineteenth century. What has changed is the way it is applied to modern society. In that respect, liberalism has changed dramatically. Today, instead of regarding government with suspicion, liberals welcome government as an instrument to serve the people. The change in philosophy began in the latter years of the nineteenth century, when businesses—once small, independent operations—began to grow into giant structures that overwhelmed individuals and sometimes even overshadowed the state in power and wealth. At that time, liberals began reconsidering their commitment to the *laissez-faire* philosophy. If the state can be an oppressor, asked liberals, can't big business also oppress people? By then, many were convinced that commercial and industrial monopolies were crushing the souls and bodies of the working classes. The state, formerly the villain, now was viewed by liberals as a potential savior. The concept of freedom was transformed into something more than a negative freedom *from;* the term began to take on a positive meaning. It meant "realizing one's full potential." Toward this end, liberals believed, the state could prove to be a valuable instrument. It could educate children, protect the health and safety of workers, help people through hard times, promote a healthy economy, and—when necessary—force business to act more humanely and responsibly. Thus was born the movement that culminated in New Deal liberalism.

New Deal Liberalism

In the United States, the argument in favor of state intervention did not win an enduring majority constituency until after the Great Depression of the 1930s began to be felt deeply. The disastrous effects of a depression that left a quarter of the workforce unemployed opened the way to a new administration—and a promise. "I pledge you, I pledge myself," Franklin D. Roosevelt said when accepting the Democratic nomination in 1932, "to a new deal for the American people." Roosevelt's New Deal was an attempt to effect relief and recovery from the Depression; it employed a variety of means, including welfare programs, public works, and business regulation—most of which involved government intervention in the economy. The New Deal liberalism relied on government to liberate people from poverty, oppression, and economic exploitation. At the same time, the New Dealers claimed to be as zealous as the classical liberals in defending political and civil liberties.

The common element in *laissez-faire* liberalism and welfare-state liberalism is their dedication to the goal of realizing the full potential of each individual. Some still questioned whether this is best done by minimizing state involvement or whether it sometimes requires an activist state. The New Dealers took the latter view, though they prided themselves on being pragmatic and experimental about their activism. During the heyday of the New Deal, a wide variety of programs were tried and—if found wanting—abandoned. All decent means should be tried, they believed, even if it meant dilution of ideological purity. The Roosevelt administration, for example, denounced bankers and businessmen in campaign rhetoric but worked very closely with them while trying to extricate the nation from the Depression. This set a pattern of pragmatism that New Dealers from Harry Truman to Lyndon Johnson emulated.

Progressive Liberalism

Progressive liberalism emerged in the late 1960s and early 1970s as a more militant and uncompromising movement than the New Deal had ever been. Its roots go back to the New Left student movement of the early 1960s. New Left students went to the South to participate in civil rights demonstrations, and many of them were bloodied in confrontations with southern police; by the mid-1960s they were confronting the authorities in the North over issues like poverty and the Vietnam War. By the end of the decade, the New Left had fragmented into a variety of factions and had lost much of its vitality, but a somewhat more respectable version of it appeared as the New Politics movement.

Many New Politics crusaders were former New Leftists who had traded their jeans for coats and ties; they tried to work within the system instead of always confronting it. Even so, they retained some of the spirit of the New Left. The civil rights slogan "Freedom Now" expressed the mood of the New Politics. The young university graduates who filled its ranks had come from an environment where "nonnegotiable" demands were issued to college deans by leaders of sit-in protests. There was more than youthful arrogance in the New Politics movement, however; there was a pervasive belief that America had lost, had compromised away, much of its idealism. The New Politics liberals sought to recover some of that spirit by linking up with an older tradition of militant reform, which went back to the time of the Revolution. These new liberals saw themselves as the authentic heirs of Thomas Paine and Henry David Thoreau, of the abolitionists, the radical populists, the suffragettes, and the great progressive reformers of the early twentieth century.

While New Deal liberals concentrated almost exclusively on bread-and-butter issues such as unemployment and poverty, the New Politics liberals introduced what came to be known as social issues into the political arena. These included: the repeal of laws against abortion, the liberalization of laws against homosexuality and pornography, the establishment of affirmative action programs to ensure increased hiring of minorities and women, and the passage of the Equal Rights Amendment. In foreign policy, too, New Politics liberals departed from the New Deal agenda. Because they had keener memories of the unpopular and (for them) unjustified war in Vietnam than of World War II, they became doves, in contrast to the general hawkishness of the New Dealers. They were skeptical of any claim that the United States must be the leader of the free world or, indeed, that it had any special mission in the world; some were convinced that America was already in decline and must learn to adjust accordingly. The real danger, they argued, came not from the Soviet Union but from the mad pace of America's arms race with the Soviets, which, as they saw it, could bankrupt the country, starve its social programs, and culminate in a nuclear Armageddon.

New Politics liberals were heavily represented at the 1972 Democratic national convention, which nominated South Dakota senator George McGovern for president. By the 1980s the New Politics movement was no longer new, and many of its adherents preferred to be called progressives. By this time their critics had another name for them: radicals. The critics saw their positions as inimical to the interests of the United States, destructive of the family, and fundamentally at odds with the views of most Americans. The adversaries of the progressives were not only conservatives but many New Deal liberals, who openly scorned the McGovernites.

This split still exists within the Democratic party, though it is now more skillfully managed by party leaders. In 1988 the Democrats paired Michael Dukakis, whose Massachusetts supporters were generally on the progressive side of the party, with New Dealer Lloyd Bentsen as the presidential and vice-presidential candidates, respectively. In 1992 the Democrats won the presidency with Arkansas governor Bill Clinton, whose record as governor seemed to put him in the moderate-to-conservative camp, and Tennessee senator Albert Gore, whose position on environmental issues could probably be considered quite liberal but whose general image was middle-of-the-road. Both candidates had moved toward liberal positions on the issues of gay rights and abortion. By 1994 Clinton was perceived by many Americans as being "too liberal," which some speculate may have been a factor in the defeat of Democrats in the congressional elections that year. Clinton immediately sought to shake off that perception, positioning himself as a "moderate" between extremes and casting the Republicans as an "extremist" party. (These two terms will be examined presently.)

Conservatism

Like liberalism, conservatism has undergone historical transformation in America. Just as early liberals (represented by Thomas Jefferson) espoused less government, early conservatives (whose earliest leaders were Alexander Hamilton and John Adams) urged government support of economic enterprise and government intervention on behalf of certain groups. But today, in reaction to the growth of the welfare state, conservatives argue strongly that more government means more unjustified interference in citizens' lives, more bureaucratic regulation of private conduct, more inhibiting control of economic enterprise, more material advantage for the less energetic and less able at the expense of those who are prepared to work harder and better, and, of course, more taxes—taxes that will be taken from those who have earned money and given to those who have not.

Contemporary conservatives are not always opposed to state intervention. They may support larger military expenditures in order to protect society against foreign enemies. They may also allow for some intrusion into private life in order to protect society against internal subversion and would pursue criminal prosecution zealously in order to protect society against domestic violence. The fact is that few conservatives, and perhaps fewer liberals, are absolute with respect to their views about the power of the state. Both are quite prepared to use the state in order to further *their* purposes. It is true that activist presidents such as Franklin Roosevelt and John Kennedy were likely to be classified as liberals. However, Richard Nixon was also an activist, and, although he does not easily fit any classification, he was far closer to conservatism than to liberalism. It is too easy to identify liberalism with statism and conservatism with antistatism: it is important to remember that it was liberal Jefferson who counseled against "energetic government" and conservative Alexander Hamilton who designed bold powers for the new central government and wrote, "Energy in the executive is a leading character in the definition of good government."

The Religious Right

Another category within the conservative movement is what is often referred to as "the religious right." Termed "the new right" when it first appeared 30 years ago, the religious right is composed of conservative Christians who are concerned not so much about high taxes and government spending as they are about the decline of traditional Judeo-Christian morality, a decline that they attribute in part to certain unwise government policies and judicial decisions.

They oppose many of the recent judicial decisions on sociocultural issues such as abortion, school prayer, pornography, and gay rights, and they were outspoken critics of the Clinton administration, citing everything from President Clinton's views on gays in the military to his sexual behavior while in the White House.

Spokesmen for progressive liberalism and the religious right stand as polar opposites: The former regard abortion as a woman's right; the latter see it as legalized murder. The former tend to regard homosexuality as a lifestyle that needs protection against discrimination; the latter are more likely to see it as a perversion. The list of issues could go on. The religious right and the progressive liberals are like positive and negative photographs of America's moral landscape. Sociologist James Davison Hunter uses the term *culture wars* to characterize the struggles between these contrary visions of America. For all the differences between progressive liberalism and the religious right, however, their styles are very similar. They are heavily laced with moralistic prose; they tend to equate compromise with selling out; and they claim to represent the best, most authentic traditions of America. This is not to denigrate either movement, for the kinds of issues they address are indeed moral issues, which do not generally admit much compromise. These issues cannot simply be finessed or ignored, despite the efforts of conventional politicians to do so. They must be aired and fought over which is why we include some of them, such as abortion (Issue 10) and homosexuality (Issue 8) in this volume.

Neoconservatism

The term *neoconservatism* came into use in the early 1970s as a designation for former New Deal Democrats who had became alarmed by what they saw as the drift of their party's foreign policy toward appeasing Communists. When Senator George McGovern, the party's presidential nominee in 1972, stated that he would "crawl to Hanoi on my knees" to secure peace in Vietnam, he seemed to them to exemplify this new tendency. They were, then, "hawks" in foreign policy, which they insisted was the historic stance of their party; they regarded themselves as the true heirs of liberal presidents such as Truman and Kennedy and liberal senators such as Henry ("Scoop") Jackson of Washington State. On domestic policy, they were still largely liberal, except for their reactions to three new liberal planks added by the "progressives": gay rights, which neoconservatives tended to regard as a distortion of civil rights; abortion, which to some degree or another went against the grain of their moral sensibilities; and affirmative action, which some compared to the "quota system" once used to keep down the number of Jews admitted to elite universities. In fact, a number of prominent neoconservatives were Jews, including Norman Podhoretz, Midge Decter, Gertrude Himmelfarb, and Irving Kristol (though others, such as Michael Novak and Daniel Patrick Moynihan, were Roman Catholics, and one, Richard John Neuhaus, was a Lutheran pastor who later converted to Catholicism and became a priest). The term *neoconservative* seemed headed for oblivion in the 1980s, when some leading neoconservatives dropped the "neo" part and classified themselves as conservatives, period. By the time the Soviet Union collapsed in 1991, it appeared that the term was no longer needed—the Cold War with "world Communism" was over. But the rise of Islamic terrorism in the 1990s, aimed at the West in general and the United States in particular, brought back alarms analogous to those of the Cold War period, with global terrorism now taking the place of world Communism. So, too, was the concern that liberal foreign policy might not be tough enough for the fight against these new, ruthless enemies of Western democracy. The concern was ratcheted up considerably after the events of 9/11, and now a new generation of neoconservatives was in the spotlight—some of its members literally the children of an earlier "neo" generation. They included Bill Kristol, John Podhoretz, Douglas Feith, Paul Wolfowitz, Richard Perle, David Brooks, and (though he was old enough to overlap with the previous generation), Bill Bennett.

Radicals, Reactionaries, and Moderates

The label *reactionary* is almost an insult, and the label *radical* is worn with pride by only a few zealots on the banks of the political mainstream. A reactionary is not a conserver but a backward-mover, dedicated to turning the clock back to better times. Most people suspect that reactionaries would restore us to a time that never was, except in political myth. For most Americans, the repeal of industrialism or universal education (or the entire twentieth century itself) is not a practical, let alone desirable, political program.

Radicalism (literally meaning "from the roots" or "going to the foundation") implies a fundamental reconstruction of the social order. Taken in that sense, it is possible to speak of right-wing radicalism as well as left-wing radicalism—radicalism that would restore or inaugurate a new hierarchical society as well as radicalism that calls for nothing less than an egalitarian society. The term is sometimes used in both of these senses, but most often the word *radicalism* is reserved to characterize more liberal change. While the liberal would effect change through conventional democratic processes, the radical is likely to be skeptical about the ability of the established machinery to bring about the needed change and might be prepared to sacrifice "a little" liberty to bring about a great deal more equality.

Moderate is a highly coveted label in America. Its meaning is not precise, but it carries the connotations of sensible, balanced, and practical. A moderate person is not without principles, but he or she does not allow principles to harden into dogma. The opposite of moderate is *extremist,* a label most American political leaders eschew. Yet there have been notable exceptions. When Arizona senator Barry Goldwater, a conservative Republican, was nominated for president in 1964, he declared, "Extremism in defense of liberty is no vice! . . . Moderation in the pursuit of justice is no virtue!" This open embrace of extremism did not help his electoral chances; Goldwater was overwhelmingly defeated. At about the same time, however, another American political leader also embraced a kind of extremism, and with better results. In a famous letter written from a jail cell in Birmingham, Alabama, the Reverend Martin Luther King, Jr., replied to the charge that he was an extremist not by denying it but by distinguishing between different kinds of extremists. The question, he wrote, "is not whether we will be extremist but what kind of extremist will we be. Will we be extremists for hate, or will we be extremists for love?" King aligned himself with the love extremists, in which category he also placed Jesus, St. Paul, and Thomas Jefferson, among others. It was an adroit use of a label that is usually anathema in America.

Pluralism

The principle of pluralism espouses diversity in a society containing many interest groups and in a government containing competing units of power. This implies the widest expression of competing ideas, and in this way, pluralism is in sympathy with an important element of liberalism. However, as James Madison and Alexander Hamilton pointed out when they analyzed the sources of pluralism in their *Federalist* commentaries on the Constitution, this philosophy springs from a profoundly pessimistic view of human nature, and in this respect it more closely resembles conservatism. Madison, possibly the single most influential member of the convention that wrote the Constitution, hoped that in a large and varied nation, no single interest group could control the government. Even if there were a majority interest, it would be unlikely to capture all of the national agencies of government—the House of Representatives, the Senate, the presidency, and the federal judiciary—each of which was chosen in a different way by a different constituency for a different term of office. Moreover, to make certain that no one branch exercised excessive power, each was equipped with "checks and balances" that enabled any agency of national government to curb the powers of the others. The clearest statement of Madison's, and the Constitution's, theory can be found in the 51st paper of the *Federalist:*

> It may be a reflection on human nature that such devices should be necessary to control the abuses of government. But what is government itself, but the greatest of all reflections on human nature? If men were angels, no government would be necessary.

This pluralist position may be analyzed from different perspectives. It is conservative insofar as it rejects simple majority rule; yet it is liberal insofar as it rejects rule by a single elite. It is conservative in its pessimistic appraisal of human nature; yet pluralism's pessimism is also a kind of egalitarianism, holding as it does that no one can be trusted with power and that majority interests no less than minority interests will use power for selfish ends. It is possible to suggest that in America pluralism represents an alternative to both liberalism and conservatism. Pluralism is antimajoritarian and antielitist and combines some elements of both.

Some Applications

Despite our effort to define the principal alignments in American politics, some policy decisions do not fit neatly into these categories. Readers will reach their own conclusions, but we suggest some alignments here in order to demonstrate the variety of viewpoints.

In Issue 1, concerning the notion of a unique American "mission," Howard Zinn expresses a view common among New Politics liberals: skepticism of any claim that the United States must be the leader of the free world or, indeed, that it has ever had any special mission in the world. Wilfred McClay's view that the "myth" of America is a noble one is still shared today by many New Deal liberals, but it is embraced more conspicuously by conservatives. In Issue 3, Mark Green favors taxpayer funding of political campaigns, based upon the progressive liberal argument that our democratic system needs not just an honest ballot count but a playing field leveled through the elimination of money as a factor in elections; John Samples adopts the conservative view that taxpayers should not be forced to fund the electoral campaigns of politicians.

In Issue 5, on courts seeking the "original meaning" of the Constitution, Supreme Court Justice Stephen Breyer believes that constitutional interpretation must reflect what he believes to be the democratic trajectory of the Constitution, a long-held liberal position, while his colleague on the bench, Justice Antonin Scalia, takes a position long argued by conservatives when he insists that the Constitution, unlike statutes, was not meant to be changed, except by amendment. Warrantless wiretapping by the president, covered in Issue 19, also taps into liberal-conservative dichotomies. Andrew McCarthy insists, as do many conservatives, that it is necessary, long practiced by presidents during wartime, and authorized by the president's wartime powers, while former Vice President Al Gore takes the liberal position that it violates essential liberties.

Affirmative action (Issue 9) has become a litmus test of the newer brand of progressive liberalism. The progressives say that it is not enough for the laws of society to be color-blind or gender-blind; they must now reach out to remedy the ills caused by racism and sexism. New Deal liberals, along with conservatives and libertarians, generally oppose affirmative action. Another issue dividing progressive liberalism from conservatism is homosexuality. Is homosexual behavior part of a "lifestyle" that deserves constitutional protection, like a person's race or gender, or does it involve behavior that states have a right to prohibit? Conservatives would urge the latter on two separate grounds: it flouts traditional Western morality, and, unlike race and gender, it is nowhere mentioned among protected categories in the Constitution. Liberals, especially progressive liberals, say that the constitutional protection of homosexual behavior between consenting adults is long overdue in America, and that it can be easily extrapolated from other rights listed in the Constitution. In Issue 8, Supreme Court justices Anthony Kennedy and Antonin Scalia clearly differ, at least on the constitutional question, when it comes to homosexual behavior.

Religious conservatives have weighed into the homosexual debate, almost always in support of Scalia's position. Not surprisingly, they have also been vocal supporters of religion in our public institutions. Liberals, at least those who would style themselves progressives, oppose any ties between religion and the state, often quoting the line from Thomas Jefferson about the need for a "wall of separation" between the two. In Issue 15, Supreme Court Justice John Paul Stevens supports that view, while Justice Scalia argues that in both the Constitution and our history there is ample support for the public acknowledgment of God's providence.

Issue 12, on whether or not the gap between the rich and the poor is increasing, points up another disagreement between liberals and conservatives. Most liberals would agree with Jeff Madrick that socioeconomic inequality is increasing and that this undermines the basic tenets of American democracy. Christopher DeMuth, representing the conservative viewpoint, maintains that Americans are becoming more equal and that virtually all people benefit from increased prosperity because it takes place in a free market. Then there is national health insurance, which liberals and conservatives have been fighting about since President Harry Truman introduced the proposal in 1945. Here is a classic liberal-conservative split, and in Issue 11 Ezra Klein takes the liberal side, arguing that health care is a right that needs to protected by the government as it is in every other developed country. John Goodman takes the conservative position that national health insurance ultimately empties the public treasury and harms the very people it is meant to serve.

Immigration, explored in Issue 14, is another issue that can sharply separate liberals from conservatives. For good historical reasons American liberals have generally welcomed immigration. The ranks of New Deal liberalism were filled by immigrants, first from Ireland, later from Southern and Eastern Europe; more recent immigrants from Latin America have been friendly to the economic program of New Deal liberalism. In recent years conservatives have also courted immigrants, realizing that many Latinos actually lean toward the conservative side of certain social issues, such as those raised by homosexuality and abortion. But the sticking point for conservatives is illegal immigration. Emphasizing their law and order credentials, conservatives, like Mark Krikorian, oppose anything resembling amnesty for undocumented aliens while liberals—in this case Frank Sharry—are more inclined to favor at least a roadway to amnesty.

There are also liberal-conservative splits in foreign policy, and they often figure into debates on national security. Both sides claim to support both civil liberties and national security, but liberals seem to emphasize the former and conservatives the latter. We can see this in the debates on Middle Eastern profiling (Issue 17), torture (Issue 18), and warrantless wiretapping (Issue 19). Since the Vietnam War, conservatives have generally leaned toward the "hawkish" side when it comes to fighting hot and cold wars, while liberals are more likely to be "doves." The symmetry is not perfect, though, as we see in the debate on China (Issue 20). Robert Kaplan, who supports a tough stance toward China because of its modernization of its military, is indeed a conservative (or "neoconservative"), but Ivan Eland, who disagrees with him, represents the CATO Institute. CATO sides with the conservatives on issues like taxing and the size of government, though it is dovish in foreign policy.

This book contains some arguments that are not easy to categorize. Issue 10, on whether or not abortion should be restricted, is one such issue. The pro-choice position, as argued by Mary Gordon, is not a traditional liberal position. Less than a generation ago legalized abortion was opposed by liberals such as Senator Edward Kennedy (D-Massachusetts) and the Reverend Jesse Jackson, and even recently some liberals, such as the late Pennsylvania governor Robert Casey and columnist Nat Hentoff, have opposed it. Nevertheless, most liberals now adopt some version of Gordon's pro-choice views. Opposing Gordon is Robert

George, whose argument here might be endorsed by liberals like Hentoff. Issue 16, on the war in Iraq and the war on terrorism, is also hard to classify. Many liberals initially favored a hard line against Saddam Hussein, endorsing economic sanctions, no-fly zones, bombing strikes, and "regime change" in Iraq in the 1990s, and later, in 2002, authorizing the president to undertake hostilities. But Robert Jervis nevertheless speaks for many liberals today in deploring what he regards as Bush's reckless unilateralism. J. R. Dunn is more in tune with conservatives in his belief that success in Iraq will lead to a healthy domino effect throughout the Middle East, thwarting the designs of the terrorists.

The arguments in Issues 6 and 7, on Congress and the president respectively, are also difficult to classify, if only because so much depends on which political party is in charge of which branch. When a party controls the White House, its members will defend, or at least acquiesce in, "executive privilege," the president's right to withhold information from congressional investigators. But when the president belongs to the other party, they fight against it. The same is true of Congress. The minority party, whether Democrat or Republican, liberal or conservative, carries on about corruption, pork-barreling, and the abuse of power by the majority, but when the minority becomes the majority, it is likely to fall silent about such practices.

Internet References . . .

In addition to the Internet sites found below, type in key worlds, such as "American mission," "American exceptionalism," "democracy fight terror," and "public financing campaigns" to find other listings.

The Federal Web Locator

Use this handy site as a launching pad for the Web sites of U.S. federal agencies, departments, and organizations. It is well organized and easy to use for informational and research purposes.

http://www.infoctr.edu/fwl/

The Library of Congress

Examine this Web site to learn about the extensive resource tools, library services/resources, exhibitions, and databases available through the Library of Congress in many different subfields of government studies.

http://www.loc.gov

U.S. Founding Documents

Through this Emory University site you can view scanned originals of the Declaration of Independence, the Constitution, and the Bill of Rights. The transcribed texts are also available, as are the *Federalist Papers.*

http://www.law.emory.edu/FEDERAL/

Hoover Institution Public Policy Inquiry: Campaign Finance

Use this Stanford University site to explore the history of campaign finance as well as the current reforms and proposals for future change.

http://www.campaignfinancesite.org

Poynter.org

This research site of the Poynter Institute. a school for journalists, provides extensive links to information and resources about the media, including media ethics and reportage techniques. Many bibliographies and Web sites are included.

http://www.poynter.org/research/index.htm

Freedom House

Founded over sixty years ago by Eleanor Roosevelt, Wendell Wike, and others concerned about the suppression of democracy in the world, Freedom House charts the progress and retrogression of freedom in the nations of the world. You can view its annual "map of freedom" to see which countries it lists each year as "free" (in green), "partly free" (in yellow) and "not free" (in blue).

http://www.freedomhouse.org

Democracy and the American Political Process

*D*emocracy *is derived from two Greek words, demos and kratia, which mean, respectively, "people" and "rule." The prerequisites for rule by the people include free speech and other vital liberties, a well-informed citizenry, a variety of available points of view, and an equal counting of votes. Does America's electoral and campaign system meet these prerequisites? Some analysts of democracy would go further and include among the prerequisites a people's belief in their nation and its unique "mission." But is that necessary? And does it pose its own dangers? In this section we address these and related issues.*

- Should Americans Believe in a Unique American "Mission"?

- Is Democracy the Answer to Global Terrorism?

- Should America Adopt Public Financing of Political Campaigns?

ISSUE 1

Should Americans Believe in a Unique American "Mission"?

YES: Wilfred M. McClay, from "The Founding of Nations," *First Things* (March 2006)

NO: Howard Zinn, from "The Power and the Glory: Myths of American Exceptionalism," *Boston Review* (Summer 2005)

ISSUE SUMMARY

YES: Humanities professor Wilfred M. McClay argues that America's "myth," its founding narrative, helps to sustain and hold together a diverse people.

NO: Historian Howard Zinn is convinced that America's myth of "exceptionalism" has served as a justification for lawlessness, brutality, and imperialism.

Take a dollar from your wallet and look at the back of it. On the left side, above an unfinished pyramid with a detached eye on top, are the words "Annuit Coeptis," Latin for, "He has favored our endeavors." The "He" is God.

Since the time of the Puritans, Americans have often thought of themselves collectively as a people whose endeavors are favored by God. "We shall be as a city upon a hill, the eyes of all people are upon us," said Puritan leader John Winthrop aboard the *Arbella*, the Puritans' flagship, as it left for the New World in 1630. Later in that century another Puritan, the Rev. Samuel Danforth, famously spoke of New England's divinely assigned "errand into the wilderness." By the eighteenth century, the role of New England had become the role of America: God had led his people to establish a new social order, a light to the nations. "Your forefathers," John Jay told New Yorkers in 1776, "came to America under the auspices of Divine Providence." For Patrick Henry, the American Revolution "was the grand operation, which seemed to be assigned by the Deity to the men of this age in our country." In his First Inaugural Address, George Washington saw an "invisible hand" directing the people of the United States. "Every step they have taken seems to have been distinguished by some token of providential agency." Even the most secular-minded founders thought of their nation in providential terms. Thomas Jefferson paid homage to the "Being . . . who led our fathers, as Israel of old, from their native land and planted them in a country flowing with all the necessaries and comforts of life; who has covered our infancy with His providence and our riper years with his wisdom and power." At the Constitutional Convention in Philadelphia, Benjamin Franklin declared that "God governs in the affairs of men," adding: "And if a sparrow cannot fall to the ground without his notice, is it probable that an empire cannot rise without his aid?"

Throughout the nineteenth and twentieth centuries, this notion of America as "a people set apart" was a perennial feature of American public discourse. Its most eloquent expression came in the speeches of Abraham Lincoln. Perhaps in deference to biblical literalists, Lincoln did not call Americans a "chosen people" (a name limited to the Jews in the Bible), but he came close: he said Americans were God's "almost chosen people." In other speeches, particularly in his Second Inaugural Address, he stressed the role of Divine Providence in directing the course of American history. Frederick Douglas, the black abolitionist leader, called the Second Inaugural "more like a sermon than a state paper."

So it has gone, down through the nation's history. Herbert Croly, the influential Progressive writer in the early twentieth century, called on Americans to realize "the promise of American life." In 1936 Franklin Roosevelt told a newer generation of Americans that they had a "rendezvous with destiny." John F. Kennedy proclaimed that "God's work must truly be our own." Martin Luther King, in his prophetic "I Have a Dream" speech identified his dream with the God-given promises of America. Ronald Reagan, paraphrasing John Winthrop's speech of 1630, saw America as a "shining city on a hill."

All of this sounds inspiring, and no doubt it did help inspire many worthy reforms, from the abolition of slavery in the 1860s to the landmark civil rights laws a century later. But is there a darker side to it? To its critics, American "exceptionalism" is a dangerous notion. They remind us that other nations, too, such as the ancient Romans, the Dutch, the Spanish, the British, and the Germans, have at various times boasted of themselves as an exceptional people, and that this has led them down the path to chauvinism, imperialism, and even genocide. To them, the invocation, "God bless America" sounds like hubris, as if God is being asked to bless whatever it is that America decides to do. Such a spirit lay behind "Manifest Destiny," a slogan from the mid-nineteenth century that was used to justify American expansion into territory claimed by Mexico, and in the 1890s American imperialists justified American expansion into Cuba and the Philippines in nearly similar language. From Indian removal at home to imperial adventures abroad, there have been few dark episodes in American history that have not found defenders ready to put them in terms of American exceptionalism.

In the selections that follow, humanities professor Wilfred M. McClay looks at the brighter side of American providentialism, while historian Howard Zinn argues that what he calls "American exceptionalism" is a dangerous idea because it has served as a justification for lawlessness, brutality, and imperialism.

YES **Wilfred M. McClay**

The Founding of Nations

Did the United States really have a beginning that can be called its "Founding"? Can any society, for that matter, be said to have a founding moment in its past that ought to be regarded as a source of guidance and support?

Much of the intellectual culture of our time stands resolutely opposed to the idea of a founding as a unique moment in secular time that has a certain magisterial authority over what comes after it. The cult of ancestors, in its many forms, is always one of the chief objects of modernity's deconstructive energies. Kant's famous command, *Sapere Aude*—"Dare to Reason," the battle cry of the Enlightenment—always ends up being deployed against arguments claiming traditional authority.

Foundings, in this view, are fairy tales that cannot be taken seriously—indeed, that it is dangerous to take seriously, since modern nation-states have used them as tools of cultural hegemony. One has a moral obligation to peek behind the curtain, and one ought to have a strong presupposition about what one will find there. There is a settled assumption in the West, particularly among the educated, that every founding was in reality a blood-soaked moment, involving the enslavement or exploitation of some for the benefit of others. Foundational myths are merely attempts to prettify this horror. Our ancestors were not the noble heroes of epic. They were the primal horde or the Oedipal usurpers, and their authority derived ultimately from their successful monopolization of violence—and then their subsequent monopolization of the way the story would be told.

The perfect expression of this view is Theodor Adorno's dictum, "There is no monument of civilization that is not at the same time a monument of barbarism." Every achievement of culture involves an elaborate concealment of the less-than-licit means that went into its making. Property is theft, in Proudhon's famous phrase, which means that legitimacy is nothing more than the preeminent force, and our systems of law are the ways that the stolen money is laundered and turned into Carnegie libraries and Vanderbilt universities and other carved Corinthian pillars of society. From this point of view, the credulous souls who speak of the American founding are merely trying to retail a heroic myth about the Founding Fathers, a group of youthful and idealistic patriarchs who somehow reached up into the heavens and pulled down a Constitution for all time.

From *First Things*, March 2006, pp. 33–39. Copyright © 2006 by Institute on Religion and Public Life. Reprinted by permission.

Admittedly, American filiopietism about the Founding can get out of hand. On the ceiling of the rotunda of the United States Capitol building—the inside of the dome which, in its external aspect, is arguably the single most recognizable symbol of American democracy—there is painted a fresco called "The Apotheosis of George Washington." It is as if the Sistine Chapel were transposed into an American key. The first president sits in glory, flanked by the Goddess of Liberty and the winged figure Fame sounding a victorious trumpet and holding aloft a palm frond. The thirteen female figures in a semi-circle around Washington represent the thirteen original states. On the outer ring stand six allegorical groups representing classical images of agriculture, arts and sciences, commerce, war, mechanics, and seafaring. This figure of a deified Washington, painted significantly enough in the year 1865, reflects a vision that appealed powerfully to the American public. But it is actually a rather disturbing image, and it cries out for debunking.

Still, debunking is a blunt instrument of limited value, despite the modern prejudice in its favor. To the question "What is a man?" André Malraux once gave the quintessential modern debunking answer: "A miserable little pile of secrets." That answer is too true to dismiss—but not quite true enough to embrace. And it is, in its way, the exact opposite number to the saccharin image of a deified and perfected George Washington dwelling in the clouds atop the Capitol dome. Such a conflict between grand moral oversimplications impoverishes our thinking and sets us a false standard of greatness—one that is too easily debunked and leaves us too easily defrauded. . . .

When we speak of American national identity, one of the chief points at issue arises out of the tension between *creed* and *culture*. This is a tension between, on the one hand, the idea of the United States as a nation built on the foundation of self-evident, rational, and universally applicable propositions about human nature and human society; and, on the other hand, the idea of the United States as a very unusual, historically specific and contingent entity, underwritten by a long, intricately evolved, and very particular legacy of English law, language, and customs, Greco-Roman cultural antecedents, and Judeo-Christian sacred texts and theological and moral teachings, without whose presences the nation's flourishing would not be possible.

All this makes a profound tension, with much to be said for both sides. And the side one comes down on will say a lot about one's stance on an immense number of issues, such as immigration, education, citizenship, cultural assimilation, multiculturalism, pluralism, the role of religion in public life, the prospects for democratizing the Middle East, and on and on.

Yet any understanding of American identity that entirely excluded either creed or culture would be seriously deficient. Any view of American life that failed to acknowledge its powerful strains of universalism, idealism, and crusading zeal would be describing a different country from the America that happens to exist. And any view of America as simply a bundle of abstract normative ideas about freedom and democracy and self-government that can flourish just as easily in any cultural and historical soil, including a multilingual, post-religious, or post-national one, takes too much for granted and will be in for a rude awakening.

◦◦◦

The antagonism of creed and culture is better understood not as a statement of alternatives but as an antinomy, one of those perpetual oppositions that can never be resolved. In fact, the two halves of the opposition often reinforce each other. The creed needs the support of the culture—and the culture, in turn, is imbued with respect for the creed. For the creed to be successful, it must be able to presume the presence of all kinds of cultural inducements— toward civility, restraint, deferred gratification, nonviolence, loyalty, procedural fairness, impersonal neutrality, compassion, respect for elders, and the like. These traits are not magically called into being by the mere invocation of the Declaration of Independence. Nor are they sustainable for long without the support of strong and deeply rooted social and cultural institutions that are devoted to the formation of character, most notably the traditional family and traditional religious institutions. But by the same token, the American culture is unimaginable apart from the influence of the American creed: from the sense of pride and moral responsibility Americans derive from being, as Walter Berns has argued, a carrier of universal values—a vanguard people.

◦◦◦

Forcing a choice between creed and culture is not the way to resolve the problem of cultural restoration. Clearly both can plausibly claim a place in the American Founding. What seems more urgent is the repair of some background assumptions about our relation to the past. It is a natural enough impulse to look back in times of turbulence and uncertainty. And it is especially natural, even obligatory, for a republican form of government to do so, since republics come into being at particular moments in secular time, through self-conscious acts of public deliberation. Indeed, philosophers from Aristotle on have insisted that republics *must* periodically recur to their first principles, in order to adjust and renew themselves through a fresh encounter with their initiating vision.

A constitutional republic like the United States is uniquely grounded in its foundational moment, its time of creation. And a founding is not merely the instant that the ball started rolling. Instead, it is a moment that presumes a certain authority over all the moments that will follow—and to speak of a founding is to presume that such moments in time are possible. It most closely resembles the moment that one takes an oath or makes a promise. One could even say that a constitutional founding is a kind of covenant, a meta-promise entered into with the understanding that it has a uniquely powerful claim on the future. It requires of us a willingness to be constantly looking back to our initiating promises and goals, in much the same way that we would chart progress or regress in our individual lives by reference to a master list of resolutions.

Republicanism means self-government, and so republican liberty does not mean living without restraint. It means, rather, living in accordance with a law that you have dictated to yourself. Hence the especially strong need of republics to recur to their founding principles and their founding narratives, is a never-ending process of self-adjustment. There should be a constant interplay between founding ideals and current realities, a tennis ball bouncing back and forth between the two.

And for that to happen, there need to be two things in place. First, founding principles must be sufficiently fixed to give us genuine guidance, to teach us something. Of course, we celebrate the fact that our Constitution was created with a built-in openness to amendment. But the fact that such ideals are open to amendment is perhaps the least valuable thing about them. A founding, like a promise or a vow, means nothing if its chief glory is its adaptability. The analogy of a successful marriage, which is also, in a sense, a res publica that must periodically recur to first principles, and whose flourishing depends upon the ability to distinguish first principles from passing circumstances, is actually a fairly good guide to these things.

Second, there needs to be a sense of connection to the past, a reflex for looking backward, and cultivating that ought to be one of the chief uses of the formal study of history. Unfortunately, the fostering of a vital sense of connection to the past is not one of the goals of historical study as it is now taught and practiced in this country. The meticulous contextualization of past events and ideas, arising out of a sophisticated understanding of the past's particularities and discontinuities with the present, is one of the great achievements of modern historiography. But we need to recognize that this achievement comes at a high cost when it emphasizes the *pastness* of the past—when it makes the past completely unavailable to us, separated from us by an impassable chasm of contextual difference.

In the case of the American Founding, a century-long assault has taken place among historians, and the sense of connection is even more tenuous. The standard scholarly accounts insist this heated series of eighteenth-century debates—among flawed, unheroic, and self-interested white men—offers nothing to which we should grant any abiding authority. That was then, and this is now.

The insistence on the pastness of the past imprisons us in the present. It makes our present antiseptically cut off from anything that might really nourish, surprise, or challenge it. It erodes our sense of being part of a common enterprise with humankind. An emphasis on scholarly precision has dovetailed effortlessly with what might be called the debunking imperative, which generally aims to discredit any use of the past to justify or support something in the present, and is therefore one of the few gestures likely to win universal approbation among historians. It is professionally safest to be a critic and extremely dangerous to be too affirmative.

Scholarly responsibility thus seems to demand the deconstruction of the American Founding into its constituent elements, thereby divesting it of any claim to unity or any heroic or mythic dimensions, deserving of our admiration or reverence. There was no coherence to what they did, and looking backward to divine what they meant by what they were doing makes no sense. The

Founders and Framers, after all, fought among themselves. They produced a document that was a compromise, that waffled on important issues, that remains hopelessly bound to the eighteenth century and inadequate to our contemporary problems, etc. And so—in much the same manner as the source criticism of the Bible, which challenges the authority of Scripture by understanding the text as a compilation of haphazardly generated redactions—the Constitution is seen as a concatenation of disparate elements, a mere political deal meant to be superseded by other political deals, and withal an instrument of the powerful. The last thing in the world you would want to do is treat it as a document with any intrinsic moral authority. Every text is merely a pretext. This is the kind of explanation one has learned to expect from the historical guild.

In this connection, it is amusing to see the extent to which historians, who are pleased to regard the Constitution as a hopelessly outdated relic of a bygone era, are themselves still crude nineteenth-century positivists at heart. They still pride themselves on their ability to puncture myths, relying on a shallow positivistic understanding of a myth as a more or less organized form of falsehood, rather than seeing myth as a structure of meaning, a manner of giving a manageable shape to the cosmos, and to one's own experience of the world, a shape that expresses cultural ideals and shared sentiments, and that guides us through the darkness of life's many perils and unanswerable questions by providing us with what Plato called a "likely story."

To be sure, there are good things to be said of a critical approach to history, and there are myths aplenty that richly deserve to be punctured. I am glad, for example, that we know beyond a shadow of a doubt that Washington, D.C., in the Kennedy years had very little in common with the legendary Camelot, aside from the ubiquity of adulterous liaisons in both places. That kind of ground-clearing is important, and we are better off without that kind of propagandistic myth. We might even be better off without the Apotheosis of George Washington sitting atop the Capitol dome.

But ground-clearing by itself is not enough. And to think otherwise is to mistake an ancillary activity for the main thing itself—as if agriculture were nothing more than the application of insecticides and weedkillers. History as debunking is ultimately an empty and fruitless undertaking, which fails to address the reasons we humans try to narrate and understand our pasts. It fails to take into account the ways in which a nation's morale, cohesion, and strength derive from a sense of connection to its past. And it fails to acknowledge how much a healthy sense of the future—including the economic and cultural preconditions for a critical historiography to ply its trade—depends on a mythic sense of the nation. The human need to encompass life within the framework of myth is not merely a longing for pleasing illusion. Myths reflect a fundamental human need for a larger shape to our collective aspirations. And it is an illusion to think that we can so ignore that need, and so cauterize our souls, that we will never again be troubled by it.

Indeed, the debunking imperative operates on the basis of its own myth. It presumes the existence of a solid and orderly substratum, a rock-solid reality lying just beneath the illusory surfaces, waiting to be revealed in all its direct and unfeigned honesty when the facades and artifices and false divisions are all stripped away. There is a remarkable complacency and naiveté about such a view. The near-universal presumption that the demise of the nation-state and the rise of international governance would be very good things has everything, except a shred of evidence, to support it. And as for the debunking of bourgeois morality that still passes for sophistication in some quarters and has been the stock-in-trade of Western intellectuals for almost two centuries now—well, this has always been a form of moral free-riding, like the radical posturing of adolescents who always know they can call Mom when they get into trouble.

⌘

One residue of the debunking heritage is the curious assumption that narratives of foundings are mere fairy tales—prettified, antiseptic flights of fancy, or wish-fulfillment fantasies, telling of superlative heroes and maidens acting nobly and virtuously to bring forth the status quo or its antecedents. I think it's fair to say that foundational narratives, including creation myths, tend to be conservative in character, in the sense that they tend to provide historical and moral support for existing regimes and social arrangements. It's hard to imagine them being any other way. But the part about their being prettifying fairy tales is demonstrably wrong. In fact, one could say that the most amazing feature of the great foundational myths is their moral complexity.

One need not even consider the appalling creation myths of Greek antiquity, such as the story of Kronos, who castrated his father Ouranos with a sickle given him by his mother, and then, in order to protect himself against the same dismal fate, swallowed his own children until his youngest child, Zeus, also aided by his mother, was able to overthrow him and assume primacy among the gods.

Consider instead the great Biblical stories of the Pentateuch, foundational texts not only for the Jewish people but for the entire family of monotheistic Abrahamic religious faiths—which is to say, those faiths that have been most constitutive of Western civilization. These Biblical texts are anything but tracts of unrelieved patriotism. In fact, one would be justified in seeing them as an exercise in collective self-humiliation. They are replete with the disreputable deeds of their imperfect and dissembling patriarchs, who pawn off their wives as sisters, deceive their fathers, cheat their brothers, murder, and commit incest—together with tales of an incorrigibly feckless people, the people of Israel, sheep-like fools who manage to forget every theophany and divine favor shown them, and prove unable and unwilling to follow the law that has been given to them.

The narrative does not blink at those things. It is itself the harshest critic of the things it describes, and every one of its human heroes is presented as deeply flawed. But what holds all this together is not the greatness of the heroes but the enduring quality of God's successive covenants with them and with His people. The God of the Hebrew Bible makes promises and keeps them, operating through covenants and laws that superintend and take precedence over the force of passing events. In that sense, the complexity of the Biblical account registers, in a remarkably accurate way, the same set of moral directives regarding the authority of the past—and the elements of pain and suffering and shame in that past—that goes into the making of any durable founding. The Passover seder, which is also the template for the Christian gospel story, is not a story of heroic triumph but of deliverance from slavery by a promise-keeping Deity. . . .

Perhaps the most interesting question about these foundational stories is why they are so complex. And the answer is surely to be found in the complexity of the mythic dimension itself, the ways in which it can register and mirror and instruct a civilization, precisely by virtue of its being a rich and truthful narrative that is widely shared. This quality can be neglected in an overly politicized or rationalized age, which wants to see the play of tangible and measurable material interests or causes always at the bottom of things. And it certainly eludes a culture that has ceased to understand the human necessity of looking backward.

⋅◆⋅

Human knowledge about human affairs always has a reflexive quality about it. It is never a matter of the tree falling unheard and unwitnessed in the forest. There is always someone listening and watching, always a feedback effect—and most prophecies tend to be either self-fulfilled or self-averted. The best social scientists understand this perfectly well (after all, they were the ones who gave us the term "self-fulfilling prophecy"), but they give us such knowledge in a vocabulary and form that are often all but self-subverting. Who, after all, wants to embrace a myth while *calling* it a myth?

But to do so may be preferable to the alternative of nineteenth-century positivism, so long as we are able to proceed with a capacious understanding of "myth," as something more than a mere tall tale, something that can be both life-giving and true. In this connection, there may be particular value in revisiting Ernest Renan's celebrated 1882 essay "What is a Nation?", a rich evocation of the nation's mythic dimension. For Renan, a nation was fundamentally "a soul, a spiritual principle," constituted not only by "present-day consent" but also by the residuum of the past, "the possession in common of a rich legacy of memories" which form in the citizen "the will to perpetuate the value of the heritage that one has received in an undivided form." He declared:

> The nation, like the individual, is the culmination of a long past of endeavors, sacrifice, and devotion. Of all cults, that of the ancestors is the most legitimate, for the ancestors have made us what we are. A heroic past, great men, glory (by which I understand genuine glory), this is the social capital upon which one bases a national idea. To have common glories in the past and

to have a common will in the present, to have performed great deeds together, to wish to perform still more—these are the essential conditions for being a people. . . . A nation is therefore a large-scale solidarity, constituted by the feeling of the sacrifices that one has made in the past and of those that one is prepared to make in the future.

Renan strongly opposed the then-fashionable view that nations should be understood as entities united by racial or linguistic or geographical or religious or material factors. None of those factors were sufficient to account for the emergence of this "spiritual principle." Active consent had to be a part of it. But it was insufficient without the presence of the past—the past in which that consent was embedded and through which it found meaning.

The ballast of the past, and our intimate connection to it, is similarly indispensable to the sense of American national identity. It forms a strain in our identity that is in some respects far less articulate (and less frequently articulated) than the universalistic principles that some writers have emphasized, precisely because it seems to conflict with American assertions of universalism, and its intellectual basis is less well-defined. But it is every bit as powerful, if not more so, and just as indispensable. And it is a very *particular* force. Our nation's particular triumphs, sacrifices, and sufferings—and our memories of those things—draw and hold us together, precisely because they are the sacrifices and sufferings, not of all humanity, but of us in particular.

No one has spoken of American national identity with greater mastery than Abraham Lincoln. In his 1838 speech on "The Perpetuation of Our Political Institutions," delivered to the Young Men's Lyceum of Springfield, Illinois, Lincoln responded to the then-raging violence directed at blacks and abolitionists in Southern and border states with an admonition that could have come from Toynbee: "If destruction be our lot, we must ourselves be its author and finisher. As a nation of freemen, we must live through all time, or die by suicide." The danger he most feared was that rampant lawlessness would dissolve the "attachment of the People" to their government. And the answer he provides to this danger is remarkable for the way it touches on the same themes that Renan recounts:

> Let every American, every lover of liberty, every well wisher to his posterity, swear by the blood of the Revolution, never to violate in the least particular, the laws of the country; and never to tolerate their violation by others. As the patriots of seventy-six did to the support of the Declaration of Independence, so to the support of the Constitution and Laws, let every American pledge his life, his property, and his sacred honor;—let every man remember that to violate the law, is to trample on the blood of his father, and to tear the character of his own, and his children's liberty. Let reverence for the laws, be breathed by every American mother, to the lisping babe, that prattles on her lap—let it be taught in schools, in seminaries, and in colleges;—let it be written in Primmers, spelling books, and in Almanacs;—let it be preached from the pulpit, proclaimed in legislative halls, and enforced in courts of justice. And, in short, let it become the

> political religion of the nation; and let the old and the young, the rich and the poor, the grave and the gay, of all sexes and tongues, and colors and conditions, sacrifice unceasingly upon its altars.

The excerpt shows Lincoln's remarkable ability to intertwine the past and the present, and evoke a sense of connection between them. The speech performs the classic republican move, back to the founding origins, connecting the public order explicitly with something so primal as a son's love of, and respect for, his father. Obedience to the law and reverence for the Constitution—these are directly connected with memory, the reverence owed to the sufferings of the patriot generation, and the blood of one's own father. Such words gesture toward his even more famous invocation of "the mystic chords of memory" in his First Inaugural Address, chords "stretching from every battlefield and patriot grave to every living heart and hearthstone all over this broad land," chords that provide the music of the Union. He performs a similar move of memorial linkage in the Gettysburg Address, beginning with the Founding Fathers and ending with a rededication and recommitment, drawn from knowledge of the "honored dead" who hallowed the ground with their sacrifice.

It is pointless to ask whether such a vision of the Union reflects an "objective" reality. The mythic reality on which such rhetoric depends, and which it helps to create and sustain, is powerful in its own right, too compelling to be dismissed or deconstructed into the language of "state formation" or "cultural hegemony." You could say that the antiseptic scholarly language offers insights that Lincoln cannot give us, and you would be right. But you could also say that Lincoln's reverent and hortatory language offers insights that the antiseptic scholars cannot provide, and you would be equally right. The real question is which language tells us more, and for what purposes.

A belief in the particularly instructive and sustaining qualities of the American Founding does not depend on a belief in the moral perfection of the Founders themselves, or the presumption that they were completely pure and disinterested regarding the measures they sought, or that they were invariably wise or prudent or far-sighted, or that they agreed in all important things, or that the Constitution they created is perfect in every way. The stories that we tell ourselves about ourselves, in order to remember who we are, should not neglect to tell us the ways we have fallen short and the ways we have suffered, both needfully and needlessly, by necessity or by chance.

We should not try to edit out those stories' strange moral complexity, because it is there for a reason. Indeed, it is precisely our encounter with the surprise of their strangeness that reminds us of how much we have yet to learn from them.

The Power and the Glory: Myths of American Exceptionalism

The notion of American exceptionalism—that the United States alone has the right, whether by divine sanction or moral obligation, to bring civilization, or democracy, or liberty to the rest of the world, by violence if necessary—is not new. It started as early as 1630 in the Massachusetts Bay Colony when Governor John Winthrop uttered the words that centuries later would be quoted by Ronald Reagan. Winthrop called the Massachusetts Bay Colony a "city upon a hill." Reagan embellished a little, calling it a "shining city on a hill."

The idea of a city on a hill is heartwarming. It suggests what George Bush has spoken of: that the United States is a beacon of liberty and democracy. People can look to us and learn from and emulate us.

In reality, we have never been just a city on a hill. A few years after Governor Winthrop uttered his famous words, the people in the city on a hill moved out to massacre the Pequot Indians. Here's a description by William Bradford, an early settler, of Captain John Mason's attack on a Pequot village.

> Those that escaped the fire were slain with the sword, some hewed to pieces, others run through with their rapiers, so as they were quickly dispatched and very few escaped. It was conceived that they thus destroyed about 400 at this time. It was a fearful sight to see them thus frying in the fire and the streams of blood quenching the same, and horrible was the stink and scent thereof; but the victory seemed a sweet sacrifice, and they gave the praise thereof to God, who had wrought so wonderfully for them, thus to enclose their enemies in their hands and give them so speedy a victory over so proud and insulting an enemy.

The kind of massacre described by Bradford occurs again and again as Americans march west to the Pacific and south to the Gulf of Mexico. (In fact our celebrated war of liberation, the American Revolution, was disastrous for the Indians. Colonists had been restrained from encroaching on the Indian territory by the British and the boundary set up in their Proclamation of 1763. American independence wiped out that boundary.)

Expanding into another territory, occupying that territory, and dealing harshly with people who resist occupation has been a persistent fact of American history from the first settlements to the present day. And this was often accompanied from very early on with a particular form of American exceptionalism: the idea that American expansion is divinely ordained. On the eve of the war with Mexico in the middle of the 19th century, just after the United States annexed Texas, the editor and writer John O'Sullivan coined the famous phrase "manifest destiny." He said it was "the fulfillment of our manifest destiny to overspread the continent allotted by Providence for the free development of our yearly multiplying millions. At the beginning of the 20th century, when the United States invaded the Philippines, President McKinley said that the decision to take the Philippines came to him one night when he got down on his knees and prayed, and God told him to take the Philippines.

Invoking God has been a habit for American presidents throughout the nation's history, but George W. Bush has made a specialty of it. For an article in the Israeli newspaper *Ha'aretz*, the reporter talked with Palestinian leaders who had met with Bush. One of them reported that Bush told him, "God told me to strike at al Qaeda. And I struck them. And then he instructed me to strike at Saddam, which I did. And now I am determined to solve the problem in the Middle East." It's hard to know if the quote is authentic, especially because it is so literate. But it certainly is consistent with Bush's oft-expressed claims. A more credible story comes from a Bush supporter, Richard Lamb, the president of the Ethics and Religious Liberty Commission of the Southern Baptist Convention, who says that during the election campaign Bush told him, "I believe God wants me to be president. But if that doesn't happen, that's okay."

Divine ordination is a very dangerous idea, especially when combined with military power (the United States has 10,000 nuclear weapons, with military bases in a hundred different countries and warships on every sea). With God's approval, you need no human standard of morality. Anyone today who claims the support of God might be embarrassed to recall that the Nazi storm troopers had inscribed on their belts, "Gott mit uns" ("God with us").

Not every American leader claimed divine sanction, but the idea persisted that the United States was uniquely justified in using its power to expand throughout the world. In 1945, at the end of World War II, Henry Luce, the owner of a vast chain of media enterprises—*Time, Life, Fortune*—declared that this would be "the American Century," that victory in the war gave the United States the right "to exert upon the world the full impact of our influence, for such purposes as we see fit and by such means as we see fit."

This confident prophecy was acted out all through the rest of the 20th century. Almost immediately after World War II the United States penetrated the oil regions of the Middle East by special arrangement with Saudi Arabia. It established military bases in Japan, Korea, the Philippines, and a number of Pacific islands. In the next decades it orchestrated right-wing coups in Iran, Guatemala, and Chile, and gave military aid to various dictatorships in the Caribbean. In an attempt to establish a foothold in Southeast Asia it invaded Vietnam and bombed Laos and Cambodia.

The existence of the Soviet Union, even with its acquisition of nuclear weapons, did not block this expansion. In fact, the exaggerated threat of "world communism" gave the United States a powerful justification for expanding all over the globe, and soon it had military bases in a hundred countries. Presumably, only the United States stood in the way of the Soviet conquest of the world.

Can we believe that it was the existence of the Soviet Union that brought about the aggressive militarism of the United States? If so, how do we explain all the violent expansion before 1917? A hundred years before the Bolshevik Revolution, American armies were annihilating Indian tribes, clearing the great expanse of the West in an early example of what we now call "ethnic cleansing." And with the continent conquered, the nation began to look overseas.

On the eve of the 20th century, as American armies moved into Cuba and the Philippines, American exceptionalism did not always mean that the United States wanted to go it alone. The nation was willing—indeed, eager—to join the small group of Western imperial powers that it would one day supersede. Senator Henry Cabot Lodge wrote at the time, "The great nations are rapidly absorbing for their future expansion, and their present defense all the waste places of the earth. . . . As one of the great nations of the world the United States must not fall out of the line of march." Surely, the nationalistic spirit in other countries has often led them to see their expansion as uniquely moral, but this country has carried the claim farthest.

American exceptionalism was never more clearly expressed than by Secretary of War Elihu Root, who in 1899 declared, "The American soldier is different from all other soldiers of all other countries since the world began. He is the advance guard of liberty and justice, of law and order, and of peace and happiness." At the time he was saying this, American soldiers in the Philippines were starting a bloodbath which would take the lives of 600,000 Filipinos.

The idea that America is different because its military actions are for the benefit of others becomes particularly persuasive when it is put forth by leaders presumed to be liberals, or progressives. For instance, Woodrow Wilson, always high on the list of "liberal" presidents, labeled both by scholars and the popular culture as an "idealist," was ruthless in his use of military power against weaker nations. He sent the navy to bombard and occupy the Mexican port of Vera Cruz in 1914 because the Mexicans had arrested some American sailors. He sent the marines into Haiti in 1915, and when the Haitians resisted, thousands were killed.

The following year American marines occupied the Dominican Republic. The occupations of Haiti and the Dominican Republic lasted many years. And Wilson, who had been elected in 1916 saying, "There is such a thing as a nation being too proud to fight," soon sent young Americans into the slaughterhouse of the European war.

Theodore Roosevelt was considered a "progressive" and indeed ran for president on the Progressive Party ticket in 1912. But he was a lover of war and a supporter of the conquest of the Philippines—he had congratulated the general who wiped out a Filipino village of 600 people in 1906. He had promulgated the 1904 "Roosevelt Corollary" to the Monroe Doctrine, which justified the occupation of small countries in the Caribbean as bringing them "stability."

During the Cold War, many American "liberals" became caught up in a kind of hysteria about the Soviet expansion, which was certainly real in Eastern Europe but was greatly exaggerated as a threat to western Europe and the United States. During the period of McCarthyism the Senate's quintessential liberal, Hubert Humphrey, proposed detention camps for suspected subversives who in times of "national emergency" could be held without trial.

After the disintegration of the Soviet Union and the end of the Cold War, terrorism replaced communism as the justification for expansion. Terrorism was real, but its threat was magnified to the point of hysteria, permitting excessive military action abroad and the curtailment of civil liberties at home.

The idea of American exceptionalism persisted as the first President Bush declared, extending Henry Luce's prediction, that the nation was about to embark on a "new American Century." Though the Soviet Union was gone, the policy of military intervention abroad did not end. The elder Bush invaded Panama and then went to war against Iraq.

The terrible attacks of September 11 gave a new impetus to the idea that the United States was uniquely responsible for the security of the world, defending us all against terrorism as it once did against communism. President George W. Bush carried the idea of American exceptionalism to its limits by putting forth in his national-security strategy the principles of unilateral war.

This was a repudiation of the United Nations charter, which is based on the idea that security is a collective matter, and that war could only be justified in self-defense. We might note that the Bush doctrine also violates the principles laid out at Nuremberg, when Nazi leaders were convicted and hanged for aggressive war, preventive war, far from self-defense.

Bush's national-security strategy and its bold statement that the United States is uniquely responsible for peace and democracy in the world has been shocking to many Americans.

But it is not really a dramatic departure from the historical practice of the United States, which for a long time has acted as an aggressor, bombing and invading other countries (Vietnam, Cambodia, Laos, Grenada, Panama, Iraq) and insisting on maintaining nuclear and non-nuclear supremacy. Unilateral military action, under the guise of prevention, is a familiar part of American foreign policy.

Sometimes bombings and invasions have been cloaked as international action by bringing in the United Nations, as in Korea, or NATO, as in Serbia, but basically our wars have been American enterprises. It was Bill Clinton's secretary of state, Madeleine Albright, who said at one point, "If possible we will act in the world multilaterally, but if necessary, we will act unilaterally." Henry Kissinger, hearing this, responded with his customary solemnity that this principle "should not be universalized." Exceptionalism was never clearer.

Some liberals in this country, opposed to Bush, nevertheless are closer to his principles on foreign affairs than they want to acknowledge. It is clear that 9/11 had a powerful psychological effect on everybody in America, and for certain liberal intellectuals a kind of hysterical reaction has distorted their ability to think clearly about our nation's role in the world.

In a recent issue of the liberal magazine *The American Prospect*, the editors write, "Today Islamist terrorists with global reach pose the greatest immediate threat to our lives and liberties. . . . When facing a substantial, immediate, and provable threat, the United States has both the right and the obligation to strike preemptively and, if need be, unilaterally against terrorists or states that support them."

Preemptively and, if need be, unilaterally; and against "states that support" terrorists, not just terrorists themselves. Those are large steps in the direction of the Bush doctrine, though the editors do qualify their support for preemption by adding that the threat must be "substantial, immediate, and provable." But when intellectuals endorse abstract principles, even with qualifications, they need to keep in mind that the principles will be applied by the people who run the U.S. government. This is all the more important to keep in mind when the abstract principle is about the use of violence by the state—in fact, about preemptively initiating the use of violence.

There may be an acceptable case for initiating military action in the face of an immediate threat, but only if the action is limited and focused directly on the threatening party—just as we might accept the squelching of someone falsely shouting "fire" in a crowded theater if that really were the situation and not some guy distributing anti-war leaflets on the street. But accepting action not just against "terrorists" (can we identify them as we do the person shouting "fire"?) but against "states that support them" invites unfocused and indiscriminate violence, as in Afghanistan, where our government killed at least 3,000 civilians in a claimed pursuit of terrorists.

It seems that the idea of American exceptionalism is pervasive across the political spectrum.

The idea is not challenged because the history of American expansion in the world is not a history that is taught very much in our educational system. A couple of years ago Bush addressed the Philippine National Assembly and said, "America is proud of its part in the great story of the Filipino people. Together our soldiers liberated the Philippines from colonial rule." The president apparently never learned the story of the bloody conquest of the Philippines.

And when the Mexican ambassador to the UN said something undiplomatic about how the United States has been treating Mexico as its "backyard" he was immediately reprimanded by then–Secretary of State Colin Powell. Powell, denying the accusation, said, "We have too much of a history that we have gone through together." (Had he not learned about the Mexican War or the military forays into Mexico?) The ambassador was soon removed from his post.

The major newspapers, television news shows, and radio talk shows appear not to know history, or prefer to forget it. There was an outpouring of praise for Bush's second inaugural speech in the press, including the so-called liberal press (*The Washington Post, The New York Times*). The editorial writers eagerly embraced Bush's words about spreading liberty in the world, as if they were ignorant of the history of such claims, as if the past two years' worth of news from Iraq were meaningless.

Only a couple of days before Bush uttered those words about spreading liberty in the world, *The New York Times* published a photo of a crouching, bleeding Iraqi girl. She was screaming. Her parents, taking her somewhere in their car, had just been shot to death by nervous American soldiers.

One of the consequences of American exceptionalism is that the U.S. government considers itself exempt from legal and moral standards accepted by other nations in the world. There is a long list of such self-exemptions: the refusal to sign the Kyoto Treaty regulating the pollution of the environment, the refusal to strengthen the convention on biological weapons. The United States has failed to join the hundred-plus nations that have agreed to ban land mines, in spite of the appalling statistics about amputations performed on children mutilated by those mines. It refuses to ban the use of napalm and cluster bombs. It insists that it must not be subject, as are other countries, to the jurisdiction of the International Criminal Court.

What is the answer to the insistence on American exceptionalism? Those of us in the United States and in the world who do not accept it must declare forcibly that the ethical norms concerning peace and human rights should be observed. It should be understood that the children of Iraq, of China, and of Africa, children everywhere in the world, have the same right to life as American children.

These are fundamental moral principles. If our government doesn't uphold them, the citizenry must. At certain times in recent history, imperial powers—the British in India and East Africa, the Belgians in the Congo, the French in Algeria, the Dutch and French in Southeast Asia, the Portuguese in Angola—have reluctantly surrendered their possessions and swallowed their pride when they were forced to by massive resistance.

Fortunately, there are people all over the world who believe that human beings everywhere deserve the same rights to life and liberty. On February 15, 2003, on the eve of the invasion of Iraq, more than ten million people in more than 60 countries around the world demonstrated against that war.

There is a growing refusal to accept U.S. domination and the idea of American exceptionalism. Recently, when the State Department issued its annual report listing countries guilty of torture and other human-rights abuses, there were indignant responses from around the world commenting on the absence of the United States from that list. A Turkish newspaper said, "There's not even mention of the incidents in Abu Ghraib prison, no mention of Guantánamo." A newspaper in Sydney pointed out that the United States sends suspects—people who have not been tried or found guilty of anything— to prisons in Morocco, Egypt, Libya, and Uzbekistan, countries that the State Department itself says use torture.

Here in the United States, despite the media's failure to report it, there is a growing resistance to the war in Iraq. Public-opinion polls show that at least half the citizenry no longer believe in the war. Perhaps most significant is that among the armed forces, and families of those in the armed forces, there is more and more opposition to it.

After the horrors of the first World War, Albert Einstein said, "Wars will stop when men refuse to fight." We are now seeing the refusal of soldiers to fight, the refusal of families to let their loved ones go to war, the insistence of the parents of high-school kids that recruiters stay away from their schools.

These incidents, occurring more and more frequently, may finally, as happened in the case of Vietnam, make it impossible for the government to continue the war, and it will come to an end.

The true heroes of our history are those Americans who refused to accept that we have a special claim to morality and the right to exert our force on the rest of the world. I think of William Lloyd Garrison, the abolitionist. On the masthead of his antislavery newspaper, *The Liberator*, were the words, "My country is the world. My countrymen are mankind."

POSTSCRIPT

Should Americans Believe in a Unique American "Mission"?

It is difficult to find much agreement between the overall views of Howard Zinn and Wilfred McClay, though both seem to share some underlying moral premises. Both would agree, for example, that it is wrong to mistreat prisoners, to massacre civilians, and to start wars without provocation, but they launch their moral arguments from very different locations. Zinn's moral premises seem to come from the eighteenth-century Enlightenment. Though claiming universal validity, its reach was limited both in time and place; it was never fully accepted outside of Western Europe and parts of North America, nor is it accepted today in large parts of the world. McClay's point of view seems to be built upon a more openly particularistic foundation: the providential foundation of America. He is no less ready than Zinn to acknowledge America's moral deviations, but he would see them as not only wrong but, in the deepest sense, un-American.

Howard Zinn's *People's History of the United States: 1492 to Present* (Harper Perennial Modern Classics, 2005) presents a more sweeping presentation of his argument here, while Stephen H. Webb make the case for a doctrine of providence in *American Providence: A Nation With a Mission* (Continuum, 2004). James H. Hutson's edited *The Founders on Religion: A Book of Quotations* (Princeton, 2005) served as the source for the quotations from the founders presented in the Introduction to this issue. Alexis de Tocqueville is credited with inventing the term "American exceptionalism," and in his classic *Democracy in America* (Knopf, 1951) he seemed to endorse the idea by stating his belief that "the people of the United States [are] that portion of the English people who are commissioned to explore the forests of the new world." Seymour Martin Lipset's *American Exceptionalism: A Double-Edged Sword* (Norton, 1997) thinks America is different not so much because of its founding narrative but because, unlike Europe, it was "born modern," with a distinct creed. Neil Baldwin, *The American Revelation: Ten Ideals That Shaped Our Country from the Puritans to the Cold War* (St. Matin's Griffin, 2006) explores the basic ideals of "fundamental Americanism," correlating them with famous Americans, from John Winthrop to George Marshall, prominently associated with them.

Samuel P. Huntington's *Who Are We?* (Simon & Schuster, 2004) highlights America's uniqueness among industrial nations today, especially in terms of its highly charged mixture of piety and patriotism. In *Hellfire Nation*, James A. Morone (Yale, 2004) finds both good and bad effects following from America's belief in its "mission"—on the one hand, utopian and reformist impulses, which he likes, and on the other hand, Victorian censoriousness, which he doesn't like.

In the 1960s the former Socialist candidate for President, Norman Thomas, admonished an angry crowd of antiwar demonstrators not to burn the flag but to wash it. Thomas was one of many critics of American policies who would insist that they love America more, not less, because they can acknowledge how far their country sometimes falls short of achieving its professed goals of "liberty and justice for all."

ISSUE 2

Is Democracy the Answer to Global Terrorism?

YES: George W. Bush, from Speech at National Defense University (March 8, 2005)

NO: F. Gregory Gause III, from "Can Democracy Stop Terrorism?" *Foreign Affairs* (September/October 2005)

ISSUE SUMMARY

YES: President George W. Bush argues that the best antidote to terrorism is the tolerance and hope generated by democracy.

NO: Political scientist Gregory Gause contends that there is no relationship between terrorism emanating from a country and the extent to which democracy is enjoyed by its citizens.

The Greek philosopher Plato characterized democracy as "an agreeable form of anarchy with plenty of variety and an equality of a peculiar kind for equals and unequals alike." Plato was contemptuous of Greek democracy because it gave equal power to citizens regardless of their intelligence, knowledge, or moral character. Until relatively recent times—in considering the merits of democracy—political thinkers have largely echoed the founder of Western philosophy. Medieval thinkers, though wary of unchecked rule by secular elites, were at least as opposed to direct rule by the people, and even during the Enlightenment Period of the eighteenth century, most major political thinkers were decidedly cool to democracy. In *The Federalist #10,* on the best kind of government for countering the dangers of a majority "faction," James Madison briefly considered what he called "pure democracy"—government by direct vote of the people. Such a governing system, he wrote, would be the worst means of controlling a majority faction because "there is nothing to check the inducements to sacrifice the weaker party or an obnoxious individual."

These concerns were still being voiced in America in the early years of the nineteenth century. But with the broadening of the suffrage, the term "democracy" acquired a more positive connotation, and by the time of Andrew Jackson's election in 1828 it was surrounded with a romantic aura.

By the end of the nineteenth century hardly anyone of importance in America questioned the ideal of democracy. If the predominant sentiment pointed anywhere, it was toward extending it. Domestically, leaders of the Progressive period sought to bring the big corporations to heel, making them more responsive to public needs and demands. Then, cautiously at first, American leaders began asking aloud whether democracy might be expanded abroad, to places still ruled by autocrats and dynastic regimes.

The question gained greater force with the outbreak of World War I in Europe, which many Americans blamed on the autocratic regimes ruling Germany and the other Central Powers. When President Woodrow Wilson finally asked Congress to declare war on them in 1917, he couched his appeal in democratic terms. "We have no quarrel with the German people," he said, "for our quarrel is only with the narrow circle of autocrats ruling Germany." Their removal was essential to the restoration of world peace, for "self-governed nations do not fill their neighbor states with spies or set the course of intrigue," permitting them to "strike and make conquest." Aggressive acts of this kind can be planned only within the narrow circles of unelected elites. "They are happily impossible where public opinion commands and insists upon full information concerning all the nation's affairs." America was to go to war, then, as a champion of the rights of mankind. Free peoples do not commit terrorist acts or aggression upon others, and so "the world must be made safe for democracy."

President George W. Bush has approached the war on terror with a somewhat similar rationale. In his Second Inaugural Address, Bush said, "The best hope for peace in the world is the expansion of freedom in the world." The theory is that terrorist groups win support from young idealists frustrated by their inability to bring about change in their countries. The classic case is Saudi Arabia, from which seventeen of the nineteen 9/11 hijackers came. There the ruling elite, stifling democracy but anxious to guard against revolution, tries to redirect the rage of militants by sponsoring Islamic clerics who turn it against the West. The belief is that we can "dry up the swamp" by encouraging the spread of democracy throughout the Middle East. If people can change their countries' policies by peaceful means they are less likely to heed the siren calls of terrorist groups.

In recent years Americans of both political parties have endorsed some version of the "dry up the swamp" theory, among them Massachusetts Senator John Kerry, Morton Halperin, President Clinton's chief State Department policy planner, and *New York Times* columnist Thomas Friedman. But it has remained for President Bush to attempt putting the theory to work. Besides seeking to establish a democratic government in Iraq, he has supported Palestinian elections and elections in Lebanon, prodded the Saudis and the Egyptians to allow greater democracy, and joined those who insisted on new elections in Ukraine in the wake of the rigged elections there.

In the following selections, President Bush spells out his theory that "the best antidote to terrorism is the tolerance and hope kindled in free societies," while political science professor F. Gregory Gause contends that there is no relationship between terrorism emanating from a country and the degree of freedom enjoyed by its citizens. He thinks that the better way to fight terror is to encourage secular, nationalist, and liberal organizations to compete with the Islamists.

President Discusses War on Terror

We meet at a time of great consequence for the security of our nation, a time when the defense of freedom requires the advance of freedom, a time with echoes in our history.

Twice in six decades, a sudden attack on the United States launched our country into a global conflict, and began a period of serious reflection on America's place in the world. The bombing of Pearl Harbor taught America that unopposed tyranny, even on far-away continents, could draw our country into a struggle for our own survival. And our reflection on that lesson led us to help build peaceful democracies in the ruins of tyranny, to unite free nations in the NATO Alliance, and to establish a firm commitment to peace in the Pacific that continues to this day.

The attacks of September the 11th, 2001 also revealed the outlines of a new world. In one way, that assault was the culmination of decades of escalating violence—from the killing of U.S. Marines in Beirut, to the bombing at the World Trade Center, to the attacks on American embassies in Africa, to the attacks on the USS Cole. In another way, September the 11th provided a warning of future dangers—of terror networks aided by outlaw regimes, and ideologies that incite the murder of the innocent, and biological and chemical and nuclear weapons that multiply destructive power.

Like an earlier generation, America is answering new dangers with firm resolve. No matter how long it takes, no matter how difficult the task, we will fight the enemy, and lift the shadow of fear, and lead free nations to victory.

Like an earlier generation, America is pursuing a clear strategy with our allies to achieve victory. Our immediate strategy is to eliminate terrorist threats abroad, so we do not have to face them here at home. The theory here is straightforward: terrorists are less likely to endanger our security if they are worried about their own security. When terrorists spend their days struggling to avoid death or capture, they are less capable of arming and training to commit new attacks. We will keep the terrorists on the run, until they have nowhere left to hide.

In three and a half years, the United States and our allies have waged a campaign of global scale—from the mountains of Afghanistan, to the border regions of Pakistan, to the Horn of Africa, to the islands of the Philippines, to the plains of North Central Iraq. The al Qaeda terror network that attacked our country still has leaders, but many of its top commanders have been

From a Speech at the National Defense University, March 8, 2005.

removed. There are still governments that sponsor and harbor terrorists, but their number has declined. There are still regimes seeking weapons of mass destruction—but no longer without attention and without consequence. Our country is still the target of terrorists who want to kill many, and intimidate us all. We will stay on the offensive against them, until the fight is won.

. . . The advance of hope in the Middle East requires new thinking in the region. By now it should be clear that authoritarian rule is not the wave of the future; it is the last gasp of a discredited past. It should be clear that free nations escape stagnation, and grow stronger with time, because they encourage the creativity and enterprise of their people. It should be clear that economic progress requires political modernization, including honest representative government and the rule of law. And it should be clear that no society can advance with only half of its talent and energy—and that demands the full participation of women.

The advance of hope in the Middle East also requires new thinking in the capitals of great democracies—including Washington, D.C. By now it should be clear that decades of excusing and accommodating tyranny, in the pursuit of stability, have only led to injustice and instability and tragedy. It should be clear that the advance of democracy leads to peace, because governments that respect the rights of their people also respect the rights of their neighbors. It should be clear that the best antidote to radicalism and terror is the tolerance and hope kindled in free societies. And our duty is now clear: For the sake of our long-term security, all free nations must stand with the forces of democracy and justice that have begun to transform the Middle East.

Encouraging democracy in that region is a generational commitment. It's also a difficult commitment, demanding patience and resolve—when the headlines are good and when the headlines aren't so good. Freedom has determined enemies, who show no mercy for the innocent, and no respect for the rules of warfare. Many societies in the region struggle with poverty and illiteracy, many rulers in the region have longstanding habits of control; many people in the region have deeply ingrained habits of fear.

For all these reasons, the chances of democratic progress in the broader Middle East have seemed frozen in place for decades. Yet at last, clearly and suddenly, the thaw has begun. The people of Afghanistan have embraced free government, after suffering under one of the most backward tyrannies on earth. The voters in Iraq defied threats of murder, and have set their country on a path to full democracy. The people of the Palestinian Territories cast their ballots against violence and corruption of the past. And any who doubt the appeal of freedom in the Middle East can look to Lebanon, where the Lebanese people are demanding a free and independent nation. In the words of one Lebanese observer, "Democracy is knocking at the door of this country and, if it's successful in Lebanon, it is going to ring the doors of every Arab regime."

Across the Middle East, a critical mass of events is taking that region in a hopeful new direction. Historic changes have many causes, yet these changes have one factor in common. A businessman in Beirut recently said, "We have removed the mask of fear. We're not afraid anymore." Pervasive fear is the foundation of every dictatorial regime—the prop that holds up all power not based on consent. And when the regime of fear is broken, and the people find their courage and find their voice, democracy is their goal, and tyrants, themselves, have reason to fear.

History is moving quickly, and leaders in the Middle East have important choices to make. The world community, including Russia and Germany and France and Saudi Arabia and the United States has presented the Syrian government with one of those choices—to end its nearly 30-year occupation of Lebanon, or become even more isolated from the world. The Lebanese people have heard the speech by the Syrian president. They've seen these delaying tactics and half-measures before. The time has come for Syria to fully implement Security Council Resolution 1559. All Syrian military forces and intelligence personnel must withdraw before the Lebanese elections, for those elections to be free and fair.

The elections in Lebanon must be fully and carefully monitored by international observers. The Lebanese people have the right to determine their future, free from domination by a foreign power. The Lebanese people have the right to choose their own parliament this spring, free of intimidation. And that new government will have the help of the international community in building sound political, economic, and military institutions, so the great nation of Lebanon can move forward in security and freedom.

Today I have a message for the people of Lebanon: All the world is witnessing your great movement of conscience. Lebanon's future belongs in your hands, and by your courage, Lebanon's future will be in your hands. The American people are on your side. Millions across the earth are on your side. The momentum of freedom is on your side, and freedom will prevail in Lebanon.

America and other nations are also aware that the recent terrorist attack in Tel Aviv was conducted by a radical Palestinian group headquartered in Damascus. Syria, as well as Iran, has a long history of supporting terrorist groups determined to sow division and chaos in the Middle East, and there is every possibility they will try this strategy again. The time has come for Syria and Iran to stop using murder as a tool of policy, and to end all support for terrorism.

In spite of attacks by extremists, the world is seeing hopeful progress in the Israel-Palestinian conflict. There is only one outcome that will end the tyranny, danger, violence and hopelessness, and meet the aspirations of all people in the region: We seek two democratic states, Israel and Palestine, living side-by-side in peace and security.

And that goal is within reach, if all the parties meet their responsibilities and if terrorism is brought to an end. Arab states must end incitement in their own media, cut off public and private funding for terrorism, stop their support for extremist education, and establish normal relations with Israel. Israel must freeze settlement activity, help the Palestinians build a thriving economy, and ensure that a new Palestinian state is truly viable, with contiguous territory on the West Bank. Palestinian leaders must fight corruption, encourage free enterprise, rest true authority with the people, and actively confront terrorist groups.

The bombing in Tel Aviv is a reminder that the fight against terrorists is critical to the search for peace and for Palestinian statehood. In an interview last week, Palestinian President Abbas strongly condemned the terrorist attack in Tel Aviv, declaring, "Ending violence and security chaos is first and foremost a Palestinian interest." He went on to say, "We cannot build the foundations of a state without the rule of law and public order."

President Abbas is correct. And so the United States will help the Palestinian Authority build the security services that current peace and future statehood require: security forces which are effective, responsive to civilian control, and dedicated to fighting terror and upholding the rule of law. We will coordinate with the government of Israel, with neighbors such as Egypt and Jordan, and with other donors to ensure that Palestinians get the training and equipment they need. The United States is determined to help the parties remove obstacles to progress and move forward in practical ways, so we can seize this moment for peace in the Holy Land.

In other parts of the Middle East, we're seeing small but welcome steps. Saudi Arabia's recent municipal elections were the beginning of reform that may allow greater participation in the future. Egypt has now—has now the prospect of competitive, multi-party elections for President in September. Like all free elections, these require freedom of assembly, multiple candidates, free access by those candidates to the media, and the right to form political parties. Each country in the Middle East will take a different path of reform. And every nation that starts on that journey can know that America will walk at its side.

Progress in the Middle East is threatened by weapons of mass destruction and their proliferation. Today, Great Britain, France, and Germany are involved in a difficult negotiation with Iran aimed at stopping its nuclear weapons program. We want our allies to succeed, because we share the view that Iran's acquisition of nuclear weapons would be destabilizing and threatening to all of Iran's neighbors. The Iranian regime should listen to the concerns of the world, and listen to the voice of the Iranian people, who long for their liberty and want their country to be a respected member of the international community. We look forward to the day when Iran joins in the hopeful changes taking place across the region. We look forward to the day when the Iranian people are free.

Iran and other nations have an example in Iraq. The recent elections have begun a process of debate and coalition building unique in Iraqi history, and it's inspiring to see. Iraq's leaders are forming a government that will oversee the next—and critical—stage in Iraq's political transition: the writing of a permanent constitution. This process must take place without external influence. The shape of Iraq's democracy must be determined by the Iraqis, themselves.

Iraq's democracy, in the long run, must also be defended by Iraqis, themselves. Our goal is to help Iraqi security forces move toward self-reliance, and they are making daily progress. Iraqi forces were the main providers of security at about 5,000 polling places in the January elections. Our coalition is providing equipment and training to the new Iraqi military, yet they bring a spirit all of their own.

Last month, when soldiers of the U.S. 7th Cavalry Regiment were on combat patrol north of Baghdad, one of their Humvees fell into a canal, and Iraqi troops came to their rescue—plunging into the water again and again, until the last American was recovered. The Army colonel in charge of the unit said, "When I saw those Iraqis in the water, fighting to save their American brothers, I saw a glimpse of the future of this country." One of the Iraqi soldiers commented, "These people have come a hundred—10,000 miles to help my country. They've left their families and their children. If we can give them something back, just a little, we can show our thanks." America is proud to defend freedom in Iraq, and proud to stand with the brave Iraqis as they defend their own freedom.

Three and a half years ago, the United States mourned our dead, gathered our resolve, and accepted a mission. We made a decision to stop threats to the American people before they arrive on our shores, and we have acted on that decision. We're also determined to seek and support the growth of democratic movements and institutions in every nation and culture, with the ultimate goal of ending tyranny in our world.

This objective will not be achieved easily, or all at once, or primarily by force of arms. We know that freedom, by definition, must be chosen, and that the democratic institutions of other nations will not look like our own. Yet we also know that our security increasingly depends on the hope and progress of other nations now simmering in despair and resentment. And that hope and progress is found only in the advance of freedom.

This advance is a consistent theme of American strategy—from the Fourteen Points, to the Four Freedoms, to the Marshall Plan, to the Reagan Doctrine. Yet the success of this approach does not depend on grand strategy alone. We are confident that the desire for freedom, even when repressed for generations, is present in every human heart. And that desire can emerge with sudden power to change the course of history.

Americans, of all people, should not be surprised by freedom's power. A nation founded on the universal claim of individual rights should not be surprised when other people claim those rights. Those who place their hope in freedom may be attacked and challenged, but they will not ultimately be disappointed, because freedom is the design of humanity and freedom is the direction of history.

In our time, America has been attacked. America has been challenged. Yet the uncertainty, and sorrow, and sacrifice of these years have not been in vain. Millions have gained their liberty; and millions more have gained the hope of liberty that will not be denied. The trumpet of freedom has been sounded, and that trumpet never calls retreat.

Before history is written in books, it is written in courage—the courage of honorable soldiers; the courage of oppressed peoples; the courage of free nations in difficult tasks. Our generation is fortunate to live in a time of courage. And we are proud to serve in freedom's cause.

May God bless you all.

F. Gregory Gause III  **NO**

Can Democracy Stop Terrorism?

What Freedom Brings

The United States is engaged in what President George W. Bush has called a "generational challenge" to instill democracy in the Arab world. The Bush administration and its defenders contend that this push for Arab democracy will not only spread American values but also improve U.S. security. As democracy grows in the Arab world, the thinking goes, the region will stop generating anti-American terrorism. Promoting democracy in the Middle East is therefore not merely consistent with U.S. security goals; it is necessary to achieve them.

But this begs a fundamental question: Is it true that the more democratic a country becomes, the less likely it is to produce terrorists and terrorist groups? In other words, is the security rationale for promoting democracy in the Arab world based on a sound premise? Unfortunately, the answer appears to be no. Although what is known about terrorism is admittedly incomplete, the data available do not show a strong relationship between democracy and an absence of or a reduction in terrorism. Terrorism appears to stem from factors much more specific than regime type. Nor is it likely that democratization would end the current campaign against the United States. Al Qaeda and like-minded groups are not fighting for democracy in the Muslim world; they are fighting to impose their vision of an Islamic state. Nor is there any evidence that democracy in the Arab world would "drain the swamp," eliminating soft support for terrorist organizations among the Arab public and reducing the number of potential recruits for them.

Even if democracy were achieved in the Middle East, what kind of governments would it produce? Would they cooperate with the United States on important policy objectives besides curbing terrorism, such as advancing the Arab-Israeli peace process, maintaining security in the Persian Gulf, and ensuring steady supplies of oil? No one can predict the course a new democracy will take, but based on public opinion surveys and recent elections in the Arab world, the advent of democracy there seems likely to produce new Islamist governments that would be much less willing to cooperate with the United States than are the current authoritarian rulers.

The answers to these questions should give Washington pause. The Bush administration's democracy initiative can be defended as an effort to spread American democratic values at any cost, or as a long-term gamble that even if

Reprinted by permission of *Foreign Affairs*, September/October 2005, pp. 62–76. Copyright © 2005 by the Council on Foreign Relations, Inc.

Islamists do come to power, the realities of governance will moderate them or the public will grow disillusioned with them. The emphasis on electoral democracy will not, however, serve immediate U.S. interests either in the war on terrorism or in other important Middle East policies.

It is thus time to rethink the U.S. emphasis on democracy promotion in the Arab world. Rather than push for quick elections, the United States should instead focus its energy on encouraging the development of secular, nationalist, and liberal political organizations that could compete on an equal footing with Islamist parties. Only by doing so can Washington help ensure that when elections finally do occur, the results are more in line with U.S. interests.

The Missing Link

President Bush has been clear about why he thinks promoting democracy in the Arab world is central to U.S. interests. "Our strategy to keep the peace in the longer term," Bush said in a speech in March 2005,

> is to help change the conditions that give rise to extremism and terror, especially in the broader Middle East. Parts of that region have been caught for generations in a cycle of tyranny and despair and radicalism. When a dictatorship controls the political life of a country, responsible opposition cannot develop, and dissent is driven underground and toward the extreme. And to draw attention away from their social and economic failures, dictators place blame on other countries and other races, and stir the hatred that leads to violence. This status quo of despotism and anger cannot be ignored or appeased, kept in a box or bought off.

. . . The numbers published by the U.S. government do not bear out claims of a close link between terrorism and authoritarianism either. Between 2000 and 2003, according to the State Department's annual "Patterns of Global Terrorism" report, 269 major terrorist incidents around the world occurred in countries classified as "free" by Freedom House, 119 occurred in "partly free" countries, and 138 occurred in "not free" countries. (This count excludes both terrorist attacks by Palestinians on Israel, which would increase the number of attacks in democracies even more, and the September 11, 2001, attacks on the United States, which originated in other countries.) This is not to argue that free countries are more likely to produce terrorists than other countries. Rather, these numbers simply indicate that there is no relationship between the incidence of terrorism in a given country and the degree of freedom enjoyed by its citizens. They certainly do not indicate that democracies are substantially less susceptible to terrorism than are other forms of government.

Terrorism, of course, is not distributed randomly. According to official U.S. government data, the vast majority of terrorist incidents occurred in only a few countries. Indeed, half of all the terrorist incidents in "not free" countries in 2003 took place in just two countries: Iraq and Afghanistan. It seems that democratization did little to discourage terrorists from operating there and may even have encouraged terrorism.

As for the "free" countries, terrorist incidents in India accounted for fully 75 percent of the total. It is fair to assume that groups based in Pakistan carried out a number of those attacks, particularly in Kashmir, but clearly not all the perpetrators were foreigners. A significant number of terrorist events in India took place far from Kashmir, reflecting other local grievances against the central government. And as strong and vibrant as Indian democracy is, both a sitting prime minister and a former prime minister have been assassinated— Indira Gandhi and her son, Rajiv Gandhi, respectively. If democracy reduced the prospects for terrorism, India's numbers would not be so high.

Comparing India, the world's most populous democracy, and China, the world's most populous authoritarian state, highlights the difficulty of assuming that democracy can solve the terrorism problem. For 2000–2003, the "Patterns of Global Terrorism" report indicates 203 international terrorist attacks in India and none in China. A list of terrorist incidents between 1976 and 2004, compiled by the National Memorial Institute for the Prevention of Terrorism, shows more than 400 in India and only 18 in China. Even if China underreports such incidents by a factor of ten, it still endures substantially fewer terrorist attacks than India. If the relationship between authoritarianism and terrorism were as strong as the Bush administration implies, the discrepancy between the number of terrorist incidents in China and the number in India would run the other way. . . .

There is, in other words, no solid empirical evidence for a strong link between democracy, or any other regime type, and terrorism, in either a positive or a negative direction. In her highly praised post-September 11 study of religious militants, *Terror in the Name of God,* Jessica Stern argues that "democratization is not necessarily the best way to fight Islamic extremism," because the transition to democracy "has been found to be an especially vulnerable period for states across the board." Terrorism springs from sources other than the form of government of a state. There is no reason to believe that a more democratic Arab world will, simply by virtue of being more democratic, generate fewer terrorists.

Flawed

There are also logical problems with the argument supporting the U.S. push for democracy as part of the war on terrorism. Underlying the assertion that democracy will reduce terrorism is the belief that, able to participate openly in competitive politics and have their voices heard in the public square, potential terrorists and terrorist sympathizers would not need to resort to violence to achieve their goals. Even if they lost in one round of elections, the confidence that they could win in the future would inhibit the temptation to resort to extra-democratic means. The habits of democracy would ameliorate extremism and focus the anger of the Arab publics at their own governments, not at the United States.

Well, maybe. But it is just as logical to assume that terrorists, who rarely represent political agendas that could mobilize electoral majorities, would reject the very principles of majority rule and minority rights on which liberal democracy is based. If they could not achieve their goals through democratic politics, why would they privilege the democratic process over those goals? It seems more likely that, having been mobilized to participate in the democratic process by a burning desire to achieve particular goals—a desire so strong that they were willing to commit acts of violence against defenseless civilians to realize it— terrorists and potential terrorists would attack democracy if it did not produce their desired results. Respect for the nascent Iraqi democracy, despite a very successful election in January 2005, has not stopped Iraqi and foreign terrorists from their campaign against the new political order.

Terrorist organizations are not mass-based organizations. They are small and secretive. They are not organized or based on democratic principles. They revolve around strong leaders and a cluster of committed followers who are willing to take actions from which the vast majority of people, even those who might support their political agenda, would rightly shrink. It seems unlikely that simply being out voted would deflect them from their path.

The United States' major foe in the war on terrorism, al Qaeda, certainly would not close up shop if every Muslim country in the world were to become a democracy. Osama bin Laden has been very clear about democracy: he does not like it. His political model is the early Muslim caliphate. In his view, the Taliban regime in Afghanistan came the closest in modern times to that model. In an October 2003 "message to Iraqis," bin Laden castigated those in the Arab world who are "calling for a peaceful democratic solution in dealing with apostate governments or with Jewish and crusader invaders instead of fighting in the name of God." He referred to democracy as "this deviant and misleading practice" and "the faith of the ignorant." Bin Laden's ally in Iraq, Abu Musab al-Zarqawi, reacted to the January 2005 Iraqi election even more directly: "The legislator who must be obeyed in a democracy is man, and not God. . . . That is the very essence of heresy and polytheism and error, as it contradicts the bases of the faith and monotheism, and because it makes the weak, ignorant man God's partner in His most central divine prerogative—namely, ruling and legislating."

Al Qaeda's leaders distrust democracy, and not just on ideological grounds: they know they could not come to power through free elections. There is no reason to believe that a move toward more democracy in Arab states would deflect them from their course. And there is no reason to believe that they could not recruit followers in more democratic Arab states—especially if those states continued to have good relations with the United States, made peace with Israel, and generally behaved in ways acceptable to Washington. Al Qaeda objects to the U.S. agenda in the Middle East as much as, if not more than, democracy. If, as Washington hopes, a democratic Middle East continued to accept a major U.S. role in the region and cooperate with U.S. goals, it is foolish to think that democracy would end Arab anti-Americanism and dry up passive support, funding sources, and recruiting channels for al Qaeda.

When it works, liberal democracy is the best form of government. But there is no evidence that it reduces or prevents terrorism. The fundamental assumption of the Bush administration's push for democracy in the Arab world is seriously flawed.

Angry Voices

It is highly unlikely that democratically elected Arab governments would be as cooperative with the United States as the current authoritarian regimes. To the extent that public opinion can be measured in these countries, research shows that Arabs strongly support democracy. When they have a chance to vote in real elections, they generally turn out in percentages far greater than Americans do in their elections. But many Arabs hold negative views of the United States. If Arab governments were democratically elected and more representative of public opinion, they would thus be more anti-American. Further democratization in the Middle East would, for the foreseeable future, most likely generate Islamist governments less inclined to cooperate with the United States on important U.S. policy goals, including military basing rights in the region, peace with Israel, and the war on terrorism. . . .

The problem with promoting democracy in the Arab world is not that Arabs do not like democracy; it is that Washington probably would not like the governments Arab democracy would produce. Assuming that democratic Arab governments would better represent the opinions of their people than do the current Arab regimes, democratization of the Arab world should produce more anti-U.S. foreign policies. In a February–March 2003 poll conducted in six Arab countries by Zogby International and the Anwar Sadat Chair for Peace and Development at the University of Maryland, overwhelming majorities of those surveyed held either a very unfavorable or a somewhat unfavorable attitude toward the United States. The Lebanese viewed the United States most favorably, with 32 percent of respondents holding a very favorable or a somewhat favorable view of the United States. Only 4 percent of Saudi respondents said the same.

The war in Iraq—which was imminent or ongoing as the poll was conducted—surely affected these numbers. But these statistics are not that different from those gathered by less comprehensive polls conducted both before and after the war. In a Gallup poll in early 2002, strong majorities of those surveyed in Jordan (62 percent) and Saudi Arabia (64 percent) rated the United States unfavorably. Only in Lebanon did positive views of the United States roughly balance negative views. In a Zogby International poll conducted in seven Arab countries at about the same time, unfavorable ratings of the United States ranged from 48 percent in Kuwait to 61 percent in Jordan, 76 percent in Egypt, and 87 percent in Saudi Arabia and the UAE. One year after the war began, a Pew Global Attitudes poll showed that 93 percent of Jordanians and 68 percent of Moroccans had a negative attitude toward the United States. . . .

The trend is clear: Islamists of various hues score well in free elections. In countries where a governing party dominates or where the king opposes political Islam, Islamists run second and form the opposition. Only in Morocco, where more secular, leftist parties have a long history and an established presence, and in Lebanon, where the Christian-Muslim dynamic determines electoral politics, did organized non-Islamist political blocs, independent of the government, compete with Islamist forces. The pattern does not look like it is about to change. According to the 2004 Zogby International-Sadat Chair poll, pluralities of those surveyed in Jordan, Saudi Arabia, and the UAE said the clergy should play a greater role in their political systems. Fifty percent of Egyptians polled said the clerics should not dictate the political system, but as many as 47 percent supported a greater role for them. Only in Morocco and Lebanon did anticlerical sentiment dominate pro-clerical feelings—51 percent to 33 percent in Morocco and 50 percent to 28 percent in Lebanon. The more democratic the Arab world gets, the more likely it is that Islamists will come to power. Even if those Islamists come to accept the rules of democracy and reject political violence, they are unlikely to support U.S. foreign policy goals in the region.

The Long Haul

The Bush administration's push for democracy in the Arab world is unlikely to have much effect on anti-American terrorism emanating from there; it could in fact help bring to power governments much less cooperative on a whole range of issues—including the war on terrorism—than the current regimes. Unfortunately, there is no good alternative at this point to working with the authoritarian Arab governments that are willing to work with the United States.

If Washington insists on promoting democracy in the Arab world, it should learn from the various electoral experiences in the region. Where there are strongly rooted non-Islamist parties, as in Morocco, the Islamists have a harder time dominating the field. The same is true in non-Arab Turkey, where the Islamist political party has moderated its message over time to contend with the power of the secular army and with well-established, more secular parties. Likewise, the diverse confessional mix of voters in Lebanon will probably prevent Hezbollah and other Islamists from dominating elections there. Conversely, where non-Islamist political forces have been suppressed, as in Saudi Arabia and Bahrain, Islamist parties and candidates can command the political field. Washington should take no comfort from the success of ruling parties in Algeria, Egypt, and Yemen over Islamist challengers: once stripped of their patronage and security apparatus, ruling parties do not fare very well in democratic transitional elections.

The United States must focus on pushing Arab governments to make political space for liberal, secular, leftist, nationalist, and other non-Islamist parties to set down roots and mobilize voters. Washington should support those groups that are more likely to accept U.S. foreign policy and emulate U.S. political values. The most effective way to demonstrate that support is to openly pressure Arab regimes when they obstruct the political activity of more liberal groups—as the administration did with Egypt after the jailing of the liberal reformers Saad Eddin Ibrahim and Ayman Nour, and as it should do with Saudi Arabia regarding the May sentencing of peaceful political activists to long prison terms. But Washington will also need to drop its focus on prompt elections in Arab countries where no strong, organized alternative to Islamist parties exists—even at the risk of disappointing Arab liberals by being more cautious about their electoral prospects than they are.

Administration officials, including President Bush, have often stated that the transition to democracy in the Arab world will be difficult and that Americans should not expect quick results. Yet whenever the Bush administration publicly defends democratization, it cites a familiar litany of Muslim-world elections—those in Afghanistan, Iraq, Lebanon, the Palestinian territories, and Saudi Arabia as evidence that the policy is working. It will take years, however, for non-Islamist political forces to be ready to compete for power in these elections, and it is doubtful that this or any other U.S. administration will have the patience to see the process through. If it cannot show that patience, Washington must realize that its democratization policy will lead to Islamist domination of Arab politics.

It is not only the focus on elections that is troubling in the administration's democracy initiative in the Arab world. Also problematic is the unjustified confidence that Washington has in its ability to predict, and even direct, the course of politics in other countries. No administration official would sign on, at least not in public, to the naive view that Arab democracy will produce governments that will always cooperate with the United States. Yet Washington's democracy advocates seem to assume that Arab democratic transitions, like the recent democratic transitions in eastern Europe, Latin America, and East Asia, will lead to regimes that support, or at least do not impede, the broad range of U.S. foreign policy interests. They do not appreciate that in those regimes, liberalism prevailed because its great ideological competitor, communism, was thoroughly discredited, whereas the Arab world offers a real ideological alternative to liberal democracy: the movement that claims as its motto "Islam is the solution." Washington's hubris should have been crushed in Iraq, where even the presence of 140,000 American troops has not allowed politics to proceed according to the U.S. plan. Yet the Bush administration displays little of the humility or the patience that such a daunting task demands. If the United States really does see the democracy-promotion initiative in the Arab world as a "generational challenge," the entire nation will have to learn these traits.

POSTSCRIPT

Is Democracy the Answer to Global Terrorism?

$\mathbf{A}$l Qaeda's leaders, Gause notes, "distrust democracy, and not just on ideological grounds: they know they could not come to power through free elections." On its face, this seems to bolster President Bush's theory of democracy as a means of fighting terror. But what Gause is getting at is that, if a pro-American or pro-Israeli regime comes to power in any Islamic country, even if it does so through democratic means, al Qaeda will have no trouble recruiting new members there. This may well be true, but the question is whether democracy may finally marginalize al Qaeda once the people realize how opposed to self-rule al Qaeda really is.

In *The Future of Freedom* (Norton, 2003), Fareed Zakaria argues that unrestrained democracy threatens vital liberties and goes so far as to suggest that "what we need in politics today is not more democracy but less." In a *New Republic* essay entitled, "The Ungreat Washed," (July 7 & 14, 2001), Robert Kagan contends that in today's world, democracy is the only practical means of protecting vital liberties. In the same vein, see Michael McFaul, "The Liberty Doctrine," *Policy Review*, April 2002. Arguing the other side is Robert D. Kaplan ("Was Democracy Just a Moment?" *Atlantic Monthly,* December 1997) who insists that not all nations enjoy conditions that allow democracy to thrive, and that some are better off without it. Morton H. Halperin's *The Democratic Advantage: How Democracies Promote Peace* (Routledge, 2004) makes the case that democracy promotes industrial development and the reduction of poverty in third-world countries. Reuel Marc Gerecht (*The Islamic Paradox*, AEI Press, 2004) agrees with the critics of democratization that democracy will probably bring even more clerical domination and anti-American rhetoric to the Middle East, but that it is actually the "least dangerous option for the United States." In *Democracy* (Cambridge University Press, 2007), Charles Tilly tries to isolate the causes of democratization in the world over the last few hundred years; he thinks "trust networks" play a central role in that process. Michael Mandelbaum, *Democracy's Good Name: The Rise and Risks of the World's Most Popular Form of Government.* (PublicAffairs, 2007) blends history, political science, and sociology to make the case that democracy "works," that is, it makes countries stronger and more stable, and teaches respect for law and liberty. One difficulty in the theory of democracy as a means of fighting terror is the possibility that a democratic election could actually bring a terrorist group to power. That this is more than hypothetical was demonstrated in the Palestinian elections of February, 2006, in which Hamas, a known terrorist group, captured control of the Palestinian Authority. Those who cling to their trust in the democratic process believe that this new power may, in time, make Hamas more mature and responsible. Henceforth, its performance in ministering to the day-to-day needs of the Palestinian people—jobs, health care, garbage collection, and so on—will be measured and judged by the people themselves, and it will be rejected by them if it fails. This will leave little time for plotting terrorism. Or so it is hoped. For now, at least, it remains a hope rather than a demonstrable fact.

ISSUE 3

Should America Adopt Public Financing of Political Campaigns?

YES: Mark Green, from *Selling Out: How Big Corporate Money Buys Elections, Rams Through Legislation, and Betrays Our Democracy* (Regan Books, 2002)

NO: John Samples, from "Taxpayer Financing of Campaigns," in John Samples, ed., *Welfare for Politicians? Taxpayer Financing of Campaigns* (Cato Institute, 2005)

ISSUE SUMMARY

YES: Political activist and author Mark Green sums up his thesis in the subtitle of his book, a work that urges adoption of public financing of election campaigns in order to make politics more honest and to reduce the dependency of elected officials on selfish interests.

NO: Cato Institute director and political scientist John Samples opposes public financing of candidates for public office because it does not achieve any of the goals of its advocates and it forces voters to underwrite the financing of candidates they do not support.

$\mathbf{A}$pproximately $4 billion was spent on the 2004 presidential and congressional elections, nearly $1 billion more than in the election four years earlier. It was the most expensive election in American history, but it will almost certainly be exceeded in 2008. Internet advertising has been added on to print, radio, television, and live campaigning, resulting not in altering how the money is spent but in adding to it.

This has occurred despite the efforts of Congress to regulate and restrict campaign expenditures. In 2000, Congress established disclosure requirements for nonparty political groups known as Section 527 organizations, which were not required to register with the Federal Elections Commission because their principle purpose was alleged to be something other than influencing federal elections. In 2002, the first important revision of federal campaign finance law in more than two decades, the Bipartisan Campaign Reform Act, was adopted. The following year, the U.S. Supreme Court upheld its major provisions: the elimination of party soft money and the regulation of candidate-specific issue advertising. Nevertheless, the presidential candidacies of President George W. Bush and Senator John Kerry inspired vaster contributions and expenditures in accordance with—and sometimes in circumvention of—the law.

What is wrong with this increased spending? A great deal, say those who believe that rampant spending on political campaigns discourages less prosperous citizens from seeking elective office, diverts office-holders from doing their jobs to seeking contributions and bending their convictions to conform to those of their contributors, exaggerates the political influence of special interests, and discourages would-be voters who conclude that money matters more than their votes.

Soft money is money that is contributed not to individual campaigns but to political parties, ostensibly for the purpose of "party-building" activities, such as get-out-the-vote drives. The Federal Election Commission (FEC), an agency created in 1974, began allowing this practice in 1978, and within a decade fundraisers in both parties began to realize its usefulness as a way around existing contribution limits. Under then-existing law, "hard money" contributions (funds contributed directly to the campaigns of particular candidates) were limited to $1,000 per person for each candidate; the assumption was that no candidate can be "bought" for a mere $1,000. But unlimited soft money allowed wealthy donors and interest groups to contribute huge sums to the parties at dinners, coffees and other such gatherings—thus subtly (or not-so-subtly) reminding them of who was buttering their bread. Another concern of those who supported the new law was what they saw as the misuse of "issue advocacy" during campaigns. Interest groups had been able to get around the legal limits on contributions by pouring millions of unregulated dollars into "attack" ads that did not explicitly ask people to vote for or against a candidate. Instead, they said something like "Call Senator Smith and tell him to stop supporting polluters."

The new law sought to plug these loopholes and to bring the existing system of federal campaign finance regulation up-to-date. Among its major provisions are the following:

- A ban on soft money contributions to the national political parties.
- An increase in hard money contribution limits. For example, limits to individual candidates were increased from $1,000 to $2,000 per candidate per election. The increase was meant to take inflation into account.
- Restrictions on the ability of corporations, labor unions, and other interest groups to run "issue ads" featuring the names or likenesses of candidates within 60 days of a general election and 30 days of a primary election.

Some critics of existing campaign finance methods believe that the recent changes do not go far enough. Mark Green, in the selection that follows, concludes that nothing less than public financing of campaigns and elections will serve the public interest and further democracy. Critics of public financing maintain that these changes in the law are contrary to democracy because they use public tax money to support views that many citizens oppose. One of these critics, John Samples, argues that the changes would have a negative effect on voter participation and would limit competition.

YES

Mark Green

Change, for Good

The evidence . . . makes it clear: our campaign finance system is broken, citizens of all persuasions want change, and successful alternatives exist.

The alibis of apologists—change helps incumbents; money is speech; money doesn't buy votes—are shallow and unpersuasive. So now the defenders of the status quo have shifted to political and free-market arguments. Voters don't really care, they say; or, as Mitch McConnell argued in 2000, they assert that no candidate has ever been elected or defeated on the issue of campaign reform, and thus it can be safely ignored. Yet McConnell's Senate nemesis, John McCain, made campaign finance reform the heart and soul of his electrifying 2000 presidential campaign. Only by vastly outspending McCain did George W. Bush squeak by him in a tight primary battle that was supposed to be a coronation—and not before soft money became a dinner-table conversation staple. That same year, Maria Cantwell believes, making campaign finance reform a centerpiece of her Washington State U.S. Senate race was a major reason for her squeaker of a victory.

Senators McCain and Cantwell ran against what big money buys for special interests—tax breaks and loopholes for big corporations, weakened environmental regulations for manufacturers, and price protections for drug companies. But they also ran against what those purchases cost Americans: higher taxes, more pollution, and expensive health care, respectively.

To be successful, a pro-democracy movement like campaign finance reform cannot be merely an abstract, good-government ideal. It must be tied to the issues that Americans care most about: affordable child care, education, health care, and housing; a clean environment and safe streets; and tax rates that are fair. Do we want children with lower rates of asthma? Then we need campaign finance reform. Do we want enough funds for smaller class sizes and qualified, well-paid teachers? Then we need campaign finance reform. Do we want seniors to have access to lifesaving medicine? Then we need campaign finance reform. Do we want to keep guns out of the hands of kids and criminals? Then we need campaign finance reform. . . .

Both Republicans and Democrats came to agree that the problem with welfare was not necessarily the result of bad people but of a very bad system that—by paying more if a recipient had no work and no husband—discouraged employment and marriage. Ditto campaign finance. The sin is the *system.* How

From *Selling Out: How Big Corporate Money Buys Elections, Rams Through Legislation, and Betrays Our Democracy,* by Mark Green (2002), excerpts pp. 269–270, 276–277, 285–288. Copyright © 2002 by Mark Green. Reprinted by permission of HarperCollins Publishers.

else can we explain how such provably honorable people as John Glenn, Alan Cranston, and John McCain felt it necessary to go to bat for the likes of a big, sleazy contributor like Charles Keating?

A comprehensive campaign finance reform program is ideally suited to achieve the conservative goals on which our economy and society are built—competition, efficiency, accountability, open markets, and market integrity. Specifically, four reforms would restore our electoral democracy by elevating voters over donors: spending limits, public financing, a restructured enforcement agency, and free broadcast time and mailings.

Limits on campaign spending are an integral part of restoring our democracy; Congress understood this fact when it included expenditure limits in the 1971 and 1974 campaign finance laws. Furthermore, the experience of the last quarter century has taught us that without caps on campaign spending to complement contribution limits, money will always find ways back into the system. But as long as *Buckley v. Valeo* remains the law, the courts are likely to strike down any attempts to place limits on campaign spending.

The Court in *Buckley* concluded that expenditures did not raise the problem of corruption in the same way contributions did. The Court's conclusion is based on two critical errors: (1) subjecting expenditure limits to a higher standard than contribution limits, and (2) considering only the anticorruption rationale while dismissing the other interests.

Why should campaign expenditures be entitled to much greater constitutional protection than campaign contributions? Neither expenditures nor contributions actually are speech; both merely facilitate expressive activities. And the argument that contributions pose a greater danger of quid pro quo corruption than expenditures seems ridiculous on its face: Are we really to believe that a $2000 contribution to a candidate will create a greater sense of obligation than millions of dollars in independent expenditures for that candidate?

And what makes preventing quid pro quo corruption so much more important than any other governmental interest? Of course, it is unacceptable for public officials to sell votes, access, or influence to the highest bidder. Why? Not because of the quid pro quo–ness of it all; we exchange money for goods and services all the time in our daily lives. Rather, it is because the sale of our government undermines the most fundamental principles of our democracy: competitive elections, effective government, and—most important of all—the guarantee that our public officials answer to their true constituents, not a handful of wealthy benefactors. Quid pro quo arrangements are surely egregious violations of these democratic norms, but they are not the only ones. . . .

Until *Buckley* falls and a spending cap is found constitutional, funding limits can only be encouraged by offering public funds to candidates who voluntarily accept them. Only spending limits can end the arms race for campaign cash and reduce the power of war chests that incumbents build to scare off competition. And only the combination of spending limits and public funds can level the political playing field.

Spending limits that are set too high tend to favor incumbents, because few others can raise the resources to compete with them. Limits that are set too low, however, also favor incumbents, since challengers need to spend enough to overcome the natural advantages that accrue to incumbents through years of constituent service, free media, and use of the franking privilege. So the porridge must not be too hot or too cold. When weighing these two considerations, a third must also be taken into account: incumbents and the well-connected will not voluntarily join a public financing program if they feel its spending limits are significantly below what they could otherwise raise. If limits are too low, so too will be participation rates, and the program's purposes will be seriously compromised.

Of these three considerations, two point toward higher spending limits, which suggests that it is better to err on the side of caution. The average House winner spent $842,245 in 2000; the average candidate who challenged an incumbent spent just $143,685. In 1988, only 22 House campaigns hit the million-dollar mark; in 2000, the number reached 176. To control costs without discouraging participation or diminishing a challenger's ability to compete, House candidates should be held to inflation-adjusted spending limits of $900,000–$450,000 each for the primary and general election. A strong argument may be made that a $900,000 limit, which memorializes a level of spending that is about the current average, does not do enough to suppress campaign spending. But to undercut opponents who will use inadequate spending limits as an excuse to oppose reform, and to ensure that challengers can spend at significant levels, it is in the reform coalition's best interests to support limits around the current average cost of a winning campaign. By definition, this amount can't be too low or too high if it's the average amount it takes to win.

Senate candidates should be able to spend $1 million, plus fifty cents for each voting-age person in the state—which would come to about $8 million (for the primary and general election combined) in New York State, $7 million in Florida, $5 million in Ohio and Pennsylvania, and $2 million in Arkansas— or about one-fourth to one-half of what's recently been spent in these states. But in comparison to House contests, Senate races have higher profiles and receive significantly more media attention, making it harder for incumbents to dominate. Consequently, spending limits lower than current averages will protect challengers from the war chests that Senate incumbents can build over six years, and still ensure—because of free media coverage—that challengers will have ample opportunity to get their message out.

For instance, in Michigan's 2000 Senate race Debbie Stabenow spent $8 million in her victory over incumbent Senator Spencer Abraham, who spent $14.5 million. Under the spending-limit formula just outlined, both candidates would have been held to about $5 million. Similarly, in Pennsylvania, a $5 million limit would have helped challenger Ron Klink, who was outspent by nearly $10 million in his losing 2000 campaign against incumbent Senator Rick Santorum.

Separate limits for the primary and general election ensure that the winner of a hard-fought primary will not be placed at a disadvantage by facing a general-election opponent who suffered no primary challenge. To ensure equity, of course, candidates without primary election opponents should be allowed to spend up to the limit in the primary election period, although no public funds should be given to candidates without serious opponents, whether in primary or general elections.

A bonus provision Again, so long as *Buckley* is the constitutional standard, legislation cannot prevent the super-rich from spending tens of millions of dollars on their campaigns. We can, however, help their opponents by eliminating the spending limit. It is unfair to keep a lid on a non-rich candidate when his or her opponent effectively says the sky's the limit. . . .

The airwaves belong to us, the public. We provide broadcasters with federal licenses—for free—on the condition that they agree to serve "the public interest, convenience, and necessity." They have not lived up to their end of the bargain.

How have they gotten away with it? (You'll never guess.) The powerful broadcast industry vehemently opposes reforms affecting their bottom lines. The industry gave $6.8 million to candidates and parties in the presidential election year of 2000, with half coming in soft money. Their annual largesse has allowed them to skirt their public duty, and then some: despite a thirty-year-old law designed to hold down campaign ad rates, broadcasters routinely gouge candidates. When the Senate included a provision in McCain-Feingold to close the loophole that allows for such price gouging, the industry went on the attack, showering both parties with hard and soft money. Their efforts paid off: the House stripped the provision from Shays-Meehan and the loophole remains.

Why is the broadcast industry unwilling to live up to its public service obligations? In the 2000 elections, broadcasters pulled down revenue from political commercials that approached $1 billion. Reducing that revenue would mean cutting into profit margins that average between 30 and 50 percent. So it makes perfect business sense for the industry to invest a relatively minute amount in contributions to candidates and parties, because the payoff is astronomical. Dan O'Connor, the general sales manager of WSYT-TV in Syracuse, New York, put it this way: Ad buyers for candidates "call you up and say, 'Can you clear $40,000 [in TV ad time] next week?' It's like, 'What? Am I dreaming? Of course I can clear that!' And they send you a check in the mail overnight. It's like Santa Claus came to town. It's a beautiful thing."

Paul Taylor, executive director of the Alliance for Better Campaigns, a nonpartisan group that advocates for free airtime, sums up the scam this way: "Let's follow the bouncing ball. Our government gives broadcasters free licenses to operate on the public airwaves on the condition that they serve the public interest. During the campaign season, broadcasters turn around and sell access to these airwaves to candidates at inflated prices. Meanwhile, many candidates sell access to the government in order to raise special-interest money to purchase access to the airwaves. It's a wonderful arrangement for the broadcasters, who reap windfall profits from political campaigns. It's a good system for incumbents, who prosper in the big-dollar, high-ante political culture of paid speech. But it's a lousy deal for the rest of us."

Walter Cronkite, the iconic American newsman, is chairman of the Alliance for Better Campaigns. According to Cronkite, "In the land of free speech, we've permitted a system of 'paid speech' to take hold during the political campaigns on the one medium we all own—our broadcast airwaves. It's long past time to turn that around. Free airtime would help free our democracy from the grip of the special interests." That's the way it is, and even Senator Mitch McConnell, the self-described Darth Vader of campaign finance reform, agrees that the broadcasters are not giving the public a fair shake. And for the rest of the world, this is a no-brainer. "America is almost alone among the Atlantic democracies in declining to provide political parties free prime time on television during elections," writes historian Arthur Schlesinger Jr. "[If it did so], it could do much both to bring inordinate campaign costs under control and revitalize the political parties."

It's time for electronic consumers to negotiate a better deal with those we give free licenses to. Cronkite's alliance is pushing an innovative and market-based proposal—first discussed in a 1982 monograph from the Democracy Project, Independent Expenditures in Congressional Campaigns: The Electronic Solution—that would provide free broadcast vouchers to candidates and parties. Here's how it would work: Qualifying candidates who win their parties' nominations would receive vouchers for use in their general election campaigns. Candidates, particularly those from urban areas who don't find it cost-effective to advertise on television or radio, could trade their vouchers to their party in exchange for funds to pay for direct mail or other forms of communication. Parties, in turn, could use the vouchers themselves or give them to other candidates. The system creates a market for broadcast vouchers that, because of pricing incentives, ensures their efficient distribution.

A comprehensive campaign finance reform program should provide candidates with a right of access to the public airwaves. Until then, the alliance's voucher proposal should be restricted to those candidates who accept spending limits. Whether vouchers were used for airtime or exchanged for party monies for direct mail, candidates would report them as expenditures. Under such a system, spending limits would retain their integrity. The value of the vouchers should be set at $250,000 for House candidates and vary by population for Senate candidates, with candidates in midsize states receiving up to $2.5 million in vouchers. As in public financing, candidates should be required to reach contribution thresholds to qualify for vouchers.

One might argue that vouchers would simply encourage the proliferation of slickly produced thirty-second advertisements. Yet the reality, for better or worse, is that political commercials are part of elections in America, and there's little chance that will change. The voucher proposal bows to that reality, but it also offers hope: candidates who accept the vouchers should be required to feature their own voices in at least 50 percent of all their ads—whether paid for by vouchers, private contributions, or public funds. There is a growing public distaste for anonymous negative advertising, and candidates, given free access to the airwaves, should be held accountable for their ads.

And there are other ways to promote civic discourse. Cronkite's alliance has put forth a complement to its voucher proposal, called "Voters' Time," that would require broadcasters to air a minimum of two hours a week of candidate discussion in the month preceding every election. At least half of the programs would have to be aired in prime time or drive time, and the formats—debates, interviews, town hall meetings—would be of the broadcasters' choosing. A voters' time requirement is necessary, because broadcasters are airing less and less campaign news and candidate discourse.

In the 2000 election campaign, despite the closest presidential election in a generation, ABC, CBS, and NBC devoted 28 percent less time to campaign coverage than in 1988. In a nationwide survey conducted two days prior to the 2000 elections, more than half the population could not answer basic questions about Bush's and Gore's positions on the issues. There are many factors contributing to that result, but two of them—the domination of election by big money interests, and the unwillingness of the broadcast industry to be a part of the solution—can be cured.

Mandating free airtime for candidates and candidate discussion would appropriately hold broadcasters to a minimal standard of what it means, under the Federal Communications Commission Act, to serve "the public interest, convenience, and necessity." But this will require a committed Congress standing up to an unusually powerful industry, one that gives big contributions and confers access to voters via the airwaves.

At a minimum, two other useful methods of encouraging civic discourse and facilitating candidate communication should be part of any reform bill. First, candidates who accept public funds should be required to debate. Kentucky, New Jersey, Los Angeles, and New York City all require debates of publicly funded candidates. Especially when the public has invested its money in public campaigns, it deserves to see the candidates in public face-to-face meetings. In March 2000, Al Gore proposed that he and George W. Bush eliminate campaign television advertisements and instead hold issue debates twice a week until the elections. Bush declined, but a CBS News poll showed that voters responded positively, with 65 percent calling it a "good idea."

Second, cities like New York and Seattle mail a voters' guide to registered voters before elections. The guides include candidate statements and biographical information, as well as information on voting. New York City's guide costs fifty cents a copy to publish and mail, a bargain by any standard. The federal government should do the same. Or it could create and promote a Web-based guide to serve as a clearing-house for candidate and election information. Before voting, citizens could log on to the site, read statements for federal candidates, and find out information about their polling stations. In the age of information technology, demology, democracy should not be left behind.

John Samples    **NO**

Taxpayer Financing of Campaigns

Candidates and parties need money to fight election campaigns. In the United States, this money comes largely from individuals and groups, not the government, that is, the taxpayers. Some critics decry such private financing of politics. They argue that private donations advance special interests and corrupt politics and government. Some of them argue that government should ban private campaign contributions in favor of public financing. Since public funding comes from everyone, they reason, it actually comes from no one, thereby precluding the influence of private interests on public affairs. That argument has found few converts at the national level. States and cities have been more willing to experiment with taxpayer support for campaigns . . . .

Proponents claim government financing of campaigns servers the public interest in three ways: it advances the integrity of elections and lawmaking, promotes political equality, and fosters electoral competitiveness.

Corruption

The Supreme Court held in *Buckley v. Valeo* that the government has a compelling interest in preventing corruption or the appearance of corruption in campaigns and policymaking, an interest that may outweigh the First Amendment rights implicated in contributing to a political campaign. Allegations of corruption thus increase the probability that a law regulating campaign finance will pass constitutional muster.

Advocates of government financing claim the current system of largely private financing of campaigns fosters corruption (or its appearance) in several ways. They say campaign contributions buy favors from elected officials, the quid-pro-quo corruption noted in *Buckley*. Others say contributors receive favorable action on policies that attract little public attention and debate. Advocates also say private money fosters more subtle forms of favoritism; for example, members of Congress may allocate their time and effort in committees to help contributors. If private money corrupts, the advocates conclude, the private financing system should be abolished in favor of government financing.

In their contribution to this volume, Jeffrey Milyo and David Primo summarize the academic studies of Congress and campaign contributions,

From *Welfare for Politicians?: Taxpayer Financing of Political Campaigns*, 2005. Copyright © 2005 by Cato Institute. Reprinted by permission.

almost all of which provide little evidence to support allegations of corruption. Having surveyed the field, even Andrew Geddis, a supporter of government financing, concludes, "One obstacle is that various studies have failed to produce the sort of evidence of a strong correlation between campaign donations and a representative's public actions needed to back up suspicions of general quid pro quo understandings." Should we not have strong evidence to uproot our current system of campaign finance, especially when money is tied to the exercise of free speech?

If corruption involves using public power for private ends, government financing itself provides an example of corruption; after all, the program takes money from everyone and gives it to particular interests. One might counter with Richard Briffault's argument that government financing cannot be corrupt because tax revenue "comes from everyone, and thus, from no one in particular." But that leaves out an important part of the story. Tax money used to finance campaigns may come from everyone, but it goes predominantly, and is designed to go predominantly, to particular interests and groups within the American polity. Government subsidies for ethanol are no less corrupt because everyone pays for them and neither are government subsidies to particular candidates.

Equality

Some Americans contribute to political campaigns, but most do not. For advocates of government financing, these differences create intolerable inequalities that are "in sharp tension with the one person-one vote principle enshrined in our civic culture and our constitutional law. Public funding is necessary to bring our campaign finance system more in line with our central value of political equality." Similarly, Public Campaign, a leading organization advocating taxpayer financing, argues that private financing "violates the rights of all citizens to equal and meaningful participation in the democratic process." The principle of one person–one vote means "one man's vote in a congressional election is to be worth as much as another's" because assigning different weights to different votes in various House districts would violate Article 1, § 2 of the Constitution. The principle applies to state elections because of the equal protection clause of the 14th Amendment. Is one person–one vote thus "our central value of political equality"? A look at American institutions suggests otherwise.

The representation of states in the U.S. Senate assigns different weights to different votes in different states. Because the Electoral College also recognizes state representation, the election of the president also accords greater weight to votes in small states compared with those in large states. Moreover, the Supreme Court has not subjected judicial elections to the principle of one person–one vote.

One person–one vote applies only to voting. No American has a right to "equal and meaningful participation in the democratic process" if that means the whole of political life. In particular, the rights of association and speech set out in the First Amendment have been explicitly protected from government efforts to compel "equal . . . participation." In *Buckley*, the Supreme Court noted that federal election law sought to equalize the influence of individuals and groups over the outcome of elections. The justices demurred:

> But the concept that government may restrict the speech of some elements of our society in order to enhance the relative voice of others is wholly foreign to the First Amendment, which was designed "to secure 'the widest possible dissemination of information from diverse and antagonistic sources,'" and "to assure unfettered interchange of ideas for the bringing about of political and social changes desired by the people."

Far from being "our central value of political equality," equal participation remains "wholly foreign to the First Amendment."

Moreover, even if the government financed all campaigns, we would not have equal participation in elections. Proponents of government financing focus on one source of political inequality: money. They ignore all other sources of inequality such as a talent for speaking, the ability to write, good looks, media ownership and access, organizational ability, and so on. The proponents do not propose to restrain the many nonmonetary sources of influence perhaps because such talents are often found among the proponents of government financing of campaigns. The leveling impulse, they imply, should not restrict such political talents; only people with money should be excluded from political influence. Sometimes in public policy what is not regulated tells you more about a piece of legislation than what is covered. So it is with government financing of campaigns. . . .

Proponents of government financing argue that public subsidies will enable new candidates to run who would otherwise be excluded from the race. They argue the candidates who now obtain funding reflect the investment and consumption preferences of wealthy and conservative individuals. They believe contributions reproduce the inequalities of wealth in the economy and lead to a government that is unrepresentative of America. This argument depends crucially on the stereotypical image of "fat cat" contributors devoted to conservative causes. Large donors may be unrepresentative of the United States as a whole—they do have more money than the average American— but that does not mean they hold vastly different political views than most Americans. In fact, a recent study indicates large contributors often identify themselves as Democrats and as liberal on the issues. That should not be so surprising. In 1998, National Election Studies found that almost one-third of the richest Americans identified themselves as liberals.

Finally, we should be clear how extensive, intrusive, and dangerous a government financing system would be. Keep in mind that the goal of equalizing financial resources in an election requires extensive control and oversight of all electoral spending. The election authority must immediately know about all spending by privately financed candidates and every dollar laid out by any group participating in an election. Public Campaign's model legislation states that government-financed candidates must use a government-issued debit card that draws solely on funds in an account created by the government. Those who believe government usually acts benevolently will not worry about such extensive oversight and control of political activity. Those who expect abuses when government takes total control over anything—and especially over campaigns—will worry.

Competition

Over the past 40 years, the percentage of the vote an incumbent member of Congress receives simply for being an incumbent has risen from 2 percent to 6 or 7 percent. Similar increases in the advantages of incumbency have been observed in executive and legislature elections in the states. Advocates of government subsidies say the need to raise large sums to challenge an incumbent explains why incumbents are hard to challenge. Government financing, they say, would overcome this barrier to entry by giving challengers tax money leading to a more competitive system.

Much depends on who designs the system of government financing. Spending levels strongly influence the competitiveness of challengers to incumbents. If a challenger can spend enough to make his name and causes known, a government financing scheme might foster more competition. If legislatures enact the system, of course, incumbents will design and pass the law. They will be tempted to set spending limits low to favor their own reelections. For example, in 1997, Congress debated a government financing proposal that included spending caps: every challenger spending less than the proposed limits in Senate campaigns in 1994 and 1996 had lost; every incumbent spending less than the limits had won. Similarly, in the House, 3 percent of the challengers spending less than the proposed limits won in 1996, while 40 percent of the incumbents under the limits won.

Such legislative design issues may explain why government financing of campaigns has not *in fact* increased the competitiveness of elections. The leading study of government financing in the states concluded, "There is no evidence to support the claim that programs combining public funding with spending limits have leveled the playing field, countered the effects of incumbency, and made elections more competitive." Believing that government financing will increase competitiveness seems to be a triumph of hope over experience. . . .

Experience indicates that government financing tends to favor certain types of candidates. The political scientists Michael Malbin and Thomas Gais found sharp partisan differences in candidate participation. They studied gubernatorial elections in 11 states from 1993 to 1996 and found that 82 percent of Democratic candidates took taxpayer funding, while only 55 percent of Republican candidates participated. Their data on legislative elections in Minnesota and Wisconsin show a similar partisan divide. Malbin and Gais attribute these partisan variations to the libertarianism of Republicans: candidates who philosophically oppose government subsidies often do not accept them. In other words, government financing in practice provides an advantage to nonlibertarian candidates.

Full government financing of campaigns in Arizona and Maine tells a similar story. In the 2000 election in Arizona, 41 percent of Democratic candidates and 50 percent of Green Party candidates received public subsidies for their campaigns; 8 percent of Republicans accepted government money in the general election, while no candidates of the Libertarian Party took the subsidy. In Maine's 2000 election, 43.4 percent of Democratic Party candidates chose government financing compared with 24 percent of Republicans.

Government financing of campaigns looks a lot like other political activity by individuals and groups that do not do well in private markets. Declining parts of the economy—say, small farmers and large steel mill owners—want government help to overcome their own mistakes or unfavorable economic changes. Similarly, candidates who have little appeal to voters and campaign contributors seek public subsidies (like farmers) and regulatory protections from competition (like steel mill owners).

Government subsidies for candidates, however, are crucially different from funding for ethanol. Government financing of campaigns takes money from taxpayers and gives it to a subset of all political candidates. For that reason, government financing seems either unnecessary or immoral. It is unnecessary if a taxpayer agrees with the candidate supported by the subsidy; the taxpayer may simply give the money directly to the candidate.

If, however, the taxpayer disagrees with the candidate, taxing him to support that candidate is immoral. An example will make clear the immorality of the policy. Imagine I had the power to force Nick Nyhart, the Executive Director of Public Campaign, to contribute to the Cato Institute, thereby supporting the writing and marketing of the very arguments against government financing you are reading right now. Such compulsion would strike most Americans as wrong. We think individuals should not be forced to support ideas that contravene their deepest commitments, whether those commitments are religious, social, or political. Government financing schemes, however, transfer money from taxpayers to political candidates and their campaigns. Inevitably they force liberals to support conservatives, Democrats to support Republicans, and vice versa.

Advocates of government financing of campaigns employ emotionally charged rhetoric at every turn. They implore us to "reform" the system to root out "corruption" and attain "clean elections." The reality of government financing belies this expansive rhetoric. Such proposals, especially the "clean elections" variant, simply transfer wealth from taxpayers to a preferred set of candidates and causes. That preferred set inevitably excludes candidates who believe forced transfers of wealth are immoral (such as Libertarians and Republican candidates with a libertarian outlook). Not surprisingly, government financing in the states has favored candidates of the left (such as Democrats and third parties like the Greens). For that reason, government financing of campaigns serves private goals through public means. Far from being a reform, government financing offers more "politics as usual," understood as the struggle to obtain special favors from government.

Those who wish to support the candidates and causes favored by government financing may do so now; they need only send their check to the candidate or cause they favor. Government financing forces all taxpayers to financially support candidates they would not otherwise support, candidates whose views they may find repugnant. On the question of government financing of campaigns, Thomas Jefferson should have the last word: "To compel a man to furnish contributions of money for the propagation of opinions which he disbelieves, is sinful and tyrannical."

POSTSCRIPT

Should America Adopt Public Financing of Political Campaigns?

There are four ways in which a country can limit the influence of money in elections: by limiting the amount of money individuals and groups may contribute to a candidate, by limiting the amount of money that can be spent by or on behalf of a candidate, by providing free access to media for candidates and political parties and restricting paid political advertisements, and by public financing of elections. Most established democracies—Great Britain and Western Europe, Canada, Australia, New Zealand, Israel, and Japan—use several of these methods; some employ them all. The United States alone employs only one—restricting contributions to candidates—and allows independent expenditures.

Critics of campaign finance reform, ranging from libertarians to the American Civil Liberties Union, maintain that the government in a free society should not restrict an individual who is prepared to put his money where his mouth is. Supporters of reform argue that every one of the other cited democracies has a much larger turnout of its citizens in national elections, and they believe that this is because citizens believe that the process is fairer when one candidate cannot vastly outspend another.

The Supreme Court decision in *Buckley v. Valeo* in 1976 came down largely on the side of critics of reform, concluding that money is speech, that candidates could not be restricted in their expenditures (although contributors to their campaigns could be restricted), and that independent expenditures (that is, by persons or groups other than the candidates and party) could not be restricted. That decision has been the focus of political debate ever since.

The first major revision of federal campaign finance law in several decades was adopted in 2002 and upheld by the Supreme Court the following year. It eliminated so-called "soft money" expenditures by the political parties that had not counted as campaign expenses because they did not expressly endorse a candidate. New campaign strategies were adopted by the parties, resulting in record expenditures in the 2004 presidential and congressional elections.

The U.S. Supreme Court in 2006 struck down Vermont's strict limits on campaign contributions. Vermont's law, approved in 1997, was the toughest in the country with regard to setting limits on the amount individuals and parties may contribute to campaigns and, perhaps more significantly, on how much candidates may spend on their campaigns.

Complaints have been filed with the Federal Election Commission concerning the raising and spending of money by organizations claiming tax exemption as "political organizations," but refusing to register as "political committees" subject to campaign finance law contribution limits, source prohibitions, and disclosure requirements. These organizations exist throughout the political spectrum. In 2006 and 2007, a number of these groups were fined for failing to abide by federal campaign finance laws during the 2004 election.

In June 2007, the Supreme Court held in *Federal Election Commission v. Wisconsin Right to Life* that the 2002 limitations on corporate and labor union funding of broadcast ads mentioning a candidate within 30 days of a primary or caucus or 60 days of a general election are unconstitutional as applied to ads susceptible of a reasonable interpretation other than as an appeal to vote for or against a specific candidate. Some election law experts believe that the new exception will render much of the law meaningless, while others believe that the new exception will be construed narrowly. The Federal Election Comission's interpretation and application of the new exception will determine the true scope and impact of the Court's decision.

Diana Dwyre and Victoria A. Farrar-Myers followed the course of campaign finance reform through Congress in *Legislative Labyrinth: Congress and Campaign Finance Reform* (Congressional Quarterly Press, 2001). The authors explored the impact of the president, interest groups, and the media, as well as the roles of congressional sponsors and opponents, providing insight into how Congress grapples with an issue of paramount importance to its members.

Most studies do not attempt to achieve objectivity, and tend to support extreme positions, as the titles of two books suggest. Darrell M. West strongly supports public finance in *Checkbook Democracy: How Money Corrupts Political Campaigns* (Northeastern University Press, 2000). In total opposition to reform, Bradley Smith offers a vigorous critique in *Unfree Speech: The Folly of Campaign Finance Reform* (Princeton University Press, 2001), contending that all restrictions on campaign contributions should be eliminated. In *Sold to the Highest Bidder: The Presidency from Dwight D. Eisenhower to George W. Bush* (Prometheus Books, 2002), Daniel M. Friedenberg contends that "money controls the actions of both the executive and legislative branches of our government on the federal and state levels."

The most comprehensive overall examination of the role of money in elections is in *The New Campaign Finance Sourcebook*, by Anthony Corrado, Thomas E. Mann, Daniel R. Ortiz, and Trevor Potter (Brookings Institution, 2005). The authors conclude that campaign finance reform will always be a work in progress, dealing with but never resolving the inherent problems of money in politics.

Internet References . . .

In addition to the Internet sites listed below, type in key words, such as "American federalism," "commerce power," "presidential appointments," and "government regulation," to find other listings.

U.S. House of Representatives

This page of the U.S. House of Representatives will lead you to information about current and past House members and agendas, the legislative process, and so on. You can learn about events on the House floor as they happen.

http://www.house.gov

The United States Senate

This page of the U.S. Senate will lead you to information about current and past Senate members and agendas, legislative activities, committees, and so on.

http://www.senate.gov

The White House

Visit the White House page for direct access to information about commonly requested federal services, the White House Briefing Room, and the presidents and vice presidents. The Virtual Library allows you to search White House documents, listen to speeches, and view photos.

http://www.whitehouse.gov/index.html

Supreme Court Collection

Open this Legal Information Institute (LII) site for current and historical information about the Supreme Court. The LII archive contains many opinions issued since May 1990 as well as a collection of nearly 600 of the most historic decisions of the Court.

http://supct.law.cornell.edu/supct/index.html

National Security Agency

Find out more about the agency that has been at the center of controversy over the President's power to intercept telecommunications in and out of the country. Its home page explains its many functions, relates its storied past in breaking the Japanese code during World War II, and boasts its continued role "in keeping the United States a step ahead of its enemies." It contains links to fourteen other federal agencies, including the C.I.A., the Defense Intelligence Agency, and the National Reconnaissance Office.

http://www.nsa.gov/about/index.cfm

The Institution of Government

*T*he Constitution divides authority between the national government and the states, delegating certain powers to the national government and providing that those not thus delegated "are reserved to the states respectively, or to the people." The national government's powers are further divided between three branches, Congress, the President, and the federal judiciary, each of which can exercise checks on the others. How vigorously and faithfully are these branches performing their respective functions? Do they remain true to the authentic meaning of the Constitution? What legitimate defenses does each branch possess against encroachment by the others? These issues have been debated since the earliest years of the Republic, and the debate continues today.

- Does the President Have Unilateral War Powers?

- Should the Courts Seek the "Original Meaning" of the Constitution?

- Is Congress a "Broken Branch"?

- Should the President Be Allowed "Executive Privilege"?

ISSUE 4

Does the President Have Unilateral War Powers?

YES: John C. Yoo, from *Memorandum Opinion for the Deputy Counsel to the President* (September 25, 2001)

NO: Michael Cairo, from "The 'Imperial Presidency' Triumphant," in Christopher S. Kelley, ed., *Executing the Constitution* (SUNY, 2006)

ISSUE SUMMARY

YES: John C. Yoo, a law professor at the University of California, Berkeley, argues that the language of the Constitution, long-accepted precedents, and the practical need for speedy action in emergencies all support broad executive power during war.

NO: Michael Cairo, lecturer in International Relations at Southern Illinois University, deplores the unilateral military actions undertaken by Presidents Clinton and Bush; he argues that the Founders never intended to grant exclusive war powers to the president.

Dramatic and bitter as they are, the current struggles between the White House and Congress over the president's unilateral authority to conduct military operations and foreign affairs are not without precedent. Episodically, they have been occurring since the administration of George Washington.

The language of the Constitution relating to war powers almost seems to invite struggles between the two branches. Congress is given the power to declare war and "to raise and support armies." The president is authorized to serve as commander-in-chief of the armed forces "when called into actual service of the United States." While the power to "declare" or authorize war rests squarely with the U.S. Congress, the Founders gave some leeway to the president when it came to war *making*. At the Constitutional Convention, some delegates wanted to give Congress the exclusive power to make war, not simply to declare it. That would have ruled out any presidential war making. But James Madison successfully argued the need for "leaving to the Executive the power to repel sudden attacks."

Down through the years, several presidents have interpreted very broadly—these emergency war-making powers. In 1801, President Jefferson ordered his navy to seize the ships of Barbary pirates in the Mediterranean, and 45 years later President Polk sent American troops into territory claimed by Mexico, thus provoking the Mexican-American War. A young congressman named Abraham Lincoln vigorously protested Polk's unilateral assertion of power, but when he came to office and faced the secession of the South, he went much further than Polk in the assertion of power, jailing people without trial, enlarging the size of the army and navy, and withdrawing money from the Treasury blockading Southern ports without authorization from Congress. In more recent times, President Truman committed America to fight in Korea without a congressional declaration, and President Kennedy ordered a naval blockade of Cuba in 1962 without even consulting Congress.

The mid-1960s marked the high-water period of unchallenged presidential war making. Between 1961 and 1963, Kennedy sent 16,000 armed "advisers" to Vietnam, and between 1964 and 1968, President Johnson escalated American involvement to 500,000 troops—all without a formal declaration of war. But that period of congressional indulgence was soon to end. By the early 1970s, Congress was starting on a course that would culminate in the cutoff of funds for Vietnam and legislative efforts to head off any more undeclared wars. In 1973, over President Nixon's veto, Congress passed the War Powers Resolution, which required the president to notify Congress within 48 hours after putting troops in harm's way, withdraw them within 60 to 90 days absent a congressional authorization, and submit periodic progress reports to Congress during that period. In practice, the War Powers Resolution has been largely ignored—by Ronald Reagan when he sent troops into Grenada, by George H. W. Bush when he sent them to Panama, and by Bill Clinton when he sent them into Somalia, Haiti, and Bosnia.

Perhaps ironically, the War Powers Resolution may even have been useful to President George W. Bush in obtaining congressional authorization for the invasion of Iraq. In October 2002, Congress passed a joint resolution giving the president the authority to use the armed forces "as he determines to be necessary and appropriate" to defend national security and enforce all U.N. resolutions against Iraq. The resolution added that this constituted "specific statutory authorization" for war within the meaning of the War Powers Resolution. Such broadly worded language has come back to haunt many members of Congress who voted for it but now wish they hadn't. The new Democratic Congress elected in 2006 is considering various options for challenging President Bush's war-making ability as it relates to Iraq, including the repeal or modification of the 2002 authorization for going to war.

In the selections that follow, John C. Yoo, a law professor at the University of California, Berkeley, argues that the language of the Constitution, long-accepted precedents, and the practical need for speedy action in emergencies all support broad executive power during war. Opposing that view is Michael Cairo, a lecturer in International Relations at Southern Illinois University, who criticizes the unilateral military actions undertaken by Presidents Clinton and Bush, arguing that the Founders never intended to grant exclusive war powers to the president.

YES

John C. Yoo

The President's Constitutional Authority to Conduct Military Operations Against Terrorists and Nations Supporting Them: Memorandum Opinion for the Deputy Counsel to the President

Our review establishes that all three branches of the Federal Government—Congress, the Executive, and the Judiciary—agree that the President has broad authority to use military force abroad, including the ability to deter future attacks.

I.

The President's constitutional power to defend the United States and the lives of its people must be understood in light of the Founders' express intention to create a federal government "cloathed with all the powers requisite to [the] complete execution of its trust." *The Federalist* No. 23 (Alexander Hamilton) Foremost among the objectives committed to that trust by the Constitution is the security of the Nation. As Hamilton explained in arguing for the Constitution's adoption, because "the circumstances which may affect the public safety are [not] reducible within certain determinate limits, . . . it must be admitted, as a necessary consequence that there can be no limitation of that authority which is to provide for the defense and protection of the community in any matter essential to its efficiency."

"It is 'obvious and unarguable' that no governmental interest is more compelling than the security of the Nation." (1981) Within the limits that the Constitution itself imposes, the scope and distribution of the powers to protect national security must be construed to authorize the most efficacious defense of the Nation and its interests in accordance "with the realistic purposes of the entire instrument." (1948) Nor is the authority to protect national security limited to actions necessary for "victories in the field." (1946) The authority

John C. Yoo, *The President's Constitutional Authority to Conduct Military Operations Against Terrorists and Nations Supporting Them*, Memorandum Opinion for the Deputy Counsel to the President, DOJ Office of Legal Counsel (2001.09.25), available at: http://www.usdoj.gov/olc/warpowers925.htm

over national security "carries with it the inherent power to guard against the immediate renewal of the conflict."

We now turn to the more precise question of the President's inherent constitutional powers to use military force.

Constitutional Text

The text, structure and history of the Constitution establish that the Founders entrusted the President with the primary responsibility, and therefore the power, to use military force in situations of emergency. Article II, Section 2 states that the "President shall be Commander in Chief of the Army and Navy of the United States, and of the Militia of the several States, when called into the actual Service of the United States." He is further vested with all of "the executive Power" and the duty to execute the laws. These powers give the President broad constitutional authority to use military force in response to threats to the national security and foreign policy of the United States. During the period leading up to the Constitution's ratification, the power to initiate hostilities and to control the escalation of conflict had been long understood to rest in the hands of the executive branch.

By their terms, these provisions vest full control of the military forces of the United States in the President. The power of the President is at its zenith under the Constitution when the President is directing military operations of the armed forces, because the power of Commander in Chief is assigned solely to the President. It has long been the view of this Office that the Commander-in-Chief Clause is a substantive grant of authority to the President and that the scope of the President's authority to commit the armed forces to combat is very broad. The President's complete discretion in exercising the Commander-in-Chief power has also been recognized by the courts. In the *Prize Cases*, (1862), for example, the Court explained that, whether the President "in fulfilling his duties as Commander in Chief" had met with a situation justifying treating the southern States as belligerents and instituting a blockade, was a question "to be *decided by him*" and which the Court could not question, but must leave to "the political department of the Government to which this power was entrusted."

Some commentators have read the constitutional text differently. They argue that the vesting of the power to declare war gives Congress the sole authority to decide whether to make war. This view misreads the constitutional text and misunderstands the nature of a declaration of war. Declaring war is not tantamount to making war—indeed, the Constitutional Convention specifically amended the working draft of the Constitution that had given Congress the power to make war. An earlier draft of the Constitution had given to Congress the power to "make" war. When it took up this clause on August 17, 1787, the Convention voted to change the clause from "make" to "declare." A supporter of the change argued that it would "leav[e] to the Executive the power to repel sudden attacks." Further, other elements of the Constitution describe "engaging" in war, which demonstrates that the Framers understood making and engaging in war to be broader than simply "declaring" war. . . . If the Framers had wanted to require congressional consent before the initiation of military hostilities, they knew how to write such provisions.

Finally, the Framing generation well understood that declarations of war were obsolete. Not all forms of hostilities rose to the level of a declared war: during the seventeenth and eighteenth centuries, Great Britain and colonial America waged numerous conflicts against other states without an official declaration of war. . . . Instead of serving as an authorization to begin hostilities, a declaration of war was only necessary to "perfect" a conflict under international law. A declaration served to fully transform the international legal relationship between two states from one of peace to one of war. Given this context, it is clear that Congress's power to declare war does not constrain the President's independent and plenary constitutional authority over the use of military force.

Constitutional Structure

Our reading of the text is reinforced by analysis of the constitutional structure. First, it is clear that the Constitution secures all federal executive power in the President to ensure a unity in purpose and energy in action. "Decision, activity, secrecy, and dispatch will generally characterize the proceedings of one man in a much more eminent degree than the proceedings of any greater number." *The Federalist* No. 70 (Alexander Hamilton). The centralization of authority in the President alone is particularly crucial in matters of national defense, war, and foreign policy, where a unitary executive can evaluate threats, consider policy choices, and mobilize national resources with a speed and energy that is far superior to any other branch. As Hamilton noted, "Energy in the executive is a leading character in the definition of good government. It is essential to the protection of the community against foreign attacks." This is no less true in war. "Of all the cares or concerns of government, the direction of war most peculiarly demands those qualities which distinguish the exercise of power by a single hand." *The Federalist* No. 74.

Second, the Constitution makes clear that the process used for conducting military hostilities is different from other government decisionmaking. In the area of domestic legislation, the Constitution creates a detailed, finely wrought procedure in which Congress plays the central role. In foreign affairs, however, the Constitution does not establish a mandatory, detailed, Congress-driven procedure for taking action. Rather, the Constitution vests the two branches with different powers—the President as Commander in Chief, Congress with control over funding and declaring war—without requiring that they follow a specific process in making war. By establishing this framework, the Framers expected that the process for warmaking would be far more flexible, and capable of quicker, more decisive action, than the legislative process. Thus, the President may use his Commander-in-Chief and executive powers to use military force to protect the Nation, subject to congressional appropriations and control over domestic legislation.

Third, the constitutional structure requires that any ambiguities in the allocation of a power that is executive in nature—such as the power to conduct military hostilities—must be resolved in favor of the executive branch. Article II, section 1 provides that "[t]he executive Power shall be vested in a President of the United States." By contrast, Article I's Vesting Clause gives Congress only the powers "herein granted." This difference in language indicates that Congress's legislative powers are limited to the list enumerated in Article I, section 8, while the President's powers include inherent executive powers that are unenumerated in the Constitution. To be sure, Article II lists specifically enumerated powers in addition to the Vesting Clause, and some have argued that this limits the "executive Power" granted in the Vesting Clause to the powers on that list. But the purpose of the enumeration of executive powers in Article II was not to define and cabin the grant in the Vesting Clause. Rather, the Framers unbundled some plenary powers that had traditionally been regarded as "executive," assigning elements of those powers to Congress in Article I, while expressly reserving other elements as enumerated executive powers in Article II. So, for example, the King's traditional power to declare war was given to Congress under Article I, while the Commander-in-Chief authority was expressly reserved to the President in Article II. Further, the Framers altered other plenary powers of the King, such as treaties and appointments, assigning the Senate a share in them in Article II itself. Thus, the enumeration in Article II marks the points at which several traditional executive powers were diluted or reallocated. Any *other*, unenumerated executive powers, however, were conveyed to the President by the Vesting Clause.

There can be little doubt that the decision to deploy military force is "executive" in nature, and was traditionally so regarded. It calls for action and energy in execution, rather than the deliberate formulation of rules to govern the conduct of private individuals. Moreover, the Framers understood it to be an attribute of the executive. "The direction of war implies the direction of the common strength," wrote Alexander Hamilton, "and the power of directing and employing the common strength forms a usual and essential part in the definition of the executive authority." *The Federalist* No. 74 (Alexander Hamilton). As a result, to the extent that the constitutional text does not explicitly allocate the power to initiate military hostilities to a particular branch, the Vesting Clause provides that it remain among the President's unenumerated powers.

Fourth, depriving the President of the power to decide when to use military force would disrupt the basic constitutional framework of foreign relations. From the very beginnings of the Republic, the vesting of the executive, Commander-in-Chief, and treaty powers in the executive branch has been understood to grant the President plenary control over the conduct of foreign relations. As Secretary of State Thomas Jefferson observed during the first Washington Administration: "the constitution has divided the powers of government into three branches [and] has declared that the executive powers shall be vested in the president, submitting only special articles of it to a negative by the senate." Due to this structure, Jefferson continued, "the transaction of business with foreign nations is executive altogether; it belongs, then, to the head of that department, except as to such portions of it as are specially submitted to the senate. Exceptions are to be construed strictly." In defending President Washington's authority to issue the Neutrality Proclamation, Alexander Hamilton came to the same interpretation of the President's foreign affairs powers. According to Hamilton, Article II "ought . . . to be considered as intended . . . to specify and regulate the principal articles implied in the definition of Executive Power; leaving the rest to flow from the general grant of that power." As future Chief Justice John Marshall famously declared a few years later, "The President is the sole organ of the nation in its external relations, and its sole representative with foreign nations. . . . The [executive] department . . . is entrusted with the whole foreign intercourse of the nation. . . ." Given the agreement of Jefferson, Hamilton, and Marshall, it has not been difficult for the executive branch consistently to assert the President's plenary authority in foreign affairs ever since. . . .

II.

Executive Branch Construction and Practice

The position we take here has long represented the view of the executive branch and of the Department of Justice. Attorney General (later Justice) Robert Jackson formulated the classic statement of the executive branch's understanding of the President's military powers in 1941:

> "Article II, section 2, of the Constitution provides that the President "shall be Commander in Chief of the Army and Navy of the United States." By virtue of this constitutional office he has supreme command over the land and naval forces of the country and may order them to perform such military duties as, in his opinion, are necessary or appropriate for the defense of the United States. These powers exist in time of peace as well as in time of war. . . .

"Thus the President's responsibility as Commander in Chief embraces the authority to command and direct the armed forces in their immediate movements and operations designed to protect the security and effectuate the defense of the United States. . . . [T]his authority undoubtedly includes the power to dispose of troops and equipment in such manner and on such duties as best to promote the safety of the country." . . .

Attorney General (later Justice) Frank Murphy, though declining to define precisely the scope of the President's independent authority to act in emergencies or states of war, stated that: "the Executive has powers not enumerated in the statutes—powers derived not from statutory grants but from the Constitution. It is universally recognized that the constitutional duties of the Executive carry with them the constitutional powers necessary for their proper performance. These constitutional powers have never been specifically defined, and in fact cannot be, since their extent and limitations are largely dependent upon conditions and circumstances. . . . The right to take specific action might not exist under one state of facts, while under another it might be the absolute duty of the Executive to take such action." . . .

Judicial Construction

Judicial decisions since the beginning of the Republic confirm the President's constitutional power and duty to repel military action against the United

States through the use of force, and to take measures to deter the recurrence of an attack. As Justice Joseph Story said long ago, "[i]t may be fit and proper for the government, in the exercise of the high discretion confided to the executive, for great public purposes, to act on a sudden emergency, or to prevent an irreparable mischief, by summary measures, which are not found in the text of the laws." (1824). The Constitution entrusts the "power [to] the executive branch of the government to preserve order and insure the public safety in times of emergency, when other branches of the government are unable to function, or their functioning would itself threaten the public safety." (1946, Stone, C.J., concurring).

If the President is confronted with an unforeseen attack on the territory and people of the United States, or other immediate, dangerous threat to American interests and security, the courts have affirmed that it is his constitutional responsibility to respond to that threat with whatever means are necessary, including the use of military force abroad. . . .

III.

The historical practice of all three branches confirms the lessons of the constitutional text and structure. The normative role of historical practice in constitutional law, and especially with regard to separation of powers, is well settled. . . . Indeed, as the Court has observed, the role of practice in fixing the meaning of the separation of powers is implicit in the Constitution itself: "'the Constitution . . . contemplates that practice will integrate the dispersed powers into a workable government.'" (1989) In addition, governmental practice enjoys significant weight in constitutional analysis for practical reasons, on "the basis of a wise and quieting rule that, in determining . . . the existence of a power, weight shall be given to the usage itself—even when the validity of the practice is the subject of investigation." (1915). . . .

The historical record demonstrates that the power to initiate military hostilities, particularly in response to the threat of an armed attack, rests exclusively with the President. As the Supreme Court has observed, "[t]he United States frequently employs Armed Forces outside this country—over 200 times in our history—for the protection of American citizens or national security." (1990). On at least 125 such occasions, the President acted without prior express authorization from Congress. Such deployments, based on the President's constitutional authority alone, have occurred since the Administration of George Washington. . . . Perhaps the most significant deployment without specific statutory authorization took place at the time of the Korean War, when President Truman, without prior authorization from Congress, deployed United States troops in a war that lasted for over three years and caused over 142,000 American casualties.

Recent deployments ordered solely on the basis of the President's constitutional authority have also been extremely large, representing a substantial commitment of the Nation's military personnel, diplomatic prestige, and financial resources. On at least one occasion, such a unilateral deployment has constituted full-scale war. On March 24, 1999, without any prior statutory authorization and in the absence of an attack on the United States, President Clinton ordered hostilities to be initiated against the Republic of Yugoslavia. The President informed Congress that, in the initial wave of air strikes, "United States and NATO forces have targeted the [Yugoslavian] government's integrated air defense system, military and security police command and control elements, and military and security police facilities and infrastructure. . . . I have taken these actions pursuant to my constitutional authority to conduct U.S. foreign relations and as Commander in Chief and Chief Executive." Bombing attacks against targets in both Kosovo and Serbia ended on June 10, 1999, seventy-nine days after the war began. More than 30,000 United States military personnel participated in the operations; some 800 U.S. aircraft flew more than 20,000 sorties; more than 23,000 bombs and missiles were used. As part of the peace settlement, NATO deployed some 50,000 troops into Kosovo, 7,000 of them American. . . .

Conclusion

In light of the text, plan, and history of the Constitution, its interpretation by both past Administrations and the courts, the longstanding practice of the executive branch, and the express affirmation of the President's constitutional authorities by Congress, we think it beyond question that the President has the plenary constitutional power to take such military actions as he deems necessary and appropriate to respond to the terrorist attacks upon the United States on September 11, 2001. Force can be used both to retaliate for those attacks, and to prevent and deter future assaults on the Nation. Military actions need not be limited to those individuals, groups, or states that participated in the attacks on the World Trade Center and the Pentagon: the Constitution vests the President with the power to strike terrorist groups or organizations that cannot be demonstrably linked to the September 11 incidents, but that, nonetheless, pose a similar threat to the security of the United States and the lives of its people, whether at home or overseas. In both the War Powers Resolution and the Joint Resolution, Congress has recognized the President's authority to use force in circumstances such as those created by the September 11 incidents. Neither statute, however, can place any limits on the President's determinations as to any terrorist threat, the amount of military force to be used in response, or the method, timing, and nature of the response. These decisions, under our Constitution, are for the President alone to make.

The "Imperial Presidency" Triumphant: War Powers in the Clinton and Bush Administrations

War Powers and the Constitution

To the casual observer, the president, as commander in chief, appears entitled to unilateral military powers when deploying and using U.S. troops and forces abroad. One of the many arguments in favor of presidential war powers is the Minority Report of the Congressional Committees Investigating the Iran-Contra Affair. According to the report, no fewer than 118 occasions of force occurred without prior legislative authorization. "The relevance of these repeated examples of the extensive use of armed force," it argues, "is that they indicate how far the President's inherent powers were assumed to have reached when Congress was silent, and even in some cases, where Congress had prohibited an action." Former Senator John Tower also argued that Congress should not encumber presidents in the foreign policy process. Robert Bork concurs, arguing that morality should be a president's guide and Congress should abstain froth decisions on the use of force. Supreme Court Justice George Sutherland presented the strongest argument on behalf of presidential war powers, however, in 1936. In his written opinion in *U.S. v. Curtiss-Wright Export Corp. et al.,* Sutherland wrote that the president is the "sole organ of the federal government in the field of international relations" and has "plenary and exclusive" power as president. Congress, he suggested, was meant to play a secondary role in U.S. foreign policy.

Presidential practice has also relegated Congress to a backseat in decisions on the use of force. Since World War II, Congress has never specifically declared war. In the Korean War, the Truman administration argued, "the President's power to send Armed Forces outside the country is not dependent on Congressional authority." Secretary of Defense Richard Cheney echoed this sentiment prior to the Persian Gulf War. Cheney explained that he did "not believe the president requires any additional authority from Congress" to engage U.S. forces abroad. During his 1992 presidential election campaign, President

From *Executing the Constitution*, Christopher S. Kelly, ed., 2006, pp. 199–218. Copyright © 2006 by State University of New York Press. Reprinted by permission.

George H. W. Bush stated that he did not need "some old goat" in Congress to evict Saddam Hussein from Kuwait.

Contrary to these arguments and presidential practice in general, the Founders did not intend to grant presidents exclusive authority in war powers. The belief that Congress should not get in the president's way when national security matters arise is clearly popular, but the Constitution contradicts this. According to the Constitution, Congress and the president are given specific foreign policy powers and each plays a role to ensure that U.S. foreign policy is effective. In fact, the Constitution grants broad power to Congress, not the president. Although the president is given the powers to nominate ambassadors, negotiate treaties, and direct the armed forces as commander in chief, the Congress is granted the powers to regulate commerce, raise and support armies, provide and maintain a navy, and declare war. Thus, the Constitution originally empowered Congress in military matters.

In drafting the Constitution, the Founders were concerned about correcting the deficiencies of the Articles of Confederation. The Articles bestowed all legislative and executive authority in the Congress. Article 6 gave Congress control over conduct of foreign affairs, and Article 9 gave Congress "the sole and exclusive right and power of determining on peace and war." Unlike the Articles, the Constitution was founded on the principle of separation of powers— a division of authority between government branches. In foreign policy, that division was ambiguous. Experience under the Articles led the Founders to favor great centralization of executive authority in the Constitution. Alexander Hamilton, writing in *Federalist 70,* explains, "energy in the Executive is a leading character in the definition of good government." When constructing the Constitution, however, the Founders favored less centralization based on their experiences with the monarchy. . . .

The Constitution thus established a shared system. This constitutional division of foreign affairs powers only served to cause confusion. Almost immediately after the founding of the new republic, the question of war powers emerged as a prominent issue of debate. In 1793 President George Washington unilaterally proclaimed U.S. neutrality in the war between France and Great Britain despite the existence of an alliance with France. Alexander Hamilton defended the action, arguing that foreign policy was an executive function and the powers of declaring war and ratifying treaties bestowed on Congress were "exceptions out of the general 'executive power' vested in the President." These powers were to be "construed strictly, and ought to be extended no further than is essential to their execution." Although Congress had the right to declare war, the president had the duty to preserve peace until the Congress did so. "The legislature," he argued, "is still free to perform its duties, according to its own sense of them; though the executive, in the exercise of constitutional powers, may establish an antecedent state of things, which ought to weigh in the legislative decision." In short, each branch had a duty to exercise its power, possessing concurrent authority.

James Madison responded to Hamilton's defense of Washington's proclamation of neutrality, denying that the powers of making wars and treaties were inherently executive. The fact that they were royal prerogative, Madison argued, did not make them presidential prerogatives. The power to declare war must include everything necessary to make that power effective, including the congressional right to judge whether the United States was obliged to declare war. According to Madison, this judgment could not be foreordained by presidential decisions. Thus, whereas Hamilton saw congressional power to declare war as limited, Madison viewed it as very powerful. . . .

The Clinton Administration and Saddam Hussein

On August 2, 1990, Saddam Hussein, the leader of Iraq, invaded and annexed Kuwait, seizing Kuwait's vast oil reserves and liquidating billions of dollars of loans provided by Kuwait during the Iran-Iraq War. Within months, the George H. W. Bush administration assembled a coalition of forces, supported by the United Nations, to remove the Iraqi army from Kuwait. On January 17, 1991, Operation Desert Storm, which was authorized by UN Resolution 678 and by a congressional vote endorsing the action, ensued.

The international coalition proved victorious and instituted UN Resolution 687, giving the UN Special Commission (UNSCOM) complete access to Iraqi facilities to search for weapons of mass destruction. In addition, the UN Security Council also passed UN Resolution 688, condemning Iraqi actions against the Kurdish population and authorizing relief organizations to provide humanitarian aid. Pursuant to these resolutions, but without specific UN Security Council authorization, a no-fly zone was established, prohibiting Iraqi flights in northern and southern Iraq.

President-elect Clinton inherited this policy toward Iraq and a hostile Hussein. Almost immediately, Clinton faced mounting tensions between the United States and Iraq. In April 1993 former President Bush visited Kuwait. Prior to his visit, the Central Intelligence Agency (CIA) and Federal Bureau of Investigation (FBI) uncovered an assassination plot against Bush and linked the Iraqi government to that plot. As a response to this plot, Clinton responded with an attack, using precision-guided missiles. Clinton justified the bombings in a statement to Congress, noting "our inherent right to self-defense as recognized in Article 51 of the United Nations Charter and pursuant to [his] constitutional authority with respect to the conduct of foreign relations and as Commander in Chief." In an address to the American public about the strikes, Clinton added, "There should be no mistake about the message we intend these actions to convey to Saddam Hussein. . . . We will combat terrorism. We will deter aggression. . . . While the cold war has ended, the world is not free of danger. And I am determined to take the steps necessary to keep our Nation secure."

In 1996 Clinton used force against Hussein in support of Iraq's Kurdish population. One Kurdish faction, the Patriotic Union of Kurdistan (PUK), accepted arms from Iran and Hussein responded by attacking the PUK's headquarters in northern Iraq, attempting to crush the opposition. In response, Clinton ordered a missile attack on targets in southern Iraq. In justifying this attack, Clinton relied on humanitarian arguments stressing UN Resolution 688 explaining, "Earlier today I ordered American forces to strike Iraq. Our missiles sent the following message to Saddam Hussein: When you abuse your own people . . . you must pay a price." During his weekly radio address, Clinton added, "America's policy has been to contain Saddam, to reduce the threat he poses to the region, and to do it in a way that makes him pay a price when he acts recklessly."

The next major crisis with Iraq occurred in 1998 when Saddam Hussein refused UNSCOM weapons inspectors access to certain sites, as the provisions of UN Resolution 687 outlined. Hussein argued that U.S. involvement in the inspections was the problem. The Clinton administration suggested that diplomacy was their main instrument in solving the crisis, but reserved the right to use force. Implicit in the administration's argument for the use of force was that the administration had the authority to do so. In an address at Tennessee State University, Secretary of State Madeleine Albright stated, "We will work for that peaceful solution as long as we can. But if we cannot get such a solution—and we do believe that the time for diplomacy is running out—then we will use force." Days before, in a statement before the House International Relations Committee, Albright remarked, "Let no one miscalculate. We have authority to do this, the responsibility to do this, the means and the will."

By the end of February, however, UN Secretary-General Kofi Annan had negotiated a diplomatic solution to the crisis. The Clinton administration responded by sponsoring a successful resolution in the UN Security Council. Resolution 1154 explained that Iraq would face the "severest consequences" if it failed to comply with UNSCOM. President Clinton made clear that the UN Security Council's decision authorized the use of force against Iraq, despite opposition from other members of the UN Security Council. In remarks the day after the UN Security Council vote on Resolution 1154, Clinton stated, "The Government of Iraq should be under no illusion. The meaning of 'severest consequences' is clear. It provides authority to act if Iraq does not turn the commitment it has now made into compliance."

In December 1998 Clinton attacked Iraq after a series of diplomatic conflicts over UNSCOM. In an address to the American public, Clinton explained that Iraq had been given numerous opportunities to comply and must face the "consequences of defying the U.N." In a letter to Congress, Clinton justified the attacks citing UN Security Council Resolutions 678 and 687, authorizing "all necessary means" to ensure Iraqi compliance. He also referred to the power granted to the president under Public Law 102–1, which authorized President Bush to use force against Iraq in 1991.

Clinton's actions toward Iraq established a pattern that continued into the George W. Bush administration. First, the Clinton administration took action with little congressional consultation. In fact, Congress remained relatively silent on each occasion. Some of this silence can be attributed to public approval of Clinton's actions. For example, in the 1993 case, 61 percent of the public approved of the action taken. Second, the Clinton administration claimed unilateral powers under the commander in chief clause of the Constitution and UN Security Council authorizations. Justifying the attacks based on UN Security Council authorization broadly defined presidential and U.S. power.

The Clinton Administration and Osama bin Laden

The Clinton administration's abuse of war powers with regard to Iraq paled in comparison to its abuse of war powers in its decision to strike the alleged terrorist bases of Osama bin Laden. The threat of terrorism became a more prominent foreign policy concern in the 1990s. In 1998, President Clinton unilaterally authorized air strikes against alleged terrorist sites. These strikes were not only conducted unilaterally, but also were executed without prior authorization from the United Nations.

Although terrorism was not considered a central threat to U.S. interests when Clinton took office, it quickly became one. By the end of the Clinton administration's first term the federal building in Oklahoma City had been bombed, the World Trade Center had been victimized by terrorists, and U.S. troops were killed in Saudi Arabia when terrorists exploded a car near a military complex. These events, among others, pushed terrorism to the center of U.S. interest. Like its predecessors, the Clinton administration attempted to deal with terrorism through multilateral, diplomatic channels. Despite these efforts, however, terrorists struck the U.S. embassies in Kenya and Tanzania on August 7, 1998. These attacks were soon attributed to Osama bin Laden and his terrorist network, al Qaeda. . . .

When the U.S. embassies in Kenya and Tanzania were bombed, 300 people were killed, including 12 Americans, and nearly 5,000 people were injured. Six days later, the Clinton administration responded with tomahawk missile attacks on alleged bin Laden bases in Afghanistan and Sudan.

In his letter to congressional leaders notifying them of the attack, he added:

> The United States acted in exercise of our inherent right of self-defense consistent with Article 51 of the United Nations Charter. These strikes were a necessary and proportionate response to the imminent threat of future terrorist attacks against U.S. personnel and facilities. . . . I directed these actions pursuant to my constitutional authority to conduct U.S. foreign relations and as Commander in Chief and Chief Executive.

Not only did Clinton rely on the UN Charter and his powers as commander in chief for his actions, but he also suggests that these actions were an inherent right of his power as chief executive. This sounds familiarly like Hamilton's argument that foreign policy was an executive function and the powers of declaring war and ratifying treaties bestowed on Congress were "exceptions out of the general 'executive power' vested in the President. Clinton was relying on the Hamiltonian interpretation of the Constitution. . . .

The Bush Administration: Increasing Risks, Increasing Power

In the George W. Bush administration, the war on terrorism and policy toward Iraq are intertwined. This became clear after the September 11, 2001, terrorist attacks on the United States. On that day, terrorists struck the World Trade

Center Twin Towers and the Pentagon, killing thousands. Following these attacks, Bush made clear his intentions vowing, "Terrorism against our nation will not stand. He further argued, "War has been waged against us by stealth and deceit and murder," granting the president full authority to defend against the threat. The policy would eventually become the Bush Doctrine, including not only terrorist groups, but rogue states.

On September 12, the UN Security Council adopted a resolution condemning the attacks, declaring that they constituted a "threat to international peace and security." In addition, the resolution recognized the "inherent right of individual or collective self-defense in accordance with the Charter. On September 28, the UN Security Council unanimously adopted a historic resolution directed toward combating terrorism and states that support, harbor, provide safe haven to, supply, finance, help recruit, or aid terrorists. The resolution required cooperation of all member states in a wide range of areas. Resolution 1373 established a comprehensive legal framework for addressing the threat of international terrorism. It also provided a basis for the Bush Doctrine.

On October 7, the U.S. ambassador to the United Nations, John Negroponte, delivered a letter to the president of the UN Security Council stating that the United States, together with other states, had "initiated actions in the exercise of its inherent right of individual and collective self defense." These actions were taken against al Qaeda terrorist camps and military installations in Afghanistan, which had a "central role in the attacks." The letter went on to state that the United States "may find that our self-defense requires further actions with respect to other organizations and other States." This letter was the birth of the Bush Doctrine, which asserted the right of the United States to use military force in "self-defense" against any state that aids, harbors, or supports international terrorism, and it had profound implications. Most significantly, Ambassador Negroponte's letter left open the possibility that a state may intervene in anticipatory self-defense, without UN Security Council authorization, in another state that is alleged to be aiding, harboring, or supporting terrorism. Secretary of Defense Donald Rumsfeld later added:

> The only way to deal with the terrorists . . . is to take the battle to them, and find them, and root them out. And that is self-defense. And there is no question but that any nation on Earth has the right of self-defense. And we do. And what we are doing is going after those people, and those organizations, and those capabilities wherever we're going to find them in the world, and stop them from killing Americans. . . . That is in effect self-defense of a preemptive nature.

In his January 2002 State of the Union address, Bush, referring to North Korea, Iran, and Iraq, argued, "States like these, and their terrorist allies, constitute an axis of evil, arming to threaten the peace of the world. . . . America will do what is necessary to ensure our nation's security. . . . I will not wait on events while dangers gather. I will not stand by as peril draws closer and closer." With this statement, the president made clear his intentions to wage war when he felt preventing threats to the United States was necessary. The United States had been attacked, and Bush believed his actions did not require congressional authority or consultation.

Although Bush had a strong argument for unilaterally exercising the decision to use force with regard to the terrorist attacks on September 11, he used that argument to extend his authority and shift U.S. foreign policy. Throughout the spring and summer 2002, the Bush administration devised its strategy for approaching the world. The national security strategy that emerged in September 2002 represents the most sweeping transformation in U.S. foreign policy since the beginning of the cold war. The strategy sets forth three tasks: "We will defend the peace by fighting terrorists and tyrants. We will preserve the peace by building good relations among great powers. We will extend the peace by encouraging free and open societies on every continent." . . .

The new strategy is proactive, rejecting the reactive strategies of containment and deterrence; its proactive stance is the basis for expanded presidential power. The strategy suggests that due to the nature of the threat a president may act alone to start a war against a perceived aggressor. The strategy presents an incontestable moral claim that in certain situations preemption is preferable to doing nothing and relies on Article 51 of the UN Charter for its legitimacy. In fact, the entire strategy is based on the presumption that a president can and must act to prevent future attacks on the United States or U.S. interests. Although such a policy may have its merits, it denies the necessity for congressional action of any kind in the use of force.

The irony of this policy is that although it does not require international support, the Bush administration has sought international support for it, using the United Nations and international law to justify the implementation of the national security strategy. On September 13, 2002, Bush addressed the UN General Assembly in New York City. He linked U.S. strategy to the purpose of the United Nations and justified using force against rogue states such as Iraq:

> The United Nations was born in the hope that survived a world war, the hope of a world moving toward justice, escaping old patterns of conflict and fear. The founding members resolved that the peace of the world must never again be destroyed by the will and wickedness of any man. . . . After generations of deceitful dictators and broken treaties and squandered lives, we dedicated ourselves to standards of human dignity . . . and to a system of security defended by all. Today, these standards and this security are challenged. . . . Above all, our principles and our security are challenged today by outlaw groups and regimes that accept no law of morality and have no limit to their violent ambitions.

Bush proceeded to make clear that the new doctrine of preemption, and the United Nations' relevancy, would be tested in Iraq. "In one place—in one regime—we find all these dangers in their most lethal and aggressive forms, exactly the kind of aggressive threat the United Nations was born to confront." Bush proceeded to lay out the case for using force against Iraq, which, he argued, had made a series of commitments to the United Nations, dating back to 1991. Furthermore, Iraq repeatedly failed to meet its commitments. . . .

The administration consequently negotiated a new UN Security Council resolution. The intent of that resolution was to prepare the way toward military action in Iraq. Resolution 1441 passed the UN Security Council unanimously on November 8, 2002, with a 15-0 vote in support of the resolution, and laid out what Iraq had to do to avoid war. The resolution cited Iraq in "material breach of its obligations under relevant resolutions." Furthermore, it offered Iraq "a final opportunity to comply with its disarmament obligations." In its final phrases, the resolution warned Iraq that it would face "serious consequences" because of continued violations of the UN Security Council resolutions.

Iraq responded to Resolution 1441 by inviting UN weapons inspectors back into the country. Throughout late 2002 and early 2003, the weapons inspectors, headed by Hans Blix and Mohammed el Baredei, pursued their task while the world watched and the United States continued to make its case that Iraqi failure to comply would be met with swift action. . . .

Bush, like Clinton before him, stressed the importance of the United Nations and used UN resolutions as a basis for using force against Iraq. . . .

On March 19, citing continued Iraqi noncompliance with international law, Bush announced that a coalition of thirty-five countries, led by the United States, began their attack on Iraq. "Our nation enters this conflict reluctantly," he told the American people, "yet our purpose is sure. The people of the United States and our friends and allies will not live at the mercy of an outlaw regime that threatens the peace with weapons of mass murder."

Following just over one month of warfare, the Iraqi regime crumbled and U.S. troops occupied Baghdad, Iraq's capital. With rebuilding efforts under way in Iraq, Bush immediately began efforts to focus on another member of the axis of evil—Iran, thus extending the Bush Doctrine of preemption. It is clear that the doctrine is firmly in place and presidential power will remain strong as long as U.S. foreign policy continues to emphasize and expand the war on terrorism. Presidential abuse of war powers is not a new phenomenon. Since World War II, however, presidential war power has vastly expanded and increased. . . . Congress is designed to be the primary check on presidential war powers. Since World War II, however, Congress has been rather ineffective in checking presidential war powers. In some cases, Congress not only fails to combat presidential war power, but also even voluntarily surrenders its legislative functions. In both the Clinton and George W. Bush administrations, Congress never declared war, but actively supported the actions each president took. . . .

[C]ontemporary presidents do not believe they need congressional approval and have substituted congressional approval with international legal sanction. Presidents Clinton and George W. Bush both relied on international legal authority in the form of UN Security Council resolutions to pursue military force. This suggests that presidents must no longer garner congressional approval when pursuing war, but must now acquire international support and must meet obligations under international law. This, as the George W. Bush case suggests, opens up the door to an even greater expansion of presidential authority and power in the use of force. . . .

POSTSCRIPT

Does the President Have Unilateral War Powers?

$\mathbf{B}$oth Yoo and Cairo were offering their views of presidential war powers at a time when President Bush was still enjoying considerable popularity. Yoo's memo is dated September 25, 2001, little more than a week after the 9/11 attacks, when the nation desperately turned to President Bush for leadership and guidance; Cairo's essay, although published in 2006, was written earlier, when Bush's job approval rating was just beginning to decline from a 60-plus level. These facts are noteworthy because, as political scientist Richard Neustadt emphasized in his seminal study of presidential power, such power is not static: It is affected by many other variables, including the president's "prestige," or standing with the public.

Neustadt's *Presidential Power: the Politics of Leadership,* originally published in 1960, has been revised under the title *Presidential Power and the Modern Presidents: The Politics of Leadership from Roosevelt to Reagan* (Free Press, 1991); it remains a useful and readable study of "personal power and its politics: what it is, how to get it, how to keep it, how to use it." For more recent studies, especially those pertinent to the immediate debate, one might begin with Yoo's book-length case for unilateral war powers, *The Powers of War and Peace: the Constitution and Foreign Affairs After 9/11* (University of Chicago, 2006). Sharply contesting that point of view is Louis Fisher's *Presidential War Power* (University Press of Kansas, 2004), which deplores what Fisher sees as the erosion of congressional war powers to a succession of modern presidents. Richard A. Posner's *Not a Suicide Pact: The Constitution in a Time of National Emergency* (Oxford, 2006) generally supports presidential emergency powers, including coercive interrogations, interception of communications within the United States, and tough laws against revealing classified information. Gerald Astor, *Presidents at War: From Truman to Bush. The Gathering of Military Powers to Our Commanders in Chief* (Wiley, 2006), traces the history and evolution of presidential war-making power in the modern era, concluding that it has gotten out of hand, especially under George W. Bush. Congressman John Murtha wrote its Foreward. Mark Brandon et al., *The Constitution in Wartime: Beyond Alarmism and Complacency* (Duke, 2005) is a collection of essays seeking a balanced view of presidential war powers.

In the 1950s and early 1960s, presidents were usually able to get their way in foreign policy and military affairs. In 1962, Congressman Carl Vinson (D-Georgia) compared Congress to an aging uncle "who complains while furiously puffing on his pipe but finally, as everyone expects, gives in and hands over the allowance." Vietnam finally ended that period of passivity. 9/11 brought it back for a time, but the results of the 2006 congressional elections appear, once again, to have stiffened congressional resistance to the president's power as commander-in-chief.

ISSUE 5

Should the Courts Seek the "Original Meaning" of the Constitution?

YES: Antonin Scalia, from Remarks at Woodrow Wilson International Center for Scholars (March 14, 2005)

NO: Stephen Breyer, from *Active Liberty: Interpreting Our Democratic Constitution* (Knopf, 2005)

ISSUE SUMMARY

YES: Supreme Court Justice Antonin Scalia rejects the notion of a "living Constitution," arguing that the judges must try to understand what the framers meant at the time.

NO: Supreme Court Justice Stephen Breyer contends that in finding the meaning of the Constitution, judges cannot neglect to consider the probable consequences of different interpretations.

On many matters the United States Constitution speaks with crystal clarity. In Article II, it says that "the Senate of the United States shall be composed of two Senators from each State." Even if it were desirable to have more than two Senators, or less, per state, there is no room for interpretation; "two" can only mean "two," and the only way of making it "one" or "three" is by constitutional amendment. (That process is itself clearly spelled out in Article V of the Constitution.) Other clauses, too, are defined in such a way as to put them beyond interpretative argument. Presidents Reagan and Clinton wanted very much to run again after their two terms, but there was no way either of them could get around the unambiguous words of the Twenty-Second amendment: "No person shall be elected to the office of President more than twice." The same clarity is found in many other provisions in the Constitution, such as the age requirements for Senators, representatives, and Presidents (Articles I and II); direct election of Senators (Amendment XVII); and both Prohibition and its repeal (Amendments XVIII and XXI).

But other clauses in the Constitution are not so clear-cut. The First Amendment states that "Congress shall make no law respecting an establishment of religion. . . ." What is an "establishment of religion"? The Constitution itself does not say. Some constitutional scholars take it to mean that the state may not single out any particular religion for state sponsorship or support; others interpret it to mean that the state may not aid any religions. Which interpretation is correct? And what method do we use to determine which is correct? The same questions have to be asked about other fuzzy-sounding phrases, such as "due process of law" (Article V and Amendment XIV), "cruel and unusual punishment" (Amendment VIII), and "commerce among the several states" (Article I). Down through the years, jurists and legal commentators have tried to devise guiding principles for interpreting these and other phrases that have been subjects of dispute in the courts.

One set of principles made headlines in the 1980s when federal Appeals Court judge Robert Bork was nominated to the Supreme Court by President Ronald Reagan. Bork was a champion of "originalism," interpreting the Constitution according to what he called the "original intent" of its framers. What the courts should do, Bork argued, is to go back to what the framers meant at the time they wrote the particular clauses in dispute. Since the effect of Bork's approach was to call into question some of the more recent decisions by the Court, such as those upholding affirmative action and abortion, his nomination provoked a tumultuous national debate, and in the end he failed to win Senate confirmation.

On its face, originalism seems to comport with common sense. In making a will, to take an analogy, people rightly expect that their will should be interpreted according to *their* intent, not what their heirs might want it to mean. The analogy, however, comes under serious strain when we consider that the Constitution is not, like a will, the product of one person, or even one generation. Its various clauses have been crafted over 220 years; they are the work of many people in various Congresses, and many, many more who ratified them in state conventions or legislatures. Each one of those people may have had a different idea of what those clauses meant. When we come to clauses like "establishment of religion" or "equal protection of the laws," how can we possibly determine what the "original intent" of these clauses was—or even if there was any single intent?

The reply of the originalists is that the goal of determining the framers' intent must be striven for even when it is not perfectly attained. Moreover, what are we going to put in its place? Surely we can't have judges simply making things up, slipping in their own personal policy preferences in place of the Constitution and statutes of the United States.

This is one of the arguments—what he calls the "killer argument"—advanced by Justice Antonin Scalia in the selections that follow. As if replying to him, Justice Stephen Breyer rises to Scalia's challenge by suggesting that in interpreting the Constitution judges should weigh the probable consequences of varying interpretations of disputed clauses in the Constitution.

YES

Antonin Scalia

Constitutional Interpretation

I am one of a small number of judges, small number of anybody: judges, professors, lawyers; who are known as originalists. Our manner of interpreting the Constitution is to begin with the text, and to give that text the meaning that it bore when it was adopted by the people. I'm not a strict constructionist, despite the introduction. I don't like the term "strict construction." I do not think the Constitution, or any text should be interpreted either strictly or sloppily; it should be interpreted reasonably. Many of my interpretations do not deserve the description "strict." I do believe, however, that you give the text the meaning it had when it was adopted.

This is such a minority position in modern academia and in modern legal circles that on occasion I'm asked when I've given a talk like this a question from the back of the room—"Justice Scalia, when did you first become an originalist?"—as though it is some kind of weird affliction that seizes some people—"When did you first start eating human flesh?"

Although it is a minority view now, the reality is that, not very long ago, originalism was orthodoxy. Everybody, at least purported to be an originalist. If you go back and read the commentaries on the Constitution by Joseph Story, he didn't think the Constitution evolved or changed. He said it means and will always mean what it meant when it was adopted.

Or consider the opinions of John Marshall in the Federal Bank case,* where he says, we must not, we must always remember it is a constitution we are expounding. And since it's a constitution, he says, you have to give its provisions expansive meaning so that they will accommodate events that you do not know of which will happen in the future.

Well, if it is a constitution that changes, you wouldn't have to give it an expansive meaning. You can give it whatever meaning you want and when future necessity arises, you simply change the meaning. But anyway, that is no longer the orthodoxy.

Oh, one other example about how not just the judges and scholars believed in originalism, but even the American people. Consider the Nineteenth Amendment, which is the amendment that gave women the vote. It was adopted by the American people in 1920. Why did we adopt a constitutional amendment for that purpose? The Equal Protection Clause existed in 1920; it was adopted right after the Civil War. And you know that if that issue of the franchise for women

---

McCulloch v. Maryland, 4 Wheat, 316 (1819). [*Eds.*]

From a Speech delivered at the Woodrow Wilson International Center for Scholars, March 14, 2005.

came up today, we would not have to have a constitutional amendment. Someone would come to the Supreme Court and say, "Your Honors, in a democracy, what could be a greater denial of equal protection than denial of the franchise?" And the Court would say, "Yes! Even though it never meant it before, the Equal Protection Clause means that women have to have the vote." But that's not how the American people thought in 1920. In 1920, they looked at the Equal Protection Clause and said, "What does it mean?" Well, it clearly doesn't mean that you can't discriminate in the franchise—not only on the basis of sex, but on the basis of property ownership, on the basis of literacy. None of that is unconstitutional. And therefore, since it wasn't unconstitutional, and we wanted it to be, we did things the good old fashioned way and adopted an amendment.

Now, in asserting that originalism used to be orthodoxy, I do not mean to imply that judges did not distort the Constitution now and then, of course they did. We had willful judges then, and we will have willful judges until the end of time. But the difference is that prior to the last fifty years or so, prior to the advent of the "Living Constitution," judges did their distortions the good old fashioned way, the honest way—they lied about it. They said the Constitution means such and such, when it never meant such and such.

It's a big difference that you now no longer have to lie about it, because we are in the era of the evolving Constitution. And the judge can simply say, "Oh yes, the Constitution didn't used to mean that, but it does now." We are in the age in which not only judges, not only lawyers, but even school children have come to learn the Constitution changes. I have grammar school students come into the court now and then, and they recite very proudly what they have been taught: "The Constitution is a living document." You know, it morphs.

Well, let me first tell you how we got to the "Living Constitution." You don't have to be a lawyer to understand it. The road is not that complicated. Initially, the Court began giving terms in the text of the Constitution a meaning they didn't have when they were adopted. For example, the First Amendment, which forbids Congress to abridge the freedom of speech. What does the freedom of speech mean? Well, it clearly did not mean that Congress, or government could not impose any restrictions upon speech. Libel laws for example, were clearly Constitutional. Nobody thought the First Amendment was *carte blanche* to libel someone. But in the famous case of *New York Times v. Sullivan*, the Supreme Court said, "But the First Amendment does prevent you from suing for libel if you are a public figure and if the libel was not malicious." That is, the person, a member of the press or otherwise, thought that what the person said was true. Well, that had never been the law. I mean, it might be a good law. And some states could amend their libel law.

It's one thing for a states to amend its libel law and say, "We think that public figures shouldn't be able to sue." That's fine. But the courts have said that the First Amendment, which never meant this before, now means that if you are a public figure, that you can't sue for libel unless it's intentional, malicious. So that's one way to do it.

Another example is: the Constitution guarantees the right to be represented by counsel; that never meant the State had to pay for your counsel. But you can reinterpret it to mean that.

That was step one. Step two, I mean, that will only get you so far. There is no text in the Constitution that you could reinterpret to create a right to abortion, for example. So you need something else. The something else is called the doctrine of "Substantive Due Process." Only lawyers can walk around talking about substantive process, inasmuch as it's a contradiction in terms. If you referred to substantive process or procedural substance at a cocktail party, people would look at you funny. But lawyers talk this way all the time.

What substantive due process is, is, is quite simple, the Constitution has a Due Process Clause, which says that no person shall be deprived of life, liberty or property without due process of law. Now, what does this guarantee? Does it guarantee life, liberty or property? No, indeed! All three can be taken away. You can be fined, you can be incarcerated, you can even be executed, but not without due process of law. It's a procedural guarantee. But the Court said, and this goes way back, in the 1920s at least, in fact the first case to do it was Dred Scott. But it became more popular in the 1920s. The Court said there are some liberties that are so important, that no process will suffice to take them away. Hence, substantive due process.

Now, what liberties are they? The Court will tell you. Be patient. When the doctrine of substantive due process was initially announced, it was limited in this way, the Court said it embraces only those liberties that are fundamental to a democratic society and rooted in the traditions of the American people.

Then we come to step three. Step three: that limitation is eliminated. Within the last twenty years, we have found to be covered by Due Process the right to abortion, which was so little rooted in the traditions of the American people that it was criminal for two hundred years; the right to homosexual sodomy, which was so little rooted in the traditions of the American people that it was criminal for two hundred years.

So it is literally true, and I don't think this is an exaggeration, that the Court has essentially liberated itself from the text of the Constitution, from the text, and even from the traditions of the American people. It is up to the Court to say what is covered by substantive due process. What are the arguments usually made in favor of the Living Constitution? As the name of it suggests, it is a very attractive philosophy, and it's hard to talk people out of it: the notion that the Constitution grows. The major argument is the Constitution is a living organism, it has to grow with the society that it governs or it will become brittle and snap.

This is the equivalent of, an anthropomorphism equivalent to what you hear from your stock broker, when he tells you that the stock market is resting for an assault on the eleven-thousand level. The stock market panting at some base camp. The stock market is not a mountain climber and the Constitution is not a living organism for Pete's sake; it's a legal document, and like all legal documents, it says some things, and it doesn't say other things.

And if you think that the aficionados of the Living Constitution want to bring you flexibility, think again. My Constitution is a very flexible Constitution. You think the death penalty is a good idea: persuade your fellow citizens and adopt it. You think it's a bad idea: persuade them the other way and eliminate it. You want a right to abortion: create it the way most rights are created in a democratic society. Persuade your fellow citizens it's a good idea, and enact it. You want the opposite, persuade them the other way. That's flexibility. But to read either result into the Constitution is not to produce flexibility, it is to produce what a constitution is designed to produce: rigidity.

Abortion, for example, is offstage, it is off the democratic stage, it is no use debating it, it is unconstitutional. I mean prohibiting it is unconstitutional. I mean it's no use debating it anymore. Now and forever, coast to coast, I guess until we amend the constitution, which is a difficult thing. So, for whatever reason you might like the Living Constitution, don't like it because it provides flexibility.That's not the name of the game.

Some people also seem to like it because they think it's a good liberal thing. That somehow this is a conservative/liberal battle. And conservatives like the old-fashioned originalist Constitution and liberals ought to like the Living Constitution. That's not true either. The dividing line between those who believe in the Living Constitution and those who don't is not the dividing line between conservatives and liberals.

Conservatives are willing to grow the Constitution to cover their favorite causes just as liberals are. And the best example of that is two cases we announced some years ago on the same day, the same morning. One case was *Romer v. Evans*, in which the people of Colorado had enacted an amendment to the State Constitution by plebiscite, which said that neither the State, nor any subdivision of the State would add to the protected statuses against which private individuals cannot discriminate. The usual ones are: race, religion, age, sex, disability and so forth. Would not add sexual preference. Somebody thought that was a terrible idea, and since it was a terrible idea, it must be unconstitutional. Brought a lawsuit, it came to the Supreme Court. And the Supreme Court said, "Yes, it is unconstitutional." On the basis of . . . I don't know. The Sexual Preference Clause of the Bill of Rights, presumably. And the liberals loved it; and the conservatives gnashed their teeth.

The very next case we announced is a case called *BMW v. [Gore]*. Not the [Gore] you think; this is another [Gore]. Mr. Gore had bought a BMW, which is a car supposedly advertised at least as having a superb finish, baked seven times in ovens deep in the Alps, by dwarfs. And his BMW apparently had gotten scratched on the way over. They did not send it back to the Alps, they took a can of spray-paint and fixed it. And he found out about this and was furious, and he brought a lawsuit. He got his compensatory damages, a couple of hundred dollars, the difference between a car with a better paint job and a worse paint job. Plus, $2 million against BMW for punitive damages for being a bad actor, which is absurd of course, so it must be unconstitutional. BMW appealed to my court, and my court said, "Yes, it's unconstitutional." In violation of, I assume, the Excessive Damages Clause of the Bill of Rights. And if excessive punitive damages are unconstitutional, why aren't excessive compensatory damages unconstitutional? So you have a federal question whenever you get a judgment in a civil case. Well, that one the conservatives liked, because conservatives don't like punitive damages, and the liberals gnashed their teeth.

I dissented in both cases because I say, "A pox on both their houses." It has nothing to do with what your policy preferences are; it has to do with what you think the Constitution is.

Some people are in favor of the Living Constitution because they think it always leads to greater freedom. There's just nothing to lose. The evolving Constitution will always provide greater and greater freedom, more and more rights. Why would you think that? It's a two-way street. And indeed, under the aegis of the Living Constitution, some freedoms have been taken away. . . .

Well, I've talked about some of the false virtues of the Living Constitution, let me tell you what I consider its, principal, vices are. Surely the greatest, you should always begin with principal, its greatest vice is its illegitimacy. The only reason federal courts sit in judgment of the constitutionality of federal legislation is not because they are explicitly authorized to do so in the Constitution. Some modern constitutions give the constitutional court explicit authority to review German legislation or French legislation for its constitutionality. Our Constitution doesn't say anything like that. But John Marshall says in *Marbury v. Madison*: look, this is lawyers' work. What you have here is an apparent conflict between the Constitution and the statute. And, all the time, lawyers and judges have to reconcile these conflicts; they try to read the two to comport with each other. If they can't, it's judges' work to decide which ones prevail. When there are two statutes, the more recent one prevails. It implicitly repeals the older one. But when the Constitution is at issue, the Constitution prevails because it is a "superstatute." I mean, that's what Marshall says: it's judges' work.

If you believe, however, that the Constitution is not a legal text, like the texts involved when judges reconcile or decide which of two statutes prevail; if you think the Constitution is some exhortation to give effect to the most fundamental values of the society as those values change from year to year; if you think that it is meant to reflect, as some of the Supreme Court cases say, particularly those involving the Eighth Amendment, if you think it is simply meant to reflect the evolving standards of decency that mark the progress of a maturing society, if that is what you think it is, then why in the world would you have it interpreted by nine lawyers? What do I know about the evolving standards of decency of American society? I'm afraid to ask.

If that is what you think the Constitution is, then *Marbury v. Madison* is wrong. It shouldn't be up to the judges, it should be up to the legislature. We should have a system like the English. Whatever the legislature thinks is constitutional is constitutional. They know the evolving standards of American society, I don't. So in principle, it's incompatible with the legal regime that America has established.

Secondly, and this is the killer argument, I mean, it's the best debater's argument. They say in politics, you can't beat somebody with nobody, it's the same thing with principles of legal interpretation. If you don't believe in originalism, then you need some other principle of interpretation. Being a non-originalist is not enough. You see, I have my rules that confine me. I know what I'm looking for. When I find it, the original meaning of the Constitution, I am handcuffed. If I believe that the First Amendment meant when it was adopted that you are entitled to burn the American flag, I have to come out that way, even though I don't like to come out that way. When I find that the original meaning of the jury trial guarantee is that any additional time you spend in prison which depends upon a fact, must depend upon a fact found by a jury, once I find that's what the jury trial guarantee means, I am handcuffed. Though I'm a law-and-order type, I cannot do all the mean conservative things I would like to do to this society. You got me.

Now, if you're not going to control your judges that way, what other criterion are you going to place before them? What is the criterion that governs the living constitutional judge? What can you possibly use, besides original meaning? Think about that. Natural law? We all agree on that, don't we? The philosophy of John Rawls? That's easy. There really is nothing else. You either tell your judges, "Look, this is a law, like all laws, give it the meaning it had when it was adopted." Or, you tell your judges, "Govern us. You tell us whether people under eighteen, who committed their crimes when they were under eighteen, should be executed. You tell us whether there ought to be an unlimited right to abortion or a partial right to abortion. You make these decisions for us."

I have put this question, you know I speak at law schools with some frequency just to make trouble, and I put this question to the faculty all the time, or incite the students to ask their living constitutional professors. "OK professor, you are not an originalist, what is your criterion?" There is none other.

And finally, this is what I will conclude with, although it is not on a happy note, the worst thing about the Living Constitution is that it will destroy the Constitution. I was confirmed, close to nineteen years ago now, by a vote of ninety-eight to nothing. The two missing were Barry Goldwater and Jake Garn, so make it a hundred. I was known at that time to be, in my political and social views, fairly conservative. But still, I was known to be a good lawyer, an honest man, somebody who could read a text and give it its fair meaning, had judicial impartiality and so forth. And so I was unanimously confirmed.

Today, barely twenty years later, it is difficult to get someone confirmed to the Court of Appeals. What has happened? The American people have figured out what is going on. If we are selecting lawyers, if we are selecting people to read a text and give it the fair meaning it had when it was adopted, yes, the most important thing to do is to get a good lawyer. If on the other hand, we're picking people to draw out of their own conscience and experience, a new constitution, with all sorts of new values to govern our society, then we should not look principally for good lawyers. We should look principally for people who agree with us, the majority, as to whether there ought to be this right, that right, and the other right. We want to pick people that would write the new constitution that we would want.

And that is why you hear in the discourse on this subject, people talking about moderate, we want moderate judges. What is a moderate interpretation of the text? Halfway between what it really means and what you'd like it to mean? There is no such thing as a moderate interpretation of the text. Would you ask a lawyer, "Draw me a moderate contract?" The only way the word has any meaning is if you are looking for someone to write a law, to write a constitution, rather than to interpret one. The moderate judge is the one who will devise the new constitution that most people would approve of. So for example, we had a suicide case some terms ago, and the Court refused to hold that there is a constitutional right to assisted suicide. We said, "We're not yet ready to say that. Stay tuned, in a few years, the time may come, but we're not yet ready." And that was a moderate decision, because I think most people would not want—if we had gone, looked into that and created a national right to assisted suicide that would have been an immoderate and extremist decision.

I think the very terminology suggests where we have arrived: at the point of selecting people to write a constitution, rather than people to give us the fair meaning of one that has been democratically adopted. And when that happens, when the Senate interrogates nominees to the Supreme Court, or to the lower courts you know, "Judge so and so, do you think there is a right to this in the Constitution? You don't? Well, my constituents think there ought to be, and I'm not going to appoint to the court someone who is not going to find that." When we are in that mode, you realize, we have rendered the Constitution useless, because the Constitution will mean what the majority wants it to mean. The senators are representing the majority. And they will be selecting justices who will devise a constitution that the majority wants.

And that of course, deprives the Constitution of its principle utility. The Bill of Rights is devised to protect you and me against, who do you think? The majority. My most important function on the Supreme Court is to tell the majority to take a walk. And the notion that the justices ought to be selected because of the positions that they will take that are favored by the majority is a recipe for destruction of what we have had for two hundred years.

Stephen Breyer

Active Liberty: Interpreting Our Democratic Constitution

My discussion sees individual constitutional provisions as embodying certain basic purposes, often expressed in highly general terms. It sees the Constitution itself as a single document designed to further certain basic general purposes as a whole. It argues that an understanding of, and a focus upon, those general purposes will help a judge better to understand and to apply specific provisions. And it identifies consequences as an important yardstick to measure a given interpretation's faithfulness to these democratic purposes. In short, focus on purpose seeks to promote active liberty by insisting on interpretations, statutory as well as constitutional, that are consistent with the people's will. Focus on consequences, in turn, allows us to gauge whether and to what extent we have succeeded in facilitating workable outcomes which reflect that will.

Some lawyers, judges, and scholars, however, would caution strongly against the reliance upon purposes (particularly abstractly stated purposes) and assessment of consequences. They ask judges to focus primarily upon text, upon the Framers' original expectations, narrowly conceived, and upon historical tradition. They do not deny the occasional relevance of consequences or purposes (including such general purposes as democracy), but they believe that judges should use them sparingly in the interpretive endeavor. They ask judges who tend to find interpretive answers in those decision-making elements to rethink the problem to see whether language, history, tradition, and precedent by themselves will not yield an answer. They fear that, once judges become accustomed to justifying legal conclusions through appeal to real-world consequences, they will too often act subjectively and undemocratically, substituting an elite's views of good policy for sound law. They hope that language, history, tradition, and precedent will provide important safeguards against a judge's confusing his or her personal, undemocratic notion of what is good for that which the Constitution or statute demands. They tend also to emphasize the need for judicial opinions that set forth their legal conclusions in terms of rules that will guide other institutions, including lower courts.

From *Active Liberty: Interpreting Our Democratic Constitution,* by Stephen Breyer (Knopf/Vintage 2005), pp. 115–124, 127, 131–132. Copyright © 2005 by Stephen Breyer. Reprinted by permission of Random House Inc.

This view, which I shall call "textualist" (in respect to statutes) or "originalist" (in respect to the Constitution) or "literalist" (shorthand for both), while logically consistent with emphasizing the Constitution's democratic objectives, is not hospitable to the kinds of arguments I have advanced. Nor is it easily reconciled with my illustrations. Why, then, does it not undercut my entire argument?

The answer, in my view, lies in the unsatisfactory nature of that interpretive approach. First, the more "originalist" judges cannot appeal to the Framers themselves in support of their interpretive views. The Framers did not say specifically what factors judges should take into account when they interpret statutes or the Constitution. This is obvious in the case of statutes. Why would the Framers have preferred (1) a system of interpretation that relies heavily on linguistic canons to (2) a system that seeks more directly to find the intent of the legislators who enacted the statute? It is close to obvious in respect to the Constitution. Why would the Farmers, who disagreed even about the necessity of *including* a Bill of Rights in the Constitution, who disagreed about the *content* of that Bill of Rights, nonetheless have agreed about *what school of interpretive thought* should prove dominant in interpreting that Bill of Rights in the centuries to come?

In respect to content, the Constitution itself says that the "enumeration" in the Constitution of some rights "shall not be construed to deny or disparage others retained by the people." Professor Bernard Bailyn concludes that the Framers added this language to make clear that "rights, like law itself, should never be fixed, frozen, that new dangers and needs will emerge, and that to respond to these dangers and needs, rights must be newly specified to protect the individual's integrity and inherent dignity." Given the open-ended nature of *content*, why should one expect to find fixed views about the nature of interpretive practice?

If, however, justification for the literalist's interpretive practices cannot be found in the Framers intentions, where can it be found—other than in an appeal to *consequences*, that is, in an appeal to the presumed beneficial consequences for the law or for the nation that will flow from adopting those practices? And that is just what we find argued. That is to say, literalist arguments often try to show that that approach will have favorable *results*, for example, that it will deter judges from substituting their own views about what is good for the public for those of Congress or for those embodied in the Constitution. They argue, in other words, that a more literal approach to interpretation will better control judicial subjectivity. Thus, while literalists eschew consideration of consequences case by case, their interpretive rationale is consequentialist in this important sense.

Second, I would ask whether it is true that judges who reject literalism necessarily open the door to subjectivity. They do not endorse subjectivity. And under their approach important safeguards of objectivity remain. For one thing, a judge who emphasizes consequences, no less than any other, is aware of the legal precedents, rules, standards, practices, and institutional understanding that a decision will affect. He or she also takes account of the way in which this system of legally related rules, institutions, and practices affects the world.

To be sure, a court focused on consequences may decide a case in a way that radically changes the law. But this is not always a bad thing. For example, after the late-nineteenth-century Court decided *Plessy v. Ferguson*, the case which permitted racial segregation that was, in principle, "separate but equal," it became apparent that segregation did not mean equality but not meant disrespect for members of a minority race and led to a segregated society that was totally unequal, a consequence directly contrary to the purpose and demands of the Fourteenth Amendment. The Court, in *Brown v. Board of Education* and later decisions, overruled *Plessy*, and the law changed in a way that profoundly affected the lives of many.

In any event, to focus upon consequences does not automatically invite frequent dramatic legal change. Judges, including those who look to consequences, understand the human need to plan in reliance upon law, the need for predictability, the need for stability. And they understand that too radical, too frequent legal change has, as a consequence, a tendency to undercut those important law-related human needs. Similarly, each judge's individual need to be consistent over time constrains subjectivity. As Justice O'Connor has explained, a constitutional judge's initial decisions leave "footprints" that the judge, in later decisions, will almost inevitably follow.

Moreover, to consider consequences is not to consider simply whether the consequences of a proposed decision are good or bad, in a particular judge's opinion. Rather, to emphasize consequences is to emphasize consequences related to the particular textual provision at issue. The judge must examine the consequences through the lens of the relevant constitutional value or purpose. The relevant values limit interpretive possibilities. If they are democratic values, they may well counsel modesty or restraint as well. And I believe that when a judge candidly acknowledges that, in addition to text, history, and precedent, consequences also guide his decision-making, he is more likely to be disciplined in emphasizing, for example, constitutionally relevant consequences rather than allowing his own subjectively held values to be outcome determinative. In all these ways, a focus on consequences will itself constrain subjectivity.

Here are examples of how these principles apply. The First Amendment says that "Congress shall make no law respecting an establishment of religion." I recently wrote (in dissent) that this clause prohibits government from providing vouchers to parents to help pay for the education of their children in parochial schools. The basic reason, in my view, is that the clause seeks to avoid among other things the "social conflict, potentially created when government becomes involved in religious education." Nineteenth- and twentieth-century immigration has produced a nation with fifty or more different religions. And that fact made the risk of "social conflict" far more serious after the Civil War and in twentieth-century America than the Framers, with their eighteenth-century experience, might have anticipated. The twentieth-century Supreme Court had held in applicable precedent that, given the changing nature of our society, in order to implement the basic value that the Framers wrote the clause to protect, it was necessary to interpret the clause more broadly than the Framers might have thought likely.

My opinion then turned to consequences. It said that voucher programs, if widely adopted, could provide billions of dollars to religious schools. At first blush, that may seem a fine idea. But will different religious groups become concerned about which groups are getting the money and how? What are the criteria? How are programs being implemented? Is a particular program biased against particular sects, say, because it forbids certain kinds of teaching? Are rival sects failing to live up to the relevant criteria, say, by teaching "civil disobedience" to "unjust laws"? How will claims for money, say, of one religious group against another, be adjudicated? In a society as religiously diverse as ours, I saw in the administration of huge grant programs for religious education the potential for religious strife. And that, it seemed to me, was the kind of problem the First Amendment's religion clauses seek to avoid.

The same constitutional concern—the need to avoid a "divisiveness based upon religion that promotes social conflict"—helped me determine whether the Establishment Clause forbade two public displays of the tables of the Ten Commandments, one inside a Kentucky state courthouse, the other on the grounds of the Texas State Capitol. It is well recognized that Establishment Clause does not allow the government to compel religious practices, to show favoritism among sects or between religion and non-religion, or to promote religion. Yet, at the same time, given the religious beliefs of most Americans, an absolutist approach that would purge all religious references from the public sphere could well promote the very kind of social conflict that the Establishment Clause seeks to avoid. Thus, I thought, the Establishment Clause cannot *automatically* forbid every public display of the Ten Commandments, despite the religious nature of its text. Rather, one must examine the context of the *particular* display to see whether, in that context, the tablets convey the kind of government-endorsed religious message that the Establishment Clause forbids.

The history of the Kentucky courthouse display convinced me and the other members of the Court's majority that the display sought to serve its sponsors' primarily religious objectives and that many of its viewers would understand it as reflecting that motivation. But the context of the Texas display differed significantly. A private civic (and primarily secular) organization had placed the tablets on the Capitol grounds as part of the organization's efforts to combat juvenile delinquency. Those grounds contained seventeen other monuments and twenty-one historical markers, none of which conveyed any religious message and all of which sought to illustrate the historical "ideals" of Texans. And the monument had stood for forty years without legal challenge. These circumstances strongly suggested that the public visiting the Capitol grounds had long considered the tablets' religious message as a secondary part of a broader moral and historical message reflecting a cultural heritage—a view of the display consistent with its promoters' basic objective.

It was particularly important that the Texas display stood uncontested for forty years. That fact indicated, as a practical matter of degree, that (unlike the Kentucky display) the Texas display was unlikely to prove socially divisive. Indeed, to require the display's removal itself would encourage disputes over the the removal of longstanding depictions of the Ten Commandments from public buildings across the nation, thereby creating the very kind of religiously based divisiveness that the Establishment Clause was designed to prevent. By way of contrast, the short and stormy history of the more contemporary Kentucky display revealed both religious motivation and consequent social controversy. Thus, in the two cases, which I called borderline cases, consideration of likely consequences—evaluated in light of the purposes or values embodied within the Establishment Clause—helped produce a legal result: The Clause allowed the Texas display, while it forbade the display in Kentucky.

I am not arguing here that I was right in any of these cases. I am arguing that my opinions sought to identify a critical value underlying the Religion Clauses. They considered how that value applied in modern-day America; they looked for consequences relevant to that value. And they sought to evaluate likely consequences in terms of that value. That is what I mean by an *interpretive approach* that emphasizes consequences. Under that approach language, precedent, constitutional values, and factual circumstances all constrain judicial subjectivity.

Third, "subjectivity" is a two-edged criticism, which the literalist himself cannot escape. The literalist's tools—language and structure, history and tradition—often fail to provide objective guidance in those truly difficult cases about which I have spoken. Will canons of interpretation provide objective answers? One canon tells the court to choose an interpretation that gives every statutory word a meaning. Another permits the court to ignore a word, treating it as surplus, if otherwise the construction is repugnant to the statute's purpose. Shall the court read the statute narrowly as in keeping with the common law or broadly as remedial in purpose? Canons to the left to them, canons to the right of them, which canons shall the judges choose to follow?

. . . Fourth, I do not believe that textualist or originalist methods of interpretation are more likely to produce clear, workable legal rules. But even were they to do so, the advantages of legal rules can be overstated. Rules must be interpreted and applied. Every law student whose class grade is borderline knows that the benefits that rules produce for cases that fall within the heartland are often lost in cases that arise at the boundaries.

. . . Fifth, textualist and originalist doctrines may themselves produce seriously harmful consequences—outweighing whatever risks of subjectivity or uncertainty are inherent in other approaches.

. . . Literalism has a tendency to undermine the Constitution's efforts to create a framework for democratic government—a government that, while protecting basic individual liberties, permits citizens to govern themselves, and to govern themselves effectively. Insofar as a more literal interpretive approach undermines this basic objective, it is inconsistent with the most fundamental original intention of the Framers themselves.

For any or all of these reasons, I hope that those strongly committed to textualist or literalist views—those whom I am almost bound not to convince—are fairly small in number. I hope to have convinced some of the rest that active liberty has an important role to play in constitutional (and statutory) interpretation.

That role, I repeat, does not involve radical change in current professional interpretive methods nor does it involve ignoring the protection the

Constitution grants fundamental (negative) liberties. It takes Thomas Jefferson's statement as a statement of goals that the Constitution now seeks to fulfill: "[A]ll men are created equal." They are endowed by their Creator with certain "unalienable Rights." "[T]o secure these Rights, Governments are instituted among Men, *deriving their just powers from the consent of the governed*." It underscores, emphasizes, or reemphasizes the final democratic part of the famous phrase. That reemphasis, I believe, has practical value when judges seek to assure fidelity, in our modern society, to these ancient and unchanging ideals.

POSTSCRIPT

Should the Courts Seek the "Original Meaning" of the Constitution?

Given their different methods of interpretation, certain cases might pose challenges for both Scalia and Breyer. For Scalia, the tough case would be *Brown v. Board of Education* (1954). Scalia is not about to defend racial segregation or seek to turn back the clock to Jim Crow days in the South. Yet, given his interpretative philosophy, how would he defend the *Brown* decision? The same Congress that passed the Fourteenth Amendment also required streetcars in the District of Columbia to be segregated, showing that the "original intent" of those legislators was certainly not to ban segregation. As for Breyer, if he is concerned about the social effects of any given interpretation, might he not want to reconsider his support for *Roe v. Wade* (1973), a decision that caused deep, bitter divisions in American society?

Ronald Dworkin also rises to Scalia's challenge to come up with a different interpretive approach if "originalism" doesn't work. Dworkin's approach is to lean toward interpretations that increase liberty and equality in America; those are his moral values and he frankly declares that they ought to be read into the Constitution. See his book, *Freedom's Law: The Moral Reading of the American Constitution* (Harvard University Press, 1996). In her book, *A Nation Under Lawyers* (Farrar, Straus, & Giroux, 1994), Mary Ann Glendon warns of the perils of what she calls "romantic judging." Jamin Raskin's *Overruling Democracy: The Supreme Court Versus the American People* (Routledge, 2003) argues that it is actually the *conservatives* who have taken the most liberties in interpreting the Constitution, offering the decision in *Bush v. Gore* (2000) as the prime example. Jeffrey Toobin, *The Nine: Inside the Secret World of the Supreme Court* (Doubleday, 2007), argues that it is not laws, the Constitution, or even ideology that move the High Court, but rather the personalities of the men and women who sit on it. Phillip J. Cooper's *Battles on the Bench: Conflict Inside the Supreme Court* (University of Kansas Press, 1995) illuminates battles behind the scenes in the Court since John Marshall's time. Jeffrey A. Segal, et al., *The Supreme Court in the Legal System* (Cambridge University Press, 2005) is a comprehensive introduction to the Supreme Court and the lower federal courts.

In the past, sitting Supreme Court Justices have typically been reticent about making strong public statements outside the Court, especially on issues that might come before it. Today that appears to be changing. In a speech before the Federalist society in February of 2006, Justice Scalia continued to criticize those who say that the Constitution is "a living document." "You would have to be an idiot to believe that," he said. In another speech the following month he criticized the idea that detainees captured in the battlefield have full rights under the Constitution or international law, even though the Court was then considering the appeal of a man formerly detained without a jury trial on grounds of being an "enemy combatant." Justice Ruth Ginsberg, too, has not been hesitant to speak her mind outside the Court, decrying Republican efforts in Congress to ban the citation of foreign law in deciding cases. They "fuel the irrational fringe," she said in a February 2006 speech in South Africa, and claimed that her life was threatened by "commandoes" who posted threats on the Internet. The line between the political and the judicial, never entirely definite, seems to be getting increasingly blurred.

ISSUE 6

Is Congress a "Broken Branch"?

YES: Thomas E. Mann and Norman J. Ornstein, from *The Broken Branch: How Congress Is Failing America and How to Get It Back on Track* (Oxford University Press, 2006)

NO: Lee H. Hamilton, from *How Congress Works* (Indiana University Press, 2004)

ISSUE SUMMARY

YES: Congressional scholars Thomas Mann and Norman Ornstein argue that Congress has become increasingly dysfunctional as a result of many self-inflicted wounds, from ethical violations to hyperpartisanship.

NO: Former representative Lee H. Hamilton contends that many of the Congress's so-called flaws are actually faithful reflections of how the American public thinks and feels.

$\mathbf{T}$hose who teach introductory American government usually look forward to the unit on the American presidency. It sets off lively class participation, especially when students talk about the actions of whoever happens to be in the White House. The same happens when the topic is the Supreme Court; students can argue about controversial decisions like school prayer, flag-burning, and abortion, and the instructor sometimes has to work hard to keep the discussion from getting too hot.

But when Congress, the third branch of the federal government, comes up for discussion, it is hard to get anything going beyond a few cynical shrugs and wisecracks. Seriously intended comments, when they finally emerge, may range from skeptical questions ("What do they *do* for their money?") to harsh pronouncements ("Bunch of crooks!").

Students today can hardly be blamed for these reactions. They are inheritors of a rich American tradition of Congress-bashing. At the end of the nineteenth century the novelist Mark Twain quipped that "there is no distinctly native American criminal class except Congress." In the 1930s the humorist Will Rogers suggested that "we have the best Congress money can buy." In the 1940s President Harry Truman coined the term *do-nothing Congress,* and Fred

Allen's radio comedy show had a loudmouth "Senator Claghorn" who did nothing but bluster. In the 1950s the *Washington Post's* "Herblock" and other cartoonists liked to draw senators as potbellied old guys chewing cigars.

Needless to say, the drafters of the U.S. Constitution did not anticipate that kind of portrayal; they wanted Congress to stand tall in power and stature. Significantly, they listed it first among the three branches, and they gave it an extensive list of powers, eighteen in all, rounding them off with the power to "make all laws which shall be necessary and proper" for executing its express powers.

Throughout the first half of the nineteenth century, Congress played a very visible role in the business of the nation, and some of its most illustrious members, like Daniel Webster, Henry Clay, and John C. Calhoun, were national superstars. Men and women crowded into to the visitors' gallery when Webster was about to deliver one of his powerful orations; during these performances they sometimes wept openly.

What, then, happened to Congress over the years to bring about this fall from grace? A number of factors have come into play, two of which can be cited immediately.

First, Congress has become a very complicated institution. In both houses, especially in the House of Representatives, legislation is not hammered out on the floor but in scores of committees and subcommittees, known to some journalists and political scientists but to relatively few others. Major bills can run hundreds of pages, and are written in a kind of lawyerspeak inaccessible to ordinary people. Congressional rules are so arcane that even a bill with clear majority support can fall through the cracks and disappear. The public simply doesn't understand all this, and incomprehension can easily sour into distrust and suspicion.

A second reason why Congress doesn't get much respect these days is connected with the increased visibility of its sometime rival, the presidency. Ever since Abraham Lincoln raised the possibility of what presidents can do during prolonged emergencies, charismatic presidents like Woodrow Wilson, Franklin Roosevelt, and Ronald Reagan, serving during such times, have aggrandized the office of the president, pushing Congress into the background. They have thus stolen much of the prestige and glamour that once attached to the legislative branch. The president has become a very visible "one" and Congress has faded into a shadowy "many." Everyone knows who the president is, but how many people can name the leaders of Congress? Can you?

These developments have emerged from long-range historical trends in America. Arguably, they might have been inevitable, beyond anyone's fault or control. But other wounds suffered by Congress might be self-inflicted. In the sections that follow, congressional scholars Thomas Mann and Norman Ornstein blame them on Congress's ethical violations, undemocratic procedures, pork-barrel legislation, intimacy with lobbyists, and hyperpartisanship. In reply, Lee H. Hamilton, a former member of Congress, contends that much of the criticism of Congress is based on misunderstandings of Congress's proper role.

YES

**Thomas E. Mann
and Norman J. Ornstein**

The Broken Branch: How Congress Is Failing America and How to Get It Back on Track

The Decline of Deliberation

When we first came to Congress, members from New York, Pennsylvania and other parts of the Northeast were notorious for their commuting schedule. Many would try to limit their time in Washington to three days, spending long "weekends" back home. They were known as the Tuesday to Thursday Club. That meant coming down to the Capitol early on Tuesday morning, during routine morning business and before the substantive legislative schedule began, and returning home late Thursday night after the last votes, or early Friday morning.

The Shrinking Schedule

Although these days the Tuesday to Thursday Club encompasses the vast majority of members, the schedule is even more attenuated. Members from all over the country straggle in late on Tuesday, insisting that there be no votes until the end of the day, and scramble to get out of town as early on Thursday as possible. Of course, it doesn't work every week—sometimes, votes actually take place on Mondays and Fridays, and sometimes emergencies or pressing business require full weeks and even occasional weekend sessions. But the change from the past—and the lack of time spent in meaningful floor debate— has been striking. For 2006, the second session of the 109th Congress, the House set a grand total of seventy-one days in which votes are scheduled to take place and an additional twenty-six days with no votes occuring before 6:30 p.m. The total number of calendar days, even if counted generously, is ninety-seven, the smallest number in sixty years. This Congress is on track to set a record-low workload for an entire Congress since the 80th—famous as, in Harry Truman's words, the "Do-Nothing Congress"—in 1947–48.

During the 1960s and 1970s, the average Congress was in session 323 days. In the 1980s and 1990s, the average declined to 278. But the days in session have since plummeted, with the likelihood that the first six years of the Bush presidency will show an average below 250 per two-year Congress.

Beyond the attenuation of meaningful action and debate on the floor, we have seen as well the decline of committees, and not only through the disappearance of oversight. Major bills that in the past would have required weeks of hearings and days of markups are now often reviewed in days of hearings and with little or no visible time spent by the committee on systematic analysis of the legislation line by line and word by word. Much of the action now takes place behind closed doors, with bills, as in the bankruptcy case, put together by a small group of leadership staff, committee staff, industry representatives, and a few majority party members and then rammed through subcommittee and committee with minimal debate. In the 1960s and 1970s, the average Congress had an average of 5,372 House committee and subcommittee meetings; in the 1980s and 1990s the average was 4,793. In the last Congress, the 108th, the number was 2,135.

The Demise of Regular Order

But the lack of interest in the admittedly arduous process of going through multiple levels and channels of discussion, debate, negotiation, and compromise that make up a robust deliberative process has been a symptom of the broader malady in the contemporary Congress—the belief, especially in the House, that deliberation, fairness, bipartisanship, and debate are impediments to the larger goal of achieving political and policy success. In other words, the credo that the ends justify the means.

The House, unlike the Senate, is a majoritarian institution. With its complete control of the Rules Committee, the majority leadership may write special rules to control debate and amendments on the House floor. As long as its party members support the Rules Committee, the leadership may waive any standing rule not specified in the Constitution, such as the requirement that conference committee reports lay over for three days before they are considered by the House. By controlling the position of presiding officer, in committee or on the floor, the majority may also adopt less formal means to advance its legislative agenda and weaken the position of the minority.

During the last decade of their forty-year control of the House, Democrats made increasing use of this power to deny the minority Republicans opportunity to participate in any meaningful fashion in the legislative process. Republicans chafed under the increasingly heavy hand of the majority. In 1993 ranking Rules Committee member David Dreier and his Republican committee colleagues issued a stinging report criticizing the tactics used by the majority to shut down "deliberative democracy." What was essential to the House but missing under the arbitrary rule of the Democrats, they argued, was a "full and free airing of conflicting opinions through hearings, debates, and amendments for the purpose of developing and improving legislation deserving of the respect and support of the people." Dreier acknowledged the majority's right to control the agenda and schedule and to structure legislation to advance its policy goals. But this can be accomplished, he asserted, without denying the minority an opportunity to be heard and have their ideas considered.

The 1994 election changed the majority party in the House but it did nothing to stem the decline of deliberative democracy. During more than a decade of Republican rule, the majority has tightened its grip on the House and the minority has been increasingly marginalized. Statistics on House rules compiled by former Republican Rules Committee staffer Donald Wolfensberger document this trend. The percentage of open or modified open rules dropped from 44 percent in the 103rd Congress (the last controlled by the Democrats) to 26 percent in the 108th Congress. During the same time span, the percentage of closed or modified closed rules jumped from 18 percent to 49 percent. Wolfensberger also documents an increasing use by the Republican majority of self-executing rules, which allow a bill to be altered without having a separate debate and direct vote on amendments, and of bills considered under suspension of the rules.

But this is only the tip of the iceberg. Committee deliberation on controversial legislation has become increasingly partisan and formalistic, with the serious work being done by the committee chair, party leadership, administration officials, and lobbyists. This pattern is repeated in conference committees, often without any pretence of a full committee mark-up with members of both political parties present. The Rules Committee routinely suspends its requirement of a 48-hour notice of meetings, invoking its authority to call an emergency meeting "at any time on any measure or matter which the Chair determines to be of an emergency nature." Those meetings, at which 60 percent of all rules during the 108th Congress were reported (a lot of emergencies), often were scheduled with little advance notice between 8 p.m. and 7 a.m. And their primary purpose was to dispense with regular order.

For example, during the 108th Congress the Rules Committee, in structuring consideration of twenty-eight conference reports, almost always in emergency session, in every case waived all points of order against the conference report and against its consideration. This action made it virtually impossible to discover what was in each conference report before voting on it. Months after the adoption of the 850-page conference report on the Medicare prescription drug bill, which was filed in the House at 1:17 a.m. on November 21, 2003, and passed at 6 a.m. on November 22, members and the public were still unraveling what was in the bill that became law.

This Rules Committee practice has been employed to facilitate the now-routine process of folding many significant issues into huge omnibus bills and bringing them to the House floor for up-or-down votes without any notice or time for members to read or absorb them. House leaders have become particularly enamored of packaging several stand-alone appropriations bills into one omnibus bill that is brought up at the end of the session, as all the members are preparing to go home and do not want to vote to shut down the government. By forgoing nearly all floor debate, they can pack these bills with numerous provisions that could never pass in separate votes.

But this form of legislating—which often means that bills are passed and laws are enacted via all-night sessions whereby staff and a few members and party leaders try to slap all the pieces together under tight deadlines—results in stealth legislation that has not really passed majority muster and frequently has embarrassing consequences. One pungent example occurred in December 2004, when it was discovered that giant appropriations bill had a provision that would allow Appropriations staff access to individual tax returns and would exempt them from criminal penalties for revealing the contents of those returns.

When a press report disclosed the provision, after the bill had passed, it was denounced by subcommittee chair Ernest Istook, who said he had no idea that language was in the bill. It turned out that the provision had surfaced between 3 and 5 a.m. during an all-night staff negotiation just before the final 3,000-page document was slapped together and sent to the floor. It does not appear that the provision was a deliberately pernicious one—it was simply that no one understood what the language actually did. No wonder; they were operating, after all, sleep-deprived in the middle of the night after a series of crash sessions to put the omnibus together. . . .

The Explosion of Earmarks

Another sign of the decline of the deliberative process is the startling rise of earmarking—legislating specific projects for specific districts or states instead of leaving the allocation of resources to professionals. Earmark fever has completely taken over the appropriations process as it earlier had consumed public works. The conservative watchdog group Citizens Against Government Waste commented in an open letter released in 2004, "Over the past ten years, pork-barrel spending has increased exponentially, from 1,430 projects totaling $10 billion in 1995 to 10,656 projects, totaling $22.9 billion, in 2004."

Scott Lilly, the longtime Democratic staff director of the House Appropriations Committee and a stellar career professional in the House, noted, "Earmarking has not simply grown in volume; the distribution of earmarks has also changed dramatically. In the 1980s, earmarks were largely rewards for Members who had persevered for years on the back benches and risen to positions of significant power on key committees. Today, earmarks are much more broadly distributed among the rank and file, and this most important advantage of incumbency affects election outcomes not just in a few districts of well-connected Members but in virtually all Congressional districts."

The most startling development on the earmark front has been in appropriations. In the definitive treatment of the appropriations committees, Richard F. Fenno's magisterial *The Power of the Purse* published in 1966, there is no reference to *earmark* in the index. That is because historically, appropriations bills have not explicitly targeted funds for particular programs in particular districts. They have shaped the direction of spending and often encouraged specific programs in report language. But appropriators avoided earmarks because they inevitably would lead to a kind of circus or bazaar, with rising pressure to add funds for each district or to use the earmark as a weapon to reward friends and punish enemies.

The House especially saw the danger in this process. The Senate was much happier to open the spigots and use the appropriations process to logroll and make each member happy. Earmarks took off in the Senate in the 1990s and have risen logarithmically, with senators of both parties eager to take advantage. Only Senator John McCain (R-AZ) has stood up strongly against the practice. In the

House, though, there were many voices opposing earmarks, including, particularly strongly, Republicans.

That is, until they took over the majority in the House. Now the House is at least as eager to use the earmarking process as the Senate, and the results are clear. In 1992, there were 892 specifically earmarked programs or projects, adding up to $2.6 billion in spending. The number more than doubled in six years (1998) to 1,000 earmarks, with spending jumping to $13.2 billion. By fiscal year 2002, the number of earmarks rose to 8,341, with spending up to $20 billion. By 2005, the number had escalated to 13,997 at a cost of $27.3 billion. The trends are obvious for almost every area of discretionary spending—$7 billion or more in defense, $1.2 billion in military construction, one hundred more pages of earmarks in the Veterans, Housing, NASA and Environmental Protection Agency appropriations than in 1995, more than $1 billion in the Labor/HHS bill, which, under Obey, had no earmarks to speak of before 1995. Among the most avid proponents and users of these earmarks has been one (ex-) House Majority Leader Tom DeLay (R-TX).

As pragmatists and students of the legislative process, we have never been ardent foes of pork barrel spending. We understand that it takes grease to make the wheels of the legislative process move and that pork itself is not evil or even necessarily bad. Some of it is the price of getting things done in Congress, and much of it is beneficial to society. But you can reach a point where all the standards fall by the wayside and scarce funds are seriously misallocated—with important programs getting diminished funding so that picayune projects can prevail. . . .

The Dominance of Machine Politics

Running the House of Representatives with an iron fist requires a high degree of unity and loyalty among members of the majority party. Indeed, strong leadership in the House is conditional on widespread agreement among rank-and-file members on major public policy issues. The growing ideological polarization between the parties set the stage for more aggressive and partisan leadership, initially while Democrats were in the majority, in the late 1970s through the early 1990s, and then more ambitiously under Republican rule. While party leaders were dependent upon policy consensus in their caucus to run the House, they sought other means of increasing loyalty among their members. Two proved to be of particular importance. The first was to play a more central role in congressional elections, especially in their financing; the second was to enlist sympathetic interest groups and their lobbyists to the partisan cause.

Money and Elections

During the rise of strong party leadership, campaign fund-raising became an essential activity of party leaders and aspiring leaders. In addition to raising funds for their own campaigns, they appeared at fund-raisers for their party colleagues in Washington and in their districts; formed leadership PACs to contribute funds to their collegues' campaigns; exhorted interest groups to contribute to the party and its members; used nonprofits to cater to the personal and electoral interests of their colleagues; and raised substantial funds for the revitalized congressional campaign committees, allowing them to play a more strategic and consequential role. With the demise of seniority, aspiring committee and subcommittee chairs were obliged to raise large sums of campaign funds just to be considered for the posts they sought. Over time parties put in place systems for redistributing campaign funds from safe to marginal districts, through both transfers to the campaign committees and member-to-member contributions.

During the 1990s, the parties and their leaders discovered new ways of spending so-called soft money—large, unregulated contributions from corporations, unions, and individuals—in congressional campaigns. President Clinton and his political adviser, Dick Morris, broke new ground in the 1996 presidential campaign by using soft money to finance sham issue ads—those designed to influence elections but that avoided words that expressly advocate the election or defeat of a candidate, which would have triggered contribution limits. Both parties quickly followed suit. Before long, congressional leaders were deeply involved in soliciting—or extorting—large contributions from CEOs, labor leaders, and wealthy individuals for their party committees and leadership PACs. These developments made a mockery of campaign finance law, and it became all too easy for congressional leaders to abuse their authority as public officials.

Immediately after the 1996 elections, the two of us joined with several colleagues to develop a reform agenda—"Five Ideas for Practical Campaign Reform"—that dealt directly with the twin problems of soft money and sham issue advocacy. Several pieces of our agenda made their way into the legislation that was ultimately enacted. Over the course of the next seven years, working with the chief sponsors as part of a sustained effort to develop, enact, and constitutionally defend the Bipartisan Campaign Reform Act of 2002 (BCRA), we had a unique vantage point from which to observe the world of money and politics on Capitol Hill. We were deeply impressed by the courage and tenacity of the prime cosponsors of the legislation, Senators John McCain (R-AZ) and Russ Feingold (D-WI), Representatives Chris Shays (R-CT) and Marty Meehan (D-MA); the resourcefulness of Senators Olympia Snowe (R-ME) and Jim Jeffords (R, I-VT) in sponsoring an amendment to more sharply define the electioneering communication that would be subject to regulation; the guts of twenty Republican House members who bucked their leadership to sign a discharge petition that allowed the Shays-Meehan legislation to be considered on the floor; and the commitment and skill of Democratic leaders Tom Daschle (D-SD) and Dick Gephardt (D-MO) in holding their party together in support of the bill. The latter was particularly notable in light of the strong opposition of Democratic election-law lawyers and political consultants, union leaders, and a number of prominent liberal interest groups.

BCRA did not reduce the amount of money in federal elections (it was never intended to) nor did it marginalize the role of congressional leaders in campaign finance. They continue to be deeply involved, a reality that fuels party polarization in both the House and the Senate. But in limiting their efforts to raising only hard money—those funds subject to restrictions on source and caps on amount—the law removed one powerful means of abusing public power. . . .

Lobbying

[Another] way of shoring up party support is to extend the whip operation beyond the halls of Congress. No one mastered this feat as well as Tom DeLay. Together with Republican strategist Grover Norquist, he started in 1995 what became a formidable political machine, especially after the 2000 elections. The K Street Project is innocuously described on the website of Norquist's Americans for Tax Reform as "a non-partisan research of the political affiliation, employment background, and political donations of members in Washington's premier lobbying firms, trade associations and industries." The collection of data is perfectly innocent, but the objective clearly is to place party loyalists in all of the key lobbying positions in Washington and then to steer the formidable resources of the organizations they represent toward support of the Republican party's legislative agenda and the election of Republican candidates to Congress. As DeLay said in 1995, "There are just a lot of people down on K Street who gained their prominence by being Democrat . . . we're just following the old adage of punish your enemies and reward your friends. We don't like to deal with people who are trying to kill the revolution. We know who they are. The word is out."

DeLay and the Republicans are hardly the first congressional majority to play hard ball with the business community in Washington. Early in the Reagan administration, Representative Tony Coelho, chairman of the Democratic Congressional Campaign Committee, reminded business lobbyists that the Democrats still controlled the House and were in a position to boost or retard their legislative priorities. He aggressively sought and achieved rough parity for his party on K Street with the Republicans, a balance that persisted until Republicans took control of Congress after their stunning 1994 election victory.

But nothing in Washington has come close to the ambition and daring of DeLay's operation. As Nicholas Confessore aptly described it, "Like the urban Democratic machines of yore, this one is built upon patronage, contracts, and one-party rule. But unlike legendary Chicago Mayor Richard J. Daley, who rewarded party functionaries with jobs in the municipal bureaucracy, the GOP is building its machine outside government, among Washington's thousands of trade associations and corporate offices, their tens of thousands of employees, and the hundreds of millions of dollars in political money at their disposal."

Joined later by Rick Santorum in the Senate and Roy Blunt in the House, DeLay had great success with his K Street strategy. He became the point man for headhunters and industry executives making hiring decisions—they knew to seek his approval. As retaliation for the Electronic Industries Association's hiring of former Democratic Representative Dave McCurdy as its president, DeLay held up two intellectual property treaties in the House that the Electronic Industries Association supported. While later admonished by the House Ethics Committee for this behavior, DeLay eventually got his way with the Electronic Industries Association (which hired two Republicans to do its lobbying), and the message was received loud and clear by other trade associations and lobbying firms. Since the late 1990s, some twenty-nine former DeLay staffers have moved to lobbying positions in Washington. No other congressional leadership office comes close. They represent about 350 energy, finance, technology, airline, auto manufacturing, tobacco, health care and pharmaceutical companies and institutions. They also represent thirteen of the biggest trade associations. DeLay alumni also work for conservative Republican organizations, including several high-powered communications firms.

The Collapse of Ethical Standards

In early 2003, the *Washington Post* reported that the staff of House Financial Services Committee chair Mike Oxley, personal and committee, had pressured the Investment Company Institute to fire its chief lobbyist, Julie Domenick, and replace her with a Republican (Domenick was a Democrat with ties to John Dingell). According to the *Post,* committee staffer Sam Geduldig "told a group of lobbyists . . . that Oxley's probe of the mutual fund industry was linked to Domenick's employment at the mutual fund group."

Following on DeLay's unethical effort to strong-arm the Electronics Industries Association, the effort to bludgeon the Investment Company Institute by threatening legislative retribution if its lobbyist were not canned made it clear that the K Street Project was more than merely another effort to extract money and jobs from interest groups.

The difference was dramatized—perhaps typified—by lobbyist Jack Abramoff, a close friend of Grover Norquist since their mutual efforts in college Republican and conservative movements and a close ally and associate of Tom DeLay (and Bob Ney, among others). Abramoff rose dramatically to visibility, power, wealth, and notoriety as a lobbyist in Tom DeLay's Washington who used his connections to DeLay and other majority insiders to represent a range of clients, most notably Indian tribes who were trying to get or keep gambling casinos—or stop other tribes from getting them—and the Northern Marianas Islands (Saipan), which was trying to keep preferential treatment for its sweatshop garment industry.

In just three years, Abramoff and his associates, including former DeLay key staffer Michael Scanlan, pulled in $82 million from the Indian tribes. This bonanza included taking fees from one tribe to prevent another from getting a casino and then taking fees from the second tribe to try to reverse the decision. Some of the money went to his law firm; but $66 million went to Scanlan's public affairs firm and to a series of nonprofits, including charities organized by Abramoff and the American International Center, a "think tank" Abramoff set up that was headquartered in the beach community of Rehoboth, Delaware, and run by a former lifeguard with no public policy experience. Some of the money was turned into fees for Grover Norquist and Ralph Reed, the former executive director of the Christian Coalition and former head of the Bush presidential campaign's Southern region, to help the Indian gambling effort by lobbying to block the licensing of rival casinos; other money was channeled to conservative organizations, including some affiliated with Norquist.

Abramoff spread his largesse around widely, hosting lavish trips abroad for members of Congress and other officials, in some cases to golf resorts in St Andrews, Scotland, where he paid greens fees that approached $5,000 a day.

DeLay and Ney were among the golfing junketeers. At the same time, Abramoff was pursuing other business ventures, including the leasing and acquisition of federal properties and the purchase of gambling boats in Florida. In each case, he enlisted lawmakers and administration officials to help.

In 2004, the Senate Indian Affairs Committee began to investigate Abramoff's alleged rip-offs of Indian tribes and other chicanery associated with them. In early 2005, Abramoff was indicted for wire fraud in his purchase of the gambling boats, amid numerous federal investigations into his other activities. . . .

Following Abramoff's plea agreement with the Department of Justice, the various investigations threatened to metastasize into a broader set of charges against many other Washington players, including prominent conservative strategists, Republican operatives, former Hill staffers, and lawmakers in both houses— with many of the players in the same constellation as Tom DeLay. All reflected a culture of greed and arrogance that had permeated Washington. It was eerily reminiscent of the Gilded Age, the era named in an 1873 novel by Mark Twain and Charles Dudley Warner that was characterized by rampant corruption involving business trusts, members of Congress, and other government officials, all in a self-reinforcing loop of sloshing money around politics to gain riches through government policy, with the money contributing to keeping in power those politicians who were getting bribed or influenced in the first place.

Some members of the 109th Congress were willing and eager to get to the bottom of this ethics embarrassment, including John McCain and others on the Indian Affairs Committee. The Senate Finance Committee began a preliminary investigation into Abramoff's use of nonprofit organizations. The approach of Congress, however, especially in Tom DeLay's House, was neither outrage nor embarrassment, but rather a concerted effort to put the lid on any investigations and to employ large-scale damage control by punishing or silencing those who wanted to sanction the miscreants.

Roots of the Problem

It is not unreasonable to ask whether these patterns of dysfunctional behavior in Congress are natural and understandable if not inevitable responses to powerful forces in its political and social environment. American democracy has been deeply affected by the rise of the most partisan era since the late nineteenth and early twentieth centuries. This is an era characterized by strong and ideologically polarized parties competing from positions of rough parity. These features of the party system are evident among elected officials in government and in the electorate. They are reinforced and strengthened by teams of aligned activists, interest groups, community organizations, and media outlets. Competition for control of the White House and Congress is intense, but it is waged on an increasingly restrictive playing field. Fewer states are up for grabs in presidential elections and the number of competitive contests for the Senate and especially for the House has dropped markedly. This environment encourages an intense struggle for control of government and an unabashed manipulation of electoral and governing institutions to achieve one's political and policy goals.

The roots of this distinctly partisan era are deep and complex. Fissures in the New Deal coalition of the Democratic Party were evident in the 1960s, with the rise of the counterculture and opposition to the war in Vietnam. The 1964 Goldwater campaign initiated a long-term struggle among party activists to develop a more distinctly conservative Republican agenda. The passage of the Voting Rights Act in 1965 and the economic development of the South broke up the uneasy coalition between blacks and conservative whites that had allowed Democrats to dominate the region for many decades and eventually led to a safe Republican South. The Supreme Court's 1973 abortion decision in *Roe v. Wade* prompted a pro-life movement that years later would form the core of the Republican Party's largest and most reliable constituency—the religious conservatives. California's tax-limiting Proposition 13 and the emergence of its governor, Ronald Reagan, on the national political scene lent the Republican Party a more distinctive economic platform. President Reagan's robust challenge to the Soviet Union added national security to the set of new issues dividing the parties.

As these developments played out over time, party platforms grew more distinctive, those recruited to Congress became more ideologically in tune with their fellow partisans, and voters increasingly sorted themselves into the two parties based on their ideological views. At the same time, voters were making residential decisions that reinforced the ideological sorting already under way. Citizens were drawn to neighborhoods, counties, and states where others shared their values and interests. This ideological sorting and geographical mobility produced many areas dominated by one party or the other, which diminished electoral competition and increased partisan polarization among elected officials. Both bipartisan and partisan gerrymanders contributed further to these effects. And they were reinforced by interest groups that increasingly aligned themselves with one party or the other and radio and cable news and talks shows that pitched to distinctive partisan and ideological audiences.

These developments in the social and political environment facilitated the actions within Congress that are chronicled in this book and that led to a broken branch. But politicians are not merely waifs amid forces. They make choices about how to organize and run their institution and how to conduct themselves personally, albeit choices constrained by the external environment and the incentives it creates. In recent decades, leaders and members of Congress acted in ways that exacerbated the partisan polarization and intensified the forces leading to institutional decline. . . .

A Final Note

A contentious, partisan, name-calling Congress is nothing new in American politics; some historians might argue that it is the norm. House Democrats went ballistic in November 2005 after freshman Republican Jean Schmidt of Ohio called veteran Democrat John Murtha (D-PA) a coward on the House floor—but that, after all, is not much compared to duels on the House floor in the early nineteenth century or a senator caned nearly to death on the Senate floor by a bitter House colleague in the middle of that century.

Still, the problems now are different and worrisome. The frontier atmosphere that characterized Congress through much of our early history occurred during a time when Congress convened almost part time and when the role of the federal government was much more limited. There was no mass mobilization, no mass media, no twenty-four-hour cable news. Now, Congress is much larger, more potent, and part of a federal government with remarkable scope and sweep. Each of its actions or inactions has more consequences. The decline in deliberation has resulted in shoddy and questionable policy—domestic and international. The unnecessarily partisan behavior of the House majority has poisoned the well enough to make any action to restrain the growth of entitlement programs and to restructure health care policy impossible and has badly strained the long tradition of bipartisanship on foreign policy at a particularly delicate time. The failure of both houses of Congress to do meaningful oversight contributed to the massive and unconscionable failures of the Department of Homeland Security and, after Hurricane Katrina, of its FEMA arm. The broken branch distresses us as long-time students of American democracy who believe Congress is the linchpin of our constitutional system. But the consequences go far beyond our sensibilities, resonating in ways that damage the country as a whole. Perhaps we can do little, as larger forces in society, driven by technological change, overwhelm any efforts to alter course. But we believe that individuals can make a difference, that every step must be taken and no stone unturned to try to mend the broken branch and restore the needed balance in our political system.

Lee H. Hamilton    **NO**

Public Criticisms of Congress

Many Americans might go along with my general explanation of how Congress works but still feel that it doesn't work particularly well. Public approval of how Congress is handling its job has typically been very low in recent decades, usually hovering around a 40 percent approval rating—sometimes going higher, sometimes falling below 30 percent.

I heard numerous criticisms of Congress while serving, often in fairly blunt terms. Many of the criticisms seemed to be quite perceptive; others were fairly far off the mark—such as when people thought that as a member of Congress I received a limousine and chauffeur, or enjoyed free medical care, or didn't pay Social Security or income taxes. Even though the attacks were sometimes unpleasant, I always felt it was important for constituents to relay their complaints about Congress, and I never took them lightly. When people are upset about Congress, it undermines public confidence in government and fosters cynicism and disengagement. In a representative democracy like ours, in which Congress must reflect the views and interests of the American people as it frames the basic laws of the land, it really does matter what people think about Congress.

This chapter will sort through several of the main public criticisms of Congress and how it works.

"Legislators Are a Bunch of Crooks"

Several years ago, I was watching the evening news on television when the anchorman announced the death of Wilbur Mills, the legendary former chairman of the House Ways and Means Committee. There was a lot he could have said. He might have recounted the central role Mills had played in creating Medicare. Or he might have talked about how Mills helped to shape the Social Security system and draft the tax code. But he didn't. Instead, he recalled how Mills's career had foundered after he had been found early one morning with an Argentinean stripper named Fanne Foxe. And then he moved on to the next story.

One of the perks of being chairman of an influential committee in Congress, as I was at the time, is that you can pick up the telephone and get

From *How Congress Works and Why You Should Care*, 2004, pp. 75–82, 85–86, 89–90, 93–95. Copyright © 2004 by Indiana University Press. Reprinted by permission.

through to television news anchors. Which I did: I chided him for summing up the man's career with a scandal. Much to my surprise, he apologized.

The fact is, though, he wasn't doing anything unusual. Americans of all stripes like to dwell on misbehavior by members of Congress. We look at the latest scandal and assume that we're seeing the *real* Congress. But we're not. People might hear repeatedly in the media about missteps, but they hear very little about the House leader who went home on weekends to pastor his local church, or the congressman who devoted decades to championing the needs of the elderly, or the senator who spent one day each month working in a local job to better understand the needs of constituents, or the many members who worked behind the scenes in a bipartisan way to reach the delicate compromises needed to make the system work.

Nor do I see members of Congress as basically out to enrich themselves at the public trough. During my time in office—when I heard numerous complaints about congressional "pay-grabs"—the salaries of members didn't even keep up with inflation. The pay I received in my last year in Congress was $20,000 *less* than if my 1965 pay had been adjusted for inflation. For most members, it is not the money that attracts them to public service; most could be making more in the private sector.

I don't want to claim that all members are saints and that their behavior is impeccable. Improper conduct does occur. Yet I agree with the assessment of historian David McCullough: "Congress, for all its faults, has not been the unbroken parade of clowns and thieves and posturing windbags so often portrayed. What should be spoken of more often, and more widely understood, are the great victories that have been won here, the decisions of courage and vision achieved."

Probity in Congress is the rule rather than the exception, and most experts on Congress agree that it has gotten better over the years. A personal example: Back in the early 1970s, I made an argument in a committee hearing one day favoring military aid for one of our allies. When I got back to my office, I discovered a delegation from that country waiting for me; they wanted to thank me with a fat honorarium, a trip to their country, and an honorary degree from one of their universities. I declined.

The point here isn't my purity. It's that at the time this happened, there was nothing improper about their offer. Today, there would be. When I arrived in Congress, members could accept lavish gifts from special interests, pocket campaign contributions in their Capitol offices, and convert their campaign contributions to personal use. And they were rarely punished for personal corruption. None of that would be tolerated now.

Things still aren't perfect. . . . But the ethical climate at the Capitol is well ahead of where it was a couple of decades ago. And, I might add, it is well ahead of the public perception. From my experience in Congress, getting to know hundreds of members of Congress well over the years, my clear impression is that the vast majority would whole-heartedly agree with Representative Barbara Jordan: "It is a privilege to serve people, a privilege that must be earned, and once earned, there is an obligation to do something good with it."

"There's Too Much Wasteful, Pork-Barrel Spending by Congress"

Some years back, I was at a public meeting in Tell City, Indiana, when one of its citizens stood up to take me and my colleagues to task for our devotion to pork-barrel spending. How in good conscience, he wanted to know, could we spend so much of the public's money on frivolous projects designed only to get us reelected?

My first instinct was to ask him to step outside—but not in the way you might think. To understand why, you have to know a little about Tell City. It is a small town in southern Indiana, founded by Swiss settlers, not far from where Abraham Lincoln ran a ferry across the mouth of the Anderson River as a young man. What you notice in Tell City, though, is a much bigger river, the Ohio, which runs along the edge of its downtown. Indeed, between the building I was standing in and thousands of cubic feet of water lay only a few yards of ground and a levee. And the levee, as you've probably guessed, was built with federal money. If it weren't for this "pork-barrel" project, a good bit of Tell City would long since have been swept away. Pork, I told my audience, is in the eye of the beholder.

The vast majority of federal spending, I would argue, goes to important, widely supported uses. After all, more than half of total federal spending each year goes just for two things—national defense and seniors programs, both very popular. Yet I would agree that you can find some mighty debatable appropriations in each year's federal budget—$1.5 million aimed at refurbishing a statue in one powerful senator's state, $650,000 for ornamental fish research, $90,000 for the National Cowgirl Museum and Hall of Fame, and millions for various memorials and special projects that, in the scheme of things, will benefit relatively few Americans. Congress never fails to provide plenty of material for groups that make it their business to uncover questionable spending.

But think for a moment about what we characterize as "pork-barrel spending." Much of it is for infrastructure: highways, canals, reservoirs, dams, and the like. There's money for erosion-control projects, federal buildings, and military installations. There's support for museums and arts centers. There's backing for academic institutions, health-care facilities, and job-training institutes. All of these have some value and indeed may prove important to lots of people. When it comes to infrastructure spending, "pork-barrel projects" are rarely worthless. Members of Congress know in considerable detail the needs of their district or state, often better than the unelected federal bureaucrat who would otherwise decide where the money goes. We shouldn't fall into the trap of thinking that simply because a senator or representative directs the money to a specific project, it's waste, whereas if a bureaucrat or even the president does, it's not.

At the same time, my scolder in Tell City was on to something. While "pork" may provide valuable support to worthy projects, it can also shore up projects that most of the country would rightly question. The problem is, Congress often doesn't do a good job of distinguishing between the two.

To begin with, pork-barrel projects are frequently inserted by powerful members in spending bills surreptitiously, literally in the dark of night. It may happen within a day of the final vote on a spending measure, and most legislators don't even notice. Nothing is more frustrating for members than to vote for major national legislation only to discover later that it also contained obscure pork-barrel items like a Lawrence Welk memorial. And when legislators do notice a particular project and have concerns about it, they are often reluctant to object, because they may have legislation or projects of their own they don't want to put at risk.

The current process frequently doesn't allow Congress to weigh the relative merit of spending projects, to look at the interests of the country as a whole, or to weigh the needs of one region against another before deciding how to spend the public's money. The problem is not so much that the spending is wasted (it usually does some good) but whether it could better be spent for other projects. Congress often ignores this question and simply provides the money at the request of a member who is powerful or whose vote is badly needed.

We do need to recognize . . . that much of what Congress passes has an important impact on our lives. But we also need to focus more on wasteful spending, going after the bad apples that get all the attention. A few years ago when I was still in Congress, a reform committee I headed up recommended requiring that no bill could be voted on until all of the funding it earmarked for individual projects was listed clearly in publicly available reports. That would force proponents to justify publicly their provisions for special projects and would help ensure that fewer wasteful projects will pass. Sunshine is still the best disinfectant for wasteful proposals. And on that, I think my critic from Tell City and I could both agree.

"Legislators Just Bicker and Never Get Anything Done"

One of the most common criticisms of Congress is that members spend too much time arguing. I must have heard it a thousand times: Why can't you folks get together?

Congress is generally perceived as the "broken branch" of government, unable to work together to carry out the nation's wishes. Sometimes the language during debates gets a little rough, such as when a member in 1875 described another as "one who is outlawed in his own home from respectable society; whose name is synonymous with falsehood; who is the champion, and has been on all occasions, of fraud; who is the apologist of thieves; who is such a prodigy of vice and meanness that to describe him would sicken imagination and exhaust invective." These comments make the recent partisan squabbling almost sound mild.

The perception of Congress as paralyzed by its own internal bickering comes up in most discussions of the institution, and it is one that matters. Surveys show it is a major factor in the American public's lack of confidence in Congress.

People get upset because they think that everyone agrees on what's right and necessary, and they can't understand why Congress doesn't simply implement the consensus. Yet the truth is that there is far less consensus in the country than is often thought. It is very difficult to get agreement among a broad cross-section of Americans on current major political issues. Most years there is little agreement on what the main issues are, let alone on what specific steps should be taken to address them. The devil—and the dispute—is often in the details.

Most bills passed by Congress actually receive fairly broad, bipartisan support. Yet dispute and delay often occur because it's a tough and tedious job making federal policy. The issues before Congress are much more numerous than in past years, often very complicated and technical, and intensely debated, with a large number of sophisticated groups knowing that key policies and millions of dollars can hinge on every word or comma. The great variety of our nation's races, religions, regional interests, and political philosophies all bring their often-conflicting views to Congress. It's the job of the House and Senate to hear all sides and to search for a broadly acceptable consensus.

There is bound to be bickering when you bring together 535 duly elected representatives and senators—all of whom feel strongly about issues, all of whom want to represent the best interests of their constituents. People shouldn't fall off their chairs because they see heated debate; that's how we thrash things out in a democratic society.

Much of what the public dislikes is part of the process. We could have chosen to have all decisions made by a single ruler at the top, but that's not the kind of government we wanted. Congress was set up as the forum in which strongly held differences would be aired; conflict is built into the system. Allowing all sides a chance to be heard on the most difficult issues facing our nation almost ensures that the debate will at times be contentious, but it also helps to keep our country from ripping apart.

Dispute is different from dysfunction, and results are what count. Intense debate doesn't mean that issues cannot be resolved. It's just that resolving them can be frustrating and time-consuming. I remember many conversations with disgruntled constituents over the years when I urged patience and suggested that they judge Congress by the final results, not by the bickering they might see during the process.

I'm not defending strongly partisan or harsh personal attacks. Certainly things can sometimes go too far and get out of hand. And Congress does have various means for handling such cases—the member in 1875 was in fact formally censured by the House for his remarks. But overall, people should expect some bickering and arguing within Congress. A democracy without conflict is not a democracy. . . .

"Congress Almost Seems Designed to Promote Total Gridlock"

People will often complain about a "do-nothing" Congress and think much of the fault lies in the basic design of Congress. When a single senator can hold up action on a popular measure, when thirty committees or subcommittees are all reviewing the same bill, when a proposal needs to move not just through both the House and Senate but also through their multilayered budget, authorization, and appropriations processes, when floor procedures are so complex that even members serving several years can still be confused by them—how can you expect to get anything done?

This feeling is magnified by the major changes American society has undergone in recent decades. The incredible increase in the speed of every facet of our lives from communication to transportation, has made many people feel that the slow, untidy, deliberate pace of Congress is not up to the demands of modern society.

It is not now, nor has it ever been, easy to pass legislation through Congress. But there is actually a method to the madness, and basic roadblocks were put into the process for a reason. We live in a great big complicated country, with enormous regional, ethnic, and economic diversity; it is, quite simply, a difficult country to govern. Moving slowly is required for responsiveness and deliberation.

The quest for consensus within Congress can be painfully slow. Issues involving spending and taxes, health care, and access to guns and abortion stir strong emotions and don't submit easily to compromise. Inside-the-Beltway scuffling annoys many Americans, but think about it: Do we really want a speedy system in which laws would be pushed through before a consensus develops? Do we really want a system in which the viewpoint of the minority gets trampled by a rush to action by the majority? Certainly reforms can be made to improve the system, but the basic process of careful deliberation, negotiation, and compromise lies at the very heart of representative democracy. Ours is not a parliamentary system; the dawdling pace comes with the territory.

We misunderstand Congress's role if we demand that it be a model of efficiency and quick action. Our country's founders never intended it to be. They clearly understood that one of the key roles of Congress is to slow down the process—to allow tempers to cool and to encourage careful deliberation, so that unwise or damaging laws do not pass in the heat of the moment and so that the views of those in the minority get a fair hearing. That basic vision still seems wise today. Proceeding carefully to develop consensus is arduous and exasperating, but it's the only way to produce policies that reflect the varied perspectives of a remarkably diverse citizenry. People may complain about the process, yet they also benefit from its legislative speed bumps when they want their views heard, their interests protected, their rights safeguarded. As Sam Rayburn used to say: "One of the wisest things ever said was, 'Wait a minute.'"

. . . I certainly recognize that sometimes there are too many roadblocks in the system and Congress needlessly gets bogged down. Some streamlining and institutional reform is often needed, and I've been involved in many of those reform efforts. Yet I still believe that the fundamental notion that the structure of Congress should contain roadblocks and barriers to hasty action and unfair action makes sense for our country and needs to be protected and preserved. . . .

"There's Too Much Money in Politics Today"

People hear the stories about all the fund-raising that members must do today, and so they believe that Congress is a "bought" institution. Often they would tell me that in our system dollars speak louder than words and that access is

bought and sold. By a four-to-one margin, Americans believe that elected officials are influenced more by pressures from campaign contributors than by
what is in the best interests of the country.

The problem of money in politics has been with us for many years. But
it has really emerged as a serious problem in recent decades with the advent of
television advertising. The biggest portion of my $1 million campaign budget—
for a largely rural seat in southern Indiana—went for television.

Having experienced it firsthand, it is clear to me that the "money chase"
has gotten out of hand. A lot of money from special interests is floating
around Capitol Hill—in fact, far too much money. I believe it's a problem we
ignore at our own peril.

To be fair, many of the claims of special interests buying influence in
Congress are overstated. I would be the last to say that contributions have no
impact on a member's voting record. But it should also be kept in mind that
most of the money comes from groups who already share your views on the
issues and want to see you reelected, rather than from groups who are hoping
to change your mind. In addition, many influences shape members' voting
decisions—including their assessment of the arguments, the opinions of experts
and colleagues, their party's position, and, most importantly, what their constituents want. In the end, members know that if their votes aren't in line
with what their constituents want, they simply won't be reelected. And that,
rather than a campaign contribution, is what is foremost in their minds.

Yet it is still an unusual member of Congress who can take thousands of
dollars from a particular group and not be affected by it at all. . . . Overall,
this is an area in which I agree that significant reform is needed. It is also,
unfortunately, an area in which there are no easy answers. . . .

"Congress Is Run by Lobbyists and Special Interests"

Americans have different views of lobbyists and special interests. Some see
them as playing an essential part in the democratic process. Others look at
them with some skepticism, but understand that they have a role to play in
developing policy. Yet most see them as sinister forces with too much control
of Congress. The recent Enron and Arthur Andersen scandals, and revelations
about those companies' extensive lobbying of Congress, have fed this cynicism about the hold that powerful private interests maintain over public policy. Americans continue to remain suspicious that Congress is manipulated by
powerful wheeler-dealers who put enormous pressure on legislators or buy
votes through extensive campaign contributions and other favors. It is not an
unfounded concern, and it is not going to go away, no matter how fervently
some might try to dismiss it.

Now, the popular view of lobbyists as nefarious fat cats smoking big
cigars and handing out $100 bills behind closed doors is wrong. These days,
lobbyists are usually principled people who recognize that their word is their
bond. They are aggressive in seeking out members of Congress, offering to
take them to dinner for a chance at a longer conversation, and operating from a
carefully worked-out game plan that takes into account who might be persuaded

to vote their way, when they ought to be approached, and whether they have interested constituents who can be used effectively to put pressure on them. Lobbying is an enormous industry today with billions of dollars riding on its outcomes. Special interest groups will often spend millions of dollars on campaigns to influence a particular decision—through political contributions, grassroots lobbying efforts, television advocacy ads, and the like—because they know they can get a lot more back than they spent. Lobbyists who can get the kind of language they want into a bill can reap very large rewards. They are very good at what they do, and members of Congress can sometimes be easily swayed by them.

The influence of lobbyists on the process is not as simple as it might appear. In the first place, "special interests" are not just the bad guys. If you're retired, or a homeowner, or use public transit, or fly on airplanes, or are concerned about religious freedom, there are people in Washington lobbying on your behalf. With an estimated 25,000 interest groups lobbying in Washington, you can be sure your views are represented in many ways. Advocacy groups help Congress understand how legislation affects their members, and they help focus the public's attention on important issues. They play a vital role in amplifying the flow of information that Thomas Jefferson called the "dialogue of democracy."

In addition, Congress often takes up controversial, attention-grabbing issues on which you'll find an entire spectrum of opinions. Public notice is high, a host of special interests are weighing in, and lobbyists as well as legislators themselves are all over the map. In these circumstances, the prospect is very small that any single interest group or lobbyist can disproportionately influence the results. Quite simply, there are too many of them involved for that to happen, and the process is too public.

Where you have to look out is when things get quiet, when measures come up that are out of the public eye. A small change in wording here, an innocuous line in a tax bill there—that's where specific groups can reap enormous benefits that might not have been granted had they been held up to close public scrutiny.

The answer, it seems to me, is not to decry lobbying or lobbyists. In our system of government, we make a lot of trade-offs, as James Madison warned more than two centuries ago when he argued that "factions" were part of the cost of maintaining a democracy. At heart, lobbying is simply people banding together to advance their interests, whether they are farmers or environmentalists or bankers. Belonging to an interest group—the Sierra Club, the AARP, the Chamber of Commerce—is one of the main ways Americans participate in public life these days.

When I was in Congress, I found that organized groups not only brought a useful perspective to the table. They also pointed out how a given measure might affect my constituents in ways I hadn't considered. Lobbyists are typically professionals with a variety of skills: They are experts in their subject, with a sophisticated knowledge of the political process and the ability to raise large sums of money and make campaign contributions. They maintain extensive contacts, can generate grassroots support, and often have experience in putting together winning coalitions. I came to think of lobbyists as an important part of the *public discussion* of policy.

I emphasize "public discussion" for a reason. Sunshine is a powerful disinfectant, and rather than trying to clamp down on lobbying, I believe we would be better off ensuring that it happens in the open and is part of the broader policy debate.

So our challenge is not to shut it down but to make sure it's a balanced dialogue and that those in power don't consistently listen to the voices of the wealthy and the powerful more intently than to others. Several legislative proposals have been made over the years that would help, including campaign finance reform, strict limits on gifts to members of Congress, travel restrictions for members and their staffs funded by groups with a direct interest in legislation, and effective disclosure of the role lobbyists play in drafting legislation. But in the end, something may be even more important: ongoing conversation between elected officials and the people they represent.

Under our system of government, there is absolutely nothing wrong with lobbyists advocating their point of view. Lobbying is a key element of the legislative process and part of the free speech guaranteed under our Constitution. Members of Congress, I would argue, have a responsibility to listen to lobbyists. But members also have a responsibility to understand where these lobbyists are coming from, to sort through what they are saying, and then to make a judgment about what is in the best interests of their constituents and the nation as a whole.

POSTSCRIPT

Is Congress a "Broken Branch"?

Though he disagrees with Thomas Mann and Norman Ornstein about Congress's dysfunctionality, Lee Hamilton concedes that there are some genuine problems. One is the practice of quietly slipping little clauses or phrases into bills that benefit particular interests instead of the nation's interest. The other has to do with money. Far too much of it comes from special interests "floating around Capital Hill," and it is "an unusual member of Congress who can take thousands of dollars from a particular group and not be affected by it." Yet, as a former representative of a small Indiana district, Hamilton knows that members of Congress can't neglect particular interests, and that money plays a vital role in their reelection campaigns. To avoid what seems to be a bit of a dilemma, he suggests that the way to prevent abuse is not to outlaw lobbyists or campaign contributions, but to shine the light of publicity on them. "Sunshine is a powerful disinfectant." But is it sufficient?

Richard Fenno's *Home Style: House Members in Their Districts* (Longman, 2002), originally published in 1978, shows how various members connect to their home districts, and reaches the unsurprising conclusion that those with the safest seats can spend most of their energies in Washington rather than back home. But in *Dilemmas of Representation: Local Politics, National Factors, and the Home Styles of Modern U.S. Congress Members* (State University of New York, 2007), Sally Friedman goes further, suggesting that the pull of national politics is even stronger now, affecting all Congress members in one way or another. Lawrence C. Dodd and Bruce Oppenheimer, *Congress Reconsidered* (CQ Press, 2004), now in its eighth edition, assesses the congressional reforms enacted during the 1970s, shows how fragile the Democratic majority became at the end of the 1980s, and traces the goings-on in Congress since the Republicans took control in 1975. Though it does not bring us quite up to date on the new Democratic majority, it lets us see how the missteps of Republicans prepared the way for the shift. Diana Evans, *Greasing the Wheels: Using Pork Barrel Projects To Build Majority Coalitions in Congress* (Cambridge University Press, 2004) defends congressional "pork-barreling," arguing—as Lee Hamilton does—that it gets a lot of good things done. Charles Bancroft Cushman's, *An Introduction to the U.S. Congress* (Shape, 2006) is a compact volume that covers the subject competently for introductory students.

Ethical violations, undemocratic procedures, pork-barrel legislation, intimacy with lobbyists, hyperpartisanship: these are among the complaints Mann and Ornstein make about Congress. Their book was published in 2006, when Congress was run by Republicans. Today, the Democrats are in charge, and so far not much has changed. Perhaps they need more time. If so, most observers think they are likely to get it, so we shall probably be able to see whether the Democrats can make good on their pledge to mend "the broken branch."

ISSUE 7

Should the President Be Allowed "Executive Privilege"?

YES: **Mark J. Rozell**, from "Pro," in Richard J. Ellis and Michael Nelson, eds., *Debating the Presidency: Conflicting Perspectives on the American Executive* (CQ Press, 2006)

NO: **David Gray Adler**, from "Con," in Richard J. Ellis and Michael Nelson, eds., *Debating the Presidency: Conflicting Perspectives on the American Executive* (CQ Press, 2006)

ISSUE SUMMARY

YES: Public policy professor Mark J. Rozell believes that executive privilege is needed for the proper functioning of the executive branch, because presidents need candid advice from their staffs.

NO: Political science professor David Gray Adler concludes that neither debate in the Constitutional Convention nor the text of the Constitution provide any support for the view that the Framers supported giving the president the power to conceal information from Congress.

Article II of the United States Constitution states: "The executive power shall be vested in a President of the United States of America." Apart from the president's power of appointment, Article II has little to add about the content and conduct of the executive power. (Even the president's power to veto legislation is described in Article I, under the powers of Congress.) Yet from the nation's beginning, presidents have extended their power, and sought to exempt it from oversight or overruling by Congress.

In 1792, when the House of Representatives requested documents relating to a failed military campaign, President George Washington decided that he would provide only such papers as the public good permitted. Four years later, Washington turned down a House request for documents relating to a recently adopted treaty. President Thomas Jefferson refused to allow two cabinet members to supply documents at the trial of Aaron Burr. President Andrew Jackson refused to give the Senate a paper he had read to executive department heads. President Abraham Lincoln refused to reveal his dispatches to a military commander.

President Dwight D. Eisenhower in 1953 was the first to call presidential defiance of Congress "executive privilege," when he refused to turn over to a Senate committee notes of his meetings with members of the U.S. Army, claiming that national security might be breached if administration officials were compelled to testify under oath.

President Richard Nixon cited executive privilege when he refused to turn over to a special prosecutor audiotapes of conversations in the Oval Office that were sought in connection with criminal charges that were being sought against members of his administration. The Supreme Court responded to Nixon's claim in 1974, when it acknowledged the validity of an appropriate claim of executive privilege, noting "the valid need for protection of communications between high government officials and those who advise and assist them in the performance of their manifold duties." The Court offered a defense of executive privilege that presidents have often since expressed: "Human experience teaches that those who expect public dissemination of their remarks may well temper candor with a concern for appearances and for their own interests to the detriment of the decision-making process."

But the Supreme Court went on to conclude that there can be no "absolute privilege," stating: "To read the Article II powers of the President as providing an absolute privilege as against a subpoena essential to enforcement of criminal statutes on no more than a generalized claim of the public interest in confidentiality of non-military and non-diplomatic discussions would upset the constitutional balance of 'a workable government' and gravely impair the role of the courts."

President Bill Clinton lost his claim of executive privilege in 1998 when a federal judge ruled that Clinton aides could be called to testify in the scandal involving the president's sexual relationship with Monica Lewinsky. Despite the ultimate rejection of executive privilege defenses by Presidents Nixon and Clinton, most presidential claims have been upheld by the courts or were not opposed by Congress.

The claim of executive privilege has been made for the vice president as well. The U.S. Supreme Court upheld Vice President Dick Cheney's refusal to reveal to Congress information regarding meetings he had with a task-force regarding energy policy.

When President George W. Bush refused to allow administration officials to testify before a House committee on the circumstances relating to the firing of eight United States attorneys, who hold their posts at the pleasure of the president, the White House counsel defended "the constitutional prerogatives of the presidency." The issue of executive privilege became most controversial for the Bush presidency when it sought to defy congressional investigation over domestic surveillance and interrogation of prisoners taken in connection with the American war in Iraq.

Professors Mark J. Rozell and David Gray Adler offer opposing interpretations regarding the constitutional status, necessity, and desirability of the president's right to withhold information from Congress.

YES

Mark J. Rozell

PRO

Controversies over executive privilege date back to the earliest years of the Republic. Although the phrase "executive privilege" was not a part of the nation's common language until the 1950s, almost every president has exercised some form of this presidential power.

Executive privilege is controversial because it is nowhere mentioned in the Constitution. That fact has led some observers to suggest that executive privilege does not exist and that the congressional power of inquiry is absolute. This view is mistaken. Executive privilege is an implied presidential power and is sometimes needed for the proper functioning of the executive branch. Presidents and their staffs must be able to deliberate without fear that their every utterance may be made public.

Granted, the power of executive privilege is not absolute. Like other constitutionally based powers, it is subject to a balancing test. Presidents and their advisers may require confidentiality, but Congress must have access to information from the executive branch to carry out its investigative function. Therefore, any claim of executive privilege must be weighed against Congress's legitimate need for information to carry out its own constitutional role. Yet the power of inquiry is also not absolute, whether it is wielded by Congress or by prosecutors.

Not all presidents have exercised executive privilege judiciously. Some have used it to cover up embarrassing or politically inconvenient information, or even outright wrongdoing. As it is with all other grants of authority, the power to do good things is also the power to do bad things. The only way to avoid the latter is to strip away the authority altogether and thereby eliminate the ability to do the former. Eliminating executive privilege would hamper the ability of presidents to discharge their constitutional duties effectively and to protect the public interest.

The Need for Candid Advice

The constitutional duties of presidents require that they be able to consult with advisers without fear that the advice will be made public. If officers of the executive branch believe their confidential advice could be disclosed, the quality of that advice could be seriously damaged. Advisers cannot be completely honest and frank in their discussions if they know that their every

From *Debating the Presidency: Conflicting Perspectives on the American Executive*, 2006, pp. 127–132. Copyright © 2006 by CQ Press, division of Congressional Quarterly, Inc. Reprinted by permission.

word might be disclosed to partisan opponents or to the public. In *United States v. Nixon* (1974), the Supreme Court recognized that the need for candid exchanges is an important basis for executive privilege:

> The valid need for protection of communications between high government officials and those who advise and assist them in the performance of their manifold duties . . . is too plain to require further discussion. Human experience teaches that those who expect public dissemination of their remarks may well temper candor with a concern for appearances and for their own interests to the detriment of the decision-making process. . . . The confidentiality of presidential communications . . . has constitutional underpinnings. . . . The privilege is fundamental to the operation of government and inextricably rooted in the separation of powers under the Constitution.

In 1979 the Court reiterated its support of executive privilege based on the need for a candid exchange of opinions among advisers. "Documents shielded by executive privilege," the Court explained, "remain privileged even after the decision to which they pertain may have been effected, since disclosure at any time could inhibit the free flow of advice, including analysis, reports and expression of opinions."

Although Congress needs access to information from the executive branch to carry out its oversight and investigative duties, it does not follow that Congress must have full access to the details of every executive branch communication. Congressional inquiry, like executive privilege, has limits. That is not to suggest that presidents can claim the need for candid advice to restrict any and all information. The president must demonstrate a need for secrecy in order to trump Congress's power of inquiry.

Limits on Congressional Inquiry

Congress's power of inquiry, though broad, is not unlimited. A distinction must be drawn between sources of information generally and those necessary to Congress's ability to perform its legislative and investigative functions. There is a strong presumption of validity to a congressional request for information relevant to these investigative functions. The presumption weakens in the case of a congressional "fishing expedition"—a broad, sweeping quest for any and all executive branch information that might be of interest to Congress for one reason or another. Indeed, Congress itself has recognized that there are limits on its power of inquiry. For example, in 1879 the House Judiciary Committee issued a report stating that neither the legislative nor the executive branch had compulsory power over the records of the other. Congress gave the executive branch the statutory authority to withhold information when it enacted the "sources and methods proviso" of the 1947 National Security Act, the implementation provision of the 1949 CIA Act, and the 1966 Freedom of Information Act.

Nevertheless, critics of executive privilege argue that Congress has an absolute, unlimited power to compel disclosure of all executive branch information. Rep. John Dingell, D-Mich., for example, said that members of Congress "have the power under the law to receive each and every item in the hands of the government." But this expansive view of congressional inquiry is as wrong as the belief that the president has the unlimited power to withhold all information from Congress. The legitimacy of the congressional power of inquiry does not confer an absolute and unlimited right to all information. The debates at the 1787 Constitutional Convention and at the subsequent ratifying conventions provide little evidence that the framers intended to confer such authority on Congress. There are inherent constitutional limits on the powers of the respective governmental branches. The common standard for legislative inquiry is whether the requested information is vital to the Congress's law-making and oversight functions.

The Other Branches and Confidentiality

Executive privilege can also be defended on the basis of accepted practices of secrecy in the other branches of government. In the legislative branch, members of Congress receive candid, confidential advice from committee staff and legislative assistants. Meanwhile, congressional committees meet on occasion in closed session to mark up legislation. Congress is not obligated to disclose information to another branch. A court subpoena will not be honored except by a vote of the legislative chamber concerned. Members of Congress enjoy a constitutional form of privilege that absolves them from having to account for certain official behavior, particularly speech, anywhere but in Congress. But as with the executive, this protection does not extend into the realm of criminal conduct.

Secrecy is found as well in the judicial branch. It is difficult to imagine more secretive deliberations than those that take place in Supreme Court conferences. Court observer David M. O'Brien refers to secrecy as one of the "basic institutional norms" of the Supreme Court. "Isolation from the Capitol and the close proximity of the justices' chambers within the Court promote secrecy, to a degree that is remarkable. . . . The norm of secrecy conditions the employment of the justices' staff and has become more important as the number of employees increases." Members of the judiciary claim immunity from having to respond to congressional subpoenas. The norm of judicial privilege also protects judges from having to testify about their professional conduct.

It is thus inconceivable that secrecy, so common to the legislative and judicial branches, would be uniquely excluded from the executive. Indeed, the executive branch regularly engages in activities that are secret in nature. George C. Calhoun explains that the executive branch "presents . . . matters to grand juries; assembles confidential investigative files in criminal matters; compiles files containing personal information involving such things as census, tax, and veterans information; and health, education and welfare benefits to name a few. All of these activities must, of necessity, generate a considerable amount of confidential information. And personnel in the executive branch . . . necessarily prepare many more confidential memoranda. Finally, they produce a considerable amount of classified information as a result of the activities of the intelligence community."

Legislative, judicial, and executive branch secrecy serves a common purpose: to arrive at policy decisions more prudent than those that would be made through an open process. And in each case, the end result is subject to scrutiny. Indeed, accountability is built into secretive decision-making processes, because elected public officials must justify the end result at some point.

Giving Executive Privilege Its Due

The dilemma of executive privilege is how to permit governmental secrecy while maintaining accountability. On the surface, the dilemma is a difficult one to resolve: how can democratically elected leaders be held accountable when they are able to deliberate in secret or to make secretive decisions?

The post-Watergate period witnessed a breakdown in the proper exercise of executive privilege. Because of former president Richard Nixon's abuses, Presidents Gerald R. Ford and Jimmy Carter avoided using executive privilege. Ford and Carter still sought to preserve presidential secrecy, but they relied on other constitutional and statutory means to achieve that goal. President Ronald Reagan tried to restore executive privilege as a presidential prerogative, but he ultimately failed when congressional committees threatened administration officials with contempt citations and adopted other retaliatory actions to compel disclosure. President George Bush, like Ford and Carter before him, avoided executive privilege whenever possible and used other strategies to preserve secrecy. President Bill Clinton exercised executive privilege more often than all of the other post-Watergate presidents combined, but often improperly, such as in the investigation into his sexual relationship with White House intern Monica Lewinsky. President George W. Bush has exercised the privilege more sparingly than his predecessor, but he also has exercised this power in some questionable circumstances, such as his attempt to deny Congress access to decades-old Justice Department documents.

Thus in the post-Watergate era either presidents have avoided uttering the words "executive privilege" and have protected secrecy through other sources of authority (Ford, Carter, G. Bush), or they have tried to restore executive privilege and failed (Reagan, Clinton, G. W. Bush). Clinton's aggressive use of executive privilege in the Lewinsky scandal served to revive the national debate over this presidential power—a debate that continued into the Bush years. It is therefore an appropriate time to discuss how to restore a sense of balance to the executive privilege debate.

First, it needs to be recognized that executive privilege is a legitimate constitutional power—not a "constitutional myth." Consequently, presidents should not be devising schemes for achieving the ends of executive privilege while avoiding any mention of this principle. Furthermore, Congress (and the courts) must recognize that the executive branch—like the legislative and judicial branches—has a legitimate need to deliberate in secret and that every assertion of executive privilege is not a devious attempt to conceal wrongdoing.

Second, executive privilege is not an unlimited, unfettered presidential power. It should be exercised rarely and only for the most compelling reasons. Congress has the right—and often the duty—to challenge presidential assertions of executive privilege.

Third, there are no clear, precise constitutional boundaries that determine, a priori, whether any particular claim of executive privilege is legitimate. The resolution to the dilemma of executive privilege is found in the political ebb and flow of the separation of powers system. Indeed, there is no need for any precise definition of the constitutional boundaries surrounding executive privilege. Such a power cannot be subject to precise definition, because it is impossible to determine in advance all of the circumstances under which presidents may have to exercise that power. The separation of powers created by the framers provides the appropriate resolution of the dilemma of executive privilege and democratic accountability.

Congress already has the institutional capability to challenge claims of executive privilege by means other than eliminating the right to withhold information or attaching statutory restrictions on the exercise of that power. For example, if members of Congress are not satisfied with the response to their demands for information, they have the option of retaliating by withholding support for the president's agenda or for the president's executive branch nominees. In one famous case during the Nixon years, a Senate committee threatened not to confirm a prominent presidential nomination until a separate access to information dispute had been resolved. That action resulted in President Nixon ceding to the senators' demands. If information can be withheld only for the most compelling reasons, it is not unreasonable for Congress to try to force the president's hand by making him weigh the importance of withholding the information against that of moving forward a nomination or piece of legislation. Presumably, information being withheld for purposes of vital national security or constitutional concerns would take precedence over pending legislation or a presidential appointment. If not, then there appears to be little justification in the first place for withholding the information.

Congress possesses many other means by which it can compel presidential compliance with requests for information. One of those is the control Congress maintains over the government's purse strings, which means that it holds formidable power over the executive branch. In addition, Congress often relies on the subpoena power and the contempt of Congress charge to compel release of withheld information. It is not merely the exercise of these powers that matters, but the threat that Congress may resort to such powers. Congress has successfully elicited information from the executive branch using both powers. During the Reagan years, for example, in several executive privilege disputes Congress prevailed and received all the information it had requested from the administration—but only after it subpoenaed documents and threatened to hold certain administration officials in contempt. The Reagan White House simply decided it was not worth the political cost to continue such battles with Congress. In these cases, the system worked as it is supposed to. Had the information in dispute been critical to national security or preserving White House candor, certainly Reagan would have taken a stronger stand to protect the documents.

In the extreme case, Congress also has the power of impeachment—the ultimate weapon with which to threaten the executive. Clearly, this congressional power cannot be routinely exercised as a means of compelling disclosure of information, and thus it will not constitute a real threat in commonplace information disputes. Nevertheless, when a scandal emerges of Watergate-like proportions and in which all other remedies have failed, Congress can threaten to exercise its ultimate power over the president. In fact, for a time in 1998 Congress considered an impeachment article against President Clinton for abuses of presidential powers, including executive privilege. Congress ultimately dropped that particular article.

In the vast majority of cases—and history verifies this point—it can be expected that the president will comply with requests for information rather than withstand retaliation from Congress. Presidential history is replete with examples of chief executives who tried to invoke privilege or threatened to do so, only to back down in the face of congressional challenges. If members of Congress believe that the executive privilege power is too formidable, the answer resides not in crippling presidential authority, but in exercising to full effect the vast array of powers already at Congress's disposal.

CON

Executive privilege—the claim that a president has the right to withhold information from Congress and the courts—has become a principal tool in the promotion of executive secrecy and deception. Executive secrecy represents a continual threat to the values and principles of the Republic. Some of the nation's darkest moments have stemmed from a presidential penchant for secrecy: the quagmire of Vietnam, the suppression of the *Pentagon Papers,* Watergate, the Iran-contra scandal, and President George W. Bush's obscurantism over the rationale for the invasion of Iraq.

The pernicious effects of executive secrecy have not deterred advocates of executive privilege from asserting its central importance to the president's performance of his constitutional responsibilities, particularly in matters of national security and foreign affairs. Yet advocates of executive privilege have been unable to document instances in which resort to executive privilege has served the interests of the nation. Nor have they been able to document any national disasters that have resulted from executive transmission of information to Congress.

Defenders of executive privilege have urged legal justifications as well, yet there is no mention of executive privilege in the Constitution. Like Topsy in *Uncle Tom's Cabin,* executive privilege "never was born. It just growed like cabbage and corn." Even if, for the sake of argument, one were to concede the occasional utility of a claim of executive privilege, that would not establish its constitutionality. As Chief Justice John Marshall wrote in *McCulloch v. Maryland,* "The peculiar circumstances of the moment may render a measure more or less wise, but cannot render it more or less constitutional."

There are a good many reasons to doubt both the constitutionality and the utility of executive privilege. When the concept of a constitutionally based executive privilege was created by the judiciary in *United States v. Nixon* (1974), it was said to be grounded in the separation of powers. Proponents of executive privilege have also sought its justification in historical precedents. In truth, both of these efforts to establish the legality of executive privilege rest on flimsy scaffolding. Moreover, whatever the legality of executive privilege it is not essential to the success of the presidency and, in fact, poses serious harms to the political system.

From *Debating the Presidency: Conflicting Perspectives on the American Executive,* 2006, pp. 132–40.
Copyright © 2006 by CQ Press, division of Congressional Quarterly, Inc. Reprinted by permission.

Constitutional Considerations

Questions of presidential authority properly begin with constitutional analysis. Where in the Constitution—in its express provisions or implied derivations—is provision made for executive privilege? Moreover, which of the president's constitutional assignments require resort to claims of executive privilege?

The framers of the Constitution made no provision for executive privilege, which is not surprising because of the framers' deep-seated fear of executive power. As the historian Charles Warren has pointed out, "Fear of a return of Executive authority like that exercised by the Royal Governors or by the King had been ever present in the states from the beginning of the Revolution." The founders assumed, as James Iredell stated at the North Carolina ratification convention, that "nothing is more fallible than human judgment." And so it was a cardinal principle of republicanism that the conjoined wisdom of the many was superior to the judgment of one. Accordingly, the founders embraced the doctrine of checks and balances as a check on executive unilateralism. In foreign affairs, too, the founders insisted on a structure of shared powers. For, as even Alexander Hamilton agreed, "The history of human conduct does not warrant that exalted opinion of human virtue which would make it wise in a nation to commit interests of so delicate and momentous a kind, as those which concerns its intercourse with the rest of the world, to the sole disposal of a magistrate created and circumstanced as would be a President of the United States."

The framers showed no sympathy for the notion of executive privilege. Speaking at the Pennsylvania ratifying convention, James Wilson, the delegate from Pennsylvania who was second in importance only to James Madison of Virginia as an architect of the Constitution, defended the Constitutional Convention's decision to establish a single presidency rather than a plural presidency. "Executive power," he explained, "is better to be trusted when it has no screen." Wilson noted the visibility and accountability of the president: "he cannot act improperly, and hide either his negligence or inattention," and although he possesses sufficient power, "not a *single privilege* is annexed to his character; far from being above the laws, he is amenable to them in his private character as a citizen, and in his public character by impeachment." The president was to be bound by the strictures of the Constitution, made amenable to the laws and the judicial process, and barred from hiding his activities. The framers' understanding, as Madison put it, that the executive power should be "confined and defined" affords no ground for the view that executive privilege was regarded as an attribute of executive power that might be advanced to conceal the president's "negligence or inattention."

The delegates' refusal to grant the president the authority to conceal information from Congress reflected more than just a generalized distrust of executive power. That decision also reflected the framers' belief that Congress, like the British Parliament, would need on occasion to pursue investigations as a prelude to impeachment. Wilson was one of many delegates to trumpet the role of the House of Commons as the "Grand Inquest of the Nation," which, he declared, has "checked the progress of arbitrary power. . . . The proudest ministers of the proudest monarchs . . . have appeared at the bar of the house to give an account of their conduct." In addition, the framers acted out of a belief that the powers vested in Congress—including its general oversight authority to supervise the enforcement of its laws and the implementation of its appropriations, as well as its broad informing function—required legislative access to information possessed by the executive.

The lone provision of the Constitution that addresses secrecy vests in Congress, not the president, the authority to conceal information from the public. Article I, Section 5, requires both houses of Congress to keep and publish journals, except "such parts as may in their judgment require secrecy." This provision proved divisive in the Constitutional Convention and in the state ratifying conventions. Wilson was one of those who objected. "The people," he insisted, "have a right to know what their Agents are doing or have done, and it should not lie in the option of the Legislature to conceal their proceedings." The framers preferred publicity over secrecy, and they understood that information and knowledge were critical to the preservation of liberty and the enterprise of self-governance.

In summary, neither the Constitutional Convention debates—in which the idea of executive privilege was never discussed—nor the text of the Constitution supports the notion that the founders intended to bestow upon the president the power to conceal information from Congress. Nor at the time of the framing was there either an inherent or implied executive power to conceal information from legislative inquiry. The framers knew how to grant power, confer immunities, and create exceptions to power, but there is no evidence to support the contention that they ascribed to the president an implied power to undercut the investigatory power of Congress.

In *United States v. Nixon,* the Supreme Court ignored the text and the architecture of the Constitution in creating the doctrine of a constitutionally based executive privilege. The Court, in an opinion written by Chief Justice Warren E. Burger, held that "a presumptive privilege for confidential communications . . . is fundamental to the operation of government and inextricably rooted in the separation of powers" and that "to the extent this interest relates to the effective discharge of a President's powers, it is constitutionally based." The Court's employment of a mere ipse dixit served to elevate executive privilege to the constitutional level for the first time. Before that ruling, executive privilege had been known only as an "evidentiary" or "presumptive" privilege— that is, one similar to the lawyer–client or doctor–patient relationship that must yield to the showing of a greater public need.

The Court's effort to ground executive privilege in the separation of powers is unpersuasive. Separation of powers does not create or grant power; rather, it constitutes a rough division of authority that serves to preserve the Constitution's enumeration of powers against acts of usurpation. The Court's claim that executive privilege is "inextricably rooted in the separation of powers" would have astonished Chief Justice Marshall, who faced the question of a presidential privilege to withhold information from the courts in 1807 in the treason trial of Aaron Burr. Burr had requested from President Thomas Jefferson a letter written to him by Gen. James Wilkinson. Jefferson's attorney, George Hay, offered to submit the letter to Marshall, "excepting such parts thereof as are, in my opinion, not material for the purposes of justice, for the defense of the accused, or pertinent to the issue. . . . The accuracy of this opinion, I am willing to refer to the judgment of the Court, by submitting the original letter for its inspection." When Jefferson submitted the letter, with certain deletions, he did not assert a right to withhold information from the court; indeed, he made no challenge to the authority of the court to demand from the president materials relevant to the trial.

Marshall said nothing at all about an executive privilege "rooted" in the separation of powers. The chief justice approached the question of a presidential power to withhold information as an evidentiary privilege, not as a constitutional power. To acknowledge a constitutionally based privilege would acknowledge the president's authority to draw the line and determine issues of disclosure. But Marshall made it clear that he, not the president, would determine the measure of a president's authority to withhold material from the Court.

No historical materials, English or American, would have given the framers an understanding of executive power that included the authority to conceal information from a legislative inquiry. The framers largely drew their understanding of separation of powers from Baron de Montesquieu, who found no grounds in separation of powers for an executive to resist a legislative inquiry. The legislature, Montesquieu wrote, "has a right, and ought to have the means, of examining in what manner its laws have been executed." That right is an attribute of the English system, unlike others, he noted, in which government officers give "no account of their administration." In short, for the framers the separation of powers did not imply an executive right to withhold information from the legislature. On the contrary, it entailed a strong belief that the legislature had a right to demand from the executive the information it deemed relevant to its inquiries.

The effort to ground executive privilege in the original understanding of separation of powers fails to withstand historical scrutiny. The case for executive privilege fares no better when early precedents are considered.

Precedents

Political scientist Mark J. Rozell has contended that "President George Washington's actions established precedents for the exercise of what is now known as executive privilege." This contention rests on the slender reed of Washington's response to a House investigation in 1792 into the disastrous military campaign of Gen. Arthur St. Clair against the Indians. The House had appointed a committee to investigate the "causes of the failure" of the campaign and had vested in it the authority to call for persons and papers to assist its investigation. For his part, Washington recognized the authority of Congress to conduct an inquiry into the conduct of an executive officer, which reflected the historic practice of parliamentary inquiries into executive actions. As president, he cooperated completely.

The assertion that Washington claimed executive privilege is drawn not so much from anything he said or did, but rests, rather, on an excerpt from

Secretary of State Jefferson's notes of a cabinet meeting. Jefferson wrote that the cabinet had agreed that the "house was an inquest, and therefore might institute inquiries," but determined that the president had discretion to refuse papers, "the disclosure of which would injure the public." There is no reason to doubt the accuracy of Jefferson's notes, but little precedential value can be gleaned from this episode. First, Washington complied with the committee's demand and supplied all materials and documents relevant to the failed expedition. He offered no separation of powers objection. Second, there is no evidence that Jefferson's notes were presented to Congress or filed with the government. In short, they formed no part of the official record; there was no assertion to Congress of an executive privilege and no statement or declaration of an executive power to withhold information from Congress. Finally, the incident's precedential value is vitiated by the fact that neither Washington nor Jefferson ever invoked the St. Clair "precedent" in subsequent episodes that allegedly involved their respective claims to executive privilege.

The early years of the Republic reflect widespread understanding of Congress's right to demand information relevant to the exercise of its constitutional powers and responsibilities. President Washington freely supplied information to Congress pursuant to investigations of the St. Clair disaster and accusations of impropriety brought against Secretary of the Treasury Alexander Hamilton. He refused demands from the House for information relative to the Jay Treaty, but not for reasons of executive privilege. Rather, he withheld the requested materials on grounds that the House has no part of the treaty power. During Washington's tenure, the question was not executive concealment from Congress, but disclosure to the public. As a consequence, as political scientist Daniel N. Hoffman has shown, information was supplied to Congress, "some on a public and some on a confidential basis." On some occasions, Congress disclosed information to the public; on others, Congress persuaded the executive to disclose information to the public. It was able to do so because Article I, Section 5, of the Constitution grants to Congress the exclusive authority to withhold information from the citizenry. At all events, what emerged from this early period was not a record of constitutionally based claims to executive privilege, but rather an institutional practice of comity between the president and Congress.

Executive Privilege and a Successful Presidency

In *United States v. Nixon,* the Court declared that executive privilege is "constitutionally based" if it "relates to the effective discharge of a President's powers." This test begs the question: which of the president's constitutional powers requires resort to concealment of information from Congress in the pursuit of a successful presidency? None. The primary purpose animating the invention of the presidency was to create an executive to enforce the laws and policies of Congress. And although the "Imperial Presidency" has soared beyond the constitutional design, it remains true that the constitutional powers and roles assigned to the president do not require the use of executive privilege. The president's constitutional duty to faithfully execute the laws requires no resort to executive privilege; indeed, it was President Nixon's resort to executive privilege that obscured his failure to faithfully enforce the laws. Moreover, the exercise of the pardon and veto powers are subject to close scrutiny and demand accountability and explanation—hardly criteria for concealment. The appointment power—a shared power, it bears reminding—cannot be carried out unless the president and the Senate cooperate, a dynamic that precludes the claim of executive privilege. In none of these areas do presidents need executive privilege to successfully carry out their constitutional duties.

The argument for executive privilege in foreign policy and national security, a favorite among extollers of a strong presidency, shatters upon close analysis. The argument assumes that executive unilateralism in foreign affairs and war making is constitutionally based. It is not. The constitutional governance of American foreign policy reflects the framers' commitment to collective decision making and their fear of executive unilateralism. As a consequence, the Constitution grants to Congress the lion's share of the nation's foreign policy powers; the president's powers pale in comparison, and they require no resort to an executive privilege. The president is commander in chief of the nation's armed forces, but in this role the president is accountable to Congress and thus possesses no authority to withhold information from it. The president is assigned the duty of receiving ambassadors from other countries, but the framers viewed the performance of this duty as a routine, administrative function, exercised in most other countries by a ceremonial head of state. The lack of discretionary or policy-making authority in this duty precludes any presidential need to conceal information from Congress. Finally, in partnership with the Senate the president appoints ambassadors and makes treaties. Because neither power can be effectuated without the consent of both parties, the claim of privilege would defy not only the text and structure of the Constitution, but also the values, policy concerns, and logic that undergird the partnership.

Nothing in the creation of the commander in chief clause justifies presidential concealment of information from Congress. The war clause vests in Congress the sole and exclusive authority to initiate military hostilities, large or small, on behalf of the American people. In his role as commander in chief, the president conducts war, as Hamilton explained at the Constitutional Convention, "once war is authorized or begun." In the capacity of "first General or Admiral," the president conducts the military campaign, but the president remains accountable to congressional supervision. As Madison explained, Congress has the sole authority to determine whether "a war ought to be commenced, continued or concluded." As a consequence, Congress is entitled to complete information about the status of military activities, a need that prohibits resort to executive concealments. At bottom, no theory of executive privilege can be adduced to subvert the express grant of the war power to Congress.

It is folly as well to assert a presidential privilege to conceal information from the Senate in matters relevant to treaty making, because the Constitution conceives the treaty power as the joint province of the president and the Senate. Under the Constitution, treaties require the advice and consent of the Senate, an arrangement that urges consultation and cooperation and renders concealment unwise and inefficacious. In *Federalist* No. 64, John Jay of New

York conveyed his understanding that negotiations with those who desired to "rely on the secrecy of the President" might arise, but he emphasized that such secrecy applied to "those preparatory and auxiliary measures which are not otherwise important in a national view, than as they tend to facilitate the attainment of the objects of the negotiations." The president may "initiate" the negotiations, which require secrecy, but the framers anticipated that the Senate would, consistent with the meaning of "advise," participate equally with the president throughout the negotiation of treaties.

In summary, the constitutional design for foreign affairs provides no basis for the assertion of a presidential power to withhold information from Congress. Rather, the Constitution reflects the understanding that Congress possesses in the realm of foreign policy the same interests, powers, and responsibilities that it has in domestic matters: an informing function, an interest in knowing how its laws and policies have been executed, a responsibility to determine that its appropriations have been effectuated, as well as a general oversight function and the power of inquiry, as prelude to impeachment.

Conclusion

Little or no evidence exists to suggest that resort to executive privilege has served the national interest. Of course, the president's interests may differ from the nation's. In that event, executive concealment may be a viable option, as it was for Richard Nixon, but it is unlikely to be worthy of emulation and likely to inflict harm on the Republic. Mark Rozell has suggested that the competitive political process will provide a sufficient safeguard against the abuse of executive privilege. That is doubtful. American history has richly affirmed the framers' understanding that the integrity of government officials will not afford a sufficient bulwark against the abuse of power. That is why the founders wrote a constitution, and it is safe to say that trust in government officials was not an animating force behind the Constitutional Convention. Convention delegates did not fail to address the issue of secrecy; rather, they chose not to clothe the president with authority to withhold information from Congress. Nothing in law or history suggested to them the wisdom of an executive power to conceal information from Congress. Nothing since—either in law or in history—has offered persuasive evidence that the framers were mistaken.

POSTSCRIPT

Should the President Be Allowed "Executive Privilege"?

Whatever the intention of the Framers, the political issue is how much executive privilege and when exercised. Historically, the two elective branches have compromised or one or the other has yielded on the extent to which the president's desire to maintain secrecy and discretion in matters involving national security, confidential communications, and sensitive political negotiations can block Congress's desire to obtain all information relevant to its resolution of a controversial issue. In a few cases, as with the Nixon tapes, the intervention of the U.S. Supreme Court has been necessary to resolve the dispute.

Neither Rozell nor Adler considers the implications of the extension of executive privilege beyond the president's term of office or, for that matter, beyond his lifetime. The Presidential Records Act changed the status of the official records of presidents from private to public and allowed for public access to these records five years after the end of an administration, although the incumbent president could invoke specific restrictions to public access for up to twelve years. President George W. Bush's Executive Order 13233 amended this Act to give current and former presidents and vice presidents and their heirs broad authority to withhold or indefinitely delay the release of presidential documents and communications. In 2007, a Democratic Congress sought to revoke this order.

In order to amend or undermine the intent of Acts of Congress, presidents have appointed administrators who were not sympathetic to Congress's intent or have issued signing statements indicating their intention to ignore particular provisions of law. No obstacle the president can impose is clearer than the exercise of executive privilege. President George W. Bush made it clear: "I have a duty to protect the executive branch from legislative encroachment. I mean, for example, when the General Accounting Office demands documents from us, we're not going to give them to them. These were privileged conversations."

The constitutional and political advantages the president possesses in maintaining confidentiality in making executive decisions and those of the Congress in obtaining the information it seeks are examined in Louis Fisher, *The Politics of Executive Privilege* (Carolina Academic Press, 2004). Fisher concludes that any fixed rules setting legislative and executive boundaries are neither realistic nor desirable, because "disputes over information invariably come with unique qualities, characteristics, and histories, both legal and political, and are not likely to be governed solely by past practices and understandings."

Many aspects of executive privilege are considered in Matthew Crenson and Benjamin Ginsberg, *Presidential Power: Unbridled and Unbalanced* (W.W.

Norton, 2007), including whether the privilege extends to conversations between the vice president and persons other than the president. Crenson and Ginsberg maintain that the federal courts have bolstered the claims of executive power, including executive privilege, at the expense of Congress.

Further scholarly commentary and analysis in the contest of the full range of presidential power can be found in Christopher S. Kelley, ed., *Executing the Constitution: Putting the President Back into the Constitution* (SUNY Press, 2006) and Katy J. Harriger, *Separation of Powers: Documents and Commentary* (CQ Press, 2003), which contains a provocative essay by Neal Devins, "Executive Privilege and Congressional and Independent Investigations."

Internet References . . .

In addition to the Internet sites listed below, type in key words, such as "gay rights," "abortion," and "affirmative action" to find other listings.

New American Studies Web

This eclectic site provides links to a wealth of Internet resources for research in American studies, including agriculture and rural development, government, and race and ethnicity.

http://www.georgetown.edu/crossroads/asw/

Public Agenda Online

Public Agenda, a nonpartisan, nonprofit public opinion research and citizen education organization, provides links to policy options for issues ranging from abortion to Social Security.

http://www.publicagenda.org

NCPA Idea House

Through this site of the National Center for Policy Analysis, access discussions on an array of topics that are of major interest in the study of American government, from regulatory policy and privatization to economy and income.

http://www.ncpa.org/iss/

U.S. Immigration and Customs Enforcement

Created in 2003, this is the largest investigative branch of the Department of Homeland Security and targets illegal immigrants: the people, money, and materials that support terrorism and other criminal activities. The site contains some interesting information on child exploitation, counter-terrorism investigations, counter-narcotics efforts, and other topics.

http://www.ice.gov

Policy Library

This site provides a collection of documents on social and policy issues submitted by different research organizations all over the world.

http://www.policylibrary.com/US/index.html

Social Change and Public Policy

*E*conomic and moral issues divide Americans. Americans appear to be increasingly divided, along a "liberal" to "conservative" spectrum, on issues as diverse as economic equality, gay rights, abortion, race relations, and national health insurance. Disagreement breaks out on the floor of Congress, in state legislatures, in the nation's courtrooms, and sometimes in the streets. These controversial issues generate intense emotions because they ask us to clarify our values and understand the consequences of the public policies America adopts in each of these areas.

- Is Homosexual Conduct Constitutionally Protected?

- Does Affirmative Action Advance Racial Equality?

- Should Abortion Be Restricted?

- Should the Government Provide National Health Insurance?

- Is America Becoming More Unequal?

- Does the Patriot Act Abridge Essential Freedom?

- Stopping Illegal Immigration: Should Border Security Come First?

- Should There Be a "Wall of Separation" Between Church and State?

ISSUE 8

Is Homosexual Conduct Constitutionally Protected?

YES: Anthony Kennedy, from the Majority Opinion, in *Lawrence v. Texas,* U.S. Supreme Court (2003)

NO: Antonin Scalia, from the Dissenting Opinion, in *Lawrence v. Texas,* U.S. Supreme Court (2003)

ISSUE SUMMARY

YES: Supreme Court Justice Anthony Kennedy argues that sodomy laws are unconstitutional because no legitimate state interest justifies intrusion into the lives of homosexuals.

NO: Supreme Court Justice Antonin Scalia believes that sodomy laws reflect long-standing traditions regarding moral behavior that have been incorporated into American law and upheld by the courts.

Although statutes in many states outlawed sodomy, defined as "any sexual act involving the sex organs of one person and the mouth or anus of another," it was enforced only in homosexual relationships, and then only accidentally, as when two men were encountered in engaging in homosexual acts in Georgia when police officers entered a home searching for drugs. Even then, the district attorney declined to prosecute, but one of the men succeeded in making this a test case. The 5-4 decision of the United States Supreme Court in *Bowers v. Hardwick* in 1986 upheld the Georgia law because in our Western tradition there is no fundamental right to engage in homosexual acts. The dissent rejected the state's right to regulate or ban sexual acts that take place in the privacy of the home.

There is clearly ambiguity (if ambiguity is ever clear) in contemporary American attitudes toward homosexuality. When resolutions expressing approval of gay rights appear on the ballot, they often are defeated. On the other hand, resolutions barring homosexuals from teaching in the public schools are also defeated. It seems to come down to widespread public disapproval of homosexuality accompanied by widespread public disapproval of penalizing people who engage in homosexual behavior. Widespread disapproval in both instances does not eliminate the deeply felt convictions of partisans on both sides.

Those who oppose sodomy laws argue if there is a constitutionally protected right of privacy, it must extend to homosexual acts, because the right to privacy is antecedent to what is privately done. Moreover, sodomy is a victimless crime, like other outlawed sexual or verbal actions that do not involve unwitting or unwilling participants. It should be noted that the Georgia statute, like most similar prohibitions, did not distinguish between heterosexual and homosexual sodomy, but the law was never applied to heterosexual acts.

In the following two decades, much has changed in American tolerance of what critics characterize as immoral speech and behavior. Mass-market motion pictures, novels, cable television, and the virtually unlimited Internet visualize and verbalize what would have been shocking and revolting to most Americans decades ago and remains unacceptable to millions of Americans today. The transmission of sexually explicit television is permitted if preceded by an announcement that the program may be offensive to many viewers, and accompanied by means of barring reception in one's own home. Preventing the entry of other objectionable material is possible if concerned adults monitor what they and their children receive.

In this changed climate, it was inevitable that another sodomy case would be heard by the U.S. Supreme Court. This became more evident when, four years after he had been a member of the majority in *Bowers v. Hardwick*, now former justice Lewis Powell told a group of university students, ""I think I probably made a mistake in that one."

In 2003, the Supreme Court reexamined the constitutionality of sodomy legislation. Once again, the intervention of police into a private home was prompted by a different complaint, this time a suspicion of a "weapons disturbance." When the policy found two men having sexual relations, they were fined for violating a Texas law banning homosexual conduct.

The Texas case, *Lawrence v. Texas*, led not only to a reappraisal of sodomy laws, but also to a consideration of the circumstances under which the Supreme Court will reject *stare decisis,* the judicial rule that precedent is binding. In 1992, refusing to overthrow *Roe v. Wade*'s defense of the right to an abortion, Justice Souter wrote: "To overrule under fire in the absence of the most compelling reason to reexamine a watershed decision would subvert the Court's legitimacy beyond any serious question." Dissenting in *Lawrence v. Texas*, Justice Souter finds less basis for overruling *Bowers* than for overruling *Roe*.

But the only "compelling reason" to overrule in the sodomy cases is that the composition of the Court has changed although the constitutional issue has not. As in the earlier case, as is still argued on other issues, the ancient religious objection to certain sexual practices confronts the modern enshrinement of a constitutional right of privacy, neither of which is found in the text of the Constitution or the debates on it.

The contrast between the majority opinion of Justice Anthony Kennedy and the dissenting opinion of Justice Antonin Scalia could not be more striking, but the opinions deserve close scrutiny. Beyond sodomy, Kennedy believes that making homosexual conduct criminal will lead to discrimination in other areas, whereas Scalia professes that he is not opposed to homosexuals urging the legal adoption of their views.

Majority Opinion: *Lawrence* v. *Texas*, 539 U.S. 558 (2003)

Justice Kennedy Delivered the Opinion of the Court

Liberty protects the person from unwarranted government intrusions into a dwelling or other private places. In our tradition the State is not omnipresent in the home. And there are other spheres of our lives and existence, outside the home, where the State should not be a dominant presence. Freedom extends beyond spatial bounds. Liberty presumes an autonomy of self that includes freedom of thought, belief, expression, and certain intimate conduct. The instant case involves liberty of the person both in its spatial and more transcendent dimensions.

I

The question before the Court is the validity of a Texas statute making it a crime for two persons of the same sex to engage in certain intimate sexual conduct.

In Houston, Texas, officers of the Harris County Police Department were dispatched to a private residence in response to a reported weapons disturbance. They entered an apartment where one of the petitioners, John Geddes Lawrence, resided. The right of the police to enter does not seem to have been questioned. The officers observed Lawrence and another man, Tyron Garner, engaging in a sexual act. The two petitioners were arrested, held in custody over night, and charged and convicted before a Justice of the Peace.

The complaints described their crime as "deviate sexual intercourse, namely anal sex, with a member of the same sex (man)." The applicable state law is Tex. Penal Code Ann. §2I.06(a) (2003). It provides: "A person commits an offense if he engages in deviate sexual intercourse with another individual of the same sex." The statute defines "[d]eviate sexual intercourse" as follows:

(A) any contact between any part of the genitals of one person and the mouth or anus of another person; or

"(B) the penetration of the genitals or the anus of another person with an object." §21.01(1).

The petitioners exercised their right to a trial *de novo* in Harris County Criminal Court. They challenged the statute as a violation of the Equal Protection Clause of the Fourteenth Amendment and of a like provision of the Texas Constitution. Tex. Const., Art. 1, §3a. Those contentions were rejected. The petitioners, having entered a plea of *nolo contendere,* were each fined $200 and assessed court costs of $141.25.

The Court of Appeals for the Texas Fourteenth District considered the petitioners' federal constitutional arguments under both the Equal Protection and Due Process Clauses of the Fourteenth Amendment. After hearing the case en banc the court, in a divided opinion, rejected the constitutional arguments and affirmed the convictions. The majority opinion indicates that the Court of Appeals considered our decision in *Bowers* v. *Hardwick* (1986), to be controlling on the federal due process aspect of the case. *Bowers* then being authoritative, this was proper.

We granted certiorari to consider three questions:

1. Whether Petitioners' criminal convictions under the Texas "Homosexual Conduct" law—which criminalizes sexual intimacy by same-sex couples, but not identical behavior by different-sex couples—violate the Fourteenth Amendment guarantee of equal protection of laws?
2. Whether Petitioners' criminal convictions for adult consensual sexual intimacy in the home violate their vital interests in liberty and privacy protected by the Due Process Clause of the Fourteenth Amendment?
3. Whether *Bowers* v. *Hardwick* should be overruled?

The petitioners were adults at the time of the alleged offense. Their conduct was in private and consensual.

II

We conclude the case should be resolved by determining whether the petitioners were free as adults to engage in the private conduct in the exercise of their liberty under the Due Process Clause of the Fourteenth Amendment to the Constitution. For this inquiry we deem it necessary to reconsider the Court's holding in *Bowers.*

There are broad statements of the substantive reach of liberty under the Due Process Clause in earlier cases but the most pertinent beginning point is our decision in *Griswold* v. *Connecticut* (1965).

In *Griswold* the Court invalidated a state law prohibiting the use of drugs or devices of contraception and counseling or aiding and abetting the use of contraceptives. The Court described the protected interest as a right to privacy and placed emphasis on the marriage relation and the protected space of the marital bedroom.

After *Griswold* it was established that the right to make certain decisions regarding sexual conduct extends beyond the marital relationship. In *Eisenstadt* v. *Baird* (1972), the Court invalidated a law prohibiting the distribution of contraceptives to unmarried persons. The case was decided under the Equal Protection Clause, but with respect to unmarried persons, the Court went on to state the fundamental proposition that the law impaired the exercise of their personal rights. It quoted from the statement of the Court of Appeals finding the law to be in conflict with fundamental human rights, and it followed with this statement of its own:

> "It is true that in *Griswold* the right of privacy in question inhered in the marital relationship. . . . If the right of privacy means anything, it is the right of the *individual*, married or single, to be free from unwarranted governmental intrusion into matters so fundamentally affecting a person as the decision whether to bear or beget a child."

The opinions in *Griswold* and *Eisenstadt* were part of the background for the decision in *Roe* v. *Wade* (1973). As is well known, the case involved a challenge to the Texas law prohibiting abortions, but the laws of other States were affected as well. Although the Court held the woman's rights were not absolute, her right to elect an abortion did have real and substantial protection as an exercise of her liberty under the Due Process Clause. The Court cited cases that protect spatial freedom and cases that go well beyond it. *Roe* recognized the right of a woman to make certain fundamental decisions affecting her destiny and confirmed once more that the protection of liberty under the Due Process Clause has a substantive dimension of fundamental significance in defining the rights of the person.

In *Carey* v. *Population Services Int'l* (1977), the Court confronted a New York law forbidding sale or distribution of contraceptive devices to persons under 16 years of age. Although there was no single opinion for the Court, the law was invalidated. Both *Eisenstadt* and *Carey*, as well as the holding and rationale in *Roe*, confirmed that the reasoning of *Griswold* could not be confined to the protection of rights of married adults. This was the state of the law with respect to some of the most relevant cases when the Court considered *Bowers* v. *Hardwick.*

The facts in *Bowers* had some similarities to the instant case. A police officer, whose right to enter seems not to have been in question, observed Hardwick, in his own bedroom, engaging in intimate sexual conduct with another adult male. The conduct was in violation of a Georgia statute making it a criminal offense to engage in sodomy. One difference between the two cases is that the Georgia statute prohibited the conduct whether or not the participants were of the same sex, while the Texas statute, as we have seen, applies only to participants of the same sex. Hardwick was not prosecuted, but he brought an action in federal court to declare the state statute invalid. He alleged he was a practicing homosexual and that the criminal prohibition violated rights guaranteed to him by the Constitution. The Court, in an opinion by Justice White, sustained the Georgia law. Chief Justice Burger and Justice Powell joined the opinion of the Court and filed separate, concurring opinions. Four Justices dissented.

The Court began its substantive discussion in *Bowers* as follows: "The issue presented is whether the Federal Constitution confers a fundamental right upon homosexuals to engage in sodomy and hence invalidates the laws of the many

States that still make such conduct illegal and have done so for a very long time." That statement, we now conclude, discloses the Court's own failure to appreciate the extent of the liberty at stake. To say that the issue in *Bowers* was simply the right to engage in certain sexual conduct demeans the claim the individual put forward, just as it would demean a married couple were it to be said marriage is simply about the right to have sexual intercourse. The laws involved in *Bowers* and here are, to be sure, statutes that purport to do no more than prohibit a particular sexual act. Their penalties and purposes, though, have more far-reaching consequences, touching upon the most private human conduct, sexual behavior, and in the most private of places, the home. The statutes do seek to control a personal relationship that, whether or not entitled to formal recognition in the law, is within the liberty of persons to choose without being punished as criminals.

This, as a general rule, should counsel against attempts by the State, or a court, to define the meaning of the relationship or to set its boundaries absent injury to a person or abuse of an institution the law protects. It suffices for us to acknowledge that adults may choose to enter upon this relationship in the confines of their homes and their own private lives and still retain their dignity as free persons. When sexuality finds overt expression in intimate conduct with another person, the conduct can be but one element in a personal bond that is more enduring. The liberty protected by the Constitution allows homosexual persons the right to make this choice.

Having misapprehended the claim of liberty there presented to it, and thus stating the claim to be whether there is a fundamental right to engage in consensual sodomy, the *Bowers* Court said: "Proscriptions against that conduct have ancient roots." In academic writings, and in many of the scholarly *amicus* briefs filed to assist the Court in this case, there are fundamental criticisms of the historical premises relied upon by the majority and concurring opinions in *Bowers*. We need not enter this debate in the attempt to reach a definitive historical judgment, but the following considerations counsel against adopting the definitive conclusions upon which *Bowers* placed such reliance.

At the outset it should be noted that there is no longstanding history in this country of laws directed at homosexual conduct as a distinct matter. Beginning in colonial times there were prohibitions of sodomy derived from the English criminal laws passed in the first instance by the Reformation Parliament of 1533. The English prohibition was understood to include relations between men and women as well as relations between men and men. Nineteenth-century commentators similarly read American sodomy, buggery, and crime-against-nature statutes as criminalizing certain relations between men and women and between men and men. The absence of legal prohibitions focusing on homosexual conduct may be explained in part by noting that according to some scholars the concept of the homosexual as a distinct category of person did not emerge until the late 19th century. Thus early American sodomy laws were not directed at homosexuals as such but instead sought to prohibit non-procreative sexual activity more generally. This does not suggest approval of homosexual conduct. It does tend to show that this particular form of conduct was not thought of as a separate category from like conduct between heterosexual persons.

Laws prohibiting sodomy do not seem to have been enforced against consenting adults acting in private. A substantial number of sodomy prosecutions and convictions for which there are surviving records were for predatory acts against those who could not or did not consent, as in the case of a minor or the victim of an assault. As to these, one purpose for the prohibitions was to ensure there would be no lack of coverage if a predator committed a sexual assault that did not constitute rape as defined by the criminal law. Thus the model sodomy indictments presented in a 19th-century treatise addressed the predatory acts of an adult man against a minor girl or minor boy. Instead of targeting relations between consenting adults in private, 19th-century sodomy prosecutions typically involved relations between men and minor girls or minor boys, relations between adults involving force, relations between adults implicating disparity in status, or relations between men and animals.

To the extent that there were any prosecutions for the acts in question, 19th-century evidence rules imposed a burden that would make a conviction more difficult to obtain even taking into account the problems always inherent in prosecuting consensual acts committed in private. Under then-prevailing standards, a man could not be convicted of sodomy based upon testimony of a consenting partner, because the partner was considered an accomplice. A partner's testimony, however, was admissible if he or she had not consented to the act or was a minor, and therefore incapable of consent. The rule may explain in part the infrequency of these prosecutions. In all events that infrequency makes it difficult to say that society approved of a rigorous and systematic punishment of the consensual acts committed in private and by adults. The longstanding criminal prohibition of homosexual sodomy upon which the *Bowers* decision placed such reliance is as consistent with a general condemnation of nonprocreative sex as it is with an established tradition of prosecuting acts because of their homosexual character.

The policy of punishing consenting adults for private acts was not much discussed in the early legal literature. We can infer that one reason for this was the very private nature of the conduct. Despite the absence of prosecutions, there may have been periods in which there was public criticism of homosexuals as such and an insistence that the criminal laws be enforced to discourage their practices. But far from possessing "ancient roots," American laws targeting same-sex couples did not develop until the last third of the 20th century. The reported decisions concerning the prosecution of consensual, homosexual sodomy between adults for the years 1880–1995 are not always clear in the details, but a significant number involved conduct in a public place.

It was not until the 1970's that any State singled out same-sex relations for criminal prosecution, and only nine States have done so. Post-*Bowers* even some of these States did not adhere to the policy of suppressing homosexual conduct. Over the course of the last decades, States with same-sex prohibitions have moved toward abolishing them.

In summary, the historical grounds relied upon in *Bowers* are more complex than the majority opinion and the concurring opinion by Chief Justice Burger indicate. Their historical premises are not without doubt and, at the very least, are overstated.

It must be acknowledged, of course, that the Court in *Bowers* was making the broader point that for centuries there have been powerful voices to condemn homosexual conduct as immoral. The condemnation has been shaped by religious beliefs, conceptions of right and acceptable behavior, and respect for the traditional family. For many persons these are not trivial concerns but profound and deep convictions accepted as ethical and moral principles to which they aspire and which thus determine the course of their lives. These considerations do not answer the question before us, however. The issue is whether the majority may use the power of the State to enforce these views on the whole society through operation of the criminal law. "Our obligation is to define the liberty of all, not to mandate our own moral code." [*Planned Parenthood of Southeastern Pa. v. Casey*, 505 (1992)]

Chief Justice Burger joined the opinion for the Court in *Bowers* and further explained his views as follows: "Decisions of individuals relating to homosexual conduct have been subject to state intervention throughout the history of Western civilization. Condemnation of those practices is firmly rooted in Judeao-Christian moral and ethical standards." As with Justice White's assumptions about history, scholarship casts some doubt on the sweeping nature of the statement by Chief Justice Burger as it pertains to private homosexual conduct between consenting adults. In all events we think that our laws and traditions in the past half century are of most relevance here. These references show an emerging awareness that liberty gives substantial protection to adult persons in deciding how to conduct their private lives in matters pertaining to sex.

This emerging recognition should have been apparent when *Bowers* was decided. In 1955 the American Law Institute promulgated the Model Penal Code and made clear that it did not recommend or provide for "criminal penalties for consensual sexual relations conducted in private." It justified its decision on three grounds: (1) The prohibitions undermined respect for the law by penalizing conduct many people engaged in; (2) the statutes regulated private conduct not harmful to others; and (3) the laws were arbitrarily enforced and thus invited the danger of blackmail. In 1961 Illinois changed its laws to conform to the Model Penal Code. Other States soon followed.

In *Bowers* the Court referred to the fact that before 1961 all 50 States had outlawed sodomy, and that at the time of the Court's decision 24 States and the District of Columbia had sodomy laws. Justice Powell pointed out that these prohibitions often were being ignored, however. Georgia, for instance, had not sought to enforce its law for decades. ("The history of nonenforcement suggests the moribund character today of laws criminalizing this type of private, consensual conduct").

The sweeping references by Chief Justice Burger to the history of Western civilization and to Judeo-Christian moral and ethical standards did not take account of other authorities pointing in an opposite direction. A committee advising the British Parliament recommended in 1957 repeal of laws punishing homosexual conduct. The Wolfenden Report: Report of the Committee on Homosexual Offenses and Prostitution (1963). Parliament enacted the substance of those recommendations 10 years later.

Of even more importance, almost five years before *Bowers* was decided the European Court of Human Rights considered a case with parallels to *Bowers* and to today's case. An adult male resident in Northern Ireland alleged he was a practicing homosexual who desired to engage in consensual homosexual conduct. The laws of Northern Ireland forbade him that right. He alleged that he had been questioned, his home had been searched, and he feared criminal prosecution. The court held that the laws proscribing the conduct were invalid under the European Convention on Human Rights. Authoritative in all countries that are members of the Council of Europe (21 nations then, 45 nations now), the decision is at odds with the premise in *Bowers* that the claim put forward was insubstantial in our Western civilization.

In our own constitutional system the deficiencies in *Bowers* became even more apparent in the years following its announcement. The 25 States with laws prohibiting the relevant conduct referenced in the *Bowers* decision are reduced now to 13, of which 4 enforce their laws only against homosexual conduct. In those States where sodomy is still proscribed, whether for same-sex or heterosexual conduct, there is a pattern of nonenforcement with respect to consenting adults acting in private. The State of Texas admitted in 1994 that as of that date it had not prosecuted anyone under those circumstances.

Two principal cases decided after *Bowers* cast its holding into even more doubt. In *Planned Parenthood of Southeastern Pa.* v. *Casey* (1992), the Court reaffirmed the substantive force of the liberty protected by the Due Process Clause. The *Casey* decision again confirmed that our laws and tradition afford constitutional protection to personal decisions relating to marriage, procreation, contraception, family relationships, child rearing, and education. In explaining the respect the Constitution demands for the autonomy of the person in making these choices, we stated as follows:

> "These matters, involving the most intimate and personal choices a person may make in a lifetime, choices central to personal dignity and autonomy, are central to the liberty protected by the Fourteenth Amendment. At the heart of liberty is the right to define one's own concept of existence, of meaning, of the universe, and of the mystery of human life. Beliefs about these matters could not define the attributes of personhood were they formed under compulsion of the State."

Persons in a homosexual relationship may seek autonomy for these purposes, just as heterosexual persons do. The decision in *Bowers* would deny them this right.

The second post-*Bowers* case of principal relevance is *Romer* v. *Evans* (1996). There the Court struck down class-based legislation directed at homosexuals as a violation of the Equal Protection Clause. *Romer* invalidated an amendment to Colorado's constitution which named as a solitary class persons who were homosexuals, lesbians, or bisexual either by "orientation, conduct, practices or relationships," and deprived them of protection under state antidiscrimination laws. We concluded that the provision was "born of animosity toward the class of persons affected" and further that it had no rational relation to a legitimate governmental purpose.

As an alternative argument in this case, counsel for the petitioners and some *amici* contend that *Romer* provides the basis for declaring the Texas statute invalid under the Equal Protection Clause. That is a tenable argument, but we conclude the instant case requires us to address whether *Bowers* itself has continuing validity. Were we to hold the statute invalid under the Equal Protection Clause some might question whether a prohibition would be valid if drawn differently, say, to prohibit the conduct both between same-sex and different-sex participants.

Equality of treatment and the due process right to demand respect for conduct protected by the substantive guarantee of liberty are linked in important respects, and a decision on the latter point advances both interests. If protected conduct is made criminal and the law which does so remains unexamined for its substantive validity, its stigma might remain even if it were not enforceable as drawn for equal protection reasons. When homosexual conduct is made criminal by the law of the State, that declaration in and of itself is an invitation to subject homosexual persons to discrimination both in the public and in the private spheres. The central holding of *Bowers* has been brought in question by this case, and it should be addressed. Its continuance as precedent demeans the lives of homosexual persons.

The stigma this criminal statute imposes, moreover, is not trivial. The offense, to be sure, is but a class C misdemeanor, a minor offense in the Texas legal system. Still, it remains a criminal offense with all that imports for the dignity of the persons charged. The petitioners will bear on their record the history of their criminal convictions. Just this Term we rejected various challenges to state laws requiring the registration of sex offenders. We are advised that if Texas convicted an adult for private, consensual homosexual conduct under the statute here in question the convicted person would come within the registration laws of a least four States were he or she to be subject to their jurisdiction. This underscores the consequential nature of the punishment and the state-sponsored condemnation attendant to the criminal prohibition. Furthermore, the Texas criminal conviction carries with it the other collateral consequences always following a conviction, such as notations on job application forms, to mention but one example.

The foundations of *Bowers* have sustained serious erosion from our recent decisions in *Casey* and *Romer*. When our precedent has been thus weakened, criticism from other sources is of greater significance. In the United States criticism of *Bowers* has been substantial and continuing, disapproving of its reasoning in all respects, not just as to its historical assumptions. The courts of five different States have declined to follow it in interpreting provisions in their own state constitutions parallel to the Due Process Clause of the Fourteenth Amendment.

To the extent *Bowers* relied on values we share with a wider civilization, it should be noted that the reasoning and holding in *Bowers* have been rejected elsewhere. The European Court of Human Rights has followed not *Bowers* but its own decision in *Dudgeon* v. *United Kingdom*. Other nations, too, have taken action consistent with an affirmation of the protected right of homosexual adults to engage in intimate, consensual conduct. The right the petitioners seek in this case has been accepted as an integral part of human freedom in many other countries.

There has been no showing that in this country the governmental interest in circumscribing personal choice is somehow more legitimate or urgent.

The doctrine of *stare decisis* is essential to the respect accorded to the judgments of the Court and to the stability of the law. It is not, however, an inexorable command. In *Casey* we noted that when a Court is asked to over-rule a precedent recognizing a constitutional liberty interest, individual or societal reliance on the existence of that liberty cautions with particular strength against reversing course. The holding in *Bowers*, however, has not induced detrimental reliance comparable to some instances where recognized individual rights are involved. Indeed, there has been no individual or societal reliance on *Bowers* of the sort that could counsel against overturning its holding once there are compelling reasons to do so. *Bowers* itself causes uncertainty, for the precedents before and after its issuance contradict its central holding.

The rationale of *Bowers* does not withstand careful analysis. In his dissenting opinion in *Bowers* Justice Stevens came to these conclusions:

> "Our prior cases make two propositions abundantly clear. First, the fact that the governing majority in a State has traditionally viewed a particular practice as immoral is not a sufficient reason for upholding a law prohibiting the practice; neither history nor tradition could save a law prohibiting miscegenation from constitutional attack. Second, individual decisions by married persons, concerning the intimacies of their physical relationship, even when not intended to produce offspring, are a form of "liberty" protected by the Due Process Clause of the Fourteenth Amendment. Moreover, this protection extends to intimate choices by unmarried as well as married persons."

Justice Stevens' analysis, in our view, should have been controlling in *Bowers* and should control here.

Bowers was not correct when it was decided, and it is not correct today. It ought not to remain binding precedent. *Bowers* v. *Hardwick* should be and now is overruled.

The present case does not involve minors. It does not involve persons who might be injured or coerced or who are situated in relationships where consent might not easily be refused. It does not involve public conduct or prostitution. It does not involve whether the government must give formal recognition to any relationship that homosexual persons seek to enter. The case does involve two adults who, with full and mutual consent from each other, engaged in sexual practices common to a homosexual lifestyle. The petitioners are entitled to respect for their private lives. The State cannot demean their existence or control their destiny by making their private sexual conduct a crime. Their right to liberty under the Due Process Clause gives them the full right to engage in their conduct without intervention of the government. "It is a promise of the Constitution that there is a realm of personal liberty which the government may not enter." [*Casey*] The Texas statute furthers no legitimate state interest which can justify its intrusion into the personal and private life of the individual.

Had those who drew and ratified the Due Process Clauses of the Fifth Amendment or the Fourteenth Amendment known the components of liberty in its manifold possibilities, they might have been more specific. They did not presume to have this insight. They knew times can blind us to certain truths and later generations can see that laws once thought necessary and proper in fact serve only to oppress. As the Constitution endures, persons in every generation can invoke its principles in their own search for greater freedom.

The judgment of the Court of Appeals for the Texas Fourteenth District is reversed, and the case is remanded for further proceedings not inconsistent with this opinion.

Antonin Scalia  **NO**

The Dissenting Opinion: *Lawrence* v. *Texas,* 539 U.S. 558 (2003)

Justice Scalia, with Whom The Chief Justice and Justice Thomas Join, Dissenting

"Liberty finds no refuge in a jurisprudence of doubt." *Planned Parenthood of Southeastern Pa.* v. *Casey* (1992). That was the Court's sententious response, barely more than a decade ago, to those seeking to overrule *Roe* v. *Wade* (1973). The Court's response today, to those who have engaged in a 17-year crusade to overrule *Bowers* v. *Hardwick*, (1986), is very different. The need for stability and certainty presents no barrier.

Most of the rest of today's opinion has no relevance to its actual holding—that the Texas statute "furthers no legitimate state interest which can justify" its application to petitioners under rational-basis review (overruling *Bowers* to the extent it sustained Georgia's anti-sodomy statute under the rational-basis test). Though there is discussion of "fundamental proposition[s] and "fundamental decisions," nowhere does the Court's opinion declare that homosexual sodomy is a "fundamental right" under the Due Process Clause; nor does it subject the Texas law to the standard of review that would be appropriate (strict scrutiny) if homosexual sodomy *were* a "fundamental right." Thus, while overruling the *outcome* of *Bowers*, the Court leaves strangely untouched its central legal conclusion: "[R]espondent would have us announce . . . a fundamental right to engage in homosexual sodomy. This we are quite unwilling to do." Instead the Court simply describes petitioners' conduct as "an exercise of their liberty"—which it undoubtedly is—and proceeds to apply an unheard-of form of rational-basis review that will have far-reaching implications beyond this case.

I

I begin with the Court's surprising readiness to reconsider a decision rendered a mere 17 years ago in *Bowers* v. *Hardwick*. I do not myself believe in rigid adherence to *stare decisis* in constitutional cases; but I do believe that we should be consistent rather than manipulative in invoking the doctrine. Today's opinions in support of reversal do not bother to distinguish—or indeed, even bother to mention—the paean to *stare decisis* coauthored by three Members of today's majority in *Planned Parenthood* v. *Casey*. There, when *stare decisis* meant preservation of judicially invented abortion rights, the widespread criticism of *Roe* was strong reason to *reaffirm* it:

> "Where, in the performance of its judicial duties, the Court decides a case in such a way as to resolve the sort of intensely divisive controversy reflected in *Roe*[,] . . . its decision has a dimension that the resolution of the normal case does not carry. . . . [T]o overrule under fire in the absence of the most compelling reason . . . would subvert the Court's legitimacy beyond any serious question."

Today, however, the widespread opposition to *Bowers*, a decision resolving an issue as "intensely divisive" as the issue in *Roe*, is offered as a reason in favor of *overruling* it. Gone, too, is any "enquiry" into whether the decision sought to be overruled has "proven 'unworkable.'"

Today's approach to *stare decisis* invites us to overrule an erroneously decided precedent (including an "intensely divisive" decision) *if:* (1) its foundations have been "eroded" by subsequent decisions; (2) it has been subject to "substantial and continuing" criticism; and (3) it has not induced "individual or societal reliance" that counsels against overturning. The problem is that *Roe* itself—which today's majority surely has no disposition to overrule—satisfies these conditions to at least the same degree as *Bowers*.

(1) A preliminary digressive observation with regard to the first factor: The Court's claim that *Planned Parenthood* v. *Casey* "casts some doubt" upon the holding in *Bowers* (or any other case, for that matter) does not withstand analysis. As far as its holding is concerned, *Casey* provided a *less* expansive right to abortion than did *Roe, which was already on the books when Bowers was decided.* And if the Court is referring not to the holding of *Casey*, but to the dictum of its famed sweet-mystery-of-life passage ("'At the heart of liberty is the right to define one's own concept of existence, of meaning, of the universe, and of the mystery of human life'"): That "casts some doubt" upon either the totality of our jurisprudence or else (presumably the right answer) nothing at all. I have never heard of a law that attempted to restrict one's "right to define" certain concepts; and if the passage calls into question the government's power to regulate *actions based on* one's self-defined "concept of existence, etc.," it is the passage that ate the rule of law.

I do not quarrel with the Court's claim that *Romer* (1996), "eroded" the "foundations" of *Bowers'* rational-basis holding. But *Roe* and *Casey* have been equally "eroded" by *Washington* v. *Glucksberg* (1997), which held that *only* fundamental rights which are "'deeply rooted in this Nation's history and tradition'" qualify for anything other than rational basis scrutiny under the doctrine of "substantive due process." *Roe* and *Casey*, of course, subjected the restriction of abortion to heightened scrutiny without even attempting to establish that the freedom to abort *was* rooted in this Nation's tradition.

(2) *Bowers*, the Court says, has been subject to "substantial and continuing [criticism], disapproving of its reasoning in all respects, not just as to its historical assumptions." Exactly what those nonhistorical criticisms are, and whether the Court even agrees with them, are left unsaid, although the Court

does cite two books. Of course, *Roe* too (and by extension *Casey*) had been (and still is) subject to unrelenting criticism, including criticism from the two commentators cited by the Court today. [Fried: "Roe was a prime example of twisted judging"]; Posner: "[The Court's] opinion in *Roe* . . . fails to measure up to professional expectations regarding judicial opinions."

(3) That leaves, to distinguish the rock-solid, unamendable disposition of *Roe* from the readily overrulable *Bowers*, only the third factor. "[T]here has been," the Court says, "no individual or societal reliance on *Bowers* of the sort that could counsel against overturning its holding. . . ." It seems to me that the "societal reliance" on the principles confirmed in *Bowers* and discarded today has been overwhelming. Countless judicial decisions and legislative enactments have relied on the ancient proposition that a governing majority's belief that certain sexual behavior is "immoral and unacceptable" constitutes a rational basis for regulation. . . . We ourselves relied extensively on *Bowers* when we concluded, in *Barnes* v. *Glen Theatre, Inc.* (1991), that Indiana's public indecency statute furthered "a substantial government interest in protecting order and morality." State laws against bigamy, same-sex marriage, adult incest, prostitution, masturbation, adultery, fornication, bestiality, and obscenity are likewise sustainable only in light of *Bowers'* validation of laws based on moral choices. Every single one of these laws is called into question by today's decision; the Court makes no effort to cabin the scope of its decision to exclude them from its holding. . . . The impossibility of distinguishing homosexuality from other traditional "morals" offenses is precisely why *Bowers* rejected the rational-basis challenge. "The law," it said, "is constantly based on notions of morality, and if all laws representing essentially moral choices are to be invalidated under the Due Process Clause, the courts will be very busy indeed."

What a massive disruption of the current social order, therefore, the overruling of *Bowers* entails. Not so the overruling of *Roe*, which would simply have restored the regime that existed for centuries before 1973, in which the permissibility of and restrictions upon abortion were determined legislatively State-by-State. *Casey*, however, chose to base its *stare decisis* determination on a different "sort" of reliance. "[P]eople," it said, "have organized intimate relationships and made choices that define their views of themselves and their places in society, in reliance on the availability of abortion in the event that contraception should fail." This falsely assumes that the consequence of overruling *Roe* would have been to make abortion unlawful. It would not; it would merely have *permitted* the States to do so. Many States would unquestionably have declined to prohibit abortion, and others would not have prohibited it within six months (after which the most significant reliance interests would have expired). Even for persons in States other than these, the choice would not have been between abortion and childbirth, but between abortion nearby and abortion in a neighboring State.

To tell the truth, it does not surprise me, and should surprise no one, that the Court has chosen today to revise the standards of *stare decisis* set forth in *Casey*. It has thereby exposed *Casey's* extraordinary deference to precedent for the result-oriented expedient that it is.

II

Having decided that it need not adhere to *stare decisis*, the Court still must establish that *Bowers* was wrongly decided and that the Texas statute, as applied to petitioners, is unconstitutional.

Texas Penal Code Ann. §21.06(a) (2003) undoubtedly imposes constraints on liberty. So do laws prohibiting prostitution, recreational use of heroin, and, for that matter, working more than 60 hours per week in a bakery. But there is no right to "liberty" under the Due Process Clause, though today's opinion repeatedly makes that claim. . . . The Fourteenth Amendment *expressly allows* States to deprive their citizens of "liberty," so long as "due process of law" is provided: "No state shall . . . deprive any person of life, liberty, or property, *without due process of law.*" (emphasis added).

Our opinions applying the doctrine known as "substantive due process" hold that the Due Process Clause prohibits States from infringing *fundamental* liberty interests, unless the infringement is narrowly tailored to serve a compelling state interest. We have held repeatedly, in cases the Court today does not overrule, that *only* fundamental rights qualify for this so-called "heightened scrutiny" protection—that is, rights which are "'deeply rooted in this Nation's history and tradition,'" . . . All other liberty interests may be abridged or abrogated pursuant to a validly enacted state law if that law is rationally related to a legitimate state interest.

Bowers held, first, that criminal prohibitions of homosexual sodomy are not subject to heightened scrutiny because they do not implicate a "fundamental right" under the Due Process Clause. Noting that "[p]roscriptions against that conduct have ancient roots," that "[s]odomy was a criminal offense at common law and was forbidden by the laws of the original 13 States when they ratified the Bill of Rights," and that many States had retained their bans on sodomy, *Bowers* concluded that a right to engage in homosexual sodomy was not "'deeply rooted in this Nation's history and tradition.'"

The Court today does not overrule this holding. Not once does it describe homosexual sodomy as a "fundamental right" or a "fundamental liberty interest," nor does it subject the Texas statute to strict scrutiny. Instead, having failed to establish that the right to homosexual sodomy is "'deeply rooted in this Nation's history and tradition,'" the Court concludes that the application of Texas's statute to petitioners' conduct fails the rational-basis test, and overrules *Bowers'* holding to the contrary, see *id.*, at 196. "The Texas statute furthers no legitimate state interest which can justify its intrusion into the personal and private life of the individual."

I shall address that rational-basis holding presently. First, however, I address some aspersions that the Court casts upon *Bowers'* conclusion that homosexual sodomy is not a "fundamental right"—even though, as I have said, the Court does not have the boldness to reverse that conclusion.

III

The Court's description of "the state of the law" at the time of *Bowers* only confirms that *Bowers* was right. The Court points to *Griswold* v. *Connecticut*

(1965). But that case *expressly disclaimed* any reliance on the doctrine of "substantive due process," and grounded the so-called "right to privacy" in penumbras of constitutional provisions *other than* the Due Process Clause. *Eisenstadt* v. *Baird* (1972), likewise had nothing to do with "substantive due process"; it invalidated a Massachusetts law prohibiting the distribution of contraceptives to unmarried persons solely on the basis of the Equal Protection Clause. Of course *Eisenstadt* contains well known dictum relating to the "right to privacy," but this referred to the right recognized in *Griswold*—a right penumbral to the *specific* guarantees in the Bill of Rights, and not a "substantive due process" right.

Roe v. *Wade* recognized that the right to abort an unborn child was a "fundamental right" protected by the Due Process Clause. The *Roe* Court, however, made no attempt to establish that this right was "'deeply rooted in this Nation's history and tradition'"; instead, it based its conclusion that "the Fourteenth Amendment's concept of personal liberty . . . is broad enough to encompass a woman's decision whether or not to terminate her pregnancy" on its own normative judgment that anti-abortion laws were undesirable. We have since rejected *Roe*'s holding that regulations of abortion must be narrowly tailored to serve a compelling state interest, and thus, by logical implication, *Roe*'s holding that the right to abort an unborn child is a "fundamental right."

After discussing the history of antisodomy laws, the Court proclaims that, "it should be noted that there is no longstanding history in this country of laws directed at homosexual conduct as a distinct matter." This observation in no way casts into doubt the "definitive [historical] conclusion," on which *Bowers* relied: that our Nation has a longstanding history of laws prohibiting *sodomy in general*—regardless of whether it was performed by same-sex or opposite-sex couples:

> "It is obvious to us that neither of these formulations would extend a fundamental right to homosexuals to engage in acts of consensual sodomy. Proscriptions against that conduct have ancient roots. *Sodomy* was a criminal offense at common law and was forbidden by the laws of the original 13 States when they ratified the Bill of Rights. In 1868, when the Fourteenth Amendment was ratified, all but 5 of the 37 States in the Union had *criminal sodomy laws*. In fact, until 1961, all 50 States outlawed *sodomy*, and today, 24 States and the District of Columbia continue to provide criminal penalties for *sodomy* performed in private and between consenting adults. Against this background, to claim that a right to engage in such conduct is 'deeply rooted in this Nation's history and tradition' or 'implicit in the concept of ordered liberty' is, at best, facetious." (emphasis added).

It is (as *Bowers* recognized) entirely irrelevant whether the laws in our long national tradition criminalizing homosexual sodomy were "directed at homosexual conduct as a distinct matter." Whether homosexual sodomy was prohibited by a law targeted at same-sex sexual relations or by a more general law prohibiting both homosexual and heterosexual sodomy, the only relevant point is that it *was* criminalized—which suffices to establish that homosexual sodomy is not a right "deeply rooted in our Nation's history and tradition." The Court today agrees that homosexual sodomy was criminalized and thus does not dispute the facts on which *Bowers actually* relied.

Next the Court makes the claim, again unsupported by any citations, that "[l]aws prohibiting sodomy do not seem to have been enforced against consenting adults acting in private." *Ante*, at 8. The key qualifier here is "acting in private"—since the Court admits that sodomy laws *were* enforced against consenting adults (although the Court contends that prosecutions were "infrequent"). I do not know what "acting in private" means; surely consensual sodomy, like heterosexual intercourse, is rarely performed on stage. If all the Court means by "acting in private" is "on private premises, with the doors closed and windows covered," it is entirely unsurprising that evidence of enforcement would be hard to come by. (Imagine the circumstances that would enable a search warrant to be obtained for a residence on the ground that there was probable cause to believe that consensual sodomy was then and there occurring.) Surely that lack of evidence would not sustain the proposition that consensual sodomy on private premises with the doors closed and windows covered was regarded as a "fundamental right," even though all other consensual sodomy was criminalized. There are 203 prosecutions for consensual, adult homosexual sodomy reported in the West Reporting system and official state reporters from the years 1880–1995. There are also records of 20 sodomy prosecutions and 4 executions during the colonial period. *Bowers'* conclusion that homosexual sodomy is not a fundamental right "deeply rooted in this Nation's history and tradition" is utterly unassailable.

Realizing that fact, the Court instead says: "[W]e think that our laws and traditions in the past half century are of most relevance here. These references show *an emerging awareness* that liberty gives substantial protection to adult persons in deciding how to conduct their private lives *in matters pertaining to sex*." (emphasis added). Apart from the fact that such an "emerging awareness" does not establish a "fundamental right," the statement is factually false. States continue to prosecute all sorts of crimes by adults "in matters pertaining to sex": prostitution, adult incest, adultery, obscenity, and child pornography. Sodomy laws, too, have been enforced "in the past half century," in which there have been 134 reported cases involving prosecutions for consensual, adult, homosexual sodomy. In relying, for evidence of an "emerging recognition," upon the American Law Institute's 1955 recommendation not to criminalize "'consensual sexual relations conducted in private,'" the Court ignores the fact that this recommendation was "a point of resistance in most of the states that considered adopting the Model Penal Code."

In any event, an "emerging awareness" is by definition not "deeply rooted in this Nation's history and tradition[s]," as we have said "fundamental right" status requires. Constitutional entitlements do not spring into existence because some States choose to lessen or eliminate criminal sanctions on certain behavior. Much less do they spring into existence, as the Court seems to believe, because *foreign nations* decriminalize conduct. The *Bowers* majority opinion *never* relied on "values we share with a wider civilization," *ante*, at 16, but rather rejected the claimed right to sodomy on the ground that such a right was not "'deeply rooted in *this Nation's* history and tradition,'" (emphasis added). *Bowers'* rational-basis holding is likewise devoid of any reliance on the views of a "wider civilization." The Court's discussion of these foreign views (ignoring, of course, the many countries that have retained criminal prohibitions on sodomy) is therefore meaningless dicta. . . .

IV

I turn now to the ground on which the Court squarely rests its holding: the contention that there is no rational basis for the law here under attack. This proposition is so out of accord with our jurisprudence—indeed, with the jurisprudence of *any* society we know—that it requires little discussion.

The Texas statute undeniably seeks to further the belief of its citizens that certain forms of sexual behavior are "immoral and unacceptable," the same interest furthered by criminal laws against fornication, bigamy, adultery, adult incest, bestiality, and obscenity. *Bowers* held that this *was* a legitimate state interest. The Court today reaches the opposite conclusion. The Texas statute, it says, "furthers *no legitimate state interest* which can justify its intrusion into the personal and private life of the individual." The Court embraces instead Justice Stevens' declaration in his *Bowers* dissent, that "the fact that the governing majority in a State has traditionally viewed a particular practice as immoral is not a sufficient reason for upholding a law prohibiting the practice." This effectively decrees the end of all morals legislation. If, as the Court asserts, the promotion of majoritarian sexual morality is not even a *legitimate* state interest, none of the above-mentioned laws can survive rational-basis review.

V

Finally, I turn to petitioners' equal-protection challenge, which no Member of the Court save Justice O'Connor embraces: On its face §21.06(a) applies equally to all persons. Men and women, heterosexuals and homosexuals, are all subject to its prohibition of deviate sexual intercourse with someone of the same sex. To be sure, §21.06 does distinguish between the sexes insofar as concerns the partner with whom the sexual acts are performed: men can violate the law only with other men, and women only with other women. But this cannot itself be a denial of equal protection, since it is precisely the same distinction regarding partner that is drawn in state laws prohibiting marriage with someone of the same sex while permitting marriage with someone of the opposite sex.

The objection is made, however, that the antimiscegenation laws invalidated in *Loving* v. *Virginia* (1967), similarly were applicable to whites and blacks alike, and only distinguished between the races insofar as the *partner* was concerned. In *Loving*, however, we correctly applied heightened scrutiny, rather than the usual rational-basis review, because the Virginia statute was "designed to maintain White Supremacy." A racially discriminatory purpose is always sufficient to subject a law to strict scrutiny, even a facially neutral law that makes no mention of race. No purpose to discriminate against men or women as a class can be gleaned from the Texas law, so rational-basis review applies. That review is readily satisfied here by the same rational basis that satisfied it in *Bowers*—society's belief that certain forms of sexual behavior are "immoral and unacceptable." This is the same justification that supports many other laws regulating sexual behavior that make a distinction based upon the identity of the partner—for example, laws against adultery, fornication, and adult incest, and laws refusing to recognize homosexual marriage.

Justice O'Connor argues that the discrimination in this law which must be justified is not its discrimination with regard to the sex of the partner but its discrimination with regard to the sexual proclivity of the principal actor. "While it is true that the law applies only to conduct, the conduct targeted by this law is conduct that is closely correlated with being homosexual. Under such circumstances, Texas' sodomy law is targeted at more than conduct. It is instead directed toward gay persons as a class."

Of course the same could be said of any law. A law against public nudity targets "the conduct that is closely correlated with being a nudist," and hence "is targeted at more than conduct"; it is "directed toward nudists as a class." But be that as it may. Even if the Texas law *does* deny equal protection to "homosexuals as a class," that denial *still* does not need to be justified by anything more than a rational basis, which our cases show is satisfied by the enforcement of traditional notions of sexual morality.

Justice O'Connor simply decrees application of "a more searching form of rational basis review" to the Texas statute. The cases she cites do not recognize such a standard, and reach their conclusions only after finding, as required by conventional rational-basis analysis, that no conceivable legitimate state interest supports the classification at issue. Nor does Justice O'Connor explain precisely what her "more searching form" of rational-basis review consists of. It must at least mean, however, that laws exhibiting "'a . . . desire to harm a politically unpopular group,'" are invalid *even though* there may be a conceivable rational basis to support them.

This reasoning leaves on pretty shaky grounds state laws limiting marriage to opposite-sex couples. Justice O'Connor seeks to preserve them by the conclusory statement that "preserving the traditional institution of marriage" is a legitimate state interest. But "preserving the traditional institution of marriage" is just a kinder way of describing the State's *moral disapproval* of same-sex couples. Texas's interest in §21.06 could be recast in similarly euphemistic terms: "preserving the traditional sexual mores of our society." In the jurisprudence Justice O'Connor has seemingly created, judges can validate laws by characterizing them as "preserving the traditions of society" (good); or invalidate them by characterizing them as "expressing moral disapproval" (bad).

❧◉❧

Today's opinion is the product of a Court, which is the product of a law-profession culture, that has largely signed on to the so-called homosexual agenda, by which I mean the agenda promoted by some homosexual activists directed at eliminating the moral opprobrium that has traditionally attached to homosexual conduct. I noted in an earlier opinion the fact that the American Association of Law Schools (to which any reputable law school *must* seek to belong) excludes from membership any school that refuses to ban from its job-interview facilities a law firm (no matter how small) that does not wish to hire as a prospective partner a person who openly engages in homosexual conduct.

One of the most revealing statements in today's opinion is the Court's grim warning that the criminalization of homosexual conduct is "an invitation to subject homosexual persons to discrimination both in the public and in the private spheres." It is clear from this that the Court has taken sides in the culture war, departing from its role of assuring, as neutral observer, that the democratic rules of engagement are observed. Many Americans do not want persons who openly engage in homosexual conduct as partners in their business, as scoutmasters for their children, as teachers in their children's schools, or as boarders in their home. They view this as protecting themselves and their families from a life style that they believe to be immoral and destructive. The Court views it as "discrimination" which it is the function of our judgments to deter. So imbued is the Court with the law profession's anti-anti-homosexual culture, that it is seemingly unaware that the attitudes of that culture are not obviously "mainstream"; that in most States what the Court calls "discrimination" against those who engage in homosexual acts is perfectly legal; that proposals to ban such "discrimination" under Title VII have repeatedly been rejected by Congress; that in some cases such "discrimination" is *mandated* by federal statute, mandating discharge from the armed forces of any service member who engages in or intends to engage in homosexual acts; and that in some cases such "discrimination" is a constitutional right, see *Boy Scouts of America* v. *Dale* (2000).

Let me be clear that I have nothing against homosexuals, or any other group, promoting their agenda through normal democratic means. Social perceptions of sexual and other morality change over time, and every group has the right to persuade its fellow citizens that its view of such matters is the best. That homosexuals have achieved some success in that enterprise is attested to by the fact that Texas is one of the few remaining States that criminalize private, consensual homosexual acts. But persuading one's fellow citizens is one thing, and imposing one's views in absence of democratic majority is something else. I would no more *require* a State to criminalize homosexual acts—or, for that matter, display *any* moral disapprobation of them—than I would *forbid* it to do so. What Texas has chosen to do is well within the range of traditional democratic action, and its hand should not be stayed through the invention of a brand-new "constitutional right" by a Court that is impatient of democratic change. It is indeed true that "later generations can see that laws once thought necessary and proper in fact serve only to oppress"; and when that happens, later generations can repeal those laws. But it is the premise of our system that those judgments are to be made by the people, and not imposed by a governing caste that knows best.

One of the benefits of leaving regulation of this matter to the people rather than to the courts is that the people, unlike judges, need not carry things to their logical conclusion. The people may feel that their disapprobation of homosexual conduct is strong enough to disallow homosexual marriage, but not strong enough to criminalize private homosexual acts—and may legislate accordingly. The Court today pretends that it possesses a similar freedom of action, so that that we need not fear judicial imposition of homosexual marriage, as has recently occurred in Canada. At the end of its opinion—after having laid waste the foundations of our rational-basis jurisprudence—the Court says that the present case "does not involve whether the government must give formal recognition to any relationship that homosexual persons seek to enter." Do not believe it. More illuminating than this bald, unreasoned disclaimer is the progression of thought displayed by an earlier passage in the Court's opinion, which notes the constitutional protections afforded to "personal decisions relating to *marriage*, procreation, contraception, family relationships, child rearing, and education," and then declares that "[p]ersons in a homosexual relationship may seek autonomy for these purposes, just as heterosexual persons do." (emphasis added). Today's opinion dismantles the structure of constitutional law that has permitted a distinction to be made between heterosexual and homosexual unions, insofar as formal recognition in marriage is concerned. If moral disapprobation of homosexual conduct is "no legitimate state interest" for purposes of proscribing that conduct; and if, as the Court coos (casting aside all pretense of neutrality), "[w]hen sexuality finds overt expression in intimate conduct with another person, the conduct can be but one element in a personal bond that is more enduring"; what justification could there possibly be for denying the benefits of marriage to homosexual couples exercising "[t]he liberty protected by the Constitution"? Surely not the encouragement of procreation, since the sterile and the elderly are allowed to marry. This case "does not involve" the issue of homosexual marriage only if one entertains the belief that principle and logic have nothing to do with the decisions of this Court. Many will hope that, as the Court comfortingly assures us, this is so.

The matters appropriate for this Court's resolution are only three: Texas's prohibition of sodomy neither infringes a "fundamental right" (which the Court does not dispute), nor is unsupported by a rational relation to what the Constitution considers a legitimate state interest, nor denies the equal protection of the laws. I dissent.

POSTSCRIPT

Is Homosexual Conduct Constitutionally Protected?

Predictably, the response of interest groups divided sharply on the Supreme Court's movement from a 5-4 majority upholding state laws against sodomy to a 6-3 majority declaring such laws unconstitutional. National Organization for Women president Kim Gandy approved: "We still have a long way to go in achieving full equality, but the Court's recognition that all women and men, regardless of their sexuality, have a constitutional right to privacy is a huge step forward." Focus on the Family's vice president of public policy disapproved: "If the people have no right to regulate sexuality then ultimately the institution of marriage is in peril, and with it, the welfare of the coming generations of children."

The evolution of the Supreme Court's decisions in which laws upholding moral principles were challenged by privacy claims goes back to *Griswold v. Connecticut* in 1965, when it struck down a law barring the use of contraceptives by married couples. The Court found the right to privacy not in any specific guarantee of the Bill of Rights, but as part of "penumbras, formed by emanations from those guarantees that help give them life and substance." Less mystical defenses have been offered by later courts, but the right has become well established, if the extent to which privacy is protected remains controversial.

Like Justice White in the majority opinion upholding sodomy laws in *Bowers v. Hardwick*, Justice Scalia argues, not in support of anti-sodomy laws but, against courts substituting their own moral judgments for those of the people's elected representatives. The larger question for both the majority and the dissenters in *Lawrence v. Texas* is whether and when legislatures may write laws based on widely held moral convictions. Americans overwhelmingly approve of laws that punish assaults on children more severely than sexual assaults on adults. They subscribe to distinctions that bar children from publicly viewing X- or R-rated movies. In another realm, courts have considered whether the death sentence is cruel or unusual punishment when it inflicts greater pain than other methods of administering it, and some Americans believe that capital punishment itself is immoral. In short, it remains true that morality matters in law.

There is a considerable literature on homosexuality. A basic source is Wayne Dynes, ed., *The Encyclopedia of Homosexuality* (Garland, 1990). Other general works include Michelangelo Signorile, *Queer in America: Sex Media, and the Closets of Power* (Random House, 1993); Didi Herman, *Rights of Passage: Struggles for Gay and Lesbian Equality* (University of Toronto Press, 1994); and Larry Gross, *Contested Closets: The Politics and Ethics of Outing* (University of

Minnesota Press, 1993). Louis Crompton, *Homosexuality and Civilization* (Belknap Press, 2006), attempts the ambitious project of relating the history of homosexuality in Europe and parts of Asia from Homer to the eighteenth century. David J. Garrow, *Liberty and Sexuality: The Right to Privacy and the Making of* Roe v. Wade (Macmillan, 1994), provides a full treatment of the earlier *Bowers* case as well as numerous other issues. Sodomy cases are placed in a larger context in Lee Epstein and Joseph F. Kobylka, *The Supreme Court and Legal Change* (University of North Carolina Press, 1992).

ISSUE 9

Does Affirmative Action Advance Racial Equality?

YES: Glenn C. Loury, from *The Anatomy of Racial Inequality* (Harvard University Press, 2002)

NO: Walter E. Williams, from "Affirmative Action Can't Be Mended," in David Boaz, ed., *Toward Liberty: The Idea That Is Changing the World* (Cato Institute, 2002)

ISSUE SUMMARY

YES: Political scientist Glenn Loury argues that the prudent use of "race-sighted" policies is essential to reducing the deleterious effects of race stigmatization, especially the sense of "racial otherness," which still remain in America.

NO: Economist Walter Williams argues that the use of racial preferences sets up a zero-sum game that reverses the gains of the civil rights movement, penalizes innocent people, and ends up harming those they are intended to help.

We didn't land on Plymouth Rock, my brothers and sisters—Plymouth Rock landed on *us!*" Malcolm X's observation is borne out by the facts of American history. Snatched from their native land, transported thousands of miles—in a nightmare of disease and death—and sold into slavery, blacks were reduced to the legal status of farm animals. Even after emancipation, blacks were segregated from whites—in some states by law, and by social practice almost everywhere. American apartheid continued for another century.

In 1954 the Supreme Court declared state-compelled segregation in schools unconstitutional, and it followed up that decision with others that struck down many forms of official segregation. Still, discrimination survived, and in most southern states blacks were either discouraged or prohibited from exercising their right to vote. Not until the 1960s was compulsory segregation finally and effectively challenged. Between 1964 and 1968 Congress passed the most sweeping civil rights legislation since the end of the Civil War.

But is that enough? Equality of condition between blacks and whites seems as elusive as ever. The black unemployment rate is double that of whites, and the percentage of black families living in poverty is nearly four times that of whites. Only a small percentage of blacks ever make it into medical school or law school.

Advocates of affirmative action have focused upon these *de facto* differences to bolster their argument that it is no longer enough just to stop discrimination. The damage done by three centuries of racism now has to be remedied, they argue, and effective remediation requires a policy of "affirmative action." At the heart of affirmative action is the use of "numerical goals." Opponents call them "racial quotas." Whatever the name, what they imply is the setting aside of a certain number of jobs or positions for blacks or other historically oppressed groups. Opponents charge that affirmative action penalizes innocent people simply because they are white, that it often results in unqualified appointments, and that it ends up harming instead of helping blacks.

Affirmative action has had an uneven history in U.S. federal courts. In *Regents of the University of California v. Allan Bakke* (1978), which marked the first time the Supreme Court directly dealt with the merits of affirmative action, a 5–4 majority ruled that a white applicant to a medical school had been wrongly excluded due to the school's affirmative action policy; yet the majority also agreed that "race-conscious" policies may be used in admitting candidates—as long as they do not amount to fixed quotas. Since *Bakke*, other Supreme Court decisions have tipped toward one side or the other, depending on the circumstances of the case and the shifting line-up of Justices. Notable among these were two cases decided by the Court on the same day in 2003, *Gratz v. Bollinger* and *Grutter v. Bollinger*. Both involved affirmative action programs at the University of Michigan, *Gratz* pertaining to undergraduate admissions and *Grutter* to the law school. The court struck down the undergraduate program in *Gratz* on grounds that it was not "narrowly tailored" enough; it awarded every black and other protected minority an extra twenty points out of a one-hundred point scale—which, the court said, amounted to a "quota." But the law school admissions criteria in *Grutter* were more flexible, using race as only one criterion among others, and so the Court refused to strike them down.

The most radical popular challenge to affirmative action was the ballot initiative endorsed by California voters in 1996. Proposition 209 banned any state program based upon racial or gender "preferences." Among the effects of this ban was a sharp decline in the numbers of non-Asian minorities admitted to the elite campuses of the state's university system, especially Berkeley and UCLA. (Asian admissions to the elite campuses either stayed the same or increased, and non-Asian minority admissions to some of the less-prestigious branches increased.)

In the following selections, political scientist Glenn Loury argues that the prudent use of "race-sighted" policies is essential to reducing the deleterious effects of race stigmatization, while economist Walter Williams contends that racial preferences reverse the gains of the civil rights movement and end up harming those they are intended to help.

YES

Glenn C. Loury

The Anatomy of Racial Inequality

Affirmative Action and the Poverty of Proceduralism

The current policy debate over racial preferences in higher education, while not the most significant racial justice question facing the nation today, is nonetheless worth considering here. I incline toward the view that the affirmative action debate receives too much attention in public discourses about racial inequality, obscuring as much as it clarifies. However, by exploring some aspects of this hotly contested public question, I hope to illustrate more incisively the conceptual distinctions that drive my larger argument. . . .

The deep question here are these: When should we explicitly undertake to reduce racial disparities, and what are the means most appropriately employed in pursuit of that end? My argument asserts an ordering of moral concerns, racial justice before race-blindness. I hold that departures from "blindness" undertaken to promote racial equality ought not be barred as a matter of principle. Instead, race-sighted policies should be undertaken, or not, as the result of prudential judgments made on a case-by-case basis. The broad acceptance of this view in U.S. society would have profound consequences. When prestigious institutions use affirmative action to ration access to their ranks, they tacitly and publicly confirm this ordering of moral priorities, in a salient and powerful way. This confirmation is the key civic lesson projected into American national life by these disputed policies. At bottom, what the argument over racial preference, in college admissions and elsewhere, is really about is this struggle for priority among competing public ideals. This is a struggle of crucial importance to the overall discourse on race and social justice in the United States.

Fundamentally, it is because these elite institutions are not "indifferent" to the racial effects of their policies that they have opted not to be "blind" to the racial identities of their applicants. If forced to be race-blind, they can pursue their race-egalitarian goals by other (in all likelihood, less efficient) means. Ought they to do so? Anyone interested in racial justice needs to answer this question. Liberal individualism provides little useful guidance here.

The priority of concerns I am asserting has far-reaching consequences. It implies, for example, that an end to formal discrimination against blacks in

From *The Anatomy of Racial Inequality* by Glenn C. Loury, pp. 130, 138–147. Copyright © 2003 by Harvard University Press. Reprinted by permission.

this post–civil rights era should in no way foreclose a vigorous public discussion about racial justice. More subtly, elevating racial equality above race-blindness as a normative concern inclines us to think critically, and with greater nuance, about the value of race-blindness. It reminds us that the demand for race-blindness—our moral queasiness about using race in public decisions—has arisen for historically specific reasons, namely slavery and enforced racial segregation over several centuries. These reasons involved the caste-like subordination of blacks—a phenomenon whose effects still linger, and one that was certainly not symmetrical as between the races. As such, taking account of race while trying to mitigate the effects of this subordination, though perhaps ill-advised or unworkable in specific cases, cannot plausibly be seen as the moral equivalent of the discrimination that produced the subjugation of blacks in the first place. To see it that way would be to mire oneself in ahistorical, procedural formalism.

Yet this is precisely what some critics of affirmative action have done, putting forward as their fundamental moral principle the procedural requirement that admissions policies be race-blind. "America, A Race-Free Zone," screams the headline from a recent article by Ward Connerly, who led the successful 1996 ballot campaign against affirmative action in California and is now at the helm of a national organization working to promote similar initiatives in other jurisdictions. Mr. Connerly wants to rid the nation of what he calls "those disgusting little boxes"—the ones applicants check to indicate their racial identities. He and his associates see the affirmative action dispute as an argument between people like themselves, who seek simply to eliminate discrimination, and people like the authors of *The Shape of the River*, who want permission to discriminate if doing so helps the right groups.

This way of casting the question is very misleading. *It obscures from view the most vital matter at stake in the contemporary debate on race and social equity—whether public purposes formulated explicitly in racial terms (that is, violating race-indifference) are morally legitimate, or even morally required.* Anti-preference advocates suggest not, arguing from the premise that an individual's race has no moral relevance to the race-indifferent conclusion that it is either wrong or unnecessary to formulate public purposes in racial terms. But this argument is a *non sequitur*. Moral irrelevance does not imply instrumental irrelevance. Nor does the conviction that an individual's race is irrelevant to an assessment of that individual's worth require the conclusion that patterns of unequal racial representation in important public venues are irrelevant to an assessment of the moral health of our society.

The failure to make these distinctions is dangerous, for it leads inexorably to doubts about the validity of discussing social justice issues in the United States in racial terms at all. Or, more precisely, it reduces such a discussion to the narrow ground of assessing whether or not certain policies are race-blind. Whatever the anti-preference crusaders may intend, and however desirable in the abstract may be their colorblind ideal, their campaign is having the effect of devaluing our collective and still unfinished efforts to achieve greater equality between the races. Americans are now engaged in deciding whether the pursuit of racial equality will continue in the century ahead to be a legitimate and vitally important purpose in our public life. Increasingly, doubts are being expressed about this. *Fervency for race-blindness has left some observers simply blind to a basic fact of American public life: We have pressing moral dilemmas in our society that can be fully grasped only when viewed against the backdrop of our unlovely racial history.*

"Figment of the Pigment" or "Enigma of the Stigma"?

Consider the stubborn social reality of race-consciousness in U.S. society. A standard concern about racial preferences in college admissions is that they promote an unhealthy fixation on racial identity among students. By classifying by race, it is said, we distance ourselves further from the goal of achieving a race-blind society. Many proponents of race-blindness as the primary moral ideal come close to equating the use of racial information in administrative practices with the continued awareness of racial identity in the broad society. They come close, that is, to collapsing the distinction between racial *information* and racial *identity.* Yet consciousness of race in the society at large is a matter of subjective states of mind, involving how people understand themselves and how they perceive others. It concerns the extent to which race is taken into account in the intimate, social lives of citizens. The implicit assumption of advocates of race-blindness is that, if we would just stop putting people into these boxes, they would oblige us by not thinking of themselves in these terms. But this assumption is patently false. Anti-preference advocates like to declare that we cannot get beyond race while taking race into account—as if someone has proven a theorem to this effect. But no such demonstration is possible.

The conservative scholars Stephen and Abigail Thernstrom, in their influential study *America in Black and White*, provide an example of this tendency of thought. They blame race-conscious public policies for what they take to be an excess of racial awareness among blacks. Affirmative action, they argue, induces blacks to seek political benefits from racial solidarity. This, in turn, encourages a belief by blacks in what they call "the figment of the pigment"—the conviction that, for African Americans, race is a trait that is inexorably and irrevocably different from European or Asian ethnicity. This gets it exactly backwards, in my view. It is not the use of race as a criterion of public action that causes blacks to nurture a sense of racial otherness. Rather, it is the historical fact and the specific nature of blacks' racial otherness that causes affirmative action—when undertaken to benefit blacks—to be so fiercely contested in contemporary American politics.

To see what I am getting at here, consider the following thought experiment. Few people, upon entering a shop with the sign "Smith and Sons" in the window to encounter a youngish proprietor at the counter, will begin to worry that they are about to be served by an unqualified beneficiary of nepotism. But I venture that a great many people, upon seeing a black as part of their treatment team at a top-flight hospital, may be led to consider the possibility that, because of affirmative action in medical school admissions, they are about to be treated by an unqualified doctor. Yet supposing that some preference had, in fact, been given in both cases and bearing in mind the incentives created by the threat of a malpractice suit, the objective probability that a customer will receive lower-quality service in the former situation is likely to be greater than the chance that a patient will receive lower-quality treatment in the latter. This difference between reality and perception has little to do with political principles, and everything to do with racial stigma.

Moreover, the ongoing experience of racial stigma is what causes many blacks to see racial solidarity as an existential necessity. Perhaps I could put it this way: It's not *the figment of the pigment,* it is *the enigma of the stigma* that causes race to be so salient for blacks today. Now mind you, I have already stipulated (in Axioms 1 and 2) that, at the most fundamental level, the "pigment" is a "figment." I have rejected racial essentialism. But I also have argued that, not withstanding the arbitrariness of racial markers, the classifying of persons on the basis of such markers is an inescapable social-cognitive activity. And I have suggested that such markers could be invested with powerful social meanings—that meaning-hungry agents could build elaborate structures of self-definition around them.

So after centuries of intensive racial classification we are now confronted with raced subjects demanding to be recognized as such. Here are selves endogenous to the historical and cultural flow, who see their social world partly through the lens of their "pigment," and the best some critics can do by way of a response is to dismiss them as deluded, confused believers in a "figment." ("Why are they so obsessed with race? Can't they see it was all a big mistake?") Would-be moralists, even some blacks, are puzzled and disturbed at the specter of African Americans being proud of the accomplishments, and ashamed of the failures, of their co-racialists. And those to whom the "wages of whiteness" flow like manna from heaven, who have a race but never have to think about it, can blithely declare, "It's time to move on."

This is simplistic social ethics and sophomoric social psychology, it seems to me. And it is an especially odd position for a liberal individualist to take. I have always supposed that the core idea of liberalism is to credit the dignity of human beings. Yet when those subjected to racial stigma, having managed to construct a more or less dignified self-concept out of the brute facts of an imposed categorization, confront us with their "true" selves—perhaps as believers in the need to carry forward a tradition of racial struggle inherited from their forebears, or as proponents of a program of racial self-help—they are written off as benighted adherents of a discredited creed. We would never tell the antagonists in a society divided by religion that the way to move forward is for the group in the minority to desist from worshiping their false god. But this, in effect, is what many critics today are saying to black Americans who simply refuse to "get over it."

The basic point needing emphasis here is this: The use of race-based instruments is typically the result, rather than the cause, of the wider awareness of racial identity in society. This is why race-blindness is such a superficial moral ideal: To forgo cognizance of race, out of fear that others will be encouraged to think in racial terms, is a bit like closing the barn door after the horses have gone. One cannot grasp the workings of the social order in which we are embedded in the United States without making use of racial categories, because these socially constructed categories are etched in the consciousness of the individuals with whom we must reckon. Because they use race to articulate their self-understandings, we must be mindful of race as we conduct our public affairs. This is a *cognitive,* not a *normative* point. One can agree with the liberal individualist claim that race is irrelevant to an individual's moral worth, that individuals and not groups are the bearers of rights, and nevertheless affirm that, to deal effectively with these autonomous individuals, account must be taken of the categories of thought in which they understand themselves.

Indeed, it is easy to produce compelling examples in which the failure to take race into account serves to exacerbate racial awareness. Consider the extent to which our public institutions are regarded as legitimate by all the people. When a public executive (like the hypothetical governor considered earlier) recognizes the link between the perceived legitimacy of institutions and their degree of racial representation, and acts on that recognition, he or she is acting so as to *inhibit,* not to *heighten,* the salience of race in public life. When the leaders of elite educational philanthropies attempt to bring a larger number of black youngsters into their ranks, so as to increase the numbers of their graduates from these communities, they are acting in a similar fashion. *To acknowledge that institutional legitimacy can turn on matters of racial representation is to recognize a basic historical fact about the American national community, not to make a moral error.* The U.S. Army has long understood this. It is absurd to hold that this situation derives from the existence of selection rules—in colleges and universities, in the military, or anywhere else—that take account of race.

So much may seem too obvious to warrant stating but, sadly, it is not. In the 5th U.S. Circuit Court of Appeals *Hopwood* opinion, Judge Smith questions the diversity rationale for using racial preferences in higher education admissions. He argues that, because a college or university exists to promote the exchange of ideas, defining diversity in racial terms necessarily entails the pernicious belief that blacks think one way, whites another. But this argument is fallacious for reasons just stated. Suppose one begins with the contrary premise, that there is no "black" or "white" way of thinking. Suppose further that conveying this view to one's students is a high pedagogic goal. The students being keenly aware of their respective racial identities, some racial diversity may be required to achieve the pedagogic goal. Teaching that "not all blacks think alike" will be much easier when there are enough blacks around to show their diversity of thought.

Walter E. Williams  **NO**

Affirmative Action Can't Be Mended

For the last several decades, affirmative action has been the basic component of the civil rights agenda. But affirmative action, in the form of racial
preferences, has worn out its political welcome. In Gallup Polls, between 1987
and 1990, people were asked if they agreed with the statement: "We should
make every effort to improve the position of blacks and other minorities even
if it means giving them preferential treatment." More than 70 percent of the
respondents opposed preferential treatment while only 24 percent supported
it. Among blacks, 66 percent opposed preferential treatment and 32 percent
supported it.

The rejection of racial preferences by the broad public and increasingly
by the Supreme Court has been partially recognized by even supporters of
affirmative action. While they have not forsaken their goals, they have begun
to distance themselves from some of the language of affirmative action. Thus,
many business, government, and university affirmative action offices have
been renamed "equity offices." Racial preferences are increasingly referred to
as "diversity multiculturalism." What is it about affirmative action that gives
rise to its contentiousness?

For the most part, post-World War II America has supported civil rights
for blacks. Indeed, if we stick to the uncorrupted concept of civil rights, we
can safely say that the civil rights struggle for blacks is over and won. Civil
rights properly refer to rights, held simultaneously among individuals, to be
treated equally in the eyes of the law, make contracts, sue and be sued, give
evidence, associate and travel freely, and vote. There was a time when blacks
did not fully enjoy those rights. With the yeoman-like work of civil rights
organizations and decent Americans, both black and white, who fought
lengthy court, legislative, and street battles, civil rights have been successfully
secured for blacks. No small part of that success was due to a morally compelling appeal to America's civil libertarian tradition of private property, rule of
law, and limited government.

Today's corrupted vision of civil rights attacks that civil libertarian tradition. Principles of private property rights, rule of law, freedom of association,
and limited government are greeted with contempt. As such, the agenda of
today's civil rights organizations conceptually differs little from yesteryear's
restrictions that were the targets of the earlier civil rights struggle. Yesteryear
civil rights organizations fought *against* the use of race in hiring, access to

From *Cato Journal*, vol. 17, no. 1, Spring/Summer 1997, pp. 1–9. Copyright © 1997 by Cato Institute.
Reprinted by permission.

public schools, and university admissions. Today, civil rights organizations fight *for* the use of race in hiring, access to public schools, and university admissions. Yesteryear, civil rights organizations fought *against* restricted association in the forms of racially segregated schools, libraries, and private organizations. Today, they fight *for* restricted associations. They use state power, not unlike the racists they fought, to enforce racial associations they deem desirable. They protest that blacks should be a certain percentage of a company's workforce or clientele, a certain percentage of a student body, and even a certain percentage of an advertiser's models.

Civil rights organizations, in their successful struggle against state-sanctioned segregation, have lost sight of what it means to be truly committed to liberty, especially the freedom of association. The true test of that commitment does not come when we allow people to be free to associate in ways we deem appropriate. The true test is when we allow people to form those voluntary associations we deem offensive. It is the same principle we apply to our commitment to free speech. What tests our commitment to free speech is our willingness to permit people the freedom to say things we find offensive.

Zero-Sum Games

The tragedy of America's civil rights movement is that it has substituted today's government-backed racial favoritism in the allocation of resources for yesterday's legal and extralegal racial favoritism. In doing so, civil rights leaders fail to realize that government allocation of resources produces the kind of conflict that does not arise with market allocation of resources. Part of the reason is that any government allocation of resources, including racial preferential treatment, is a zero-sum game.

A zero-sum game is defined as any transaction where one person's gain necessarily results in another person's loss. The simplest example of a zero-sum game is poker. A winner's gain is matched precisely by the losses of one or more persons. In this respect, the only essential difference between affirmative action and poker is that in poker participation is voluntary. Another difference is the loser is readily identifiable, a point to which I will return later.

The University of California, Berkeley's affirmative action program for blacks captures the essence of a zero-sum game. Blacks are admitted with considerably lower average SAT scores (952) than the typical white (1232) and Asian student (1254).* Between UCLA and UC Berkeley, more than 2,000 white and Asian straight A students are turned away in order to provide spaces for black and Hispanic students. The admissions gains by blacks are exactly matched by admissions losses by white and Asian students. Thus, any preferential treatment program results in a zero-sum game almost by definition.

More generally, government allocation of resources is a zero-sum game primarily because government has no resources of its very own. When government gives some citizens food stamps, crop subsidies, or disaster relief payments,

---

*This practice was outlawed in California in 1996 with the passage of proposition 209. [*Editors*]

the recipients of the largesse gain. Losers are identified by asking: where does government acquire the resources to confer the largesse? In order fix government to give to some citizens, it must through intimidation, threats, and coercion take from other citizens. Those who lose the rights to their earnings, to finance government largesse, are the losers.

Government-mandated racial preferential treatment programs produce a similar result. When government creates a special advantage for one ethnic group, it necessarily comes at the expense of other ethnic groups for whom government simultaneously creates a special disadvantage in the form of reduced alternatives. If a college or employer has X amount of positions, and R of them have been set aside for blacks or some other group, that necessarily means there are $(X - R)$ fewer positions for which other ethnic groups might compete. At a time when there were restrictions against blacks, that operated in favor of whites, those restrictions translated into a reduced opportunity set for blacks. It is a zero-sum game independent of the race or ethnicity of the winners and losers.

Our courts have a blind-sided vision of the zero-sum game. They have upheld discriminatory racial preferences in hiring but have resisted discriminatory racial preferences in job layoffs. An example is the U.S. Supreme Court's ruling in *Wygant v. Jackson Board of Education* (1986), where a teacher union's collective-bargaining agreement protected black teachers from job layoffs in order to maintain racial balance. Subsequently, as a result of that agreement, the Jackson County School Board laid off white teachers having greater seniority while black teachers with less seniority were retained.

A lower court upheld the constitutionality of the collective bargaining agreement by finding that racial preferences in layoffs were a permissible means to remedy societal discrimination. White teachers petitioned the U.S. Supreme Court, claiming their constitutional rights under the Equal Protection clause were violated. The Court found in their favor. Justice Lewis F. Powell delivered the opinion saying, "While hiring goals impose a diffuse burden, only closing one of several opportunities, layoffs impose the entire burden of achieving racial equity on particular individuals, often resulting in serious disruption of their lives. The burden is too intrusive."

In *Wygant,* the Supreme Court recognized the illegitimacy of creating a special privilege for one citizen (a black teacher) that comes at the expense and disadvantage of another citizen (a white teacher). However, the Court made a false distinction when it stated that "hiring goals impose a diffuse burden [while] . . . layoffs impose the entire burden . . . on particular individuals."

There is no conceptual distinction in the outcome of the zero-sum game whether it is played on the layoff or the hiring side of the labor market. If a company plans to lay off X amount of workers and decides that R of them will have their jobs protected because of race, that means the group of workers that may be laid off have $(X - R)$ fewer job retention opportunities. The diffuseness to which Justice Powell refers is not diffuseness at all. It is simply that the victims of hiring preferencas are less visible than victims of layoff preferences as in the case of *Wygant.* The petitioners in *Wygant* were identifiable people who could not be covered up as "society." That differs from the cases of hiring and college admissions racial preferences where those who face a reduced opportunity set tend to be unidentifiable to the courts, other people, and even to themselves. Since they are invisible victims, the Supreme Court and others can blithely say racial hiring goals (and admission goals) impose a diffuse burden.

Tentative Victim Identification

In California, voters passed the California Civil Rights Initiative of 1996 (CCRI) that says: "The state shall not discriminate against, or grant preferential treatment to, any individual or group on the basis of race, sex, color, ethnicity, or national origin in the operation of public employment, public education, or public contracting." Therefore, California public universities can no longer have preferential admission policies that include race as a factor in deciding whom to admit. As a result, the UCLA School of Law reported accepting only 21 black applicants for its fall 1997 class—a drop of 80 percent from the previous year, in which 108 black applicants were accepted. At the UC Berkeley Boalt Hall School of Law, only 14 of the 792 students accepted for the fall 1997 class are black, down from 75 the previous year. At the UCLA School of Law, white enrollment increased by 14 percent for the fall 1997 term and Asian enrollment rose by 7 percent. At UC Berkeley, enrollment of white law students increased by 12 percent and Asian law students increased by 18 percent.

For illustrative purposes, let us pretend that CCRI had not been adopted and the UCLA School of Law accepted 108 black students as it had in 1996 and UC Berkeley accepted 75. That being the case, 83 more blacks would be accepted to UCLA Law School for the 1997–98 academic year and 61 more blacks would be accepted to UC Berkeley's Law School. Clearly, the preferential admissions program, at least in terms of being accepted to these law schools, benefits blacks. However, that benefit is not without costs. With preferential admission programs in place, both UCLA and UC Berkeley law schools would have had to turn away 144 white and Asian students, with higher academic credentials, in order to have room for black students.

In the case of UC Berkeley's preferential admissions for blacks, those whites and Asians who have significantly higher SAT scores and grades than the admitted blacks are victims of reverse discrimination. However, in the eyes of the courts, others, and possibly themselves, they are invisible victims. In other words, no one can tell for sure who among those turned away would have gained entry to UC Berkeley were it not for the preferential treatment given to blacks.

The basic problem of zero-sum games (those of an involuntary nature) is that they are politically and socially unstable. In the case of UCLA and UC Berkeley, two of California's most prestigious universities, one would not expect parents to permanently tolerate seeing their children work hard to meet the university's admission standards only to be denied admission because of racial preference programs. Since the University of California is a taxpayer-subsidized system, one suspects that sooner or later parents and others would begin to register complaints and seek termination of racial preferences in admissions. That is precisely much of the political motivation behind Proposition 209.

Affirmative Action and Supply

An important focus of affirmative action is statistical underrepresentation of different racial and ethnic groups on college and university campuses. If the percentages of blacks and Mexican-Americans, for example, are not at a level deemed appropriate by a court, administrative agency, or university administrator, racial preference programs are instituted. The inference made from the underrepresentation argument is that, in the absence of racial discrimination, groups would be represented on college campuses in proportion to their numbers in the relevant population. In making that argument, little attention is paid to the supply issue—that is, to the pool of students available that meet the standards or qualifications of the university in question.

In 1985, fewer than 1,032 blacks scored 600 and above on the verbal portion of the SAT and 1,907 scored 600 and above on the quantitative portion of the examination. There are roughly 58 elite colleges and universities with student body average composite SAT scores of 1200 and above. If blacks scoring 600 or higher on the quantitative portion of the SAT (assuming their performance on the verbal portion of the examination gave them a composite SAT score of 1200 or higher) were recruited to elite colleges and universities, there would be less than 33 black students available per university. At none of those universities would blacks be represented according to their numbers in the population.

There is no evidence that suggests that university admissions offices practice racial discrimination by turning away blacks with SAT scores of 1200 or higher. In reality, there are not enough blacks to be admitted to leading colleges and universities on the same terms as other students, such that their numbers in the campus population bear any resemblance to their numbers in the general population.

Attempts by affirmative action programs to increase the percent of blacks admitted to top schools, regardless of whether blacks match the academic characteristics of the general student body, often produce disastrous results. In order to meet affirmative action guidelines, leading colleges and universities recruit and admit black students whose academic qualifications are well below the norm for other students. For example, of the 317 black students admitted to UC Berkeley in 1985, all were admitted under affirmative action criteria rather than academic qualifications. Those students had an average SAT score of 952 compared to the national average of 900 among all students. However, their SAT scores were well below UC Berkeley's average of nearly 1200. More than 70 percent of the black students failed to graduate from UC Berkeley.

Not far from UC Berkeley is San Jose State University, not one of the top-tier colleges, but nonetheless respectable. More than 70 percent of its black students fail to graduate. The black students who might have been successful at San Jose State University have been recruited to UC Berkeley and elsewhere

where they have been made artificial failures. This pattern is one of the consequences of trying to use racial preferences to make a student body reflect the relative importance of different ethnic groups in the general population. There is a mismatch between black student qualifications and those of other students when the wrong students are recruited to the wrong universities.

There is no question that preferential admissions is unjust to both white and Asian students who may be qualified but are turned away to make room for less-qualified students in the "right" ethnic group. However, viewed from a solely black self-interest point of view, the question should be asked whether such affirmative action programs serve the best interests of blacks. Is there such an abundance of black students who score above the national average on the SAT, such as those admitted to UC Berkeley, that blacks as a group can afford to have those students turned into artificial failures in the name of diversity, multiculturalism, or racial justice? The affirmative action debate needs to go beyond simply an issue of whether blacks are benefited at the expense of whites. Whites and Asians who are turned away to accommodate blacks are still better off than the blacks who were admitted. After all, graduating from the university of one's second choice is preferable to flunking out of the university of one's first choice.

To the extent racial preferences in admission produce an academic mismatch of students, the critics of California's Proposition 209 may be unnecessarily alarmed, assuming their concern is with black students actually graduating from college. If black students, who score 952 on the SAT, are not admitted to UC Berkeley, that does not mean that they cannot gain admittance to one of America's 3,000 other colleges. It means that they will gain admittance to some other college where their academic characteristics will be more similar to those of their peers. There will not be as much of an academic mismatch. To the extent this is true, we may see an *increase* in black graduation rates. Moreover, if black students find themselves more similar to their white peers in terms of college grades and graduation honors, they are less likely to feel academically isolated and harbor feelings of low self-esteem.

Affirmative Action and Justice

Aside from any other question, we might ask what case can be made for the morality or justice of turning away more highly credentialed white and Asian students so as to be able to admit more blacks? Clearly, blacks as a group have suffered past injustices, including discrimination in college and university admissions. However, that fact does not spontaneously yield sensible policy proposals for today. The fact is that a special privilege cannot be created for one person without creating a special disadvantage for another. In the case of preferential admissions at UCLA and UC Berkeley, a special privilege for black students translates into a special disadvantage for white and Asian students. Thus, we must ask what have those individual white and Asian students done to deserve punishment? Were they at all responsible for the injustices, either in the past or present, suffered by blacks? If, as so often is the case, the justification for preferential treatment is to redress past grievances, how just is it to have a policy where a black of today is helped by punishing a white of today for what a white of yesterday did to a black of yesterday? Such an idea becomes even more questionable in light of the fact that so many whites and Asians cannot trace the American part of their ancestry back as much as two or three generations.

Affirmative Action and Racial Resentment

In addition to the injustices that are a result of preferential treatment, such treatment has given rise to racial resentment where it otherwise might not exist. While few people support racial resentment and its manifestations, if one sees some of affirmative action's flagrant attacks on fairness and equality before the law, one can readily understand why resentment is on the rise.

In the summer of 1995, the Federal Aviation Administration (FAA) published a "diversity handbook" that said, "The merit promotion process is but one means of filling vacancies, which need not be utilized if it will not promote your diversity goals." In that spirit, one FAA job announcement said, "Applicants who meet the qualification requirements . . . cannot be considered for this position. . . . Only those applicants who do not meet the Office of Personnel Management requirements . . . will be eligible to compete."

According to a General Accounting Office report that evaluated complaints of discrimination by Asian-Americans, prestigious universities such as UCLA, UC Berkeley, MIT, and the University of Wisconsin have engaged in systematic discrimination in the failure to admit highly qualified Asian students in order to admit relatively unqualified black and Hispanic students.

In Memphis, Tennessee, a white police officer ranked 59th out of 209 applicants for 75 available positions as police sergeant, but he did not get promoted. Black officers, with lower overall test scores than he, were moved ahead of him and promoted to sergeant. Over a two-year period, 43 candidates with lower scores were moved ahead of him and made sergeant.

There is little need to recite the litany of racial preference instances that are clear violations of commonly agreed upon standards of justice and fair play. But the dangers of racial preferences go beyond matters of justice and fair play. They lead to increased group polarization ranging from political backlash to mob violence and civil war as seen in other countries. The difference between the United States and those countries is that racial preferences have not produced the same level of violence. However, they have produced polarization and resentment.

Affirmative action proponents cling to the notion that racial discrimination satisfactorily explains black/white socioeconomic differences. While every vestige of racial discrimination has not been eliminated in our society, current social discrimination cannot begin to explain all that affirmative action proponents purport it explains. Rather than focusing our attention on discrimination, a higher payoff can be realized by focusing on real factors such as fraudulent education, family disintegration, and hostile economic climates in black neighborhoods. Even if affirmative action was not a violation of justice and fair play, was not a zero-sum game, was not racially polarizing, it is a poor cover-up for the real work that needs to be done.

POSTSCRIPT

Does Affirmative Action Advance Racial Equality?

Much of the argument between Loury and Williams turns on the question of "color blindness." To what extent should our laws be color-blind? During the 1950s and early 1960s, civil rights leaders were virtually unanimous on this point. Martin Luther King, Jr., in a speech given at a civil rights march on Washington, said, "I have a dream that my four little children will one day live in a nation where they will not be judged by the color of their skin but by the content of their character." This was the consensus view in 1963, but today it may need to be qualified: In order to *bring about* color blindness, it may be necessary to become temporarily color-conscious. But for how long? And is there a danger that this temporary color consciousness may become a permanent policy?

Linda Chavez, a columnist and president of the Center for Equal Opportunity, an organization opposing affirmative action, develops her argument against it in "Promoting Racial Harmony," an essay published in George E. Curry, ed., *The Affirmative Action Debate* (Perseus, 1996); Mary Francis Berry, former chair of the U.S. Civil Rights Commission, argues for it ("Affirmative Action: Why We Need It, Why It Is Under Attack") in the same volume. An article by Richard H. Sander in the November, 2004 *Stanford Law Review* caused a stir in legal education circles. Sander argued that reduced admission standards for blacks entering law school leads to their receiving "lower grades and less learning," which in turn produce "higher attrition rates, lower pass rates on the bar," and "problems in the job market." The following spring (May 2005) the *Review* published four rebuttals to Sanders, together with Sander's reply. Columnist Jim Sleeper's *Liberal Racism* (Viking, 1997) is critical of affirmative action and other race-based programs, as is a book by *ABC News* reporter Bob Zelnick, *Backfire: A Reporter's Look at Affirmative Action* (Regnery, 1996). Barbara Bergmann supports affirmative action in *In Defense of Affirmative Action* (Basic Books, 1996), while Stephan Thernstrom and Abigail Thernstrom, in their comprehensive survey of racial progress in America entitled *America in Black and White: One Nation, Indivisible* (Simon & Schuster, 1997), argue that it is counterproductive. In *Collision Course: The Strange Convergence of Affirmative Action and Immigration Policy in America* (Oxford University Press, 2002), Hugh David Graham maintains that affirmative action is now at loggerheads with America's expanded immigration policies, in that employers use affirmative action to hire new immigrants at the expense of American blacks. Peter Schmidt, *Color and Money: How Rich White Kids Are Winning the War over College Affirmative Action* (Palgrave Macmillan, 2007) summarizes the history of government policy, court decisions, and politics as they affect affirmative action in America and concludes that they ill-serve poor and working-class students of all colors.

Affirmative action is one of those issues, like abortion, in which the opposing sides seem utterly intransigent. But there may be a large middle sector of opinion that is simply weary of the whole controversy and may be willing to support any expedient solution worked out by pragmatists in the executive and legislative branches of the government.

ISSUE 10

Should Abortion Be Restricted?

YES: Robert P. George, from *The Clash of Orthodoxies: Law, Religion, and Morality in Crisis* (ISI Books, 2001)

NO: Mary Gordon, from "A Moral Choice," *The Atlantic Monthly* (March 1990)

ISSUE SUMMARY

YES: Legal philosopher Robert P. George asserts that, since each of us was a human being from conception, abortion is a form of homicide and should be banned.

NO: Writer Mary Gordon maintains that having an abortion is a moral choice that women are capable of making for themselves, that aborting a fetus is not killing a person, and that antiabortionists fail to understand female sexuality.

Until 1973 the laws governing abortion were set by the states, most of which barred legal abortion except where pregnancy imperiled the life of the pregnant woman. In that year, the U.S. Supreme Court decided the controversial case *Roe v. Wade*. The *Roe* decision acknowledged both a woman's "fundamental right" to terminate a pregnancy before fetal viability and the state's legitimate interest in protecting both the woman's health and the "potential life" of the fetus. It prohibited states from banning abortion to protect the fetus before the third trimester of a pregnancy, and it ruled that even during that final trimester, a woman could obtain an abortion if she could prove that her life or health would be endangered by carrying to term. (In a companion case to *Roe,* decided on the same day, the Court defined *health* broadly enough to include "all factors—physical, emotional, psychological, familial, and the woman's age—relevant to the well-being of the patient.") These holdings, together with the requirement that state regulation of abortion had to survive "strict scrutiny" and demonstrate a "compelling state interest," resulting in later decisions striking down mandatory 24-hour waiting periods, requirements that abortions be performed in hospitals, and so-called informed consent laws.

The Supreme Court did uphold state laws requiring parental notification and consent for minors (though it provided that minors could seek permission from a judge if they feared notifying their parents). And federal courts have affirmed the right of Congress not to pay for abortions. Proabortion groups, proclaiming the "right to choose," have charged that this and similar action at the state level discriminates against poor women because it does not inhibit the ability of women who are able to pay for abortions to obtain them. Efforts to adopt a constitutional amendment or federal law barring abortion have failed, but antiabortion forces have influenced legislation in many states.

Can legislatures and courts establish the existence of a scientific fact? Opponents of abortion believe that it is a fact that life begins at conception and that the law must therefore uphold and enforce this concept. They argue that the human fetus is a live human being, and they note all the familiar signs of life displayed by the fetus: a beating heart, brain waves, thumb sucking, and so on. Those who defend abortion maintain that human life does not begin before the development of specifically human characteristics and possibly not until the birth of a child. As Justice Harry A. Blackmun put it in 1973, "There has always been strong support for the view that life does not begin until live birth."

Antiabortion forces sought a court case that might lead to the overturning of *Roe v. Wade.* Proabortion forces rallied to oppose new state laws limiting or prohibiting abortion. In *Webster v. Reproductive Health Services* (1989), with four new justices, the Supreme Court upheld a Missouri law that banned abortions in public hospitals and abortions that were performed by public employees (except to save a woman's life). The law also required that tests be performed on any fetus more than 20 weeks old to determine its viability. In the later decision of *Planned Parenthood v. Casey* (1992), however, the Court affirmed what it called the "essence" of the constitutional right to abortion while permitting some state restrictions, such as a 24-hour waiting period and parental notification in the case of minors.

In 2000, a five-to-four decision of the Supreme Court in *Stenberg v. Carhart* overturned a Nebraska law that outlawed "partial birth" abortions. The law defined "partial birth abortion" as a procedure in which the doctor "partially delivers vaginally a living child before killing" the child, further defining the process as "intentionally delivering into the vagina a living unborn child, or a substantial portion thereof, for the purpose of performing a procedure that the [abortionist] knows will kill the child." The Court's stated reason for striking down the law was that it lacked a "health" exception. Critics complained that the Court has defined "health" so broadly that it includes not only physical health but also "emotional, psychological," and "familial" health, and that the person the Court has authorized to make these judgments is the attendant physician, that is, the abortionist himself.

In the following selections, Robert P. George contends that, since each of us was a human being from conception, abortion is a form of homicide and should be banned. Mary Gordon asserts that the fetus removed in most abortions may not be considered a person and that women must retain the right to make decisions regarding their sexual lives.

YES

Robert P. George

God's Reasons

In his contributions to the February 1996 issue of *First Things* magazine—contributions in which what he has to say (particularly in his critique of liberalism) is far more often right than wrong—Stanley Fish of Duke University cites the dispute over abortion as an example of a case in which "incompatible first assumptions [or] articles of opposing faiths"—make the resolution of the dispute (other than by sheer political power) impossible. Here is how Fish presented the pro-life and pro-choice positions and the shape of the dispute between their respective defenders:

> A pro-life advocate sees abortion as a sin against God who infuses life at the moment of conception; a pro-choice advocate sees abortion as a decision to be made in accordance with the best scientific opinion as to when the beginning of life, as we know it, occurs. No conversation between them can ever get started because each of them starts from a different place and they could never agree as to what they were conversing *about*. A pro-lifer starts from a belief in the direct agency of a personal God, and this belief, this religious conviction, is not incidental to his position; it is his position, and determines its features in all their detail. The "content of a belief" is a *function* of its source, and the critiques of one will always be the critique of the other.

It is certainly true that the overwhelming majority of pro-life Americans are religious believers and that a great many pro-choice Americans are either unbelievers or less observant or less traditional in their beliefs and practice than their fellow citizens. Indeed, although most Americans believe in God, polling data consistently show that Protestants, Catholics, and Jews who do not regularly attend church or synagogue are less likely than their more observant co-religionists to oppose abortion. And religion is plainly salient politically when it comes to the issue of abortion. The more secularized a community, the more likely that community is to elect pro-choice politicians to legislative and executive offices.

Still, I don't think that Fish's presentation of the pro-life and pro-choice positions, or of the shape of the dispute over abortion, is accurate. True, inasmuch as most pro-life advocates are traditional religious believers who, as such, see gravely unjust or otherwise immoral acts as sins—and understand sins precisely as offenses against God—"a pro-life advocate sees abortion as a sin

From *The Clash of Orthodoxies: Law, Religion, and Morality in Crisis*, 2001, pp. 66–74. Copyright © 2001 by ISI Books. Reprinted by permission.

against God." But most pro-life advocates see abortion as a sin against God *precisely because it is the unjust taking of innocent human life.* That is their reason for opposing abortion; and that is God's reason, as they see it, for opposing abortion and requiring that human communities protect their unborn members against it. And, they believe, as I do, that this reason can be identified and acted on even independently of God's revealing it. Indeed, they typically believe, as I do, that the precise content of what God reveals on the subject ("in thy mother's womb I formed thee") cannot be known without the application of human intelligence, by way of philosophical and scientific inquiry, to the question.

Fish is mistaken, then, in *contrasting* the pro-life advocate with the pro-choice advocate by depicting (only) the latter as viewing abortion as "a decision to be made in accordance with the best scientific opinion as to when the beginning of life . . . occurs." First of all, supporters of the pro-choice position are increasingly willing to sanction the practice of abortion even where they concede that it constitutes the taking of innocent human life. Pro-choice writers from Naomi Wolfe to Judith Jarvis Thomson have advanced theories of abortion as "justifiable homicide." But, more to the point, people on the pro-life side *insist* that the central issue in the debate is the question "as to when the beginning of life occurs." And they insist with equal vigor that this question is not a "religious" or even "metaphysical" one: it is rather, as Fish says, "scientific." In response to this insistence, it is pro-choice advocates who typically want to transform the question into a "metaphysical" or "religious" one. It was Justice Harry Blackmun who claimed in his opinion for the Court legalizing abortion in *Roe v. Wade* (1973) that "at this point in man's knowledge" the scientific evidence was inconclusive and therefore could not determine the outcome of the case. And twenty years later, the influential pro-choice writer Ronald Dworkin went on record claiming that the question of abortion is inherently "religious." It is pro-choice advocates, such as Dworkin, who want to distinguish between when a human being comes into existence "in the biological sense and when a human being comes into existence" in the moral sense. It is they who want to distinguish a class of human beings "with rights" from pre- (or post-) conscious human beings who "don't have rights." And the reason for this, I submit, is that, short of defending abortion as "justifiable homicide," the pro-choice position collapses if the issue is to be settled purely on the basis of scientific inquiry into the question of when a new member of Homo sapiens comes into existence as a self-integrating organism whose unity, distinctiveness, and identity remain intact as it develops without substantial change from the point of its beginning through the various stages of its development and into adulthood.

All this was, I believe, made wonderfully clear at a debate at the 1997 meeting of the American Political Science Association between Jeffrey Reiman of American University, defending the pro-choice position, and John Finnis of Oxford and Notre Dame, defending the pro-life view. That debate was remarkable for the skill, intellectual honesty, and candor of the interlocutors. What is most relevant to our deliberations, however, is the fact that it truly was a debate Reiman and Finnis did not talk past each other. They did not proceed from "incompatible first assumptions." They *did* manage to agree as to what they were talking *about*—and it was not about whether or when life was infused by God. It was precisely about the *rational* (i.e., scientific and philosophical) grounds, if any, available for distinguishing a class of human beings "in the moral sense" (with rights) from a class of human beings "in the (merely) biological sense" (without rights). Finnis did not claim any special revelation to the effect that no such grounds existed. Nor did Reiman claim that Finnis's arguments against his view appealed implicitly (and illicitly) to some such putative revelation. Although Finnis is a Christian and, as such, believes that the new human life that begins at conception is in each and every case created by God in His image and likeness, his argument never invoked, much less did it "start from a belief in the direct agency of a personal God." It proceeded, rather, by way of point-by-point philosophical challenge to Reiman's philosophical arguments. Finnis marshaled the scientific facts of embryogenesis and intrauterine human development and defied Reiman to identify grounds, compatible with those facts, for denying a right to life to human beings in the embryonic and fetal stages of development.

Interestingly, Reiman began his remarks with a statement that would seem to support what Fish said in *First Things*. While allowing that debates over abortion were useful in clarifying people's thinking about the issue, Reiman remarked that they "never actually cause people to change their minds." It is true, I suppose, that people who are deeply committed emotionally to one side or the other are unlikely to have a road-to-Damascus type conversion after listening to a formal philosophical debate. Still, any open-minded person who sincerely wishes to settle his mind on the question of abortion—and there continue to be many such people, I believe—would find debates such as the one between Reiman and Finnis to be extremely helpful toward that end. Anyone willing to consider the *reasons* for and against abortion and its legal prohibition or permission would benefit from reading or hearing the accounts of these reasons proposed by capable and honest thinkers on both sides. Of course, when it comes to an issue like abortion, people can have powerful motives for clinging to a particular position even if they are presented with conclusive reasons for changing their minds. But that doesn't mean that such reasons do not exist.

I believe that the pro-life position is superior to the pro-choice position precisely because the scientific evidence, considered honestly and dispassionately, fully supports it. A human being is conceived when a human sperm containing twenty-three chromosomes fuses with a human egg also containing twenty-three chromosomes (albeit of a different kind) producing a single-cell human zygote containing, in the normal case, forty-six chromosomes that are mixed differently from the forty-six chromosomes as found in the mother or father. Unlike the gametes (that is, the sperm and egg), the zygote is genetically unique and distinct from its parents. Biologically, it is a separate organism. It produces, as the gametes do not, specifically human enzymes and proteins. It possesses, as they do not, the active capacity or potency to develop itself into a human embryo, fetus, infant, child, adolescent, and adult.

Assuming that it is not conceived *in vitro*, the zygote is, of course, in a state of dependence on its mother. But independence should not be confused with distinctness. From the beginning, the newly conceived human being, not its mother, directs its integral organic functioning. It takes in nourishment and converts it to energy. Given a hospitable environment, it will, as Dianne Nutwell Irving says, "develop continuously without any biological interruptions, or gaps, throughout the embryonic, fetal, neo-natal, childhood and adulthood stages—until the death of the organism."

❦

Some claim to find the logical implication of these facts—that is, that life begins at conception—to be "virtually unintelligible." A leading exponent of that point of view in the legal academy is Jed Rubenfeld of Yale Law School, author of an influential article entitled "On the Legal Status of the Proposition that 'Life Begins at Conception.'" Rubenfeld argues that, like the zygote, *every* cell in the human body is "genetically complete"; yet nobody supposes that every human cell is a distinct human being with a right to life. However, Rubenfeld misses the point that there comes into being at conception, not a mere clump of human cells, but a distinct, unified, self-integrating organism, which develops itself, truly himself or herself, in accord with its own genetic "blueprint." The significance of genetic completeness for the status of newly conceived human beings is that no outside genetic material is required to enable the zygote to mature into an embryo, the embryo into a fetus, the fetus into an infant, the infant into a child, the child into an adolescent, the adolescent into an adult. What the zygote needs to function as a distinct self-integrating human organism, a human being, it already possesses.

At no point in embryogenesis, therefore, does the distinct organism that came into being when it was conceived undergo what is technically called "substantial change" (or a change of natures). It is human and will remain human. This is the point of Justice Byron White's remark in his dissenting opinion in *Thornburgh v. American College of Obstetricians & Gynecologists* that "there is no non-arbitrary line separating a fetus from a child." Rubenfeld attacks White's point, which he calls "[t]he argument based on the gradualness of gestation," by pointing out that, "[n]o non-arbitrary line separates the hues of green and red. Shall we conclude that green is red?"

White's point, however, was *not* that fetal development is "gradual," but that it is *continuous* and is the (continuous) development of a single lasting (fully human) being. The human zygote that actively develops itself is, as I have pointed out, a genetically complete organism directing its own integral organic functioning. As it matures, *in utero* and *ex utero,* it does not "become" a human being, for it is a human being *already,* albeit an immature human being, just as a newborn infant is an immature human being who will undergo quite dramatic growth and development over time.

These considerations undermine the familiar argument, recited by Rubenfeld, that "the potential" of an *unfertilized* ovum to develop into a whole human being does not make it into "a person." The fact is, though, that an ovum is not a whole human being. It is, rather, a part of another human being (the woman whose ovum it is) with merely the potential to give rise to, in interaction with a part of yet another human being (a man's sperm cell), a new and whole human being. Unlike the zygote, it lacks both genetic distinctness and completeness, as well as the active capacity to develop itself into an adult member of the human species. It is living human cellular material, but, left to itself, it will never become a human being, however hospitable its environment may be. It will "die" as a human ovum, just as countless skin cells "die" daily as nothing more than skin cells. If successfully fertilized by a human sperm, which, like the ovum (but dramatically unlike the zygote), lacks the active potential to develop into an adult member of the human species, then *substantial* change (that is, a change of *natures*) will occur. There will no longer be merely an egg, which was part of the mother, sharing her genetic composition, and a sperm, which was part of the father, sharing his genetic composition; instead, there will be a genetically complete, distinct, unified, self-integrating human organism, whose nature differs from that of the gametes—not mere human material, but a human being.

These considerations also make clear that it is incorrect to argue (as some pro-choice advocates have argued) that, just as "I" was never a week-old sperm or ovum, "I" was likewise never a week-old embryo. It truly makes no sense to say that "I" was once a sperm (or an unfertilized egg) that matured into an adult. Conception was the occasion of substantial change (that is, change from one complete individual entity to another) that brought into being a distinct self-integrating organism with a specifically human nature. By contrast, it makes every bit as much sense to say that I was once a week-old embryo as to say that I was once a week-old infant or a ten-year-old child. It was the new organism created at conception that, without itself undergoing any change of substance, matured into a week-old embryo, a fetus, an infant, a child, an adolescent, and, finally, an adult.

But Rubenfeld has another argument: "Cloning processes give to non-zygotic cells the potential for development into distinct, self-integrating human beings; thus to recognize the zygote as a human being is to recognize all human cells as human beings, which is absurd."

It is true that a distinct, self-integrating human organism that came into being by a process of cloning would be, like a human organism that comes into being as a monozygotic twin, a human being. That being, no less than human beings conceived by the union of sperm and egg, would possess a human nature and the active potential to mature as a human being. However, even assuming the possibility of cloning human beings from non-zygotic human cells, the non-zygotic cell must be activated by a process that effects substantial change and not mere development or maturation. Left to itself, apart from an activation process capable of effecting a change of substance or natures, the cell will mature and die as a human cell, not as a human being.

⟡

The scientific evidence establishes the fact that each of us was, from conception, a human being. Science, not religion, vindicates this crucial premise of the pro-life claim. From it, there is no avoiding the conclusion that deliberate feticide is a form of homicide. The only real questions remaining are moral and political, not scientific: Although I will not go into the matter here, I do not see how direct abortion can even be considered a matter of "justified homicide." It is important to recognize, however, as traditional moralists always have recognized, that not all procedures that foreseeably result in fetal death are, properly speaking, abortions. Although any procedure whose precise objective is the destruction of fetal life is certainly an abortion, and cannot be justified, some procedures result in fetal death as an unintended, albeit foreseen and accepted, side effect. Where procedures of the latter sort are done for very grave reasons, they may be justifiable. For example, traditional morality recognizes that a surgical operation to remove a life-threateningly cancerous uterus, even in a woman whose pregnancy is not far enough along to enable the child to be removed from her womb and sustained by a life support system, is ordinarily morally permissible. Of course, there are in this area of moral reflection, as in others, "borderline" cases that are difficult to classify and evaluate. Mercifully, modern medical technology has made such cases exceptionally rare in real life. Only in the most extraordinary circumstances today do women and their families and physicians find it necessary to consider a procedure that will result in fetal death as the only way of preserving maternal life. In any event, the political debate about abortion is not, in reality, about cases of this sort; it is about "elective" or "social indication" abortions, viz., the deliberate destruction of unborn human life for nontherapeutic reasons.

A final point: In my own experience, conversion from the pro-choice to the pro-life cause is often (though certainly not always) a partial cause of religious conversion rather than an effect. Frequently, people who are not religious, or who are only weakly so, begin to have doubts about the moral defensibility of deliberate feticide. Although most of their friends are pro-choice, they find that position increasingly difficult to defend or live with. They perceive practical inconsistencies in their, and their friends', attitudes toward the unborn depending on whether the child is "wanted" or not. Perhaps they find themselves arrested by sonographic (or other even more sophisticated) images of the child's life in the womb. So the doubts begin creeping in. For the first time, they are really prepared to listen to the pro-life argument (often despite their negative attitude toward people—or "the kind of people"—who are pro-life); and somehow, it sounds more compelling than it did before. Gradually, as they become firmly pro-life, they find themselves questioning the whole philosophy of life—in a word, secularism—associated with their former view. They begin to understand the reasons that led them out of the pro-choice and into the pro-life camp as God's reasons, too.

A Moral Choice

I am having lunch with six women. What is unusual is that four of them are in their seventies, two of them widowed, the other two living with husbands beside whom they've lived for decades. All of them have had children. Had they been men, they would have published books and hung their paintings on the walls of important galleries. But they are women of a certain generation, and their lives were shaped around their families and personal relations. They are women you go to for help and support. We begin talking about the latest legislative act that makes abortion more difficult for poor women to obtain. An extraordinary thing happens. Each of them talks about the illegal abortions she had during her young womanhood. Not one of them was spared the experience. Any of them could have died on the table of whatever person (not a doctor in any case) she was forced to approach, in secrecy and in terror, to end a pregnancy that she felt would blight her life.

I mention this incident for two reasons: first as a reminder that all kinds of women have always had abortions; second because it is essential that we remember that an abortion is performed on a living woman who has a life in which a terminated pregnancy is only a small part. Morally speaking, the decision to have an abortion doesn't take place in a vacuum. It is connected to other choices that a woman makes in the course of an adult life.

Anti-choice propagandists paint pictures of women who choose to have abortions as types of moral callousness, selfishness, or irresponsibility. The woman choosing to abort is the dressed-for-success yuppie who gets rid of her baby so that she won't miss her Caribbean vacation or her chance for promotion. Or she is the feckless, promiscuous ghetto teenager who couldn't bring herself to just say no to sex. A third, purportedly kinder, gentler picture has recently begun to be drawn. The woman in the abortion clinic is there because she is misinformed about the nature of the world. She is having an abortion because society does not provide for mothers and their children, and she mistakenly thinks that another mouth to feed will be the ruin of her family, not understanding that the temporary truth of family unhappiness doesn't stack up beside the eternal verity that abortion is murder. Or she is the dupe of her husband or boyfriend, who talks her into having an abortion because a child will be a drag on his life-style. None of these pictures created by the anti-choice movement assumes that the decision to have an abortion is made responsibly, in the context of a morally lived life, by a free and responsible moral agent.

The Ontology of the Fetus

How would a woman who habitually makes choices in moral terms come to the decision to have an abortion? The moral discussion of abortion centers on the issue of whether or not abortion is an act of murder. At first glance it would seem that the answer should follow directly upon two questions: Is the fetus human? and Is it alive? It would be absurd to deny that a fetus is alive or that it is human. What would our other options be—to say that it is inanimate or belongs to another species? But we habitually use the terms "human" and "live" to refer to parts of our body—"human hair," for example, or "live red-blood cells"—and we are clear in our understanding that the nature of these objects does not rank equally with an entire personal existence. It then seems important to consider whether the fetus, this alive human thing, is a *person,* to whom the term "murder" could sensibly be applied. How would anyone come to a decision about something so impalpable as personhood? Philosophers have struggled with the issue of personhood, but in language that is so abstract that it is unhelpful to ordinary people making decisions in the course of their lives. It might be more productive to begin thinking about the status of the fetus by examining the language and customs that surround it. This approach will encourage us to focus on the choosing, acting woman, rather than the act of abortion—as if the act were performed by abstract forces without bodies, histories, attachments.

This focus on the acting woman is useful because a pregnant woman has an identifiable, consistent ontology, and a fetus takes on different ontological identities over time. But common sense, experience, and linguistic usage point clearly to the fact that we habitually consider, for example, a seven-week-old fetus to be different from a seven-month-old one. We can tell this by the way we respond to the involuntary loss of one as against the other. We have different language for the experience of the involuntary expulsion of the fetus from the womb depending upon the point of gestation at which the experience occurs. If it occurs early in the pregnancy, we call it a miscarriage; if late, we call it a stillbirth.

We would have an extreme reaction to the reversal of those terms. If a woman referred to a miscarriage at seven weeks as a stillbirth, we would be alarmed. It would shock our sense of propriety; it would make us uneasy; we would find it disturbing, misplaced—as we do when a bag lady sits down in a restaurant and starts shouting, or an octogenarian arrives at our door in a sailor suit. In short, we would suspect that the speaker was mad. Similarly, if a doctor or a nurse referred to the loss of a seven-month-old fetus as a miscarriage, we would be shocked by that person's insensitivity: could she or he not understand that a fetus that age is not what it was months before?

Our ritual and religious practices underscore the fact that we make distinctions among fetuses. If a woman took the bloody matter—indistinguishable from a heavy period—of an early miscarriage and insisted upon putting it in a tiny coffin and marking its grave, we would have serious concerns about her mental health. By the same token, we would feel squeamish about flushing a seven-month-old fetus down the toilet—something we would quite normally do with an early miscarriage. There are no prayers for the matter of a miscarriage, nor do we feel there should be. Even a Catholic priest would not baptize the issue of an early miscarriage.

The difficulties stem, of course, from the odd situation of a fetus's ontology: a complicated, differentiated, and nuanced response is required when we are dealing with an entity that changes over time. Yet we are in the habit of making distinctions like this. At one point we know that a child is no longer a child but an adult. That this question is vexed and problematic is clear from our difficulty in determining who is a juvenile offender and who is an adult criminal and at what age sexual intercourse ceases to be known as statutory rape. So at what point, if any, do we on the pro-choice side say that the developing fetus is a person, with rights equal to its mother's?

The anti-choice people have one advantage over us; their monolithic position gives them unity on this question. For myself, I am made uneasy by third-trimester abortions, which take place when the fetus could live outside the mother's body, but I also know that these are extremely rare and often performed on very young girls who have had difficulty comprehending the realities of pregnancy. It seems to me that the question of late abortions should be decided case by case, and that fixation on this issue is a deflection from what is most important: keeping early abortions, which are in the majority by far, safe and legal. I am also politically realistic enough to suspect that bills restricting late abortions are not good-faith attempts to make distinctions about the nature of fetal life. They are, rather, the cynical embodiments of the hope among anti-choice partisans that technology will be on their side and that medical science's ability to create situations in which younger fetuses are viable outside their mothers' bodies will increase dramatically in the next few years. Ironically, medical science will probably make the issue of abortion a minor one in the near future. The RU-486 pill, which can induce abortion early on, exists, and whether or not it is legally available (it is not on the market here, because of pressure from anti-choice groups), women will begin to obtain it. If abortion can occur through chemical rather than physical means, in the privacy of one's home, most people not directly involved will lose interest in it. As abortion is transformed from a public into a private issue, it will cease to be perceived as political; it will be called personal instead.

An Equivocal Good

But because abortion will always deal with what it is to create and sustain life, it will always be a moral issue. And whether we like it or not, our moral thinking about abortion is rooted in the shifting soil of perception. In an age in which much of our perception is manipulated by media that specialize in the sound bite and the photo op, the anti-choice partisans have a twofold advantage over us on the pro-choice side. The pro-choice moral position is more complex, and the experience we defend is physically repellent to contemplate.

None of us in the pro-choice movement would suggest that abortion is not a regrettable occurrence. Anti-choice proponents can offer pastel photographs of babies in buntings, their eyes peaceful in the camera's gaze. In answer, we can't offer the material of an early abortion, bloody, amorphous in a paper cup, to prove that what has just been removed from the woman's body is not a child, not in the same category of being as the adorable bundle in an adoptive mother's arms. It is not a pleasure to look at the physical evidence of abortion, and most of us don't get the opportunity to do so.

The theologian Daniel Maguire, uncomfortable with the fact that most theological arguments about the nature of abortion are made by men who have never been anywhere near an actual abortion, decided to visit a clinic and observe abortions being performed. He didn't find the experience easy, but he knew that before he could in good conscience make a moral judgment on abortion, he needed to experience through his senses what an aborted fetus is like: he needed to look at and touch the controversial entity. He held in his hand the bloody fetal stuff; the eight-week-old fetus fit in the palm of his hand, and it certainly bore no resemblance to either of his two children when he had held them moments after their birth. He knew at that point what women who have experienced early abortions and miscarriages know: that some event occurred, possibly even a dramatic one, but it was not the death of a child.

Because issues of pregnancy and birth are both physical and metaphorical, we must constantly step back and forth between ways of perceiving the world. When we speak of gestation, we are often talking in terms of potential, about events and objects to which we attach our hopes, fears, dreams, and ideals. A mother can speak to the fetus in her uterus and name it; she and her mate may decorate a nursery according to their vision of the good life; they may choose for an embryo a college, a profession, a dwelling. But those of us who are trying to think morally about pregnancy and birth must remember that these feelings are our own projections onto what is in reality an inappropriate object. However charmed we may be by an expectant father's buying a little football for something inside his wife's belly, we shouldn't make public policy based on such actions, nor should we force others to live their lives conforming to our fantasies.

As a society, we are making decisions that pit the complicated future of a complex adult against the fate of a mass of cells lacking cortical development. The moral pressure should be on distinguishing the true from the false, the real suffering of living persons from our individual and often idiosyncratic dreams and fears. We must make decisions on abortion based on an understanding of how people really do live. We must be able to say that poverty is worse than not being poor, that having dignified and meaningful work is better than working in conditions of degradation, that raising a child one loves and has desired is better than raising a child in resentment and rage, that it is better for a twelve-year-old not to endure the trauma of having a child when she is herself a child.

When we put these ideas against the ideas of "child" or "baby," we seem to be making a horrifying choice of life-style over life. But in fact we are telling the truth of what it means to bear a child, and what the experience of abortion really is. This is extremely difficult, for the object of the discussion is hidden, changing, potential. We make our decisions on the basis of approximate and inadequate language, often on the basis of fantasies and fears. It will always be crucial to try to separate genuine moral concern from phobia, punitiveness, superstition, anxiety, a desperate search for certainty in an uncertain world.

One of the certainties that is removed if we accept the consequences of the pro-choice position is the belief that the birth of a child is an unequivocal good. In real life we act knowing that the birth of a child is not always a good thing: people are sometimes depressed, angry, rejecting, at the birth of a child. But this is a difficult truth to tell; we don't like to say it, and one of the fears preyed on by anti-choice proponents is that if we cannot look at the birth of a child as an unequivocal good, then there is nothing to look toward. The desire for security of the imagination, for typological fixity, particularly in the area of "the good," is an understandable desire. It must seem to some anti-choice people that we on the pro-choice side are not only murdering innocent children but also murdering hope. Those of us who have experienced the birth of a desired child and felt the joy of that moment can be tempted into believing that it was the physical experience of the birth itself that was the joy. But it is crucial to remember that the birth of a child itself is a neutral occurrence emotionally: the charge it takes on is invested in it by the people experiencing or observing it.

The Fear of Sexual Autonomy

These uncertainties can lead to another set of fears, not only about abortion but about its implications. Many anti-choice people fear that to support abortion is to cast one's lot with the cold and technological rather than with the warm and natural, to head down the slippery slope toward a brave new world where handicapped children are left on mountains to starve and the old are put out in the snow. But if we look at the history of abortion, we don't see the embodiment of what the anti-choice proponents fear. On the contrary, excepting the grotesque counterexample of the People's Republic of China (which practices forced abortion), there seems to be a real link between repressive anti-abortion stances and repressive governments. Abortion was banned in Fascist Italy and Nazi Germany; it is illegal in South Africa and in Chile. It is paid for by the governments of Denmark, England, and the Netherlands, which have national health and welfare systems that foster the health and well-being of mothers, children, the old, and the handicapped.

Advocates of outlawing abortion often refer to women seeking abortion as self-indulgent and materialistic. In fact these accusations mask a discomfort with female sexuality, sexual pleasure, and sexual autonomy. It is possible for a woman to have a sexual life unriddled by fear only if she can be confident that she need not pay for a failure of technology or judgment (and who among us has never once been swept away in the heat of a sexual moment?) by taking upon herself the crushing burden of unchosen motherhood.

It is no accident, therefore, that the increased appeal of measures to restrict maternal conduct during pregnancy—and a new focus on the physical autonomy of the pregnant woman—have come into public discourse at precisely the time when women are achieving unprecedented levels of economic and political autonomy. What has surprised me is that some of this new anti-autonomy talk comes to us from the left. An example of this new discourse is an article by Christopher Hitchens that appeared in *The Nation* last April, in which the author asserts his discomfort with abortion. Hitchens's tone is impeccably British: arch, light, we're men of the left.

> Anyone who has ever seen a sonogram or has spent even an hour with a text-book on embryology knows that the emotions are not the deciding factor. In order to terminate a pregnancy, you have to still a heartbeat, switch off a developing brain, and whatever the method, break some bones and rupture some organs. As to whether this involves pain on the "Silent Scream" scale, I have no idea. The "right to life" leadership, again, has cheapened everything it touches. ["Silent Scream" refers to Dr. Bernard Nathanson's widely debated antiabortion film *The Silent Scream*, in which an abortion on a 12-week-old fetus is shown from inside the uterus.—Eds.]

"It is a pity," Hitchens goes on to say, "that . . . the majority of feminists and their allies have stuck to the dead ground of 'Me Decade' possessive individualism, an ideology that has more in common than it admits with the prehistoric right, which it claims to oppose but has in fact encouraged." Hitchens proposes, as an alternative, a program of social reform that would make contraception free and support a national adoption service. In his opinion, it would seem, women have abortions for only two reasons: because they are selfish or because they are poor. If the state will take care of the economic problems and the bureaucratic messiness around adoption, it remains only for the possessive individualists to get their act together and walk with their babies into the communal utopia of the future. Hitchens would allow victims of rape or incest to have free abortions, on the grounds that since they didn't choose to have sex, the women should not be forced to have the babies. This would seem to put the issue of volition in a wrong and telling place. To Hitchens's mind, it would appear, if a woman chooses to have sex, she can't choose whether or not to have a baby. The implications of this are clear. If a woman is consciously and volitionally sexual, she should be prepared to take her medicine. And what medicine must the consciously sexual male take? Does Hitchens really believe, or want us to believe, that every male who has unintentionally impregnated a woman will be involved in the lifelong responsibility for the upbringing of the engendered child? Can he honestly say that he has observed this behavior—or, indeed, would want to see it observed—in the world in which he lives?

Real Choices

It is essential for a moral decision about abortion to be made in an atmosphere of open, critical thinking. We on the pro-choice side must accept that there are indeed anti-choice activists who take their position in good faith. I believe, however, that they are people for whom childbirth is an emotionally overladen topic, people who are susceptible to unclear thinking because of their unrealistic hopes and fears. It is important for us in the pro-choice movement to be open in discussing those areas involving abortion which are nebulous and unclear. But we must not forget that there are some things that we know to be undeniably true. There are some undeniable bad consequences of a woman's being forced to bear a child against her will. First is the trauma of going through a pregnancy and giving birth to a child who is not desired, a trauma more long-lasting than that experienced by some (only some) women who experience an early abortion. The grief of giving up a child at its birth—and at nine months it is a child whom one has felt move inside one's body—is underestimated both by anti-choice partisans and by those for whom access to adoptable children is important. This grief should not be forced on any woman—or, indeed, encouraged by public policy.

We must be realistic about the impact on society of millions of unwanted children in an overpopulated world. Most of the time, human beings have sex not because they want to make babies. Yet throughout history sex has resulted in unwanted pregnancies. And women have always aborted. One thing that is not hidden, mysterious, or debatable is that making abortion illegal will result in the deaths of women, as it has always done. Is our historical memory so short that none of us remember aunts, sisters, friends, or mothers who were killed or rendered sterile by septic abortions? Does no one in the anti-choice movement remember stories or actual experiences of midnight drives to filthy rooms from which aborted women were sent out, bleeding, to their fate? Can anyone genuinely say that it would be a moral good for us as a society to return to those conditions?

Thinking about abortion, then, forces us to take moral positions as adults who understand the complexities of the world and the realities of human suffering, to make decisions based on how people actually live and choose, and not on our fears, prejudices, and anxieties about sex and society, life and death.

POSTSCRIPT

Should Abortion Be Restricted?

The real issue dividing George and Gordon is whether or not the fetus is fully human, in the sense of being entitled to the treatment that civilized society gives to human beings. Their respective arguments use different methods of proof. George reasons from the biological premise that sperm and egg, each with 23 chromosomes, produce a fertilized human organism with the human's full 46 chromosomes; what occurs after that is simply human growth, which no one has the right to interrupt. Gordon reasons from the appearance of the fetus and how people normally react to it. Since even pro-lifers do not conduct funeral services and memorials for the "bloody matter" resulting from an early miscarriage, Gordon reasons, the Supreme Court was right to exclude early fetuses from legal protection. Such reactions, in George's view, proceed from emotion rather than reason.

Barbara Hinkson Craig and David M. O'Brien, *Abortion and American Politics* (Chatham House, 1993) is a historical treatment of the abortion controversy in America. An interesting examination of the political factors that have influenced the abortion debate can be found in William Saletan, *Bearing Right: How Conservatives Won the Abortion War* (University of California Press, 2000). Saletan concludes that, although abortion remains legal, antiabortion forces have largely won by eliminating most public financing of anything related to abortion or family planning. Peter Charles Hoffer, ed., *The Abortion Rights Controversy in America: A Legal Reader* (University of North Carolina Press, 2004) brings together a wide variety of legal briefs, oral arguments, court opinions, newspaper reports, and contemporary essays. In *What* Roe v. Wade *Should Have Said*, edited by Jack M. Balkin (New York University Press, 2005), eleven leading constitutional scholars of varying viewpoints have rewritten the opinions in *Roe v. Wade* with the insights acquired by three decades of experience. Francis J. Beckwith, *Defending Life: A Moral and Legal Case Against Abortion Choice* (Cambridge University Press, 2007) offers a comprehensive philosophical defense of the prolife position; in the process, it takes on *Roe v. Wade* and its leading defenders, offering rebuttals to their arguments.

President Clinton twice vetoed federal bills outlawing "partial-birth" abortions, but President Bush signed a nearly similar bill in 2003. In February of 2006 the Supreme Court agreed to hear arguments on its constitutionality. In the meantime, President Bush had appointed two new members of the Court, Chief Justice John Roberts and Justice Samuel Alito, the latter replacing Justice Sandra Day O'Connor, who had voted to strike down the earlier Nebraska ban on that procedure. Perhaps anticipating a friendlier reception by the Court to legislative bans on abortion, South Dakota in 2006 passed a law outlawing all abortions except where the woman's life is endangered.

ISSUE 11

Should the Government Provide National Health Insurance?

YES: Ezra Klein, from "The Health of Nations," *The American Prospect* (May 2007)

NO: John C. Goodman, from "Health Care in a Free Society: Rebutting the Myths of National Health Insurance," *Policy Analysis* (January 27, 2005)

ISSUE SUMMARY

YES: Political essayist Ezra Klein argues that Canada, France, Great Britain, and Germany provide better health care for everyone at less cost than the United States.

NO: Political analyst John C. Goodman believes that none of the claims made for universal health coverage in other countries withstands objective analysis.

There is widespread agreement that the United States has been a world leader in providing the highest quality medical research and education. Since World War II, more than one-and-a-half times more Nobel prizes in physiology and medicine have been awarded to physicians and medical scientists working in the United States than in the rest of the world. It is widely acknowledged that the training and education of medical personnel in the United States is the best in the world. The latest medical technology is more widely available in the United States than anywhere else. It is no surprise that when wealthy people in other countries have a disease that requires the newest and most sophisticated methods of treatment, they often seek treatment in the United States.

There is also widespread agreement that the United States falls short of providing high-quality medical coverage and treatment for all Americans. It is estimated that more than 45 million Americans have no medical coverage and perhaps as many as another 100 million are not adequately insured for major or long-term illness or disability. This is true despite the fact that more than one trillion dollars a year is currently spent on health care in the United States, a per capita expenditure much higher than in other countries. Public financing of health expenditures is now a little less than half (46 percent in 2005) of that total, compared with nearly three-fourths in other industrial nations.

In 1965 the national government recognized and sought to remedy the problems of coverage and the availability of medical care by establishing Medicare, which provides some government-sponsored medical care for older people, and Medicaid, which provides medical coverage for the poor. Nevertheless, the rising cost of private medical care increasingly puts it beyond the means of millions of Americans. Dental and optical care are scarcely covered by public and many private insurance systems.

Although there is widespread conviction that something should be done to make medical care more available to more Americans, there is no agreement as to what and how. What are the alternatives? We can continue to rely on the free market, complemented by tax credits and medical vouchers for poor people. We can require insurance companies to accept all potential buyers, including those with preexisting medical conditions, with the increased costs that this would entail. We can require that employers provide medical coverage (although more are moving away from such benefits) or contribute to a fund that would pay coverage for those not otherwise insured. More sweeping would be the adoption of national health insurance, in which all individuals would have access to alternative means of health insurance. Most comprehensive would be the federal adoption of a universal single-payer system, under which every American (or every person) would be guaranteed medical coverage.

Those who advocate the most far-reaching reforms argue that, despite the fact that medical costs in the United States are higher per capita than in other industrially advanced countries, too many people receive inadequate or no medical service. They point out that every other industrial nation has some form of national health insurance that covers everyone, and the overall cost is less than in the United States.

Opponents of a national system of health insurance counter that experience demonstrates that a government bureaucracy regulating health care would do a poor job, deny individuals the right to choose their own physicians, and make the system much more costly. In Canada, where there is no private option, there are often long waits for elective medical care. In Great Britain, those who elect private care are promptly treated, whereas those who remain in the National Health Service, must endure long delays.

Ezra Klein believes that other industrial countries and America's Veterans Health Administration have demonstrated that better health care coverage can be provided for everyone at lower cost than in the United States today. John Goodman rebuts twelve "myths" of national health insurance, concluding that free-market reforms are preferable to the inevitable failures of socialized medicine.

YES

Ezra Klein

How Europe, Canada, and Our Own VA Do Health Care Better?

Medicine may be hard, but health insurance is simple. The rest of the world's industrialized nations have already figured it out, and done so without leaving 45 million of their countrymen uninsured and 16 million or so underinsured, and without letting costs spiral into the stratosphere and severely threaten their national economies.

Even better, these successes are not secret, and the mechanisms not unknown. Ask health researchers what should be done, and they will sigh and suggest something akin to what France or Germany does. Ask them what they think can be done, and their desperation to evade the opposition of the insurance industry and the pharmaceutical industry and conservatives and manufacturers and all the rest will leave them stammering out buzzwords and workarounds, regional purchasing alliances and health savings accounts. The subject's famed complexity is a function of the forces protecting the status quo, not the issue itself.

So let us, in these pages, shut out the political world for a moment, cease worrying about what Aetna, Pfizer, and Grover Norquist will say or do, and ask, simply: What should be done? To help answer that question, we will examine the best health-care systems in the world: those of Canada, France, Great Britain, Germany, and the U.S. Veterans Health Administration (VHA), whose inclusion I'll justify shortly.

Putting aside the VHA, America's annual per person health expenditures are about twice what anyone else spends. That actually understates the difference, as our 45 million uninsured citizens have radically restricted access to care, and so the spending on the median insured American is actually quite a bit higher. Canada, France, Great Britain, and Germany all cover their entire populations, and they do so for far less money than we spend. Indeed, Canada, whose system is the most costly of the group, spends only 52 percent per capita what we do.

While comparing outcomes is difficult because of various lifestyle and demographic differences in the populations served, none of the systems mentioned betray any detectable disadvantage in outcomes when compared with the United States, and a strong case can be made that they in fact perform better. Here, however, I largely restrict myself to comparisons of efficiency and equity. With that said, off we go.

Oh, Canada!

As described by the American press, Canada's health-care system takes the form of one long queue. The line begins on the westernmost edge of Vancouver, stretches all the way to Ottawa, and the overflow are encouraged to wait in Port Huron, Michigan, while sneering at the boorish habits of Americans. Nobody gets to sit.

Sadly for those invested in this odd knock against the Canadian system, the wait times are largely hype. A 2003 study found that the median wait time for elective surgeries in Canada was a little more than four weeks, while diagnostic tests took about three (with no wait times to speak of for emergency surgeries). By contrast, Organisation for Economic Co-operation and Development data from 2001 found that 32 percent of American patients waited more than a month for elective surgery, and 5 percent waited more than four months. That, of course, doesn't count the millions of Americans who never seek surgery, or even the basic care necessary for a diagnosis, because they lack health coverage. If you can't see a doctor in the first place, you never have to wait for treatment.

Canada's is a single-payer, rather than a socialized, system. That means the government is the primary purchaser of services, but the providers themselves are private. (In a socialized system, the physicians, nurses, and so forth are employed by the government.) The virtue of both the single-payer and the socialized systems, as compared with a largely private system, is that the government can wield its market share to bargain down prices—which, in all of our model systems, including the VHA, it does.

A particularly high-profile example of how this works is Canadian drug reimportation. The drugs being bought in Canada and smuggled over the border by hordes of lawbreaking American seniors are the very same pharmaceuticals, made in the very same factories, that we buy domestically. The Canadian provinces, however, bargain down the prices (Medicare is barred from doing the same) until we pay 60 percent more than they do.

Single-payer systems are also better at holding down administrative costs. A 2003 study in *The New England Journal of Medicine* found that the United States spends 345 percent more per capita on health administration than our neighbors up north. This is largely because the Canadian system doesn't have to employ insurance salespeople, or billing specialists in every doctor's office, or underwriters. Physicians don't have to negotiate different prices with dozens of insurance plans or fight with insurers for payment. Instead, they simply bill the government and are reimbursed.

The downside of a single-payer system in the Canadian style is that it constructs a system with a high floor and a low ceiling. If you don't like the government's care options, there's no real alternative. In this, Canada is rare. As we'll see with both France and Germany, other countries are able to preserve a largely nationalized system with universal access while allowing private options at the upper levels.

France

It's a common lament among health-policy wonks that the world's best health-care system resides in a country Americans are particularly loath to learn from. Yet France's system is hard to beat. Where Canada's system has a high floor and a low ceiling, France's has a high floor and *no* ceiling. The government provides basic insurance for all citizens, albeit with relatively robust co-pays, and then encourages the population to also purchase supplementary insurance— which 86 percent do, most of them through employers, with the poor being subsidized by the state. This allows for as high a level of care as an individual is willing to pay for, and may help explain why waiting lines are nearly unknown in France.

France's system is further prized for its high level of choice and responsiveness—attributes that led the World Health Organization to rank it the finest in the world (America's system came in at No. 37, between Costa Rica and Slovenia). The French can see any doctor or specialist they want, at any time they want, as many times as they want, no referrals or permissions needed. The French hospital system is similarly open. About 65 percent of the nation's hospital beds are public, but individuals can seek care at any hospital they want, public or private, and receive the same reimbursement rate no mat-ter its status. Given all this, the French utilize more care than Americans do, averaging six physician visits a year to our 2.8, and they spend more time in the hospital as well. Yet they still manage to spend half per capita than we do, largely due to lower prices and a focus on preventive care.

That focus is abetted by the French system's innovative response to one of the trickier problems bedeviling health-policy experts: an economic concept called "moral hazard." Moral hazard describes people's tendency to overuse goods or services that offer more marginal benefit without a proportionate mar-ginal cost. Translated into English, you eat more at a buffet because the refills are free, and you use more health care because insurers generally make you pay up front in premiums, rather than at the point of care. The obvious solution is to shift more of the cost away from premiums and into co-pays or deduct-ibles, thus increasing the sensitivity of consumers to the real cost of each unit of care they purchase.

This has been the preferred solution of the right, which has argued for a move toward high-deductible care, in which individuals bear more financial risk and vulnerability. As the thinking goes, this increased exposure to the economic consequences of purchasing care will create savvier health-care con-sumers, and individuals will use less unnecessary care and demand better prices for what they do use.

Problem is, studies show that individuals are pretty bad at distinguish-ing necessary care from unnecessary care, and so they tend to cut down on mundane-but-important things like hypertension medicine, which leads to far costlier complications. Moreover, many health problems don't lend themselves to bargain shopping. It's a little tricky to try to negotiate prices from an ambulance gurney.

A wiser approach is to seek to separate cost-effective care from unproven treatments, and align the financial incentives to encourage the former and discourage the latter. The French have addressed this by creating what amounts to a tiered system for treatment reimbursement. As Jonathan Cohn explains in his new book, *Sick*:

> In order to prevent cost sharing from penalizing people with serious medical problems—the way Health Savings Accounts threaten to do—the [French] government limits every individual's out-of-pocket expenses. In addition, the government has identified thirty chronic conditions, such as diabetes and hypertension, for which there is usually no cost sharing, in order to make sure people don't skimp on preventive care that might head off future complications.

The French do the same for pharmaceuticals, which are grouped into one of three classes and reimbursed at 35 percent, 65 percent, or 100 percent of cost, depending on whether data show their use to be cost effective. It's a wise straddle of a tricky problem, and one that other nations would do well to emulate.

Great Britain

I include Great Britain not because its health system is very good but because its health system is very cheap. Per capita spending in Great Britain hovers around 40 percent what it is in the United States, and outcomes aren't noticeably worse. The absolute disparity between what we pay and what they get illuminates a troublesome finding in the health-care literature: Much of the health care we receive appears to do very little good, but we don't yet know how to separate the wheat from the chaff. Purchasing less of it, however, doesn't appear to do much damage.

What's interesting is that many of the trade-offs that our health-care system downplays, the English system emphasizes. Where our medical culture encourages near-infinite amounts of care, theirs subtly dissuades lavish health spending, preferring to direct finite funds to other priorities.

This sort of national prioritizing is made easier because Great Britain has a socialized system, wherein the government directly employs most of the providers. Great Britain contains costs in part by paying doctors through capitation, which gives doctors a flat monthly sum for every patient in their practice. Since most patients don't need care in a given month, the payments for the healthy subsidize the needs of the sick. Crucially, though, the fixed pool of monthly money means doctors make more for offering less treatment. With traditional fee-for-service arrangements, like ours, doctors gain by treating more. The British system, by contrast, lowers total costs by lowering the quantity of prescribed care. As University of San Francisco professors Thomas Bodenheimer and Kevin Grumbach write, "British physicians simply do less of nearly everything—perform fewer surgeries, prescribe fewer medications, and order fewer x-rays."

That may sound strange, but it also means that society pays for fewer of those surgeries, fewer of those medications, and fewer of those X-rays—and as far as we can tell, the English aren't suffering for it. Indeed, a 2006 study published in *The Journal of the American Medical Association* found that, on average, English people are much healthier than Americans are; they suffer from lower rates of diabetes, hypertension, heart disease, heart attack, stroke, lung disease, and cancer. According to the study's press release, the differences are vast enough that "those in the top education and income level in the U.S. had similar rates of diabetes and heart disease as those in the bottom education and income level in Great Britain."

Great Britain's example proves that it is possible to make economy a guiding virtue of a health system. We could do that on the supply side, through policies like capitation that would change the incentives for doctors, or on the demand side, by making patients pay more up front—or both, or neither. Americans may not want that system, in the same way that the owner of a Range Rover may not want a Corolla, but we should at least recognize that we have chosen to make health care a costly priority, and were we to decide to prioritize differently, we could.

Germany

The German system offers a possible model for those who want to retain the insurance industry but end its ability to profit by pricing out the sick and shifting financial risk onto individuals. The German system's insurers are 300 or so different "sickness funds" that act both as both payers and purchasers for their members' care. Originally, each fund covered only a particular region, profession, or company, but now each one has open enrollment. All, however, are heavily regulated, not for profit, and neither fully private nor publicly owned. The funds can't charge different prices based on age or health status, and they must continue covering members even when the members lose the job or status that got them into the fund in the first place. The equivalent would be if you could retain membership in your company's health-care plan after leaving the company.

The move toward open enrollment was an admission that interfund competition could have some positive effects. The fear, however, was that the funds would begin competing for the healthiest enrollees and maneuvering to avoid the sickest, creating the sort of adverse selection problems that bedevil American insurance. To avoid such a spiral, the government has instituted exactly the opposite sort of risk profiling that we have in the United States. Rather than identifying the unhealthy to charge them higher rates, as our insurers do, the government compels sickness funds with particularly healthy applicants to pay into a central fund; the government then redistributes those dollars to the funds with less-healthy enrollees. In other words, the government pays higher rates to sickness funds with unhealthy enrollees in order to level the playing field and make the funds compete on grounds of price and efficiency. In this way, the incentive to dump the sick and capture the well is completely erased. The burdens of bad luck and ill health are spread across the populace, rather than remaining confined to unlucky individuals.

The system works well enough that even though Germans are allowed to opt-out of the sickness funds, they largely don't. Those with incomes of more than $60,000 a year are not required to join a sickness fund; about 10 percent of these citizens purchase private insurance and .02 percent choose to eschew coverage entirely. The retention of a private insurance option ensures that Germans have an escape hatch if the sickness funds cease providing responsive and comprehensive coverage; it also clears a channel for experimentation and the rapid introduction of new technologies. And the mix of private-public competition works to spur innovation: By 2005, Germany had spent $21.20 per capita wiring its system with health-information technology; America, meanwhile, had spent a mere 43 cents per capita, and most U.S. hospitals still have no systems to speak of.

What the German system has managed to achieve is competition without cruelty, deploying market forces without unleashing capitalism's natural capriciousness. They have not brought the provision of health care completely under the government's control, but neither have they allowed the private market, with its attendant and natural focus on profits, to have its way with their health system. It's a balance the United States has been unable to strike.

The Veterans Health Administration

The mistreatment and poor conditions at the Walter Reed Army Medical Center were a front-page story recently, and they were rather conclusive in showing the system's inadequacy. But don't be confused: Walter Reed is a military hospital, not a VHA hospital. Poor reporting inaccurately smeared the quietly remarkable reputation of the best medical system in America.

Over the last decade or two, the VHA system has become a worldwide leader in both the adoption and the invention of health-information technology, and it has leveraged its innovations into quantifiable gains in quality of care. As Harvard's Kennedy School noted when awarding the VHA its prestigious Innovations in American Government prize:

> [The] VHA's complete adoption of electronic health records and performance measures have resulted in high-quality, low-cost health care with high patient satisfaction. A recent RAND study found that VHA outperforms all other sectors of American health care across the spectrum of 294 measures of quality in disease prevention and treatment. For six straight years, VHA has led private-sector health care in the independent American Customer Satisfaction Index.

Indeed, the VHA's lead in care quality isn't disputed. A *New England Journal of Medicine* study from 2003 compared the VHA with fee-for-service Medicare on 11 measures of quality. The VHA came out "significantly better" on every single one. *The Annals of Internal Medicine* pitted the VHA against an array of managed-care systems to see which offered the best treatment for diabetics. The VHA triumphed in all seven of the tested metrics. The National Committee for Quality Assurance, meanwhile, ranks health plans on 17 different care metrics, from hypertension treatment to adherence to evidence-based treatments. As Phillip Longman, the author of *Best Care Anywhere*, a book chronicling the VHA's remarkable transformation, explains: "Winning NCQA's seal of approval is the gold standard in the health-care industry. And who do you suppose is the highest ranking health care system? Johns Hopkins? Mayo Clinic? Massachusetts General? Nope. In every single category, the veterans health care system outperforms the highest-rated non-VHA hospitals."

What makes this such an explosive story is that the VHA is a truly socialized medical system. The unquestioned leader in American health care is a government agency that employs 198,000 federal workers from five different unions, and nonetheless maintains short wait times and high consumer satisfaction. Eighty-three percent of VHA hospital patients say they are satisfied with their care, 69 percent report being seen within 20 minutes of scheduled appointments, and 93 percent see a specialist within 30 days.

Critics will say that the VHA is not significantly cheaper than other American health care, but that's misleading. In fact, the VHA is also proving far better than the private sector at controlling costs. As Longman explains, "Veterans enrolled in [the VHA] are, as a group, older, sicker, poorer, and more prone to mental illness, homelessness, and substance abuse than the population as a whole. Half of all VHA enrollees are over age 65. More than a third smoke. One in five veterans has diabetes, compared with one in 14 U.S. residents in general." Yet the VHA's spending per patient in 2004 was $540 less than the national average, and the average American is healthier and younger (the nation includes children; the VHA doesn't).

The VHA's advantages come in part from its development of the health-information software VistA, which was created at taxpayer expense and is now distributed for free to any health systems that wish to use it. It's a remarkably adaptive program that helps in virtually every element of care delivery, greatly aiding efforts to analyze symptoms and patient reactions in order to improve diagnoses and treatments, reduce mistaken interventions, and eliminate all sorts of care redundancies.

The VHA also benefits from the relative freedoms of being a public, socialized system. It's a sad reality that in the American medical system, doctors make money treating the sick, not keeping patients well. Thus, we encourage intervention-based, rather than prevention-based, medicine. It's telling, for instance, that hospital emergency rooms, where we handle traumas, are legally required to treat the poor, but general practitioners, who can manage conditions and catch illnesses early and cheaply, can turn away the destitute.

Moreover, patients are transient, so early investments in their long-term health will offer financial rewards to other providers. And which HMO wants to be known as the one that's really good at treating diabetes? Signing up a bunch of diabetes patients is no way to turn a profit.

As Longman details, the VHA suffers from none of these problems. Its patients are patients for life, so investing early and often in their long-term health is cost-effective; the system was set up to deal with the sick, so the emphasis is on learning how to best manage diseases rather than avoid the diseased; and the doctors are salaried, so they have no incentives to either over- or undertreat patients. Moreover, the VHA is not only empowered to bargain down drug costs; it also uses formularies (lists of covered drugs), and so is actually empowered to walk away from a pharmaceutical company that won't meet its offer.

The results have been clear. "Between 1999 and 2003," writes Longman, "the number of patients enrolled in the VHA system increased by 70 percent, yet funding (not adjusted for inflation) increased by only 41 percent. So the VHA has not only become the health-care industry's best quality performer, it has done so while spending less and less on each patient." Pretty good for socialized medicine.

The goal of health care is to get everyone covered, at the lowest possible cost, with the highest possible quality. But in the United States, there is another element in the equation that mucks up the outcome: Our system seeks to get everyone covered, at the lowest possible cost, with the highest possible quality, while generating the maximum possible profits. Within that context, the trade-offs and outcomes all seem to benefit the last goal, and so we tolerate 45 million uninsured Americans, unbelievably high prices, and a fractured system that lacks the proper incentives to deliver high-quality care.

This makes it hard to move toward a preventive system, as Canada has, because preventive medicine pays less. It makes it hard to address moral-hazard issues wisely, as the French have, because it's unprofitable to insure diabetics, and less profitable still to make their care essentially free. It makes it hard to institute the cost savings that Great Britain has, because with less money flowing into the system, there would be far less profit to be made. It makes it hard to harness market forces while protecting against individual risk, as Germany has, because insurer business models are predicated on shifting risk to employers and individuals, and profits are made when insurers can keep that risk from being shifted back onto them. And it is impossible to implement the practices that have so improved the VHA, because doing so would require a single, coherent health system that stuck with its members through their life cycles rather than an endlessly fractured structure in which insurers pawn off their members as they grow old, ill, or unemployed.

That's not to say that there's no room for profit within the American health-care system, but that it's time the discussion stopped focusing on how to preserve the interests of moneyed stakeholders and started asking how to deliver the best care, for the lowest cost, at the highest quality—to every American. Such a system will probably still have private insurers (at least at the high end of care), pay enough to encourage pharmaceutical innovation, and allow for choice and competition and market pressures. But it will take as its guiding principle the health of the populace, rather than that of the providers. That, in the end, is what all the model health-care systems have in common. Except ours.

John C. Goodman

 **NO**

Health Care in a Free Society: Rebutting the Myths of National Health Insurance

Almost everyone agrees that the U.S. health care system is in dire need of reform. But there are differing opinions on what kind of reform would be best. Some on the political left would like to see us copy one of the government-run "single-payer" systems that exist in Western Europe, Canada, and New Zealand, among other places. Proponents of socialized medicine point to other countries as examples of health care systems that are superior to our own. They insist that government will make health care available on the basis of need rather than ability to pay. The rich and poor will have equal access to care. And more serious medical needs will be given priority over less serious needs.

Unfortunately, those promises have not been borne out by decades of studies and statistics from nations with single-payer health care. Reports from those governments contradict many of the common misperceptions held by supporters of national health insurance in the United States. Wherever national health insurance has been tried, rationing by waiting is pervasive, putting patients at risk and keeping them in pain. Single-payer systems tend to leave rationing choices up to local bureaucracies that, for example, fill hospital beds with chronic patients, while acute patients wait for care. Access to health care in single-payer systems is far from equitable; in fact, it often correlates with income—with rich and well-connected citizens jumping the queue for treatment. Democratic political pressures (i.e., the need for votes) dictate the redistribution of health care dollars from the few to the many. In particular, the elderly, racial minorities, and those in rural areas are discriminated against when it comes to expensive treatments. And patients in countries with national health insurance usually have less access to critical medical procedures, modern medical technology, and lifesaving drugs than patients in the United States.

Far from being accidental byproducts of government-run health care systems that could be solved with the right reforms, these are the natural and inevitable consequences of placing the market for health care under the control

From *Policy Analysis*, no. 532, January 27, 2005, pp. 1–26. Copyright © 2005 by Cato Institute. Reprinted by permission.

of politicians. The best remedy for all countries' health care crises is not increasing government power, but increasing patient power instead.

Despite overwhelming evidence that singlepayer health care systems do not provide high-quality care to all citizens regardless of ability to pay, proponents of socialized medicine tout such systems as models for the United States to emulate. Ironically, over the course of the past decade almost every European country with a national health care system has introduced market-oriented reforms and turned to the private sector to reduce health costs and increase the value, availability, and effectiveness of treatments. In making such changes, more often than not those countries looked to the United States for guidance. About seven million people in Britain now have private health insurance, and since the Labor government assumed power, the number of patients paying out of pocket for medical treatment has increased by 40 percent.

To reduce its waiting lists, the British National Health Service recently announced that it will treat some patients in private hospitals, reversing a long-standing policy of using only public hospitals; the NHS has even contracted with HCA International, America's largest health care provider, to treat 10,000 NHS cancer patients at HCA facilities in Britain. Australia has turned to the private sector to reform its public health care system to such an extent that it is now second only to the United States among industrialized nations in the share of health care spending that is private.

Since 1993, the German government has experimented with American-style managed competition by giving Germans the right to choose among the country's competing sickness funds (insurers). The Netherlands also has American-style managed competition, with an extensive network of private health care providers, and slightly more than one-third of the population is insured privately. Sweden is introducing reforms that will allow private providers to deliver more than 40 percent of all health care services and about 80 percent of primary care in Stockholm. Even Canada has changed, using the United States as a partial safety valve for its overtaxed health care system; provincial governments and patients spend more than $1 billion a year on U.S. medical care.

In each of these countries, growing frustration with government health programs has led to a reexamination of the fundamental principles of health care delivery. Through bitter experience, many of the countries that once touted the benefits of government control have learned that the surest remedy for their countries' health care crises is not increasing government power, but increasing patient power instead. . .

Myth No. 1: In Countries with National Health Insurance Systems, People Have a Right to Health Care

In fact, no country with national health insurance has established a right to health care. Citizens of Canada, for example, have no right to any particular health care service. They have no right to an MRI scan. They have no right to heart surgery.

They do not even have the right to a place in line. The 100th person waiting for heart surgery is not entitled to the 100th surgery. Other people can and do jump the queue. . . .

Countries with national health insurance limit health care spending by limiting supply. They do so primarily by imposing global budgets on hospitals and area health authorities and skimping on high-tech equipment. The result is rationing by waiting. . . .

Myth No. 2: Countries with National Health Insurance Systems Deliver High-Quality Health Care

In countries with national health insurance, governments often attempt to limit demand for medical services by having fewer physicians. Because there are fewer physicians, they must see larger numbers of patients for shorter periods of time. U.S. physicians see an average of 2,222 patients per year, but physicians in Canada and Britain see an average of 3,143 and 3,176, respectively. Family practitioners in Canada bear even higher patient loads—on the average, more than 6,000 per year. Thus it is not surprising that 30 percent of American patients spend more than 20 minutes with their doctor on a visit, compared to 20 percent in Canada and only 5 percent in Britain. . . .

Although critics of the U.S. health care system claim that we have too much technology, all the evidence suggests that our counterparts have too little—as a result of the conscious decisions of government officials. . . .

Many health authorities ration cancer drugs, and some are unwilling to fund certain drugs. Such practice leads to similar patients being treated differently depending on where they reside, resulting in a wide variation in clinical outcomes.

Myth No. 3: Countries with National Health Insurance Make Health Care Available on the Basis of Need Rather Than Ability to Pay

"The United States alone treats health care as a commodity distributed according to the ability to pay, rather than as a social service to be distributed according to medical need," claims Physicians for Single-Payer National Health Insurance. The idea that national health insurance makes health care available on the basis of need rather than ability to pay is an article of faith among supporters of socialized medicine.

But is it really true that national health insurance systems make care available on the basis of need alone? Precisely because of rationing, inefficiencies, and quality problems, patients in countries with national health insurance often spend their own money on health care when they are given an opportunity to do so. In fact, private-sector health care is the fastest-growing part of the health care system in many of these countries. . . .

The almost seven million people in Britain covered by private health insurance account for two-thirds of all patients in private hospitals. . . .

Despite British claims that health care is a right and is not conditioned on the ability to pay, large numbers of patients waited for care while 10,000 private-pay patients—about half of whom were foreigners—received preferential treatment in top NHS hospitals in 2001. . . .

Myth No. 4: Although the United States Spends More per Capita on Health Care Than Countries with National Health Insurance, Americans Do Not Get Better Health Care

This myth is often supported by reference to two facts: (1) that life expectancy is not much different among the developed countries and (2) that the U.S. infant mortality rate is one of the highest among developed countries. If the United States spends more than other countries, why don't we rate higher than the others by these indices of health outcomes? The answer is that neither statistic is a good indicator of the quality of a country's health care system. Other indicators are much more telling.

Average life expectancy tells us almost nothing about the efficacy of health care systems because, throughout the developed world, there is very little correlation between health care spending and life expectancy. While a good health care system may, by intervention, extend the life of a small percentage of a population, it has very little to do with the average life span of the whole population. Instead, the number of years a person will live is primarily a result of genetic and social factors, including lifestyle, environment, and education. . . .

The infant mortality rate in the United States is higher than the average among developed countries, at 7.2 deaths per 1,000 live births in 1998, compared to an average of about 5.0. Why does the United States have a much higher infant mortality rate than countries with comparable living standards? Like the life expectancy rate, the U.S. infant mortality rate is a composite average. Overall, the chances that an infant will die at birth vary widely according to such factors as race, geography, income, and education. . . .

These factors have nothing to do with the quality of (or access to) health care.

A better measure of a country's health care system is mortality rates for those diseases that modern medicine can treat effectively. Take cancer, for example. In New Zealand and the United Kingdom nearly half of all women diagnosed with breast cancer die of the disease. In Germany and France, almost one in three dies of the disease. By contrast, in the United States only one in four women diagnosed with breast cancer dies of the disease. This is among the lowest rates of any industrial country.

Similarly, in the United States the mortality rate for prostate cancer is lower than in most other OECD countries. Slightly fewer than one in five men in the United States diagnosed with prostate cancer dies of the disease. In the United Kingdom, 57 percent die. France and Germany fare slightly better at 49 percent and 44 percent, respectively. At 30 percent and 25 percent, respectively, death rates from prostate cancer in New Zealand and Canada are still well above that of the United States.

The relatively high incidence of prostate and breast cancer in the United States may be the result of lifestyle and diet as well as genetics. This, of course, puts greater demands on the U.S. health care system. Yet patients diagnosed with either of these diseases have a better chance of survival.

Myth No. 5: Countries with National Health Insurance Create Equal Access to Health Care

One of the most surprising features of national health insurance systems is the enormous amount of rhetoric devoted to the notion of equality and the importance of achieving it—especially in relation to the tiny amount of progress that appears to have been made. Aneurin Bevan, father of the NHS, declared that "everyone should be treated alike in the matter of medical care." But more than 30 years into the program (in the 1980s), an official task force (the Black Report) found little evidence that access to health care was any more equal than when the NHS was started. Almost 20 years later, a second task force (the Acheson Report) found evidence that access had become *less equal* in the years between the two studies. Across a range of indices, NHS performance figures have consistently shown widening gaps between the best-performing and worst-performing hospitals and health authorities, as well as vastly different survival rates for different types of illness, depending on where patients live. The problem of unequal access is so well known in Britain that the press refers to the NHS as a "postcode lottery" in which a person's chances for timely, high-quality treatment depend on the neighborhood or "postcode" in which he or she lives. . . .

Myth No. 6: Countries with National Health Insurance Hold Down Costs by Operating More Efficient Health Care Systems

A widely used measure of hospital efficiency is average length of stay (LOS). By this standard, U.S. hospitals are ahead of their international counterparts. The average length of a hospital stay in the United States is 5.4 days compared to 6.2 days in Australia, 9.0 in the Netherlands, and 9.6 in Germany. Whereas patients from other countries routinely convalesce in a hospital, American patients are more likely to recover at home.

It is an inefficient use of resources to fill an acute care hospital bed with a patient waiting for nonemergency care, a geriatric patient waiting to transfer to a nonacute facility, or simply because the hospital has not gotten around to discharging that patient. This is especially true when there are lengthy waiting lists for hospital admission. Generally, the more efficient the hospital, the more quickly it will admit and discharge patients. . . .

Myth No. 7: National Health Insurance Would Benefit the Elderly and Racial Minorities

It is frequently argued that national health insurance would benefit the elderly and reduce racial health disparities that exist in the United States. Empirical studies show this not to be the case. Minorities are often discriminated against under national health insurance. In a market where prices are used to allocate resources, goods and services are rationed by price. Willingness to pay determines which individuals utilize resources. In a nonmarket system, things are very different. Unable to discriminate on the basis of price, suppliers of services must discriminate among potential customers on the basis of other factors. Race and ethnic background are invariably among those factors. . . .

If the experience of other countries is any guide, the elderly have the most to lose under a national health insurance system. In general, when health care is rationed, the young get preferential treatment, while older patients get pushed to the rear of the waiting lines.

In Britain, many elderly do not receive the treatment and specialized care they need. Although more than one-third of all diagnosed cancers occur in patients 75 years of age or older, most cancer-screening programs in the NHS do not include people over age 65. Only one in 50 lung cancer patients over age 75 receives surgery. . . .

Although there is very little relationship between health care spending and life expectancy at birth in OECD countries, at age 80 there is a significant correlation. An 80-year-old U.S. female can expect to live almost a year longer than her British counterpart. An 80-year-old U.S. male can expect to live a half-year longer than his British counterpart.

Myth No. 8: Countries with National Health Insurance Systems Have Been More Successful Than the United States in Controlling Health Care Costs

The United States spends more on health care than any other country in the world, both in dollars per person and as a percentage of GDP. Does that mean that our predominantly private health care system is less able to control spending than developed countries with national health insurance? Not necessarily.

Almost without exception, international comparisons show that wealthier countries spend a larger proportion of their GDP on health care. In his classic 1977 and 1981 studies, health economist Joseph Newhouse found that

90 percent of the variation in health care spending among developed countries is based on income alone. . . .

Myth No. 9: Single-Payer National Health Insurance Would Reduce the Cost of Prescription Drugs for Americans

Advocates of single-payer insurance maintain that it would provide all Americans with full coverage for necessary drugs and control drug costs by establishing a national formulary—a list of drugs available to patients under the national health plan—and negotiating drug prices with manufacturers "based on their costs (excluding marketing and lobbying)." However, access to new, more effective (and more expensive) prescription drugs is often restricted in countries with national health insurance.

Drug development is costly. Only one in five drugs tested ever reaches the public, and the cost of bringing a new drug to market now averages $900 million. A government facing rising health care costs is tempted to negotiate prices just above the costs of production, ignoring the research and development (R&D) costs. Countries with single-payer systems thus reap the benefits of new drugs without sharing the burden of their development. As a result, many pharmaceutical firms based in single-payer countries have gone abroad to recoup their costs, and drug innovation is limited.

One way that single-payer countries control their drug spending is by delaying the introduction of the newest, most expensive drugs or by restricting access to them. In Britain, many drugs that are available to private pay patients are not available to NHS patients. Each local health board decides which drugs will be covered, and expensive drugs are often left off the lists because of budget constraints. For example, Dr. Edward Newlands, the British doctor who codeveloped the brain cancer drug Temodal, cannot prescribe it to his patients. Fewer than one-third of British patients who suffer a heart attack have access to beta-blockers used by 75 percent of patients in the United States, despite the fact that post–heart attack use of the drug reduces the risk of sudden death from a subsequent heart attack by 20 percent.

The American news media often feature stories about buses of elderly Americans who travel to Canada to buy cheaper prescription drugs. Less publicized, however, is the fact that some Canadians travel to the United States to buy drugs not available at any price in Canada. . . .

Despite the fact that countries with single-payer systems go to great lengths to limit both price and availability of prescription drugs, they don't appear to be all that successful at holding down drug spending. OECD data from 1992 showed that when per capita spending on medications was adjusted for purchasing power parity, the United States spent less than France, Germany, and Japan. It spent a few dollars more than Canada and substantially more than Britain. . . .

Myth No. 10: Under National Health Insurance, Funds Are Allocated So That They Have the Greatest Impact on Health

The one characteristic of foreign health care systems that strikes American observers as the most bizarre is the way in which limited resources are allocated. Foreign governments do not merely deny life-saving medical technology to patients under national insurance schemes. They also take money that could be spent saving lives and curing disease and spend it serving people who are not seriously ill. Often, the spending has little if anything to do with health care.

The British National Health Service's emphasis on "caring" rather than "curing" marks a radical difference between British and American health care. The tendency throughout the NHS is to divert funds from expensive care for the small number who are seriously ill toward the large number who seek relatively inexpensive services for minor ills. Take British ambulance service, for example. British "patients" take between 18 million and 19 million ambulance rides each year—about one ride for every three people in Britain. Almost 80 percent of these rides are for such nonemergency purposes as taking an outpatient to a hospital or a senior to a pharmacy and amount to little more than free taxi service. . . .

Myth No. 11: A Single-Payer National Health Care System Would Lower Health Care Costs Because Preventive Health Services Would Be More Widely Available

Proponents of national health insurance often argue that because care is "free" at the point of service, people will be more likely to seek preventive services. Thus, money will be saved when doctors catch conditions in their early stages before they develop into expensive-to-treat diseases. Yet the evidence shows that patients in government-run health care systems do not get more preventive care than Americans do, and even if they did, such care would not save the government money.

Preventive care may even be less available under a single-payer system *because* care is free. A comparison of American and British physicians in the 1990s found that the British saw a physician almost as often as Americans (roughly six times a year). Yet when Americans did see a doctor, the consultation was six times as likely to last more than 20 minutes. A recent survey of 200 British GPs and more than 2,000 consumers found that 87 percent of smokers want more advice and help in quitting from their GPs, but 93 percent of GPs say they lack the time to give such advice. Moreover, British physicians have much less access to diagnostic equipment and must send their patients to hospitals for chest X-rays and simple blood tests. In Canada, fee structures are designed to discourage physicians from providing office-based procedures. Doctors can only bill for the time they spend examining and evaluating patients, not for diagnostic tests. Access to preventive care—which is often costly in itself—is tacitly discouraged by cash-strapped health care bureaucracies.

If anything, the amount of preventive care people get under single-payer systems seems to be based more on socioeconomic status and education than on whether medical care is "free" or not. . . .

Myth No. 12: The Defects of National Health Insurance Schemes in Other Countries Could Be Remedied by a Few Reforms

The characteristics described above are not accidental byproducts of government-run health care systems. They are the natural and inevitable consequences of placing the market for health care under the control of politicians. Health care delivery in countries with national health insurance does not just happen to be as it is. In many respects, it could not be otherwise.

Why are low-income patients so frequently discriminated against under national health insurance? Because such insurance is almost always a middle-class phenomenon. Prior to its introduction, every country had some government-funded program to meet the health care needs of the poor. The middle-class working population not only paid for its own health care but also paid taxes to fund health care for the poor. National health insurance extends the "free ride" to those who pay taxes to support it. Such systems respond to the political demands of the middle-class population, and they serve the interests of this population.

Why do national health insurance schemes skimp on expensive services to the seriously ill while providing so many inexpensive services to those who are only marginally ill? Because the latter services benefit millions of people (read: millions of voters), while acute and intensive care services concentrate large amounts of money on a handful of patients (read: small numbers of voters). Democratic political pressures in this case dictate the redistribution of resources from the few to the many.

Why are sensitive rationing decisions and other issues of hospital management left to hospital bureaucracies? Because the alternative—to have those decisions made by politicians—is politically impossible. As a practical matter, no government can make it a national policy to let 25,000 of its citizens die from lack of the best cancer treatment every year. Nor can any government announce that some people must wait for surgery so that the elderly can use hospitals as nursing homes, or that elderly patients must be moved so that surgery can proceed. These decisions are so emotionally loaded that no elected official could afford to claim responsibility for them. Important decisions on who will receive care and how that care will be delivered are left to the hospital bureaucracy because no other course is politically possible.

Why do the rich and the powerful manage to jump the queues and obtain care that is denied to others? Because they are the people with the power to change the system. If they had to wait in line for their care like ordinary people, the system would not last for a minute. For example, the president of the Canadian Medical Association, Dr. Victor Dirnfeld, suggested in 1998 that the Canadian system is in fact a two-tiered system, and said that he knew of seven prominent political figures in British Columbia and Ontario who received special treatment. "Instead of waiting three months for an MRI," he said, "they will have it done in three or four days." More recently, Canada's Health Minister, Allan Rock, underwent a successful surgery after he was diagnosed with prostate cancer in January 2001. Rock was sharply criticized by other Canadian prostate cancer patients who waited much longer for treatment—often more than a year between diagnosis and surgery.

Conclusion

The realities of national health insurance documented in this paper—waiting lines, rationing, lack of cutting-edge medical technology, restricted access to the latest prescription drugs, inequitable distribution of care—are not accidental. Such problems flow inexorably from the fact that politicians and bureaucrats—not patients and doctors—are given the authority to allocate limited health care resources.

Yet proponents of socialized medicine insist that a single-payer health care system is the only way to solve the structural problems of the U.S. health care system. They conveniently ignore or explain away the flaws of single-payer systems, arguing that we could design a better system and spend more money than Britain and Canada, thus getting better results. But the failures of socialized medicine are evident in every country that implements it, and there is no reason to believe that a single-payer system in the United States would be any different. Advocates of national health insurance would do well to look at how countries like Germany, Sweden, and Australia are choosing free-market reforms to alleviate the problems of their national health systems. Through painful experience, many of the countries that once heralded the benefits of government control have learned that the best remedy for their countries' health care crises is not increasing government power, but increasing patient power instead.

POSTSCRIPT

Should the Government Provide National Health Insurance?

Both Ezra Klein and John Goodman recognize that the cost of health care continues to rise. Intense public debate centers on the role of government in meeting that cost. Almost daily we learn of new treatments and drugs that may extend the life of sick premature infants, terminally ill people, or ordinary healthy individuals, but there is always a limit as to what society is prepared to pay. Rationing health care is an unpopular prospect, but not doing so is unrealistic. Rationing exists today in America, it exists in nations that have created national health insurance, and it will exist in any country that is unwilling to bankrupt itself by paying whatever it must in order to provide unlimited health care to meet the demands of its citizens.

Because there are limits, every proposal implicitly involves the rationing of health care. The difference comes down to whether the government establishes a cut-off point below which it will not pay for expensive or rare or experimental medical procedures, or whether individuals and their insurers determine the price beyond which they will not go to provide additional health care. In *The Challenge of Rationing Health Care* by Henry J. Aaron and William B. Schwartz, with Melissa Cox (Brookings Institution, 2005), the claim is made that sensible rationing can both improve health care and save money.

Julius Richmond and Rashi Fein, in *The Health Care Mess: How We Got Into It and What it Will Take to Get Out* (Harvard, 2005) oppose a decentralized system of health insurance containing a variety of insurance methods, because private companies pass on their costs either to the government or their employees, and the young and healthy opt out of mass coverage plans, preventing their contributions from being spent on the aged and infirm.

The perspectives of patients in five English-speaking countries are examined in *Mirror, Mirror on the Wall: Looking at the Quality of American Health Care Through the Patient's Lens* (The Commonwealth Fund, 2004), a study by Karen Davis, president of The Commonwealth Fund and five physicians and medical scholars. The United States ranked first in the timeliness of hospital admissions and elective surgery, but last in reporting the most medical or medication errors and Americans were more likely not to undertake recommended care because of the cost.

Health care policy and public health experts consider the impact of socioeconomic disadvantage, obesity, tobacco policy, gun violence, medical errors, the nursing shortage, and other factors in a series of essays in *Political Challenges in Modern Health Care,* edited by David Mechanic and others (Rutgers, 2005). Michael F. Cannon and Michael D. Tanner, *What's Holding Back Health*

Care and How to Free It (Cato Institute, 2005), believe that consumer choice and competition deliver the highest quality at the lowest price. Jill Quadagno, *One Nation, Uninsured: Why the U.S. Has No National Health Insurance* (Oxford, 2005), disagrees, concluding that powerful medical and drug interests have blocked health reform.

ISSUE 12

Is America Becoming More Unequal?

YES: Jeff Madrick, from "Inequality and Democracy," in George Packer, ed., *The Fight Is for Democracy* (Perennial, 2003)

NO: Christopher C. DeMuth, from "The New Wealth of Nations," *Commentary* (October 1997)

ISSUE SUMMARY

YES: Editor and author Jeff Madrick maintains that the striking recent increase in income and wealth inequality reflects increasing inequality of opportunity and threatens the civil and political rights of less wealthy Americans.

NO: American Enterprise Institute president Christopher C. DeMuth asserts that Americans have achieved an impressive level of wealth and equality and that a changing economy ensures even more opportunities.

There has always been a wide range in real income in the United States. In the first three decades after the end of World War II, family incomes doubled, income inequality narrowed slightly, and poverty rates declined. Prosperity declined in the mid-1970s, when back-to-back recessions produced falling average incomes, greater inequality, and higher poverty levels. Between the mid-1980s and the late 1990s, sustained economic recovery resulted in a modest average growth in income, but high poverty rates continued.

Defenders of the social system maintain that, over the long run, poverty has declined. Many improvements in social conditions benefit virtually all people and, thus, make us more equal. The increase in longevity (attributable in large measure to advances in medicine, nutrition, and sanitation) affects all social classes. In a significant sense, the U.S. economy is far fairer now than at any time in the past. In the preindustrial era, when land was the primary measure of wealth, those without land had no way to improve their circumstances. In the industrial era, when people of modest means needed physical strength and stamina to engage in difficult and hazardous labor in mines, mills, and factories, those who were too weak, handicapped, or too old stood little chance of gaining or keeping reasonable jobs.

In the postindustrial era, many of the manufactured goods that were once "Made in U.S.A.," ranging from clothing to electronics, are now made by cheaper foreign labor. Despite this loss, America achieved virtually full employment in the 1990s, largely because of the enormous growth of the information and service industries. Intelligence, ambition, and hard work—qualities that cut across social classes—are likely to be the determinants of success.

In the view of the defenders of the American economic system, the sharp increase in the nation's gross domestic product has resulted in greater prosperity for most Americans. Although the number of superrich has grown, so has the number of prosperous small business owners, middle-level executives, engineers, computer programmers, lawyers, doctors, entertainers, sports stars, and others who have gained greatly from the longest sustained economic growth in American history. For example, successful young pioneers in the new technology and the entrepreneurs whose capital supported their ventures have prospered, and so have the technicians and other workers whom they hired. Any change that mandated more nearly equal income would greatly diminish the incentives for invention, discovery, and risk-taking enterprises. As a result, the standard of living would be much lower and rise much more slowly, and individual freedom would be curtailed by the degree of state interference in people's private lives.

None of these objections satisfies those who deplore what they characterize as an increasing disparity in the distribution of income and wealth. In 2002 the U.S. Census Bureau concluded that the relative prosperity of the 1990s left poverty virtually unchanged, with 8 percent of American families earning less than $17,600, the income level below which a family of four is considered to be living in poverty. One in five households was broke, with nothing to tide them over when confronted with unemployment or a health crisis—not to mention being unable to save for college or retirement. Contrary to the popular cliché, a rising tide does not lift all boats; it does not lift the leaky boats or those who have no boat. *Business Week* reported that the pay gap between top executives and production workers in the 362 largest U.S. companies soared from a ratio of 42 to 1 to 475 to 1 in 1989. The financial wealth of the top 1 percent of households now exceeds the combined household financial wealth of the bottom 98 percent.

Advocates of more nearly equal income argue that a reduced pay gap would lead to less social conflict, less crime, more economic security, and better and more universal social services. Also, more nearly egalitarian societies (Scandinavia and Western Europe, for example) offer more nearly equal access to education, medical treatment, and legal defense. What happens to democracy, some ask, when more money means better access to those who write and administer the laws and to the very offices of political power themselves?

In the following selections, Jeff Madrick examines the causes and consequences of income and wealth inequality, while Christopher C. DeMuth outlines a number of forces that have reduced inequality.

YES

Jeff Madrick

Inequality and Democracy

When I was a boy in the 1950s, "equality" was central to the public discourse. The word was seemingly everywhere. Equality before the law was widely thought of as an unquestioned good, charged with positive associations. Equality was an unquestioned component of American greatness, and of its democracy. We experienced it directly. Almost all of us went to public schools, drove on free and quite extraordinary public highways, and got our federally subsidized polio shots. Our GI parents went to college on the government dole and our teachers got federal subsidies for their education after Russia launched Sputnik.

Not all was ideal. Inequality of health care was never adequately or objectively discussed. That millions of African Americans were originally, and for a long time thereafter, excluded from this equality was still the nation's stunning hypocrisy. But in the 1950s, America was at least beginning to address this central tragedy more directly. "Separate but equal," the prevailing idea that justified legalizing school segregation, was disturbing because it clearly meant separate but unequal to a nation committed in its traditions to equality as a principle. Without that tradition, legal racism would have had an even more extended life.

But if equal rights before the law was an accepted principle of democracy, what can we say about economic equality and democracy? In this period, political and economic equality unmistakably went hand in hand. In fact, the association between political and economic equality made the very idea of equality fine and noble for us. In the 1950s, for example, civil rights clearly implied equality of economic opportunity, and equal economic opportunity implied a middle class life. It was a glorious time for the economy. Incomes grew for all levels of workers on average in America in these years, and the income distribution, which narrowed significantly during World War II, remained that way and even improved slightly for the next twenty-five years. The benefits of this most rapid period of growth in American history—at the least, on a par with the more uneven growth of the late 1800s—accrued to a new middle class.

Naïveté still abounded about how widespread prosperity was. In 1962 Michael Harrington's landmark book, *The Other America,* awakened the nation to convincing evidence that a large proportion of the population was still poor. Much of the nation was in truth appalled precisely because equality was a central American value. With the rise of a counterculture and eventual antagonism toward the prosecution of the Vietnam War, America was no longer thought blemish-free, and the fight for equality, or at least rough fairness, became imperative in many spheres. Relatively few disputed that poverty implied unequal opportunity. The majority increasingly favored programs that were outright grants to the poor, which went against the grain of much of American history. In the past, we typically (with a few exceptions) only gave money to those who already worked or sacrificed for their country—Social Security, unemployment insurance, and war veterans. Now, there were new programs, such as expanded welfare and Medicaid, that simply handed out money with relatively few qualifications. The commitment to equality in these years extended to the new feminists, marked by a threshold book, *The Feminine Mystique,* and it was again not confined to matters of civil rights for women. The wide gap in pay for the same work became a key issue in the struggle for equality.

Times are entirely different today, and regrettably so. Political discussion about economic equality has essentially become a taboo. Social Security is no longer the third rail of politics; equality is. Congressmen and senators are cautioned against discussing it because it sounds like class warfare to the public. A wide range of people believe they are put at an unfair disadvantage by affirmative action, welfare, a minimum wage, and other social programs designed to level the playing field. Ironically, the aversion to discussing equality intensified as inequality of incomes and wealth increased over twenty years to levels not seen since the 1920s.

Where does income and wealth inequality start to impinge on civil and political rights, and on America's long commitment to equality of economic opportunity? Where does it both reflect a failure of democracy and contribute to its weakening? There is a good argument to be made that we are already there.

The past few decades are not the first period in which the nation devalued equality. In the second half of the 1800s and in the 1920s, economic inequality rose rapidly. It was accompanied by a contraction of American ideology that limited the nation's focus to the individualistic components and excluded the egalitarian aspects of the national character. Social Darwinism was the simplistic individualistic philosophy of the day in the late 1800s. Survival of the fittest was a natural law with which government should not interfere, its advocates argued. In the 1920s, there was again a momentary return to rough individualism. Rates for the relatively new income tax were slashed, for example.

In the national mythology, if Americans are left to their own devices, to fall and rise according to their talents, the simple values of early America will reassert themselves and all will be well. If there is more inequality as a result, that merely reflects the abilities and tenacity of individuals, not a failure of the nation. The dominant ideological tenet of the time held that, left to their own devices, most Americans would do well.

Was this ever true? There was plenty of poverty in early America, a strong landed plutocracy, and by any modern standards, times were difficult for most. But compared to conditions in the Old World, the romantic notions about opportunity in early America were based in a large measure of fact. Equal rights did mean in the 1700s and early 1800s, to a greater extent than ever before, equal economic opportunity, even if mere self-sufficiency for most. And self-sufficiency meant political independence that was entirely new for most whites. Many people today fail to realize that equality was a reigning principle of the early 1800s and even the colonial years. . . .

Today, . . . America accepts its growing inequality equably. Yet the increase in income and wealth inequality since the late 1970s is striking. In 1979 the top 5 percent of earners made eleven times more than those in the bottom 20 percent. Now they earn nineteen times what the bottom quintile earns. The top 10 percent earn 40 percent of total income in America: They earned only about 30 percent from the 1940s to the late 1970s. We are now back to the income-distribution levels of the 1920s. In terms of wealth—homes and financial assets such as stocks and bonds (less debt)—the top 1 percent have 40 percent of all assets, again about the same as in the 1920s.

Some of the skewing toward the wealthy has been the result of capital gains on stocks during the extraordinary bull market of the late 1990s, which are temporary. If we include only wages, salaries, government payments, rent, dividends, and interest, however, we find that income became highly unequal, anyway. Families in the top 20 percent earned ten and a half times what families in the bottom quintile earned in the 1970s.

Forbes magazine's four hundred richest Americans were almost ten times richer in 2002, on average, even after the market crash, than the four hundred richest were in 1982. The economy grew by only three times over this period, and typical family incomes only doubled. In 1982, when the list was started, it required only $50 million to make it; in 2002, it required $550 million. The average net worth was almost $2.2 billion. Kevin Phillips, author most recently of *Wealth and Democracy,* figures that ten thousand families in 2000, at the height of the market, were worth $65 million. A quarter of a million may have been worth $10 million or more.

The CEOs, of course, ate their cake and had it, too. In the late 1970s, the average CEO made twenty-five times what the average worker made each year. By 1988, that ratio had soared with the stock market and the enormous Reagan tax cuts. The CEO now made nearly one hundred times what the typical worker made. By 2000, with stock options and a bull market like no other, the CEO made five hundred times on average what the typical worker made.

Phillips and others point out that the last twenty years or so are a period much like the late 1800s, the era of the robber barons. But, in fact, there is a disturbing difference. When such fabulous wealth accrued in the past, such as in the late 1880s and the 1920s, the economy grew rapidly. Wages on average rose handsomely, even if unevenly, over these years for most levels of workers. So did the typical family's net worth. Rising revenues enabled the nation to afford a federal government that ultimately minimized worker abuses and established new regulations for trade and markets. A case could at least be made that rising inequality was a price worth paying for rapid economic growth—a case I nevertheless think is wrong. Had incomes been more equal and abuse less prevalent, I believe that the economy would have grown still faster.

Since the rise of inequality in the recent era, however, the economy grew unusually slowly with the exception of the late 1990s. Even including the rise in wages in the late 1990s, average wages in 2002 were still only slightly higher than they were in 1973. Male workers bore the brunt of this decline. As they grew older and more experienced, nearly half of them lost ground over twenty years and another 10 percent made almost no gain—an extraordinary failure unprecedented in American history over so long a period of time. Women, by contrast, experienced fairly rapid wage increases, but they were still earning less than men, often when they were doing the same job. Businesses clearly substituted lower-wage women for men in these years. But this did not explain the decline in the average wage for all workers. And, even with so many spouses working, family income rose at an unusually slow rate. It could no longer be argued that rising inequality was worth the price, as it could have been argued in the late 1800s and the 1920s, because the economy raised the standard of living for all others. In the last quarter century, this was not true.

Arguably, the accrual of individual wealth in this period was as extreme as in the Gilded Age, although comparisons are difficult to draw. By the late 1990s, the great fortunes were surely much larger than they were, comparatively speaking, in the 1920s or 1960s when the American economy as a whole did far better. When we analyze the data further, we find more disheartening news. Average retirement wealth rose over this period, but highly unequally. The economist Edward Wolff calculates that retirement wealth actually fell between 1983 and 1998 for well more than half of America's families. Childhood poverty rates are simply alarming. Every way they can be calculated, whether in absolute terms or by comparison to median or high incomes, a higher proportion of children live in poverty in America than in any other developed nation. Nearly one out of five children grow up in poverty in America, compared to one in twelve in much of Europe. Moreover, the gap between better off and poor children, according to economist Timothy Smeeding, was significantly wider in America than almost everywhere else in comparably advanced nations. Only British children were almost as disadvantaged.

The pressures of inequality are by now quite severe. The strain on working people and on family life, as spouses have gone to work in dramatic numbers, has become significant. VCRs and television sets are cheap, but higher education, health care, public transportation, drugs, housing, and cars have risen faster in price than typical family incomes and in many cases, such as higher education, health care, and drugs, much faster. Life has grown neither calm nor secure for most Americans, by any means. Only in the late 1990s did all levels of workers do well, but they still had not compensated for falling behind in the prior twenty-odd years.

Some argue that Americans did better all along than the data indicated. For a while, some even argued that inequality did not rise, a claim now totally discredited. But the data are clear and, furthermore, anecdotal evidence vastly supports the stagnating economic indicators.

Yet most Americans have accepted slow-growing or stagnating wages and widening inequality with little complaint about the economy, business, or the traditional guarantees of equal opportunity before the law. A key question is: *Why?*

There are a few possible explanations. By the 1970s, America was exhausted by the modern liberal social policies of Presidents Kennedy and Johnson, even though they worked better than was recognized. Welfare programs created dependencies, but poverty was dramatically reduced, racism was seriously circumscribed, good education was made widely available, Medicare was created, and under President Nixon, Social Security was seriously enhanced. Incomes had become much more equal over these early post–World War II decades.

The bigger source of moral exhaustion was probably the Vietnam War, a mostly liberal venture. By the time it ended, the nation seemed tired of government. And the prosecution of the war was not equal. As noted, it fell largely on young working-class men to fight. The educated easily escaped the draft.

But set against this moral political exhaustion, I think it was mostly slow economic growth, high inflation and interest rates, and lost jobs that turned the nation against its long-standing progressive attitudes. The nation had to apportion a pie that was growing much more slowly—that was simply much smaller than Americans had come to expect it would be, based on their history and traditions. Government was now easily portrayed as the cause of, not the solution to, economically tightened conditions. To many, equality now meant taking from those who worked to give to those who didn't, taking from the working class who were not disposed to higher education to give to those advantaged young people who were, helping people of color at the expense of people who were white. In the past, equality meant that most people's opportunities were expanded. But working people were now suffering, and they needed a scapegoat or two. Business escaped blame partly because government had dominated the previous period. We were tired of government. It did indeed wage an unpopular war and develop expensive new social programs. Moreover, businesspeople were not making fortunes in the 1970s. Profits in general were poor. The stock market stagnated at 1960s levels. There was less obvious cause to direct anger at them.

Ultimately, financially straitened workers did not want to pay more taxes; to the contrary, they wanted to pay less. Beginning in the difficult 1970s, victimized by both high inflation and deep recession, and before Ronald Reagan's large tax cut of 1981, the electorate rewarded politicians who promised tax cuts. . . .

A fundamental question for Americans is whether the inequality in outcomes since the 1980s reflected an inequality in opportunity in these decades. In other words, did it amount to a direct challenge to one of our basic ideals? I think it did. What stands out most is childhood poverty. When one out of five children is so disadvantaged, and another one in five is nearly poor, one simply cannot argue that opportunity is equal in America. The parents of these children are typically at work, they do not get decent childcare, and early education is out of the question. Their standard primary schools are almost always below average. Measures of education quality across America are not as bad as they are often reported to be. But there are huge pockets of inadequate education in poorer and working-class neighborhoods. Some other economies also produce large numbers of poor children. In France, for example, as high a proportion of children are poor as in America. But their significant government social programs raise the lower levels to acceptable standards. Because schools are financed locally in America, poverty and poor education have become a vicious circle. Money matters. As the Nobel Prize–winning economist George Akerlof points out, the evidence is considerable that money spent in these schools has productive results.

Further, as economies become more complex and change in other ways, burdens on people change as well, and they fall on them unequally. Not only the poor, but those in the middle now bear these burdens, and slow-growing incomes for the wide middle of America make opportunity unequal. In recent times, the so-called New Economy of the 1990s placed even more emphasis on education. This economy has created greater need for public childcare because spouses have to go to work. Its demand for worker flexibility means that as workers lose jobs, they also lose pension and health-care benefits. These are all "dis-equalizing" circumstances to which the government should respond but has not.

To the contrary, it has gone energetically in the other direction, creating inequalities rather than ameliorating them. Consider the litany. The rise of defined-contribution pension plans, which supplanted old-style defined-benefits plans, helped corporations reduce their contributions but, it turns out, only the better-off were better off with them. The middle- and lower-income workers did worse. If Social Security is privatized, elderly incomes will become significantly more unequal. The march toward deregulation and privatization—partly, but only partly, necessary—often favored the well-off at the expense of middle- and lower-income workers. The nation in these years steadfastly refused to raise the minimum wage until relatively recently. America did not seriously enforce worker-safety regulations. It did not support laws to enable labor unions to organize. It found no way to provide health insurance for the nearly 20 percent of people who were not covered. It did not strengthen accounting regulations, even when the Securities and Exchange Commission tried to, beaten back by angry legislators who were lectured to by their investment-banking and accounting-industry campaign supporters. CEOs took tens of millions of dollars, workers lost their savings. The government did not adopt new protective regulations, even after the debacle of Long-Term Capital Management. It wholeheartedly supported regulation-free capital flows around the world, even when they were a primary cause of the Asian financial crisis. It reduced the coverage of unemployment insurance significantly. It reduced tax rates dramatically for upper-income workers. In general, as noted, it allowed a financial movement on Wall Street to emphasize job cuts as the best path to profitability; taking on debt was not discouraged. Many economists exalted the restraint on wages but said nothing about overinvestment in high technology and telecommunications and absurdly romantic securities speculation. The Federal Reserve under Alan Greenspan was far more concerned about wage increases than about a stock-market bubble.

Let me be clear that some of these changes were necessary. Profits were probably too low in the 1960s and '70s, wages too high. Some federal programs were poorly thought out. Private business had become more sophisticated and government direction and sometimes even oversight were often no longer necessary. Some social programs will inevitably get more expensive, especially as the population ages, and therefore the nation has to deal with how to pay for them. International competition had toughened, and required leaner and more flexible companies. In general, tax revenues no longer grow as rapidly because the economy grows more slowly, so ultimately we can afford less. But the movement was carried too far, and government's role as a protector of equal opportunity and equal rights was often abandoned. The results showed up in falling wages, slow-growing family incomes, and rising inequality. It is not just the bottom 10 percent who have fared poorly. The lower 50 percent have, and in some ways, even the lower three-quarters are more strained than at any time in the post–World War II era. International competition from low-wage nations, a more sophisticated workplace, and slow growth all contributed to inequality. But government did not perform its traditional role of a counterforce to balance these other factors, and often exacerbated inequality in the name of self-reliance and limiting regulation in general.

What, then, is the case for equality in a democracy? Equal political rights may remain the most important issue. They are an end in themselves. But in practice, fairly equal economic outcomes have helped guarantee equal political rights. Nowhere has this been more true than in the American experience. The original source of political equality was not a simple social contract arrived at through agreement or revolution. Of course, John Locke's ideas mattered, and the European Enlightenment emboldened the Western world and valued the individual and his or her rights. But in America, the primary source of political equality was access to land. It was not an accident that Jefferson promised land to the thousandth generation when he purchased the Louisiana Territory. Land was not an issue of wealth to him but an issue of spreading political power.

Our current acceptance of inequality is dangerous for at least four reasons. First, it is unjust socially and may eventually generate spreading, if unarticulated, discontent, which will seek further scapegoats. Second, contrary to much conventional wisdom, inequality undermines economic growth because it limits the strength of demand, the optimism of a nation, and the capacity for people to educate themselves. Even now, only 60 percent of families own a PC; in contrast, by 1955, 90 percent of families had a television set, which was relatively much more expensive then. Wages were not sufficient to support booming demand in the late 1990s; consumers borrowed at record levels. Contrary to conventional wisdom of the moment, high levels of inequality imply generally low wages, and low-wage economies are generally inimical to growth. They do not create an internal market for goods and services on a sufficient scale to make production efficient. In *Why Economies Grow,* I argue that, historically, growing internal markets are a major source of economic growth, and perhaps the most important source. In fact, almost all economies that have taken off historically, such as those of the Netherlands in the 1600s or Britain in the 1700s, have been more egalitarian than those of their competitors. These domestic markets are themselves often the most important stimulants to capital investment and technological innovation. As British economic historian J.H. Habakkuk argued long ago, low wages do not provide incentives for business to invest in modern equipment or to train and provide private services for their workers. America's South, as economist Gavin Wright has shown time and again, beginning with his book *Old South, New South,* is still dominated by low-wage industries. Slow growth, in turn, invariably hurts lower-level workers more than the rest.

Third, unequal incomes can in themselves mean unequal opportunity. Poor families and even median-income families often cannot afford to live in neighborhoods that will provide their children with a decent education; they cannot get quality childcare when they have to work, and they cannot get adequate health care for the family. Costs of being middle class today—the costs of health care, education, transportation, and housing—have far outrun the incomes of the typical family, not merely those of the poor. Serious inequality of incomes and wealth already reflect unequal opportunity. Today, more than ever before, opportunity means a competitive education, and typically a decent higher education. But America probably has the most unequal education system in the developed world, supported by local tax revenues that reflect the incomes of the community. Vouchers are typical of the current response: They will save a few and discourage many, and on balance, will lead to more inequality. Those in the bottom half of America also cannot afford the best health care. They have jobs that do not provide health benefits. Poor health undermines equality of opportunity as well.

Fourth, inequality can lead to a skewing of political power toward elite interests. The congressional turn toward deregulation and lower taxes, many observers argue, is a function of the growing importance of money in politics. New well-financed think tanks supported by conservatives spread an ideology about the unimportance of equality and the dangers of government. Reforms, even of accounting principles, are beaten back by aggressive lobbyists with millions of dollars of campaign funds. Rightist foundations spend tens of millions of dollars to fight ideological battles. Most distressing, the growing numbers of those who do not vote in America are dominated by the least well off.

In my view, inequality means exclusion, and the nation needs something like a new social contract that emphasizes both inclusiveness and change. New programs should include a higher minimum wage, a still more expansive earned income tax credit, and serious savings subsidies for college. Efforts to universalize health care are critical, yet hardly addressed. Serious public investment must be directed toward equalizing education locally. Ideally, open discussion of how a high-wage economy can promote rather than impede growth will begin to change social norms about the expendability of workers. Campaign-finance reform should be enacted to minimize the growing political power of rich people and corporations.

The nation must also recognize that times change. Americans used to look forward, not backward. We built canals, railroads, primary and then high schools, public universities, vast public health systems to sanitize cities; we regulated business and put down a vast highway system. In retrospect, we think all this was inevitable, that the decisions made were obvious. But they were all reactions to change by an open and optimistic society. Now we scorn government responses to change. We look back, unwilling to risk. If we confronted change, we would emphasize new ideas. This means family-friendly policies like flexible hours and high quality day care. In a changing economy, with an increasingly expendable labor force, corporate benefits should be made portable.

A new New Deal? Of sorts, yes. Can we afford it? There are limits. But such programs can enhance economic growth, while reinforcing our long-held beliefs in equality. After a period of soaring income for the wealthy, higher progressive rates on very high incomes are entirely in order to pay for part of what we need.

The preponderance of economic research suggests high marginal rates do not impede economic growth by undermining incentives for the wealthy.

But none of this is politically possible without a reinvigoration of fundamental principles. Our democracy is no longer working as it should. The influence of moneyed corporations has never been higher. But the most vigorous democracies are essentially about equality—in the case of America, about equality of civil rights and equality of economic opportunity in a complex and changing environment. Democracy is not about making economic outcomes equal. Americans want everyone and anyone to be able to make a fortune. But when outcomes are as skewed as they have been, it is clear that something in the process is badly wrong. Sustaining democracy may now depend on maintaining a vibrant spirit of national equality. If equality—let's call it inclusion, because that is what it is—were again the passion of the people, as it was two centuries ago, we might accomplish what is necessary. I doubt there is any true democracy without such a passion.

Christopher C. DeMuth    **NO**

The New Wealth of Nations

The Nations of North America, Western Europe, Australia, and Japan are wealthier today than they have ever been, wealthier than any others on the planet, wealthier by far than any societies in human history. Yet their governments appear to be impoverished—saddled with large accumulated debts and facing annual deficits that will grow explosively over the coming decades. As a result, government spending programs, especially the big social-insurance programs like Social Security and Medicare in the United States, are facing drastic cuts in order to avert looming insolvency (and, in France and some other European nations, in order to meet the Maastricht treaty's criteria of fiscal rectitude). American politics has been dominated for several years now by contentious negotiations over deficit reduction between the Clinton administration and the Republican Congress. This past June, first at the European Community summit in Amsterdam and then at the Group of Eight meeting in Denver, most of the talk was of hardship and constraint and the need for governmental austerity ("Economic Unease Looms Over Talks at Denver Summit," read the *New York Times* headline).

These bloodless problems of governmental accounting are said, moreover, to reflect real social ills: growing economic inequality in the United States; high unemployment in Europe; an aging, burdensome, and medically needy population everywhere; and the globalization of commerce, which is destroying jobs and national autonomy and forcing bitter measures to keep up with the bruising demands of international competitiveness.

How can it be that societies so surpassingly wealthy have governments whose core domestic-welfare programs are on the verge of bankruptcy? The answer is as paradoxical as the question. We have become not only the richest but also the freest and most egalitarian societies that have ever existed, and it is our very wealth, freedom, and equality that are causing the welfare state to unravel.

•❦•

That we have become very rich is clear enough in the aggregate. That we have become very equal in the enjoyment of our riches is an idea strongly resisted by many. Certainly there has been a profusion of reports in the media and political speeches about increasing income inequality: the rich, it is said, are getting richer, the poor are getting poorer, and the middle and working classes are under the relentless pressure of disappearing jobs in manufacturing and middle management.

Although these claims have been greatly exaggerated, and some have been disproved by events, it is true that, by some measures, there has been a recent increase in income inequality in the United States. But it is a very small tick in the massive and unprecedented leveling of material circumstances that has been proceeding now for almost three centuries and in this century has accelerated dramatically. In fact, the much-noticed increase in measured-income inequality is in part a result of the increase in real social equality. Here are a few pieces of this important but neglected story.

• First, progress in agriculture, construction, manufacturing, and other key sectors of economic production has made the material necessities of life—food, shelter, and clothing—available to essentially everyone. To be sure, many people, including the seriously handicapped and the mentally incompetent, remain dependent on the public purse for their necessities. And many people continue to live in terrible squalor. But the problem of poverty, defined as material scarcity, has been solved. If poverty today remains a serious problem, it is a problem of individual behavior, social organization, and public policy. This was not so 50 years ago, or ever before.

• Second, progress in public health, in nutrition, and in the biological sciences and medical arts has produced dramatic improvements in longevity, health, and physical well-being. Many of these improvements—resulting, for example, from better public sanitation and water supplies, the conquest of dread diseases, and the abundance of nutritious food—have affected entire populations, producing an equalization of real personal welfare more powerful than any government redistribution of income.

The Nobel prize-winning economist Robert Fogel has focused on our improved mastery of the biological environment—leading over the past 300 years to a doubling of the average human life span and to large gains in physical stature, strength, and energy—as the key to what he calls "the egalitarian revolution of the 20th century." He considers this so profound an advance as to constitute a distinct new level of human evolution. Gains in stature, health, and longevity are continuing today and even accelerating. Their outward effects may be observed, in evolutionary fast-forward, in the booming nations of Asia (where, for example, the physical difference between older and younger South Koreans is strikingly evident on the streets of Seoul).

• Third, the critical *source* of social wealth has shifted over the last few hundred years from land (at the end of the 18th century) to physical capital (at the end of the 19th) to, today, human capital—education and cognitive ability. This development is not an unmixed gain from the standpoint of economic equality. The ability to acquire and deploy human capital is a function of intelligence, and intelligence is not only unequally distributed but also, to a significant degree, heritable. As Charles Murray and the late Richard J. Herrnstein argue in *The Bell Curve,* an economy that rewards sheer brain-power replaces one old source of inequality, socioeconomic advantage with a new one, cognitive advantage.

But an economy that rewards human capital also tears down far more artificial barriers than it erects. For most people who inhabit the vast middle range of the bell curve, intelligence is much more equally distributed than land or physical capital ever was. Most people, that is, possess ample intelligence to pursue all but a handful of specialized callings. If in the past many were held back by lack of education and closed social institutions, the opportunities to use one's human capital have blossomed with the advent of universal education and the erosion of social barriers.

Furthermore, the material benefits of the knowledge-based economy are by no means limited to those whom Murray and Herrnstein call the cognitive elite. Many of the newest industries, from fast food to finance to communications, have succeeded in part by opening up employment opportunities for those of modest ability and training—occupations much less arduous and physically much less risky than those they have replaced. And these new industries have created enormous, widely shared economic benefits in consumption; I will return to this subject below.

• Fourth, recent decades have seen a dramatic reduction in one of the greatest historical sources of inequality: the social and economic inequality of the sexes. Today, younger cohorts of working men and women with comparable education and job tenure earn essentially the same incomes. The popular view would have it that the entry of women into the workforce has been driven by falling male earnings and the need "to make ends meet" in middleclass families. But the popular view is largely mistaken. Among married women (as the economist Chinhui Juhn has demonstrated), it is wives of men with high incomes who have been responsible for most of the recent growth in employment.

• Fifth, in the wealthy Western democracies, material needs and desires have been so thoroughly fulfilled for so many people that, for the first time in history, we are seeing large-scale voluntary reductions in the amount of time spent at paid employment. This development manifests itself in different forms: longer periods of education and training for the young; earlier retirement despite longer life spans; and, in between, many more hours devoted to leisure, recreation, entertainment, family, community and religious activities, charitable and other nonremunerative pursuits, and so forth. The dramatic growth of the sports, entertainment, and travel industries captures only a small slice of what has happened. In Fogel's estimation, the time devoted to nonwork activities by the average male head of household has grown from 10.5 hours per week in 1880 to 40 hours today, while time per week at work has fallen from 61.6 hours to 33.6 hours. Among women, the reduction in work (including not only outside employment but also household work, food preparation, childbearing and attendant health problems, and child rearing) and the growth in nonwork have been still greater.

There is a tendency to overlook these momentous developments because of the often frenetic pace of modern life. But our busy-ness actually demonstrates the point: time, and not material things, has become the scarce and valued commodity in modern society.

ᴇᴬᴼᴾ

One implication of these trends is that in very wealthy societies, income has become a less useful gauge of economic welfare and hence of economic equality. When income becomes to some degree discretionary, and when many peoples' incomes change from year to year for reasons unrelated to their life circumstances, *consumption* becomes a better measure of material welfare. And by this measure, welfare appears much more evenly distributed: people of higher income spend progressively smaller shares on consumption, while in the bottom ranges, annual consumption often exceeds income. (In fact, government statistics suggest that in the bottom 20 percent of the income scale, average annual consumption is about twice annual income—probably a reflection of a substantial underreporting of earnings in this group.) According to the economist Daniel Slesnick, the distribution of consumption, unlike the distribution of reported income, has become measurably *more* equal in recent decades.

If we include leisure-time pursuits as a form of consumption, the distribution of material welfare appears flatter still. Many such activities, being informal by definition, are difficult to track, but Dora Costa of MIT has recently studied one measurable aspect—expenditures on recreation—and found that these have become strikingly more equal as people of lower income have increased the amount of time and money they devote to entertainment, reading, sports, and related enjoyments.

Television, videocassettes, CD's, and home computers have brought musical, theatrical, and other entertainments (both high and low) to everyone, and have enormously narrowed the differences in cultural opportunities between wealthy urban centers and everywhere else. Formerly upper-crust sports like golf, tennis, skiing, and boating have become mass pursuits (boosted by increased public spending on parks and other recreational facilities as well as on environmental quality), and health clubs and full-line book stores have become as plentiful as gas stations. As some of the best things in life become free or nearly so, the price of pursuing them becomes, to that extent, the "opportunity cost" of time itself.

The substitution of leisure activities for income-producing work even appears to have become significant enough to be contributing to the recently much-lamented increase in inequality in measured income. In a new AEI study, Robert Haveman finds that most of the increase in earnings inequality among U.S. males since the mid-1970's can be attributed not to changing labor-market opportunities but to voluntary choice—to the free pursuit of nonwork activities at the expense of income-producing work.

Most of us can see this trend in our own families and communities. A major factor in income inequality in a wealthy knowledge economy is age—many people whose earnings put them at the top of the income curve in their late fifties were well down the curve in their twenties, when they were just getting out of school and beginning their working careers. Fogel again: today the average household in the top 10 percent might consist of a professor or accountant married to a nurse or secretary, both in their peak years of earning. As for the stratospheric top 1 percent, it includes not only very rich people like Bill Cosby but also people like Cosby's fictional Huxtable family:

an obstetrician married to a corporate lawyer. All these individuals would have appeared well down the income distribution as young singles, and that is where their young counterparts appear today.

That more young people are spending more time in college or graduate school, taking time off for travel and "finding themselves," and pursuing interesting but low- or non-paying jobs or apprenticeships before knuckling down to lifelong careers is a significant factor in "income inequality" measured in the aggregate. But this form of economic inequality is in fact the social equality of the modern age. It is progress, not regress, to be cherished and celebrated, not feared and fretted over.

❧

Which brings me back to my contention that it is our very wealth and equality that are the undoing of the welfare state. Western government today largely consists of two functions. One is income transfers from the wages of those who are working to those who are not working: mainly social-security payments to older people who have chosen to retire rather than go on working and education subsidies for younger people who have chosen to extend their schooling before beginning work. The other is direct and indirect expenditures on medical care, also financed by levies on the wages of those who are working. It is precisely these aspects of life—nonwork and expenditures on medical care and physical well-being—that are the booming sectors of modern, wealthy, technologically advanced society.

When the Social Security program began in America in the 1930's, retirement was still a novel idea: most men worked until they dropped, and they dropped much earlier than they do today. Even in the face of our approaching demographic crunch, produced by the baby boom followed by the baby bust, we could solve the financial problems of the Social Security program in a flash by returning to the days when people worked longer and died younger. Similarly, a world without elaborate diagnostic techniques, replaceable body parts, and potent pharmaceutical and other means of curing or ameliorating disease—a world where medical care consisted largely of bed rest and hand-holding—would present scant fiscal challenge to government as a provider of health insurance.

Our big government-entitlement programs truly are, as conservatives like to call them, obsolete. They are obsolete not because they were terrible ideas to begin with, though some of them were, but because of the astounding growth in social wealth and equality and because of the technological and economic developments which have propelled that growth. When Social Security was introduced, not only was retirement a tiny part of most people's lives but people of modest means had limited ability to save and invest for the future. Today, anyone can mail off a few hundred dollars to a good mutual fund and hire the best investment management American finance has to offer.

In these circumstances it is preposterous to argue, as President Clinton has done, that privatizing Social Security (replacing the current system of income transfers from workers to retirees with one of individually invested retirement savings) would be good for Warren Buffett but bad for the little guy. Private savings—through pension plans, mutual funds, and personal investments in housing and other durables—are *already* a larger source of retirement income than Social Security transfers. Moreover, although there is much talk nowadays about the riskiness of tying retirement income to the performance of financial markets, the social developments I have described suggest that the greater risk lies in the opposite direction. The current Social Security program ties retirement income to the growth of wage earners' payrolls; that growth is bound to be less than the growth of the economy as a whole, as reflected in the financial markets.

Similarly, Medicare is today a backwater of old-fashioned fee-for-service medicine, hopelessly distorted by a profusion of inefficient and self-defeating price-and-service controls. Over the past dozen years, a revolution has been carried out in the private financing and organization of medical care. The changes have not been unmixed blessings; nor could they be, so long as the tax code encourages people to overinsure for routine medical care. Yet substantial improvements in cost control and quality of service are now evident throughout the health-care sector—except under Medicare. These innovations have not been greeted by riots or strikes at the thousands of private organizations that have introduced them. Nor will there be riots in the streets if, in place of the lame-brained proposals for Medicare "spending cuts" and still more ineffective price controls currently in fashion in Washington, similar market-based innovations are introduced to Medicare.

In sum, George Bush's famous statement in his inaugural address that "we have more will than wallet" was exactly backward. Our wallets are bulging; the problems we face are increasingly problems not of necessity, but of will. The political class in Washington is still marching to the tune of economic redistribution and, to a degree, "class warfare." But Washington is a lagging indicator of social change. In time, the progress of technology and the growth of private markets and private wealth will generate the political will to transform radically the redistributive welfare state we have inherited from an earlier and more socially balkanized age.

There are signs, indeed, that the Progressive-era and New Deal programs of social insurance, economic regulation, and subsidies and protections for farming, banking, labor organization, and other activities are already crumbling, with salutary effects along every point of the economic spectrum. Anyone who has been a business traveler since the late 1970's, for example, has seen firsthand how deregulation has democratized air travel. Low fares and mass marketing have brought such luxuries as foreign travel, weekend getaways to remote locales, and reunions of far-flung families—just twenty years ago, pursuits of the wealthy—to people of relatively modest means. Coming reforms, including the privatization of Social Security and, most of all, the dismantling of the public-school monopoly in elementary and secondary education, will similarly benefit the less well-off disproportionately, providing them with opportunities enjoyed today primarily by those with high incomes.

I venture a prediction: just as airline deregulation was championed by Edward Kennedy and Jimmy Carter before Ronald Reagan finished the job, so the coming reforms will be a bipartisan enterprise. When the political class catches on (as Prime Minister Tony Blair has already done in England), the Left will compete vigorously and often successfully with the Right for the allegiance of the vast new privileged middle class. This may sound implausible at a moment when the Clinton administration has become an energetic agent of traditional unionism and has secured the enactment of several new redistributive tax provisions and spending programs. But the watershed event of the Clinton years will almost certainly be seen to be not any of these things but rather the defeat of the President's national health-insurance plan in the face of widespread popular opposition.

The lesson of that episode is that Americans no longer wish to have the things they care about socialized. What has traditionally attracted voters to government as a provider of insurance and other services is not that government does the job better or more efficiently or at a lower cost than private markets; it is the prospect of securing those services through taxes paid by others. That is why today's advocates of expanding the welfare state are still trying to convince voters to think of themselves as members of distinct groups that are net beneficiaries of government: students, teachers, women, racial minorities, union members, struggling young families, retirees, and so forth. But as the material circumstances of the majority become more equal, and as the proficiency and social reach of private markets increasingly outstrip what government can provide, the possibilities for effective redistribution diminish. The members of an egalitarian, middle-class electorate cannot improve their lot by subsidizing one another, and they know it.

With the prospects dimming for further, broad-based socialization along the lines of the Clinton health-care plan, the private supply of important social services will continue to exist and, in general, to flourish alongside government programs. Defenders of the welfare state will thus likely be reduced to asserting that private markets and personal choice may be fine for the well-off, but government services are more appropriate for those of modest means. This is the essence of President Clinton's objection to privatizing Social Security and of the arguments against school choice for parents of students in public elementary and high schools. But "capitalism for the rich, socialism for the poor" is a highly unpromising banner for liberals to be marching under in an era in which capitalism has itself become a profound egalitarian force.

⋅❦⋅

Where, then, will the battlegrounds be for the political allegiance of the new middle class? Increasingly, that allegiance will turn on policies involving little or no redistributive cachet but rather society-wide benefits in the form of personal amenity, autonomy, and safety: environmental quality and parks, medical and other scientific research, transportation and communications infrastructure, defense against terrorism, and the like. The old welfare-state debates between Left and Right will be transformed into debates over piece-meal incursions into private markets that compete with or replace government services. Should private insurers be required to cover annual mammograms for women in their forties? Should retirement accounts be permitted to invest in tobacco companies? Should parents be permitted to use vouchers to send their children to religious schools? Thus transformed, these debates, too, will tend to turn on considerations of general social advantage rather than on the considerations of social justice and economic desert that animated the growth of the welfare state.

Political allegiance will also turn increasingly on issues that are entirely nonmaterial. I recently bumped into a colleague, a noted political analyst, just after I had read the morning papers, and asked him to confirm my impression that at least half the major political stories of the past few years had something to do with sex. He smiled and replied, "Peace and prosperity."

What my colleague may have had in mind is that grave crises make all other issues secondary: President Roosevelt's private life received less scrutiny than has President Clinton's, and General Eisenhower's private life received less scrutiny than did that of General Ralston (whose nomination to become chairman of the Joint Chiefs of Staff was torpedoed by allegations of an extra-marital affair). There is, however, another, deeper truth in his observation. The stupendous wealth, technological mastery, and autonomy of modern life have freed man not just for worthy, admirable, and self-improving pursuits but also for idleness and unworthy and self-destructive pursuits that are no less a part of his nature.

And so we live in an age of astounding rates of divorce and family breakup, of illegitimacy, of single teenage motherhood, of drug use and crime, of violent and degrading popular entertainments, and of the "culture of narcissism"—and also in an age of vibrant religiosity, of elite universities where madrigal singing and ballroom dancing are all the rage and rampant student careerism is a major faculty concern, and of the Promise Keepers, over a million men of all incomes and races who have packed sports stadiums around the United States to declare their determination to be better husbands, fathers, citizens, and Christians. Ours is an age in which obesity has become a serious public-health problem—and in which dieting, fitness, environmentalism, and self-improvement have become major industries.

It is true, of course, that the heartening developments are in part responses to the disheartening ones. But it is also true that *both* are the results of the economic trends I have described here. In a society as rich and therefore as free as ours has become, the big question, in our personal lives and also in our politics, is: what is our freedom for?

POSTSCRIPT

Is America Becoming More Unequal?

Almost from the day of its publication, *The Bell Curve: Intelligence and Class Structure in American Life* by Richard J. Herrnstein and Charles Murray (Free Press, 1994) became the basic text against equality in America. Murray insists that the book is about intelligence; his critics say that it is about race. It is about both, but above all it is about equality, why it does not exist (people are very unequal intellectually), why it cannot exist (intelligence is largely a product of inheritance), and why we should reconcile ourselves to its absence (because income differences and intermarriage among intelligent people will widen the gap).

The enormous publicity and sales generated by *The Bell Curve* led to the publication of books and essays rejecting its thesis. A large number of critical essays (by biologist Stephen Jay Gould, philosopher Alan Ryan, educator Howard Gardner, psychologist Leon J. Kamin, and others) purporting to refute what the authors call the unwarranted premises, shaky statistics, and pseudoscience of *The Bell Curve* have been gathered together in Russell Jacoby and Naomi Glauberman, eds., *The Bell Curve Debate: History, Documents, Opinions* (Times Books, 1995).

In an effort to deal with educational inequality and its later economic and social consequences, the No Child Left Behind Act of 2001 required that every public school abolish social class differences in achievement, but that hope is contradicted by a U.S. Department of Education study that sees a close correlation between socioeconomic status and educational achievement in most countries including the United States, according to Richard Rothstein, *Class and Schools: Using Social, Economic, and Educational Reform to Close the Black-White Achievement Gap* (The Economic Policy Institute and Teachers College Press, 2004). A "culture of underachievement" is fostered and enforced by the absence of a literate and conversational family environment, peer pressure, and discrimination in school and workplace.

Kevin Phillips, in *Wealth and Democracy: A Political History of the American Rich* (Broadway Books, 2002), argues that American wealth owes as much to government and influence as to free markets and free competition. He concludes that "the imbalance of wealth and democracy in the United States is unsustainable." Leslie McCall examines changing public attitudes in "The Rising Risks of Rising Economic Inequality: Do Americans Care?," a Social Science Research Council paper (June 7, 2006).

The central question that Madrick an DeMuth consider remains: How much and what kinds of equality—educational, income, and legal—are necessary for democracy to exist and thrive?

ISSUE 13

Does the Patriot Act Abridge Essential Freedom?

YES: Nat Hentoff, from *The War on the Bill of Rights and the Gathering Resistance* (Seven Stories Press, 2003)

NO: Heather Mac Donald, from "Straight Talk on Homeland Security," *City Journal* (Summer 2003)

ISSUE SUMMARY

YES: *Village Voice* columnist Nat Hentoff opposes the Patriot Act as an unjustified invasion of private belief and behavior, in the conviction that the sacrifice of liberty for security will result in the loss of both.

NO: Manhattan Institute fellow Heather Mac Donald believes that, since the new terrorism poses an unprecedented threat to America's survival, the Patriot Act is an appropriate response and contains adequate protection of fundamental liberties.

$\mathbf{T}$en days before the Declaration of Independence was adopted, the Continental Congress recommended that all colonies adopt laws punishing as treasonous persons those who levy war on the colonies or adhere to the king of Great Britain and other enemies. When independence was won, treason was the only crime against the nation mentioned in the Constitution, and it was defined as providing "aid and comfort" to an enemy.

Eleven years later, the threat of war with France led Congress to adopt and President John Adams to support the Sedition Act, which punished "whoever shall by word or act support or favor the cause of any country with which the United States is at war or by word or act oppose the cause of the United States therein." In 1918, when the United States was engaged in the First World War, another Sedition Act punished anyone who would "willfully utter, print, write or publish any disloyal, profane, scurrilous, or abusive language" about our form of government. The Second World War and the Cold War waged against the Soviet Union led to the passage of the Internal Security Act and Communist Control Act, which reacted in similar ways to perceived threats to national security. All of these measures were accompanied by efforts to punish, intern, or expel suspected aliens.

Wars inspire a response to strengthen internal security, and the declaration of a war against terrorism is no different. The most far-reaching reaction to the 9/11 attack on the United States was the quick passage of the USA Patriot Act. (The official title is The Uniting and Strengthening America by Providing Appropriate Tools Required to Intercept and Obstruct Terrorism Act.) The USA Patriot Act permits tracking Web sites and e-mails if the law enforcement agency certifies that it relates to an ongoing investigation; searching a business or residence with a warrant but without notifying the owner that the search has been conducted until some later time; installing wiretaps to be granted against individuals, instead of a particular phone, allowing government wiretaps of public phones used by suspected persons; seizing voice-mail messages under a warrant; detaining non-citizens without a hearing; denying entry to non-citizens based on their speech or deportation based on support of a terrorist group, even if that support is unrelated to terrorist activity, and a variety of other measures.

Less controversially, the Act encourages the exchange of information among the FBI, the CIA, and other law enforcement groups. Many critics had blamed the poor communications between the FBI and CIA for America's failure to put together pieces of information that might have alerted the nation to the terrorist threat before 9/11.

To its critics, the very title of the USA Patriot Act implicitly suggests that those who oppose it are less than patriotic, or at least are dangerously foolish. As proof, they cite this statement of Attorney General John Ashcroft: "To those who pit Americans against immigrants, citizens against non-citizens, to those who scare peace-loving people with phantoms of lost liberty, my message is this: Your tactics only aid terrorists for they erode our national unity and diminish our resolve. They give ammunition to America's enemies and pause to America's friends. They encourage people of good will to remain silent in the face of evil." They oppose the law's increase in the surveillance and investigative powers of law enforcement because they believe that it sacrifices the checks and balances vital to safeguarding civil liberties.

To its defenders, the Patriot Act is essential to the nation's security. The 9/11 acts were part of a war against the United States unlike any fought before. The enemy, bent upon the mass slaughter of civilians, is hidden on American soil and must be ferreted out—for which the techniques used for catching bank robbers and other traditional criminals are totally inadequate. From the perspective of its defenders, then, the Patriot Act is a modest step toward dealing with the new reality of massive terrorist strikes within this country. But what of the dangers the Patriot Act poses to civil liberties? Its defenders charge that the critics ignore the many safeguards for civil liberties built into the law, such as the fact that before FBI agents can demand records of any citizen they must first obtain judicial approval.

In the following selections, Nat Hentoff deplores the fact that, under this law, there is no need to show probable cause that a crime has been or is about to be committed, and that there is no effective check upon the executive power. Heather Mac Donald believes that civil liberties have been safeguarded, but that terrorist "acts of war" require new weapons in dealing with unidentified combatants within the United States.

YES

Nat Hentoff

How We Began to Lose Our Liberties

Two nights after the September 11 attack, the Senate swiftly, by voice vote after thirty minutes of debate, attached to a previously written appropriations bill an amendment making it much easier for the government to wiretap computers of terrorism suspects without having to go to various courts to get multiple search warrants. The bipartisan bill was introduced by Senators Orrin Hatch, Republican of Utah, and Dianne Feinstein, Democrat of California. "Terrorism" was not defined.

That was the beginning of the steamroller. Attorney General John Ashcroft then got his way with his originally titled Anti-Terrorism Act of 2001, which coolly contradicted the earnest assertions of the president and the secretary of defense that necessary security measures would not violate our fundamental liberties because our freedom is what we are fighting for. The final legislation passed the Senate on October 25 by a vote of 98 to 1, with only Russ Feingold, Democrat of Wisconsin, dissenting. In the House, the bill passed 356 to 66.

The law permits government agents to search a suspect's home without immediately notifying the object of the search. In J. Edgar Hoover's day, this was known as a "black bag job." The FBI then never bothered to get a search warrant for such operations. Now, a warrant would be required, but very few judges would turn a government investigator down in this time of fear. Ashcroft's "secret searches" provision can now extend to *all* criminal cases and can include taking photographs, the contents of your hard drive, and other property. This is now a permanent part of the law, not subject to any "sunset" review by Congress.

Ashcroft also asked for roving wiretaps—a single warrant for a suspect's telephone must include any and all types of phones he or she uses in any and all locations, including pay phones. If a suspect uses a relative's phone or your phone, that owner becomes part of the investigative database. So does anyone using the same pay phone or any pay phone in the area.

Ashcroft neglected to tell us, however, that roving wiretaps already became law under the Clinton Administration in 1998. At that time, only Congressman Bob Barr, Republican of Georgia, spoke against it in Congress, while the media paid little attention to this revision of the Fourth Amendment.

But Ashcroft demanded and received a radical extension of these roving wiretaps: a one-stop *national* warrant for wiretapping these peripatetic phones. Until now, a wiretap warrant was valid only in the jurisdiction in which it was issued. But now, the government won't have to waste time by having to keep going to court to provide a basis for each warrant in each locale.

The expansion of wiretapping to computers, and thereby the Internet, makes a mockery of Internet champion John Perry Barlow's 1996 "Declaration of the Independence of Cyberspace":

> Governments of the industrial world, on behalf of the future, I ask you of the past to leave us alone. . . . You have no sovereignty where we gather . . . nor do you possess any methods of enforcement we have true reason to fear. Cyberspace does not lie within your borders.

This government invasion of cyberspace fulfills the prophecy of Justice Louis Brandeis, who warned, in his dissent in the first wiretapping case before the Supreme Court, *Olmstead v. United States* (1928), "Ways may some day be developed by which the Government, without removing papers from secret drawers, can reproduce them in court, and by which it will be enabled to expose to a jury the most intimate occurrences of the home."

This has come to pass. The government now has access to bank records, credit card purchases, what has been searched for on the Internet, and a great deal more data from those who have "supported," or are suspected of, terrorism.

Moreover, as Brandon Koerner, a fellow at the New America Foundation, has pointed out in the *Village Voice,* the bill that Congress passed so hastily on the night of September 13—and that is now part of the law—"lowers the legal standards necessary for the FBI to deploy its infamous Carnivore surveillance system." Without showing—as the Fourth Amendment requires—probable cause that a crime has been committed or is about to be committed, the government invades your privacy through Carnivore.

The fearful name "Carnivore" disturbed some folks, and so it has been renamed DCS1000. Carnivore, Koerner notes, is "a computer that the Feds attach to an Internet service provider. Once in place, it scans e-mail traffic for 'suspicious' subjects which, in the current climate, could be something as innocent as a message with the word 'Allah' in the header." Or maybe: "SAVE THE FOURTH AMENDMENT FROM TYRANTS!" Carnivore also records other electronic communications.

There was resistance to the assault on the Bill of Rights. In Congress, such previously unlikely alliances between Maxine Waters and Bob Barr, Barney Frank and Dick Armey, helped hold back Ashcroft's rush to enact his antiterrorism weapons within a week, as he had demanded. In the Senate, Patrick Leahy, chairman of the Judiciary Committee, also tried to allow some deliberation, but Majority Leader Tom Daschle usurped and undermined Leahy's authority. Leahy ultimately caved and declared the law signed by Bush on October 26 "a good bill that protects our liberties."

The House Judiciary Committee did pass by a 36-to-0 vote a bipartisan bill that restored some mention of the Bill of Rights to Ashcroft's proposals. But, late at night, that bill was scuttled behind closed doors by Speaker of the House Dennis Hastert and other Republican leaders, along with emissaries from the White House.

As a result, on October 12, the House, 337 to 39, approved a harsh bill that most of its members had not had time even to read. David Dreier, chairman of the Committee on Rules, often seen being smoothly disingenuous on television, said casually that it was hardly the first time bills had been passed that House members had not read.

Democrat David Obey of Wisconsin accurately described the maneuver as "a back-room quick fix."

And Barney Frank made the grim point that this subversion of representative government was "the least democratic process for debating questions fundamental to democracy I have ever seen. A bill drafted by a handful of people in secret, subject to no committee process, comes before us immune from amendment."

Among those voting against the final bill were Barney Frank, John Conyers, David Bonior, Barbara Lee, Cynthia McKinney, John Dingell, Jesse Jackson Jr., Jerrold Nadler, Melvin Watt, and Maxine Waters. Unaccountably, Bob Barr voted for the bill.

But House Judiciary Committee Chairman James Sensenbrenner, as reported on National Public Radio, assured us all that this steamrollered bill did not diminish the freedom of "innocent citizens."

Providing, of course, that the presumption of innocence holds. (Sensenbrenner was later to change his mind.)

Also late at night, on October 11, the Senate, in a closed-door session attended only by Senate leaders and members of the Administration, created a similar, expansive antiterrorism bill that the Senate went on to pass by a vote of ninety-six to one. Only Russ Feingold, a Wisconsin Democrat, had the truly patriotic courage to vote against this attack on the Bill of Rights that the president and the secretaries of state and defense have said we are fighting for.

As Feingold had said while the Senate was allegedly deliberating the bill, "It is crucial that civil liberties in this country be preserved. Otherwise I'm afraid terror will win this battle without firing a shot."

In essence, the new law will, as the *Wall Street Journal* noted, "make it easier for government agents to track e-mail sent and Web sites visited by someone involved in an investigation; to collect call records for phones such a person might use; and to share information between the Federal Bureau of Investigation and the Central Intelligence Agency."

Until now, the CIA was not legally allowed to spy on Americans. Also, previously secret grand jury proceedings will now be shared among law enforcement and intelligence agencies.

In addition, the new law subverts the Fourth Amendment's standards of reasonable searches and seizures by allowing antiterrorism investigations to obtain a warrant not on the basis of previously defined "probable cause," as has been required in domestic criminal probes, but on the much looser basis that the information is "relevant to an ongoing criminal investigation" somehow linked to alleged terrorism.

The new law has a "sunset clause," requiring it to be reviewed in December 2005, to determine if these stringent measures are still needed. But before this collusion in reducing our liberties was effected, George W. Bush had assured us that the war on worldwide terrorism will be of indeterminate length. A Congress that so overwhelmingly passed this antiterrorism bill is hardly likely to expunge parts of it unless there is rising citizen resistance. And even if it did, evidence gathered in the first four years could be used in prosecutions after that. Moreover, not every part of the PATRIOT ACT is subject to the sunset clause. There are sections that are now part of our permanent laws.

In self-defense, all of us should be interested in how terrorism is defined in this historic legislation. As summarized by the ACLU, the language in the final bill said: A person "commits the crime of domestic terrorism if within the U.S., activity is engaged in that involves acts dangerous to human life that violate the laws of the United States or any State, and appear to be intended to: (1) intimidate or coerce a civilian population; (2) influence the policy of a government by intimidation or coercion; or (3) affect the conduct of the government by mass destruction, assassination, or kidnapping." (Note the words: "appear to be intended to" and "intimidate.")

Considering the loose language of the first two provisions, the ACLU points out that "this over-broad terrorism definition would sweep in people who engage in acts of political protest if those acts were dangerous to human life. People associated with organizations such as Operation Rescue and the Environmental Liberation Front, and the World Trade Organization protesters, have engaged in activities that should subject them to prosecution as terrorists."

Furthermore, "once the government decides that conduct is 'domestic terrorism,' law enforcement agents have the authority to charge anyone who provides assistance to that person, even if the assistance is an act as minor as providing lodging. They would have the authority to wiretap the home of anyone who is providing assistance."

"Assistance" includes "support." So, contributions to any group later charged with domestic terrorism—even if the donor was unaware of its range of activities—could lead to an investigation of those giving "support."

As Judge Learned Hand once said, "Liberty lies in the hearts of men and women; when it dies there, no constitution, no law, no court can even do much to help it. While it lies there, it needs no constitution, no law, no court to save it."

We and the Constitution have survived the contempt for the Bill of Rights in the Alien and Sedition Acts of 1798; Abraham Lincoln's suspension of *habeas corpus*, and the jailing of editors and other dissenters during the Civil War; Woodrow Wilson's near annihilation of the First Amendment in the First World War; and the Red Scares of 1919 and the early 1920s when Attorney General A. Mitchell Palmer and his enthusiastic aide, J. Edgar Hoover, rounded up hundreds of "radicals," "subversives," and "Bolsheviks" in thirty-three cities and summarily deported many of them. And we also survived Joe McCarthy. But will liberty still survive "in the hearts" of Americans?

This will be one of our severest tests yet to rescue the Constitution from our government. Benjamin Franklin has been quoted a lot since the USA PATRIOT Act and its progeny. "They that can give up essential liberty to obtain a little temporary safety deserve neither liberty nor safety."

On October 11, 2001, Senator Russ Feingold, dissenting to the PATRIOT Act, said on the floor of the Senate:

> There is no doubt that if we lived in a police state, it would be easier to catch terrorists. If we lived in a country where the police were allowed to search your home at any time for any reason; if we lived in a country where the government is entitled to open your mail, eavesdrop on your phone conversations, or intercept our e-mail communications; if we lived in a country where people could be held in jail indefinitely based on what they write or think, or based on mere suspicion that they are up to no good, the government would probably, discover and arrest more terrorists or would-be terrorists, just as it would find more lawbreakers generally.
>
> But that wouldn't be a country in which we would want to live, and it wouldn't be a country for which we could, in good conscience, ask our young people to fight and die. In short, that country wouldn't be America.
>
> I think it is important to remember that the Constitution was written in 1789 by men who had recently won the Revolutionary War . . . They wrote the Constitution and the Bill of Rights to protect individual liberties in times of war as well as in times of peace.
>
> There have been periods in our nation's history when civil liberties have taken a back seat to what appeared at the time to be legitimate exigencies of war. Our national consciousness still bears the stain and the scars of those events.
>
> We must not allow this piece of our past to become prologue. Preserving our freedom is the reason we are now engaged in this new war on terrorism. We will lose that war without a shot being fired if we sacrifice the liberties of the American people in the belief that by doing so we will stop the terrorists.

Russ Feingold predicted much of what was to come.

⤷◉⤶

During the fierce debates in the new America on whether the Constitution, written in 1787, should be ratified, there was fear among the dissenters that a national federal government would be too powerful. During that debate, the proposed Constitution, which did not yet have a Bill of Rights, was attacked by Robert Yates, writing under the pseudonym "Brutus."

In Bernard Bailyn's *To Begin the World Anew* (Knopf, 2003), Brutus, much concerned with the new government's power to tax, predicted that this federal government "will introduce itself into every corner of the city and country. It [the national government] will wait upon the ladies at their toilett, and will not leave them in any of their domestic concerns; it will accompany them to the ball, the play, the assembly . . . it will enter the house of every gentlemen . . . it will take cognizance of the professional man in his office, or his study . . . it will follow the mechanic to his shop, and in his work, and will haunt him in his family, in his bed . . . it will penetrate into the most obscure cottage; and finally, it will light upon the head of every person in the United States."

It was as if "Brutus" could have foreseen beyond the power to tax, Admiral John Poindexter's Terrorism Information Awareness System in the Pentagon, or the ever increasing electronic surveillance of the citizenry by John Ashcroft. Soon after the hasty passage of the USA PATRIOT Act in the immediate wake of 9/11, Mindy Tucker, then the spokesperson for the Justice Department, promised: "This is just the first step. There will be additional items to come." . . .

In the April 11, 2003, issue of *The Chronicle of Higher Education*, the authoritative source of news and analysis concerning college and university affairs, Judith Grant, an associate professor of political science and women's studies at the University of Southern California, wrote in an article titled "Uncle Sam Over My Shoulder":

> I am now experiencing what American legal scholars call 'a chilling effect,' and I was indeed aware of it as a sort of chill running up my spine—a half-second of anxiety, almost subconscious, the moment I heard that the [USA PATRIOT] Act had been passed.
>
> I feel that chill again when I realize that I now pause a moment before I write almost anything. I think about how a government official might read my writing if he or she were trying to build a (completely unjustified) case against me. I worried even while I wrote that last sentence, then I worried about my worry. Might someone in the Justice Department ask: "Why would she be worried if she were doing nothing wrong?"

In the April 20, 2003, Letters section of the *New York Times*, Tina Rosan of Cambridge, Massachusetts, comments on a previous *Times* story, "Muslims Hesitating on Gifts as U.S. Scrutinizes Charities":

> Of course Muslims in the United States are "hesitating" to give money to charities because they are afraid . . . Many have been detained without trial. Given this environment, Muslims are trying to stay under the radar. They don't want a contribution to a charity to put them on a suspect list or cause them to end up in jail. Unfortunately the news media have not been paying attention to the severe violation of civil liberties at home. The real truth is much deeper and darker.

In the April 21, 2003, *Newsday*, columnist Sheryl McCarthy told of a twenty-six-year-old mechanical engineer, Daniel Ueda, and twenty-eight-year-old Carey Larsen, who were arrested in a demonstration "outside the offices of The Carlyle Group, a private investment house with holdings in the defense industry":

> At police headquarters both Ueda and Larsen were asked questions that seemed strange, considering the minor offenses with which they were charged. Questions like: how many protests had they participated in, what groups were they affiliated with, how they heard about the demonstrations . . . how they felt about the war with Iraq and whether they thought the United States should have entered World War II. Yes, really.
>
> When they balked at answering the political questions, they were warned they'd be held longer if they didn't cooperate.

When *New York Times* columnist Joyce Purnick (April 21) asked the New York City Police Department if the information obtained from such questioning could be used to infiltrate political groups, the Police Department's chief spokesman, Michael O'Looney, said: "I'm going to leave it with that." He refused to answer the question that brought back my memories of the days of J. Edgar Hoover's COINTELPRO, when the FBI, at will, infiltrated and disrupted entirely lawful groups.

Donna Lieberman, executive director of the New York Civil Liberties Union, is aware of the history of COINTELPRO, and she told Joyce Purnick: "When people are asked about their political affiliations, it's intimidation. It's discouraging people from exercising their fundamental right to criticize government."

So when Judith Grant feels "a chilling effect" when she writes for *The Chronicle of Higher Education,* she may not be entirely without reason to be somewhat intimidated by the environment that John Ashcroft has created.

Sam Adams, the eighteenth-century patriot, once said of this new sweet land of liberty: "Driven from every other corner of the earth, freedom of thought and the right of private judgement in matters of conscience, direct their course to this happy country as their last asylum."

Like "Brutus," Sam Adams did not foresee the Bush-Ashcroft omnivorous surveillance of the residents of this "last asylum."

Sam Adams was overly sanguine about the future of freedom of conscience here. In 1858, Abraham Lincoln, speaking in Edwardsville, Illinois—before assuming the powers of the presidency—spoke to a truth that George W. Bush would do well to keep in mind:

> What constitutes the bulwark of our own liberty and independence? It is not our frowning battlements, our bristling seacoasts, our army and navy. These are not our reliance against tyranny . . . Our reliance is the love of liberty . . . Destroy this spirit and you have planted the seeds of despotism at your door.

This was the same Abraham Lincoln who suspended *habeas corpus,* imprisoned many Americans who dissented from his policies, and set up military tribunals to dispose of citizens of contrary views—even though the civilian courts were still open.

Then there was Franklin Delano Roosevelt, who earnestly told the nation:

> We must scrupulously guard the civil liberties of all citizens, whatever their background. We must remember that any oppression, any injustice, any hatred, is a wedge designed to attack our civilization.

It was the same Franklin Delano Roosevelt who signed Executive Order No. 9066 that sent Japanese-Americans into detention camps, which they rightly regarded as concentration camps.

When, in August 2002, Federal Judge Damon J. Keith, writing for the Sixth Circuit Court of Appeals, ruled against the Bush administration's closing of all deportation hearings to the press and the public, though the Third Circuit voted the other way, he emphasized:

> Democracies die behind closed doors. The only safeguard on this extraordinary government power is in the public, deputizing the press as the guardians of their liberty. An informed public is the most potent of all restraints on government . . . the First Amendment, through a free press, protects the people's right to know that their government acts fairly, lawfully, and accurately.

But veteran journalist Jack Nelson, retired Washington bureau chief of the *Los Angeles Times,* told a First Amendment Center conference on March 12, 2003:

> President Bush has gone beyond just being extremely secretive about the conduct of the government's business. In the name of fighting terrorism, he has amassed powers and wrapped them in a cloak of resilience to normal oversight by Congress and the judiciary. *No president since I've been a reporter has so tried to change the very structure of government to foster secrecy.* (Emphasis added.)

Even the Fourth Circuit Court of Appeals—the most conservative Federal appellate court in the country—rebuked the Bush administration in the case of Zacarias Moussaoui, accused of involvement in a terrorist conspiracy. Reported the April 2, 2003, *Washington Post:*

> The court chided the government for "simultaneously prosecuting the defendant and attempting to restrict his ability to use information [in court] that he feels is necessary to defend himself against the prosecution . . .
>
> Courts must not be remiss in protecting a defendant's right to a full and meaningful presentation of his claim to innocence."

Concerning this case, Donald Rehkopf, chairman of the Military Law Committee of the National Association of Criminal Defense Lawyers, accused the government of "inventing the law as they go along. The Constitution," he reminded the administration—echoing the Supreme Court in the 1866 *Milligan* case—"is not suspended, even during time of war."

And when the government proposed, in "Patriot Act II," to strip Americans of their citizenship if they give "support" to an organization cited by the administration as implicated in terrorism—even if the accused American is unaware of that part of the group's activities—human rights attorney Joanne Mariner noted in an article on . . . ("Patriot II's Attack on Citizenship", March 3, 2003) how Ashcroft and Bush also invent the law in proposing to take away the most essential of all American rights, our citizenship. Professor Mariner wrote:

> If you help fund an orphanage administered by one of the three Chechen separatist groups that the government has labeled as terrorist, or if you give pharmaceutical supplies to a medical outpost run by the East Turkestan Islamic Movement, or if you are on the wrong side of any of a number of

other political conflicts in the world, you are vulnerable to the loss of your citizenship.

Although you "would be able to challenge this determination in court," she continued, you would "not necessarily succeed." Particularly, if during the limitless war on terrorism, our courts keep deferring to the government, bypassing the separation of powers in the Constitution.

Through the years, I have often quoted a warning by Supreme Court Justice Louis Brandeis that resonates throughout a study of American history. It is especially relevant now:

> Experience should teach us to be most on our guard to protect liberty when the government's purposes are beneficent. Men born to freedom are naturally alert to repel invasion of their liberty by evil-minded rulers. The greatest dangers to liberty lurk in insidious encroachment by men of zeal, well-meaning but without understanding.

Brandeis's warning was part of his dissent in the first wiretapping case, *Olmstead v. the United States* (1928). The year before, in a less often quoted but even more profound definition of the spirit that has enabled this country to remain the freest in the world—despite severe misunderstandings of the Constitution by past administrations—Justice Brandeis again spoke to us now.

The case, *Whitney v. California,* concerned the prosecution of Charlotte Anita Whitney for violating the Criminal Syndication Act of California. That law, as constitutional scholar Louis Fisher noted, penalized "efforts of trade union and industrial workers to gain control of production through general strikes, sabotage, violence, or other criminal means."

Whitney "was found guilty of having organized and participated in a group assembled to advocate, teach, aid, and abet criminal syndicalism." In 1919, at a convention in Oakland, California, held to organize a California branch of the Communist Labor Party, Charlotte Whitney, as a member of the Resolutions Committee, signed this statement: "The Communist Labor Party proclaims and insists that the capture of political power, locally or nationally by the revolutionary working class, can be of tremendous assistance to the workers in their struggle for emancipation."

The Supreme Court upheld California's Criminal Syndication Act. But, in a concurring opinion, which was really a dissent, Brandeis wrote:

> A State is ordinarily denied the power to prohibit the dissemination of social, economic, and political doctrine [even though] a vast majority of its citizens believes [it] to be false and fraught with evil consequence . . . It is . . . always open to Americans to challenge a law abridging free speech and assembly by showing that there was no emergency justifying [its abridgement.]

That is precisely what the continually growing number of Bill of Rights Defense Committees around the nation are doing in challenging the USA PATRIOT Act and the other violations of the Bill of Rights by Ashcroft and

Bush. However, what Brandeis also said in *Whitney v. California* underlines this book's celebration of the gathering resistance to the war on the Bill of Rights:

> Those who won our independence . . . believed that the greatest menace to freedom is an inert people . . . They knew that order cannot be secured merely through fear of punishment for its infraction . . . that fear breeds repression; that repression breeds hate; that hate menaces stable government . . .
>
> Believing in the power of reason as applied through public discussion, they eschewed silence coerced by law—the argument of force in its worst form . . .
>
> Fear of serious injury cannot alone justify suppression of free speech and assembly. Men feared witches and burnt women [as in the Salem witchcraft trials] . . .
>
> *Those who won our independence by revolution were not cowards . . . They did not exalt order at the cost of liberty.* (Emphasis added.)

The challenge to Americans now is to act with the determination of those who won our independence because what we do now to recover the Bill of Rights will decide for years to come—as Justice William Brennan used to say—whether those words "will come off the page and into the very lives of the American people."

Straight Talk on Homeland Security

The backlash against the Bush administration's War on Terror began on 9/11 and has not let up since. Left- and right-wing advocacy groups likened the Bush administration to fascists, murderers, apartheid ideologues, and usurpers of basic liberties. Over 120 cities and towns have declared themselves "civil liberties safe zones"; and the press has amplified at top volume a recent report by the Justice Department's inspector general denouncing the government's handling of suspects after 9/11. Even the nation's librarians are shredding documents to safeguard their patrons' privacy and foil government investigations.

The advocates' rhetoric is both false and dangerous. Lost in the blizzard of propaganda is any consciousness that 9/11 was an act of war against the U.S. by foreign enemies concealed within the nation's borders. If the media and political elites keep telling the public that the campaign against those terrorist enemies is just a racist power grab, the most essential weapon against terror cells—intelligence from ordinary civilians—will be jeopardized. A drumbeat of ACLU propaganda could discourage a tip that might be vital in exposing an al-Qaida plot.

It is crucial, therefore, to demolish the extravagant lies about the anti-terror initiatives. Close scrutiny of the charges and the reality that they misrepresent shows that civil liberties are fully intact. The majority of legal changes after September 11 simply brought the law into the twenty-first century. In those cases where the government has its powers—as is inevitable during a war—important judicial and statutory safeguards protect the rights of law-abiding citizens. And in the one hard case where a citizen's rights appear to have been curtailed—the detention of a suspected American al-Qaida operative without access to an attorney—that detention is fully justified under the laws of war.

The anti–War on Terror worldview found full expression only hours after the World Trade Center fell, in a remarkable e-mail that spread like wildfire over the Internet that very day. Sent out by Harvard Law School research fellow John Perry Barlow, founder of the cyber-libertarian Electronic Freedom Foundation, the message read: "Control freaks will dine on this day for the rest of our lives. Within a few hours, we will see beginning the most vigorous efforts to end what remains of freedom in America. . . . I beg you to begin NOW to do whatever you can . . . to prevent the spasm of control mania from destroying the dreams that far more have died for over the last two hundred twenty-five years than died this morning. Don't let the terrorists or (their natural allies) the fascists win. Remember that the goal of terrorism is to create increasingly paralytic totalitarianism in the government it attacks. Don't give them the satisfaction. . . . And, please, let us try to forgive those who have committed these appalling crimes. If we hate them, we will become them."

Barlow, a former lyricist for the Grateful Dead, epitomizes the rise of the sixties counterculture into today's opinion elite, for whom no foreign enemy could ever pose as great a threat to freedom as the U.S. For Barlow, the problem isn't the obvious evil of Islamic terrorism but the imputed evil of the American government—an inversion that would characterize the next two years of anti-administration jeremiads. In this spirit, critics would measure each legal change not against the threat it responded to, but in a vacuum. Their verdict: "increasingly paralytic totalitarianism."

Right-wing libertarians soon joined forces with the Left. A few months after the Twin Towers fell, the Rutherford Institute, a Christian think tank concerned with religious liberty, added the final piece to the anti-administration argument: the 9/11 attacks were not war but, at most, a crime. Rutherford president John Whitehead denounced the Bush administration's characterization of the terror strikes as "acts of war by foreign aggressors," without however offering a single argument to support his view. Since that characterization has produced, in Whitehead's view, growing "police statism" that is destroying Americans' freedom, the characterization must be false.

In fact, of course, the 9/11 bombings were classic decapitation strikes, designed to take out America's political and financial leadership. Had a state carried them out, no one could possibly deny that they were acts of war, as John Yoo and James Ho point out in a forthcoming *Virginia Journal of International Law* article. The aim of the 19 foreign terrorists and their backers was not criminal but ideological: to revenge U.S. policies in the Middle East with mass destruction. — 9/11 wasn't a crime.

Recognizing that the World Trade Center and Pentagon attacks were acts of war entails certain consequences. First, the campaign against al-Qaida and other Islamic terror organizations is really war, not a metaphor, like the "war on drugs." Second, it is a war unlike any the U.S. has ever fought. The enemy, mostly but not exclusively foreign, is hidden on American soil in the civilian population, with the intention of slaughtering as many innocent noncombatants as possible. The use of military force abroad, while necessary, is by no means sufficient: domestic counterterrorism efforts by the FBI and other domestic law enforcement agencies are at least as essential to defeating the enemy.

When these agencies are operating against Islamic terrorists, they are operating in an unprecedented war mode—but most of the rules that govern them were designed for crime fighting. The tension between the Justice Department's and FBI's traditional roles as law enforcement agencies and their new roles as terror warriors lies at the heart of the battle over the Bush administration's post-9/11 homeland-security policies: critics refuse to recognize the reality of the war and thus won't accept the need for expanded powers to prosecute it.

Most of the changes in the law that the Justice Department sought after 9/11 concern the department's ability to gather intelligence on terror strikes before they happen—its key responsibility in the terror war. Yet the libertarian lobby will not allow the department to budge from the crime paradigm, refusing to admit that surveillance and evidence-gathering rules designed to protect the rights of suspected car thieves and bank robbers may need modification when the goal is preventing a suitcase bomb from taking out JFK. But of course the libertarians rarely acknowledge that suitcase bombs and the like are central to this debate.

Ironically, none of the changes instituted by Attorney General Ashcroft comes anywhere near what the government *could* ask for in wartime, such as the suspension of *habeas corpus,* as Lincoln ordered during the Civil War. The changes preserve intact the entire criminal procedural framework governing normal FBI and police actions, and merely tinker around the edges. But the left and right civil libertarians are having none of it.

The charges they have brought against the War on Terror have been so numerous, impugning every single administration action since 9/11, that it would take hundreds of pages to refute them all. But the following analysis of only the main charges will amply illustrate the range of duplicitous strategies that the anti-government forces deploy.

Strategy #1: Hide the Judge

Jan O'Rourke, a librarian in Bucks County, Pennsylvania, is preparing for the inevitable post-9/11 assault: She is destroying all records of her patrons' book and Internet use and is advising other Bucks County libraries to do the same. The object of her fear? The U.S. government. O'Rourke is convinced that federal spooks will soon knock on her door to spy on her law-abiding clients' reading habits. So, like thousands of librarians across the country, she is making sure that when that knock comes, she will have nothing to show. "If we don't have the information, then they can't get it," she explains.

O'Rourke is suffering from Patriot Act hysteria, a malady approaching epidemic levels. The USA-PATRIOT Act, which President Bush signed in October 2001, is a complex measure to boost the federal government's ability to detect and prevent terrorism. Its most important provision relaxed a judge-made rule that, especially after Clinton administration strengthening, had prevented intelligence and law enforcement officials from sharing information and collaborating on investigations (see "Why the FBI Didn't Stop 9/11," Autumn 2002). But the act made many other needed changes too: updating surveillance law to take into account new communications technology, for instance, enhancing the Treasury Department's ability to disrupt terrorist financing networks, and modestly increasing the attorney general's power to detain and deport suspected terrorist aliens.

From the moment the administration proposed the legislation, defenders of the status quo started ringing the tyranny alarm. When the law passed, the Electronic Privacy Information Center depicted a tombstone on its website, captioned: "The Fourth Amendment: 1789–2001." The *Washington Post* denounced the bill as "panicky." And the ever touchy American Library Association decided that a particular provision of the Patriot Act—section 215—was a "present danger to the constitutional rights and privacy of library users," though the section says not a word about libraries.

The furor over section 215 is a case study in Patriot Act fear-mongering. Section 215 allows the FBI to seek business records in the hands of third parties—the enrollment application of a Saudi national in an American flight school, say—while investigating terrorism. The section broadens the categories of institutions whose records and other "tangible items" the government may seek in espionage and terror cases, on the post-9/11 recognition that lawmakers cannot anticipate what sorts of organizations terrorists may exploit. In the past, it may have been enough to get hotel bills or storage-locker contracts (two of the four categories of records covered in the narrower law that section 215 replaced) to trace the steps of a Soviet spy; today, however, gumshoes may find they need receipts from scuba-diving schools or farm-supply stores to piece together a plot to blow up the Golden Gate Bridge. Section 215 removed the requirement that the records must concern an "agent of a foreign power" (generally, a spy or terrorist), since, again, the scope of an anti-terror investigation is hard to predict in advance.

From this tiny acorn, Bush administration foes have conjured forth a mighty assault on the First Amendment. The ACLU warns that with section 215, "the FBI could spy on a person because they don't like the books she reads, or because they don't like the websites she visits. They could spy on her because she wrote a letter to the editor that criticized government policy." Stanford Law School dean Kathleen Sullivan calls section 215 "threatening." And librarians, certain that the section is all about them, are scaring library users with signs warning that the government may spy on their reading habits.

These charges are nonsense. Critics of section 215 deliberately ignore the fact that any request for items under the section requires judicial approval. An FBI agent cannot simply walk into a flight school or library and demand records. The bureau must first convince the court that oversees anti-terror investigations (the Foreign Intelligence Surveillance Act, or FISA, court) that the documents are relevant to protecting "against international terrorism on clandestine intelligence activities." The chance that the FISA court will approve a 215 order because the FBI "doesn't like the books [a person] reads . . . or because she wrote a letter to the editor that criticized government policy" is zero. If the bureau can show that someone using the Bucks County library computers to surf the web and send e-mails has traveled to Pakistan and was seen with other terror suspects in Virginia, on the other hand, then the court may well grant an order to get the library's Internet logs.

Moreover, before the FBI can even approach the FISA court with any kind of request, agents must have gone through multiple levels of bureaucratic review just to open an anti-terror investigation. And to investigate a U.S. citizen (rather than an alien) under FISA, the FBI must show that he is knowingly engaged in terrorism or espionage.

Ignoring the Patriot Act's strict judicial review requirements is the most common strategy of the act's critics. Time and again, the Cassandras will hold up a section from the bill as an example of rampaging executive power—without ever mentioning that the power in question is overseen by federal judges who will allow its use only if the FBI can prove its relevance to a bona fide terror (or sometimes criminal) investigation. By contrast, in the few cases where a law enforcement power does not require judicial review, the jackboots-are-coming brigade screams for judges as the only trustworthy check on executive tyranny.

Strategy #2: Invent New Rights

A running theme of the campaign against section 215 and many other Patriot Act provisions is that they violate the Fourth Amendment right to privacy. But there is no Fourth Amendment privacy right in records or other items disclosed to third parties. A credit-card user, for example, reveals his purchases to the seller and to the credit-card company. He therefore has no privacy expectations in the record of those purchases that the Fourth Amendment would protect. As a result, the government, whether in a criminal case or a terror investigation, may seek his credit-card receipts without a traditional Fourth Amendment showing to a court that there is "probable cause" to believe that a crime has been or is about to be committed. Instead, terror investigators must convince the FISA court that the receipts are "relevant."

Despite librarians' fervent belief to the contrary, this analysis applies equally to library patrons' book borrowing or Internet use. The government may obtain those records without violating anyone's Fourth Amendment rights, because the patron has already revealed his borrowing and web browsing to library staff, other readers (in the days of handwritten book checkout cards), and Internet service providers. Tombstones declaring the death of the Fourth Amendment contain no truth whatsoever.

What's different in the section 215 provision is that libraries or other organizations can't challenge the FISA court's order and can't inform the target of the investigation, as they can in ordinary criminal proceedings. But that difference is crucial for the Justice Department's war-making function. The department wants to know if an al-Qaida suspect has consulted maps of the Croton reservoir and researched the toxic capacities of cyanide in the New York Public Library not in order to win a conviction for poisoning New York's water supply but to preempt the plot before it happens. The battleground is not the courtroom but the world beyond, where speed and secrecy can mean life or death.

Strategy #3: Demand Antiquated Laws

The librarians' crusade against section 215 has drawn wide media attention and triggered an ongoing congressional battle, led by Vermont socialist Bernie Sanders, to pass a law purporting to protect the "Freedom to Read." But the publicity that administration-hostile librarians were able to stir up pales in comparison to the clout of the Internet privacy lobby. The day the Patriot Act became law, the Center for Democracy and Technology sent around a warning that "privacy standards" had been "gutt[ed]." The Electronic Freedom Foundation declared that the "civil liberties of ordinary Americans have taken a tremendous blow." Jeffrey Rosen of *The New Republic* claimed that the law gave the government "essentially unlimited authority" to surveil Americans. The ACLU asserted that the FBI had suddenly gained "wide powers of phone and internet surveillance." And the Washington Post editorialized that the act made it "easier" to wiretap by "lowering the standard of judicial review."

The target of this ire? A section that merely updates existing law to modern technology. The government has long had the power to collect the numbers dialed from, or the incoming numbers to, a person's telephone by showing a court that the information is "relevant to an ongoing criminal investigation." Just as in section 215 of the Patriot Act, this legal standard is lower than traditional Fourth Amendment "probable cause," because the phone user has already forfeited any constitutional privacy rights he may have in his phone number or the number he calls by revealing them to the phone company.

A 1986 federal law tried to extend the procedures for collecting phone-number information to electronic communications, but it was so poorly drafted that its application to e-mail remained unclear. Section 216 of the Patriot Act resolves the ambiguity by making clear that the rules for obtaining phone numbers apply to incoming and outgoing e-mail addresses as well. The government can obtain e-mail headers—but not content—by showing a court that the information is "relevant to an ongoing criminal investigation." Contrary to cyber-libertarian howls, this is not a vast new power to spy but merely the logical extension of an existing power to a new form of communication. Nothing else has changed: the standard for obtaining information about the source or destination of a communication is the same as always.

Section 216 made one other change to communications surveillance law. When a court issues an order allowing the collection of phone numbers or e-mail headers, that order now applies nationally. Before, if a phone call was transmitted by a chain of phone companies headquartered in different states, investigators needed approval from a court in each of those states to track it. This time-consuming procedure could not be more dangerous in the age of terror. As Attorney General John Ashcroft testified in September 2001, the "ability of law enforcement officers to trace communications into different jurisdictions without obtaining an additional court order can be the difference between life and death for American citizens." Yet the ACLU has complained that issuing national warrants for phone and e-mail routing information marginalizes the judiciary and gives law enforcement unchecked power to search citizens.

The furor over this section of the Patriot Act employs the same deceptions as the furor over section 215 (the business records provision). In both cases, Patriot Act bashers ignore the fact that a court must approve the government's access to information. Despite the *Washington Post's* assertion to the contrary, section 216 does not lower any standards of judicial review. Both the anti-216 and anti-215 campaigns fabricate privacy rights where none exists. And neither of these anti-government campaigns lets one iota of the reality of terrorism intrude into its analyses of fictional rights violations—the reality that communications technology is essential to an enemy that has no geographical locus, and whose combatants have mastered the Internet and every form of modern communications, along with methods to defeat surveillance, such as using and discarding multiple cell phones and communicating from Internet cafés. The anti–Patriot Act forces would keep anti-terror law enforcement in the world of Ma Bell and rotary phones, even as America's would-be destroyers use America's most sophisticated technology against it.

Strategy #4: Conceal Legal Precedent

Section 213 of the Patriot Act allows the FBI (with court approval) to delay notifying a property owner that his property will be or has been searched, if notice would have an "adverse result": if he might flee the country, for example, or destroy documents or intimidate witnesses before agents can acquire sufficient evidence to arrest him. In such cases, the court that issues the search warrant may grant a delay of notice for a "reasonable period" of time.

The advocates dubbed Section 213 the "sneak-and-peek" section and have portrayed it as one of the most outrageous new powers seized by Attorney General John Ashcroft. The ACLU's fund-raising pitches warn: "Now, the government can secretly enter your home while you're away . . . rifle through your personal belongings . . . download your computer files . . . and seize any items at will. . . . And, because of the Patriot Act, you may never know what the government has done." Richard Leone, president of the Century Foundation and editor of *The War on Our Freedoms: Civil Liberties in an Age of Terrorism*, cites the fact that the Patriot Act "allows the government to conduct secret searches without notification" to support his hyperbolic claim that the act is "arguably the most far-reaching and invasive legislation passed since the espionage act of 1917 and the sedition act of 1918."

These critics pretend not to know that, long before anyone imagined such a thing as Islamic terrorism, federal judges have been granting "sneak-and-peak" warrants in criminal cases under identical standards those of section 213. The possibility of seeking delayed notice is a long-standing law enforcement prerogative, sanctioned by numerous courts. Section 213 merely codified the case law to make the process uniform across different jurisdictions. Portraying section 213 as a new power is simple falsehood, and portraying it as an excessive and unnecessary power is extraordinarily ignorant. Delayed notice under life-threatening conditions is not just reasonable but absolutely imperative.

Strategy #5: Keep the FBI off the Web

In May 2002, Attorney General Ashcroft announced that FBI agents would for the first time be allowed to surf the web, just like hundreds of millions of people across the globe. Previously, the Internet was strictly off-limits to federal law enforcement, unless agents had already developed evidence that a crime was under way. In other words, although a 12-year-old could sit in on a *jihadi*

[handwritten marginal note: Seems sarcastic + not really supporting, but argumentative, deceptive, provoking]

chat room where members were praising Usama bin Ladin, visit sites teaching bombmaking, or track down the links for the production of anthrax—all information essential to mapping out the world of Islamic terrorists or finding out how much terrorists might know—intelligence officials couldn't inspect those same public sites until they had already discovered a terror plot. But for an FBI agent in Arizona to wait for specific information about a conspiracy before researching his local biochem lab to see if it might have any connection to the Washington anthrax attacks, or might be a target for sabotage, is not the best strategy for fighting terrorism.

But Ashcroft's critics say the bureau *should* wait. According to the Electronic Privacy Information Center, for instance, the new guidelines "threaten Fourth Amendment rights" because they permit the FBI to "engage in prospective searches without possessing any evidence of suspicious behavior." But there are no Fourth Amendment rights in the web. Far from expecting privacy on a website, its designers hope for the greatest possible exposure to all comers. The Internet is more public even than a newspaper, since it is free and unbound by geography; it is the most exhibitionistic communication medium yet designed. To require the FBI to be the one entity on earth that may not do general web searches, as the civil libertarians have demanded, makes no sense.

In fact, the new guidelines are unduly narrow. They prohibit searches by an individual's name—Usama bin Ladin, say—unless agents have cause to suspect him of involvement in a terror plot. But since millions of web users may conduct searches of Usama bin Ladin's name or of any other individual without violating anyone's privacy rights, it is hard to discern a basis for barring the government from also obtaining that information in preliminary criminal or terror investigations. Law enforcement agencies need to survey as much information as possible about Islamic terrorism before, not after, attacks happen, so that they can recognize an early warning sign or pattern in what an uninformed observer may see as an innocuous set of events.

Opening the web to the FBI, common sense for any criminal investigation, is particularly essential in fighting Islamic terrorism, because the web is the most powerful means of spreading jihad. Rohan Gunaratna, an al-Qaida expert at Scotland's Saint Andrews University, argues that unless the authorities shut down jihadist sites, "we will not able to end terrorism." But even if the U.S. can't shut down web pages celebrating mass destruction in the name of holy war, it should at least be able to visit them to learn what's out there.

The May guidelines also permit agents to attend public meetings for the first time since 1976 in order to "detect or prevent terrorist activities." Let's say a Moroccan imam at a Brooklyn mosque regularly preaches vengeance against America for its support of Israel. The imam was banished from Morocco for his agitation against the secular government. Visitors from Saudi Arabia known to associate with radical fundamentalists regularly visit.

Under previous guidelines, the FBI could not attend public worship at the mosque to learn more about the imam's activities unless it had actual evidence that he was planning to release sarin in the subways, say. But most of the preparations leading up to a terror attack—such as casing transportation systems, attending crop-dusting school, or buying fertilizer—are legal. Only intelligence gathering and analysis can link them to terrorist intent. To require evidence before permitting the intelligence gathering that would produce it is a suicidal Catch-22.

Yet the civil libertarian lobby would keep the FBI in the dark about public events until the last minute. The Electronic Privacy Information Center brands the public-meeting rule a "serious threat to the right of individuals to speak and assemble freely without the specter of government monitoring." But the First Amendment guarantees free speech and assembly, not freedom from government attendance at public meetings. Even so, the new guidelines narrow the government's power anyway, by allowing agents to participate in public meetings only for a terror investigation, not for criminal investigations.

Strategy #6: Exploit Hindsight

Early this June, anti–War on Terror advocates and journalists pulled out all the stops to publicize a report by the Justice Department's inspector general criticizing the department's detention of illegal immigrants suspected of terrorist ties. Headlines blared: DETAINEES ABUSED, CIVIL RIGHTS OF POST-SEPT. 11 DETAINEES VIOLATED, REPORT FINDS (*Washington Post*); U.S. FINDS ABUSES OF 9/11 DETAINEES; JUSTICE DEPT. INQUIRY REVEALS MANY VIOLATIONS OF IMMIGRANTS' RIGHTS (*Los Angeles Times*); THE ABUSIVE DETENTIONS OF SEPT. 11 (*New York Times* editorial). Advocacy groups declared full vindication of their crusade against the Bush administration.

These headlines exaggerated the report only modestly. To be sure, Inspector General Glenn Fine did not declare any rights violations in the Justice Department's policies or practices, but he did decry "significant problems in the way the 9/11 detainees were treated." He charged that the investigation and clearance of terror suspects took too long, that the Justice Department did not sufficiently differentiate moderately suspicious detainees from highly suspect ones, and that the conditions in one New York City detention center, where guards were charged with taunting detainees and slamming them against walls, were unduly.

Fine's report, however measured its language, is ultimately as much a misrepresentation of the government's post-9/11 actions as the shrillest press release from Amnesty International. While it pays lip service to the "difficult circumstances confronting the department in responding to the terror attacks," it fails utterly to understand the terrifying actuality of 9/11. Fine's cool and sensible recommendations—"timely clearance process, timely service of immigration charges, careful consideration of where to house detainees . . . ; better training of staff . . . ; and better oversight"—read, frankly, like a joke, in light of the circumstances at the time.

Recall what the Justice Department and FBI were facing on 9/11: an attack by an invisible, previously unsuspected enemy on a scale unprecedented in this country, with weapons never imagined. Utter uncertainty prevailed about what the next hour or day or week might bring: if these 19 men had remained undetected while plotting their assault with such precision, who else was ready to strike next, and with what weapons? In New York, the FBI office, seven blocks from Ground Zero, had to evacuate on 9/11 to a temporary command center set up in a parking garage; the New York INS evacuated its processing center downtown as well. Electricity and other utilities were down, as was delivery and express mail service. One week after the attacks, 96,000 leads had flooded in to FBI offices around the country; tens of thousands more would soon follow, requiring round-the-clock operations at FBI headquarters, with thousands of agents following up the leads. Recriminations over the government's failure to prevent the catastrophe also flooded in: Why hadn't the intelligence community "connected the dots"? Why didn't the CIA and FBI communicate better? How had the State Department and INS let in foreign terrorists bent on destroying America?

Given the magnitude of the carnage and the depth of the uncertainty, the government would have failed in its duty had it not viewed suspects as serious risks. These were, possibly, enemy combatants, not car thieves or muggers. Justice Department officials declared that any suspect picked up in the course of a terror investigation, if an illegal immigrant, would be held in detention until the FBI cleared him of any possible terror connections. Moreover, if agents, following a lead, were looking for a particular individual and discovered half a dozen illegal immigrants at his apartment, all seven would be detained as suspects, since the FBI had no way of knowing who might be an accomplice of the wanted man. In another safeguard against letting a terrorist go, FBI headquarters ruled that it needed to sign off on all clearances, since only bureau brass possessed the full national picture of developing intelligence. Finally, the FBI mandated CIA background checks on all detainees.

These policies are eminently reasonable. That they ended up delaying clearance for an average of 80 days for the 762 illegal aliens detained after 9/11 does not discredit their initial rationale. (That delay is not unlawful, since the government can hold illegal aliens for an undefined period under emergency circumstances.) Justice Department officials expected to release innocent detainees in days, or at most several weeks, and they were concerned as the process stretched out; memos about the need to speed things up flew around the department daily. Officials worried about staying within the law and not violating anyone's rights (which they did not), but they also worried—and for good reason—about releasing even one deadly person. Even in retrospect, this calculus is unimpeachable: the costs of being legally held as an illegal alien and terror suspect for three months without ultimate conviction, while huge for the person held, pale in comparison to the costs of allowing terrorists to go free. (That some prison guards may have abused about 20 detainees is deplorable but does not invalidate the detention policy.)

The inspector general has plenty of good-government suggestions for how to make sure that, after the next terror attack, suspects are efficiently processed, but he is silent on the paramount questions that will face the government should a bomb go off in the nation's capital or a biological weapon in the subway at rush hour: how to find out who did it and who is waiting in the wings, and how to protect the country in the face of grossly inadequate knowledge. Should the country experience another attack on the scale of 9/11, the aftermath undoubtedly will not follow administrative law procedures perfectly. As long as the government does not deliberately or flagrantly abuse suspects' rights, it need have no apology for the slow functioning of bureaucracy through the crisis. . . .

Strategy #7: Treat War as a Continuation of Litigation by Other Means

The Bush bashers are correct that the Padilla case, with its serious liberty issues weighing against serious national peril, has pushed the law where it has never gone before. But that is because the threat the country is facing is without precedent, not because the administration is seizing unjustified power.

When the War on Terror's opponents intone, "We need not trade liberty for security," they are right—but not in the way they think. Contrary to their slogan's assumption, there is no zero-sum relationship between liberty and security. The government may expand its powers to detect terrorism without diminishing civil liberties one iota, as long as those powers remain subject to traditional restraints: statutory prerequisites for investigative action, judicial review, and political accountability. So far, these conditions have been met.

But the larger fallacy at the heart of the elites' liberty-versus-security formula is its blindness to all threats to freedom that do not emanate from the White House. Nothing the Bush administration has done comes close to causing the loss of freedom that Americans experienced after 9/11, when air travel shut down for days, and fear kept hundreds of thousands shut up in their homes. Should al-Qaida strike again, fear will once again paralyze the country far beyond the effects of any possible government restriction on civil rights. And that is what the government is trying to forestall, in the knowledge that preserving security is essential to preserving freedom.

POSTSCRIPT

Does the Patriot Act Abridge Essential Freedoms?

Those who deplore the USA Patriot Act are likely to share Nat Hentoff's conviction, expressed in quotations from Benjamin Franklin and Supreme Court Justice Louis Brandeis, that security cannot be obtained by the sacrifice of essential liberty. Defenders of the law will agree with Heather Mac Donald that liberty can be preserved while adopting new weapons in dealing with a new kind of threat to national security, and liberty will be lost if we do not respond effectively.

With the stakes so high and passions so great, it appears to be difficult for partisans on either side to retain civility in assessing the appropriate balance of civil liberty and national security. If we accept the accusations on both sides, rational discussion is impossible. Americans who favor the USA Patriot Act have been accused of being totalitarians who are enemies of civil liberty and individual privacy. Those who oppose many provisions of the law have been slandered in turn as implicitly unpatriotic and blind to all threats that do not originate with the American government.

Elaine Scarry, in "Resolving to Resist" (*Boston Review,* February–March 2004), sympathetically examines the opposition of more than 200 communities whose local governments have in different ways resolved not to assist the federal government in enforcing this law. A series of essays critical of the government's response to terrorism, largely but not exclusively focused on the USA Patriot Act, appear in the Winter 2002 issue of *Human Rights,* published by the American Bar Association. John Podesta, in "USA Patriot Act: The Good, the Bad, and the Sunset," acknowledges that some provisions are necessary, but others infringe on civil liberties and lack protective mechanisms to prevent abuse by the executive.

Robert H. Bork, in "Civil Liberties After 9/11" (*Commentary,* July–August 2003), points out that lawful prisoners of war are held without the right to a lawyer, and unlawful enemy combatants are entitled to even fewer rights. "A judicial system with rights of due process is crucial to a free society, but it is not designed for the protection of enemies engaged in armed conflict against us." Because some controversial features of the law are due to expire, debate will be vigorously renewed.

Renewal of the USA Patriot Act has not ended debate. David Horowitz and John Perazzo warn against what they characterize as "The Unholy Alliance of American Radicals and Islamic Terrorists Against the Patriot Act," in FrontPageMagazine.com, on June 27, 2005. In opposition to the revised law, Paul Craig Roberts opposes the creation of a new federal police force that can arrest without a warrant and other "Unfathomed Dangers in Patriot Act Reauthorization, in Anti-War.com on January 24, 2006.

In September 2007, a federal district court struck down two provisions of the Patriot Act dealing with searches and intelligence gathering, concluding that they violated the Fourth Amendment's protection against unreasonable searches and seizures.

ISSUE 14

Stopping Illegal Immigration: Should Border Security Come First?

YES: Mark Krikorian, from "Comprehensive Immigration Reform II," Testimony Before Senate Committee on the Judiciary (October 18, 2005)

NO: Frank Sharry, from "Comprehensive Immigration Reform II," Testimony Before Senate Committee on the Judiciary (October 18, 2005)

ISSUE SUMMARY

YES: Mark Krikorian, executive director of the Center for Immigration Studies, argues that we have not seriously tried to enforce the laws against illegal aliens, and recommends shrinking the illegal population through consistent and equitable law enforcement.

NO: Frank Sharry, executive director of the National Immigration Forum, contends that the "enforcement only" approach ignores the fact that the United States has an increasingly integrated labor market with Latin America, and recommends a comprehensive approach combining border control with expanded legal channels.

In 1949 a delegation of Native Americans went to Washington to tell lawmakers about the plight of America's original occupants. After meeting with Vice President Alben Barkley, one old Sioux chief delivered a parting word to the vice president. "Young fellow," he said, "let me give you a little advice. Be careful with your immigration laws. We were careless with ours." As America prospered and offered the hope of opportunity and freedom, increasing numbers of immigrants came to the United States.

Between 1870 and 1920, more than 26 million people came to live in the United States. The National Origins Act was adopted in 1924 to restrict the number of new immigrants, ban East Asian immigration, and establish a European quota based on the population of the United States in 1890, when there had been far fewer new arrivals from eastern and southern Europe. In 1965 the national origins formula was abandoned, but strict limits on the number of immigrants were retained. The end of quotas spurred a dramatic increase of immigrants from Central and South America and Asia. Today, Mexico and the rest of Latin America account for the largest number of illegal immigrants. Approximately 57 percent of undocumented immigrants come from Mexico; the rest of Latin America (mainly Central America) accounts for just under 25 percent, while 10 percent come from Asia.

The growing number of illegal immigrants in the 1980s prompted congressional passage of the Immigration Reform and Control Act (IRCA) of 1986, which beefed up border controls, made it illegal for employers to hire undocumented immigrants, and required employers to confirm the legal status of their employees; at the same time, undocumented workers who had entered the United States before 1982 were granted immunity. It was hoped that IRCA's combination of carrots and sticks—tougher border controls, penalties for hiring illegal immigrants, and amnesty for those already here—would bring the illegals "out of the shadows," making them taxpayers and eventually citizens, while at the same time "de-magnifying" the United States as an attraction for further illegal immigration. Unfortunately, events didn't work out that way. At the time of IRCA's passage there were about 5 million illegal immigrants in the United States; today the figure is somewhere between 10 and 12 million.

What went wrong? It depends on whom you ask. For some, the main problem was the amnesty, which, they say, taught those already here that they could break the law with impunity and tempted others in the other side of the border to do the same. For other critics, however, the main problem was that IRCA never properly took account of the huge demand for low-skilled work in certain areas.

Both sides in this debate became increasingly vocal in 2005 and 2006 as Congress wrestled anew with the problem of illegal immigration. Everyone seemed to agree that border controls needed to be strengthened, but those supporting a route to legalization for the millions of undocumented immigrants already here argued that there also needed to be expanded legal channels for those seeking temporary employment in the United States, as well as some means of granting legal recognition for immigrants who had illegally crossed the border years earlier and were now living, working, and raising families in the United States. Critics of these latter proposals were quick to note that they sounded like the failed amnesty provisions of IRCA, but this was disputed by the proponents. They were not calling for *carte blanche* forgiveness, they said, but for fines, a requirement to learn English, and waiting periods of various length before the undocumented could become legalized.

Whatever the outcome of the congressional debate, neither of the clashing positions is likely to fade away any time soon. In the following selections, Mark Krikorian, Executive Director of the Center for Immigration Studies, argues that the best approach is to rigorously enforce the laws against illegal aliens and provide stiff punishments for employers who hire them, while Frank Sharry, Executive Director of the National Immigration Forum, contends that the "enforcement only" approach ignores the fact that the United States has an increasingly integrated labor market with Latin America; he recommends an expanded effort to keep illegal aliens out, together with expanded legal channels for those who are already here.

YES

Mark Krikorian

Comprehensive Immigration Reform II

T here is broad dissatisfaction with the current state of our immigration policy. We have in our country 11 or 12 million illegal aliens among a total immigrant population of 35 million, the largest number in our nation's history and soon to be the largest percentage of the population in our history. Despite misleading reports to the contrary, the pace of immigration is not abating; in the past five years, eight million people from abroad have settled in the United States, about half of them illegally.

How should we deal with the illegal aliens who are here? How should we structure future immigration policy to prevent this situation from recurring? There are two major proposals before this house attempting to answer these questions, one by Senators Kyl and Cornyn, the other from Senators Kennedy and McCain. In addition, there are at least two comprehensive proposals before the other house. And, of course, the Administration has its own proposal. The plans differ widely, but most have some form of legalization (i.e., amnesty) for illegal aliens already here, plus provisions to import large numbers of foreign workers in the future, whether through guestworker programs or large increases in permanent immigration.

Rather than examine the minutiae of the various measures, I want to address some of the fallacies that pervade the discussion of immigration in general, and of amnesty and foreign-worker schemes in particular, in order to offer some principles by which to judge the soundness of the various proposals.

Immigration Is Not Inevitable

The bedrock assumption underlying most of the immigration plans being offered is that the flow of workers from Mexico and elsewhere is unstoppable—a natural phenomenon like the weather or the tides, which we are powerless to influence. Therefore, it is said, managing the flow in an orderly and lawful manner is preferable to the alternative.

On the surface, the flow of Mexican immigration may indeed seem inevitable; it is very large, rapidly growing, and spreading throughout the country. But a longer view shows that this flow has been created in large part by

Hearing on "Comprehensive Immigration Reform II", October 18, 2005. Senate Committee on the Judiciary.

government policies, both in the United States and Mexico. And, government policy having created the migration flows, government policy can interrupt the flows, though a social phenomenon like this is naturally more difficult to stop than to start.

Migration is often discussed in terms of pushes and pulls—poverty, corruption, oppression, and general societal dysfunction impel people to leave their homelands, while high wages and expanded economic and social opportunities attract people to this country. While true, this analysis is incomplete because it overlooks the connection between the sending country and the receiving country.

No one wakes up in Timbuktu and says, "Today I will move to Milwaukee!"—migration takes place by way of networks of relatives, friends, acquaintances, and fellow countrymen, and few people immigrate to a place where these connections are absent. Consider two countries on the other side of the planet—the Philippines and Indonesia. These neighbors both have large, poor populations and share many cultural similarities, yet there are more than one million Filipino immigrants in the United States and only a handful of Indonesians, and annual immigration from the Philippines is routinely 40–50 times greater than immigration from Indonesia. Why? Because the ties between the United States and the Philippines are numerous and deep, our having ruled the country for 50 years and maintained an extensive military presence there for another 50 years. On the other hand, the United States has very few ties to Indonesia, whose people tend to migrate to the Netherlands, its former colonial ruler.

At the end of the Mexican War in 1848, there were only a small number of Mexican colonists living in the Southwest, many of whom soon returned to Mexico with the Mexican government's assistance. The immigration of Mexican workers began in a small way with the construction of the railroads beginning in the 1870s and later with the expansion of other industries. But the process of mass migration northward to the United States, and the development of the networks which made further immigration possible, began in earnest during the Mexican Revolution of 1910–1920. The Cristero rebellion of the late 1920s was the last major armed conflict in Mexico and was centered in the states of west-central Mexico; partly to prevent further trouble, the newly consolidated Mexico City regime adopted a policy of encouraging emigration from these very states. The power of government-fostered migration networks is clear from the fact that even today these same states account for a disproportionate share of Mexican immigrants to the United States.

On the U.S. side, federal policies that established migration networks between the United States and Mexico arguably began in the 1920s, when Congress specifically excluded the Western Hemisphere from the newly enacted immigration caps so as not to limit the flow of Mexican immigrants. Then in 1942, the Bracero Program to import Mexican farmworkers was started under the cover of World War II, and it continued until 1964. About 4.6 million contracts were issued to Mexican workers (many were repeat contracts for workers who returned several times, so that an estimated one to two million individuals participated). By creating vast new networks connecting the United States and Mexico, the Bracero Program launched the mass illegal immigration we are still experiencing today. Illegal immigration networks were reinforced by the IRCA amnesty of 1986, which granted legal status to nearly three million illegal aliens, at least two-thirds of whom were Mexican. This new legal status conferred by the federal government generated even more immigration, legal and illegal, as confirmed by a 2000 INS report. And the federal government's effective abandonment of interior immigration enforcement has served to further promote immigration from Mexico.

As a result of this series of government decisions, the flow of Mexican immigration to the United States is very large. The Mexican immigrant population ballooned from less than 800,000 in 1970 to nearly eight million in 2000, and is more than 10 million today, most having arrived since 1990. This rapid growth has created a snowball effect through the reinforcement of old networks and the establishment of new ones. If present trends continue, within a few years Mexico will have sent more immigrants to the United States in 100 years than Germany (currently the leading historical source of immigrants) has in more than 300 years.

Far from being an inevitable process with deep historical roots, then, mass immigration from Mexico is a relatively recent phenomenon created by government policies. The same is true for most other sources of immigration to the United States, such as Cuba, India, Central America, Russia, Vietnam, and elsewhere.

We Have Not Seriously Tried to Enforce the Law

A supporter of a guestworker/amnesty program might respond that while interrupting immigration flows may be possible in theory, it cannot be accomplished in practice, and the proof of that is that we have tried to enforce our immigration laws and failed.

We have done no such thing. Increases in immigration enforcement over the past decade have been confined almost exclusively to patrolling the border; as important as that is, enforcement of the immigration laws inside the country has declined precipitously, and without such a combined strategy, success is impossible. In particular, enforcement of the ban on hiring illegal aliens, the centerpiece of any effort to regain control of our chaotic immigration system, has been all but abandoned. We might date the abandonment from INS raids in Georgia during the Vidalia onion harvest in 1998, which caused large numbers of illegal aliens—knowingly hired by the farmers—to abandon the fields to avoid arrest. By the end of the week, both of the state's senators and three congressmen had sent an outraged letter to Washington complaining that the INS "does not understand the needs of America's farmers," and that was the end of that.

So, the INS tried out a "kinder, gentler" means of enforcing the law, which fared no better. Rather than conduct raids on individual employers, Operation Vanguard in 1998–99 sought to identify illegal workers at all meat-packing plants in Nebraska through audits of personnel records. The INS then asked to interview those employees who appeared to be unauthorized—and the illegals ran off. The procedure was remarkably successful, and was meant to be repeated every two or three months until the plants were weaned from their dependence on illegal labor.

Local law enforcement officials were very pleased with the results, but employers and politicians vociferously criticized the very idea of enforcing the immigration law. Gov. Mike Johanns organized a task force to oppose the operation; the meat packers and the ranchers hired former Gov. Ben Nelson to lobby on their behalf; and, in Washington, Sen. Chuck Hagel (R-Neb.) pressured the Justice Department to stop. They succeeded, the operation was ended, and the senior INS official who had thought it up in the first place was forced into early retirement.

The INS got the message and developed a new interior enforcement policy that gave up trying to actually control immigration and focused almost entirely on the important, but narrow, issues of criminal aliens and smugglers. As INS policy director Robert Bach told *The New York Times* in a March 9, 2000, story appropriately entitled "I.N.S. Is Looking the Other Way as Illegal Immigrants Fill Jobs": "It is just the market at work, drawing people to jobs, and the INS has chosen to concentrate its actions on aliens who are a danger to the community."

The enforcement statistics tell the story in a nutshell: According to the GAO, even in 1999, only 417 notices of intent to fine were levied against employers who knowingly hired illegal aliens; but in 2004, the number of employer fines was 3. That's "three". Nationwide.

Tony Blankley, the *Washington Times'* editorial-page editor, summed it up last year:

> I might agree with the president's proposals if they followed, rather than preceded, a failed Herculean, decades-long national effort to secure our borders. If, after such an effort, it was apparent that we simply could not control our borders, then, as a practical man I would try to make the best of a bad situation. But such an effort has not yet been made.

Amnesties and Foreign-Worker Programs Can't Stop Illegal Immigration

Even if it is possible to enforce the law, wouldn't accommodating the immigration flow through a guestworker program or increased issuance of green cards (plus an amnesty for those already here) be another way of eliminating illegal immigration?

No.

Putting aside their other effects, amnesties and increased immigration (whether permanent or "temporary") simply cannot eliminate illegal immigration. To begin with expansions in immigration: The sense seems to be that the economy demands a certain amount of foreign labor each year, but that the various legal channels only admit a portion of the needed flow, with the rest entering illegally. It would follow, then, that establishing a legal means for those foreign workers "forced" to come illegally would all but eliminate ordinary illegal immigration.

This represents a simplistic understanding of both the economy and of immigration. Immigration always creates more immigration and, as the discussion above about Bracero Program made clear, the proliferation of connections created by the arrival of workers from abroad will continually expand the pool of people who have the means to come here, leading to more immigration, legal and illegal. In fact, a large body of sociological research shows that one of the best predictors of a person's likelihood to immigrate to the United States illegally is whether he has legal immigrant family members already here.

This is why the momentum of immigration continues regardless of economic circumstances; the economy today no longer serves as a regulator of immigration levels. For instance, if we examine the four years before and after 2000, we see that the first period, 1996–2000, was a time of dramatic job growth and rapid expansion, while 2000–2004 saw slower economic growth and weaker labor demand. Immigrant unemployment grew significantly during that period, as did the number of unemployed immigrants. And yet immigration actually increased slightly, from 5.5 million arrivals during the first period and 6.1 million new immigrants during the second.

The experience with amnesties is no different. About 2.7 million people were legalized in the late 1980s and early 1990s as a result of the amnesties contained in the Immigration Reform and Control Act (IRCA) of 1986. But INS figures show that by the beginning of 1997 those former illegal aliens had been entirely replaced by new illegal aliens, and that the unauthorized population again stood at more than 5 million, just as before the amnesty.

In fact, INS estimates show that the 1986 amnesty almost certainly increased illegal immigration, as the relatives of newly legalized illegals came to the United States to join their family members. The flow of illegals grew dramatically during the years of the amnesty to more than 800,000 a year, before dropping back down to "only" 500,000 a year.

To sum up: If increased admission of foreign workers served to limit illegal immigration, how can it be that all three—legal immigration, "temporary" work visas, and illegal immigration—have all mushroomed together? In 1974, legal immigration was less than 400,000; in 2004, it was nearly 1 million. In 1981, about 45,000 "temporary workers and trainees" were admitted; in 2004, the number was 684,000. Twenty years ago, the illegal population was estimated to be 5 million; today it is 11–12 million, even after nearly 3 million illegals were amnestied.

Whatever other arguments might be made for them, neither amnesties nor foreign-worker programs are a solution to illegal immigration. . . .

No Amnesty or Foreign-Worker Program Is Administratively Feasible

In any large government program, plans on paper must translate into policies on the ground. Any amnesty or foreign-worker program would require extensive background checks as well as simple management of the program—processing applications, interviewing applicants, checking arrivals, tracking whether a worker is still employed, enforcing the departure of those who are supposed to leave. Supporters of the various amnesty and foreign-worker proposals have assumed that administering these programs would not be a problem.

But it is not explained how the immigration bureaus within the Department of Homeland Security, already choking on massive workloads, are supposed to be able to accomplish these goals. The GAO has reported that the backlog of pending immigration applications of various kinds was at 6.2 million at the end of FY 2003, up 59 percent from the beginning of FY 2001. It has since shrunk to "only" 4.1 million.

Because of the enormity of the backlog, the immigration service often issues work permits and travel documents to green-card applicants right when they submit their forms, knowing that it will be years before anyone actually reads the application. What's more, the immigration bureaus are trying to implement vast new tracking systems for foreign students and foreign visitors. The crush of work has been so severe, that many important statutory deadlines have been missed.

And the context for all this is a newly created Department of Homeland Security, which incorporates pieces of the old Immigration and Naturalization Service and many other agencies in various combinations. To add to DHS's well-known management problems, all three immigration bureaus are currently without a head.

The registration and screening and tracking of millions of additional aliens for amnesty or foreign-worker programs would result in complete institutional paralysis and breakdown. After all, the workload created by any such program would be larger than the total number of visas issued annually worldwide by the State Department (approximately 5 million), and many, many times larger than the total number of green cards issued each year by DHS (around 1 million). None of this is to pin blame on the bureaucrats charged with implementing congressional mandates. Rather, the immigration proposals themselves are the problem, because they are not based on any real-world assessment of the administrative capacity of the immigration agencies.

Massive Fraud Is a Security Threat

In addition to widespread paralysis, overloading administrative agencies with the vast and complicated new responsibilities of an amnesty and foreign-worker program would cause staggering levels of fraud, as overworked bureaucrats are pressured to rubber-stamp applications.

In fact, even without the tsunami of paperwork that new immigration programs would cause, fraud is already dangerously widespread. Stephen Dinan of *The Washington Times* reported earlier this month that internal investigators at U.S. Citizenship and Immigration Services (USCIS) have uncovered thousands of cases of misconduct, including bribery, exchanging immigration benefits for sex, and being influenced by foreign governments. And new charges are being added at the rate of 50 per week.

Nor is this a new development. A January 2002 GAO report addressed the consequences of such administrative overload. It found that the crush of work has created an organizational culture in the immigration services bureau where "staff are rewarded for the timely handling of petitions rather than for careful scrutiny of their merits." The pressure to move things through the system has led to "rampant" and "pervasive" fraud, with one official estimating that 20 to 30 percent of all applications involve fraud. The GAO concluded that "the goal of providing immigration benefits in a timely manner to those who are legally entitled to them may conflict with the goal of preserving the integrity of the legal immigration system."

This last point was reinforced in an especially lurid way by the last big amnesty program, which was part of the Immigration Reform and Control Act (IRCA) of 1986. As Paul Virtue, then general counsel of the INS, testified before Congress in 1999, "the provisions of IRCA were subject to widespread abuse, especially the Special Agricultural Worker (SAW) program." There were nearly 1.3 million applications for the SAW amnesty—double the total number of foreign farm workers usually employed in the United States in any given year, and up to six times as many applicants as congressional sponsors of the scheme assured skeptics would apply. INS officials told *The New York Times* that the majority of applicants in certain offices were clearly fraudulent, but that they didn't have the means to prove the fraud. Some women came to interviews with long, painted nails, while others claimed to have picked strawberries off trees. One woman in New Jersey who owned a five-acre garden plot certified that more than 1,000 illegal aliens had worked on her land.

This is a problem not just because it offends our sensibilities but because ineligible people will get legal status—people like Mahmud Abouhalima, a cabbie in New York, who got amnesty as a farmworker under the 1986 law and went on to help lead the first World Trade Center attack. Having an illegal-alien terrorist in your country is bad; having one with legal status is far worse, since he can work and travel freely, as Abouhalima did, going to Afghanistan to receive terrorist training only after he got amnesty.

And we cannot safely assume that at least those illegal aliens who have snuck across the Mexican border are no threat, since they want only to wash our dishes. For example, Iraqi-born smuggler George Tajirian pled guilty in 2001 to forging an alliance with a Mexican immigration officer to smuggle "Palestinian, Jordanian, Syrian, Iraqi, Yemeni, and other illegal aliens through Mexico and into the United States." And in late 2003, the former Mexican consul in Beirut was arrested for her involvement in a similar enterprise.

Another amnesty or large foreign-worker program is guaranteed—guaranteed—to give legal residence to a future terrorist.

A Third Way—Neither Roundups Nor Amnesty

The final selling point for supporters of amnesty and foreign-worker programs is that there are only two options available to us—either massive roundups and a huge burst of deportations, or some form of legalization. And since it's clear there's no way we can remove 11 million people all at once, the only option available to us is amnesty, however it might be labeled or camouflaged.

But there is a third way that rejects this false choice, and it is the only approach that can actually work: Shrink the illegal population through consistent, across-the-board enforcement of the immigration law. By limiting the settlement of new illegals, by increasing deportations to the extent possible, and, most importantly, by increasing the number of illegals already here who give up and deport themselves, the United States can bring about an annual decrease in the illegal-alien population, rather than allowing it to continually increase. The result would be attrition of the illegal population, shrinking it over a period of several years to a manageable nuisance, rather than today's looming crisis. This is analogous to the approach a corporation might take to downsizing a bloated workforce: a hiring freeze, some layoffs, plus new incentives to encourage excess workers to leave on their own.

Churn in the illegal population. This strategy of attrition is not a pipe dream, or the idle imaginings of a policy wonk. The central insight is that there is already significant churn in the illegal population, which can be used to speed the decline in overall numbers. According to a 2003 report from the Immigration and Naturalization Service, thousands of people are subtracted from the illegal population each year. From 1995 to 1999, an average of 165,000 a year went back home on their own after residing here for at least a year; the same number got some kind of legal status, about 50,000 were deported, and 25,000 died, for a total of more than 400,000 people each year subtracted from the resident illegal population. The problem is that the average annual inflow of new illegal aliens over that same period was nearly 800,000, swamping the outflow and creating an average annual increase of close to 400,000.

A strategy of attrition would seek to reverse this relationship, so that the outflow from the illegal population is much larger than the number of new illegal settlers from abroad. This would be a measured approach to the problem, one that doesn't aspire to an immediate, magical solution to a long-brewing crisis, but also does not simply surrender, as the amnesty and foreign-worker proposals do.

There are a number of real-world examples of successful enforcement. During the first several years after the passage of the IRCA, illegal crossings from Mexico fell precipitously, as prospective illegals waited to see if we were serious. Apprehensions of aliens by the Border Patrol—an imperfect measure but the only one available—fell from more than 1.7 million in FY 1986 to under a million in 1989. But then the flow began to increase again as the deterrent effect of the hiring ban dissipated, when word got back that we were not serious about enforcement and that the system could be easily evaded through the use of inexpensive phony documents.

That showed that reducing new illegal immigration is possible; but what about increasing the number of illegals already here who give up and leave? That, too, has already been demonstrated. After the 9/11 attacks, immigration authorities undertook a "Special Registration" program for visitors from Islamic countries. The affected nation with the largest illegal-alien population was Pakistan, with an estimated 26,000 illegals here in 2000. Once it became clear that the government was getting more serious about enforcing the immigration law—at least with regard to Middle Easterners—Pakistani illegals started leaving on their own in large numbers. The Pakistani embassy estimated that more than 15,000 of its illegal aliens left the United States, and the *Washington Post* reported the "disquieting" fact that in Brooklyn's Little Pakistan the mosque was one-third empty, business was down, there were fewer want ads in the local Urdu-language paper, and "For Rent" signs sprouted everywhere.

And in an inadvertent enforcement initiative, the Social Security Administration in 2002 sent out almost a million "no-match" letters to employers who filed W-2s with information that was inconsistent with SSA's records. The intention was to clear up misspellings, name changes, and other mistakes that had caused a large amount of money paid into the system to go uncredited. But, of course, most of the problem was caused by illegal aliens lying to their employers, and thousands of illegals quit or were fired when they were found out. The effort was so successful at denying work to illegals that business and immigrant-rights groups organized to stop it and won a 90 percent reduction in the number of letters to be sent out.

A policy of attrition through enforcement would have two main components: an increase in conventional enforcement—arrests, prosecutions, deportations, asset seizures, etc.—plus expanded use of verification of legal status at a variety of important points, to make it as difficult and unpleasant as possible to live here illegally.

Conventional enforcement. As to the first, the authorities—from the White House on down—need to make an unambiguous commitment to immigration enforcement. There must be an end to the climate of impunity for border-jumping, and illegal employment, and fake documents, and immigration fraud. To use only one example of the longstanding lack of commitment, aliens who repeatedly sneak across the border are supposed to be prosecuted and jailed, and the Border Patrol unveiled a new digital fingerprint system in the mid '90s to make tracking of repeat crossers possible. The problem is that short-staffed U.S. attorneys' offices kept increasing the number of apprehensions needed before they would prosecute, to avoid actually having to prosecute at all.

It would be hard to exaggerate the demoralizing effect that such disregard for the law has on immigration enforcement agents. Conversely, the morale of immigration workers would soar in the wake of a real commitment to law enforcement.

Among measures that would facilitate enforcement: hiring more U.S. Attorneys and judges in border areas, to allow for more prosecutions; expanding our laughably small Border Patrol which, even with recent increases, is barely one-quarter the size of the New York Police Department and is only able to deploy an average of one agent per mile along the Mexican border during any given shift; promoting enhanced cooperation between federal immigration authorities and state and local police; and seizing the assets, however modest, of apprehended illegal aliens; expanding detention capacity; streamlining the immigration appeals process to deport aliens more quickly.

Firewalls. Even if we were somehow to increase deportations ten-fold, most of the decline in the illegal population would have to come through self-deportation, illegal aliens giving up and going home. Unlike at the visa office or the border crossing, once aliens are inside the United States, there's no physical site to exercise control, no choke point at which to examine whether someone should be admitted. The solution is to create "virtual choke points"—events that are necessary for life in a modern society but are infrequent enough not to bog down everyone's daily business. Another analogy for this concept is to firewalls in computer systems—filters that people could pass through only if their legal status is verified. The objective is not mainly to identify illegal aliens for arrest (though that will always be a tool) but rather to make it as difficult as possible for illegal aliens to live a normal life here.

This is the rationale for the prohibition against employing illegal aliens—people have to work, so requiring proof of legal status upon starting a job would serve as an important firewall. Congress instituted this firewall tactic in 1986 when in prohibited the employment of illegal aliens; but in the absence of a mandatory verification mechanism, such a system could not succeed. The immigration service has already developed a verification system which has proven both workable and popular with participating businesses (including my own Center for Immigration Studies). Building on this fledgling system, we need to find other instances in which legal status might be verified, and thus illegals barred, such as getting a driver's license, registering an automobile, opening a bank account, applying for a car loan or a mortgage, getting a business or occupational license, and obtaining government services of any kind.

An important element in this firewall tactic is secure documentation. By enacting the Real ID Act, Congress has already taken a step toward establishing uniform standards for state driver's licenses, which serve as our nation's de facto national identification system. At least as important is to formally prohibit acceptance of consular registration cards, chiefly Mexico's "matricula consular" card, which functions as an illegal-alien ID; when accepted by U.S. jurisdictions and companies as a valid ID, it enables illegal aliens to pass through many firewalls.

An important point about using verification of legal status as a way to downsize the illegal population is that its effects would be felt gradually, rather than all at once. A new, functional verification system for employment, for instance, would be applied mainly to new hires (though employers should have the option of checking existing employees as well). The same is true for getting a driver's license or a mortgage—these are not things people do every day, so the effects of verifying legal status would unfold over a period of time.

Mr. Chairman, you and your colleagues should deliberate on immigration policy secure in the knowledge that reasserting control over immigration requires no land mines, no machine guns, no tattoos—none of the cartoonish images invoked by opponents of tight immigration controls. All that is needed is the consistent application of ordinary law-enforcement tools—plus a rejection of measures that would undermine enforcement, such as amnesties or expanded foreign-worker programs. I look forward to any questions you might have.

Frank Sharry

 **NO**

Comprehensive Immigration Reform II

The American people are right to demand that Congress and the Administration take effective action to restore the rule of law to our nation's immigration system. The evidence of the system's dysfunction is all around us: young men and women die gruesome deaths in southwestern deserts as they attempt to enter the U.S. in search of work; fake document merchants and criminal smugglers turn huge profits in networks that one day might be exploited not by those seeking work in our economy but by those seeking to attack our nation; local community tensions simmer and sometimes explode as housing gets stretched, schools experience change, and language differences emerge; immigrant families remain divided for years, even decades, by restrictive admissions policies and inefficient processing; immigrant workers afraid of being discovered and deported are subject to abuse and exploitation by unscrupulous employers seeking to gain an unfair advantage over law-abiding competitors; meanwhile, public frustration mounts as the federal government seems incapable of mobilizing the political leadership and enacting the policy changes to fix the system once and for all.

Mr. Chairman, I urge you and the Committee to lead the way and take effective action in this Congress. The country is crying out for leadership on this issue and a solution to this problem. Immigration policy is fundamentally and constitutionally a matter for the federal government. States and local communities are understandably frustrated with the effects of a broken immigration system, but they cannot and do not set national immigration policy. It is up to Congress and the Administration to rise to the occasion. . . .

Fixing the broken immigration system requires sizing up its complexity and its dimensions. The numbers tell part of the story. Some 11 million undocumented immigrants now live and work in the United States. That means that almost one-third of all the immigrants in America lives here without government authorization. Fourteen million people, including some 5 million kids, live in households headed by an undocumented immigrant. One out of 20 workers in the nation's labor force is living and working here illegally. Two-thirds of them have arrived in the last decade. More than half are from Mexico. More than 80% are from Latin America and the Caribbean. America's backyard is showing up on America's front porch.

Hearing on "Comprehensive Immigration Reform II", October 18, 2005. Senate Committee on the Judiciary.

Illegal immigration is no longer a niche issue affecting a handful of gateway states and cities. It has gone nationwide. Consider the five states with the fastest growing populations of undocumented immigrants: North Carolina, Utah, Colorado, Arizona, and Idaho. In fact, a wide swath of the nation's heartland, from the old South stretching up through the Mountain states to the Northwest, is undergoing a remarkable demographic transformation with little to no recent experience to draw on to respond to it.

Moreover, most new undocumented immigrants appear to be here to stay. The vast majority no longer fit the stereotype of the migrant male on his own here to do temporary work before returning home. Today, 70% live with spouses and/or children. And only 3% work in agriculture. The vast majority are employed in year-round service sector jobs. After all, the jobs are plentiful. More than half the new jobs created in the American economy require hard work, not multiple diplomas. Meanwhile, young native-born workers are smaller in number, better educated than ever, and more interested in office work than manual labor. Consequently, much of the nation's demand for housekeepers, childcare workers, landscapers, protein processors, busboys, cooks, janitors, dry wallers, and construction workers is met by a steady flow of some 500,000 undocumented migrants who enter and settle in America each year.

Which begs the question: Since the U.S. has a legal immigration system, why don't these workers from Mexico and elsewhere simply wait in line and enter with legal visas? Answer: what legal visas? There are virtually none available for these workers. While the labor market demands an estimated 500,000 full-time low-skilled service jobs a year, our immigration laws supply just 5,000 permanent visas for workers to fill these jobs. And this tiny category is so backlogged it has been rendered useless. As the Immigration Policy Center recently pointed out, of the other 15 immigrant visa categories available for employment and training, only two are available to industries that require little or no formal training. These two categories (H2A and H2B) are small and seasonal. In addition to the enormous mismatch between labor market realities and our government's immigration policy, our family visa lines are so backlogged that it can take a decade for spouses to be reunited, legally. Not surprisingly, many stop waiting and cross the border illegally in order to reunite with their loved ones.

What to do? Some argue that the solution is to simply enforce the laws we already have on the books. And while we certainly need tighter, more targeted, and more effective enforcement as part of a comprehensive overhaul, the fact is that over the past two decades the "enforcement only" approach has failed miserably. . . . Since 1986 the border patrol budget has increased tenfold in value. This beefing up of border enforcement has been augmented by tough restrictions on immigrant access to employment, public services, and due process protections.

And yet this unprecedented increase in enforcement has coincided with an unprecedented increase in illegal immigration.

Why hasn't "enforcement only" worked to stem illegal immigration? Because our current approach to immigration and border security policy fails to recognize that the United States has an increasingly integrated labor market with Latin America. In much the same way that we used to see workers from rural areas in the South migrate to the urban North to fill manufacturing jobs, we now see workers from rural areas south of the border migrating to all areas of the U.S. to fill service jobs. Our failure to account for this fact of life leads to a failure of policy. Instead of building a workable regulatory regime to govern what is essentially a market-driven labor migration, we keep legal channels severely restricted and then wonder why workers and their families have nowhere to go but into the clutches of a migration black market dominated by smugglers, fake document merchants, and unscrupulous employers.

Dan Griswold of the Cato Institute sums it up this way: "Demand for low-skilled labor continues to grow in the United States while the domestic supply of suitable workers inexorably declines—yet U.S. immigration law contains virtually no legal channel through which low-skilled immigrant workers can enter the country to fill that gap. The result is an illegal flow of workers characterized by more permanent and less circular migration, smuggling, document fraud, deaths at the border, artificially depressed wages, and threats to civil liberties." He adds, "American immigration laws are colliding with reality, and reality is winning."

Griswold is right. We will not be able to restore respect for the rule of law in our immigration system until we restore respect for the law of supply and demand. Instead of "enforcement only" or "enforcement first," we need an "enforcement plus" approach.

I recall the first time I came face to face with the reality of an integrated labor market and the futility of an "enforcement only" strategy. In the late 1990's I accompanied a delegation that visited Tixla ("Teesh-la"), a "sending community" located in Mexico. Most of its sons and daughters had left and migrated illegally to Chicago to fill available service jobs in construction, landscaping, hospitality, and childcare. Those left behind consisted mostly of women, children, and the elderly. The workers used to come back and forth, at least for visits, but this had mostly stopped due to the press of their multiple jobs up north and the risks associated with re-crossing the border illegally. The townspeople were proud to show us the new school and basketball court which had recently been built with pooled remittances. And there, right there in the middle of the basketball court, was a huge replica of the logo for the Chicago Bulls.

That's when it hit me. Tixla, a dusty, rural town south of Mexico City, is a bedroom community for Chicago. We may not think of it that way, but it is a 21st century fact. The town produces the workers needed to fill newly-created service sector jobs in the Chicago area. There is plenty of work available just up the road, and these workers are willing to risk their lives to make the commute.

Needed: A New Perspective and a Comprehensive Strategy

Like so many other public policy debates, the highly-charged immigration debate is often polarized and paralyzed by an "either/or" framework. The tit-for-tat goes something like this: you are either for immigrants or for control;

you are either for higher levels or lower levels; you are either for closed borders or open borders; you are either for lax policies or tough policies. This narrow and lopsided framework is a trap that obscures realistic solutions.

What's needed is a "both/and" approach that recognizes the reality of an integrated labor market with Latin America and the legitimate U.S. demand for operational control of its borders in a post 9/11 world. Such an approach seeks to integrate seemingly contradictory elements into a comprehensive package; a package that combines expanded enforcement strategies and expanded legal channels for those entering the U.S. to work and join families and expanded pathways to legal status and citizenship for undocumented immigrants already living and working in the U.S. We need to change our immigration laws so that they are enforceable and enforce them effectively.

Senator Edward Kennedy put it this way in recent testimony before this Committee: "The past debate has long been polarized between those who want more enforcement and those who want more visas. But to repair what's broken, we need to combine increased enforcement and increased legality. Better border control and better treatment of immigrants are not inconsistent—they are two sides of the same coin."

This new perspective was first promoted and popularized by Presidents Bush and Fox in their 2001 migration negotiations. The two presidents imagined a system based on improved border security and widened legal channels. The idea was, and is, to recognize, regularize, and regulate the status of workers who are either coming from south of the border to jobs in the U.S. or already here working and contributing to our economy. The goal? Make the healthy, positive, and predictable movement of workers to available jobs safe, legal, and orderly.

The President deserves considerable credit for getting this "big idea" and sticking with it. In January 2004 he announced principles for immigration reform that, although somewhat vague and incomplete, captured this new perspective. And this vision of immigration reform has spawned two significant immigration reform proposals in the Senate. One is authored by Senators McCain and Kennedy. The other is authored by Senators Cornyn and Kyl. Both proposals are serious and go beyond an "enforcement only" approach. However, in our view only the McCain-Kennedy bill is both fully comprehensive and workable. That is why the organization I direct has joined with constituencies from across the political spectrum and across the country to endorse the Secure America and Orderly Immigration Act of 2005.

Secure America: A Cure for What Ails Us

Secure America is not perfect, but it is an excellent draft that should serve as the basis for fixing our broken immigration system. Specifically, the bill combines 1) enhanced enforcement to ensure the reformed immigration system is effectively policed; 2) widened legal channels for the future flow of workers and families; 3) a workable solution for the 11 million undocumented immigrants currently working and living in the United States; and 4) support for the successful integration of newcomers in the communities where they settle.

The key to effective enforcement is to augment our border enforcement efforts with a system that ensures that all workers hired in the United States are in our country legally. The bill accomplishes this by building an electronic worker verification system (the bill contemplates credit card swipe machines, but for social security cards, drivers' licenses, or immigration documents, and only at the point of hire) combined with tough sanctions for employers who attempt to end-run the new system. I predict that responsible employers will support it as long as the verification system is functional and the new system is combined with legal channels for workers here and those needed in the future. I predict that unscrupulous employers—those that benefit from the dysfunctional status quo—will oppose it.

The keys to making the admissions system realistic, controlled, and workable are a) to provide enough visas for the expected future flow of workers and families; and b) to avoid the exploitation and abuses of old-style guest worker programs. Secure America accomplishes the first by creating 400,000 worker visas a year and increasing family reunification visas so that the current illegal flow will be funneled into a legal one while being fair to those from around the world. It tackles the second by requiring employers to pay newly admitted workers the same wages as similarly-situated workers, and by mostly de-linking workers' status from employer say-so. For example, workers on temporary visas (three year visas, renewable) will be able to "vote with their feet" and change jobs without threatening their immigration status. After four years in the country, such workers will be able to self-petition for permanent residence—rather than having to ask for the blessing of a particular employer.

The key to putting migration on legal footing once and for all is finding a way for the 11 million or so undocumented immigrants to come out of the shadows voluntarily and transition to legal status. Secure America addresses this controversial issue head on. It offers incentives for undocumented immigrants already here to come forward, register with the government, submit to criminal, security, and health screenings, pay a hefty fine, study English and civics, and clear up their taxes as a way to eventually earn permanent residency. Immigrants who meet these requirements can apply for permanent residence after six years, and become eligible for citizenship in 11 years at the earliest. And this component interacts with the family reunification provisions such that those waiting in the queue outside the U.S. secure permanent residence before those previously undocumented immigrants who obtain temporary status.

Critics label this process of registration and earned legalization an "amnesty." Senator Kennedy rightly objects that "there is no free pass, no automatic pardon, no trip to the front of the line." The *Wall Street Journal* editorial page, which I suspect rarely lines up with the senior Massachusetts Senator, agrees: "This amnesty charge may be potent as a political slogan, but it becomes far less persuasive when you examine its real-world implications. If paying a fine isn't good enough for illegals already here, what are the restrictionists proposing? Mass arrests, raids on job-creating businesses, or deportations? . . . . Those who wave the 'no amnesty' flag are actually encouraging a larger underground illegal population. The only reform that has a chance to succeed is one that recognizes the reality that 10 or so million illegal aliens already work in the U.S. and are vital to the economy and their communities."

Finally, the bill promotes the successful integration of new immigrants into local communities. Immigration to America has worked throughout our history because newcomers have been encouraged to become new Americans. Secure America takes steps to renew this commitment by increasing English classes for adult immigrants, citizenship promotion and preparation, and the legal security immigrant workers need to move up the economic ladder. In fact, it's worth noting that when 3 million undocumented immigrants became legal immigrants some 20 years ago, their wages increased by 14% over 5 years— they were no longer afraid to speak up or change jobs—and their productivity increased dramatically—they studied English and improved their skills through training. The bill also deals with a longstanding and legitimate complaint from state and local governments by reimbursing costs related to health care and other public services.

The bill certainly has its faults and its critics. The immigration enforcement provisions are strong but will need to be strengthened if we are to ensure immigrant workers and families use widened legal channels and no others. Similarly, the bill aims to construct a temporary worker program that adequately protects both native and immigrant workers alike, but will probably need to be tweaked to fully realize this objective. After all, the goal of immigration reform should be nothing less than to restore the rule of law—both to our immigration system and to low-wage labor markets. And unfortunately, the bill does not adequately address the acknowledged long-term solution to the migration challenge: economic development in sending nations and communities. It is my hope that this session's immigration reform debate will serve as a stepping stone to, if not a venue for, a much-needed review of trade, aid, and development policies in the Americas.

Overall, though, the bill's premise is brilliant and its promise viable: take migration out of the black market and bring it under the rule of law; funnel the illegal flow into legal channels; increase the legality of the migration that is occurring, rather than increase the numbers of those who enter; get control of the flow so we get control of our border; bring undocumented immigrants out of the shadows and under the protection of our laws; know who is in our country and who is entering it; shift from repressing migration ineffectively to regulating migration intelligently; turn the broken status quo into a functioning, regulated system; drain the swamp of fake documents and criminal smugglers; vetted airport arrivals instead of deaths in the desert; families united rather than divided for decades; verification mechanisms that work and fake documents that don't; legal workers and an equal playing field for honest employers; equal labor rights for all rather than a race to the bottom for most. In sum, this bill represents a 21st century solution for a 21st century challenge.

The Cornyn-Kyl Bill: Right Direction, But Falls Short

The proposal introduced recently by Senators John Cornyn and Jon Kyl is a serious bill. And Senator Cornyn in particular has distinguished himself recently by his eloquent diagnosis of our broken immigration system. He has repeatedly said that the only way to solve the immigration dilemma is to combine tougher enforcement with a legal regime that deals realistically both with those entering our nation and those already here.

Unfortunately, the bill as introduced is not workable. Instead of offering carrots to draw the 11 million out of the shadows so they register with the government, submit to screenings, pay a fine, and get in line for eventual permanent residency, it presents mostly sticks that would end up with most undocumented immigrants opting to remain in the shadows. Instead of reuniting families in a more timely fashion and keeping nuclear families together, the bill fails to address existing backlogs and instead would most likely result in more families split between different countries for longer periods of time. Instead of ensuring that immigrant workers are treated equally so that both low-wage workers and law-abiding employers benefit, the bill would likely end up favoring employers who undercut their competitors by hiring short-term guest workers. Instead of providing for a stable workforce and promoting citizenship, the bill threatens to force workers out of the country or out of their jobs, and provides no meaningful path to citizenship.

Nevertheless, the authors have rightly steered clear of an "enforcement only" or "enforcement first" approach and have developed a number of ideas worthy of consideration and inclusion in a Senate Judiciary Committee bill. It is my hope and recommendation that this Committee, led by its Chairman, will start with the McCain-Kennedy template and include the best of the proposals before it in a way that builds momentum and support in the full Senate for workable comprehensive reform.

Final Remarks

We at the National Immigration Forum have been working on challenges related to immigration policy for more than 20 years. We understand how hard it is to fashion immigration reform that can pass Congress and work on the ground once enacted. We are fully prepared to support and fight for a combination of tough and smart enforcement measures if combined with simultaneous reforms to our admissions policies that bring undocumented immigrants out of the shadows and provide a sufficient number of worker and family reunification visas for the future flow. But we cannot and will not support proposals that have no realistic chance of working once implemented. Our stand is that we not only get it done, but that we get it done right.

But we are optimistic. We believe this is our generation's best shot at enacting workable reform. As a nation we seem poised to moved beyond the old debate—characterized by simplistic and shallow prescriptions of the past, the non-solution, sound bite-driven "get tough and be done with it" approach. The nation is ready to take part in a new debate, one that takes all of the moving parts into full consideration and at the same time. The old debate suggests that we have to choose between being a nation of immigrants or a nation of laws. The new debate recognizes that the only way to be either is to be both.

POSTSCRIPT

Stopping Illegal Immigration: Should Border Security Come First?

Few issues arouse such contradictory emotions as does immigration. Americans are proud of their immigrant past because they are all immigrants or the descendants of immigrants. Yet they are also concerned about how the newest immigrants, especially those who are coming here illegally, may affect American culture and values. Will their presence and growing numbers encourage others to break the law? Will they live in ethnic enclaves, finding it unnecessary to learn English or respect American traditions? Or will their experience parallel that of most immigrants in the last century, men and women who came to America to work hard, live decent lives, and raise their children to become good citizens?

In *Who Are We? The Challenges to America's National Identity* (Simon & Schuster, 2004), Samuel P. Huntington presents an alarming view of the new immigrants, particularly those from Mexico. He worries that they are forming their own transnational culture in the United States, adversely affecting America's work ethnic and its sense of national identity. In a similar vein is Georgie Anne Geyer's *Americans No More* (Atantic Monthly Press, 1996). Geyer is not so much concerned about immigration per se but about the recent tendencies of even legal immigrants to resist assimilation. In *Whatever It Takes: Illegal Immigration, Border Security and the War on Terror* (Regnery, 2006), former U.S. Representative J. D. Hayworth expresses indignation that illegal immigrants actually get support from local officials and mindless bureaucratic practices. Opposing those views is Sanford J. Ungar's *In Fresh Blood: The New American Immigrants* (Simon & Schuster, 1995). "To be American," Ungar writes, "means being part of an ever more heterogeneous people and participating in the constant redefinition of a complex, evolving cultural fabric." Somewhere in between multiculturalists like Ungar and assimilationists like Brimelow and Geyer is Peter D. Salins. In *Assimilation, American Style* (Basic Books, 1997), Salins argues that the naturalization process is the best means for absorbing the flood of immigrants who arrive in America each year.

Often forgotten in these debates are the experiences of the immigrants themselves. Newer immigrants to America have recounted some of these experiences in recent books by and about them. In *Becoming American: Personal Essays by First Generation Immigrant Women* (Hyperion, 2000), Ghanaian American writer Meri Nana-Ama Danquah brings together the personal recollections and reflections by immigrant women from Europe, Latin America, Africa, Asia, and the Caribbean. In *American by Choice: The Remarkable Fulfillment of an Immigrant's Dreams* (Thomas Nelson, 1998), Sam Moore describes his rise in America from a poor Lebanese immigrant to president and CEO of

Thomas Nelson Publishers, a major religious publishing house. A more troubling account of the immigrant experience is that of Mary C. Waters, in *Black Identities: West Indian Immigrant Dreams and American Realities* (Harvard University Press, 2000). Waters finds that when West Indian immigrants first arrive, their skills, knowledge of English, and general optimism carry them forward, but later on, a variety of influences, from racial discrimination to low wages and poor working conditions, tend to erode their self-confidence.

Attitudes toward immigration change with time and circumstances. September 11, 2001, was one of those times. The terrorist attacks on the World Trade Center have increased the fear that many Americans have of all foreigners. Tamar Jacoby examines the changing circumstances in "Too Many Immigrants?" *Commentary* (April 2002).

The literature on immigration seems to grow as rapidly as immigration itself. Christopher Jencks has assessed this literature in two long essays entitled "Who Should Get In?" *New York Review of Books* (November 29 and December 20, 2001). Among the controversial issues that he examines is whether or not permanent status can be granted to illegal immigrants who are presently residing in the United States without encouraging the influx of many more and, if so, how. In 2004, President Bush proposed an amnesty program for illegal aliens. Mark Krikorian, in "Amnesty Again" (*The National Review*, January 26, 1994), criticizes the plan because it would lead to the permanent importation of thousands of new workers.

Americans confront a choice. On the one hand, there are the ethical and political consequences of restricting immigration into a country whose attraction to poor or persecuted people is as great as its borders are vast. On the other hand, there are the problems of absorbing new, generally non-English-speaking populations into an economy that may have to provide increasing public support and into a society whose traditions and values may clash with those of the newcomers.

ISSUE 15

Should There Be a "Wall of Separation" Between Church and State?

YES: John Paul Stevens, from Dissenting Opinion in *Van Orden v. Perry*, 545 U.S. 677 (June 27, 2005)

NO: Antonin Scalia, from Dissenting Opinion in *McCreary County, et al., v. American Civil Liberties Union of Kentucky, et al.*, 545 U.S. 844 (June 27, 2005)

ISSUE SUMMARY

YES: United States Supreme Court Justice John Paul Stevens believes that the Constitution creates "a wall of separation" between church and state that can be rarely broached and only insofar as the state recognition of religion does not express a bias in support of particular religious doctrines.

NO: United States Supreme Court Justice Antonin Scalia believes that both the Constitution and American history support the sympathetic acknowledgement of the nearly universal American belief in monotheistic religion as reflected in presidential proclamations, public oaths, public monuments, and other displays.

The first words of the First Amendment to the United States Constitution are "Congress shall make no law respecting an establishment of religion." (This prohibition was later extended to the states by the Fourteenth Amendment to the Constitution.) It has proved to be one of the most controversial clauses, and as shown in the extracts from the two cases considered here, its meaning has never been clearly resolved.

In Virginia, opposition to the established Anglican Church owed less to abstract belief in tolerance than to the increasing number of members of dissenting faiths. Virginia's disestablishment in 1786 was echoed in Article VI of the U.S. Constitution written the following year that "no religious test shall ever be required as a qualification" for any public office. Other states soon abolished their religious establishments and tests.

It may seem a contradiction to some, but not to most Americans, that a nation that disestablished religion may also be the most religious democratic nation, as measured by its high proportion of believers in God and attendance at church services. Because of such deep feelings, sharp disagreement exists as to the meaning of the establishment clause when considering laws *regarding* an establishment of religion.

Government proclamations regarding religion have tended to be general. Presidents have often invoked a Supreme Being, with modern presidents often concluding a public address with "God bless America." In 1864, Congress passed a law to allow "In God We Trust" to appear on coins, and it has appeared on all U.S. coins since 1938. In 1956, "In God We Trust" became the official national motto of the United States. A similar phrase ("And this be our motto, 'In God is our trust'") is in the fourth stanza of "The Star-Spangled Banner," adopted as the national anthem in 1931. The Ninth U.S. Circuit Court of Appeals concluded in 1970 that the spiritual, psychological, and inspirational value of the phrase "has nothing whatsoever to do with the establishment of religion."

The closest the Supreme Court has come to creating a standard for permissible state acknowledgment of and support for religion was when, in 1971 in *Lemon v. Kurtzman,* it established a three-pronged test to escape invalidation under the Establishment Clause: Governmental action must (1) have a secular purpose that neither endorses nor disapproves of religion, (2) have an effect that neither advances nor inhibits religions, and (3) avoid creating a relationship between religion and government that entangles either in the internal affair of the other. The *Lemon* criteria have been interpreted to reach contradictory conclusions, and often have been ignored.

The division is best illustrated by the two cases considered here that were decided on the same day in 2005. In *McCreary County,* a 5-4 majority rejected a courthouse display of the Ten Commandments as "an unmistakably religious statement." In *Van Orden,* a 5-4 majority concluded that a Ten Commandments monument on the Texas capitol grounds served "a mixed but primarily nonreligious purpose." The differences between the two cases are considered in the dissenting opinions excerpted here, but they served only to affect the decision of Justice Stephen Breyer, who in one case voted with the four justices who are most supportive of state acknowledgment of religious influence and in the other voted with the four justices who are most hostile to such state support. His switch was motivated by a conclusion he alone held, that the display had a primarily religious purpose in one case, but not in the other. The other justices divided 4-4, but none was moved by the different circumstances that influenced Breyer.

The selections that follow are from the dissenting opinion of Justice John Paul Stevens in *Van Orden v. Perry,* in which he endorses Jefferson's "wall of separation" as an expression of the constitutional principle and the dissenting opinion of Justice Antonin Scalia in *McCreary County v. American Civil Liberties Union of Kentucky*, in which he rejects Jefferson's wall as a misleading metaphor that contradicts the intention of the Framers.

YES

John Paul Stevens

Dissenting Opinion

The sole function of the monument on the grounds of Texas' State Capitol is to display the full text of one version of the Ten Commandments. The monument is not a work of art and does not refer to any event in the history of the State. It is significant because, and only because, it communicates the following message:

> "I AM the LORD thy God.
> "Thou shalt have no other gods before me.
> "Thou shalt not make to thyself any graven images.
> "Thou shalt not take the Name of the Lord thy God in vain.
> "Remember the Sabbath day, to keep it holy.
> "Honor thy father and thy mother, that thy days may be long upon the land which the Lord thy God giveth thee.
> "Thou shalt not kill.
> "Thou shalt not commit adultery.
> "Thou shalt not steal.
> "Thou shalt not bear false witness against thy neighbor.
> "Thou shalt not covet thy neighbor's house.
> "Thou shalt not covet thy neighbor's wife, nor his manservant, nor his maidservant, nor his cattle, nor anything that is thy neighbor's."

Viewed on its face, Texas' display has no purported connection to God's role in the formation of Texas or the founding of our Nation; nor does it provide the reasonable observer with any basis to guess that it was erected to honor any individual or organization. The message transmitted by Texas' chosen display is quite plain: This State endorses the divine code of the "Judeo-Christian" God.

For those of us who learned to recite the King James version of the text long before we understood the meaning of some of its words, God's Commandments may seem like wise counsel. The question before this Court, however, is whether it is counsel that the State of Texas may proclaim without violating the Establishment Clause of the Constitution. If any fragment of Jefferson's metaphorical "wall of separation between church and State" is to be preserved—if there remains any meaning to the "wholesome 'neutrality' of which this Court's [Establishment Clause] cases speak"—a negative answer to that question is mandatory.

Van Orden v. Perry, 545 U.S. 677 (2005), Justice John Paul Stevens, dissenting.

I

In my judgment, at the very least, the Establishment Clause has created a strong presumption against the display of religious symbols on public property. The adornment of our public spaces with displays of religious symbols and messages undoubtedly provides comfort, even inspiration, to many individuals who subscribe to particular faiths. Unfortunately, the practice also runs the risk of "offend[ing] nonmembers of the faith being advertised as well as adherents who consider the particular advertisement disrespectful."

Government's obligation to avoid divisiveness and exclusion in the religious sphere is compelled by the Establishment and Free Exercise Clauses, which together erect a wall of separation between church and state. This metaphorical wall protects principles long recognized and often recited in this Court's cases. The first and most fundamental of these principles, one that a majority of this Court today affirms, is that the Establishment Clause demands religious neutrality—government may not exercise a preference for one religious faith over another. This essential command, however, is not merely a prohibition against the government's differentiation among religious sects. We have repeatedly reaffirmed that neither a State nor the Federal Government "can constitutionally pass laws or impose requirements which aid all religions as against nonbelievers, and neither can aid those religions based on a belief in the existence of God as against those religions founded on different beliefs." This principle is based on the straightforward notion that governmental promotion of orthodoxy is not saved by the aggregation of several orthodoxies under the State's banner.

Acknowledgments of this broad understanding of the neutrality principle are legion in our cases. Strong arguments to the contrary have been raised from time to time. Powerful as [Chief Justice Rehnquist's] argument was, we squarely rejected it and thereby reaffirmed the principle that the Establishment Clause requires the same respect for the atheist as it does for the adherent of a Christian faith. As we wrote, "the Court has unambiguously concluded that the individual freedom of conscience protected by the Constitution embodies the right to select any religious faith or none at all."

In restating this principle, I do not discount the importance of avoiding an overly strict interpretation of the metaphor so often used to define the reach of the Establishment Clause. The plurality is correct to note that "religion and religious traditions" have played a "strong role . . . throughout our nation's history." This Court has often recognized "an unbroken history of official acknowledgment . . . of the role of religion in American life." Given this history, it is unsurprising that a religious symbol may at times become an important feature of a familiar landscape or a reminder of an important event in the history of a community. The wall that separates the church from the State does not prohibit the government from acknowledging the religious beliefs and practices of the American people, nor does it require governments to hide works of art or historic memorabilia from public view just because they also have religious significance.

This case, however, is not about historic preservation or the mere recognition of religion. The issue is obfuscated rather than clarified by simplistic commentary on the various ways in which religion has played a role in American life, and by the recitation of the many extant governmental "acknowledgments" of the role the Ten Commandments played in our Nation's heritage. Surely, the mere compilation of religious symbols, none of which includes the full text of the Commandments and all of which are exhibited in different settings, has only marginal relevance to the question presented in this case. . . .

II

The State may admonish its citizens not to lie, cheat or steal, to honor their parents and to respect their neighbors' property; and it may do so by printed words, in television commercials, or on granite monuments in front of its public buildings. Moreover, the State may provide its schoolchildren and adult citizens with educational materials that explain the important role that our forebears' faith in God played in their decisions to select America as a refuge from religious persecution, to declare their independence from the British Crown, and to conceive a new Nation. The message at issue in this case, however, is fundamentally different from either a bland admonition to observe generally accepted rules of behavior or a general history lesson.

The reason this message stands apart is that the Decalogue is a venerable religious text. As we held 25 years ago, it is beyond dispute that "[t]he Ten Commandments are undeniably a sacred text in the Jewish and Christian faiths." For many followers, the Commandments represent the literal word of God as spoken to Moses and repeated to his followers after descending from Mount Sinai. The message conveyed by the Ten Commandments thus cannot be analogized to an appendage to a common article of commerce ("In God we Trust") or an incidental part of a familiar recital ("God save the United States and this honorable Court"). Thankfully, the plurality does not attempt to minimize the religious significance of the Ten Commandments. . . . Attempts to secularize what is unquestionably a sacred text defy credibility and disserve people of faith.

The profoundly sacred message embodied by the text inscribed on the Texas monument is emphasized by the especially large letters that identify its author: "I AM the LORD thy God." It commands present worship of Him and no other deity. It directs us to be guided by His teaching in the current and future conduct of all of our affairs. It instructs us to follow a code of divine law, some of which has informed and been integrated into our secular legal code ("Thou shalt not kill"), but much of which has not ("Thou shalt not make to thyself any graven images. . . . Thou shalt not covet"). . . .

The Establishment Clause, if nothing else, forbids government from "specifying details upon which men and women who believe in a benevolent, omnipotent Creator and Ruler of the world are known to differ." . . . Given that the chosen text inscribed on the Ten Commandments monument invariably places the State at the center of a serious sectarian dispute, the display is unquestionably unconstitutional under our case law. . . .

Even if, however, the message of the monument, despite the inscribed text, fairly could be said to represent the belief system of all Judeo-Christians, it would still run afoul of the Establishment Clause by prescribing a compelled code of conduct from one God, namely a Judeo-Christian God, that is rejected by prominent polytheistic sects, such as Hinduism, as well as nontheistic religions, such as Buddhism. . . . And, at the very least, the text of the Ten Commandments impermissibly commands a preference for religion over irreligion. . . . Any of those bases, in my judgment, would be sufficient to conclude that the message should not be proclaimed by the State of Texas on a permanent monument at the seat of its government.

I do not doubt that some Texans, including those elected to the Texas Legislature, may believe that the statues displayed on the Texas Capitol grounds, including the Ten Commandments monument, reflect the "ideals . . . that compose Texan identity." . . . Texas, like our entire country, is now a much more diversified community than it was when it became a part of the United States or even when the monument was erected. Today there are many Texans who do not believe in the God whose Commandments are displayed at their seat of government. Many of them worship a different god or no god at all. Some may believe that the account of the creation in the Book of Genesis is less reliable than the views of men like Darwin and Einstein. The monument is no more an expression of the views of every true Texan than was the "Live Free or Die" motto that the State of New Hampshire placed on its license plates in 1969 an accurate expression of the views of every citizen of New Hampshire. . . .

Recognizing the diversity of religious and secular beliefs held by Texans and by all Americans, it seems beyond peradventure that allowing the seat of government to serve as a stage for the propagation of an unmistakably Judeo-Christian message of piety would have the tendency to make nonmonotheists and nonbelievers "feel like [outsiders] in matters of faith, and [strangers] in the political community." . . .

Even more than the display of a religious symbol on government property, . . . displaying this sectarian text at the state capitol should invoke a powerful presumption of invalidity. . . . The physical setting in which the Texas monument is displayed—far from rebutting that presumption—actually enhances the religious content of its message. . . . The monument's permanent fixture at the seat of Texas government is of immense significance. The fact that a monument: "is installed on public property implies official recognition and reinforcement of its message. That implication is especially strong when the sign stands in front of the seat of government itself. The 'reasonable observer' of any symbol placed unattended in front of any capitol in the world will normally assume that the sovereign—which is not only the owner of that parcel of real estate but also the lawgiver for the surrounding territory—has sponsored and facilitated its message." . . .

Critical examination of the Decalogue's prominent display at the seat of Texas government, rather than generic citation to the role of religion in American life, unmistakably reveals on which side of the "slippery slope," . . . this display must fall. God, as the author of its message, the Eagles, as the donor of the monument, and the State of Texas, as its proud owner, speak with one voice for a common purpose—to encourage Texans to abide by the divine code of a "Judeo-Christian" God. If this message is permissible, then the shining principle of neutrality to which we have long adhered is nothing more than mere shadow.

III

The plurality relies heavily on the fact that our Republic was founded, and has been governed since its nascence, by leaders who spoke then (and speak still) in plainly religious rhetoric. The Chief Justice cites, for instance, George Washington's 1789 Thanksgiving Proclamation in support of the proposition that the Establishment Clause does not proscribe official recognition of God's role in our Nation's heritage. . . . Further, the plurality emphatically endorses the seemingly timeless recognition that our "institutions presuppose a Supreme Being." . . . Many of the submissions made to this Court by the parties and *amici*, in accord with the plurality's opinion, have relied on the ubiquity of references to God throughout our history.

The speeches and rhetoric characteristic of the founding era, however, do not answer the question before us. I have already explained why Texas' display of the full text of the Ten Commandments, given the content of the actual display and the context in which it is situated, sets this case apart from the countless examples of benign government recognitions of religion. But there is another crucial difference. Our leaders, when delivering public addresses, often express their blessings simultaneously in the service of God and their constituents. Thus, when public officials deliver public speeches, we recognize that their words are not exclusively a transmission from *the* government because those oratories have embedded within them the inherently personal views of the speaker as an individual member of the polity. The permanent placement of a textual religious display on state property is different in kind; it amalgamates otherwise discordant individual views into a collective statement of government approval. Moreover, the message never ceases to transmit itself to objecting viewers whose only choices are to accept the message or to ignore the offense by averting their gaze. . . . In this sense, although Thanksgiving Day proclamations and inaugural speeches undoubtedly seem official, in most circumstances they will not constitute the sort of governmental endorsement of religion at which the separation of church and state is aimed.

The plurality's reliance on early religious statements and proclamations made by the Founders is also problematic because those views were not espoused at the Constitutional Convention in 1787 nor enshrined in the Constitution's text. Thus, the presentation of these religious statements as a unified historical narrative is bound to paint a misleading picture. It does so here. In according deference to the statements of George Washington and John Adams, The Chief Justice and Justice Scalia . . . fail to account for the acts and publicly espoused views of other influential leaders of that time. Notably absent from their historical snapshot is the fact that Thomas Jefferson refused to issue the Thanksgiving proclamations that Washington had so readily embraced based on the argument that to do so would violate the Establishment Clause. The Chief Justice and Justice Scalia disregard the substantial debates that took place regarding the constitutionality of the early proclamations and acts they cite, . . . and paper over the fact that Madison more than once repudiated the views attributed to him by many, stating unequivocally that with respect to government's involvement with religion, the "'tendency to a usurpation on one side, or the other, or to a corrupting coalition or alliance between them, will be best guarded against by an entire abstinence of the Government from interference, in any way whatever, beyond the necessity of preserving public order, & protecting each sect against trespasses on its legal rights by others.'"

These seemingly nonconforming sentiments should come as no surprise. Not insignificant numbers of colonists came to this country with memories of religious persecution by monarchs on the other side of the Atlantic. Others experienced religious intolerance at the hands of colonial Puritans, who regrettably failed to practice the tolerance that some of their contemporaries preached. . . . The Chief Justice and Justice Scalia ignore the separationist impulses—in accord with the principle of "neutrality"—that these individuals brought to the debates surrounding the adoption of the Establishment Clause.

Ardent separationists aside, there is another critical nuance lost in the plurality's portrayal of history. Simply put, many of the Founders who are often cited as authoritative expositors of the Constitution's original meaning understood the Establishment Clause to stand for a *narrower* proposition than the plurality, for whatever reason, is willing to accept. Namely, many of the Framers understood the word "religion" in the Establishment Clause to encompass only the various sects of Christianity.

The evidence is compelling. Prior to the Philadelphia Convention, the States had begun to protect "religious freedom" in their various constitutions. Many of those provisions, however, restricted "equal protection" and "free exercise" to Christians, and invocations of the divine were commonly understood to refer to Christ. That historical background likely informed the Framers' understanding of the First Amendment. Accordingly, one influential thinker wrote of the First Amendment that "'[t]he meaning of the term "establishment" in this amendment unquestionably is, the preference and establishment given by law to one sect of Christians over every other.'" Jasper Adams, The Relation of Christianity to Civil Government in the United States (Feb. 13, 1833) (quoted in Dreisbach 16). That definition tracked the understanding of the text Justice Story adopted in his famous Commentaries, in which he wrote that the "real object" of the Clause was:

> "not to countenance, much less to advance Mahometanism, or Judaism, or infidelity, by prostrating Christianity; but to exclude all rivalry among Christian sects, and to prevent any national ecclesiastical establishment, which should give to an hierarchy the exclusive patronage of the national government. It thus sought to cut off the means of religious persecution, (the vice and pest of former ages,) and the power of subverting the rights of conscience in matters of religion, which had been trampled upon almost from the days of the Apostles to the present age." . . .

Along these lines, for nearly a century after the Founding, many accepted the idea that America was not just a *religious* nation, but "a Christian nation." . . .

The original understanding of the type of "religion" that qualified for constitutional protection under the Establishment Clause likely did not include those followers of Judaism and Islam who are among the preferred "monotheistic" religions Justice Scalia has embraced in his *McCreary County* opinion. The inclusion of Jews and Muslims inside the category of constitutionally favored religions surely would have shocked Chief Justice Marshall and Justice Story. Indeed, Justice Scalia is unable to point to any persuasive historical evidence or entrenched traditions in support of his decision to give specially preferred constitutional status to all monotheistic religions. Perhaps this is because the history of the Establishment Clause's original meaning just as strongly supports a preference for Christianity as it does a preference for monotheism. Generic references to "God" hardly constitute evidence that those who spoke the word meant to be inclusive of all monotheistic believers; nor do such references demonstrate that those who heard the word spoken understood it broadly to include all monotheistic faiths. Justice Scalia's inclusion of Judaism and Islam is a laudable act of religious tolerance, but it is one that is unmoored from the Constitution's history and text, and moreover one that is patently arbitrary in its inclusion of some, but exclusion of other (*e.g.,* Buddhism), widely practiced non-Christian religions. Given the original understanding of the men who championed our "Christian nation"—men who had no cause to view anti-Semitism or contempt for atheists as problems worthy of civic concern—one must ask whether Justice Scalia "has not had the courage (or the foolhardiness) to apply [his originalism] principle consistently."

Indeed, to constrict narrowly the reach of the Establishment Clause to the views of the Founders would lead to more than this unpalatable result; it would also leave us with an unincorporated constitutional provision—in other words, one that limits only the *federal* establishment of "a national religion." Under this view, not only could a State constitutionally adorn all of its public spaces with crucifixes or passages from the New Testament, it would also have full authority to prescribe the teachings of Martin Luther or Joseph Smith as *the* official state religion. Only the Federal Government would be prohibited from taking sides, (and only then as between Christian sects).

A reading of the First Amendment dependent on either of the purported original meanings expressed above would eviscerate the heart of the Establishment Clause. It would replace Jefferson's "wall of separation" with a perverse wall of exclusion—Christians inside, non-Christians out. It would permit States to construct walls of their own choosing—Baptists inside, Mormons out; Jewish Orthodox inside, Jewish Reform out. A Clause so understood might be faithful to the expectations of some of our Founders, but it is plainly not worthy of a society whose enviable hallmark over the course of two centuries has been the continuing expansion of religious pluralism and tolerance. . . .

Unless one is willing to renounce over 65 years of Establishment Clause jurisprudence and cross back over the incorporation bridge, appeals to the religiosity of the Framers ring hollow. But even if there were a coherent way to embrace incorporation with one hand while steadfastly abiding by the Founders' purported religious views on the other, the problem of the selective use of history remains. As the widely divergent views espoused by the leaders

of our founding era plainly reveal, the historical record of the preincorpora-
tion Establishment Clause is too indeterminate to serve as an interpretive
North Star.

It is our duty, therefore, to interpret the First Amendment's command
that "Congress shall make no law respecting an establishment of religion" not
by merely asking what those words meant to observers at the time of the
founding, but instead by deriving from the Clause's text and history the broad
principles that remain valid today. As we have said in the context of statutory
interpretation, legislation "often [goes] beyond the principal evil [at which
the statute was aimed] to cover reasonably comparable evils, and it is ultimately the provisions of our laws rather than the principal concerns of our
legislators by which we are governed." In similar fashion, we have construed
the Equal Protection Clause of the Fourteenth Amendment to prohibit segregated schools, even though those who drafted that Amendment evidently
thought that separate was not unequal. We have held that the same Amendment prohibits discrimination against individuals on account of their gender,
despite the fact that the contemporaries of the Amendment "doubt[ed] very
much whether any action of a State not directed by way of discrimination
against the negroes as a class, or on account of their race, will ever be held to
come within the purview of this provision." And we have construed "evolving
standards of decency" to make impermissible practices that were not considered "cruel and unusual" at the founding. . . .

To reason from the broad principles contained in the Constitution does
not, as Justice Scalia suggests, require us to abandon our heritage in favor of
unprincipled expressions of personal preference. The task of applying the
broad principles that the Framers wrote into the text of the First Amendment
is, in any event, no more a matter of personal preference than is one's selection between two (or more) sides in a heated historical debate. We serve our
constitutional mandate by expounding the meaning of constitutional provisions with one eye towards our Nation's history and the other fixed on its
democratic aspirations. Constitutions, after all,

> "are not ephemeral enactments, designed to meet passing occasions. They
> are, to use the words of Chief Justice Marshall, 'designed to approach
> immortality as nearly as human institutions can approach it.' The future
> is their care and provision for events of good and bad tendencies of which
> no prophecy can be made. In the application of a constitution, therefore,
> our contemplation cannot be only of what has been but of what may be.
> Under any other rule a constitution would indeed be as easy of application
> as it would be deficient in efficacy and power. Its general principles would
> have little value and be converted by precedent into impotent and lifeless
> formulas." . . .

The principle that guides my analysis is neutrality. The basis for that
principle is firmly rooted in our Nation's history and our Constitution's text.
I recognize that the requirement that government must remain neutral
between religion and irreligion would have seemed foreign to some of the
Framers; so too would a requirement of neutrality between Jews and Christians.

Fortunately, we are not bound by the Framers' expectations—we are bound by the legal principles they enshrined in our Constitution. Story's vision that States should not discriminate between Christian sects has as its foundation the principle that government must remain neutral between valid systems of belief. As religious pluralism has expanded, so has our acceptance of what constitutes valid belief systems. The evil of discriminating today against atheists, "polytheists[,] and believers in unconcerned deities," (Scalia, dissenting), is in my view a direct descendent of the evil of discriminating among Christian sects. The Establishment Clause thus forbids it and, in turn, forbids Texas from displaying the Ten Commandments monument the plurality so casually affirms.

IV

. . . The judgment of the Court in this case stands for the proposition that the Constitution permits governmental displays of sacred religious texts. This makes a mockery of the constitutional ideal that government must remain neutral between religion and irreligion. If a State may endorse a particular deity's command to "have no other gods before me," it is difficult to conceive of any textual display that would run afoul of the Establishment Clause.

The disconnect between this Court's approval of Texas's monument and the constitutional prohibition against preferring religion to irreligion cannot be reduced to the exercise of plotting two adjacent locations on a slippery slope. Rather, it is the difference between the shelter of a fortress and exposure to "the winds that would blow" if the wall were allowed to crumble. . . . That wall, however imperfect, remains worth preserving.

Antonin Scalia

Dissenting Opinion

I shall discuss first, why the Court's oft repeated assertion that the government cannot favor religious practice is false; second, why today's opinion extends the scope of that falsehood even beyond prior cases; and third, why even on the basis of the Court's false assumptions the judgment here is wrong.

I

[In] a model spread across Europe by the armies of Napoleon, . . . [r]eligion is to be strictly excluded from the public forum. This is not, and never was, the model adopted by America. George Washington added to the form of Presidential oath prescribed by Art. II, § 1, cl. 8, of the Constitution, the concluding words "so help me God." . . . The Supreme Court under John Marshall opened its sessions with the prayer, "God save the United States and this Honorable Court." . . . The First Congress instituted the practice of beginning its legislative sessions with a prayer. The same week that Congress submitted the Establishment Clause as part of the Bill of Rights for ratification by the States, it enacted legislation providing for paid chaplains in the House and Senate. The day after the First Amendment was proposed, the same Congress that had proposed it requested the President to proclaim "a day of public thanksgiving and prayer, to be observed, by acknowledging, with grateful hearts, the many and signal favours of Almighty God." President Washington offered the first Thanksgiving Proclamation shortly thereafter, devoting November 26, 1789 on behalf of the American people "'to the service of that great and glorious Being who is the beneficent author of all the good that is, that was, or that will be,'" . . . thus beginning a tradition of offering gratitude to God that continues today. The same Congress also reenacted the Northwest Territory Ordinance of 1787, . . . Article III of which provided: "Religion, morality, and knowledge, being necessary to good government and the happiness of mankind, schools and the means of education shall forever be encouraged." And of course the First Amendment itself accords religion (and no other manner of belief) special constitutional protection.

These actions of our First President and Congress and the Marshall Court were not idiosyncratic; they reflected the beliefs of the period. Those who wrote the Constitution believed that morality was essential to the well-being of society and that encouragement of religion was the best way to foster

McCreary County, Kentucky v. American Civil Liberties Union of Kentucky, 545 U.S. 844 (2005), Justice Antonin Scalia, dissenting.

morality. . . . President Washington opened his Presidency with a prayer, and reminded his fellow citizens at the conclusion of it that "reason and experience both forbid us to expect that National morality can prevail in exclusion of religious principle." . . . President John Adams wrote to the Massachusetts Militia, "we have no government armed with power capable of contending with human passions unbridled by morality and religion. . . . Our Constitution was made only for a moral and religious people. It is wholly inadequate to the government of any other." . . . Thomas Jefferson concluded his second inaugural address by inviting his audience to pray: "I shall need, too, the favor of that Being in whose hands we are, who led our fathers, as Israel of old, from their native land and planted them in a country flowing with all the necessaries and comforts of life; who has covered our infancy with His providence and our riper years with His wisdom and power and to whose goodness I ask you to join in supplications with me that He will so enlighten the minds of your servants, guide their councils, and prosper their measures that whatsoever they do shall result in your good, and shall secure to you the peace, friendship, and approbation of all nations."

James Madison, in his first inaugural address, likewise placed his confidence "in the guardianship and guidance of that Almighty Being whose power regulates the destiny of nations, whose blessings have been so conspicuously dispensed to this rising Republic, and to whom we are bound to address our devout gratitude for the past, as well as our fervent supplications and best hopes for the future."

Nor have the views of our people on this matter significantly changed. Presidents continue to conclude the Presidential oath with the words "so help me God." Our legislatures, state and national, continue to open their sessions with prayer led by official chaplains. The sessions of this Court continue to open with the prayer "God save the United States and this Honorable Court." Invocation of the Almighty by our public figures, at all levels of government, remains commonplace. Our coinage bears the motto "IN GOD WE TRUST." And our Pledge of Allegiance contains the acknowledgment that we are a Nation "under God." As one of our Supreme Court opinions rightly observed, "We are a religious people whose institutions presuppose a Supreme Being." . . .

With all of this reality (and much more) staring it in the face, how can the Court *possibly* assert that "'the First Amendment mandates governmental neutrality between . . . religion and nonreligion,'" and that "[m]anifesting a purpose to favor . . . adherence to religion generally" is unconstitutional? Who says so? Surely not the words of the Constitution. Surely not the history and traditions that reflect our society's constant understanding of those words. Surely not even the current sense of our society, recently reflected in an Act of Congress adopted *unanimously* by the Senate and with only 5 nays in the House of Representatives, criticizing a Court of Appeals opinion that had held "under God" in the Pledge of Allegiance unconstitutional. . . . Nothing stands behind the Court's assertion that governmental affirmation of the society's belief in God is unconstitutional except the Court's own say-so, citing as support only the unsubstantiated say-so of earlier Courts going back no farther than the mid-20th century. . . . And it is, moreover, a thoroughly discredited say-so. It is discredited, to begin with, because a majority of the Justices on the current Court (including at least one Member of today's majority) have, in separate opinions, repudiated the brain-spun "*Lemon* test" that embodies the supposed principle of neutrality between religion and irreligion. . . . And it is discredited because the Court has not had the courage (or the foolhardiness) to apply the neutrality principle consistently.

What distinguishes the rule of law from the dictatorship of a shifting Supreme Court majority is the absolutely indispensable requirement that judicial opinions be grounded in consistently applied principle. That is what prevents judges from ruling now this way, now that—thumbs up or thumbs down—as their personal preferences dictate. Today's opinion forthrightly (or actually, somewhat less than forthrightly) admits that it does not rest upon consistently applied principle. In a revealing footnote, the Court acknowledges that the "Establishment Clause doctrine" it purports to be applying "lacks the comfort of categorical absolutes." What the Court means by this lovely euphemism is that sometimes the Court chooses to decide cases on the principle that government cannot favor religion, and sometimes it does not. The footnote goes on to say that "[i]n special instances we have found good reason" to dispense with the principle, but "[n]o such reasons present themselves here." . . . It does not identify all of those "special instances," much less identify the "good reason" for their existence.

I have cataloged elsewhere the variety of circumstances in which this Court—even *after* its embrace of *Lemon*'s stated prohibition of such behavior—has approved government action "undertaken with the specific intention of improving the position of religion." . . . Suffice it to say here that when the government relieves churches from the obligation to pay property taxes, when it allows students to absent themselves from public school to take religious classes, and when it exempts religious organizations from generally applicable prohibitions of religious discrimination, it surely means to bestow a benefit on religious practice—but we have approved it. . . . Indeed, we have even approved (post-*Lemon*) government-led prayer to God. In *Marsh v. Chambers,* the Court upheld the Nebraska State Legislature's practice of paying a chaplain to lead it in prayer at the opening of legislative sessions. The Court explained that "[t]o invoke Divine guidance on a public body entrusted with making the laws is not . . . an 'establishment' of religion or a step toward establishment; it is simply a tolerable acknowledgment of beliefs widely held among the people of this country." (Why, one wonders, is not respect for the Ten Commandments a tolerable acknowledgment of beliefs widely held among the people of this country?) . . .

Besides appealing to the demonstrably false principle that the government cannot favor religion over irreligion, today's opinion suggests that the posting of the Ten Commandments violates the principle that the government cannot favor one religion over another. That is indeed a valid principle where public aid or assistance to religion is concerned, or where the free exercise of religion is at issue, but it necessarily applies in a more limited sense to public acknowledgment of the Creator. If religion in the public forum had to be entirely nondenominational, there could be no religion in the public forum at all. One cannot say the word "God," or "the Almighty," one cannot offer public supplication or thanksgiving, without contradicting the beliefs of some people that there are many gods, or that God or the gods pay no attention to human affairs. With respect to public acknowledgment of religious belief, it is entirely clear from our Nation's historical practices that the Establishment Clause permits this disregard of polytheists and believers in unconcerned deities, just as it permits the disregard of devout atheists. The Thanksgiving Proclamation issued by George Washington at the instance of the First Congress was scrupulously nondenominational—but it was monotheistic. . . .

Historical practices thus demonstrate that there is a distance between the acknowledgment of a single Creator and the establishment of a religion. . . . The three most popular religions in the United States, Christianity, Judaism, and Islam—which combined account for 97.7% of all believers—are monotheistic. All of them, moreover (Islam included), believe that the Ten Commandments were given by God to Moses, and are divine prescriptions for a virtuous life. Publicly honoring the Ten Commandments is thus indistinguishable, insofar as discriminating against other religions is concerned, from publicly honoring God. Both practices are recognized across such a broad and diverse range of the population—from Christians to Muslims—that they cannot be reasonably understood as a government endorsement of a particular religious viewpoint. . . .

I have relied primarily upon official acts and official proclamations of the United States or of the component branches of its Government, including the First Congress' beginning of the tradition of legislative prayer to God, its appointment of congressional chaplains, its legislative proposal of a Thanksgiving Proclamation, and its reenactment of the Northwest Territory Ordinance; our first President's issuance of a Thanksgiving Proclamation; and invocation of God at the opening of sessions of the Supreme Court. The only mere "proclamations and statements" of the Founders I have relied upon were statements of Founders who occupied federal office, and spoke in at least a quasi-official capacity—Washington's prayer at the opening of his Presidency and his Farewell Address, President John Adams' letter to the Massachusetts Militia, and Jefferson's and Madison's inaugural addresses. The Court and Justice Stevens, by contrast, appeal to no official or even quasi-official action in support of their view of the Establishment Clause—only James Madison's Memorial and Remonstrance Against Religious Assessments, written before the federal Constitution had even been proposed, two letters, written by Madison long after he was President, and the quasi-official *inaction* of Thomas Jefferson in refusing to issue a Thanksgiving Proclamation. The Madison Memorial and Remonstrance, dealing as it does with enforced contribution to religion rather than public acknowledgment of God, is irrelevant; one of the letters is utterly ambiguous as to the point at issue here, and should not be read to contradict Madison's statements in his first inaugural address, quoted earlier; even the other letter does not disapprove public acknowledgment of God, unless one posits (what Madison's own actions as President would contradict) that reference to God contradicts "the equality of *all* religious sects." And as to Jefferson: the notoriously self-contradicting Jefferson did not choose to have his nonauthorship of a Thanksgiving Proclamation inscribed on his tombstone. What he did have inscribed was his authorship of the Virginia Statute for Religious Freedom, a governmental act which begins "Whereas Almighty God hath created the mind free. . . ."

It is no answer for Justice Stevens to say that the understanding that these official and quasi-official actions reflect was not "enshrined in the Constitution's text." The Establishment Clause, upon which Justice Stevens would rely, *was* enshrined in the Constitution's text, and these official actions show *what it meant.* There were doubtless some who thought it should have a broader meaning, but those views were plainly rejected. Justice Stevens says that reliance on these actions is "bound to paint a misleading picture," but it is hard to see why. What is more probative of the meaning of the Establishment Clause than the actions of the very Congress that proposed it, and of the first President charged with observing it?

Justice Stevens also appeals to the undoubted fact that some in the founding generation thought that the Religion Clauses of the First Amendment should have a *narrower* meaning, protecting only the Christian religion or perhaps only Protestantism. I am at a loss to see how this helps his case, except by providing a cloud of obfuscating smoke. (Since most thought the Clause permitted government invocation of monotheism, and some others thought it permitted government invocation of Christianity, he proposes that it be construed not to permit any government invocation of religion at all.) At any rate, those narrower views of the Establishment Clause were as clearly rejected as the more expansive ones. Washington's First Thanksgiving Proclamation is merely an example. *All* of the actions of Washington and the First Congress upon which I have relied, virtually all Thanksgiving Proclamations throughout our history, and *all* the other examples of our Government's favoring religion that I have cited, have invoked God, but not Jesus Christ. Rather than relying upon Justice Stevens' assurance that "[t]he original understanding of the type of 'religion' that qualified for constitutional protection under the First amendment certainly did not include . . . followers of Judaism and Islam," . . . I would prefer to take the word of George Washington, who, in his famous Letter to the Hebrew Congregation of Newport, Rhode Island, wrote that, "All possess alike liberty of conscience and immunities of citizenship. It is now no more that toleration is spoken of, as if it was by the indulgence of one class of people, that another enjoyed the exercise of their inherent natural rights." The letter concluded, by the way, with an invocation of the one God: "May the father of all mercies scatter light and not darkness in our paths, and make us all in our several vocations useful here, and in his own due time and way everlastingly happy." . . .

Justice Stevens argues that original meaning should not be the touchstone anyway, but that we should rather "expoun[d] the meaning of constitutional provisions with one eye toward our Nation's history and the other fixed on its democratic aspirations." This is not the place to debate the merits of the "living Constitution," though I must observe that Justice Stevens' quotation from *McCulloch v. Maryland* (1819), refutes rather than supports that approach. Even assuming, however, that the meaning of the Constitution ought to change according to "democratic aspirations," why are those aspirations to be found in Justices' notions of what the Establishment Clause ought to mean, rather than in the democratically adopted dispositions of our current society? As I have observed above, numerous provisions of our laws and numerous continuing practices of our people demonstrate that the government's invocation of God (and hence the government's invocation of the Ten Commandments) is unobjectionable—including a statute enacted by Congress almost unanimously less than three years ago, stating that "under God" in the Pledge of Allegiance is constitutional. To ignore all this is not to give effect to "democratic aspirations" but to frustrate them.

Finally, I must respond to Justice Stevens' assertion that I would "marginaliz[e] the belief systems of more than 7 million Americans" who adhere to religions that are not monotheistic. Surely that is a gross exaggeration. The beliefs of those citizens are entirely protected by the Free Exercise Clause, and by those aspects of the Establishment Clause that do not relate to government acknowledgment of the Creator. Invocation of God despite their beliefs is permitted not because nonmonotheistic religions cease to be religions recognized by the religion clauses of the First Amendment, but because governmental invocation of God is not an establishment. Justice Stevens fails to recognize that in the context of public acknowledgments of God there are legitimate *competing* interests: On the one hand, the interest of that minority in not feeling "excluded"; but on the other, the interest of the overwhelming majority of religious believers in being able to give God thanks and supplication *as a people*, and with respect to our national endeavors. Our national tradition has resolved that conflict in favor of the majority. It is not for this Court to change a disposition that accounts, many Americans think, for the phenomenon remarked upon in a quotation attributed to various authors, including Bismarck, but which I prefer to associate with Charles de Gaulle: "God watches over little children, drunkards, and the United States of America."

II

As bad as the *Lemon* test is, it is worse for the fact that, since its inception, its seemingly simple mandates have been manipulated to fit whatever result the Court aimed to achieve. Today's opinion is no different. In two respects it modifies *Lemon* to ratchet up the Court's hostility to religion. First, the Court justifies inquiry into legislative purpose, not as an end itself, but as a means to ascertain the appearance of the government action to an "'objective observer.'" Because in the Court's view the true danger to be guarded against is that the objective observer would feel like an "outside[r]" or "not [a] full membe[r] of the political community," its inquiry focuses not on the *actual purpose* of government action, but the "purpose apparent from government action." Under this approach, even if a government could show that its actual purpose was not to advance religion, it would presumably violate the Constitution as long as the Court's objective observer would think otherwise. . . .

I have remarked before that it is an odd jurisprudence that bases the unconstitutionality of a government practice that does not *actually* advance religion on the hopes of the government that it *would* do so. But that oddity pales in comparison to the one invited by today's analysis: the legitimacy of a government action with a wholly secular effect would turn on the *misperception* of an imaginary observer that the government officials behind the action had the intent to advance religion.

Second, the Court replaces *Lemon's* requirement that the government have "*a* secular . . . purpose," with the heightened requirement that the secular purpose "predominate" over any purpose to advance religion. The Court treats this extension as a natural outgrowth of the longstanding requirement that the government's secular purpose not be a sham, but simple logic shows the two to be unrelated. If the government's proffered secular purpose is not genuine, then the government has no secular purpose at all. The new demand that secular purpose predominate contradicts *Lemon's* more limited requirement, and finds no support in our cases. In all but one of the five cases in which this Court has invalidated a government practice on the basis of its purpose to benefit religion, it has first declared that the statute was motivated entirely by the desire to advance religion. . . .

I have urged that *Lemon's* purpose prong be abandoned, because . . . even an *exclusive* purpose to foster or assist religious practice is not necessarily invalidating. But today's extension makes things even worse. By shifting the focus of *Lemon's* purpose prong from the search for a genuine, secular motivation to the hunt for a predominantly religious purpose, the Court converts what has in the past been a fairly limited inquiry into a rigorous review of the full record. Those responsible for the adoption of the Religion Clauses would surely regard it as a bitter irony that the religious values they designed those Clauses to *protect* have now become so distasteful to this Court that if they constitute anything more than a subordinate motive for government action they will invalidate it.

III

Even accepting the Court's *Lemon*-based premises, the displays at issue here were constitutional.

. . . . [W]hen the Ten Commandments appear alongside other documents of secular significance in a display devoted to the foundations of American law and government, the context communicates that the Ten Commandments are included, not to teach their binding nature as a religious text, but to show their unique contribution to the development of the legal system. This is doubly true when the display is introduced by a document that informs passersby that it "contains documents that played a significant role in the foundation of our system of law and government."

The same result follows if the Ten Commandments display is viewed in light of the government practices that this Court has countenanced in the past. The acknowledgment of the contribution that religion in general, and the Ten Commandments in particular, have made to our Nation's legal and governmental heritage is surely no more of a step towards establishment of religion than was the practice of legislative prayer we approved in *Marsh v.*

Chambers, 463 U. S. 783 (1983), and it seems to be on par with the inclusion of a crèche or a menorah in a "Holiday" display that incorporates other secular symbols, see *Lynch*. The parallels between this case and *Marsh* and *Lynch* are sufficiently compelling that they ought to decide this case, even under the Court's misguided Establishment Clause jurisprudence.

Acknowledgment of the contribution that religion has made to our Nation's legal and governmental heritage partakes of a centuries-old tradition. Members of this Court have themselves often detailed the degree to which religious belief pervaded the National Government during the founding era. Display of the Ten Commandments is well within the mainstream of this practice of acknowledgment. Federal, State, and local governments across the Nation have engaged in such display. The Supreme Court Building itself includes depictions of Moses with the Ten Commandments in the Courtroom and on the east pediment of the building, and symbols of the Ten Commandments "adorn the metal gates lining the north and south sides of the Courtroom as well as the doors leading into the Courtroom." Similar depictions of the Decalogue appear on public buildings and monuments throughout our Nation's Capital. The frequency of these displays testifies to the popular understanding that the Ten Commandments are a foundation of the rule of law, and a symbol of the role that religion played, and continues to play, in our system of government.

Perhaps in recognition of the centrality of the Ten Commandments as a widely recognized symbol of religion in public life, the Court is at pains to dispel the impression that its decision will require governments across the country to sandblast the Ten Commandments from the public square. The constitutional problem, the Court says, is with the Counties' *purpose* in erecting the Foundations Displays, not the displays themselves. The Court adds in a footnote: "One consequence of taking account of the purpose underlying past actions is that the same government action may be constitutional if taken in the first instance and unconstitutional if it has a sectarian heritage."

. . . Displays erected in silence (and under the direction of good legal advice) are permissible, while those hung after discussion and debate are deemed unconstitutional. Reduction of the Establishment Clause to such minutiae trivializes the Clause's protection against religious establishment; indeed, it may inflame religious passions by making the passing comments of every government official the subject of endless litigation. . . .

The Court has in the past prohibited government actions that "proselytize or advance any one, or . . . disparage any other, faith or belief," or that apply some level of coercion (though I and others have disagreed about the form that coercion must take). The passive display of the Ten Commandments, even standing alone, does not begin to do either. . . .

Nor is it the case that a solo display of the Ten Commandments advances any one faith. They are assuredly a religious symbol, but they are not so closely associated with a single religious belief that their display can reasonably be understood as preferring one religious sect over another. The Ten Commandments are recognized by Judaism, Christianity, and Islam alike as divinely given. . . .

Turning at last to the displays actually at issue in this case, the Court faults the Counties for not *repealing* the resolution expressing what the Court believes to be an impermissible intent. Under these circumstances, the Court says, "no reasonable observer could swallow the claim that the Counties had cast off the objective so unmistakable in the earlier displays." Even were I to accept all that the Court has said before, I would not agree with that assessment. To begin with, of course, it is unlikely that a reasonable observer *would even have been aware* of the resolutions, so there would be nothing to "cast off." The Court implies that the Counties may have been able to remedy the "taint" from the old resolutions by enacting a new one. But that action would have been wholly unnecessary in light of the explanation that the Counties included *with the displays themselves*: A plaque next to the documents informed all who passed by that each display "contains documents that played a significant role in the foundation of our system of law and government." Additionally, there was no reason for the Counties to repeal or repudiate the resolutions adopted with the hanging of the second displays, since they related *only to the second displays*. After complying with the District Court's order to remove the second displays "immediately," and erecting new displays that in content and by express assertion reflected a *different* purpose from that identified in the resolutions, the Counties had no reason to believe that their previous resolutions would be deemed to be the basis for their actions. After the Counties discovered that the sentiments expressed in the resolutions could be attributed to their most recent displays (in oral argument before this Court), they repudiated them immediately.

In sum: The first displays did not necessarily evidence an intent to further religious practice; nor did the second displays, or the resolutions authorizing them; and there is in any event no basis for attributing whatever intent motivated the first and second displays to the third. Given the presumption of regularity that always accompanies our review of official action, the Court has identified no evidence of a purpose to advance religion in a way that is inconsistent with our cases. The Court may well be correct in identifying the third displays as the fruit of a desire to display the Ten Commandments, but neither our cases nor our history support its assertion that such a desire renders the fruit poisonous.

POSTSCRIPT

Should There Be a "Wall of Separation" Between Church and State?

Contradictions abound in church-state relations. The Supreme Court has justified the practice of opening congressional sessions with prayer. On the other hand, a U.S. Circuit Court of Appeals found the opening of court sessions with a prayer unconstitutional, because the practice had no long-standing tradition. Congress's 1954 inclusion of "under God" in the Pledge of Allegiance was upheld by the Seventh U.S. Circuit Court of Appeals in 1992 and rejected by the Ninth Circuit in 2002. In 2004, the U.S. Supreme Court overturned the Ninth Circuit Court on technical grounds without reaching the First Amendment merits of the case. Other examples of governmental support of religion include prayers at presidential inaugurations, the use of the Bible in public oaths, the dating of public documents "in the year of our Lord," and the proclamation of Thanksgiving and Christmas holidays.

Strict separation is defended in William Lee Miller, *The First Liberty: America's Foundation in Religious Freedom* (Georgetown University Press, expanded edition, 2003), which traces the development of the establishment clause in the words of Roger Williams, Thomas Jefferson, and James Madison, in contradiction to the positions of those who believe that the United States is a Christian Nation.

David Limbaugh charges that judicial interpretation of the establishment clause has led to bias against religion, particularly against Christianity. In *Persecution: How Liberals Are Waging War Against Christianity* (Regnery, 2003), he writes, "Christian expression is treated as profanity and worse in many public schools and certain federal courts across the nation." In justifying this harsh criticism, Limbaugh cites barring children from praying before football games, Hollywood caricatures of Christians as fanatics, and the suppression of criticism of Darwinian evolution in colleges.

Christopher L. Eisgruber and Lawrence G. Sager, in *Religious Freedom and the Constitution* (Harvard University Press, 2007), create a principle of "equal liberty" to reconcile opposing views. Donald L. Drakeman comes close to providing an objective account of leading church-state cases in *Church-State Constitutional Issues: Making Sense of the Establishment Clause* (Greenwood Press, 1991). Drakeman concludes that the intentions of the Founding Fathers provide inadequate guidance for understanding the establishment clause. He concludes that the fairest balance can be found in a religiously nonprofessional endorsement doctrine in which religion is not given special treatment by the government, nor is it singled out as a type of charitable organization ineligible for government benefits. In *The Founding Fathers and the Place of*

Religion in America (Princeton University Press, 2006), Frank Lambert provides an overview of how America's Founders thought religion should be treated in the new nation.

Given the passionate commitments of those holding opposed positions, compromise often seems impossible in disputes about faith-based social services, public money for religious schools, the Pledge of Allegiance, Ten Commandments monuments, the theory of evolution, abortion rights, stem cell research, and many other topics. Like the subject of religious preferences, discussion of church-state relations appears to be off-limits in polite society. Nonsectarian schools shy away from any serious discussion of religion for fear of giving offense. Teachers, including those who may be qualified to explain different religions and irreligion, are wary of risking unemployment or worse, and prudently avoid offending the sensitivities of others. Thoughtful explanations of the belief systems held by others is rare, and when it takes place is open to charges of bias. The consequence is that most Americans have acquired little knowledge of religious beliefs other than their own, and are ill-equipped to deal sympathetically with other positions.

Internet References . . .

In addition to the Internet sites listed below, type in key words, such as "China military threat, "American world leadership," "torture," or "Middle Eastern profiling" to find other listings.

U.S. State Department

View this site for understanding into the workings of a major U.S. executive branch department. Links explain exactly what the department does, what services it provides, and what it says about U.S. interests around the world, as well as provide other information.

http://www.state.gov

Marketplace of Political Ideas/University of Houston Libraries

Here is a valuable collection of links to campaign, conservative/liberal perspectives, and political party sites. There are general political sites, Democratic sites, Republican sites, third-party sites, and much more.

http://info.lib.uh.edu/politics/markind:htm

United States Senate Committee on Foreign Relations

This site is an excellent up-to-date resource for information about the United States' reaction to events regarding foreign policy.

http://www.senate.gov/~foreign/

Woodrow Wilson School of Public and International Affairs

This center of scholarship in public and international affairs, based at Princeton University, sponsors more than twenty research centers. Among its many links is the Princeton Center for Globalization and Governance, which explores the academic and policy dimensions of globalization and international governance.

http://www.wws.princeton.edu/mission/mission.html

American Diplomacy

American Diplomacy is an online journal of commentary, analysis, and research on U.S. foreign policy and its results around the world.

http://www.unc.edu/depts/diplomat/

Foreign Affairs

This page of the well-respected foreign policy journal *Foreign Affairs* is a valuable research tool. It allows users to search the journal's archives and provides Indexed access to the field's leading publications, documents, online resources, and so on. Link to dozens of other related Web sites from here too.

http://www.foreignaffairs.org

America and the World

*A*t one time the United States could isolate itself from much of the *world, and it did. That possibility disappeared long before the terrorist attack of September 11, 2001. Today America's unsurpassed wealth and military power mean that it cannot escape influencing and being influenced by world events. What methods are morally justified in protecting the American homeland against further attacks? Is America's war in Iraq helping to defeat al-Qaida? Besides the threat of terrorism, what about the potential danger from aggressive superpowers? Will China, to take the most prominent example, soon become a threat to this nation's security? These are among the issues that any serious student of American policy will have to consider in the years to come.*

- Does the War in Iraq Help the War Against Terrorism?
- Is "Middle Eastern" Profiling Ever Justified?
- Is the Use of Torture Against Terrorist Suspects Ever Justified?
- Is Warrantless Wiretapping in Some Cases Justified to Protect National Security?
- Is China a Military Threat to the United States?
- Must America Exercise World Leadership?
- Should Federal Taxes Be Increased?
- Does Conservatism Get the World Wrong?

ISSUE 16

Does the War in Iraq Help the War Against Terrorism?

YES: J. R. Dunn, from "Prospects of Terror," *The American Thinker* (March 21, 2006)

NO: Robert Jervis, from "Why the Bush Doctrine Cannot Be Sustained," *Political Science Quarterly* (Fall 2005)

ISSUE SUMMARY

YES: J. R. Dunn, a military editor and author, believes that the radical Islamists are losing the support of the Iraqi people, that Iraq is moving toward democracy, and that the war against terror is being won. In the same fashion, America and its allies will thwart Iran's quest for nuclear weapons.

NO: Robert Jervis, a professor of international relations, maintains that the war in Iraq distracted the United States from the war against terrorism, that preventive war risks grave errors of judgment, and that victory in Iraq will not necessarily result in more democracy or less terrorism.

On September 11, 2001, four commercial aircraft were hijacked after leaving New York and Boston airports on transcontinental flights. Two were directed into the World Trade Center, the two tallest buildings in New York City, one was directed into the Pentagon, the United States Defense Department headquarters in Washington, and a fourth crashed in a Pennsylvania field after passengers resisted the hijackers. All aboard the four planes and many of those in the struck buildings were killed. The continental United States had never suffered such a violent attack.

Since the end of the Gulf War in 1991, in which Iraq was driven out of Kuwait and United Nations forces defeated Iraq, Iraq was viewed as a potential breeding ground for terrorism directed against Western democracies, particularly the United States. Hostility toward Iraq was heightened by its failure to respond to United Nations' resolutions demanding an accounting of its weapons of mass destruction. Members of the administration of President Bush stated that there was a link between Saddam Hussein, the tyrannical head of the Iraqi government, and international terrorism, although fifteen of the nineteen hijackers came from Saudi Arabia and none from Iraq.

In 1998, the U.S. Congress appropriated funds to support a democratic opposition movement in Iraq. Later that year the United States and United Kingdom bombarded Iraq. In 2002, Congress authorized President George W. Bush to "use any means necessary" to "defend the national security of the United States against the continuing threat posed by Iraq." The success of the American invasion of Afghanistan, known to be the training ground for Al Qaeda, the Islamic radical group that had masterminded the attack of September 11, 2001 (now known simply as 9/11), inspired the invasion of Iraq on March 20, 2003 by the United States and Great Britain, which supplied 98 percent of the invading forces.

Smaller nations offered token forces, but France, Germany, Russia, and other major allies opposed the invasion. Despite the fact that Iraq had ignored United Nations' resolutions to reveal their weapons and weapons capacity, U.N. Secretary General Kofi Annan called the invasion "illegal." The military victory over the Iraqi armed forces was swift, but opposition by Iraqi insurgents to the American occupation, bolstered by the influx of anti-American terrorists, has not relented.

Saddam Hussein has been captured, free elections have been held, some terrorists have been killed or captured, and some vital services have been restored. But more than three years later, Osama bin Laden, the leader of Al Qaeda, is still at large, and no stockpiles of weapons of mass destruction have been found. In spring of 2006, after months of delay, a "unity government" was formed, but whether the actual unity of Sunnis, Shiites, and Kurds could be effected was by no means certain. The economy has not yet been restored and the military struggle continues, with two thousand Americans and an estimated tens of thousands of Iraqis among the fatalities.

President Bush maintains that Iraq can be reshaped as a democratic nation, that terrorism can be defeated, and that the two objectives are intimately intertwined. Foreign policy analysts and others who agree with the president believe that the democratization of Iraq will set an example in the Middle East, leading that troubled region to greater freedom and peaceful relations with other nations. Military historian J. R. Dunn states that America must take a long view, looking beyond temporary setbacks to recognize the inevitable defeat of the Islamic terrorists and the benefits this will bring to the United States and the free world.

Critics of the Bush administration, far from sharing this optimism, see the United States as having entered a morass from which it can extricate itself only at great cost. They believe that America's Iraqi policy has created wider distrust of government among citizens who feel deceived by government claims that have been disproved, as well as alienating public opinion among its natural allies. International relations professor Robert Jarvis is among those critics who believe that, far from combating terrorism, the invasion of Iraq resulted in the recruitment of more anti-American terrorists in Iraq and elsewhere.

YES

J. R. Dunn

Prospects of Terror

The first campaigns of the Long War are drawing to a close. The Jihadis have lost the opening rounds. What next?

There's an unconscious conviction that what happens next is . . . nothing. We go back to everyday life, the way things were before all that unpleasantness in lower Manhattan and Washington those long years ago. We shut out the harmful, hateful world once again, go our own way, and forget about jihads, and suicide belts, and dirty bombs, and beheadings, and all the other nightmares that have filled our days since 2001.

Unfortunately, that doesn't seem to be in the cards.

What happened on 9/11 was not an earthquake, over and done quickly, but a long, slow and complete reshuffling of the tectonic plates that comprise human civilization; something comparable to the deaths of empires and the passing of eras. Such events are not over in a day, or a year, or a decade. They take their time. And when it ends at last the world will be a different place, in ways that we now have no way of knowing. But the part we have played in it will, in some shape or form, match our position when it's all over, American or European or Arab, Muslim or Christian or Secular.

We are still amid early days, roughly the days of Midway and Guadalcanal and El Alamein in a previous great struggle. "Not the beginning of the end," as Churchill put it, "but the end of the beginning."

The Jihadis have lost Iraq and Afghanistan. It's true that fighting continues in both countries, but at this point it's effectively theater. It can't be repeated often enough that the type of war we are involved in is as much political as it is military. By any political measure, the Jihadis have been routed. Their only chance of prevailing was to appeal to the Iraqis and Afghans as a viable alternative to elected democratic governments. No such attempt was ever made. Instead, the Jihadis have relentlessly made the Iraqis and Afghans suffer. Their final chance in Iraq lay in derailing the political process last year. They failed at this, and now it is over. Not the violence—there will be car bombs going off in Iraq for years to come, unfortunately. But any opportunity of a Jihadi victory is gone.

(Skepticism on this point is understandable, considering the circumstances. Doubters are encouraged to read any of the myriad milblogs written by soldiers on the spot, or the recent reportage from Iraq by Victor Davis Hanson and Ralph Peters. It's a sad comment on the nature of the times that anyone relying solely on the legacy media knows next to nothing of what's going on in Iraq, Afghanistan, or in truth most other areas of the world.)

The Islamists now have a choice of either changing or fading out the way the Anarchists did early in the last century. Like the Jihadis, the Anarchist followers of Bakunin and Galliani, no more than a vague memory today, were an international terror network bent on converting the world to their ideology. They had a good long run, set off a lot of bombs, and killed a lot of people, but they disappeared at last in the 1920s leaving behind only a legend far more romantic in tone that it deserves to be.

It's doubtful that the Jihadis will fade out yet, not after spending over twenty years organizing and laying the groundwork. They may be hurt, but they still have a punch. According to the Defense Department, at least eighteen distinct groups, active throughout the Islamic world, are currently operating under the Al-Queda umbrella. Organizing has been detected in Europe and elsewhere. Al-Queda has settled into Gaza (and probably the West Bank), and has been detected in Beirut. A lot of activity in a lot of places, in no way emblematic of a movement ready to give up.

But if the Jihadis want to continue, they'll need to adopt a strategy. Not modify the current one—they have never, up to this point, displayed the least signs of ever having one. Osama bin Laden's concept of action appears to have been to make his move, then sit back and wait for Allah to handle the rest. Allah has been disinclined to do any such thing. (In fact, if ObL actually believed that Allah's will is revealed in the course of events, he'd more than likely be devoting the rest of his days to prayer and repentance above all else.)

His followers and disciples have acted on the same principle, carrying out isolated actions in London, Madrid, or Bali, uncoordinated with each other and with a steadily decreasing effect. This randomness has been so striking as to lead some observers to postulate a deep and ornate plan beneath the surface irregularity. But after four years with no sign of such a thing, it's safe to say that a Jihadi uberplan does not exist.

This may change in the future. The intercepted letter from Ayman al-Zawahiri to Abu Musab al-Zarqawi suggests that deep thinking has been going on concerning the trend of Islamist fortunes. Many of the movement's wild men have been killed off by U.S. and Coalition action. The remainder will be more thoughtful, balanced, and cautious. Some will have had actual military training and experience. These last will be unwilling to take action only out of religious zeal, without a workable goal and a clear method of getting there—a strategy.

Actually, they would need three strategies, since their major targets—the Middle East, Europe, and the U.S.—differ so much as to require separate plans for each.

What follows is not a prediction, or advice, but something of the nature of what Einstein called a "thought experiment." An attempt to envision the strategies a Jihadi and his allies might choose for the Long War's next campaign, and what moves should be taken to counteract them.

I should mention here that you will find little concerning "4th Generation Warfare"—usually abbreviated to "4GW"—or "Asymmetrical Warfare." Both have deteriorated into fads with more noise than content. 4GW has gotten a lot of mileage by claiming, on little evidence, that terrorism is something other than what it actually is. Asymmetrical Warfare addresses a real phenomenon but the term has in recent years been abused to the point of near meaninglessness.

The first campaign has been a complete, if not unqualified success for the West. But this war will continue for a long time, and to assure that the campaigns to come end the same way, we must be well prepared. Because the Islamists certainly will be.

> If you know the enemy and know yourself, you need not fear the result of a hundred battles. If you know yourself but not the enemy, for every victory gained you will suffer a defeat. If you know neither the enemy nor yourself, you will succumb in every battle.
>
> —Sun Tzu, *The Art of War*

The Iraq War has been a serious embarrassment for the Jihadis. They had two goals in Iraq: to hand the U.S. a Vietnam-style humiliation and to prevent the creation of a working government. They have failed at both.

The roots of this failure lie in the fact that terror is not a strategy. That, in a nutshell, is what went wrong with the Islamist effort in Iraq. If killing a lot of people in novel ways was a war-winning plan, the Jihadis would have prevailed. Fortunately, there's a little more to it.

Terror has its uses in the type of campaign being fought in Iraq. But it also has limitations, overlooked for many years, limitations that the Jihadi leadership, in particular Osama bin Laden and Abu Musab al-Zarqawi, have been slow to recognize.

Iraqi insurgents transferred the Palestinian Intifada model of random bombings intact to Iraq (Zarqawi himself is a Palestinian), evidently expecting similar results. But conditions in Iraq were not quite the same. Unlike helpless Israeli civilians, many of the targets in Iraq were able to shoot back, and the resulting losses to no effect forced a switch to the roadside bomb or IED, the Jihadi's single innovation.

The IED reduced Jihadi strategy to one of pure attrition. IEDs were effective at causing casualties but little else. They were not adaptable to any other role besides the booby trap, and despite occasional spectacular hits, were useless at maneuver, engaging the enemy, taking and holding territory, or anything else a military asset is expected to do. (Early attempts at ambushes and holding cities and neighborhoods were dropped after it became apparent that Jihadi forces could not stand up against conventional infantry.) Nor did the insurgents see anything wrong with this. They viewed warfare as a terror operation writ large. And there was no one, evidently, not even Saddam Hussein's ex-army officers, to tell them otherwise.

The Western media, as ignorant of military affairs as the Islamists, played a large role in Jihadi self-deception by covering each explosion as if it were Stalingrad in and of itself. By this time, the insurgents must know better. But it's too late to do anything about it. (The destruction of Samarra's Golden Mosque has all the qualities of a last-ditch desperation move, and may well turn out to be exactly that.) Dependence on the IED deprived the Jihadis of any opportunity of adapting their tactics to the actual situation.

Another drawback of relying on the Palestinian model involved the Jihadis' lack of a political goal. Ouster of the Israelis, by any means necessary, was a goal shared by virtually all Palestinians, creating a level of support that Zarqawi's gangs could only dream of. Al Fatah and Hamas could persuade anyone from fathers of young families to teenage schoolgirls to sacrifice themselves in suicide bombings. In contrast, the Baathists and Al-Queda were operating in an environment where support was a wasting asset, with each attack further eroding the trust of the populace. (Victor Davis Hanson points out that much of the "insurgent" violence occurring in Iraq actually originates with the 100,000 criminals released by Saddam Hussein just prior to his downfall. The fact that Zarqawi allowed Jihadi actions to become identified with criminal activity, to a point where no differentiation was possible, speaks volumes about Jihadi political judgment.)

What, precisely, could the Baathists and Al-Queda offer the Iraqi people? A return to Saddamist dictatorship, or a Taliban-style theocracy? The lack of a viable political program crippled the insurgency. Mao's theory of people's war, which formed the basis of every successful revolutionary movement of the late 20th century, emphasizes a struggle's political aspect over the military. A successful insurgency cultivates and holds on to popular support, as occurred in Algeria and Vietnam. Similar efforts were conspicuous in Iraq by their absence. (The Center for Combating Terrorism's report on Al-Queda states that since Zarqawi's aims were limited, he ". . . does not need to be as careful about whom [he] inflicts casualties upon." Clearly an error, in light of how the war has progressed.)

The U.S., on the other hand, was carrying out an exercise in grand strategy. What is the distinction between grand strategy and strategy *per se*? Grand strategy is the strategy of the long view, derived from national policy, involving a nation's long-term goals, its ideals, and its place in the world. As defined by B. H. Liddell-Hart, grand strategy involves

> the actual direction of military force, as distinct from the policy governing
> its employment, and combining it with other weapons: economic, political,
> psychological.

Grand strategy sets the goals; strategy fulfills them. Harry Truman was engaging in grand strategy with the Truman Doctrine, as was Ronald Reagan in his proactive campaign that finally defeated the USSR. George W. Bush's grand strategy for defeating terrorism is of the same order: to remake the region, replacing dictatorships with democracies in order to deprive terrorists of support—in Maoist terms, "drying up the water in which the insurgent fish swim."

It is a bold concept, as sweeping as anything that has occurred in the Middle East since the collapse of the Ottomans. Its execution will require years, if not decades—it's no accident that the administration has taken to calling the effort "the Long War."

This political goal set the agenda for the conduct of operations. The Coalition made few of the errors customary for a large army enmeshed in an insurgency—the mistakes of Vietnam were not repeated. Iraqis did not become "gooks"; their customs and culture remained respected. No free-fire zones were set up in the countryside. Apart from isolated imbecilities like Abu Ghraib, there was no brutality. Reprisals were avoided, as were deliberate attacks on civilians.

The Coalition displayed considerable adaptability once it became clear that insurgency was not simply gangs of stay-behinds but a broad and well-organized threat. Critics of the Coalition's performance in Iraq rarely mention that U.S. forces switched with no preparation or warning from a maneuver warfare campaign to a urban combat scenario (known by the unlovely acronym MOUT—Military Operations in Urbanized Terrain), and in truth one of the most difficult—battling an insurrection hiding among a friendly civilian population. The credit for this generally smooth transition goes to outstanding training and excellent commanders—the success of Gen. David Petraeus of the 101st Airborne in pacifying Mosul and that of Col. H. R. McMaster's 3rd Armored Combat Regiment in Tal Afar will be studied for years to come.

By locking himself into a strategy of attrition, Zarqawi enabled U.S. forces to vary their tactics in a search for what would work in the novel and complex Iraqi environment, an approach that might have been fatal against a nimbler opponent. Failed initiatives (e.g., the useless "Fallujah Brigade") were dropped, and the final strategy of "clear and hold," introduced in Fallujah in November 2004, began to pay off in 2005 as the appearance of capable Iraqi troops enabled the Coalition to clean out the Euphrates corridor and its "ratlines" to Syria. The recent "sand berm" technique, in which isolated towns are surrounded by sand walls to prevent both infiltration and escape by Jihadi forces, is an fine example of adapting imaginative tactics to a novel environment.

The Jihadi response was an increase in bomb size and what the Germans call *"Schrecklicheit"* (frightfulness—literally, "shriekmaking"). The list of potential victims expanded to include children, hospital patients, and members of funeral processions. Men seeking to join the police or military became particular targets, and were murdered in batches of a hundred at a time.

As 2005 progressed, the operations of Al-Qaeda in Iraq took on a form chillingly suggestive of the "disorderly" phase of psychopathic breakdown, with killings occurring with no rhyme or reason, as if the sole purpose was to pile the bodies high. When Zarqawi's allies among the Sunnis began to distance themselves, he struck out at them as well, assassinating four respected sheiks in Anbar Province, his stronghold, along with others elsewhere, in the process triggering feuds that continue to this day. The bloody *walpurgisnacht* culminated in an inexplicable attack on three Jordanian hotels (one of which was hosting a wedding party), resulting in near-universal obloquy throughout the Middle East. Lost amid all the bloodshed was any sign of the strategy that many onlookers claimed to detect—an attempt to trigger a civil war between Sunni and Shi'ite factions.

Faced with a choice between men who killed children and men who built schools, the Iraqis made the rational decision. The triple votes—two elections and a constitutional referendum—comprising the Purple Revolution were carried out peacefully, on schedule, and with acceptable results. Territory and bases were turned over to the newly formed Iraqi military, and the police force, long the

Achilles' heel of government efforts, began to come together. As 2006 opens, the Coalition's political program is achieving its goals, as revealed by the response to the Golden Mosque bombing, in which security forces stood firm and Sunnis, Shi'ites, and Kurds joined to halt a potential catastrophic break. (It's telling that even the thuggish Moqtada al-Sadr, whose militias were responsible for most of the killings that occurred, felt compelled to make overtures to his Sunni foes.) Recent reports tell of Sunni tribal fighters working with government troops to clean out the more troublesome provinces, which could well mean the end of Al-Queda in Iraq as a viable force. The Coalition effort has not been without errors and setbacks, but has been considerably more successful than critics are willing to grant.

Having failed in their two primary aims, the single Jihadi alternative is to roll back the Coalition program at any cost. What are their chances of bringing this off?

The Jihadis now face a serious dilemma. Their chosen weapon, the bomb, in its various manifestations, is losing effectiveness as Iraqi forces begin taking the lead. In short order, they'll be killing only Muslims, which is unacceptable to the Iraqi populace. (Recent polls among Iraqis reveal that up to 94% oppose attacks on Iraqi security forces while 97% oppose attacks on civilians. Oposition to attacks on foreigners is much lower.)

But fight on they must, or give up their dream of a new caliphate, of a return to a 'purified' Islam, of a world in which they are dominant. The Zawahiri letter touches gingerly on this problem. (How else would one reproach a man like Zarqawi?)

> "You know well," wrote Zawahiri, "that purity of faith and the correct way of living are not connected necessarily to success in the field unless you take into consideration the reasons and practices which events are guided by." The rest of Zawahiri's advice—some of which is excellent—can be summed up by the ancient saying that "tragedy in politics is when what is necessary is no longer possible."

So what possibilities are left? None open to the Jihadis acting on their own. Like guerillas, terrorists cannot prevail without intervention from an outside force. A coup or an invasion are the sole methods of destroying the budding Iraqi state (apart from the Iraqi's own errors). Both would require the cooperation of the Jihadis' local allies, and it's not at all certain that this would be forthcoming. The Baathist remnants almost certainly have a coup plan worked out and infiltrators in place within the government, army, and police, and Syria and Iran would both be eager to send troops across the border to rescue their lost Islamic brethren.

But Iraq will, for the foreseeable future, remain a protege of the United States, with a U.S. garrison maintained within the country's borders. Complete withdrawal is a fantasy—at least one base (and probably more) will remain, most likely in Kurdistan, with its America-loving population. Such a base would serve a large number of purposes that can't possibly be covered otherwise—air support and logistics, training of Iraqi forces, an intelligence window on Syria and Iran (and possibly a staging area for covert missions), and not the least, a barrier to prevent interference with the fledgling Iraqi state.

So the Jihadi problem may have no easy solution—which may explain why others in the region have been striking out on their own.

Two of the most surprising developments in the Middle East over the past year may well be responses to American success in Iraq.

The Iranian electoral system is one that fools a lot of people, almost all of whom are eager to claim that the election of Mahmoud Ahmadinejad "proves" something. In practice, a council of ayatollahs, answerable to no one, selects the candidates, using criteria known only to themselves. In Ahmadinejad's case, they went on to instruct local mullahs to order their flocks to vote for him. That may be an "election" in some sense of the term, but none that we recognize in this hemisphere.

The question remains as to why. The Iranian president is a figurehead, a mask for a theocratic despotism. Why go to such effort to elect a figurehead?

Iranian internal politics, the endless battles between "moderates" and "hard-liners," can't be ruled out. But we also can't overlook the Iranian view of international affairs. They have not forgotten the phrase "Axis of Evil," or the fact that Iran is number two on that list behind Saddam Hussein's Iraq. Everywhere they look, Kuwait, Dubai, Uzbekistan, Afghanistan, and Iraq, they find the U.S. military looking back. Under those circumstances, watching American forces at work in Axis Number One only a five-minute Tomahawk flight across the Persian Gulf must have been a sobering experience, particularly as Iraqi progress in 2005 began to free the most powerful land force in the world for potential duties elsewhere.

But the Iranians were also aware of the use to which Axis Number Three, North Korea (with which they had closely collaborated in the development of ballistic missiles), had put their nuclear weapons program. So they reached down into the country's political structure, plucked out the loudest, noisiest blusterer they could find (an ex-Revolutionary Guard and a "Twelver" to boot), one who could be depended on not to wilt under the spotlight, and threw him in front of the cameras.

It's interesting how closely the Iranian propaganda effort has matched that of North Korea's—the same stop and start activities with their nuclear programs, the same empty multinational negotiations, the same headline threats followed by back-door concessions. So far it has worked as well for Iran as it has for North Korea—Iran has become a problem, but, since the problem involves nuclear weapons, one that must be handled with caution.

Soviet premier Nikita Khrushchev did much the same thing in the 1950s, boasting that the Soviets were turning out nuclear-armed rockets "like sausages" and were simply blazing to fire some and see what they could do. This had results—it dampened any vague Western impulses toward aiding the Hungarian rebels in October 1956, and at the same time raised second thoughts concerning the Suez incursion.

It even had an effect on U.S. presidential politics, through the notorious "missile gap" that played a large role in the 1960 election.

But in the long run, it didn't work out well for the USSR—the U.S. response was a crash ICBM program, which succeeded in deploying over 1,000 missiles by the mid-60s. Something similar is likely for Iran. Ahmadinejad has succeeded in uniting not only the U.S. and Europe, but also, *mirabile dictu*, the UN. By any rational analysis, Iran is in a worse position than it held last year. But from the point of view of the Iranians, they have bought some time.

The other development is the Danish cartoon jihad. Despite inept mass media coverage, it's now widely understood that the scandal was a put-up job from first to last. But it's still unrecognized how broad-based the operation was. According to Amir Taheri, it involved the Arab League, the Muslim Brotherhood (the granddaddy of all Islamic terror organizations), the Islamic Liberation Party, the Movement of the Exiles, Al Jazeera, half a dozen Middle Eastern governments, and the Syrian and Iranian secret police. And the web may very well extend farther—Abu Laban, the Danish mullah who got the ball rolling, is an old associate of Ayman al Zawahiri.

This is an outlandishly large conspiracy for the sole purpose of embarrassing the mighty Danes. So the question arises once again: why? Why dig up a four-month-old provocation from a paper in Denmark, of all the innocuous places, and turn it into an international, umma-wide cause celebre? What got all these important figures involved? Why all the effort?

Taheri points out that the Syrians and Iranians had their reasons: Syria is under investigation for the Hariri assassination in Lebanon, while Denmark will be chairing the Security Council at the same time nuclear sanctions recommendations against Iran are making their way through the UN bureaucracy. But both were also late getting on the bandwagon. Iran originally dismissed Laban's troupe as Sunni pests, while Syria, these days, does nothing unless Iran moves first. Neither country got involved until the effort was well along.

A glance at the Middle Eastern timeline for late last year offers an explanation: what was the major event in the region between late September, when the cartoons first appeared to a universal yawn, and late January, when the mobs began howling? The answer: the December 15 parliamentary elections in Iraq, the keystone of U.S. efforts in the Middle East.

Clearly, the Danish cartoons are a pretext. Any other insult would have worked just as well. The actual target is the liberation of Iraq, and all that it portends for the region. The intended audience not the West, but the Muslim umma.

Viewed from that angle, it's no surprise that such heavy hitters became involved. American strategy embodies a threat to them all, Jihadis, religious throwbacks, and secular dictators alike. The advent of democracy marks the end of their way of doing business. What better method of forcing it back than to call on Muslim religious solidarity? Portraying the cartoons as an attack on Islam undercuts the attractions of democracy, drives an even wider wedge between Muslim states and the West, and characterizes the new Iraqi government as deluded servants of the Infidel, while the U.S. slips into its customary role as the Great Satan.

Several observers, among them Professor Sari Hanafi of American University in Beirut, concur, viewing the scandal as an attempt to limit the spread of democracy: ". . . you had regimes taking advantage saying, 'Look, this is the democracy they're talking about.'"

(The cartoon uproar scarcely registered in Iraq. The sole responses, some defiant talk from the minister of transport and a single demonstration in Baghdad,

were instigated by Moqtadr al-Sadr, a man who would throw himself into a vol-
cano if that would get him into the papers.)

There's an endless number of ways such campaigns can be played. More
public scandals can be cooked up (or else pulled from the Western media—recall
the Koran-in-the-toilet uproar, which may well have inspired Laban in the first
place), each portraying democracy and the West at large as inveterate enemies of
the Muslim umma, aided by the fact that Europe-based Muslims like Laban know
exactly what buttons to push on both sides. The Iraqi insurrection can be characterized as a battle to save Iraqi Muslims from a depraved, secular West, with the
Jihadis taking the role of defenders of Islam.

The sole drawbacks are that such campaigns are obviously a sign of
Muslim weakness, not strength. It's also doubtful how far they can be taken—
there's no such thing as keeping a population at constant fever pitch. Eventually
the effort will reach a point of diminishing returns.

But these examples do suggest that the struggle in the Middle East has
mutated, with the Islamists and their allies—the Arab nationalists and the old
regimes—adapting a new strategy: the struggle to halt reform in the Middle East
is no longer, for the moment, a military effort, but a political one.

A political attack requires a political response. Not that military efforts can
be dropped—not while the Jihadis remain active in Iraq and the Iranians still
present a threat. But the major effort for the near future will occur on the political plane. As for countermoves, three approaches suggest themselves.

The first is a more effective method of fighting public convulsions of the
cartoon intifada type. The cartoon tempest was essentially a conspiracy involving
individuals, NGOs, and governments. All of them can be targeted in one way or
another, to clarify the point that any repetition will have a price. A first step would
be the immediate expulsion of Abu Laban, who at last report was still roaming
around Copenhagen. News comes today that Denmark has arrested Fadi Abdullatif
for threatening the government for distributing a leaflet urging Muslims to
"eliminate" rulers that prevent them from joining the Iraq insurgency.

Also advisable would be the defunding of Yusuf al Qaradawi, the popular
mullah (he has his own show on Al Jazeera) who signed the fatwa against
Denmark, and whose branch of the Muslim Brotherhood is financed by none
other than the EU. (I have racked my brains for some rational explanation for
this, and have come up with nothing.)

Above all, the response must be consistent. This was not a conspiracy
against Denmark, but against the West and all its values. The only way to face
such provocations is with a united front. European attitudes toward such
matters—the mixture of frivolity, fatalism, and avarice that has marked all their
recent dealings with the Middle East—must in particular be brought up short.
This may in fact be occurring in response to events.

The second approach should be engagement of Middle Eastern governments and ruling classes to persuade them that democracy is coming, that it cannot be stopped, and that it is not a threat. Apart from the mullahs, these people
are the major roadblock to serious reform. They view democracy with deep
suspicion, and with some reason. The shabby fate of the Hindu nobility, who

willingly gave up their ancestral holdings to the Indian government only to have the promised subsidies cut off a few years later, must always be before their eyes. But other examples do exist: buried in the uproar elsewhere in the Gulf is the fact that Bahrain became a constitutional monarchy in February 2002, thanks to a wise decision by King Hamad. Some people are prepared to take the step. On the other hand, Iranian ex-president Mohamed Khatami's recent call for democracy should be viewed with caution—it's doubtful that he means the same as we do in the West. (This is also true of the results of the Palestinian election, taken by many observers as evidence that the Bush strategy is empty. There is simply no rational way that a contest between two murderous terror organizations can be considered a "democratic election.")

The recently-released *Quadrennial Defense Review* envisions a second stage in the war against terror involving active undercutting of AQAM's (al-Qaeda and Affiliated Movements, the military term) appeal to the Muslim populace. Condeleezza Rice's "transformational diplomacy," in which crucial assets of the U.S. Foreign Service will be shifted to the Middle East from Europe, is aimed at implementing a democratic program. But it can't simply be left to the Defense and State Departments. (I keep trying to picture Joseph C. Wilson IV carrying out the assignment, but the image simply won't gel.) Such a campaign of influence and persuasion seems tailor-made for NGOs and trade associations in business, the sciences, and the arts and entertainment. It's dismaying to consider how few of this country's resources have actually been brought to bear against the terrorist threat. Many people would be willing to act but lack necessary direction. Some effort must be made to provide this.

The third and most difficult task involves getting through to the Muslim masses. To read the Middle Eastern media is an exercise in despair. Absolutely nothing of the Western or American case gets through. The Muslim worldview is a sad morass of conspiracy theories, ethnic and religious hatreds, and paranoia. (Only a handful of exceptions exist—the Saudi *Arab News* and the *Beirut Daily Star* among them.)

Last year's roadshow led by Karen Hughes was supposed to help correct this, but went nowhere. Which doesn't mean that it should not be reattempted, with more in the way of resources and imagination. There are plenty of successful, happy, and well-integrated American Muslims. We need to recruit from among them to speak to people of their own backgrounds about the America that they themselves know. More sophisticated approaches can be worked out by bringing together Western figures familiar with the culture and politics of the Middle East, such as Mansoor Ijaz, Salim Mansur, Amir Taheri, Fouad Ajami, Ayaan Hirsi Ali, Wafa Sultan, and for that matter, Bernard Lewis and David Pryce-Jones. The U.S. has a lot to tell the people of the Muslim world. Some, at least, will listen. Everyone who does is one less supporter of jihad.

A political solution is necessary to secure the military victories already won. This strategy will require patience, understanding, and willingness to overcome setbacks. Things are going to happen that we do not like. There will be disappointments and failures. These are not products of policy, but aspects of the human condition. None of them will be any reason to turn back or abandon the effort. Errors can [be] corrected, failures can be overcome. And it should never be forgotten that, in the words of Churchill, the ongoing liberation of the Middle East remains "one of the great unsordid acts of history."

As it stands, there is little likelihood that the Jihadis will turn back U.S. gains. Al-Qaeda and it allies are paying the price of a flawed strategy. The Jihadis went into this war convinced that terror would carry all before it—a thesis disproven for all time. There is no practical action they can take to recover. (They might begin by replacing Zarqawi, but who would volunteer to bell that cat?) A nuclear-armed Iran would open new vistas, but that's the very reason, among many others, that Iran will not be allowed to procure them in the first place. The Iranian situation is an example of the type that Curtis LeMay used to dismiss with the words, "No alternative, so no problem."

Paradoxically, the Jihadi field of action is more constricted in their own backyard, the Middle East, than elsewhere. Iraq has been a trap for the Islamist cause, costing them well over 50,000 casualties and prisoners. It's difficult to conceive a set of circumstances where it will ever be anything else. The Jihadis, and their allies, are always going to be in a position where resistance will cost them more than they're able to pay. And that's the way you want a war to go.

And besides, there are better targets elsewhere.

Robert Jervis

 **NO**

Why the Bush Doctrine Cannot Be Sustained

With the reelection of George W. Bush, the apparent progress of democracy in Iraq and other countries in the Middle East, and the agreement of allies that Iran and North Korea should not be permitted to gain nuclear weapons, the prospects for what can be called the Bush Doctrine seem bright. I believe this impression is misleading, however, and politics within the United States and abroad is more likely to conspire against the course that Bush has set.

The Bush Doctrine, set out in numerous speeches by the President and other high-level officials and summarized in the September 2002 "National Security Strategy of the United States," consists of four elements. First and perhaps most importantly, democracies are inherently peaceful and have common interests in building a benign international environment that is congenial to American interests and ideals. This means that the current era is one of great opportunity because there is almost universal agreement on the virtues of democracy. Second, this is also a time of great threat from terrorists, especially when linked to tyrannical regimes and weapons of mass destruction (WMD). A third major element of the Bush Doctrine is that deterrence and even defense are not fully adequate to deal with these dangers and so the United States must be prepared to take preventive actions, including war, if need be. In part because it is difficult to get consensus on such actions, and in part because the United States is so much stronger than its allies, the United States must be prepared to act unilaterally. Thus the fourth element of the Doctrine is that although the widest possible support should be sought, others cannot have a veto on American action. . . .

The Bush Doctrine combines a war on terrorism with the strong assertion of American hegemony. Although elements arguably reinforced each other in the overthrow of the Taliban, it is far from clear that this will be the case in the future. Rooting out terrorist cells throughout the world calls for excellent information, and this requires the cooperation of intelligence services in many countries. American power allows it to deploy major incentives to induce cooperation, but there may come a point at which opposition to U.S. dominance will hamper joint efforts. The basic unilateralism of the U.S. behavior that goes with assertive hegemony as exemplified by the war in Iraq has strained the alliance bonds in a way that can make fighting terrorism more difficult.

Iraq highlights a related tension in the Bush Doctrine. The administration argued that overthrowing Saddam Hussein was a part of the war on terrorism because of the danger that he would give WMD to terrorists. Bush calls Iraq the "the central front" in the counterterrorist effort, and he rhetorically asks, "If America were not fighting terrorists in Iraq, . . . what would these thousands of killers do, suddenly begin leading productive lives of service and charity?"

I join many observers in finding this line of argument implausible and in believing that the war was, at best, a distraction from the struggle against al Qaeda. To start with, diplomatic, military, and intelligence resources that could have been used to seek out terrorists, especially in Afghanistan, were redeployed against Iraq. In perhaps an extreme case, in June of 2002, the White House vetoed a plan to attack a leading terrorist and his poison laboratory in northern Iraq because it might have disturbed the efforts to build a domestic and international coalition to change the regime, and Abu Musab al-Zarqawi later emerged as the most important insurgent in Iraq and second only to Osama bin Laden on the overall most-wanted list. More generally, thanks to the war, the United States is now seen as a major threat to peace, and in many countries, George Bush is more disliked than bin Laden. Of course, foreign policy is not a popularity contest, but these views eventually will be reflected in reduced support for and cooperation with the United States. Finally and most importantly, if the United States is fighting terrorists in Iraq, the main reason is not that they have flocked to that country to try to kill Americans but that the occupation has recruited large numbers of people to the terrorist cause. Although evidence, let alone proof, is of course elusive, it is hard to avoid the inference that the war has created more terrorists than it has killed, has weakened the resolve of others to combat them, and has increased the chance of major attacks against the West.

Even without the stimulus of the American occupation of Iraq, the highly assertive American policy around the world may increase the probability that it will be the target of terrorist attacks, inasmuch as others attribute most of the world's ills to America. Whether terrorists seek vengeance, publicity, or specific changes in policy, the dominant state is likely to be the one they seek to attack. American power, then, produces American vulnerability. If the United States wanted to place priority on reducing its attractiveness as a target for terrorism, it could seek a reduced role in world politics. The real limits to what could be done here should not disguise the tension between protection from terror and hegemony.

The Bush Doctrine argues that combatting terrorism and limiting proliferation go hand in hand. They obviously do in some cases. The danger that a rogue state could provide terrorists with WMD, although implausible in the case of Iraq, is not fictitious, and controlling the spread of nuclear weapons and nuclear material contributes to American security. But this does not mean that there are no trade-offs between nonproliferation and rooting out terrorism. Most obviously, Iraq's drain on American military resources, time and energy, and on the support from the international community means that the ability to deal with Iran and North Korea has been reduced. These two countries figured prominently in administration fears before September 11 and are more dangerous and perhaps more likely to provide weapons to terrorists than was Iraq. But the way the Bush administration interpreted the war on terror has hindered its ability to deal with these threats, and, in an added irony, if Iran gets nuclear weapons, the United States may be forced to provide a security guarantee for Iraq or permit that country to develop its own arsenal. Furthermore, even if better conceived, combating terrorism can call for alliances with regimes that seek or even spread nuclear weapons. The obvious example is Pakistan, a vital American ally that has been the greatest facilitator of proliferation. The United States eventually uncovered A. Q. Kahn's network and forced President Pervez Musharraf to cooperate in rolling it up, but it might have moved more quickly and strongly had it not needed Pakistan's support against al Qaeda. This compromise is not likely to be the last, and the need to choose between these goals will continue to erode the Bush Doctrine's coherence.

Despite its *realpolitik* stress on the importance of force, the Bush Doctrine also rests on idealistic foundations—the claim for the centrality of universal values represented by America, the expected power of positive example, the belief in the possibility of progress. What is important is that these have power through their acceptance by others, not through their imposition by American might. They require that others change not only their behavior but their outlook, if not their values, as well. For this to happen, the United States has to be seen as well-motivated and exemplifying shared ideals. America's success in the Cold War derived in part from its openness to allied voices, its articulation of a common vision, and a sense of common interest. Although we should not idealize this past or underestimate the degree to which allies, let alone neutrals, distrusted U.S. power and motives, neither should we neglect the ways that enabled influence to be exercised relatively cheaply and allowed the West to gain a much greater degree of unity and cooperation than many contemporary observers had believed possible.

Then, as now, the United States needed not only joint understandings but also multilateral institutions to provide for cooperation on a wide range of issues, especially economic ones. Perhaps the United States can ignore or diminish them in the security area without affecting those such as the World Trade Organization (WTO) on which it wants to continue to rely, but the possibility of undesired spillovers is not to be dismissed. If others do not expect the United States to respect limits that rules might place on it, they are less apt to see it as a trustworthy partner.

Just as the means employed by the Bush Doctrine contradict its ends, so also the latter, by being so ambitious, invite failure. Not only is it extremely unlikely that terror can ever be eradicated, let alone the world be rid of evil, but the fact that Saddam lost the war in Iraq does not mean that the United States won it. Ousting his regime was less important in itself than as a means to other objectives: reducing terrorism, bringing democracy to Iraq, transforming the Middle East, and establishing the correctness and the legitimacy of the Bush Doctrine. Although the effects of the invasion have not yet fully played out, it is hard to see it as a success in these terms. Indeed, despite the fact that the January 2005 elections in Iraq were relatively successful, the political outlook for the country is not good. Ironically, the dramatic and disabling insurgency has distracted American if not Iraqi attention from what is probably the even less-tractable problem of establishing a political settlement among those who have not (yet) resorted to arms. Overly ambitious goals invite not only defeat, but disillusion; if the experiment in Iraq does not yield satisfactory results, it will be hard to sustain support for the Doctrine in the future.

Finally, the Bush Doctrine is vulnerable because although it rests on the ability to deploy massive force, its army, despite being capable of great military feats, is not large enough to simultaneously garrison a major country and attack another adversary, and may not even be sufficient for the former task over a prolonged period. Thanks to the occupation of Iraq, the United States could not now use ground force against Iran or North Korea, and, indeed, the occupation appears to be gravely damaging the system of a volunteer-army, reserves, and national guard that has proven so successful since the draft was abolished more than a quarter-century ago. . . .

Public opinion, the structure of the U.S. government, and domestic politics make it difficult to sustain the Bush Doctrine or any other clear policy. "It seems that the United States was a very difficult country to govern," Charles de Gaulle is said to have told British Prime Minister Harold Macmillan when explaining why it was hard to count on the United States. The General was correct: democracies, and especially the United States, do not find it easy to sustain a clear line of policy when the external environment is not compelling. Domestic priorities ordinarily loom large, and few Americans think of their country as having an imperial mission. Wilsonianism may provide a temporary substitute for the older European ideologies of a *mission civilisatrice* and "the white man's burden," but because it rests on the assumption that its role will be not only noble but also popular, I am skeptical that it will endure if it meets much opposition from those who are supposed to benefit from it. . . .

At first glance, it would seem that much as the experts criticize the Bush Doctrine for its unilateralism, on this score, at least, it rests on secure domestic foundations. The line that drew the most applause in the President's 2004 State of the Union address was: "America will never seek a permission slip to defend the security of our country." In fact, the public is, sensibly, ambivalent. Although few would argue that the lack of international support should stop the United States from acting when a failure to do so would endanger the country, polls taken in the run-up to the war in Iraq indicated that international endorsement would have added as much as 20 percentage points to support for attacking. Even in a country with a strong tradition of unilateralism, people realize that international support translates into a reduced burden on the United States and increased legitimacy that can both aid the specific endeavor at hand and strengthen the patterns of cooperation that serve American interests. Furthermore, many people take endorsement by allies as an indication that the American policy is sensible. This is a great deal of the reason why Tony Blair's support for Bush was so important domestically, and this means that the Bush Doctrine is particularly vulnerable to British defection.

In summary, although the combination of Bush's preferences and the attack of September 11 have produced a coherent doctrine, domestic support is likely to erode. Congress will become increasingly assertive as the war continues, especially if it does not go well; the Democrats, although lacking a consistent policy of their own, have not accepted the validity of Bush's strategy; and although the public is united in its desire to oppose terrorism, the way to do so is disputed. The United States remains a very difficult country to govern.

It is particularly difficult for the Bush Doctrine to maintain public support, because preventive wars require more-accurate assessment of the international environment than intelligence can provide. The basic idea of nipping threats in the bud, of acting when there is still time, implies a willingness to accept false positives in order to avoid more-costly false negatives. That is, the United States must act on the basis of far from complete information, because if it hesitates until the threat is entirely clear, it will be too late: it cannot afford to wait until the smoking gun is a mushroom cloud, to use the phrase the administration favored before the Iraq war. In principle, this is quite reasonable. The costs of a WMD attack are so high that a preventive war could be rational even if retrospect were to reveal that it was not actually necessary.

Even if this approach is intellectually defensible, however, it is not likely to succeed politically. The very nature of a preventive war means that the evidence is ambiguous and the supporting arguments are subject to rebuttal. If Britain and France had gone to war with Germany before 1939, large segments of the public would have believed that the war was not necessary. If the war had gone well, public opinion might still have questioned its wisdom; had it gone badly, the public would have been inclined to sue for peace. At least as much today, the cost of a war that is believed to be unnecessary will be high in terms of both international and domestic opinion and will sap the support for the policy. (Indeed, in the case of Iraq, the administration chose not to admit that the war was not forced on it despite the clear evidence that the central claims used to justify it were incorrect.) Even if the public does not judge that the administration should be turned out of power for its mistake, it is not likely to want the adventure to be repeated.

Preventive war, then, asks a great deal of intelligence. It does not bode well for the Bush Doctrine that not only did the war in Iraq involve a massive intelligence failure concerning WMD (which is different from saying that it was caused by this failure), but also the United States started the war two days ahead of schedule because agents incorrectly claimed to know the whereabouts of Saddam Hussein and his sons. The amazing accuracy of the munitions that destroyed the location only underlined the falsity of the information.

The case for preventive war against Iraq turned on the claim that it had active WMD programs, and so, in retrospect, the question is often posed as to whether the intelligence was faulty or whether the Bush administration distorted it. I think the former was dominant but the latter should not be ignored. . . .

Despite the fact that the United States has more room to maneuver now that it does not have to worry about a new regime allying with a major enemy state, there appears to be a great deal of continuity between the U.S. policy during the Cold War, what it did in the first decade after it, and Bush's actions. While the United States hopes to replace hostile dictatorships with democracies, only rarely does it push for democracy when doing so could destabilize friendly regimes. It would be tiresome to recount the sorry but perhaps sensible history of U.S. policies toward Egypt, Pakistan, and Saudi Arabia, and I will just note that when the latter arrested reformers who had called for a constitutional monarchy and independent human rights monitoring, Colin Powell said that "each nation has to find its own path and follow that path at its own speed." Over the past year, Bush and his colleagues have taken a somewhat stronger position, but the depth of the American commitment still remains unclear.

Ironically, the war on terrorism, although accompanied by greater stress on the value of democracy, has increased the costs of acting accordingly by increasing the American need for allies throughout the globe. Without the war, the United States might have put more pressure on the nondemocratic states of the former Soviet Union, or at least not supported them. But the need for bases in Central Asia has led the United States to embrace a particularly unsavory set of regimes. The pressure to democratize Pakistan is similarly minimal, in part because of the fear that greater responsiveness to public opinion would lead to an unacceptable Islamic regime. This danger, and that of any kind of instability, is magnified because of Pakistan's nuclear arsenal. Although Egypt lacks nuclear weapons, instability in such a powerful and centrally placed country is also greatly to be feared. In other parts of the Middle East and areas such as the Caspian basin, it is the need for a secure flow of oil that leads the United States to support nondemocratic regimes. . . .

Furthermore, the Bush administration appears to be driven more by the politics of the regimes it is dealing with than by an abstract commitment to democracy, as is shown by its stance toward if not its role in the opposition (constitutional or otherwise) to, Hugo Chavez in Venezuela and Jean-Bertrand Aristide in Haiti. In a continuation of the Cold War pattern, leftist governments are seen as dangerous and authoritarian regimes of the right are acceptable. On other occasions, it is the specific policies of a leader that make him unacceptable despite his popular approval. The American refusal to treat Yasser Arafat as the Palestinians' leader was rooted in the belief that he was unwilling to stop terrorism, not in his inability to win an election, and the United States withdrew its recognition of President Rauf Denktash in Turkish Cyprus when he opposed proposals for reunifying the island.

But even vigorous support for democracy might not produce that outcome. The fate of Iraq may not yet be determined, and, at this writing, anything appears to be possible, from a partially democratic regime to a civil war to the return of a national strongman to the loss of national unity. But it is hard to believe that the foreseeable future will see a full-fledged democracy, with extensive rule of law, open competition, a free press, and checks and balances. The best that can be hoped for would be a sort of semi-democracy, such as we see in Russia or Nigeria, to take two quite different countries.

The Bush administration's position is much more optimistic, however, arguing that for democracy to flourish, all that is needed is for repression to be struck down. With a bit of support, all countries can become democratic; far from being the product of unusually propitious circumstances, a free and pluralist system is the "natural order" that will prevail unless something special intervenes. President Bush devoted a full speech to this subject, saying: "Time after time, observers have questioned whether this country, or that people, or this group, are 'ready' for democracy—as if freedom were a prize you win for meeting our own Western standards of progress. In fact, the daily work of democracy is itself the path of progress." This means that for him, the prospects for Iraq are bright. In his view, although it is true that you cannot force people to be democratic, this is not necessary. All that is needed is to allow people to be democratic.

We would all like this vision to be true, but it probably is not. Even if there are no conditions that are literally necessary for the establishment of democracy, this form of government is not equally likely to flourish under all conditions. Poverty, deep divisions, the fusion of secular and religious authority, militaristic traditions and institutions, and a paucity of attractive careers for defeated politicians all inhibit democracy. Although Bush is at least partly right in arguing that some of these conditions arise out of authoritarian regimes, they are causes as well and there is no reason to expect the United States to be able to make most countries democratic even if it were to bend all its efforts to this end. Indeed, movements for reform and democracy may suffer if they are seen as excessively beholden to the United States. As Colin Powell noted after one American attempt of this type had to be abandoned in the face of cries of U.S. bullying, "I think we are now getting a better understanding with the Arab nations that it has to be something that comes from them. If you don't want us to help, you don't want us to help."

Is it even true that the world would be safer and the United States better off if many more countries were democratic? The best-established claim that democracies rarely, if ever, fight each other is not entirely secure, and the more sophisticated versions of this theory stress that joint democracy will not necessarily produce peace unless other factors, especially economic interdependence and a commitment to human rights, are present as well. This makes sense, because democracy is compatible with irreconcilable conflicts of interest. Furthermore, even if well-established democracies do not fight each other, states that are undergoing transitions to democracy do not appear to be similarly pacifistic. Putting these problems aside, there is no reason to expect democracies to be able to get along well with nondemocracies, which means that establishing democracy in Iraq or in any other country will not make the world more peaceful unless its neighbors are similarly transformed.

The Bush administration has also argued that other countries are much more likely to support American foreign policy objectives if they are democratic. The basic point that democracies limit the power of rulers has much to be said for it, but it is far from clear how far this will translate into shared foreign policy goals. After all, at bottom, democracy means that a state's policy will at least roughly reflect the objectives and values of the population, and there is no reason to believe that these should be compatible between one country and another. Why would a democratic Iraq share American views on the Arab–Israeli dispute, for example? Would a democratic Iran be a closer ally than the Shah's regime was? If Pakistan were truly democratic, would it oppose Islamic terrorism? In many cases, if other countries become more responsive to public opinion, they will become more anti-American. In the key Arab states of Jordan, Egypt, and Saudi Arabia, cooperation with the United States could not be sustained if the public had greater influence; the elections in Pakistan in September of 2002 reduced the regime's stability and complicated the efforts to combat al Qaeda, results that would have been magnified had the elections been truly free; in Europe, the public is even more critical of the United States than are the leaders. . . .

Turning to what is already clear from events since September 11, the Bush Doctrine and the war in Iraq have weakened Western unity and called into question the potency of deterrence by claiming that the United States could not have contained a nuclear-armed Saddam. I think this belief was incorrect, but because deterrence rests on potential challengers' understanding that the defender is confident of its deterrent threats, the American demonstration of its lack of faith in this instrument will diminish its utility. Even if future administrations adopt a different stance and affirm the role of deterrence, some damage may be permanent.

The largely unilateral overthrow of Saddam has set in motion even more important irreversible changes in relations with allies. Before Bush came to power, the emerging consensus was that the United States was committed to multilateralism. This is not to say that it would never act without the consent of its leading allies, but that on major issues, it would consult fully, listen carefully, and give significant weight to allied views. International institutions, deeply ingrained habits, the sense of shared values and interests, close connections at the bureaucratic levels, public support for this way of proceeding, and the understanding that long-run cooperation was possible only if the allies had faith that the United States would not exploit its superior power position all led to a structure that inhibited American unilateralism. This partial world order, it was argued, served American interests as well as those of its partners, because it induced the latter to cooperate with each other and with the United States, reduced needless frictions, and laid the foundations for prosperity and joint measures to solve common problems. This way of doing business had such deep roots that it could absorb exogenous shocks and the election of new leaders.

Recent events have shown that although the argument may have been correct normatively, it was not correct empirically. It is quite possibly true that it would have been wise for the United States to have continued on the multilateral path, to have maintained a broad coalition, and to have given its allies more influence over the way it fought terrorism. But we can now see that it was wrong to conclude that the international system and U.S. policy had evolved to a point that compelled this approach.

This does not mean that the United States is now firmly set on a new course. Indeed, I do not think that the Bush Doctrine can be sustained. Bush's domestic support rests on the belief that he is making the United States safer, not on an endorsement of a wider transformationist agenda. Especially in the absence of a clear political victory in Iraq, support for assertive hegemony is limited at best. But if Bush is forced to retract, he will not revert to the sort of coalition-building that Clinton favored. Of course there will be a new president elected in 2008, but even if he or she wanted to pick up where Clinton left off, this will not be possible. Although allies would meet the United States more than halfway in their relief that policy had changed, they would realize that the permanence of the new American policy could not be guaranteed. The familiar role of anarchy in limiting the ability of states to bind themselves has been highlighted by Bush's behavior and will not be forgotten.

The United States and others, then, face a difficult task. The collapse of the Bush foreign policy will not leave clear ground on which to build: new policies and forms of cooperation will have to be jury-rigged above the rubble of the recent past. The Bush administration having asserted the right (and the duty) to maintain order and provide what it believes to be collective goods, an American retraction will be greeted with initial relief by many, but it is also likely to produce disorder, unpredictability, and opportunities for others.

Machiavelli famously asked whether it is better to be feared or to be loved. The problem for the United States is that it is likely to be neither. Bush's unilateralism and perceived bellicosity have weakened ties to allies, dissipated much of the sympathy that the United States had garnered after September 11, and convinced many people that America was seeking an empire with little room for their interests or values. It will be very hard for any future administration to regain the territory that has been lost. At best, the policy is a gigantic gamble that a stable and decent regime can be established in Iraq and that this can produce reform in the other countries and a settlement between Israel and the Palestinians. In this case, the United States might gain much more support and approval, if not love. But anything less will leave the United States looking neither strong nor benign, and we may find that the only thing worse than a successful hegemon is a failed one. We are headed for a difficult world, one that is not likely to fit any of our ideologies or simple theories.

POSTSCRIPT

Does the War in Iraq Help the War Against Terrorism?

Whether the prosecution of the war in Iraq helps to defeat the war against terrorism or results in an increase in terrorist activity is bound to be a critical question—perhaps the decisive question—in the presidential election of 2008. Some of the almost-certain themes in that election are sounded in the preceding selections by J. R. Dunn and Robert Jervis.

Two of the most prominent essayists supporting the war in Iraq and the war on terror are William Kristol, editor of *The Weekly Standard,* and Robert Kagan, senior associate at the Carnegie Endowment for International Peace. Separately and together, they have written many books and articles dealing with America's role in the world. In a book they co-edited, *Present Dangers: Crisis and Opportunity in America's Foreign and Defense Policy* (Encounter Books, 2000), Kristol and Kagan call for a foreign policy of "benevolent hegemony" in order to secure peace and advance American ideals throughout the world. In their essay in that volume, "National Interest and Global Responsibility," they maintain that it would be dangerous and less congenial to democracy and liberty to share world dominance with other nations.

Norman Podhoretz, editor of *Commentary,* in which other defenses of the Bush doctrine have appeared, has written "The Panic Over Iraq" (*Commentary,* January 2006), in which he provides support for both the invasion of Iraq and the war on terror. James Fallows deplores what he called "Bush's Lost Year," *The Atlantic Monthly,* October 2004, because the president did not reconstruct Afghanistan, did not deal with the threats posed by North Korea and Iran, and did not wage an effective war on terror.

William Blum has compiled his harshly critical essays in *Freeing the World to Death: Essays on the American Empire* (Common Courage Press, 2005). Blum maintains that the United States vastly understates the resistance of ordinary Iraqi citizens who are not terrorists, but oppose being invaded, bombed, occupied, and humiliated by an invading power. We are losing the war on terror, according to Daniel Benjamin and Steven Simon, both former staff members of the National Security Council. In their book, *The Next Attack: The Failure of the War on Terror and a Strategy for Getting It Right* (Henry Holt, 2005), they argue that the invasion of Iraq radicalized large numbers of Iraqis and other Muslims. On the contrary, Richard A. Falkenrath asserts in "Grading the War on Terrorism," in *Foreign Affairs,* January/February 2006, Iraq has been more of a burial ground than a breeding ground for Islamic terrorists.

Richard A. Clarke, who was the National Security Council's antiterrorism chief under Presidents Clinton and Bush, wrote *Against All Enemies: Inside America's War on Terror* (Free Press, 2004), in which he charges that he could not persuade National Security Advisor Condoleezza Rice to schedule meetings to plan how to deal with al Qaeda and that President Bush himself urged Clarke to find a relationship between Iraq and the 9/11 attack on the United States.

The Council on Foreign Relations has published a transcript of a 2005 debate on *The Law of War in the War on Terrorism: A Council on Foreign Relations Debate.* The participants were University of California, Berkeley law professor John Yoo, defending the Bush administration's anti-terror policy, and Human Right Watch executive director Kenneth Roth, opposing that policy.

The United States Department of State issues an annual report on terrorism. The 2007 report (issued before the increase in American troops in Iraq in what President Bush described as a "surge") concluded that international counterterrorism cooperation is improving, but new terrorist tactics and a spike in Iraqi violence led to a worldwide increase in terrorist incidents in 2006. The report declared that al Qaeda, although weakened, remains "the most immediate national security threat to the United States."

Hearings in 2007 before the Armed Services Committee of the House of Representatives resulted in conflicting testimony as to whether the war in Iraq helped or hurt the war against terrorism. Tony Blankley believes that the stakes could not be higher in *The West's Last Chance: Will We Win the Clash of Civilizations?* (Regnery, 2005). If the United States and its allies do not defeat revolutionary Islam in Iraq, they will have to fight it elsewhere, and there is a genuine basis for fearing that militant Islam and terrorism will prevail in Europe.

F. Gregory Gause asks "Can Democracy Stop Terrorism?" in *Foreign Affairs* (September/October 2005), and concludes that a push for democracy in the Muslim world will not improve American national security. On the contrary, there is no evidence that democracy reduces terrorism. In fact, a democratic Middle East would probably result in Islamist governments unwilling to cooperate with the United States. This raises the question as to what policies the United States should pursue in Iraq in order to combat terrorism.

ISSUE 17

Is "Middle Eastern" Profiling Ever Justified?

YES: Daniel Pipes, from "Fighting Militant Islam, Without Bias," *City Journal* (November 2001)

NO: David A. Harris, from "'Flying While Arab,' Immigration Issues, and Lessons from the Racial Profiling Controversy," Testimony before the U.S. Commission on Civil Rights (October 12, 2001)

ISSUE SUMMARY

YES: Daniel Pipes, director of the Middle East Forum, argues that "heightened scrutiny" of Muslims and Middle Eastern–looking people is justified because, while not all Muslims are Islamic extremists, all Islamic extremists are Muslims.

NO: Law professor David A. Harris opposes profiling people of Middle Eastern appearance because, like racial profiling, it compromises civil liberties and actually damages our intelligence efforts.

T he word "stereotype" was introduced into political and social discourse by journalist-philosopher Walter Lippmann in *Public Opinion,* a book he published in 1922. Lippmann called stereotypes the "pictures in our heads," images of reality that we have in our minds even before sense data arrive there. Often these *a priori* definitions produce hasty, distorted generalizations of what is "out there" in the real world. He gives as an example, news reports describing the appearance of "radical" gatherings:

> There is, of course, some connection between the scene outside and the mind through which we watch it, just as there are some long-haired men and short-haired women in radical gatherings. But to the hurried observer a slight connection is enough. If there are two bobbed heads and four beards in the audience, it will be a bobbed and bearded audience to the reporter who knows beforehand that such gatherings are composed of people with these tastes in the management of their hair.

A reporter who consistently brings these stereotypes into news coverage is doing the readers a disservice, but at least they are free to check the reports for accuracy by comparing them to those in another news source. The case is different, though, if the stereotyping is being done by a government official. Government has a monopoly of coercive powers, so when an official engages in stereotyping, a perfectly innocent man or woman may be forced to submit to heightened scrutiny, or humiliating searches, or long interrogations, simply because of the person's appearance. This raises serious issues about civil liberties and civil rights.

Yet the issues are not easy to resolve. We tend to think of stereotyping as invariably wrong, but that was not Lippmann's view. First of all, he insisted, stereotyping cannot be avoided. We do not innocently perceive all the "facts" around us—we decide *which* facts are relevant and then combine them in our own ways. "A report is the joint product of the knower and known, in which the role of the observer is always selective and usually creative." Secondly, he contended, stereotypes are essential if we are to make sense of our world. A stereotype, then, is not unlike a road map, providing a simplified, schematic picture of what is otherwise an impossibly complicated set of facts.

How might Lippmann's observations, made in 1922, apply to the case of Middle Eastern profiling in the twenty-first century? If Lippmann were right to say that stereotyping is inevitable and even necessary to make sense of the world, then perhaps a case can be made for such profiling. Should we require an 82-year-old grandmother to remove her shoes at the airline gate, simply because we just asked a 25-year-old single man from Yemen to do the same? Our stereotype tells us that she is far less likely to have a bomb in her shoe; our common sense tells us that we can more efficiently use resources by concentrating our attention on people like him.

Notice, however, that our stereotype is more complicated than it may seem at first. The Middle Easterner in this hypothetical case is also male, unmarried, and in his twenties. This invites us to complicate the picture a little more. Remembering that Timothy McVeigh, the Oklahoma City bomber, and John Walker Linde, who consorted with the Taliban in Afghanistan, were Caucasian Americans, suppose we compare an 82-year-old Middle Eastern grandmother to a young white American man who has just bought a one-way ticket and looks nervous and shifty-eyed. Which of the two passengers deserves closer scrutiny? If we agree that in this case it would be the American, then there would seem to be qualitative differences among stereotypes; some are better than others. That was Lippmann's view. We need to put "more inclusive patterns" in our stereotypes, and, realizing that they *are* only stereotypes, "to hold them lightly, to modify them gladly."

In these dangerous times, we must somehow strike a balance between liberty and security.

In the following selections, Daniel Pipes, director of the Middle East Forum, argues that in the post–9/11 world, "heightened scrutiny" of Muslims and Middle Eastern–looking people is justified because, while not all Muslims are Islamic extremists, all Islamic extremists are Muslims. Law professor David A. Harris opposes profiling people of Middle Eastern appearance because, like racial profiling, it compromises civil liberties and actually damages our intelligence efforts.

327

YES

Daniel Pipes

Fighting Militant Islam, Without Bias

The whole country, and New York especially, has to face an urgent question in the wake of the September 11 attacks, organized by a militant Islamic network and carried out by Arabic-speaking Muslims resident in North America: how should Americans now view and treat the Muslim populations living in their midst?

Initial reactions have differed widely. Elite opinion, as voiced by President Bush, rushed to deny any connection between the acts of war and the resident Muslim population. "Islam is peace," Bush assured Americans, adding, "we should not hold one who is a Muslim responsible for an act of terror." Attorney General Ashcroft, Governor Pataki, and Mayor Giuliani closely echoed these comments. Secretary of State Powell went further still, declaring that the attacks "should not be seen as something done by Arabs or Islamics; it is something that was done by terrorists"—as though Arabs and Muslims by definition can't be terrorists.

This approach may have made sense as a way to calm the public and prevent attacks against Muslims, but it clearly failed to convince everyone. Rep. John Cooksey (R-La.) told a radio interviewer that anyone wearing "a diaper on his head and a fan belt wrapped around the diaper" should be "pulled over" for extra questioning at airports. And survey research shows that Americans overwhelmingly tie Islam and Muslims to the horrifying events of September. One poll found that 68 percent of respondents approved of "randomly stopping people who may fit the profile of suspected terrorists." Another found that 83 percent of Americans favor stricter controls on Muslim entry into the country and 58 percent want tighter controls on Muslims traveling on planes or trains. Remarkably, 35 percent of New Yorkers favor establishing internment camps for "individuals who authorities identify as being sympathetic to terrorist causes." Nationally, 31 percent of Americans favor detention camps for Arab-Americans, "as a way to prevent terrorist attacks in the United States."

What in fact are the connections between the atrocities and the Muslim minority resident in the United States and Canada? And what policies can protect the country from attack while protecting the civil rights of Muslims?

The problem at hand is not the religion of Islam but the totalitarian ideology of Islamism. As a faith, Islam has meant very different things over

14 centuries and several continents. What we can call "traditional Islam," forged in the medieval period, has inspired Muslims to be bellicose and quiescent, noble and not: one can't generalize over such a large canvas. But one can note two common points: Islam is, more than any other major religion, deeply political, in the sense that it pushes its adherents to hold power; and once Muslims do gain power, they feel a strong impetus to apply the laws of Islam, the shari`a. So Islam does, in fact, contain elements that can justify conquest, theocracy, and intolerance.

In the course of the twentieth century, a new form of Islam arose, one that now has great appeal and power. Militant Islam (or Islamism—same thing) goes back to Egypt in the 1920s, when an organization called the Muslim Brethren first emerged, though there are other strains as well, including an Iranian one, largely formulated by Ayatollah Khomeini, and a Saudi one, to which the [formerly] ruling Taliban in Afghanistan and Usama bin Ladin both belong. Islamism differs in many ways from traditional Islam. It is faith turned into ideology, and radical ideology at that. When asked, "Do you consider yourself a revolutionary?" Sudanese Islamist politician Hasan al-Turabi replied, "Completely." Whereas traditional Islam places the responsibility on each believer to live according to God's will, Islamism makes this duty something for which the state is responsible. Islam is a personal belief system that focuses on the individual; Islamism is a state ideology that looks to the society. Islamists constitute a small but significant minority of Muslims in the U.S. and worldwide, perhaps 10 to 15 percent.

Apologists would tell us that Islamism is a distortion of Islam, or even that it has nothing to do with Islam, but that is not true; it emerges out of the religion, while taking features of it to a conclusion so extreme, so radical, and so megalomaniacal as to constitute something new. It adapts an age-old faith to the political requirements of our day, sharing some key premises of the earlier totalitarianisms, fascism and Marxism-Leninism. It is an Islamic-flavored version of radical utopianism. Individual *Islamists may* appear law-abiding and reasonable, but they are part of a totalitarian movement, and as such, all must be considered potential killers.

Traditional Muslims, generally the first victims of Islamism, understand this ideology for what it is and respond with fear and loathing, as some examples from northern Africa suggest. Naguib Mahfouz, Egypt's Nobel Prize-winning novelist, said to his country's prime minister and interior minister as they were suppressing Islamism: "You are fighting a battle for the sake of Islam." Other traditional Egyptian Muslims concur with Mahfouz, with one condemning Islamism as "the barbaric hand of terrorism" and another calling for all extremists to be "hanged in public squares." In Tunisia, Minister of Religion Ali Chebbi says that Islamists belong in the "garbage can." Algeria's interior minister, Abderrahmane Meziane-Cherif, likewise concludes: "You cannot talk to people who adopt violence as their credo; people who slit women's throats, rape them, and mutilate their breasts; people who kill innocent foreign guests." If Muslims feel this way, non-Muslims may join them without embarrassment: being against Islamism in no way implies being against Islam.

Islamists of all stripes have a virulent attitude toward non-Muslims and have a decades-long history of fighting with British and French colonial rulers, as well as with such non-Muslim governments as those of India, Israel, and the Philippines. They also have had long and bloody battles against Muslim governments that reject the Islamist program: in Egypt, Pakistan, Syria, Tunisia, and Turkey, for instance—and, most spectacularly, in Algeria, where 100,000 persons so far are estimated to have lost their lives in a decade of fighting.

Islamist violence is a global phenomenon. During the first week of April, [2001], for example, I counted up the following incidents, relying only on news agency stories, which are hardly exhaustive: deaths due to violent Islamist action occurred in Algeria (42 victims), Kashmir (17), the southern Philippines (3), Bangladesh (2), and the West Bank (1); assorted violence broke out in many other countries, including Afghanistan, Indonesia, Nigeria, and Sudan; courts handed down judgments against radical Muslims in France, Germany, Italy, Jordan, Turkey, the United States, and Yemen. Islamists are well organized: fully 11 of the 29 groups that the State Department calls "foreign terrorist organizations" are Islamist, as are 14 out of 21 groups outlawed by Britain's Home Office.

Starting in 1979, Islamists have felt confident enough to extend their fight against the West. The new militant Islamic government of Iran assaulted the U.S. embassy in Tehran at the end of that year and held nearly 60 Americans captive for 444 days. Eight American soldiers (the first casualties in this war) died in the failed U.S. rescue attempt in 1980. Violence against Americans began in earnest in 1983 with an attack on the U.S. embassy in Lebanon, killing 63. Then followed a long sequence of assaults on Americans in embassies, ships, planes, barracks, schools, and elsewhere.

Islamists have also committed at least eight lethal attacks on the soil of the United States prior to September 11, 2001: the July 1980 murder of an Iranian dissident in the Washington area; the January 1990 murder of an Egyptian Islamic freethinker in Tucson; the November 1990 assassination of Rabbi Meir Kahane in New York; the January 1993 assault on CIA personnel, killing two, outside the agency's Langley, Virginia, headquarters; the February 1993 World Trade Center bombing, killing six; the March 1994 shooting attack on a van full of Orthodox Jewish boys driving over the Brooklyn Bridge, killing one; the February 1997 murder of a Danish tourist at the top of the Empire State Building; and the deliberate October 1999 crash of an EgyptAir flight by the Egyptian pilot into the Atlantic near New York City, killing 217. All but one of these murders took place near or in New York City or Washington, D.C. This partial list doesn't include a number of fearsome near misses, including the "day of terror" planned for June 1993 that would have culminated with the simultaneous bombing of the United Nations and the Lincoln and Holland Tunnels, and a thwarted plot to disrupt Seattle's millennial celebrations.

In short, the massacre of upward of 6,000 Americans in September 2001 was not the start of something new but the intensification of an Islamist campaign of violence against the U.S. that has been raging for more than two decades.

No one knows exactly how many Muslims live in the United States—the estimates, prone to exaggeration, range widely—but their numbers clearly range in the several millions. The faithful divide into two main groups, immigrants and converts, with immigrants two to three times more numerous than converts. The immigrants come from all over the world, but especially from South Asia, Iran, and the Arabic-speaking countries; converts tend overwhelmingly to be African-American.

This community now faces a profound choice: either it can integrate within the United States or it can be Islamist and remain apart. It's a choice with major implications for both the U.S. and the Muslim world.

Integrationist Muslims—some pious, others not—can live simultaneously as patriotic Americans and as committed Muslims. Such Muslims have no problem giving their allegiance to a non-Muslim government. Integrationists believe that what American culture calls for—hard work, honesty, tolerance—is compatible with Islamic beliefs, and they even see Islam as reaffirming such classic American values. They accept that the United States is not a Muslim country, and they seek ways to live successfully within its Constitutional framework. Symbolic of this positive outlook, the Islamic Supreme Council of America proudly displays an American flag on its Internet home page.

American Muslims who go the Islamist route, however, reject American civilization, based as it is on a mix of Christian and Enlightenment values that they find anathema. Islamists believe that their ways are superior to America's, and they want to impose these on the entire country. In the short term, they promote Islam as the solution to the nation's social and moral ills. Over time, however, and much more radically, they want to transform the United States into a Muslim country run along strict Islamist lines. Giving expression to this radical view, Zaid Shakir, a former Muslim chaplain at Yale University, argues that Muslims cannot accept the legitimacy of the existing American order, since it "is against the orders and ordainments of Allah." "[T]he orientation of the Quran," he adds, "pushes us in the exact opposite direction." However outlandish a political goal this might seem, it is widely discussed in Islamist circles, and the events of September 11 should make clear just how seriously U.S. authorities must take this ambition.

The great debate among Islamists is, in fact, not over the desirability or plausibility of transforming the U.S. into a Muslim nation but whether to work toward this goal in a legal but slow way, through conversion, or by taking a riskier but swifter illegal path that would require violence. Shamim A. Siddiqi, a Pakistani immigrant, expects that vast numbers of Americans will peacefully convert to Islam in what he calls a "Rush-to-Islam." Omar Abdel Rahman, the blind sheikh behind the 1993 World Trade Center bombing, wants Muslims to "conquer the land of the infidels." These two approaches can and do overlap, with some pinstripe-suited lobbyists in Washington doing things that help terrorists, such as closing down the practice of profiling Middle Eastern–looking airline passengers.

Integrationists tend to be thankful to live in the United States, with its rule of law, democracy, and personal freedoms. Islamists despise these achievements and long to bring the ways of Iran or Afghanistan to America.

Integrationists seek to create an American Islam and can take part in American life. Islamists, who want an Islamic America, cannot.

The good news is that integrationists far outnumber Islamists. The bad news—and this poses a real and still largely unacknowledged problem for the United States—is that Islamists are much more active in Muslim affairs than integrationists and control nearly all of the nation's Muslim institutions: mosques, schools, community centers, publications, websites, and national organizations. It is the Islamists who receive invitations to the White House and the State Department. It was primarily Islamists with whom President Bush, in gestures intended to reassure American Muslims, met with twice after September 11.

What must Americans do to protect themselves from Islamists while safeguarding the civil rights of law-abiding Muslims? The first and most straightforward thing is not to allow any more Islamists into the country. Each Islamist who enters the United States, whether as a visitor or an immigrant, is one more enemy on the home front. Officials need to scrutinize the speech, associations, and activities of potential visitors or immigrants for any signs of Islamist allegiances and keep out anyone they suspect of such ties. Some civil libertarian purists will howl, as they once did over similar legislation designed to keep out Marxist-Leninists. But this is simply a matter of national self-protection.

Laws already on the books allow for such a policy, though excercising them these days is extremely difficult, requiring the direct involvement of the secretary of state. . . . Though written decades before Islamism appeared on the U.S. scene, for example, the 1952 McCarren-Walter Act permits the exclusion of anyone seeking to overthrow the U.S. government. Other regulations would keep out people suspected of terrorism or of committing other acts with "potentially serious adverse foreign policy consequences." U.S. officials need greater leeway to enforce these laws.

Keeping Islamists out of the country is an obvious first step, but it will be equally important to watch closely Islamists already living here as citizens or residents. Unfortunately, this means all Muslims must face heightened scrutiny. For the inescapable and painful fact is that, while anyone might become a fascist or communist, only Muslims find Islamism tempting. And if it is true that most Muslims aren't Islamists, it is no less true that all Islamists are Muslims. Muslims can expect that police searching for suspects after any new terrorist attack will not spend much time checking out churches, synagogues, or Hindu temples but will concentrate on mosques. Guards at government buildings will more likely question pedestrians who appear Middle Eastern or wear headscarves.

Because such measures have an admittedly prejudicial quality, authorities in the past have shown great reluctance to take them, an attitude Islamists and their apologists have reinforced, seeking to stifle any attempt to single out Muslims for scrutiny. When Muslims have committed crimes, officials have even bent over backward to disassociate their motives from militant Islam. For example, the Lebanese cabdriver who fired at a van full of Orthodox Jewish boys on the Brooklyn Bridge in 1994, leaving one child dead, had a well-documented fury at Israel and Jews—but the FBI ascribed his motive to "road rage." Only after a persistent campaign by the murdered boy's mother did the FBI finally classify the attack as "the crimes of a terrorist," almost seven years after the killing. Reluctance to come to terms with militant Islam might have been understandable before September 11—but no longer.

Heightened scrutiny of Muslims has become de rigueur at the nation's airports and must remain so. Airline security personnel used to look hard at Arabs and Muslims, but that was before the relevant lobbies raised so much fuss about "airline profiling" as a form of discrimination that the airlines effectively abandoned the practice. The absence of such a commonsense policy meant that 19 Muslim Arab hijackers could board four separate flights on September 11 with ease.

Greater scrutiny of Muslims also means watching out for Islamist "sleepers"—individuals who go quietly about their business until, one day, they receive the call from their controllers and spring into action as part of a terrorist operation. The four teams of September 11 hijackers show how deep deception can go. As one investigator, noting the length of time the 19 terrorists spent in the United States, explained, "These weren't people coming over the border just to attack quickly. . . . They cultivated friends, and blended into American society to further their ability to strike." Stopping sleepers before they are activated and strike will require greater vigilance at the nation's borders, good intelligence, and citizen watchfulness.

Resident Muslim aliens who reveal themselves to be Islamist should be immediately expelled from the country before they have a chance to act. Citizen Islamists will have to be watched very closely and without cease.

Even as the nation monitors the Muslim world within its borders more closely for signs of Islamism, it must continue, of course, to protect the civil rights of law-abiding American Muslims. Political leaders should regularly and publicly distinguish between Islam, the religion of Muslims, and Islamism, the totalitarian ideology. In addition, they should do everything in their power to make sure that individual Muslims, mosques, and other legal institutions continue to enjoy the full protection of the law. A time of crisis doesn't change the presumption of innocence at the core of our legal system. Police should provide extra protection for Muslims to prevent acts of vandalism against their property or their persons.

Thankfully, some American Muslims (and Arab-Americans, most of whom actually are Christian) understand that by accepting some personal inconvenience—and even, let's be honest, some degree of humiliation—they are helping to protect both the country and themselves. Tarek E. Masoud, a Yale graduate student, shows a good sense that many of his elders seem to lack: "How many thousands of lives would have been saved if people like me had been inconvenienced with having our bags searched and being made to answer questions?" he asks. "People say profiling makes them feel like criminals. It does—I know this firsthand. But would that I had been made to feel like a criminal a thousand times over than to live to see the grisly handiwork of real criminals in New York and Washington."

A third key task will be to combat the totalitarian ideology of militant Islam. That means isolating such noisy and vicious Islamist institutions as the

American Muslim Council, the Council on American-Islamic Relations, and the Muslim Public Affairs Council. Politicians, the press, corporations, voluntary organizations, and society as a whole—all must shun these groups and grant them not a shred of legitimacy. Tax authorities and law enforcement should watch them like hawks, much as they watch the Teamsters.

Fighting Islamist ideology will also require shutting down Internet sites that promote Islamist violence, recruit new members to the terrorist campaign against the West, and raise money for militant Islamic causes ("Donate money for the military Jihad," exhorts one such website). The federal government began to take action even before September 11, closing InfoCom, a Dallas-based host for many Islamist organizations, some of them funneling money to militant Islamic groups abroad.

Essential, too, in the struggle against Islamist ideology will be reaching out to moderate non-Islamist Muslims for help. These are the people unfairly tarred by Islamist excesses, after all, and so are eager to stop this extremist movement. Bringing them on board has several advantages: they can provide valuable advice, they can penetrate clandestine Islamist organizations, and their involvement in the effort against Islamism blunts the inevitable charges of "Islamophobia."

Further, experts on Islam and Muslims—academics, journalists, religious figures, and government officials—must be held to account for their views. For too long now, they have apologized for Islamism rather than interpreted it honestly. As such, they bear some responsibility for the unpreparedness that led to September's horror. The press and other media need to show greater objectivity in covering Islam. In the past, they have shamefully covered up for it. The recent PBS documentary *Islam: Empire of Faith* is a case in point, offering, as the *Wall Street Journal* sharply put it, an "uncritical adoration of Islam, more appropriate to a tract for true believers than a documentary purporting to give the American public a balanced account." Islamists in New York City celebrated the destruction on September 11 at their mosques, but journalists refused to report the story for fear of offending Muslims, effectively concealing this important information from the U.S. public.

Taking these three steps—keeping Islamists out, watching them within the nation's borders without violating the civil liberties of American Muslims, and delegitimating extremists—permits Americans to be fair toward the moderate majority of Muslims while fighting militant Islam. It will be a difficult balancing act, demanding sensitivity without succumbing to political correctness. But it is both essential and achievable.

David A. Harris

"Flying While Arab," Immigration Issues, and Lessons from the Racial Profiling Controversy

What changes in the law might we see? We know that we are a nation of immigrants—that, in many ways, immigrants built our great nation. We know that the immigrant experience has, in many ways, been at the core of the American experience, and that the diversity that these people have brought to our country has been, and continues to be, our greatest strength. But we also know that we have sometimes dealt harshly and unfairly with them, especially in times of national emergency and crisis. Thus the Commission does exactly the right thing by inquiring into these issues now, even as new legislative proposals continue to unfold in the Congress. In short, we seek to understand what the implications will be of the changes that will surely come because of the events of September 11—changes in the very idea of what America is, and what it will be in the future.

History

I said earlier that our history gives us reason to feel concern at such a critical juncture. Any serious appraisal of American history during the some of the key periods of the twentieth century would counsel an abundance of caution; when we have faced other national security crises, we have sometimes overreacted—or at the very least acted more out of emotion than was wise. In the wake of World War I, the infamous Palmer Raids resulted in the rounding up of a considerable number of immigrants. These people were deported, often without so much as a scintilla of evidence. During the Second World War, tens of thousands of Japanese—immigrants and native born, citizens and legal residents—were interned in camps, their property confiscated and sold off at fire-sale prices. To its everlasting shame, the U.S. Supreme Court gave the internment of the Japanese its constitutional blessing in the infamous Korematsu case. It took the United States government decades, but eventually it apologized and paid reparations to the Japanese. And during the 1950s, the Red Scare resulted in the ruining of lives and careers and the jailing of citizens, because they had had the temerity to exercise their constitutionally protected rights to free association by becoming members of the Communist Party years before.

Categorical Thinking

We must hope that we have learned the lessons of this history—that the emotions of the moment, when we feel threatened, can cause us to damage our civil liberties and our fellow citizens, and that this is particularly true for our immigrant populations. And it is this legacy that should make us think now, even as we engage in a long and detailed investigation of the September 11 terror attacks. As we listen to accounts of that investigation, reports indicate that the investigation has been strongly focused on Arab Americans and Muslims. What's more, private citizens have made Middle Eastern appearance an important criterion in deciding how to react to those who look different around them. Many of these reports have involved treatment of persons of Middle Eastern descent in airports.

In itself, this is not really surprising. We face a situation in which there has been a catastrophic terrorist attack by a small group of suicidal hijackers, and as far as we know, all of those involved were Arabs and Muslims and had Arabic surnames. Some or all had entered the country recently. Given the incredibly high stakes, some Americans have reacted to Middle Easterners as a group, based on their appearance. In a way, this is understandable. We seldom have much information on any of the strangers around us, so we tend to think in broad categories. It is a natural human reaction to fear to make judgments concerning our safety based on these broad categories, and to avoid those who arouse fear in us. This may translate easily into a type of racial and ethnic profiling, in which—as has been reported in the last few weeks—passengers on airliners refuse to fly with other passengers who have a Middle Eastern appearance.

Use of Race and Ethnic Appearance in Law Enforcement

The far more worrying development, however, is the possibility that profiling of Arabs and Muslims will become standard procedure in law enforcement. Again, it is not hard to understand the impulse; we want to catch and stop these suicidal hijackers, every one of whom fits the description of Arab or Muslim. So we stop, question, and search more of these people because we believe it's a way to play the odds. If all the September 11 terrorists were Middle Easterners, then we get the biggest bang for the enforcement buck by questioning, searching, and screening as many Middle Easterners as possible. This should give us the best chance of finding those who helped the terrorists or those bent on creating further havoc.

But as we embark in this new world, a world changed so drastically by the events of September 11, we need to be conscious of some of the things that we have learned over the last few years in the ongoing racial profiling controversy. Using race or ethnic appearance as part of a *description* of particular suspects may indeed help an investigation; using race or ethnic appearance as a broad *predictor* of who is involved in crime or terrorism will likely hurt our investigative efforts. All the evidence indicates that profiling Arab Americans or Muslims would be an ineffective waste of law enforcement resources that would damage our intelligence efforts while it compromises basic civil liberties. If we want to do everything we can to secure our country, we have to be smart about the steps we take.

As we think about the possible profiling of Arabs and Muslims, recall that much the same argument has been made for years about domestic efforts against drugs and crime. African Americans and Latinos are disproportionately involved in drug crime, the reasoning goes; therefore concentrate on them. Many state and local police agencies, led by the federal Drug Enforcement Administration, did exactly that from the late 1980s on. We now know that police departments in many jurisdictions used racial profiling, especially in efforts to get drugs and guns off the highways and out of the cities. But as we look back, what really stands out is how ineffective this profile-based law enforcement was. In departments that focused on African Americans, Latinos, and other minorities, the "hit rates"—the rates of successful searches—were actually *lower* for minorities than they were for whites, who were not apprehended by using a racial or ethnic profile. That's right: when these agencies used race or ethnic appearance as a factor—not as *the only* factor but *one factor among many*—they did not get the higher returns on their enforcement efforts that they were expecting.

This is because race and ethnic appearance are very poor predictors of behavior. Race and ethnicity describe people well, and there is absolutely nothing wrong with using skin color or other features to describe known suspects. But since only a very small percentage of African Americans and Latinos participate in the drug trade, race and ethnic appearance do a bad job identifying the *particular* African Americans and Latinos in whom police should be interested. Racial and ethnic profiling caused police to spread their enforcement net far too widely and indiscriminately.

The results of this misguided effort have been disastrous for law enforcement: constant efforts to stop, question, and search people who "look like" suspects, the vast majority of whom are hard working, tax paying citizens. This treatment has alienated African Americans, Latinos, and other minorities from the police—a critical strategic loss in the fight against crime, since police can only win this fight if they have the full cooperation and support of those they serve. And it is precisely this lesson we ought to think about now, as the cry goes up to use profiling and intensive searches against people who look Middle Eastern or Muslim.

Even if the hijackers share a particular ethnic appearance or background, subjecting *all* Middle Easterners to intrusive questioning, stops, or searches will have a perverse and unexpected effect: it will spread our enforcement and detection efforts over a huge pool of people who we would not otherwise think worthy of any police attention. Profiling will drain enforcement efforts and resources away from more worthy investigative efforts and tactics that focus on the close observation of behavior—like the buying of expensive one-way tickets with cash just a short time before takeoff, as some of the World Trade Center hijackers did. Focusing on race and ethnicity keeps police attention on a set of surface details that tell us very little, and draw officers' attention away from what is much more important and concrete: conduct.

At least as important, one of the most crucial tools we can use against terrorism is intelligence. And if we are concerned about terrorists of Middle Eastern origin, among the most fertile places from which to gather intelligence will be the Arab American and Muslim communities. If we adopt a security policy that stigmatizes every member of these groups in airports and other public places with intrusive stops, questioning, and searches, we will alienate them from the enforcement efforts at precisely the time we need them most. And the larger the population we subject to this treatment, the greater the total amount of damage we inflict on law-abiding persons.

And of course the profiling of Arabs and Muslims assumes that we need worry about only one type of terrorist. We must not forget that, prior to the attacks on September 11, the most deadly terrorist attack on American soil was carried out not by Middle Easterners with Arabic names and accents, but by two very average American white men: Timothy McVeigh, a U.S. Army veteran from upstate New York, and Terry Nichols, a farmer from Michigan. Yet we were smart enough in the wake of McVeigh and Nichols' crime not to call for a profile emphasizing the fact that the perpetrators were white males. The unhappy truth is that we just don't know what the next group of terrorists might look like.

Treatment of Immigrants

The numbers from the 2000 census of our country's population tell us that the 1990s were a time of considerable immigration to the United States. Some of this immigration came from Asia and the Middle East. These immigrants helped many of our older cities make population gains not seen in some time, and helped the American economy to achieve unprecedented growth and prosperity. This was especially true in the high technology sector, which has become a crucial mainstay of growth over the last ten years despite a shortage of American workers to fill computer-oriented positions. Immigrants stepped into the breach for us, bolstering our high-tech labor force just when we needed it.

Yet under the antiterrorism proposal now circulating in the U.S. Senate, immigrants could suffer treatment that smacks strongly of racial profiling and associated practices. Popularly referred to as the USA Act, S. 1510 allows the unlimited detention of noncitizens whom the Attorney General moves to deport or charge criminally, when the Attorney General "reasonably believes" these noncitizens to be engaged in certain terrorist activities. If none of the specifically mentioned activities applies, the Attorney General can still detain the noncitizens based on his or her own determination that the noncitizen "is engaged in any other activity that endangers the national security of the United States." . . .

The Attorney General is empowered to hold these noncitizens even in the face of a court's determination that they are not terrorists. And if the government attempts to deport them and no nation will take them, the legislation appears to allow the Attorney General to detain them indefinitely. The slippery slope here is obvious; the dangers of abuse are easy to see. The basic structure of Section 412 allows the Attorney General to make the decision of who is a terrorist suspect, and to continue to detain these people even in the face of contrary judicial review. The checks and balances built into our basic system of government vanish under this scheme—a worrisome development under any circumstances.

Conclusion

The terrorist attacks in New York and Washington present us with many difficult choices that will test our resolve and our abilities. We must find effective ways to secure ourselves without giving up what is best about our country; the proper balance will often be difficult to discern. But we should not simply repeat the mistakes of the past as we take on this new challenge. Nobody would gain from that—except those who would destroy us.

POSTSCRIPT

Is "Middle Eastern" Profiling
Ever Justified?

Both David Harris and Daniel Pipes tend to use "Muslim" and "Middle Eastern" interchangeably. This is understandable, since the Middle East is predominantly Muslim, but it conflates terms that are quite distinct. Muslim refers to a religion, that of Islam. In this case, the religion is relevant, since al Qaeda and other terrorist groups claim to be acting in the name of it. But a person's religion (absent some religious insignia) is invisible to the eye, so the tendency is to shift one's attention into something connected with appearance, such as skin color or facial features. The result can be confusing—and unfair. There are tan-complexioned Catholics from the Middle East and blond Chechnyan Muslims. Who are more likely to be scrutinized at the airport?

In his testimony, Harris makes reference to his earlier book, *Profiles in Injustice: Why Racial Profiling Cannot Work* (New Press, 2003), an analysis of racial profiling, its uses, and, he believes, its ultimate failure in crime prevention. In Daniel Pipes's *Militant Islam Reaches America* (Norton, 2003), one of the dozen or so he has published on the Middle East and what he calls "Islamism," he portrays it as the greatest threat to the United States since the end of the Cold War. While not directly addressing the issue of profiling, Samuel P. Huntington's seminal *The Clash of Civilizations and the Remaking of the World Order* (Touchstone Books, 1998) still remains as a powerful challenge to those who hope that "modernization" will bring Western-style democracy to the Middle East. Bernard Lewis's *What Went Wrong: The Clash Between Islam and Modernity in the Middle East* (Perennial, 2003) and his more recent *From Babel to Dragomans; Interpreting the Middle East* (Oxford, 2004) reach back far into the history of the Middle East and attempt to demonstrate his long-held contention that Islam presents a formidable obstacle to modernization. Michael Wolfe, ed., *Taking Back Islam: American Muslims Reclaim Their Faith* (Rodale Press, 2002) is a collection of writings from several American Muslims, including Yusuf Islam (Cat Stevens) and newer voices such as Aasma Khan, all of whom claim to represent a silent majority of "progressive" Muslims determined to divest their religion of its associations with terrorism and sexism.

Brian L. Wuthrow's *Racial Profiling: From Rhetoric to Reason* (Prentice-Hall, 2005) is an attempt to take the issue of profiling beyond the superheated exchanges one sees in the media; Wuthrow summarizes some of the conclusions of social science analysts on the subject. In a similar vein is *Racial Profiling: Issues, Data and Analysis,* edited by Steven J. Muffler (Nova Science Publications, 2006). Richard C. Leone and Greg Anrig, Jr., eds., *The War on Our Freedoms: Civil Liberties in an Age of Terrorism* (PublicAffairs, 2003) is a collection of essays by scholars and journalists critical of U.S. anti-terrorist policies.

The arguments for and against profiling are likely to continue as long as the threat of terror remains, which would appear to be indefinitely. But perhaps some sort of compromise is possible between the contending points of view. The case of Richard Reid, the would-be "shoe bomber," is instructive. Reid's attempt to ignite the explosive charge in his shoe was first detected by a flight attendant, who smelled the sulfur from his burning match, and he was wrestled to the ground by quick-thinking passengers. The lesson is that suspicious *actions* may be a better indication of the potential for terrorism than anything having to do with appearance—though, judging from the menacing photos of Reid, it is possible to speculate that the flight attendant was already keeping an eye on him.

ISSUE 18

Is the Use of Torture Against Terrorist Suspects Ever Justified?

YES: Charles Krauthammer, from "The Truth About Torture," *The Weekly Standard* (December 5, 2005)

NO: Andrew Sullivan, from "The Abolition of Torture," *The New Republic* (December 19, 2005)

ISSUE SUMMARY

YES: Charles Krauthammer argues that the legal protections for prisoners of war and civilians do not apply to terrorist suspects captured abroad, and in certain extreme cases torture may be used to extract information from them.

NO: Andrew Sullivan contends that any nation that uses torture infects itself with the virus of totalitarianism, belies its claim of moral superiority to the terrorists, and damages its chances of persuading the Arab world to adopt Western-style democracy.

Under Saddam Hussein, Iraq's former dictator, Abu Ghraib prison was a place where tens of thousands were routinely subjected to torture and execution. After the fall of the dictatorship following the invasion of Iraq, it was turned into a U.S. military prison. In December 2003, after hearing complaints about the treatment of prisoners at Abu Ghraib, the Army launched a major investigation. At its conclusion in February, 2004, the chief investigator's confidential report—later leaked to journalists—charged that numerous instances of "sadistic, blatant, and wanton criminal abuses" had occurred at Abu Ghraib. A few months later, photographs taken by some of those engaged in the abuses began circulating through the Internet, and some were shown on CBS's "60 Minutes." Soon the pictures were repeatedly shown throughout worldwide media. They have become iconic representations of abuse and oppression by Americans who were sent to liberate a country from abuse and oppression.

The Army and the Defense Department attributed these abuses largely to criminal behavior by a few low-level G.I.s and dereliction of duty by the officers in charge. Nevertheless, critics charge that constant demands by officials in the Defense Department and the C.I.A. for fresh information set the stage for the abuses, and the aggressive interrogating procedures used by the Army at Guantanamo Bay, Cuba, set an example that needed only a slight degree of amplification to become full-fledged torture.

What is torture? The 1994 U.N. Convention Against Torture, of which the United States is a signatory, defines it as "any act by which severe pain, whether physical or mental, is intentionally inflicted" to gain information. But since people have different thresholds of pain, it is hard to get the subjectivity out of this definition. The 1949 Geneva Conventions (also signed by the United States) require prisoners to be "treated humanly" and outlaw acts such as "violence to life and person," "mutilation, cruel treatment," and "outrages upon personal dignity." But the Geneva Conventions were meant to apply to uniformed soldiers captured in war and noncombatant civilians; whether they should be extended to suspected terrorists remains in dispute.

Shortly after 9/11 a team of Justice Department lawyers sought to formulate an unambiguous definition of "torture," but their attempt stirred controversy when it was publicized. To constitute "torture," they wrote, an act "must inflict pain that is difficult to endure"; it must be "equivalent in intensity to the pain accompanying serious physical injury, such as organ failure, impairment of bodily functions, or even death." Once this "torture memo," as some of its critics called it, came to light, the Bush administration distanced itself from it. Through various spokesmen, including the President himself, the administration has repeatedly condemned the use of torture. "Torture anywhere is an affront to human dignity anywhere," Bush stated in 2003. "Freedom from torture is an inalienable human right." Yet some critics contend that the administration has permitted and even facilitated practices that have culminated in torture, citing in particular the policy of "rendition," in which terrorist suspects apprehended in Western Europe are sent to other countries for interrogation. The policy of rendition began in the mid-1990s, during the Clinton administration, but since 9/11, according to some reports, it has come into more frequent use. A probe by a committee of the European Parliament has not found any human rights violations, and the Bush administration has neither confirmed nor denied the policy of rendition. The facts behind the rendition controversy thus remain murky. At some point, probably, the full truth will emerge, but uncovering it may require a few more drafts of history.

Whatever the validity of the charges, the larger question haunting Americans in the present era is not an empirical but a moral one: Are there *any* circumstances in which it could be morally permissible to apply pain or other extreme measures to prisoners in order to extract information from them? The immediate, almost reflexive answer of decent people is "no, never." But what of circumstances, say, in which an Al Qaeda prisoner knows that a nuclear device will soon go off somewhere in Manhattan but refuses to say where? The "ticking time bomb" has become the classic defense of torture, and in the following selections columnist and commentator Charles Krauthammer elaborates upon it. Opposing him is Andrew Sullivan, also a columnist and commentator, who argues against the legitimacy of torture even in extreme circumstances.

YES

Charles Krauthammer

The Truth About Torture

During the last few weeks in Washington the pieties about torture have lain so thick in the air that it has been impossible to have a reasoned discussion. The McCain amendment that would ban "cruel, inhuman, or degrading" treatment of any prisoner by any agent of the United States sailed through the Senate by a vote of 90–9. The Washington establishment remains stunned that nine such retrograde, morally inert persons—let alone senators—could be found in this noble capital.

Now, John McCain has great moral authority on this issue, having heroically borne torture at the hands of the North Vietnamese. McCain has made fine arguments in defense of his position. And McCain is acting out of the deep and honorable conviction that what he is proposing is not only right but is in the best interest of the United States. His position deserves respect. But that does not mean, as seems to be the assumption in Washington today, that a critical analysis of his "no torture, ever" policy is beyond the pale.

Let's begin with a few analytic distinctions. For the purpose of torture and prisoner maltreatment, there are three kinds of war prisoners: First, there is the ordinary soldier caught on the field of battle. There is no question that he is entitled to humane treatment. Indeed, we have no right to disturb a hair on his head. His detention has but a single purpose: to keep him *hors de combat*. The proof of that proposition is that if there were a better way to keep him off the battlefield that did not require his detention, we would let him go. Indeed, during one year of the Civil War, the two sides did try an alternative. They mutually "paroled" captured enemy soldiers, i.e., released them to return home on the pledge that they would not take up arms again. (The experiment failed for a foreseeable reason: cheating. Grant found that some paroled Confederates had reenlisted.)

Because the only purpose of detention in these circumstances is to prevent the prisoner from becoming a combatant again, he is entitled to all the protections and dignity of an ordinary domestic prisoner—indeed, more privileges, because, unlike the domestic prisoner, he has committed no crime. He merely had the misfortune to enlist on the other side of a legitimate war. He is therefore entitled to many of the privileges enjoyed by an ordinary citizen—the right to send correspondence, to engage in athletic activity and intellectual

From *The Weekly Standard*, by Charles Krauthammer, December 5, 2005, pp. 21–25. Copyright © 2005 by Charles Krauthammer. Reprinted by permission.

pursuits, to receive allowances from relatives—except, of course, for the freedom to leave the prison.

Second, there is the captured terrorist. A terrorist is by profession, indeed by definition, an unlawful combatant: He lives outside the laws of war because he does not wear a uniform, he hides among civilians, and he deliberately targets innocents. He is entitled to no protections whatsoever. People seem to think that the postwar Geneva Conventions were written only to protect detainees. In fact, their deeper purpose was to provide a deterrent to the kind of barbaric treatment of civilians that had become so horribly apparent during the first half of the 20th century, and in particular, during the Second World War. The idea was to deter the abuse of civilians by promising combatants who treated noncombatants well that they themselves would be treated according to a code of dignity if captured—and, crucially, that they would be denied the protections of that code if they broke the laws of war and abused civilians themselves.

Breaking the laws of war and abusing civilians are what, to understate the matter vastly, terrorists do for a living. They are entitled, therefore, to nothing. Anyone who blows up a car bomb in a market deserves to spend the rest of his life roasting on a spit over an open fire. But we don't do that because we do not descend to the level of our enemy. We don't do that because, unlike him, we are civilized. Even though terrorists are entitled to no humane treatment, we give it to them because it is in our nature as a moral and humane people. And when on rare occasions we fail to do that, as has occurred in several of the fronts of the war on terror, we are duly disgraced.

The norm, however, is how the majority of prisoners at Guantanamo have been treated. We give them three meals a day, superior medical care, and provision to pray five times a day. Our scrupulousness extends even to providing them with their own Korans, which is the only reason alleged abuses of the Koran at Guantanamo ever became an issue. That we should have provided those who kill innocents in the name of Islam with precisely the document that inspires their barbarism is a sign of the absurd lengths to which we often go in extending undeserved humanity to terrorist prisoners.

Third, there is the terrorist with information. Here the issue of torture gets complicated and the easy pieties don't so easily apply. Let's take the textbook case. Ethics 101: A terrorist has planted a nuclear bomb in New York City. It will go off in one hour. A million people will die. You capture the terrorist. He knows where it is. He's not talking.

Question: If you have the slightest belief that hanging this man by his thumbs will get you the information to save a million people, are you permitted to do it? Now, on most issues regarding torture, I confess tentativeness and uncertainty. But on this issue, there can be no uncertainty: Not only is it permissible to hang this miscreant by his thumbs. It is a moral duty. Yes, you say, but that's an extreme and very hypothetical case. Well, not as hypothetical as you think. Sure, the (nuclear) scale is hypothetical, but in the age of the car-and suicide-bomber, terrorists are often captured who have just set a car bomb to go off or sent a suicide bomber out to a coffee shop, and you only have minutes to find out where the attack is to take place. This "hypothetical" is common enough that the Israelis have a term for precisely that situation: the ticking time bomb problem.

And even if the example I gave were entirely hypothetical, the conclusion—yes, in this case even torture is permissible—is telling because it establishes the principle: Torture is not always impermissible. However rare the cases, there are circumstances in which, by any rational moral calculus, torture not only would be permissible but would be required (to acquire life-saving information). And once you've established the principle, to paraphrase George Bernard Shaw, all that's left to haggle about is the price. In the case of torture, that means that the argument is not *whether* torture is ever permissible, but *when*—i.e., under what obviously stringent circumstances: how big, how imminent, how preventable the ticking time bomb. That is why the McCain amendment, which by mandating "torture never" refuses even to recognize the legitimacy of any moral calculus, cannot be right. There must be exceptions. The real argument should be over what constitutes a legitimate exception.

Let's take an example that is far from hypothetical. You capture Khalid Sheikh Mohammed in Pakistan. He not only has already killed innocents, he is deeply involved in the planning for the present and future killing of innocents. He not only was the architect of the 9/11 attack that killed nearly three thousand people in one day, most of them dying a terrible, agonizing, indeed tortured death. But as the top al Qaeda planner and logistical expert he also knows a lot about terror attacks to come. He knows plans, identities, contacts, materials, cell locations, safe houses, cased targets, etc. What do you do with him?

We have recently learned that since 9/11 the United States has maintained a series of "black sites" around the world, secret detention centers where presumably high-level terrorists like Khalid Sheikh Mohammed have been imprisoned. The world is scandalized. Black sites? Secret detention? Jimmy Carter calls this "a profound and radical change in the . . . moral values of our country." The Council of Europe demands an investigation, calling the claims "extremely worrying." Its human rights commissioner declares "such practices" to constitute "a serious human rights violation, and further proof of the crisis of values" that has engulfed the war on terror. The gnashing of teeth and rending of garments has been considerable.

I myself have not gnashed a single tooth. My garments remain entirely unrent. Indeed, I feel reassured. It would be a gross dereliction of duty for any government *not* to keep Khalid Sheikh Mohammed isolated, disoriented, alone, despairing, cold and sleepless, in some godforsaken hidden location in order to find out what he knew about plans for future mass murder. What are we supposed to do? Give him a nice cell in a warm Manhattan prison, complete with Miranda rights, a mellifluent lawyer, and his own website? Are not those the kinds of courtesies we extended to the 1993 World Trade Center bombers, then congratulated ourselves on how we "brought to justice" those responsible for an attack that barely failed to kill tens of thousands of Americans, only to discover a decade later that we had accomplished nothing—indeed, that some of the disclosures at the trial had helped Osama bin Laden avoid U.S. surveillance?

Have we learned nothing from 9/11? Are we prepared to go back with complete amnesia to the domestic-crime model of dealing with terrorists, which allowed us to sleepwalk through the nineties while al Qaeda incubated and grew and metastasized unmolested until on 9/11 it finished what the first World Trade Center bombers had begun?

Let's assume (and hope) that Khalid Sheikh Mohammed has been kept in one of these black sites, say, a cell somewhere in Romania, held entirely incommunicado and subjected to the kind of "coercive interrogation" that I described above. McCain has been going around praising the Israelis as the model of how to deal with terrorism and prevent terrorist attacks. He does so because in 1999 the Israeli Supreme Court outlawed all torture in the course of interrogation. But in reality, the Israeli case is far more complicated. And the complications reflect precisely the dilemmas regarding all coercive interrogation, the weighing of the lesser of two evils: the undeniable inhumanity of torture versus the abdication of the duty to protect the victims of a potentially preventable mass murder.

In a summary of Israel's policies, Glenn Frankel of the *Washington Post* noted that the 1999 Supreme Court ruling struck down secret guidelines established 12 years earlier that allowed interrogators to use the kind of physical and psychological pressure I described in imagining how KSM might be treated in America's "black sites."

"But after the second Palestinian uprising broke out a year later, and especially after a devastating series of suicide bombings of passenger buses, cafes and other civilian targets," writes Frankel, citing human rights lawyers and detainees, "Israel's internal security service, known as the Shin Bet or the Shabak, returned to physical coercion as a standard practice." Not only do the techniques used "command widespread support from the Israeli public," but "Israeli prime ministers and justice ministers with a variety of political views," including the most conciliatory and liberal, have defended these techniques "as a last resort in preventing terrorist attacks."

Which makes McCain's position on torture incoherent. If this kind of coercive interrogation were imposed on any inmate in the American prison system, it would immediately be declared cruel and unusual, and outlawed. How can he oppose these practices, which the Israelis use, and yet hold up Israel as a model for dealing with terrorists? Or does he countenance this kind of interrogation in extreme circumstances—in which case, what is left of his categorical opposition to inhuman treatment of any kind?

But let us push further into even more unpleasant territory, the territory that lies beyond mere coercive interrogation and beyond McCain's self-contradictions. How far are we willing to go? This "going beyond" need not be cinematic and ghoulish. (Jay Leno once suggested "duct tape" for Khalid Sheikh Mohammed.) Consider, for example, injection with sodium pentathol. (Colloquially known as "truth serum," it is nothing of the sort. It is a barbiturate whose purpose is to sedate. Its effects are much like that of alcohol: disinhibiting the higher brain centers to make someone more likely to disclose information or thoughts that might otherwise be guarded.) Forcible sedation is a clear violation of bodily integrity. In a civilian context it would be considered assault. It is certainly impermissible under any prohibition of cruel, inhuman, or degrading treatment.

Let's posit that during the interrogation of Khalid Sheikh Mohammed, perhaps early on, we got intelligence about an imminent al Qaeda attack. And we had a very good reason to believe he knew about it. And if we knew what he knew, we could stop it. If we thought we could glean a critical piece of information by use of sodium pentathol, would we be permitted to do so?

Less hypothetically, there is waterboarding, a terrifying and deeply shocking torture technique in which the prisoner has his face exposed to water in a way that gives the feeling of drowning. According to CIA sources cited by ABC News, Khalid Sheikh Mohammed "was able to last between 2 and 2 1/2 minutes before begging to confess." Should we regret having done that? Should we abolish by law that practice, so that it could never be used on the next Khalid Sheikh Mohammed having thus gotten his confession?

And what if he possessed information with less imminent implications? Say we had information about a cell that he had helped found or direct, and that cell was planning some major attack and we needed information about the identity and location of its members. A rational moral calculus might not permit measures as extreme as the nuke-in-Manhattan scenario, but would surely permit measures beyond mere psychological pressure.

Such a determination would not be made with an untroubled conscience. It would be troubled because there is no denying the monstrous evil that is any form of torture. And there is no denying how corrupting it can be to the individuals and society that practice it. But elected leaders, responsible above all for the protection of their citizens, have the obligation to tolerate their own sleepless nights by doing what is necessary—and only what is necessary, nothing more—to get information that could prevent mass murder.

Given the gravity of the decision, if we indeed cross the Rubicon—as we must—we need rules. The problem with the McCain amendment is that once you have gone public with a blanket ban on all forms of coercion, it is going to be very difficult to publicly carve out exceptions. The Bush administration is to be faulted for having attempted such a codification with the kind of secrecy, lack of coherence, and lack of strict enforcement that led us to the McCain reaction.

What to do at this late date? Begin, as McCain does, by banning all forms of coercion or inhuman treatment by anyone serving in the military— an absolute ban on torture by all military personnel everywhere. We do not want a private somewhere making these fine distinctions about ticking and slow-fuse time bombs. We don't even want colonels or generals making them. It would be best for the morale, discipline, and honor of the Armed Forces for the United States to maintain an absolute prohibition, both to simplify their task in making decisions and to offer them whatever reciprocal treatment they might receive from those who capture them—although I have no illusion that any anti-torture provision will soften the heart of a single jihadist holding a knife to the throat of a captured American soldier. We would impose this restriction on ourselves for our own reasons of military discipline and military honor.

Outside the military, however, I would propose, contra McCain, a ban against all forms of torture, coercive interrogation, and inhuman treatment, except in two contingencies: (1) the ticking time bomb and (2) the slower-fuse high-level terrorist (such as KSM). Each contingency would have its own set of rules. In the case of the ticking time bomb, the rules would be relatively simple: Nothing rationally related to getting accurate information would be ruled out. The case of the high-value suspect with slow-fuse information is more complicated. The principle would be that the level of inhumanity of the measures used (moral honesty is essential here—we would be using measures that are by definition inhumane) would be proportional to the need and value of the information. Interrogators would be constrained to use the least inhumane treatment necessary relative to the magnitude and imminence of the evil being prevented and the importance of the knowledge being obtained.

These exceptions to the no-torture rule would not be granted to just any nonmilitary interrogators, or anyone with CIA credentials. They would be reserved for highly specialized agents who are experts and experienced in interrogation, and who are known not to abuse it for the satisfaction of a kind of sick sadomasochism Lynndie England and her cohorts indulged in at Abu Ghraib. Nor would they be acting on their own. They would be required to obtain written permission for such interrogations from the highest political authorities in the country (cabinet level) or from a quasi-judicial body modeled on the Foreign Intelligence Surveillance Court (which permits what would ordinarily be illegal searches and seizures in the war on terror). Or, if the bomb was truly ticking and there was no time, the interrogators would be allowed to act on their own, but would require post facto authorization within, say, 24 hours of their interrogation, so that they knew that whatever they did would be subject to review by others and be justified only under the most stringent terms.

One of the purposes of these justifications would be to establish that whatever extreme measures are used are for reasons of nothing but information. Historically, the torture of prisoners has been done for a variety of reasons apart from information, most prominently reasons of justice or revenge. We do not do that. We should not do that. Ever. Khalid Sheikh Mohammed, murderer of 2,973 innocents, is surely deserving of the most extreme suffering day and night for the rest of his life. But it is neither our role nor our right to be the agents of that suffering. Vengeance is mine, sayeth the Lord. His, not ours. Torture is a terrible and monstrous thing, as degrading and morally corrupting to those who practice it as any conceivable human activity including its moral twin, capital punishment.

If Khalid Sheikh Mohammed knew nothing, or if we had reached the point where his knowledge had been exhausted, I'd be perfectly prepared to throw him into a nice, comfortable Manhattan cell and give him a trial to determine what would be fit and just punishment. But as long as he had useful information, things would be different.

Very different. And it simply will not do to take refuge in the claim that all of the above discussion is superfluous because torture never works anyway. Would that this were true. Unfortunately, on its face, this is nonsense. Is one to believe that in the entire history of human warfare, no combatant has ever received useful information by the use of pressure, torture, or any other kind of inhuman treatment? It may indeed be true that torture is not a reliable tool. But that is very different from saying that it is *never* useful.

The monstrous thing about torture is that sometimes it does work. In 1994, 19-year-old Israeli corporal Nachshon Waxman was kidnapped by Palestinian terrorists. The Israelis captured the driver of the car used in the kidnapping and tortured him in order to find where Waxman was being held. Yitzhak Rabin, prime minister and peacemaker, admitted that they tortured him in a way that went even beyond the '87 guidelines for "coercive interrogation" later struck down by the Israeli Supreme Court as too harsh. The driver talked. His information was accurate. The Israelis found Waxman. "If we'd been so careful to follow the ['87] Landau Commission [which *allowed* coercive interrogation]," explained Rabin, "we would never have found out where Waxman was being held."

In the Waxman case, I would have done precisely what Rabin did. (The fact that Waxman's Palestinian captors killed him during the Israeli rescue raid makes the case doubly tragic, but changes nothing of the moral calculus.) Faced with a similar choice, an American president would have a similar obligation. To do otherwise—to give up the chance to find your soldier lest you sully yourself by authorizing torture of the person who possesses potentially lifesaving information—is a deeply immoral betrayal of a soldier and countryman. Not as cosmically immoral as permitting a city of one's countrymen to perish, as in the Ethics 101 case. But it remains, nonetheless, a case of moral abdication—of a kind rather parallel to that of the principled pacifist. There is much to admire in those who refuse on principle ever to take up arms under any conditions. But that does not make pure pacifism, like no-torture absolutism, any less a form of moral foolishness, tinged with moral vanity. Not reprehensible, only deeply reproachable and supremely impracticable. People who hold such beliefs are deserving of a certain respect. But they are not to be put in positions of authority. One should be grateful for the saintly among us. And one should be vigilant that they not get to make the decisions upon which the lives of others depend.

Which brings us to the greatest irony of all in the torture debate. I have just made what will be characterized as the pro-torture case contra McCain by proposing two major exceptions carved out of any no-torture rule: the ticking time bomb and the slow-fuse high-value terrorist. McCain supposedly is being hailed for defending all that is good and right and just in America by standing foursquare against any inhuman treatment. Or is he?

According to *Newsweek*, in the ticking time bomb case McCain says that the president should disobey the very law that McCain seeks to pass—under the justification that "you do what you have to do. But you take responsibility for it." But if torturing the ticking time bomb suspect is "what you have to do," then why has McCain been going around arguing that such things must never be done?

As for exception number two, the high-level terrorist with slow-fuse information, Stuart Taylor, the superb legal correspondent for *National Journal*, argues that with appropriate legal interpretation, the "cruel, inhuman, or degrading" standard, "though vague, is said by experts to codify . . . the commonsense principle that the toughness of interrogation techniques should be calibrated to the importance and urgency of the information likely to be obtained." That would permit "some very aggressive techniques . . . on that small percentage of detainees who seem especially likely to have potentially life-saving information." Or as Evan Thomas and Michael Hirsh put it in the *Newsweek* report on McCain and torture, the McCain standard would "presumably allow for a sliding scale" of torture or torture-lite or other coercive techniques, thus permitting "for a very small percentage—those High Value Targets like Khalid Sheikh Mohammed—some pretty rough treatment."

But if that is the case, then McCain embraces the same exceptions I do, but prefers to pretend he does not. If that is the case, then his much-touted and endlessly repeated absolutism on inhumane treatment is merely for show. If that is the case, then the moral preening and the phony arguments can stop now, and we can all agree that in this real world of astonishingly murderous enemies, in two very circumscribed circumstances, we must all be prepared to torture. Having established that, we can then begin to work together to codify rules of interrogation for the two very unpleasant but very real cases in which we are morally permitted—indeed morally compelled—to do terrible things.

Andrew Sullivan  **NO**

The Abolition of Torture

Why is torture wrong? It may seem like an obvious question, or even one beneath discussion. But it is now inescapably before us, with the introduction of the McCain Amendment banning all "cruel, inhuman, and degrading treatment" of detainees by American soldiers and CIA operatives anywhere in the world. The amendment lies in legislative limbo. It passed the Senate in October by a vote of 90 to nine, but President Bush has vowed to veto any such blanket ban on torture or abuse; Vice President Cheney has prevailed upon enough senators and congressmen to prevent the amendment—and the defense appropriations bill to which it is attached—from moving out of conference; and my friend Charles Krauthammer, one of the most respected conservative intellectuals in Washington (and a *New Republic* contributing editor) has written a widely praised cover essay for *The Weekly Standard* endorsing the legalization of full-fledged torture by the United States under strictly curtailed conditions. We stand on the brink of an enormously important choice—one that is critical, morally as well as strategically, to get right.

This debate takes place after three years in which the Bush administration has defined "torture" in the narrowest terms and has permitted coercive, physical abuse of enemy combatants if "military necessity" demands it. It comes also after several internal Pentagon reports found widespread and severe abuse of detainees in Afghanistan, Iraq, and elsewhere that has led to at least two dozen deaths during interrogation. Journalistic accounts and reports by the International Committee of the Red Cross paint an even darker picture of secret torture sites in Eastern Europe and innocent detainees being murdered. Behind all this, the grim images of Abu Ghraib—the worst of which have yet to be released—linger in the public consciousness.

In this inevitably emotional debate, perhaps the greatest failing of those of us who have been arguing against all torture and "cruel, inhuman, and degrading treatment" of detainees is that we have assumed the reasons why torture is always a moral evil, rather than explicating them. But, when you fully ponder them, I think it becomes clearer why, contrary to Krauthammer's argument, torture, in any form and under any circumstances, is both antithetical to the most basic principles for which the United States stands and a profound impediment to winning a wider war that we cannot afford to lose.

From *The New Republic*, December 19, 2005, pp. 19–23. Copyright © 2005 by New Republic. Reprinted by permission.

Torture is the polar opposite of freedom. It is the banishment of all freedom from a human body and soul, insofar as that is possible. As human beings, we all inhabit bodies and have minds, souls, and reflexes that are designed in part to protect those bodies: to resist or flinch from pain, to protect the psyche from disintegration, and to maintain a sense of selfhood that is the basis for the concept of personal liberty. What torture does is use these involuntary, self-protective, self-defining resources of human beings against the integrity of the human being himself. It takes what is most involuntary in a person and uses it to break that person's will. It takes what is animal in us and deploys it against what makes us human. As an American commander wrote in an August 2003 e-mail about his instructions to torture prisoners at Abu Ghraib, "The gloves are coming off gentlemen regarding these detainees, Col. Boltz has made it clear that we want these individuals broken."

What does it mean to "break" an individual? As the French essayist Michel de Montaigne once commented, and Shakespeare echoed, even the greatest philosophers have difficulty thinking clearly when they have a toothache. These wise men were describing the inescapable frailty of the human experience, mocking the claims of some seers to be above basic human feelings and bodily needs. If that frailty is exposed by a toothache, it is beyond dispute in the case of torture. The infliction of physical pain on a person with no means of defending himself is designed to render that person completely subservient to his torturers. It is designed to extirpate his autonomy as a human being, to render his control as an individual beyond his own reach. That is why the term "break" is instructive. Something broken can be put back together, but it will never regain the status of being unbroken—of having integrity. When you break a human being, you turn him into something subhuman. You enslave him. This is why the Romans reserved torture for slaves, not citizens, and why slavery and torture were inextricably linked in the antebellum South.

What you see in the relationship between torturer and tortured is the absolute darkness of totalitarianism. You see one individual granted the most complete power he can ever hold over another. Not just confinement of his mobility—the abolition of his very agency. Torture uses a person's body to remove from his own control his conscience, his thoughts, his faith, his selfhood. The CIA's definition of "waterboarding"—recently leaked to ABC News— describes that process in plain English: "The prisoner is bound to an inclined board, feet raised and head slightly below the feet. Cellophane is wrapped over the prisoner's face and water is poured over him. Unavoidably, the gag reflex kicks in and a terrifying fear of drowning leads to almost instant pleas to bring the treatment to a halt." The ABC report then noted, "According to the sources, CIA officers who subjected themselves to the waterboarding technique lasted an average of 14 seconds before caving in. They said Al Qaeda's toughest prisoner, Khalid Sheikh Mohammed, won the admiration of interrogators when he was able to last between two and two and a half minutes before begging to confess."

Before the Bush administration, two documented cases of the U.S. Armed Forces using "waterboarding" resulted in courts-martial for the soldiers implicated. In Donald Rumsfeld's post–September 11 Pentagon, the technique is approved and, we recently learned, has been used on at least eleven detainees, possibly many more. What you see here is the deployment of a very basic and inescapable human reflex—the desire not to drown and suffocate—in order to destroy a person's autonomy. Even the most hardened fanatic can only endure two and a half minutes. After that, he is indeed "broken."

⊷⊙⊶

The entire structure of Western freedom grew in part out of the searing experience of state-sanctioned torture. The use of torture in Europe's religious wars of the sixteenth and seventeenth centuries is still etched in our communal consciousness, as it should be. Then, governments deployed torture not only to uncover perceived threats to their faith-based autocracies, but also to "save" the victim's soul. Torturers understood that religious conversion was a difficult thing, because it necessitated a shift in the deepest recesses of the human soul. The only way to reach those depths was to deploy physical terror in the hopes of completely destroying the heretic's autonomy. They would, in other words, destroy a human being's soul in order to save it. That is what burning at the stake was—an indescribably agonizing act of torture that could be ended at a moment's notice if the victim recanted. In a state where theological doctrine always trumped individual liberty, this was a natural tactic.

Indeed, the very concept of Western liberty sprung in part from an understanding that, if the state has the power to reach that deep into a person's soul and can do that much damage to a human being's person, then the state has extinguished all oxygen necessary for freedom to survive. That is why, in George Orwell's totalitarian nightmare, the final ordeal is, of course, torture. Any polity that endorses torture has incorporated into its own DNA a totalitarian mutation. If the point of the U.S. Constitution is the preservation of liberty, the formal incorporation into U.S. law of the state's right to torture—by legally codifying physical coercion, abuse, and even, in Krauthammer's case, full-fledged torture of detainees by the CIA—would effectively end the American experiment of a political society based on inalienable human freedom protected not by the good graces of the executive, but by the rule of law.

The founders understood this argument. Its preeminent proponent was George Washington himself. As historian David Hackett Fischer memorably recounts in his 2004 book, *Washington's Crossing*: "Always some dark spirits wished to visit the same cruelties on the British and Hessians that had been inflicted on American captives. But Washington's example carried growing weight, more so than his written orders and prohibitions. He often reminded his men that they were an army of liberty and freedom, and that the rights of humanity for which they were fighting should extend even to their enemies. . . . Even in the most urgent moments of the war, these men were concerned about ethical questions in the Revolution."

Krauthammer has described Washington's convictions concerning torture as "pieties" that can be dispensed with today. He doesn't argue that torture is not evil. Indeed, he denounces it in unequivocal moral terms: "[T]orture is a terrible and monstrous thing, as degrading and morally corrupting to those who practice it as any conceivable human activity including its moral twin, capital punishment." But he maintains that the nature of the Islamofascist enemy after September 11 radically altered our interrogative options and that we are now not only permitted, but actually "morally compelled," to torture.

This is a radical and daring idea: that we must extinguish human freedom in a few cases in order to maintain it for everyone else. It goes beyond even the Bush administration's own formal position, which states that the United States will not endorse torture but merely "coercive interrogation techniques." (Such techniques, in the administration's elaborate definition, are those that employ physical force short of threatening immediate death or major organ failure.) And it is based on a premise that deserves further examination: that our enemies actually *deserve* torture; that some human beings are so depraved that, in Krauthammer's words, they "are entitled to no humane treatment."

Let me state for the record that I am second to none in decrying, loathing, and desiring to defeat those who wish to replace freedom with religious tyranny of the most brutal kind—and who have murdered countless innocent civilians in cold blood. Their acts are monstrous and barbaric. But I differ from Krauthammer by believing that monsters remain human beings. In fact, to reduce them to a subhuman level is to exonerate them of their acts of terrorism and mass murder—just as animals are not deemed morally responsible for killing. Insisting on the humanity of terrorists is, in fact, critical to maintaining their profound responsibility for the evil they commit.

And, if they are human, then they must necessarily not be treated in an inhuman fashion. You cannot lower the moral baseline of a terrorist to the subhuman without betraying a fundamental value. That is why the Geneva Conventions have a very basic ban on "cruel treatment and torture," and "outrages upon personal dignity, in particular humiliating and degrading treatment"—even when dealing with illegal combatants like terrorists. That is why the Declaration of Independence did not restrict its endorsement of freedom merely to those lucky enough to find themselves on U.S. soil—but extended it to all human beings, wherever they are in the world, simply because they are human.

꿈

Nevertheless, it is important to address Krauthammer's practical points. He is asking us to steel ourselves and accept that, whether we like it or not, torture and abuse may be essential in a war where our very survival may be at stake. He presents two scenarios in which he believes torture is permissible. The first is the "ticking bomb" scenario, a hypothetical rarity in which the following conditions apply: a) a terrorist cell has planted a nuclear weapon or something nearly as devastating in a major city; b) we have captured someone in this cell; c) we know for a fact that he knows where the bomb is. In practice, of course, the likelihood of such a scenario is extraordinarily remote. Uncovering a terrorist plot is hard enough; capturing a conspirator involved in that plot is even harder; and realizing in advance that the person knows the whereabouts of the bomb is nearly impossible. (Remember, in the war on terrorism, we have already detained—and even killed—many innocents. Pentagon reports have acknowledged that up to 90 percent of the prisoners at Abu Ghraib, many of whom were abused and tortured, were not guilty of anything.) But let us assume, for the sake of argument, that all of Krauthammer's conditions apply. Do we have a right to torture our hypothetical detainee?

According to Krauthammer, *of course* we do. No responsible public official put in that position would refuse to sanction torture if he believed it could save thousands of lives. And, if it's necessary, Krauthammer argues, it should be made legal. If you have conceded that torture may be justified in one case, Krauthammer believes, you have conceded that it may be justified in many more. In his words, "Once you've established the principle, to paraphrase George Bernard Shaw, all that's left to haggle about is the price."

But this is too easy and too glib a formulation. It is possible to concede that, in an extremely rare circumstance, torture may be used without conceding that it should be legalized. One imperfect but instructive analogy is civil disobedience. In that case, laws are indeed broken, but that does not establish that the laws should be broken. In fact, civil disobedience implies precisely that laws should *not* be broken, and protesters who engage in it present themselves promptly for imprisonment and legal sanction on exactly those grounds. They do so for demonstrative reasons. They are not saying that laws don't matter. They are saying that laws do matter, that they should be enforced, but that their conscience in this instance demands that they disobey them.

In extremis, a rough parallel can be drawn for a president faced with the kind of horrendous decision on which Krauthammer rests his entire case. What should a president do? The answer is simple: He may have to break the law. In the Krauthammer scenario, a president might well decide that, if the survival of the nation is at stake, he must make an exception. At the same time, he must subject himself—and so must those assigned to conduct the torture—to the consequences of an illegal act. Those guilty of torturing another human being must be punished—or pardoned ex-post-facto. If the torture is revealed to be useless, if the tortured man is shown to have been innocent or ignorant of the information he was tortured to reveal, then those responsible must face the full brunt of the law for, in Krauthammer's words, such a "terrible and monstrous thing." In Michael Walzer's formulation, if we are to have dirty hands, it is essential that we show them to be dirty.

What Krauthammer is proposing, however, is not this compromise, which allows us to retain our soul as a free republic while protecting us from catastrophe in an extremely rare case. He is proposing something very different: that our "dirty hands" be wiped legally clean before and after the fact. That is a Rubicon we should not cross, because it marks the boundary between a free country and an unfree one.

Krauthammer, moreover, misses a key lesson learned these past few years. What the hundreds of abuse and torture incidents have shown is that, once you permit torture for someone somewhere, it has a habit of spreading. Remember that torture was originally sanctioned in administration memos only for use against illegal combatants in rare cases. Within months of that decision, abuse and torture had become endemic throughout Iraq, a theater of war in which, even Bush officials agree, the Geneva Conventions apply. The extremely coercive interrogation tactics used at Guantánamo Bay "migrated" to Abu Ghraib. In fact, General Geoffrey Miller was sent to Abu Ghraib specifically to replicate Guantánamo's techniques. According to former Brigadier General Janis Karpinski, who had original responsibility for the prison, Miller ordered her to treat all detainees "like dogs." When Captain Ian Fishback, a West Point graduate and member of the 82nd Airborne, witnessed routine beatings and abuse of detainees at detention facilities in Iraq and Afghanistan, often for sport, he tried to stop it. It took him a year and a half to get any response from the military command, and he had to go to Senator John McCain to make his case.

In short, what was originally supposed to be safe, sanctioned, and rare became endemic, disorganized, and brutal. The lesson is that it is impossible to quarantine torture in a hermetic box; it will inevitably contaminate the military as a whole. Once you have declared that some enemies are subhuman, you have told every soldier that every potential detainee he comes across might be exactly that kind of prisoner—and that anything can therefore be done to him. That is what the disgrace at Abu Ghraib proved. And Abu Ghraib produced a tiny fraction of the number of abuse, torture, and murder cases that have been subsequently revealed. The only way to control torture is to ban it outright. Everywhere. Even then, in wartime, some "bad apples" will always commit abuse. But at least we will have done all we can to constrain it.

⚜

Krauthammer's second case for torture is equally unpersuasive. For "slow-fuse" detainees—high-level prisoners like Khalid Sheikh Mohammed with potentially, if not immediately, useful intelligence—Krauthammer again takes the most extreme case and uses it to establish a general rule. He concedes that torture, according to almost every careful student and expert, yields highly unreliable information. Anyone can see that. If you are screaming for relief after a few seconds of waterboarding, you're likely to tell your captors anything, true or untrue, to stop the agony and terror. But Krauthammer then argues that, unless you can prove that torture *never* works, it should always be retained as an option. "It may indeed be true that torture is not a reliable tool," he argues. "But that is very different from saying that it is *never* useful." And if it cannot be deemed always useless, it must be permitted—even when an imminent threat is not in the picture.

The problem here is an obvious one. You have made the extreme exception the basis for a new rule. You have said that, if you cannot absolutely rule out torture as effective in every single case, it should be ruled in as an option for many. Moreover, if allowing torture even in the "ticking bomb" scenario makes the migration of torture throughout the military likely, this loophole blows the doors wide open. And how do we tell good intelligence from bad intelligence in such torture-infested interrogation? The short answer is: We cannot. By allowing torture for "slow-fuse" detainees, you sacrifice a vital principle for intelligence that is uniformly corrupted at best and useless at worst.

In fact, the use of torture and coercive interrogation by U.S. forces in this war may have contributed to a profound worsening of our actionable intelligence. The key to intelligence in Iraq and, indeed, in Muslim enclaves in the West, is gaining the support and trust of those who give terrorists cover but who are not terrorists themselves. We need human intelligence from Muslims and Arabs prepared to spy on and inform on their neighbors and friends and even family and tribe members. The only way they will do that is if they perceive the gains of America's intervention as greater than the costs, if they see clearly that cooperating with the West will lead to a better life and a freer world rather than more of the same.

What our practical endorsement of torture has done is to remove that clear boundary between the Islamists and the West and make the two equivalent in the Muslim mind. Saddam Hussein used Abu Ghraib to torture innocents; so did the Americans. Yes, what Saddam did was exponentially worse. But, in doing what we did, we blurred the critical, bright line between the Arab past and what we are proposing as the Arab future. We gave Al Qaeda an enormous propaganda coup, as we have done with Guantánamo and Bagram, the "Salt Pit" torture chambers in Afghanistan, and the secret torture sites in Eastern Europe. In World War II, American soldiers were often tortured by the Japanese when captured. But FDR refused to reciprocate. Why? Because he knew that the goal of the war was not just Japan's defeat but Japan's transformation into a democracy. He knew that, if the beacon of democracy—the United States of America—had succumbed to the hallmark of totalitarianism, then the chance for democratization would be deeply compromised in the wake of victory.

No one should ever underestimate the profound impact that the conduct of American troops in World War II had on the citizens of the eventually defeated Axis powers. Germans saw the difference between being liberated by the Anglo-Americans and being liberated by the Red Army. If you saw an American or British uniform, you were safe. If you didn't, the terror would continue in different ways. Ask any German or Japanese of the generation that built democracy in those countries, and they will remind you of American values—not trumpeted by presidents in front of handpicked audiences, but *demonstrated* by the conduct of the U.S. military during occupation. I grew up in Great Britain, a country with similar memories. In the dark days of the cold war, I was taught that America, for all its faults, was still America. And that America did not, and constitutively could not, torture anyone.

If American conduct was important in Japan and Germany, how much more important is it in Iraq and Afghanistan. The entire point of the war on terrorism, according to the president, is to advance freedom and democracy in the Arab world. In Iraq, we had a chance not just to tell but to show the Iraqi people how a democracy acts. And, tragically, in one critical respect, we failed. That failure undoubtedly contributed to the increased legitimacy of the insurgency and illegitimacy of the occupation, and it made collaboration between informed Sunnis and U.S. forces far less likely. What minuscule intelligence we might have plausibly gained from torturing and abusing detainees is vastly outweighed by the intelligence we have forfeited by alienating many otherwise sympathetic Iraqis and Afghans, by deepening the divide between the democracies, and by sullying the West's reputation in the Middle East. Ask yourself: Why does Al Qaeda tell its detainees to claim torture regardless of what happens to them in U.S. custody? Because Al Qaeda knows that one of America's greatest weapons in this war is its reputation as a repository of freedom and decency. Our policy of permissible torture has handed Al Qaeda this weapon—to use against us. It is not just a moral tragedy. It is a pragmatic disaster. Why compound these crimes and errors by subsequently legalizing them, as Krauthammer (explicitly) and the president (implicitly) are proposing?

Will a ban on all "cruel, inhuman, and degrading treatment" render interrogations useless? By no means. There are many techniques for gaining intelligence from detainees other than using their bodies against their souls. You can start with the 17 that appear in the Army Field Manual, tested by decades of armed conflict only to be discarded by this administration with barely the blink of an eye. Isolation, psychological disorientation, intense questioning, and any number of other creative techniques are possible. Some of the most productive may well be those in which interrogators are so versed in Islamic theology and Islamist subcultures that they win the confidence of prisoners and pry information out of them—something the United States, with its dearth of Arabic speakers, is unfortunately ill-equipped to do.

꒰◍꒱

Enemy combatants need not be accorded every privilege granted legitimate prisoners of war; but they must be treated as human beings. This means that, in addition to physical torture, wanton abuse of their religious faith is out of bounds. No human freedom is meaningful without religious freedom. The fact that Koran abuse has been documented at Guantánamo; that one prisoner at Abu Ghraib was forced to eat pork and drink liquor; that fake menstrual blood was used to disorient a strict Muslim prisoner at Guantánamo—these make winning the hearts and minds of moderate Muslims far harder. Such tactics have resulted in hunger strikes at Guantánamo—perhaps the ultimate sign that the coercive and abusive attempts to gain the cooperation of detainees has completely failed to achieve the desired results.

The war on terrorism is, after all, a religious war in many senses. It is a war to defend the separation of church and state as critical to the existence of freedom, including religious freedom. It is a war to persuade the silent majority of Muslims that the West offers a better way—more decency, freedom, and humanity than the autocracies they live under and the totalitarian theocracies waiting in the wings. By endorsing torture—on anyone, anywhere, for any reason—we help obliterate the very values we are trying to promote. You can see this contradiction in Krauthammer's own words: We are "morally compelled" to commit "a terrible and monstrous thing." We are obliged to destroy the village in order to save it. We have to extinguish the most basic principle that defines America in order to save America.

No, we don't. In order to retain fundamental American values, we have to banish from the United States the totalitarian impulse that is integral to every act of torture. We have to ensure that the virus of tyranny is never given an opening to infect the Constitution and replicate into something that corrupts as deeply as it wounds. We should mark the words of Ian Fishback, one of the heroes of this war: "Will we confront danger and adversity in order to preserve our ideals, or will our courage and commitment to individual rights wither at the prospect of sacrifice? My response is simple. If we abandon our ideals in the face of adversity and aggression, then those ideals were never really in our possession. I would rather die fighting than give up even the smallest part of the idea that is 'America.'" If we legalize torture, even under constrained conditions, we will have given up a large part of the idea that is America. We will have lost the war before we have given ourselves the chance to win it.

POSTSCRIPT

Is the Use of Torture Against Terrorist Suspects Ever Justified?

Despite their obvious disagreements, there is an *almost* meeting of the minds between Sullivan and Krauthammer. Krauthammer admits that torture is a "terrible and monstrous thing," which is the essence of Sullivan's objection to it. Sullivan, for his part, concedes that, "in an extremely rare circumstance, torture may be used," though he refuses to allow its legalization. He compares it to civil disobedience, in which a principled law-breaker accepts the penalty for breaking the law. And so with torture: the decision to do it would have to be personally approved by the president, and he "must" then suffer the legal consequences. But if a president "must" be punished for doing something that he "may" do, isn't that unfair? Without directly answering this question, Sullivan opens up a loophole for the president: he can always be pardoned *ex post facto*.

Seymour Hersh, famous for breaking the story twenty-four years earlier on the Mai Lai massacre by American soldiers in Vietnam, has written an account of the mistreatment of prisoners at Abu Ghraib, based largely on a copy of the Army's own confidential report. See his "Torture at Abu Ghraib," *The New Yorker,* May 10, 2004. In another *New Yorker* article Jane Mayer has written on the "rendition" program, claiming that it amounts to American complicity in torture. See "Outsourcing Torture," *The New Yorker,* February 14, 2005.

Historian Alfred W. McCoy has traced what he characterizes as the historical and institutional continuity of torture in American wars in *A Question of Torture: CIA Interrogation, from the Cold War to the War on Terror* (Metropolitan Books, 2006). He concludes that the American use of torture during interrogations has been deliberate and systematic, not accidental. Kenneth Roth has edited *Torture: Does It Make Us Safe? Is It Ever OK?: A Human Rights Perspective* (New Press, 2005). As the subtitle suggests, the contributors offer negative answers to both questions.

Are there extraordinary circumstances under which opponents of torture will defend it, or at least overlook its use? Would you refrain if you knew that the known terrorist now in your custody could prevent a horrific tragedy if he revealed to you within the next thirty minutes the location of a bomb that he has planted? Sam Harris poses these questions in "In Defense of Torture," in *The Huffington Post,* October 17, 2005 on the Internet. In *Why Terrorism Works: Understanding the Threat, Responding to the Challenge* (Yale University Press, 2003), Alan M. Dershowitz offers a qualified defense of interrogation procedures ranging from sleep deprivation to the insertion of needles under fingernails.

Those who, going beyond the morality of torture, maintain that the confession elicited by torture is unreliable have a point: There is a considerable chance that the confession is false and may not prevent disaster. It is also true that there is considerable likelihood that a bomb dropped from an airplane may miss its intended target and instead kill hundreds of innocent people, but the bomb is dropped because there is a reasonable possibility that it will produce the desired result. That is the rationale for torture.

President Bush signed a law in 2005 prohibiting "cruel, inhuman, or degrading treatment or punishment" of detainees. However, neither the law nor the president, spelled out what punishments constituted such treatment. Michael Mukasey, upon his nomination in 2007 by President Bush to become attorney general, the nation's chief law enforcement official, was asked if he condoned or condemned waterboarding, a technique that simulates drowning, in questioning terrorist suspects. Mukasey replied, "If it amounts to torture, then it is not constitutional." But he would not answer a direct question as to whether it did amount to torture.

The debate continues. What is torture? When, if ever, is its use justified?

ISSUE 19

Is Warrantless Wiretapping in Some Cases Justified to Protect National Security?

YES: Andrew C. McCarthy, from "How to 'Connect the Dots'," *National Review* (January 30, 2006)

NO: Al Gore, from "Restoring the Rule of Law," from a Speech Presented to The American Constitution Society for Law and Policy and The Liberty Coalition (January 15, 2006)

ISSUE SUMMARY

YES: Former federal prosecutor Andrew C. McCarthy supports the National Security Agency program of surveillance without a warrant as an effective means of protecting national security that employs the inherent power of the president to protect the country against subversion.

NO: Former vice president Al Gore views the warrantless wiretapping of American citizens as a brazen violation of the Constitution and of specific acts of Congress that have spelled out the circumstances under which a president may receive judicial permission to wiretap or otherwise invade the privacy of citizens.

Americans overwhelmingly believe in the right to privacy. They subscribe to the old adage that a man's home is his castle (adding that a woman's home is hers). Yet the Constitution makes no explicit mention of a right to privacy. Controversy revolves not around the right to privacy but under what circumstances there are conflicting societal interests that would curtail it.

As it has on earlier occasions, privacy rights became a political issue when, shortly after the terrorist attack on September 11, 2001, on the World Trade Center in New York and the Pentagon in Washington, D.C., President Bush issued a secret executive order authorizing the National Security Agency to conduct warrantless electronic surveillance of telecommunications into and out of the United States of persons who might be linked to al Qaeda or other terrorist organizations. Some NSA surveillance involved persons in the United States.

The classified presidential authorization was made known to select members of the congressional leadership and intelligence committees, but was concealed from public knowledge until *The New York Times* reported it in December 2005, more than a year after it acquired information regarding it. (President Bush's administration had sought to have the newspaper not publish the article.)

The 1978 Foreign Intelligence Surveillance Act (FISA) had barred electronic surveillance of persons within the United States without the approval of a newly established Foreign Intelligence Surveillance Court. Before the public revelation of warrantless wiretapping, President Bush stated, with regard to domestic surveillance, "Constitutional guarantees are in place when it comes to doing what is necessary to protect our homeland, because we value the Constitution." He later maintained that warrantless surveillance was justified in dealing with international communications that threaten nation security, and that such surveillance was implicitly authorized by the 2001 congressional Authorization for Use of Military Force adopted days after 9/11. Supporting the president, some legal authorities argued that Congress cannot interfere with the means and methods the president uses to engage an enemy.

Critics of warrantless wiretapping hold that FISA established a clear and exclusive procedure for authorizing emergency wiretaps. They charge that such wiretaps by the president, when based upon the claim of "inherent authority," risk unauthorized government recording of the communications of a wholly domestic character.

Publication by the *Times* precipitated widespread public debate regarding the right to privacy and the legality of warrantless electronic surveillance of American citizens. Despite later revelations by the *Times* and the *Washington Post*, details of the extent of wiretapping or other secret interception of messages have not been revealed. Defending this silence, White House Press Secretary Scott McClellan said, "There's a reason we don't get into discussing ongoing intelligence activities, because it could compromise our efforts to prevent attacks from happening."

As for the success of warrantless wiretapping, General Michael Hayden, Principal Deputy Director for National Intelligence, stated, "The program has been successful in detecting and preventing attacks inside the United States." Along with administration officials, General Hayden has asserted, "Had this program been in effect prior to 9/11, it is my professional judgment that we would have detected some of the 9/11 Al Qaeda operatives in the United States, and we would have identified them as such."

Many members of both parties disagreed with the president's secret executive action. It is unlikely that all the facts regarding the extent of the program or what it achieved will be known for years, but the constitutional questions require answers.

Former federal prosecutor Andrew McCarthy defends secret surveillance as having been widely used (although sometimes abused) and wholly within the president's power. Former presidential candidate Al Gore believes that this activity is dangerous, unnecessary, and violates the rule of law.

YES

Andrew C. McCarthy

How to 'Connect the Dots'

Washington's scandal *du jour* involves a wartime surveillance program President Bush directed the National Security Agency to carry out after al-Qaeda killed nearly 3,000 Americans on September 11, 2001. The idea that there is anything truly scandalous about this program is absurd. But the outcry against it is valuable, highlighting as it does the mistaken assumption that criminal-justice solutions are applicable to national-security challenges.

The intelligence community has identified thousands of al-Qaeda operatives and sympathizers throughout the world. After Congress overwhelmingly authorized the use of military force immediately following the 9/11 attacks, the president, as part of the war effort, ordered the NSA to intercept the enemy's international communications, even if those communications went into and out of the United States and thus potentially involved American citizens. According to reports from the *New York Times*, which shamefully publicized leaks of the program's existence in mid-December 2005, as many as 7,000 suspected terrorists overseas are monitored at any one time, as are up to 500 suspects inside the U.S.

As is typical of such wartime operations, the NSA program was classified at the highest level of secret information. It was, nevertheless, completely different from the kind of rogue intelligence operations of which the Nixon era is emblematic (though by no means the only case). The Bush administration internally vetted the program, including at the Justice Department, to confirm its legal footing. It reviewed (and continues to review) the program every 45 days. It briefed the bipartisan leadership of Congress (including the intelligence committees) at least a dozen times. It informed the chief judge of the federal Foreign Intelligence Surveillance Court (FISC), the tribunal that oversees domestic national-security wiretapping. And it modified the program in mid-2004 in reaction to concerns raised by the chief judge, national-security officials, and government lawyers.

Far from being a pretextual use of war powers to spy on political opponents and policy dissenters, the NSA program has been dedicated to national security. More to the point, it has saved lives, helping break up at least one al-Qaeda conspiracy to attack New York City and Washington, D.C., in connection with which a plotter named Lyman Faris was sentenced to 20 years' imprisonment.

As potential scandal fodder, so unremarkable did the NSA program seem that the *Times* sat on the story for a year—and a year, it is worth noting, during which it transparently and assiduously sought to exploit any opportunity to discredit the administration and cast it as a mortal threat to civil liberties. The leak was not sprung until the eleventh hour of congressional negotiations over renewal of the Patriot Act—at which point it provided ammunition to those who would gut Patriot's crucial post-9/11 domestic surveillance powers and simultaneously served as a marketing campaign for *Times* reporter James Risen, who just happened to be on the eve of publishing a book about, among other things, Bush's domestic "spying."

In fact, so obviously appropriate was wartime surveillance of the enemy that Rep. Jane Harman, the ranking Democrat on the House Intelligence Committee, issued a statement right after the *Times* exposed the program, saying: "I have been briefed since 2003 on a highly classified NSA foreign collection program that targeted Al-Qaeda. I believe the program is essential to US national security and that its disclosure has damaged critical intelligence capabilities." (With partisan "scandal" blowing in the wind, Harman changed her tune two weeks later, suddenly deciding that the "essential" program was probably illegal after all.)

꧁꧂

If President Bush's reelection is any indication, what most Americans will care about is that we are monitoring the enemy. Chances are they won't be overly interested in knowing whether that monitoring is done on the president's own constitutional authority or in accordance with a statutory scheme calling for judicial imprimatur. Nevertheless, the Left is already indulging in loose talk about impeachment. Even some Republican "moderates," such as Arlen Specter, say the domestic-spying allegations are troubling enough that hearings are warranted. So it's worth asking: What is all the fuss about?

At bottom, it is about a power grab that began nearly three decades ago. Ever since it became technologically possible to intercept wire communications, presidents have done so. All of them, going back to FDR, claimed that the powers granted to the chief executive under Article II of the Constitution allowed them to conduct such wiretapping for national-security purposes. Particularly in wartime, this power might be thought indisputable. The president is the commander in chief of the armed forces, and penetrating enemy communications is as much an incident of war-fighting as bombing enemy targets is.

But surveillance power has been abused—and notoriously by President Nixon, whose eavesdropping on political opponents was the basis of a draft article of impeachment. Watergate-era domestic-spying controversies dovetailed with important developments in the law of electronic surveillance. In 1967, the Supreme Court, in *Katz* v. *United States*, held that Fourth Amendment protection against unreasonable searches extended to electronic surveillance—meaning that eavesdropping without a judicial warrant was now presumptively unconstitutional. Congress followed by enacting a comprehensive scheme, known as "Title III," that required law-enforcement agents to obtain a court warrant for probable cause of a crime before conducting electronic surveillance. Yet both *Katz* and Title III recognized inherent presidential authority to conduct *national-security* monitoring without being bound by the new warrant requirement.

The Supreme Court undertook to circumscribe this inherent authority in its 1972 *Keith* decision. It held that a judicial warrant was required for national-security surveillance if the target was a purely *domestic* threat—the Vietnam-era Court giving higher priority to the free-speech interests of "those suspected of unorthodoxy in their political beliefs" than to the safety of those who might be endangered by domestic terrorists. Still, the Court took pains to exempt from its ruling the "activities of *foreign* powers or their agents" (emphasis added).

The true power grab occurred in 1978, when Congress enacted the Foreign Intelligence Surveillance Act. FISA attempted to do in the national-security realm what Title III had done in law enforcement: erect a thoroughgoing legal regime for domestic eavesdropping. And therein lies the heart of the current dispute. If the president has inherent authority to conduct national-security wiretapping, it is a function of his constitutional warrant. It is not a function of Congress's having failed until 1978 to flex its own muscles. A constitutional power cannot be altered or limited by statute. Period.

But limiting presidential authority is precisely what FISA purports to do. It ostensibly prohibits national-security eavesdropping (and, since 1994, physical searches) unless the executive branch can satisfy a federal judge—one of eleven who sit on a specially created Foreign Intelligence Surveillance Court—that there is probable cause that the subject it seeks to monitor is an "agent of a foreign power" (generally either a spy or a member of a foreign terrorist organization).

FISA does not aim to restrict the power to eavesdrop on *all* conversations. Communications that are entirely foreign—in that they involve aliens communicating overseas, for example—are exempted, as are conversations that *unintentionally* capture "U.S. persons" (generally, American citizens and permanent resident aliens), as long as these communications are intercepted outside the U.S. But where it does apply, FISA holds that the president—the constitutional officer charged with the nation's security—is powerless to eavesdrop on an operative posing a threat to the United States unless a judge—who need not possess any national-security expertise—is persuaded that the operative is a genuine threat. One suspects that such a system would astonish the Founders.

◦⟨◉⟩◦

Does the NSA program violate FISA? That question is difficult to answer with certainty. The program remains highly classified, and many of its details are not publicly known, nor should they be. Much has been made of the fact that FISA approval is required to intercept calls into or out of the United States if an American is intentionally being targeted. But scant attention has been given to FISA's caveat that such conversations are protected only if their participants have a *reasonable expectation of privacy*. It is difficult to imagine that Americans who make or receive calls to war zones in, say, Afghanistan or Iraq, or to al-Qaeda operatives anywhere, can reasonably expect that no one is listening in.

Nevertheless, it would not be surprising to learn that at least some of the NSA monitoring transgresses the bounds of FISA. For example, the statute mandates—without qualification about the reasonable expectation of privacy— that the government seek a judicial warrant before eavesdropping on any international call to or from the U.S., if that call is intercepted *inside* our borders. A distinction based on where a call is intercepted made sense in 1978. Back then, if a conversation was intercepted inside our borders, its partici- pants were almost certain to include at least one U.S. person. But modern technology has since blurred the distinction between foreign and domestic telephony. Packets of digital information are now routed through switches inside countries (including, predominately, the U.S.) where neither the sender nor the recipient of the call is located. The NSA has capitalized on this evolu- tion, and is now able, from within the U.S., to seize calls between Tikrit and Kabul, or between Peshawar and Hamburg. If done without a warrant, those intercepts present no FISA problem, because all the speakers are overseas. But it's hard to believe that the NSA is using this technology *only* to acquire all- foreign calls, while intercepting calls between, say, New York and Hamburg only from locations *outside* the U.S.

Perhaps that is why the Bush administration's defense has been light on the abstruse details of FISA and heavy on the president's inherent Article II power—although carefully couched to avoid offending Congress and the FISC with suggestions that FISA is at least partly unconstitutional. Essentially, the administration argues that FISA is beneficial in ordinary times and for long-term investigations, but that it did not and cannot repeal the president's independent constitutional obligation to protect the country: an obligation that was explicitly reserved even by President Carter, who signed FISA; that has been claimed by every president since; and that is uniquely vital in a war against thousands of stateless, stealthy terrorists, in which both a "probable cause" requirement and a sclerotic bureaucracy for processing warrant applications would be dan- gerously impractical.

In advancing this argument, the administration finds much support in the one and only decision ever rendered by the Foreign Intelligence Court of Review—the appellate court created by FISA to review FISC decisions. That decision came in 2002, after a quarter-century of FISA experience. Tellingly, its context was a brazen effort by the FISC to reject the Patriot Act's disman- tling of the "wall" that prevented intelligence agents and criminal investiga- tors from pooling information. In overruling the FISC, the Court of Review observed that "all the other courts to have decided the issue [have] held that the President did have inherent authority to conduct warrantless searches to obtain foreign intelligence information." Notwithstanding FISA, the Court thus pronounced: "We take for granted that the President does have that authority."

The administration has also placed great stock in Congress's post-9/11 authorization of "all necessary and appropriate force" against those behind the terrorist attacks. While this resolution did not expressly mention penetrating enemy communications, neither did it explicitly include the detention of enemy combatants, which the Supreme Court, in its 2004 *Hamdi* decision, found implicit in the use-of-force authorization because it is a "fundamental incident of waging war." Capturing intelligence, of course, is as much a component of waging war as capturing operatives. Any other conclusion would lead to the absurdity of the president's having full discretion to kill terrorists but needing a judge's permission merely to eavesdrop on them.

FISA aside, the administration stresses that the NSA program fits comfortably within the Fourth Amendment. That Amendment proscribes *unreasonable* searches, not warrantless ones—and it is thus unsurprising that the Supreme Court has recognized numerous exceptions to the warrant requirement that are of far less moment than the imperative to protect the country from attack. Plainly, there is nothing unreasonable about intercepting potential enemy communications in wartime. Moreover, the courts have long held that searches conducted at the border are part of the sovereign right of self-protection, and thus require neither probable cause nor a warrant. Cross-border communications, which might well be triggers of terror plots, are no more deserving of constitutional protection.

ᴄ◖०⟩०

Critics have made much of a lengthy analysis published on January 6, 2006, by the Congressional Research Service that casts doubt on the administration's core contentions. Media have treated the report as bearing special weight because the CRS is a nonpartisan entity. But that does not mean the CRS is *objective*. "The sole mission of CRS," it explains on its website, "is to serve the United States Congress." Yet the issue at stake is precisely a separation-of-powers dispute.

While the CRS study is an impressive compilation of the relevant law, it resorts to a fairly standard tactic for marginalizing executive power: reliance on the concurring opinion by Supreme Court Justice Robert Jackson in a 1952 case involving President Truman's failed effort to seize steel mills—a move Truman justified by referring to the exigencies of the Korean War. Jackson saw executive power as waxing or waning along a three-stage scale, depending on whether a president acted with the support, the indifference, or the opposition of Congress. On this theory, a statute like FISA could curb a president's inherent constitutional authority. The fatal problem with the Jackson construct, however, has always been that it makes Congress, not the Constitution, the master of presidential authority. It disregards the reality that the executive is a coequal branch whose powers exist whether Congress acts or not. But the CRS prefers Jackson's conveniently airy formula, which failed to command a Court majority, to relevant opinions that don't go Congress's way, such as that of the Foreign Intelligence Court of Review—which, unlike the Supreme Court, was actually considering FISA.

Frustrated by its inability to move public opinion, the Left is now emphasizing the large "volume of information harvested from telecommunication data and voice networks," as the *Times* breathlessly put it, "without court-approved warrants." But this is pure legerdemain. When we refer to "information" from "telecommunication data," we are talking about something that, legally, is worlds apart from the content of telephone calls or e-mail messages.

These data do not include the substance of what people privately say to one another in conversations, but rather comprise statistical facts about the use of telecommunications services (for example, what phone number called another number, the date and time of the call, how long it lasted, etc.). Court warrants have never been required for the acquisition of such information because, as the Supreme Court explained over a quarter-century ago in *Smith* v. *Maryland*, telecommunications data do not implicate the Fourth Amendment. All phone and e-mail users know this information is conveyed to and maintained by service providers, and no one expects it to be private.

Analyzing such data is clearly different from monitoring the calls and e-mails themselves. For our own protection, we should want the government to collect as many of these data as possible (since doing so affects no one's legitimate privacy interests) in order to develop investigative leads. That's how a country manages to go four years without a domestic terror attack.

Yet the Left's rage continues, despite the public's evident disinterest in the mind-numbingly technical nature of the dispute, and despite the obvious truth that the NSA program was a bona fide effort to protect the nation from harm, not to snoop on Americans—only a tiny fraction of whom were affected, and those with apparent good reason. The controversy is a disquieting barometer of elite commitment to the War on Terror. As recently as two years ago, when "connecting the dots" was all the rage, liberals ignored eight years of Clintonian nonfeasance and portrayed the Bush administration as asleep at the switch while terrorists ran amok. Now they ignore President Clinton's insistence on the very same executive surveillance power that the current administration claims and caricature Bush as the imperial president, shredding core protections of civil liberties by exaggerating the terror threat. Either way you slice it, national security becomes a game in which necessary decisions by responsible adults become political grist, and, if they get enough traction, phony scandals. What remains real, though, is the danger to Americans implicit in any system that can't tell a war from a crime.

 **NO**

Restoring the Rule of Law

The Executive Branch of the government has been caught eavesdropping on huge numbers of American citizens and has brazenly declared that it has the unilateral right to continue without regard to the established law enacted by Congress to prevent such abuses.

It is imperative that respect for the rule of law be restored.

So, many of us have come here to Constitution Hall to sound an alarm and call upon our fellow citizens to put aside partisan differences and join with us in demanding that our Constitution be defended and preserved.

It is appropriate that we make this appeal on the day our nation has set aside to honor the life and legacy of Dr. Martin Luther King, Jr., who challenged America to breathe new life into our oldest values by extending its promise to all our people.

On this particular Martin Luther King Day, it is especially important to recall that for the last several years of his life. Dr. King was illegally wiretapped—one of hundreds of thousands of Americans whose private communications were intercepted by the U.S. government during this period.

The FBI privately called King the "most dangerous and effective negro leader in the country" and vowed to "take him off his pedestal." The government even attempted to destroy his marriage and blackmail him into committing suicide.

This campaign continued until Dr. King's murder. The discovery that the FBI conducted a long-running and extensive campaign of secret electronic surveillance designed to infiltrate the inner workings of the Southern Christian Leadership Conference, and to learn the most intimate details of Dr. King's life, helped to convince Congress to enact restrictions on wiretapping.

The result was the Foreign Intelligence and Surveillance Act (FISA), which was enacted expressly to ensure that foreign intelligence surveillance would be presented to an impartial judge to verify that there is a sufficient cause for the surveillance. I voted for that law during my first term in Congress and for almost thirty years the system has proven a workable and valued means of according a level of protection for private citizens, while permitting foreign surveillance to continue.

Yet, just one month ago, Americans awoke to the shocking news that in spite of this long settled law, the Executive Branch has been secretly spying on large numbers of Americans for the last four years and eavesdropping on "large

From a speech by former Vice President Al Gore, "Restoring the Rule of Law," January 16, 2006. The event was co-sponsored by The American Constitution Society for Law and Policy and The Liberty Coalition. Reprinted by permission.

volumes of telephone calls, e-mail messages, and other Internet traffic inside the United States." The New York Times reported that the President decided to launch this massive eavesdropping program "without search warrants or any new laws that would permit such domestic intelligence collection."

During the period when this eavesdropping was still secret, the President went out of his way to reassure the American people on more than one occasion that, of course, judicial permission is required for any government spying on American citizens and that, of course, these constitutional safeguards were still in place.

But surprisingly, the President's soothing statements turned out to be false. Moreover, as soon as this massive domestic spying program was uncovered by the press, the President not only confirmed that the story was true, but also declared that he has no intention of bringing these wholesale invasions of privacy to an end.

At present, we still have much to learn about the NSA's domestic surveillance. What we do know about this pervasive wiretapping virtually compels the conclusion that the President of the United States has been breaking the law repeatedly and persistently.

A president who breaks the law is a threat to the very structure of our government. Our Founding Fathers were adamant that they had established a government of laws and not men. Indeed, they recognized that the structure of government they had enshrined in our Constitution—our system of checks and balances—was designed with a central purpose of ensuring that it would govern through the rule of law. As John Adams said: "The executive shall never exercise the legislative and judicial powers, or either of them, to the end that it may be a government of laws and not of men."

An executive who arrogates to himself the power to ignore the legitimate legislative directives of the Congress or to act free of the check of the judiciary becomes the central threat that the Founders sought to nullify in the Constitution—an all-powerful executive too reminiscent of the King from whom they had broken free. In the words of James Madison, "the accumulation of all powers, legislative, executive, and judiciary, in the same hands, whether of one, a few, or many, and whether hereditary, self-appointed, or elective, may justly be pronounced the very definition of tyranny."

Thomas Paine, whose pamphlet, "On Common Sense" ignited the American Revolution, succinctly described America's alternative. Here, he said, we intended to make certain that "the law is king."

Vigilant adherence to the rule of law strengthens our democracy and strengthens America. It ensures that those who govern us operate within our constitutional structure, which means that our democratic institutions play their indispensable role in shaping policy and determining the direction of our nation. It means that the people of this nation ultimately determine its course and not executive officials operating in secret without constraint.

The rule of law makes us stronger by ensuring that decisions will be tested, studied, reviewed and examined through the processes of government that are designed to improve policy. And the knowledge that they will be reviewed prevents over-reaching and checks the accretion of power.

A commitment to openness, truthfulness and accountability also helps our country avoid many serious mistakes. Recently, for example, we learned from recently classified declassified documents that the Gulf of Tonkin Resolution, which authorized the tragic Vietnam war, was actually based on false information. We now know that the decision by Congress to authorize the Iraq War, 38 years later, was also based on false information. America would have been better off knowing the truth and avoiding both of these colossal mistakes in our history. Following the rule and law makes us safer, not more vulnerable.

The President and I agree on one thing. The threat from terrorism is all too real. There is simply no question that we continue to face new challenges in the wake of the attack on September 11th and that we must be ever-vigilant in protecting our citizens from harm.

Where we disagree is that we have to break the law or sacrifice our system of government to protect Americans from terrorism. In fact, doing so makes us weaker and more vulnerable.

Once violated, the rule of law is in danger. Unless stopped, lawlessness grows. The greater the power of the executive grows, the more difficult it becomes for the other branches to perform their constitutional roles. As the executive acts outside its constitutionally prescribed role and is able to control access to information that would expose its actions, it becomes increasingly difficult for the other branches to police it. Once that ability is lost, democracy itself is threatened and we become a government of men and not laws.

The President's men have minced words about America's laws. The Attorney General openly conceded that the "kind of surveillance" we now know they have been conducting requires a court order unless authorized by statute. The Foreign Intelligence Surveillance Act self-evidently does not authorize what the NSA has been doing, and no one inside or outside the Administration claims that it does. Incredibly, the Administration claims instead that the surveillance was implicitly authorized when Congress voted to use force against those who attacked us on September 11th.

This argument just does not hold any water. Without getting into the legal intricacies, it faces a number of embarrassing facts. First, another admission by the Attorney General: he concedes that the Administration knew that the NSA project was prohibited by existing law and that they consulted with some members of Congress about changing the statute. Gonzalez says that they were told this probably would not be possible. So how can they now argue that the Authorization for the Use of Military Force somehow implicitly authorized it all along? Second, when the Authorization was being debated, the Administration did in fact seek to have language inserted in it that would have authorized them to use military force domestically—and the Congress did not agree. Senator Ted Stevens and Representative Jim McGovern, among others, made statements during the Authorization debate clearly restating that that Authorization did not operate domestically.

When President Bush failed to convince Congress to give him all the power he wanted when they passed the AUMF, he secretly assumed that power anyway, as if congressional authorization was a useless bother. But as Justice

Frankfurter once wrote: "To find authority so explicitly withheld is not merely to disregard in a particular instance the clear will of Congress. It is to disrespect the whole legislative process and the constitutional division of authority between President and Congress."

This is precisely the "disrespect" for the law that the Supreme Court struck down in the steel seizure case.

It is this same disrespect for America's Constitution which has now brought our republic to the brink of a dangerous breach in the fabric of the Constitution. And the disrespect embodied in these apparent mass violations of the law is part of a larger pattern of seeming indifference to the Constitution that is deeply troubling to millions of Americans in both political parties. . . .

Whenever power is unchecked and unaccountable it almost inevitably leads to mistakes and abuses. In the absence of rigorous accountability, incompetence flourishes. Dishonesty is encouraged and rewarded.

Last week, for example, Vice President Cheney attempted to defend the Administration's eavesdropping on American citizens by saying that if it had conducted this program prior to 9/11, they would have found out the names of some of the hijackers.

Tragically, he apparently still doesn't know that the Administration did in fact have the names of at least 2 of the hijackers well before 9/11 and had available to them information that could have easily led to the identification of most of the other hijackers. And yet, because of incompetence in the handling of this information, it was never used to protect the American people.

It is often the case that an Executive Branch beguiled by the pursuit of unchecked power responds to its own mistakes by reflexively proposing that it be given still more power. Often, the request itself it used to mask accountability for mistakes in the use of power it already has.

Moreover, if the pattern of practice begun by this Administration is not challenged, it may well become a permanent part of the American system. Many conservatives have pointed out that granting unchecked power to this President means that the next President will have unchecked power as well. And the next President may be someone whose values and belief you do not trust. And this is why Republicans as well as Democrats should be concerned with what this President has done. If this President's attempt to dramatically expand executive power goes unquestioned, our Constitutional design of checks and balances will be lost. And the next President or some future President will be able, in the name of national security, to restrict our liberties in a way the framers never would have thought possible.

The same instinct to expand its power and to establish dominance characterizes the relationship between this Administration and the courts and the Congress.

In a properly functioning system, the Judicial Branch would serve as the constitutional umpire to ensure that the branches of government observed their proper spheres of authority, observed civil liberties and adhered to the rule of law. Unfortunately, the unilateral executive has tried hard to thwart the ability of the judiciary to call balls and strikes by keeping controversies out of its hands—notably those challenging its ability to detain individuals without legal process—by appointing judges who will be deferential to its exercise of power and by its support of assaults on the independence of the third branch.

The President's decision to ignore FISA was a direct assault on the power of the judges who sit on that court. Congress established the FISA court precisely to be a check on executive power to wiretap. Yet, to ensure that the court could not function as a check on executive power, the President simply did not take matters to it and did not let the court know that it was being bypassed. . . .

The Executive Branch, time and again, has co-opted Congress' role, and often Congress has been a willing accomplice in the surrender of its own power.

Look for example at the Congressional role in "overseeing" this massive four year eavesdropping campaign that on its face seemed so clearly to violate the Bill of Rights. The President says he informed Congress, but what he really means is that he talked with the chairman and ranking member of the House and Senate intelligence committees and the top leaders of the House and Senate. This small group, in turn, claimed that they were not given the full facts, though at least one of the intelligence committee leaders handwrote a letter of concern to VP Cheney and placed a copy in his own safe.

Though I sympathize with the awkward position in which these men and women were placed, I cannot disagree with the Liberty Coalition when it says that Democrats as well as Republicans in the Congress must share the blame for not taking action to protest and seek to prevent what they consider a grossly unconstitutional program. . . .

Fear drives out reason. Fear suppresses the politics of discourse and opens the door to the politics of destruction. Justice Brandeis once wrote: "Men feared witches and burnt women."

The founders of our country faced dire threats. If they failed in their endeavors, they would have been hung as traitors. The very existence of our country was at risk.

Yet, in the teeth of those dangers, they insisted on establishing the Bill of Rights.

Is our Congress today in more danger than were their predecessors when the British army was marching on the Capitol? Is the world more dangerous than when we faced an ideological enemy with tens of thousands of missiles poised to be launched against us and annihilate our country at a moment's notice? Is America in more danger now than when we faced worldwide fascism on the march—when our fathers fought and won two World Wars simultaneously?

It is simply an insult to those who came before us and sacrificed so much on our behalf to imply that we have more to be fearful of than they. Yet they faithfully protected our freedoms and now it is up to us to do the same. . . .

A special counsel should immediately be appointed by the Attorney General to remedy the obvious conflict of interest that prevents him from investigating what many believe are serious violations of law by the President. We have had a fresh demonstration of how an independent investigation by a special counsel with integrity can rebuild confidence in our system of justice. Patrick Fitzgerald has, by all accounts, shown neither fear nor favor in pursuing allegations that the Executive Branch has violated other laws.

Republican as well as Democratic members of Congress should support the bipartisan call of the Liberty Coalition for the appointment of a special counsel to pursue the criminal issues raised by warrantless wiretapping of Americans by the President.

Second, new whistleblower protections should immediately be established for members of the Executive Branch who report evidence of wrongdoing—especially where it involves the abuse of Executive Branch authority in the sensitive areas of national security.

Third, both Houses of Congress should hold comprehensive—and not just superficial—hearings into these serious allegations of criminal behavior on the part of the President. And, they should follow the evidence wherever it leads.

Fourth, the extensive new powers requested by the Executive Branch in its proposal to extend and enlarge the Patriot Act should, under no circumstances be granted, unless and until there are adequate and enforceable safeguards to protect the Constitution and the rights of the American people against the kinds of abuses that have so recently been revealed.

Fifth, any telecommunications company that has provided the government with access to private information concerning the communications of Americans without a proper warrant should immediately cease and desist their complicity in this apparently illegal invasion of the privacy of American citizens.

Freedom of communication is an essential prerequisite for the restoration of the health of our democracy.

It is particularly important that the freedom of the Internet be protected against either the encroachment of government or the efforts at control by large media conglomerates. The future of our democracy depends on it.

I mentioned that along with cause for concern, there is reason for hope. As I stand here today, I am filled with optimism that America is on the eve of a golden age in which the vitality of our democracy will be re-established and will flourish more vibrantly than ever. Indeed I can feel it in this hall.

As Dr. King once said, "Perhaps a new spirit is rising among us. If it is, let us trace its movements and pray that our own inner being may be sensitive to its guidance, for we are deeply in need of a new way beyond the darkness that seems so close around us."

POSTSCRIPT

Is Warrantless Wiretapping in Some Cases Justified to Protect National Security?

The opposing positions of Andrew McCarthy and Al Gore raise several questions. Does the president have the inherent power to engage in secret surveillance or is that authority dependent upon an explicit delegation by Congress? Is there a difference between presidential interception of communications involving foreigners and those involving American citizens? Can national security curtail individual rights or is there no conflict between them?

These questions came to the fore after the December 2005 revelation of President Bush's creation of a warrantless wiretapping program in the National Security Agency. Testimony by Attorney General Alberto Gonzalez on February 6, 2006 before the U.S. Senate Committee on the Judiciary took the position that presidents have always employed enemy surveillance in support of the president's constitutional authority to protect the safety of all Americans. Gonzalez insists that the president must be capable of acting promptly, "rather than wait until it is too late." A group of scholars of constitutional law and former government officials rejected these arguments in an open letter to Congress addressed February 9, 2006, stating that domestic spying was explicitly prohibited by the Foreign Intelligence Surveillance Act.

In August 2006, U.S. District Court Judge Anna Diggs Taylor declared unconstitutional the warrantless wiretapping of calls between Americans and alleged foreign terrorists. Judge Taylor ordered a nationwide injunction to end the once-secret program as a violation of both constitutional rights and the 1978 Foreign Intelligence Surveillance Act that required court warrants for electronic surveillance related to terrorism or espionage.

One year later in August 2007, Congress passed and President Bush signed a surveillance law allowing the government to monitor telephone calls and e-mails without a warrant. The new law requires communications companies to make their facilities available for government wiretaps, grants them immunity from lawsuits for complying, and allows government agencies to conduct surveillance of all international calls and e-mails, including those with Americans, provided the intelligence-gathering is "directed at a person reasonably believed to be outside the United States." There is no requirement that either caller be a ...d terrorist, spy, or criminal. While those who favor the new law argued ...is vital to prevent potential terrorist attacks, those who oppose it contend ... erodes fundamental American liberties and privacy rights.

J. Michael McConnell, director of national intelligence, told Congress in ...ptember 2007 that there has been no recent electronic surveillance without court-approved warrants. Nevertheless, McConnell echoed President Bush's objective to make permanent the law allowing warrantless wiretapping. The opposition of leading congressional Democrats ensures that this will provoke passionate debate.

Jonathan White has written extensively on national security, and his *Terrorism and Homeland Security*, Fifth Edition (Wadsworth, 2005) is considered the leading work in the field. Ellen Frankel Paul, Fred D. Miller, Jr., and Jeffrey Paul have edited *The Right to Privacy* (Cambridge University Press, 2000), a series of wide-ranging essays by philosophers and academic lawyers, examining various aspects of privacy, including its role in American constitutional law and the ways it influences public policy.

Privacy is the ability of an individual or group to keep their lives and personal affairs out of public view, or to stop information about themselves from becoming known to people other than those to whom they choose to give the information. Americans believe that a man's or woman's home is his or her castle, and it should not ordinarily be entered by others without permission.

Brief reflection will lead most Americans, except those firm libertarians who oppose all government action that impinges upon their lives, to conclude that there are trade-offs between privacy and liberty. The government needs to collect personal census information in order to determine appropriations for particular programs, and it needs to know the income of persons in order to assess income taxes, while individuals need to believe that this knowledge will not be widely circulated because it can be used in illegal and improper ways. Medical information is deemed to be private communication between physician and patient, yet moral issues arise, such as whether an HIV-positive individual should reveal that condition before having relations with a prospective sexual partner. Similarly, the introduction of a universal identity card could have substantial social benefits, but it also raises the risks of unfair discrimination and identity theft.

The difficulty the government has in striking an appropriate balance between individual freedom and national security is mirrored in the close division in public sentiment. A CNN/USA Today/Gallup poll in January 2006 showed 46 to 50 percent support for warrantless wiretapping. Five months later, the figures were reversed and the program was opposed, 46 to 50 percent. It is likely that the relationship and possible conflict between personal liberty and national security will never be definitively resolved.

ISSUE 20

Is China a Military Threat
to the United States?

YES: Robert D. Kaplan, from "How We Would Fight China," *The Atlantic.Com* (June 2005)

NO: Ivan Eland, from "Is Chinese Military Modernization a Threat to the United States?" *Policy Analysis* (January 23, 2003)

ISSUE SUMMARY

YES: Robert Kaplan, senior associate for the Carnegie Endowment for International Peace, notes that China is poised to achieve political-strategic parity with the United States by planning asymmetric warfare with America and cultivating a series of pragmatic alliances with America's enemies.

NO: Ivan Eland, director of policy studies at the Cato Institute, contends that China's ongoing military modernization is still far behind that of the United States—the gap is actually widening—and that its purpose is to merely to protect Chinese interests in the area.

$\mathbf{W}$ith over a billion people, China is the world's most populous nation, and one of the world's oldest civilizations, dating back more than six millennia. China was already an advanced and powerful kingdom during Europe's Dark Ages, having invented paper, the compass, gunpowder, and printing. But in the modern era it suffered great humiliation at the hands of Western powers, as trading companies and military adventurers forced their way into the country, forcing it into signing a number of unfavorable treaties. Its last ruling dynasty fell in 1911 and a republic was proclaimed, but a long series of regional struggles between warlords ensued, plunging the nation into a prolonged civil war.

Japan seized Manchuria in 1931 and invaded China proper a few years later, an extraordinary brutal occupation that lasted until the defeat of the Japanese in 1945. Resisting the occupation was an uneasy coalition of Chinese Nationalists, led by Chaing Kai-shek, and the Communists, led by Mao Zedong. The coalition quickly dissolved in 1946, and after a three-year civil war, Mao's Communists triumphed and renamed the country the People's Republic of China (PRC). Chaing's forces retreated to the offshore island of Taiwan.

Mao ruled China with an ideology that combined radical communism with traditional Chinese nationalism. Sometimes the radicalism dominated, as during Mao's "Great Leap Forward" (1958–1960), when peasants were forced into a massive experiment in backyard industrialization, costing the lives of at least 20 million people, and the Cultural Revolution (1966–1976), which targeted intellectuals as "social parasites" and encouraged popular violence against them. All this time, Mao's propaganda boasted that China was taking the "true path," remaining loyal to the authentic spirit of Marx and Lenin as opposed to its erstwhile ally, the Soviet Union.

For much of this period, U.S.-Chinese relations remained tense. At first the United States refused to recognize the Communist mainland, insisting that the "real" China was that of the defeated Nationalist forces in Taiwan. The Communists insisted that Taiwan was part of the PRC and hinted that they would force its reunion if necessary.

Then, unexpectedly and from a surprising source, a breakthrough in Sino-American relations occurred. Early in 1972 President Richard Nixon, who had long been seen as a hard-liner in the Cold War, announced that he would visit China. For a week he met with Chinese officials, including Mao himself, and both sides agreed to seek a "normalization" of relations, a peaceful resolution of the Taiwan controversy, and new trade agreements. The warming trend accelerated in the post-Mao era, and by the time of the Clinton administration, China was regarded as a "strategic partner" of the United States.

Today, visitors to China have been impressed by the proliferation of consumer goods and entertainments in a land that once scorned Western "decadence." In 2004, China held its first European-style Formula 1 car race on a brand-new $320-million track, held an NBA exhibition game, and staged its first Spanish bullfight to cheering crowds. More recently it opened its first Hooters restaurant, hundreds of Starbucks coffeehouses, and even an adult-products expo displaying various sex aids. China, it would seem, is beginning to take on the appearance of the nations of North America or of any Western European country. Could a nation of Hooters and bullfights really represent a threat to the United States?

Despite these appearances, many observers regard China warily. China is ruled by a small clique of men whose intentions are largely unknown even within China, much less to the outside world. Its press—even its Internet—is carefully monitored by bureaucrats who answer to the regime, and, as was shown at Tiananmen Square in 1989, it is capable of using the most brutal methods to crush dissent. What is more, the same prosperity that provides new consumer goods also permits the development or purchase of modern, sophisticated weaponry. Concerned China-watchers, largely in the United States (the European Union still regards China as a "strategic partner") view with alarm the spike in Chinese arms spending since the end of the 1990s, the extension of its influence in the region, and its acquisition of high-tech missiles and other modern weapons. In the following selections, scholar and commentator Robert Kaplan expresses some of these concerns. Opposing Kaplan's view is that of Cato Institute director Ivan Eland, who contends that the Chinese have their own legitimate concerns that need protection and have spent only moderately to modernize their military.

YES

Robert D. Kaplan

How We Would Fight China

For some time now no navy or air force has posed a threat to the United States. Our only competition has been armies, whether conventional forces or guerrilla insurgencies. This will soon change. The Chinese navy is poised to push out into the Pacific—and when it does, it will very quickly encounter a U.S. Navy and Air Force unwilling to budge from the coastal shelf of the Asian mainland. It's not hard to imagine the result: a replay of the decades-long Cold War, with a center of gravity not in the heart of Europe but, rather, among Pacific atolls that were last in the news when the Marines stormed them in World War II. In the coming decades China will play an asymmetric back-and-forth game with us in the Pacific, taking advantage not only of its vast coastline but also of its rear base— stretching far back into Central Asia—from which it may eventually be able to lob missiles accurately at moving ships in the Pacific.

In any naval encounter China will have distinct advantages over the United States, even if it lags in technological military prowess. It has the benefit, for one thing, of sheer proximity. Its military is an avid student of the competition, and a fast learner. It has growing increments of "soft" power that demonstrate a particular gift for adaptation. While stateless terrorists fill security vacuums, the Chinese fill economic ones. All over the globe, in such disparate places as the troubled Pacific Island states of Oceania, the Panama Canal zone, and out-of-the-way African nations, the Chinese are becoming masters of indirect influence—by establishing business communities and diplomatic outposts, by negotiating construction and trade agreements. Pulsing with consumer and martial energy, and boasting a peasantry that, unlike others in history, is overwhelmingly literate, China constitutes the principal conventional threat to America's liberal imperium.

How should the United States prepare to respond to challenges in the Pacific? To understand the dynamics of this second Cold War—which will link China and the United States in a future that may stretch over several generations— it is essential to understand certain things about the first Cold War, and about the current predicament of the North Atlantic Treaty Organization, the institution set up to fight that conflict. This is a story about military strategy and tactics, with some counterintuitive twists and turns. . . .

The first thing to understand is that the alliance system of the latter half of the twentieth century is dead. Warfare by committee, as practiced by NATO, has simply become too cumbersome in an age that requires light and lethal strikes. During the fighting in Kosovo in 1999 (a limited air campaign against a toothless enemy during a time of Euro-American harmony; a campaign, in other words, that should have been easy to prosecute) dramatic fissures appeared in the then-nineteen-member NATO alliance. The organization's end effectively came with the U.S. invasion of Afghanistan, in the aftermath of which, despite talk of a broad-based coalition, European militaries have usually done little more than patrol and move into areas already pacified by U.S. soldiers and Marines—a job more suggestive of the United Nations. NATO today is a medium for the expansion of bilateral training missions between the United States and formerly communist countries and republics: the Marines in Bulgaria and Romania, the Navy in Albania, the Army in Poland and the Czech Republic, Special Operations Forces in Georgia—the list goes on and on. Much of NATO has become a farm system for the major-league U.S. military.

The second thing to understand is that the functional substitute for a NATO of the Pacific already exists, and is indeed up and running. It is the U.S. Pacific Command, known as PACOM. Unencumbered by a diplomatic bureaucracy, PACOM is a large but nimble construct, and its leaders understand what many in the media and the policy community do not: that the center of gravity of American strategic concern is already the Pacific, not the Middle East. PACOM will soon be a household name, as CENTCOM (the U.S. Central Command) has been in the current epoch of Middle Eastern conflict—an epoch that will start to wind down, as far as the U.S. military is concerned, during the second Bush administration.

The third thing to understand is that, ironically, the vitality of NATO itself, the Atlantic alliance, could be revived by the Cold War in the Pacific—and indeed the re-emergence of NATO as an indispensable war-fighting instrument should be America's unswerving aim. In its posture toward China the United States will look to Europe and NATO, whose help it will need as a strategic counterweight and, by the way, as a force to patrol seas more distant than the Mediterranean and the North Atlantic. That is why NATO's current commander, Marine General James L. Jones, emphasizes that NATO's future lies in amphibious, expeditionary warfare.

Let me describe our military organization in the Pacific—an area through which I have traveled extensively during the past three years. PACOM has always been the largest, most venerable, and most interesting of the U.S. military's area commands. (Its roots go back to the U.S. Pacific Army of the Philippines War, 1899–1902.) Its domain stretches from East Africa to beyond the International Date Line and includes the entire Pacific Rim, encompassing half the world's surface and more than half of its economy. The world's six largest militaries, two of which (America's and China's) are the most rapidly modernizing, all operate within PACOM's sphere of control. PACOM has—in addition to its many warships and submarines—far more dedicated troops than CENTCOM. Even though the military's area commands do not *own* troops today in the way they used to, these statistics matter, because they demonstrate that the United States has chosen to locate the bulk of its forces in the Pacific, not in the Middle East. CENTCOM fights wars with troops essentially borrowed from PACOM.

Quietly in recent years, by negotiating bilateral security agreements with countries that have few such arrangements with one another, the U.S. military has formed a Pacific military alliance of sorts at PACOM headquarters, in Honolulu. This is where the truly interesting meetings are being held today, rather than in Ditchley or Davos. The attendees at those meetings, who often travel on PACOM's dime, are military officers from such places as Vietnam, Singapore, Thailand, Cambodia, and the Philippines.

Otto von Bismarck, the father of the Second Reich in continental Europe, would recognize the emerging Pacific system. In 2002 the German commentator Josef Joffe appreciated this in a remarkably perceptive article in *The National Interest*, in which he argued that in terms of political alliances, the United States has come to resemble Bismarck's Prussia. Britain, Russia, and Austria needed Prussia more than they needed one another, Joffe wrote, thus making them "spokes" to Berlin's "hub"; the U.S. invasion of Afghanistan exposed a world in which America can forge different coalitions for different crises. The world's other powers, he said, now need the United States more than they need one another.

Unfortunately, the United States did not immediately capitalize on this new power arrangement, because President George W. Bush lacked the nuance and attendant self-restraint of Bismarck, who understood that such a system could endure only so long as one didn't overwhelm it. The Bush administration did just that, of course, in the buildup to the invasion of Iraq, which led France, Germany, Russia, and China, along with a host of lesser powers such as Turkey, Mexico, and Chile, to unite against us.

In the Pacific, however, a Bismarckian arrangement still prospers, helped along by the pragmatism of our Hawaii-based military officers, five time zones removed from the ideological hothouse of Washington, D.C. In fact, PACOM represents a much purer version of Bismarck's imperial superstructure than anything the Bush administration created prior to invading Iraq. As Henry Kissinger writes in *Diplomacy* (1994), Bismarck forged alliances in all directions from a point of seeming isolation, without the constraints of ideology. He brought peace and prosperity to Central Europe by recognizing that when power relationships are correctly calibrated, wars tend to be avoided.

Only a similarly pragmatic approach will allow us to accommodate China's inevitable re-emergence as a great power. The alternative will be to turn the earth of the twenty-first century into a battlefield. Whenever great powers have emerged or re-emerged on the scene (Germany and Japan in the early decades of the twentieth century, to cite two recent examples), they have tended to be particularly assertive—and therefore have thrown international affairs into violent turmoil. China will be no exception. Today the Chinese are investing in both diesel-powered and nuclear-powered submarines—a clear signal that they intend not only to protect their coastal shelves but also to expand their sphere of influence far out into the Pacific and beyond.

This is wholly legitimate. China's rulers may not be democrats in the literal sense, but they are seeking a liberated First World lifestyle for many of their 1.3 billion people—and doing so requires that they safeguard sea-lanes for the transport of energy resources from the Middle East and elsewhere. Naturally, they do not trust the United States and India to do this for them. Given the stakes, and given what history teaches us about the conflicts that emerge when great powers all pursue legitimate interests, the result is likely to be the defining military conflict of the twenty-first century: if not a big war with China, then a series of Cold War-style standoffs that stretch out over years and decades. And this will occur mostly within PACOM's area of responsibility.

To do their job well, military officers must approach power in the most cautious, mechanical, and utilitarian way possible, assessing and reassessing regional balances of power while leaving the values side of the political equation to the civilian leadership. This makes military officers, of all government professionals, the least prone to be led astray by the raptures of liberal internationalism and neo-conservative interventionism.

The history of World War II shows the importance of this approach. In the 1930s the U.S. military, nervous about the growing strength of Germany and Japan, rightly lobbied for building up our forces. But by 1940 and 1941 the military (not unlike the German general staff a few years earlier) was presciently warning of the dangers of a two-front war; and by late summer of 1944 it should have been thinking less about defeating Germany and more about containing the Soviet Union. Today Air Force and Navy officers worry about a Taiwanese declaration of independence, because such a move would lead the United States into fighting a war with China that might not be in our national interest. Indonesia is another example: whatever the human-rights failures of the Indonesian military, PACOM assumes, correctly, that a policy of non-engagement would only open the door to Chinese-Indonesian military cooperation in a region that represents the future of world terrorism. (The U.S. military's response to the Asian tsunami was, of course, a humanitarian effort; but PACOM strategists had to have recognized that a vigorous response would gain political support for the military-basing rights that will form part of our deterrence strategy against China.) Or consider Korea: some Pacific-based officers take a reunified Korean peninsula for granted, and their main concern is whether the country will be "Finlandized" by China or will be secure within an American-Japanese sphere of influence.

PACOM's immersion in Asian power dynamics gives it unusual diplomatic weight, and consequently more leverage in Washington. And PACOM will not be nearly as constrained as CENTCOM by Washington-based domestic politics. Our actions in the Pacific will not be swayed by the equivalent of the Israel lobby; Protestant evangelicals will care less about the Pacific Rim than about the fate of the Holy Land. And because of the vast economic consequences of misjudging the power balance in East Asia, American business and military interests are likely to run in tandem toward a classically conservative policy of deterring China without needlessly provoking it, thereby amplifying PACOM's authority. Our stance toward China and the Pacific, in other words, comes with a built-in stability—and this, in turn, underscores the notion of a new Cold War that is sustainable over the very long haul. Moreover, the complexity of the many political and military relationships managed by PACOM will give the command considerably greater influence than that currently exercised by CENTCOM—which, as a few military experts have disparagingly put it to me, deals only with a bunch of "third-rate Middle Eastern armies."

The relative shift in focus from the Middle East to the Pacific in coming years—idealistic rhetoric notwithstanding—will force the next American president, no matter what his or her party, to adopt a foreign policy similar to those of moderate Republican presidents such as George H. W. Bush, Gerald Ford, and Richard Nixon. The management of risk will become a governing ideology. Even if Iraq turns out to be a democratic success story, it will surely be a from-the-jaws-of-failure success that no one in the military or the diplomatic establishment will ever want to repeat—especially in Asia, where the economic repercussions of a messy military adventure would be enormous. "Getting into a war with China is easy," says Michael Vickers, a former Green Beret who developed the weapons strategy for the Afghan resistance in the 1980s as a CIA officer and is now at the Center for Strategic and Budgetary Assessments, in Washington. "You can see many scenarios, not just Taiwan—especially as the Chinese develop a submarine and missile capability throughout the Pacific. But the dilemma is, How do you *end* a war with China?"

Like the nations involved in World War I, and unlike the rogue states everyone has been concentrating on, the United States and China in the twenty-first century would have the capacity to keep fighting even if one or the other lost a big battle or a missile exchange. This has far-reaching implications. "Ending a war with China," Vickers says, "may mean effecting some form of regime change, because we don't want to leave some wounded, angry regime in place." Another analyst, this one inside the Pentagon, told me, "Ending a war with China will force us to substantially reduce their military capacity, thus threatening their energy sources and the Communist Party's grip on power. The world will not be the same afterward. It's a very dangerous road to travel on."

The better road is for PACOM to deter China in Bismarckian fashion, from a geographic hub of comparative isolation—the Hawaiian Islands—with spokes reaching out to major allies such as Japan, South Korea, Thailand, Singapore, Australia, New Zealand, and India. These countries, in turn, would form secondary hubs to help us manage the Melanesian, Micronesian, and Polynesian archipelagoes, among other places, and also the Indian Ocean. The point of this arrangement would be to dissuade China so subtly that over time the rising behemoth would be drawn into the PACOM alliance system without any large-scale conflagration—the way NATO was ultimately able to neutralize the Soviet Union.

Whatever we say or do, China will spend more and more money on its military in the coming decades. Our only realistic goal may be to encourage it to make investments that are defensive, not offensive, in nature. Our efforts will require particular care, because China, unlike the Soviet Union of old (or Russia today, for that matter), boasts soft as well as hard power. Businesspeople love the idea of China; you don't have to beg them to invest there, as you do in Africa and so many other places. China's mixture of traditional authoritarianism and market economics has broad cultural appeal throughout Asia and other parts of the world. And because China is improving the material well-being of hundreds of millions of its citizens, the plight of its dissidents does not have quite the same market allure as did the plight of the Soviet Union's Sakharovs and Sharanskys. Democracy is attractive in places where tyranny has been obvious, odious, and unsuccessful, of course, as in Ukraine and Zimbabwe. But the world is full of gray areas—Jordan and Malaysia, for example—where elements of tyranny have ensured stability and growth. . . .

China has committed itself to significant military spending, but its navy and air force will not be able to match ours for some decades. The Chinese are therefore not going to do us the favor of engaging in conventional air and naval battles, like those fought in the Pacific during World War II. The Battle of the Philippine Sea, in late June of 1944, and the Battle of Leyte Gulf and the Surigao Strait, in October of 1944, were the last great sea battles in American history, and are very likely to remain so. Instead the Chinese will approach us asymmetrically, as terrorists do. In Iraq the insurgents have shown us the low end of asymmetry, with car bombs. But the Chinese are poised to show us the high end of the art. That is the threat. There are many ways in which the Chinese could use their less advanced military to achieve a sort of political-strategic parity with us. According to one former submarine commander and naval strategist I talked to, the Chinese have been poring over every detail of our recent wars in the Balkans and the Persian Gulf, and they fully understand just how much our military power depends on naval projection—that is, on the ability of a carrier battle group to get within proximity of, say, Iraq, and fire a missile at a target deep inside the country. To adapt, the Chinese are putting their fiber-optic systems underground and moving defense capabilities deep into western China, out of naval missile range—all the while developing an offensive strategy based on missiles designed to be capable of striking that supreme icon of American wealth and power, the aircraft carrier. The effect of a single Chinese cruise missile's hitting a U.S. carrier, even if it did not sink the ship, would be politically and psychologically cata-strophic, akin to al-Qaeda's attacks on the Twin Towers. China is focusing on missiles and submarines as a way to humiliate us in specific encounters. Their long-range-missile program should deeply concern U.S. policymakers.

With an advanced missile program the Chinese could fire hundreds of mis-siles at Taiwan before we could get to the island to defend it. Such a capability, combined with a new fleet of submarines (soon to be a greater undersea force than ours, in size if not in quality), might well be enough for the Chinese to coerce other countries into denying port access to U.S. ships. Most of China's seventy current submarines are past-their-prime diesels of Russian design; but these vessels could be used to create mobile minefields in the South China, East China, and Yellow Seas, where, as the *Wall Street Journal* reporter David Lague has written, "uneven depths, high levels of background noise, strong currents and shifting thermal layers" would make detecting the submarines very difficult. Add to this the seventeen new stealthy diesel submarines and three nuclear ones that the Chinese navy will deploy by the end of the decade, and one can imagine that China could launch an embarrassing strike against us, or against one of our Asian allies. Then there is the whole field of ambiguous coercion—for example, a series of non-attributable cyberattacks on Taiwan's electrical-power grids, designed to gradually demoralize the population. This isn't science fiction; the Chinese have invested significantly in cyberwarfare training and technology. Just because the Chinese are not themselves democratic doesn't mean they are not expert in manipulating the psychology of a democratic electorate. . . .

The first part of the twenty-first century will be not nearly as stable as the second half of the twentieth, because the world will be not nearly as bipolar as it was during the Cold War. The fight between Beijing and Washington over the Pacific will not dominate all of world politics, but it will be the most important of several regional struggles. Yet it will be the organizing focus for the U.S. defense posture abroad. If we are smart, this should lead us back into concert with Europe. No matter how successfully our military adapts to the rise of China, it is clear that our current dominance in the Pacific will not last. The Asia expert Mark Helprin has argued that while we pursue our democratization efforts in the Middle East, increasingly befriending only those states whose internal systems resemble our own, China is poised to reap the substantial benefits of pursuing its interests amorally—what the United States did during the Cold War. The Chinese surely hope, for example, that our chilly attitude toward the brutal Uzbek dictator, Islam Karimov, becomes even chillier; this would open up the possibility of more pipeline and other deals with him, and might persuade him to deny us use of the air base at Karshi-Khanabad. Were Karimov to be toppled in an uprising like the one in Kyrgyzstan, we would immediately have to stabilize the new regime or risk losing sections of the country to Chinese influence.

We also need to realize that in the coming years and decades the moral distance between Europe and China is going to contract considerably, especially if China's authoritarianism becomes increasingly restrained, and the ever expanding European Union becomes a less-than-democratic superstate run in imperious regulatory style by Brussels-based functionaries. Russia, too, is headed in a decidedly undemocratic direction: Russia's president, Vladimir Putin, reacted to our support of democracy in Ukraine by agreeing to "massive" joint air and naval exercises with the Chinese, scheduled for the second half of this year. These unprecedented joint Russian-Chinese exercises will be held on Chinese territory.

Therefore the idea that we will no longer engage in the "cynical" game of power politics is illusory, as is the idea that we will be able to advance a foreign policy based solely on Wilsonian ideals. We will have to continually play various parts of the world off China, just as Richard Nixon played less than morally perfect states off the Soviet Union. This may well lead to a fundamentally new NATO alliance, which could become a global armada that roams the Seven Seas. Indeed, the Dutch, the Norwegians, the Germans, and the Spanish are making significant investments in fast missile-bearing ships and in landing-platform docks for beach assaults, and the British and the French are investing in new aircraft carriers. Since Europe increasingly seeks to avoid conflict and to reduce geopolitics to a series of negotiations and regulatory disputes, an emphasis on sea power would suit it well. Sea power is intrinsically less threatening than land power. It allows for a big operation without a large onshore footprint. Consider the tsunami effort, during which Marines and sailors returned to their carrier and destroyers each night. Armies invade; navies make port visits. Sea power has always been a more useful means of realpolitik than land power. It allows for a substantial military presence in areas geographically remote from states themselves—but without an overtly belligerent effect. Because ships take so long to get somewhere, and are less threatening than troops on the ground, naval forces allow diplomats to ratchet up pressure during a crisis in a responsible—and reversible—way. Take the Cuban Missile Crisis, in 1962. As the British expert H. P. Willmott has written, "The use of naval power by the Americans was the least dangerous option that presented itself, and the slowness with which events unfolded at sea gave time for both sides to conceive and implement a rational response to a highly dangerous situation."

Submarines have been an exception to this rule, but their very ability to operate both literally and figuratively below the surface, completely off the media radar screen, allows a government to be militarily aggressive, particularly in the field of espionage, without offending the sensibilities of its citizenry. Sweden's neutrality is a hard-won luxury built on naval strength that many of its idealistic citizens may be incompletely aware of. Pacifistic Japan, the ultimate trading nation, is increasingly dependent on its burgeoning submarine force. Sea power protects trade, which is regulated by treaties; it's no accident that the father of international law, Hugo Grotius, was a seventeenth-century Dutchman who lived at the height of Dutch naval power worldwide. Because of globalization, the twenty-first century will see unprecedented sea traffic, requiring unprecedented regulation by diplomats and naval officers alike. And as the economic influence of the European Union expands around the globe, Europe may find, like the United States in the nineteenth century and China today, that it has to go to sea to protect its interests. . . .

The ships and other naval equipment being built now by the Europeans are designed to slot into U.S. battle networks. And European nations, which today we conceive of as Atlantic forces, may develop global naval functions; already, for example, Swedish submarine units are helping to train Americans in the Pacific on how to hunt for diesel subs. The sea may be NATO's and Europe's best chance for a real military future. And yet the alliance is literally and symbolically weak. For it to regain its political significance, NATO must become a military alliance that no one doubts is willing to fight and kill at a moment's notice. That was its reputation during the Cold War—and it was so well regarded by the Soviets that they never tested it. Expanding NATO eastward has helped stabilize former Warsaw Pact states, of course, but admitting substandard militaries to the alliance's ranks, although politically necessary, has been problematic. The more NATO expands eastward, the more superficial and unwieldy it becomes as a fighting force, and the more questionable becomes its claim that it will fight in defense of any member state. Taking in yet more substandard militaries like Ukraine's and Georgia's too soon is simply not in NATO's interest. We can't just declare an expansion of a defense alliance because of demonstrations somewhere in support of democracy. Rather, we must operate in the way we are now operating in Georgia, where we have sent in the Marines for a year to train the Georgian armed forces. That way, when a country like Georgia does make it into NATO, its membership will have military as well as political meaning. Only by making it an agile force that is ready to land on, say, West African beaches at a few days' or hours' notice can we save NATO.

And we need to save it. NATO is ours to lead—unlike the increasingly powerful European Union, whose own defense force, should it become a reality, would inevitably emerge as a competing regional power, one that might align itself with China in order to balance against us. Let me be even clearer about something that policymakers and experts often don't want to be clear about. NATO and an autonomous European defense force cannot both prosper. Only one can—and we should want it to be the former, so that Europe is a military asset for us, not a liability, as we confront China.

The Chinese military challenge is already a reality to officers and sailors of the U.S. Navy. I recently spent four weeks embedded on a guided-missile destroyer, the USS *Benfold*, roaming around the Pacific from Indonesia to Singapore, the Philippines, Guam, and then Hawaii.

During my visit the *Benfold* completed a tsunami-relief mission (which consisted of bringing foodstuffs ashore and remapping the coastline) and then recommenced combat drills, run from the ship's combat-information center—a dark and cavernous clutter of computer consoles. Here a tactical action officer led the response to what were often hypothetical feints or attacks from China or North Korea.

Observing the action in the combat-information center, I learned that although naval warfare is conducted with headphones and computer keyboards, the stress level is every bit as acute as in gritty urban combat. A wrong decision can result in a catastrophic missile strike, against which no degree of physical toughness or bravery is a defense.

Sea warfare is cerebral. The threat is over the horizon; nothing can be seen; and everything is reduced to mathematics. The object is deception more than it is aggression—getting the other side to shoot first, so as to gain the political advantage, yet not having to absorb the damage of the attack.

As enthusiastic as the crew members of the *Benfold* were in helping the victims of the tsunami, once they left Indonesian waters they were just as enthusiastic about honing their surface and subsurface warfare skills. I even picked up a feeling, especially among the senior chief petty officers (the iron grunts of the Navy, who provide the truth unvarnished), that they might be tested in the western Pacific to the same degree that the Marines have been in Iraq. The main threat in the Persian Gulf to date has been asymmetric attacks, like the bombing of the *Cole*. But the Pacific offers all kinds of threats, from increasingly aggressive terrorist groups in the Islamic archipelagoes of Southeast Asia to cat-and-mouse games with Chinese subs in the waters to the north. Preparing to meet all the possible threats the Pacific has to offer will force the Navy to become more nimble, and will make it better able to deal with unconventional emergencies, such as tsunamis, when they arise.

Welcome to the next few decades. As one senior chief put it to me, referring first to the Persian Gulf and then to the Pacific, "The Navy needs to spend less time in that salty little mud puddle and more time in the pond."

Ivan Eland  **NO**

Is Chinese Military Modernization a Threat to the United States?

Executive Summary

The ongoing modernization of the Chinese military poses less of a threat to the United States than recent studies by the Pentagon and a congressionally mandated commission have posited. Both studies exaggerate the strength of China's military by focusing on the modest improvements of specific sectors rather than the still-antiquated overall state of Chinese forces.

The state of the Chinese military and its modernization must also be put in the context of U.S. interests in East Asia and compared with the state and modernization of the U.S. military and other militaries in East Asia, especially the Taiwanese military. Viewed in that context, China's military modernization does not look especially threatening.

Although not officially calling its policy in East Asia "containment," the United States has ringed China with formal and informal alliances and a forward military presence. With such an extended defense perimeter, the United States considers as a threat to its interests any natural attempt by China—a rising power with a growing economy—to gain more control of its external environment by increasing defense spending. If U.S. policymakers would take a more restrained view of America's vital interests in the region, the measured Chinese military buildup would not appear so threatening. Conversely, U.S. policy may appear threatening to China. Even the Pentagon admits that China accelerated hikes in defense spending after the United States attacked Yugoslavia over the Kosovo issue in 1999.

The United States still spends about 10 times what China does on national defense—$400 billion versus roughly $40 billion per year—and is modernizing its forces much faster. In addition, much of the increase in China's official defense spending is soaked up by expenses not related to acquiring new weapons. Thus, China's spending on new armaments is equivalent to that of a nation that spends only $10 billion to $20 billion per year on defense. In contrast, the United States spends well over $100 billion per year to acquire new weapons.

Even without U.S. assistance, Taiwan's modern military could probably dissuade China from attacking. Taiwan does not have to be able to win a conflict; it needs only to make the costs of any attack unacceptable to China. The informal U.S. security guarantee is unneeded.

From *Policy Analysis*, no. 465, January 23, 2003, pp. 1–6, 8–9, 12–13. Copyright © 2003 by Cato Institute. Reprinted by permission. References omitted.

Introduction

Both the Pentagon and a congressionally mandated commission recently issued studies on the Chinese military that overstated the threat to the United States posed by that force. The pessimism of both studies was understandable. The Department of Defense's study—the *Annual Report on the Military Power of the People's Republic of China*—was issued by a federal bureaucracy that has an inherent conflict of interest in developing assessments of foreign military threats. Because the department that is creating the threat assessments is the same one that is lobbying Congress for money for weapons, personnel, fuel, and training to combat threats, its threat projections tend to be inflated. Because China, with an economy that is seemingly growing rapidly, is the rising great power on the horizon that should shape the future posture of American conventional forces (the brushfire wars needed to combat terrorism are likely to require only limited forces), the threat from China's armed forces is critical for bringing additional money into the Pentagon. The U.S.-China Security Review Commission's work—*The National Security Implications of the Economic Relationship between the United States and China*—drew at least partially on the Pentagon's effort and was written by anti-China hawks and those with a desire to restrict commerce with China.

In contrast, this paper attempts to place the modernizing Chinese military in the context of a more balanced and limited view of U.S. strategic interests in East Asia. In addition, when the distorting perspectives of both studies are removed—that is, their focus on recent improvements in Chinese military capabilities rather than on the overall state of the Chinese military—the threat from the Chinese armed forces is shown to be modest. The bone-crushing dominance of the U.S. military remains intact. In fact, the Chinese military does not look all that impressive when compared even to the Taiwanese armed forces.

Putting the Modernizing Chinese Military in Context

Frequently, improvements in the Chinese military are reported in the world press without any attention to context. That is, those "flows" are highlighted but the "stock"—the overall state of the Chinese military—is ignored. The state of the Chinese military and how rapidly it is likely to improve will be examined in the second half of this paper. But first, additional context is needed.

Pockets of the Chinese military are now modernizing more rapidly than in the past, but compared to what? Both the modernization and the actual state of the Chinese military must be compared with those of the U.S. military and other militaries in the East Asian region (especially Taiwan's armed forces). In addition, the geopolitical and strategic environment in which Chinese military modernization is occurring needs to be examined. Western students of the Chinese military often speak abstractly about when growing Chinese military power will adversely affect "U.S. interests." It is very important to concretely define such interests because the wider the definition, the more likely even small increments of additional Chinese military power will threaten them.

U.S. Interests in East Asia

Even before President Bush's expansive new national security strategy was published, the United States perceived that it had a vital interest in maintaining in East Asia a continuous military presence that was deployed far forward. Despite the end of the Cold War, the United States has maintained Cold War–era alliances that encircle China; indeed, it has actually strengthened them. The United States has formal alliances with Japan, South Korea, Thailand, the Philippines, and Australia. In addition, the United States has an informal alliance with Taiwan—China's arch enemy—and a friendly strategic relationship with Singapore and New Zealand. In the post–Cold War era, as the military threat to East Asia decreased, the United States strengthened its alliance with Japan by garnering a Japanese commitment to provide logistical support to the United States during any war in the theater. The Bush administration came into office with an even stronger predilection to enhance security alliances (especially the one with Japan) than its predecessor.

Also, using the war on terrorism as part of its rationale, the Bush administration has expanded U.S. military presence in the areas surrounding China. Citing the need to fight the war on terrorism, the United States sent special forces to fight Abu Sayaf—a tiny group of bandits with only a tangential connection to the al-Qaeda terrorist movement—in order to strengthen the U.S. security relationship with the government of the Philippines. That security relationship had been diminished when the Philippine government ejected the U.S. military from its bases in the early 1990s. During the war against terrorism in Afghanistan, the United States established a "temporary" military presence on bases in Central Asian nations on China's western border. Given the Bush administration's use of the war on terrorism as a cover for deploying troops to Georgia and the Philippines and the history of the U.S. military presence in Japan, Germany, and South Korea, the U.S. military presence in those Central Asian nations will likely become permanent.

Before the September 11, 2001, terrorist attacks and the ensuing war in Afghanistan slowed the process, the administration was seeking better relations with India so as to use that country as a counterweight to a rising China. Finally, the war on terrorism has fostered a newly cooperative U.S.-Russian relationship, thus completing the encirclement of China. Moreover, the Pentagon is increasing the number of U.S. warships in the Pacific region.

Of course, the U.S. government does not admit to a policy of containing China, as it did with the Soviet Union during the Cold War. But in Asia the ring of U.S.-led alliances (formal and informal), a forward U.S. military presence, and closer American relationships with great powers capable of acting to balance against a rising China constitute a de facto containment policy. Such a policy is unwarranted by the current low threat posed by China and may actually increase the threat that it is designed to contain. . . .

The extended defense perimeter that the United States continues to maintain in East Asia to carry out that containment policy shows a failure to recognize China's security concerns. Although China remains an authoritarian state (it is no longer a totalitarian state because the government no longer has total control over the economic sphere, and the average Chinese citizen is probably more free economically and politically than at any time since the communist government took power in 1949), conflict might be avoided if some understanding of the calculus of a potential adversary were shown. If a foreign nation had ringed the United States with alliances, friendships with potential adversaries, and an increasing military presence, the United States would feel very threatened—as was the case, for example, when the Soviets attempted to place nuclear missiles in nearby Cuba during the 1960s.

The United States fears any attempt by China to increase its influence in East or Southeast Asia. Yet, as the Chinese economy grows and China becomes a great power, it will naturally seek more control over its external environment. As Michael O'Hanlon and Bates Gill, both then at the Brookings Institution, perceptively noted, most of China's ambitions are not global and are no longer ideological; they are territorial and confined to exerting more regional influence over the islands and waterways to the south and southeast of its borders. The United States could accommodate such limited ambitions as long as they did not snowball— an unlikely scenario—into a conflict that drastically altered the power balance in East Asia. China has given no indication that it would like to make an attempt at imperial conquest of East Asia.

In the past, wars occurred when an established power refused to acknowledge the great power status of a rising nation—for example, Britain's refusal to acknowledge the kaiser's Germany in the late 1800s and early 1900s. The United States should not make the same mistake with a rising China. China should be allowed, as all great powers do, to develop a sphere of influence in its own region—that is, East Asia. Within limits, an expanded sphere of Chinese influence should not threaten U.S. vital interests, if defined less grandiosely than at present.

Unfortunately, the United States regards even the smallest change in the status quo in East Asia (unless the change expands the already overextended U.S. defense perimeter) with suspicion. The United States does have a vital interest in ensuring a diffusion of power in East Asia so that no hegemonic great power—like imperial Japan in the 1930s—arises. But, unlike the situation before World War II, when China was weak and the French and British colonial powers were spread too thin, centers of power in East Asia other than the United States exist to balance a rising China. Japan, alone or in combination with South Korea, Taiwan, Australia, and the Association of Southeast Asian Nations, could balance against China. The United States, instead of maintaining Cold War–era alliances and a forward military presence in the region, should gradually withdraw its forces from East Asia and allow those nations to be the first line of defense against China. Currently, those nations fail to spend enough on their security because the United States spends huge amounts on its military and is willing to subsidize their security for them (the effects of this ill-advised policy in perpetuating Taiwan's insufficient defense spending are discussed below).

Only if the balance of power in East Asia broke down with the advent of an aggressive hegemonic power should the United States intervene militarily in the affairs of the region. That policy would be called a "balancer-of-last-resort" strategy. Such a strategy would minimize the danger of a confrontation with China.

U.S. Military Capabilities Compared with Those of China

The Bush administration's national security-strategy attempts to ensure American primacy by outspending other nations on defense many times over, thus dissuading them from competing with the United States. The United States is already more powerful militarily relative to other nations of the world than the Roman, Napoleonic, or British Empire was at its height. According to the national security strategy, "Today, the United States enjoys a position of unparalleled military strength and great economic and political influence." And the Bush administration would like to keep such U.S. military dominance by profligate spending on military might that is deployed around the world. The history of international relations indicates that this strategy has little chance of succeeding. Historically, when threatened by a country that had become too powerful, nations banded together to balance against it. Of course, administration officials claim that the United States is a benevolent power and that other nations will feel no need to balance against it. Such countries as Russia, India, and especially China might disagree. For example, China accuses the United States of maintaining a policy of containment, and Russia has protested the expansion of the NATO alliance up to its borders. A good place for more sustainable and less threatening U.S. policies to start is in East Asia.

Forces and Defense Spending. Currently, the United States maintains about 100,000 military personnel in East Asia. That military presence is centered in Japan (41,000), South Korea (37,000), and afloat (19,000). At sea, the United States stations one carrier battle group and one Marine amphibious group forward in the region and will now ensure that a second carrier group will be there more of the time. The United States will also augment the number of nuclear submarines stationed in Guam. That military presence seems small compared to the military forces of China, which has active forces of 2.3 million.

Yet the U.S. military presence deployed forward in East Asia is only the tip of the iceberg. That presence is a symbol of U.S. interest in the region and of the world-dominant U.S. military juggernaut that could be brought to bear against the large, but largely antiquated, Chinese military during any war between the two nations.

The United States spends about $400 billion a year on national defense and alone accounts for about 40 percent of the world's defense spending. There is some dispute about how much China spends because not all of its defense spending (for example, funds for weapons research and procurement of foreign weapons) is reflected in the official Chinese defense budget. David Shambaugh, a prominent academic authority on the Chinese military, estimates total Chinese defense spending at about $38 billion per year. In the same ballpark, the International Institute of Strategic Studies' Military Balance estimates such spending at $47 billion per year. In contrast, the U.S. Department of Defense's estimate is predictably much higher—noting that annual Chinese military spending "*could* total $65 billion." Because Shambaugh and the IISS do not build weapon systems to combat threats and thus have no inherent conflict of interest, their independent estimates are probably less prone to threat inflation than is DoD's estimate.

China has had real (inflation-adjusted) increases in defense spending only since 1997. Chinese military expenditures are constrained by limits on the ability of China's central government to collect revenues and the concomitant budget deficit. Moreover, increases in military spending have been surpassed by rapid Chinese economic growth, leading to declines in defense spending as a proportion of gross domestic product.

The $38 billion to $47 billion range is roughly what other medium powers, such as Japan, France, and the United Kingdom, spend on defense. But the militaries of those other nations are much smaller and more modern than the obsolete Chinese military, which needs to be completely transformed from a guerrilla-style Maoist people's army into a modern force that emphasizes projection of power on the sea and in the air. (Since the early 1990s, the Chinese have reoriented their military doctrine from "fighting a people's war under modern conditions" to fighting and winning a high-technology war against a modern opponent.) So the Chinese must spend much of their increases in official defense funding to prop up their sagging, oversized force and slowly convert it to a force that can project power, to meet escalating payroll requirements to compete with the thriving Chinese private sector, and to compensate the military for "off-the-books" revenues lost when the Chinese political leadership ordered the armed forces to stop running commercial businesses.

Consequently, China's spending to acquire weapons is equivalent only to that of countries with total defense budgets of $10 billion to $20 billion. Given that the United States, with a gargantuan budget for the research, development, and procurement of weapons—well over $100 billion per year—is leaving its rich NATO allies behind in technology (there is fear in NATO that U.S. capabilities are so far advanced that the U.S. armed forces would not be able to operate with allied militaries), it most surely is leaving China in the dust. . . .

A Massive Military Buildup? David Shambaugh maintains that the Chinese are not engaged in a massive Soviet-style military buildup. Even the Defense Intelligence Agency and high-ranking U.S. military officials seem to agree with that assessment. According to the Defense Intelligence Agency, by 2010, even the best 10 percent of the Chinese military will have equipment that is more than 20 years behind the capabilities of the U.S. military (equivalent to U.S. equipment in the late 1980s). The other 90 percent of the Chinese military will have even more outdated equipment. Gen. William J. Begert, the commander of U.S. Pacific Air Forces, asserted that Chinese military modernization was a "matter of concern" but not alarming. His boss, Adm. Dennis Blair, the commander of all U.S. forces in the Pacific, noted in 1999 that China would not pose a serious strategic threat to the United States for at least two decades. O'Hanlon and Gill also conclude that the Chinese military lags behind U.S. forces by at least 20 years and that it will be that long before China's armed forces could significantly challenge the United States and allied nations in East Asia. Even DoD has admitted that "the PLA [People's Liberation Army] is still decades from possessing a comprehensive capability to engage and defeat a modern adversary beyond China's boundaries."

The assessments of DoD, Blair, and O'Hanlon and Gill are most likely predicated on the excessively expansive conception of U.S. interests in East Asia that currently holds sway in U.S. foreign policy circles. If a more restrained view of U.S. interests in the region were adopted, the slow Chinese military modernization would be even less threatening to the United States.

Chinese leaders have clearly learned a lesson from the implosion of the Soviet regime, which was largely caused by the dysfunctional socialist economy sagging under the weight of excessive military spending. Even the Pentagon admits that the Chinese leadership is focused primarily on economic development and has given the modernization of China's military a priority below development in industry, agriculture, and science and technology. DoD acknowledges that the Chinese military is modernizing selectively rather than massively:

> Rather than shifting priority resources from civil infrastructure and economic reform programs to an across-the-board modernization of the PLA, Beijing is focused on those programs and assets which will give China the most effective means for exploiting vulnerabilities in an adversary's military capabilities.

The Pentagon has also conceded that the additional funding the Chinese leadership provided to the military for modernization accelerated after the U.S.-led attack in Kosovo in 1999. Thus, provocative U.S. actions lead to precisely the Chinese response that the United States would most like to avoid.

Although in the last few years the Chinese have been modernizing their military more rapidly than in the past, recent hikes in the U.S. budget for national defense have been extraordinary. The increase in the U.S. budget for national defense in 2003 alone is of approximately the same magnitude as the entire Chinese defense budget (if the most probable estimates are accepted). And much of the increase in official Chinese defense spending is allocated to maintaining a bloated Chinese military until it can be transformed, escalating payroll requirements to attempt to stay apace with the salaries in the booming Chinese private sector, and compensating the Chinese armed forces for off-the-books revenues lost when the Chinese leadership forced the divestiture of military holdings in private businesses—rather than to new weapons research, development, and production. The United States spends more than $40 billion a year on research and development for weapons (again, roughly equal to total annual Chinese defense spending) and more than $60 billion yearly on weapons procurement. Thus, the speed of U.S. military modernization dwarfs the pace of improvements in parts of the antiquated Chinese forces. In fact, U.S. military modernization is outpacing even that of wealthy NATO allies—the next most capable militaries on the planet. In the war in Afghanistan, U.S. military commanders were reluctant to operate with allied militaries because of the disparity in capabilities.

In conclusion, even though the Chinese military is modernizing more rapidly than in the past, the speed of the modernization is less than that of the modernization of the already vastly superior U.S. force. In other words, despite all of the clamor in the press and in the U.S. government about Chinese military modernization, the U.S. military is way ahead and the gap is actually widening (the same situation holds when U.S. armed forces are compared with all of the other militaries in the world). When pressed, even anti-China hawks admit that Chinese military capabilities are far behind those of the United States. . . .

Conclusion

Although many alarmist articles in the press have trumpeted improvements in the Chinese military, those enhancements are pockets of modernization in a largely antiquated force. China's military modernization is more rapid than before but is not a massive Soviet-style military buildup. As the Chinese economy grows and China becomes a great power, the United States should accept that it, like other great powers, will want more influence over its region. If kept within bounds, that increased sphere of influence should not threaten vital U.S. interests.

But the United States, especially under the Bush administration's new expansive national security strategy of primacy and preemption, sees any change in the status quo in East Asia as a threat to its expansive list of vital interests. If the United States unnecessarily maintains, or even continues to expand, its defense perimeter to surround and contain China, the rising power and the status quo power—both armed with nuclear weapons—may come into needless conflict. The United States must take a less grandiose view of its vital interests, redraw its defense perimeter, abrogate its Cold War–era alliances (including the informal alliance with nonstrategic Taiwan), and reverse its military buildup. Currently, the United States is unnecessarily modernizing its armed forces faster than is China, which is starting from an extremely low level of military modernity. China, whose highest priority is economic development, is now reacting to the expansion of the U.S. defense perimeter and the U.S. military buildup by increasing its own defense budget more rapidly. Thus, U.S. policy may be engendering the threat it most fears.

POSTSCRIPT

Is China a Military Threat to the United States?

Kaplan and Eland have this much in common: They both seem to belong to the "realist" school of foreign policy. Realists try to keep universal moral imperatives out of foreign policy debates. What counts, for them, are vital national "interests," which all nations have a right to protect. Eland defends China's military buildup in part because he believes that China is entitled to exert "regional influence over the islands and waterways" near its borders; the United States should "accommodate" those interests. Kaplan, though warning that China's military buildup must be watched carefully, refers to the same extension of Chinese interest in the region and remarks, "This is wholly legitimate." Where the two differ is largely in the area of how realism should be pursued by the United States.

China may not yet be a first-rate military power, but Aaron L. Friedberg, in "Arming China Against Ourselves," *Commentary* (July–August 1999), argues that China continues to increase its armed forces and has shown an alarming interest in American thermonuclear devices. In *China, Inc.: How the Rise of the Next Superpower Challenges America and the World* (Scribner, 2005), Ted C. Fishman turns his attention to Chinese economic expansion, which helps it to acquire "geopolitical clout" and "strategic presence" in the world. A more benign view of Chinese trade policy is advanced by James Fallows, "Why China's Rise Is Good for Us," *The Atlantic* (July/August 2007). A standard short history of American-Chinese relations can be found in Warren I. Cohen, *America's Response to China: A History of Sino-American Relations* (Columbia University Press, 2000). Nicholas R. Lardy, *Integrating China into the Global Economy* (Brookings Institution Press, 2002), offers a comprehensive examination of different scenarios of China's future relationship with the rest of the world.

In *Common Sense*, the fiery pamphlet that helped launch the American Revolution, Thomas Paine wrote that "commerce diminishes the spirit both of patriotism and military defense." Is it possible that China's commercial boom may diminish its appetite for warships and missiles? At the moment that seems quite unlikely, but history is full of surprises.

ISSUE 21

Must America Exercise World Leadership?

YES: Robert J. Lieber, from *The American Era: Power and Strategy for the 21st Century* (Cambridge University Press, 2005)

NO: Niall Ferguson, from "An Empire in Denial," *Harvard International Review* (Fall 2003)

ISSUE SUMMARY

YES: International relations professor Robert J. Lieber believes that the United States, as the world's sole superpower, is uniquely capable of providing leadership against the threats of terrorism and weapons of mass destruction, as well as extending the rule of law and democracy.

NO: Author Niall Ferguson maintains that despite America's military and economic dominance, it lacks both the long-term will and the capital and human investment that would be necessary to sustain its dominance.

$\mathbf{F}$or centuries, great empires conquered and exploited distant colonies. All this changed with World War II, from which the United States emerged as the greatest military and economic power the world had ever known, without creating a network of colonies.

How was that power to be employed, if it was to be used at all? Before 1940, the United States avoided involvement in international relations beyond the Americas. This sentiment went back to the warning in President Washington's farewell address to avoid "entangling alliances." As long as the United States felt separated from most of the rest of the world by two great oceans, it thought it was impregnable and remained out of the League of Nations. Isolation no longer seemed possible after World War II, and an international role became inescapable as a consequence of instant communications, rapid transportation, increasing dependence on international trade, and the development of weapons of mass destruction (WMD).

For forty-five years after World War II, the supremacy of the United States was challenged by the military expansionism of the Soviet Union.

Confronted by this threat, liberal internationalism took the place of isolationism as the world seemed to divide between two superpowers, both capable of building and employing nuclear and other WMDs. Only the prospect of what seemed the certainty of what was dubbed Mutual Assured Destruction (MAD) kept both nations from using these weapons. The United States relied on the doctrine of containment to confine communist power. This policy called for the participation of allies in multinational treaties, United Nations resolutions, the North Atlantic Treaty Organization (NATO), and other political and military alliances.

This liberal internationalism was identified with the advocacy of self-determination, democracy, and human rights. The United States sometimes fell short of such ideals when it embraced anti-communist regimes that were not democratic or overlooked gross abuses of human rights, but it never discarded its moral posture in opposition to what President Reagan called "the evil empire" of the Soviet Union. The disintegration of the Soviet empire as a threat to Western democracy left the United States as the sole superpower.

Since the 9/11 attack, the United States has assumed a mantle of world leadership. If America is a new empire (as both authors in the following selections agree), it is different from empires of the past, without vast colonies, but with unparalleled military and economic strength, as well as unprecedented cultural and technological impact. The clearest official statement of the Bush foreign policy is found in "The National Security Strategy of the United States of America," issued by the National Security Council in 2002 (available on the Internet), which proclaims America's world leadership in fighting terrorism, preempting threats, and spreading democracy, development, free markets, and free trade throughout the world.

Where this differs most significantly from that of previous administrations is in its unilateralism. The U.S. government proclaimed a commitment to act on behalf of America's best interests irrespective of the objections or reservations of its allies or the United Nations. Contrast the unwillingness of President George H. W. Bush in 1991 to have the American army enter Baghdad and overthrow the regime of Saddam Hussein, because it would alienate some of America's allies, with the determination of President George W. Bush in 2003 to engage in the second war against Iraq despite the failure of the United Nations or many nominal allies to support that action.

An unwillingness to compromise the American government's perception of its best interests led the second President Bush to reject treaties on land mines, nuclear proliferation, biological and chemical warfare, the International Criminal Court, and other international agreements, and to justify preemptive strikes in the absence of an attack upon the United States or a treaty ally.

The differences between Robert J. Lieber and others who are prepared to have America act alone and Niall Ferguson and others who insist on international cooperation are differences as to what needs to be done, what the United Nations can do, and whether the United States can long sustain responsibility for world peace and security.

YES

Robert J. Lieber

The American Era:
Power and Strategy
for the 21st Century

References to America's unmatched power have become common-place, not only among those who welcome it, but especially by those who disdain it. The assessment made some years ago by a former French foreign minister is worth quoting, the more so because he spent so much of his time trying to stimulate a counterbalancing coalition, "The United States of America today predominates on the economic level, on the monetary level, on the military level, on the technological level, and in the cultural area in the broad sense of the word. It is not comparable, in terms of power and influence, to anything known in modern history."

All the same, it is well worth contemplating what this preponderance means in practice. Consider, first, the military realm. In material terms, no other country or group of countries comes close to approaching America's capacity in warfare and in virtually every dimension of modern military technology. Nor does any other country have a comparable ability to project power and to deploy and sustain large and effective forces abroad.

Air power provides a compelling illustration. A single American aircraft carrier with its high technology and precision munitions is capable of striking 700 targets in a single day. There are few, if any, air forces in the world that can muster such power, yet the United States possesses not one but twelve of these carriers and their battle groups. Military spending, too, dwarfs that of any other country and is roughly equivalent to that of the rest of the world combined. Yet at slightly more than 4 percent of GDP annually, this defense burden ought to be relatively manageable compared with levels during the Cold War. (At the height of the Reagan defense buildup in the mid-1998s, the figure was 6.6%, and at times during the 1950s and 1960s it was more than 10%.) Paul Kennedy has previously referred to America's ability to sustain the costs of its world role by observing, "Being Number One at great cost is one thing; being the world's single superpower on the cheap is astonishing."

From *The American Era : Power and Strategy for the 21st Century,* 2005, pp. 1, 15–17, 25–27, 42–44, 49–50, 51–52, 54, 57–59. Copyright © 2005 by Cambridge University Press. Reprinted by permission.

Other dimensions of American power are impressive in their own right. The most important of these is economic. The United States, with less than 5 percent of the world's population, accounts for more than 30 percent of world GDP. By contrast, in 1914 when Britain was widely regarded as the world's foremost imperial power, its economy amounted to approximately 8 percent of world GDP. In addition, the United States is responsible for more than 40 percent of the world's spending on research and development, and—with Singapore and Finland—is consistently ranked as one of the top three countries in terms of global competitiveness. Moreover, the United States possesses dozens of major research universities, produces the lion's share of Nobel prizewinners in science, medicine, and economics, and exerts a remarkable cultural influence that, for example, accounts for more than 80 percent of world movie box office receipts. The unique traits of American society make the United States adaptable, dynamic, and—despite the impact of post-9/11 visa regulations—a magnet for talented immigrants from around the world. In the words of the *Economist* magazine of London, "The clamour of Indians, Chinese, Guatemalans and millions more to go to America to work or be educated is not merely a mercenary reaction to its wealth. It is a reaction to the blend of opportunity, knowledge and freedom that America provides and that nowhere else comes close to matching."

All in all, American primacy is both robust and unlikely to be challenged in the near future. It is robust because it rests on preponderance across all the realms—military, economic, technological, wealth, and size—by which we measure power. And with the possible exception of China, no other country or group of countries is likely to emerge as an effective global competitor in the coming decades. This unique status is evident when we consider other possible contenders. . . .

After the end of the Cold War, the absence of a single, overarching, and unambiguous threat had the effect of relegating global concerns to a low priority for most Americans, thus making it harder for any administration to gain support for a coherent foreign policy or allocation of substantial resources for that purpose. Abroad, despite allied collaboration in the 1991 Gulf War against Iraq and ultimately in dealing with the civil war in Bosnia and ethnic cleansing in Kosovo, the collapse of the Soviet Union made cooperation more difficult because there no longer seemed to be an Imperative for collective action in the face of a common enemy.

It is no exaggeration to describe September 11, 2001, as the start of a new era in American strategic thinking. The attacks of that morning had an effect comparable to the Pearl Harbor attack on December 7, 1941, which propelled the United States into World War II. In an instant, the events of September 11 transformed the international security environment. The threats from terrorism and weapons of mass destruction that had seemed distant and hypothetical suddenly became a dominant reality, and responding to them necessitated a new grand strategy. Terrorism was no longer one among a number of assorted dangers to the United States but a fundamental threat to America, its way of life, and its vital interests. The al-Qaeda terrorists who masterminded the use of hijacked jumbo jets to attack the Pentagon and to destroy the twin towers of the World Trade Center were carrying out mass murder as a means of political intimidation.

The gravity of this danger was amplified by two additional factors. First, the cold-blooded willingness to slaughter thousands of innocent civilians without the slightest moral compunction raised fears about potential use of WMD. Given the terrorists' conduct and statements by their leaders, as well as evidence that state sponsors of terrorism were seeking to acquire chemical, biological, and nuclear weapons, there was a risk that WMD might be used directly against the United States as well as its friends and allies abroad.

Second, in view of the fact that the nineteen terrorists in the four hijacked aircraft committed suicide in carrying out their attacks, the precepts of deterrence were now called into question. By contrast, even at the height of the Cold War, American strategists could make their calculations based on the assumed rationality of Soviet leaders and the knowledge that they would not willingly commit nuclear suicide by initiating a massive attack against the United States or its allies. September 11, however, undermined that key assumption. We thus live at a time when deterrence, which has often worked in confronting hostile states, cannot be relied on in facing non-state actors with millenarian aims and potentially equipped with devastating weapons. Though the threat had been developing for some time, 9/11 demonstrated that this peril is now quite real. Nor is the danger unique to America, as shown by the March 11, 2004, terrorist attack in Madrid—Spain's equivalent of 9/11. As a result there is good reason to act decisively against the most lethal threats, rather than to hope to be able to deter them or to retaliate following a mass casualty attack.

Mechanisms of international law and organization can at times be effective, but international law is not self-enforcing. We continue to live not in a world of global governance, but in a world of states—some of which are benign, others malevolent or even failed. In reality, neither the U.N. nor other international institutions including the European Union are capable of intervening quickly and effectively on life and death matters. Thus, in its own interest, but also in terms of sustaining wider values of liberal democracy and economic openness, the United States can neither allow itself to be subject to an international veto nor disengage from the wider world. Nor should Americans be apologetic about the necessity or capacity of the United States to act. . . .

The terrorism of 9/11 dramatically altered the sense of complacency that had prevailed during the 1990s and provided the impetus for a new grand strategy. In the wake of the attacks, President Bush and his administration were explicit in saying that the war against terror would not be completed quickly, and in January 2002, speaking to a joint session of Congress, Bush outlined what quickly became known as the Bush Doctrine:

> [W]e will shut down terrorist camps, disrupt terrorist plans and bring terrorists to justice. And . . . we must prevent the terrorists and regimes who seek chemical, biological, or nuclear weapons from threatening the United States and the world. . . .

> Yet time is not on our side. I will not wait on events while dangers gather. I will not stand by as peril draws closer and closer. *The United States of America will not permit the world's most dangerous regimes to threaten us with the world's most destructive weapons.*

Two elements were crucial to the doctrine. The first was a sense of urgency, reflected in the words that "time is not on our side." The second was that the unique danger created by weapons of mass destruction required the United States to be prepared to take swift, decisive, and preemptive action. Both of these imperatives reflected the calculation that whatever the risks of acting, the risks of *not* acting were more ominous. These features foreshadowed the elaboration of a grand strategy, published just over a year after the September 11 attacks.

The National Security Strategy of the United States of America (NSS) was released by the White House on September 17, 2002, and immediately attracted wide attention, including both praise as a determined and far-reaching response to the grave dangers America now faced and criticism as a radical and even dangerous departure from foreign policy tradition. In its thirty-two pages, the document provided a candid, ambitious, and far-reaching proclamation of national objectives. First, it called for preemptive military action against hostile states and terrorist groups seeking to develop weapons of mass destruction. Second, it announced that the United States would not allow its global military strength to be challenged by any hostile foreign power. Third, it expressed a commitment to multilateral international cooperation but made clear that the United States "will not hesitate to act alone, if necessary" to defend national interests and security. Fourth, it proclaimed the goal of spreading democracy and human rights around the globe, especially in the Muslim world. . . .

The Bush NSS was not just about power and security. It also committed the United States to spread democracy worldwide and to promote the development of "free and open societies on every continent." To this end, the document called for a comprehensive public information campaign—"a struggle of ideas"—to help foreigners, especially in the Muslim world, learn about and understand America and the core ideas it stands for.

This aspiration embodied deep-seated themes within American history and evoked long-standing beliefs about foreign policy. In particular, the idea that the exercise of American power goes hand in hand with the promotion of democratic principles can be found in the policy pronouncements of U.S. Presidents from Woodrow Wilson to John F. Kennedy, Ronald Reagan, and Bill Clinton (whose 1993 inaugural address proclaimed, "Our hopes, our hearts, our hands, are with those on every continent who are building democracy and freedom. Their cause is America's"). This combination of values reflects both a belief in universal ideals ("The United States," the NSS declares, "must defend liberty and justice because these principles are right and true for all people everywhere") and a judgment that promoting these principles abroad not only benefits citizens of other countries, but also increases U.S. national security by making foreign conflicts less likely because democracies are unlikely to attack one another.

The National Security Strategy committed the United States to "actively work to bring the hope of democracy, development, free markets, and free trade to every corner of the world." This objective was driven by the belief that the fundamental cause of radical Islamic terrorism lies in the absence of democracy, the prevalence of authoritarianism, and the lack of freedom and opportunity in the Arab world. In the past, this idea might have been dismissed as political rhetoric. But after September 11, even the United Nations in its 2002 *Arab Human Development Report* and in subsequent reports in 2003 and 2005, defined the problem similarly and called for the extension of representative institutions and basic human freedoms to the Muslim Middle East. A Bush speech to the National Endowment for Democracy in November 2003 provided an elaboration that was both moral and strategic in its commitment to democratization, while criticizing half a century of policies that had failed to make this a priority: "Sixty years of Western nations excusing and accommodating the lack of freedom in the Middle East did nothing to make us safe, because in the long run stability cannot be purchased at the expense of liberty."

The commitment to democratization was Wilsonian in its scope and ambition, but the practicality of this aspiration was daunting. The difficulties of reconstruction and political stabilization in Afghanistan and Iraq were sobering, and the American emphasis on democratization in the wider Middle East drew extensive criticism from domestic and European critics, who saw these efforts as overly ambitious and potentially destabilizing, and from Arab authoritarian governments, who depicted the approach as an imperialistic imposition of American and Western values. Media criticisms in the Arab world often struck similar notes, but a smaller number of Arab authors and political figures did speak up—often at great personal risk—to defend such initiatives as a means of breaking the tenacious hold of authoritarian rule throughout the region. . . .

The commitment to spread democracy "to every corner of the world" does remain an ideal and a long-term goal, one reiterated by president Bush in his second inaugural address, in acknowledging that the "great objective of ending tyranny" is "the concentrated work of generations." Often, external encouragement of liberalization is likely to be the most feasible course of action, yet remarkable achievements have been evident in the Middle East, not only in countries where the United States has led military intervention, but elsewhere as well. In Afghanistan and Iraq, the first free elections have taken place, drawing large voter turnouts even in the face of violence and intimidation by those opposed to democratization. In Gaza and the West Bank, Palestinians voted to elect a president, and in Gaza they held genuinely free local elections. These are initial steps in the face of serious obstacles, but they are noteworthy achievements and there are signs of ferment elsewhere in the region, both on the part of those seeking change and by existing regimes feeling more pressure to liberalize.

꒰◉꒱

The United States possesses the military and economic means to act assertively on a global basis, but *should* it do so, and if so, how? In short, if the

United States conducts itself in this way, will the world be safer and more stable, and is such a role in America's national interest? Here, the anarchy problem is especially pertinent. The capacity of the United Nations to act, especially in coping with the most urgent and deadly problems, is severely limited, and in this sense, the demand for "global governance" far exceeds the supply. Since its inception in 1945, there have only been two occasions (Korea in 1950 and Kuwait in 1991) when the U.N. Security Council authorized the use of force, and in both instances the bulk of the forces were provided by the United States.

In the most serious cases, especially those involving international terrorism, the proliferation of weapons of mass destruction, ethnic cleansing, civil war, and mass murder, if America does not take the lead, no other country or organization is willing or able to respond effectively. The deadly cases of Bosnia (1991–95) and Rwanda (1994) make this clear, in their own way, so did the demonstrations by the people of Liberia calling for American intervention to save them from the ravages of predatory militias in a failed state. And the weakness of the international reaction to ethnic cleansing, rape, and widespread killing in the Darfur region of Western Sudan provides a more recent example.

International society, as Michael Walzer has observed, does not function in any way comparable to domestic society, whether in the use of force, rule of law, or effectiveness of its common institutions. As cases in point, North Korean violations of the Nuclear Non-Proliferation Treaty, the funding by former Liberian President Charles Taylor of guerrilla armies in Sierra Leone and the Ivory Coast, and Saddam Hussein's violations of the U.N. sanctions and weapons inspections regime did not meet with effective enforcement by the international community. All too often, meaningful responses to challenges of this kind require ad hoc efforts, and for the most part that means leadership by a major power. . . .

American preponderance is a fact of life by the criteria that are commonly used in measuring national power. But could this primacy prove to be short-lived? After all, there have been other periods in which judgments about the relative strength or weakness of the United States have proved to be overstated. For example, in the aftermath of the Cuban missile crisis of October 1962 and into the mid-1960s, foreign policymakers embraced overly ambitious notions of American power and influence. Conversely, during the late 1970s and early 1980s, in reaction to a series of adverse events (the loss of South Vietnam, fall of the American-supported Shah of Iran, Soviet advances in parts of Africa and in Afghanistan, energy crises, and lagging economic performance), talk of American decline became widespread but proved to be exaggerated. Instead, the decade of the 1990s saw the collapse of the Soviet Union and provided comprehensive evidence of American strength.

One of the most common contemporary warnings concerns imperial over-extension, in which a great power finds that the cost of maintaining its foreign commitments increasingly exceeds its resources. The process has been described elsewhere, most notably by Paul Kennedy, in his work on the rise and fall of great powers. And Robert Jervis has cautioned, "Avoiding this imperial temptation will be the greatest challenge that the United States faces." Might this happen to the United States? Here it is worth pondering possibilities of military risk, entanglement in a foreign quagmire, erosion of domestic support, and economic decline. . . .

Other developments that are unpredictable but have the potential to weigh on the economy might include, for example, a severe and prolonged interruption of oil imports or terrorist attacks with WMD that result in serious economic disruption and loss of life. Possible longer term causes over the course of a generation or more could include serious deterioration of public primary and secondary education, curtailment in the flow of foreign scientists, engineers, and students working or studying in the United States, difficulty in coping with the steeply rising costs of retirement, disability, and medical benefits, or an unexpected erosion in society's ability to absorb large immigrant populations. However, other than China, which has the potential to become a formidable challenger, the U.S. economy is likely to maintain its edge over Japan, Russia, and Europe, all of whom lag behind the United States in competitiveness and face far more serious demographic pressures involving low birth rates, aging populations, and a declining ratio of those in the active work force compared with retirees.

⤞◉⤝

How a grand strategy is put into practice can be as important as the substance of that strategy. Here, the interplay between power and diplomacy is crucial. As Stanley Hoffmann has observed, diplomacy without power is impotent, but power without diplomacy is blind. A wise choice of priorities is equally essential, since the range of possible foreign commitments is vast.

Critics of an assertive grand strategy incorporate varying assumptions. Realists overstate the likelihood of other countries effectively balancing against American power and are too sanguine about what would occur if the United States really did disengage from its principal foreign commitments. Liberal internationalists, on the other hand, often exaggerate the effectiveness and cohesion of international institutions and idealize the motives of other countries who actually seek to use international organizations to constrain the United States rather than to achieve collective goals. And ultimately, neither realists nor liberal internationalists give sufficient weight to the implications of 9/11 and the gravity of the threats to American national security that it represents.

All the same, the risks of over-commitment are real. In the mid-1960s, when both the power and purpose of the United States seemed unparalleled, the Kennedy and Johnson administrations found themselves drawn into Vietnam. At the time, a sense of benign invincibility shaped foreign policy-making in an atmosphere where our purposes seemed noble and our capacity to achieve those purposes unlimited. Decisions about the American role in Indochina thus unfolded without sufficient regard to priorities and limits. In the end, the United States was unable to achieve its objectives and withdrew after costly expenditures of lives, material resources, political capital, and domestic consensus. This experience means not that intervention and the use of force must not be undertaken, but that decisions about these issues need to be prioritized, carefully weighed, and skillfully implemented.

The United States today possesses unique strengths, but its ability to achieve desired outcomes is not infinite. It is thus essential that the application of power, including political commitments and military engagement, be focused on those cases in which American national interest is most squarely at stake. This dictates a focus on those places where nuclear proliferation and radical Islamist terrorism pose particular threats, and hence American grand strategy must be framed with such compelling priorities in mind.

Niall Ferguson  **NO**

An Empire in Denial: The Limits of U.S. Imperialism

It used to be only foreigners and those on the fringes of US politics who referred to the "American Empire." Invariably, they did so in order to criticize the United States. Since the attack on the World Trade Center in September 2001, however, there has been a growing volume of more serious writing on the subject of an American empire. The phrase is now heard both in polite academic company and in mainstream public debate. The striking thing is that not all those who now openly use the term "empire" do so pejoratively. A number of commentators—notably Max Boot, Thomas Donnelly, Robert Kaplan, and Charles Krauthammer—seem to relish the idea of a US imperium. "Today there is only one empire." James Kurth of Swarthmore College declared in a recent article in the *National Interest*, "the global empire of the United States."

Officially, however, the United States remains an empire in denial. In the words of US President George Bush during his presidential election campaign in 2000: "America has never been an empire. We may be the only great power in history that had the chance, and refused—preferring greatness to power, and justice to glory." Freud defined denial as a primitive psychological defense mechanism against trauma. Perhaps it was therefore inevitable that, in the aftermath of the September 11 attacks, US citizens would deny their country's imperial character more vehemently than ever. It may nevertheless be therapeutic to determine the precise nature of this American Empire—since empire it is, in all but name.

Imperial denial may simply be a matter of semantics. Many post-war writers about US power have used words like "hegemon" to convey the idea that US overseas influence is great but not imperial. There are other useful alternatives to the term "empire," including "unipolarity," global "leadership," and "the only superpower." Define the term "empire" narrowly enough, and the United States can easily be excluded from the category. Suppose empire is taken to mean "the forcible military occupation and governance of territory whose citizens remain permanently excluded from political representation." By that definition, the American Empire is laughably small. The United States accounts for around 6.5 percent of the world's surface, but its 14 formal dependencies add up to a mere 0.007 percent. In demographic terms, the United States and its dependencies account for barely five percent of the world's population, whereas the British ruled between one-fifth and one-quarter of the world's population at the zenith of their empire.

Yet this narrow definition of empire is as simplistic as it is convenient. To begin with, the expansion of the original 13 US states westwards and southwards in the course of the 19th century was itself a quintessentially imperialist undertaking. In both the US and British empires, indigenous populations were vanquished, expropriated and marginalized. The people living in the newer states were all ultimately enfranchised, but so were the settler populations of large tracts of the British Empire: "responsible government" was, after all, granted to Canada, Australia, New Zealand, and South Africa. The only substantial difference between the two processes of white settlement was that the United States absorbed most of its new territories—even Alaska and Hawaii—into its federal system, whereas the British never did more than toy with the idea of imperial federation.

In any case, the US empire is—and can afford to be—much less concerned with the acquisition of large areas of overseas territory than Britain's was. The United States has few formal colonies, but it possesses a great many small areas of territory within nationally sovereign states that serve as bases for its armed services. Before the deployment of troops for the invasion of Iraq, the US military had around 752 military installations located in more than 130 countries. New wars have meant new bases, like Camp Bondsteel in Kosovo, acquired during the 1999 war against Yugoslavia, and the Bishkek airbase in Kyrgyzstan, an "asset" picked up during the war against the Taliban regime in Afghanistan.

When the full extent of US military presence overseas is made plain, then the claim that the United States is not an empire rings hollow indeed. Nor should it be forgotten what formidable military technology can be unleashed from these bases. Commentators like to point out that the Pentagon's budget equals the combined military expenditures of the next 12 to 15 states. Such fiscal measures nevertheless understate the quantitative and qualitative lead currently enjoyed by US armed forces. In military terms, the British Empire did not dominate the full spectrum of military capabilities, as the United States does today; it was never so far ahead of its imperial rivals. If military power is the *sine qua non* of an empire, then it is hard to deny the imperial character of the United States today. The US sphere of military influence is now quite literally global.

It is, of course, conventional wisdom that large-scale overseas military commitments can have deleterious economic effects. Yet the United States seems a very long way from the kind of "overstretch" Paul Kennedy warned against in the late 1980s. According to one estimate, "America's 31 percent share of world product (at market prices) is equal to the next four countries (Japan, Germany, Britain, and France) combined," which exceeds the highest share of global output ever achieved by Great Britain by a factor of three. In terms of raw resources, then, the United States is already a vastly more powerful empire than Britain ever was. The rapid growth of the US economy since the late 1980s partly explains how the United States has managed to achieve a unique revolution in military affairs while at the same time substantially reducing the share of defense expenditures as a proportion of gross domestic product (GDP). The Defense Department Green Paper published in March 2003 forecast total expenditure on national defense to remain at 3.5 percent of GDP for at least three years, compared with an average figure during the Cold War of seven percent. Bearing in mind Paul Kennedy's "formula" that "if a particular nation is allocating *over the long term* more than 10 percent of gross national product (GNP) to armaments, that is likely to limit its growth rate," there seems little danger of imminent "overstretch."

In short, in terms of military capability and economic resources the United States not only resembles the last great Anglophone empire but exceeds it. Nor are its goals so very different. In September 2002, the Office of the President produced a document on "National Security Strategy" that explicitly states that it is a goal of US foreign policy "to extend the benefits of freedom . . . to every corner of the world." There are those who argue that such altruism is quite different from the more self-serving aims of British imperialism, but this betrays an ignorance of the comparably liberal ethos of the Victorian Empire. In any case, the National Security Strategy also asserts that the United States reserves the right, if the President should deem it necessary, to take pre-emptive military action against any state perceived as a threat to US security. If the US population still refuses to acknowledge that they have become an empire, the doctrine of pre-emption suggests—by way of a compromise—a possible neologism. Perhaps the United States today should be characterized as a pre-empire.

City on a Hill

One argument sometimes advanced to distinguish US "hegemony" from British Empire is qualitative. US power, it is argued, consists not just of military and economic power but also of "soft" power. According to Joseph Nye, "A country may obtain the outcomes it wants in world politics because other countries want to follow it, admiring its values, emulating its example, aspiring to its level of prosperity and openness." Soft power, in other words, is getting what you want without sticks or carrots. In the case of the United States, "it comes from being a shining 'city upon a hill'"—an enticing New Jerusalem of economic and political liberty. Nye is not so naïve as to assume that the US way is inherently attractive to everyone, everywhere. But he does believe that making it attractive matters more than ever before because of the global spread of information technology. To put it simply, soft power can reach the parts of the world that hard power cannot.

But does this really make US power so very different from imperial power? On the contrary. If anything, it illustrates how very like the last Anglophone empire the United States has become. The British Empire, too, sought to make its values attractive to others, though initially the job had to be done by "men on the spot." British missionaries, businessmen, administrators, and schoolmasters fanned out across the globe to "entice and attract" people toward British values.

These foot-slogging efforts were eventually reinforced by technology. It was the advent of wireless radio—and specifically the creation of the British Broadcasting Corporation (BBC)—which really ushered in the age of soft power in Nye's sense of the term. Within six years, the BBC had launched its first foreign language service—in Arabic, significantly—and, by the end of 1938, it was broadcasting around the world in all the major languages of continental Europe.

In some ways, the soft power that Britain could exert in the 1930s was greater than the soft power of the United States today. In a world of newspapers, radio receivers, and cinemas—where the number of content-supplying corporations (often national monopolies) was relatively small—the overseas broadcasts of the BBC could hope to reach a relatively large number of foreign ears. Yet whatever soft power Britain thereby wielded did nothing to halt the precipitous decline of British power after the 1930s.

This raises the question of how much US soft power really matters today. If the term is to denote anything more than cultural background music to more traditional forms of dominance, it surely needs to be demonstrated that the United States can secure what it wants from other countries without coercing or suborning them, but purely because its cultural exports are seductive. One reason for skepticism about the extent of US soft power today is the very nature of the channels of communication for US culture, the various electronic media through which US culture is currently transmitted tend to run from the United States to Western Europe, Japan, and in the case of television, Latin America. It would be too much to conclude that US soft power is abundant where it is least needed, for it may well be that a high level of exposure to US cinema and television is one of the reasons why Western Europe, Japan, and Latin America are on the whole less hostile to the United States than countries in the Middle East and Asia. But the fact remains that the *range* of US soft power in Nye's sense is more limited than is generally assumed.

One important qualification applies. Whatever the critics of the United States may say, the United States is indeed a very attractive place—and its

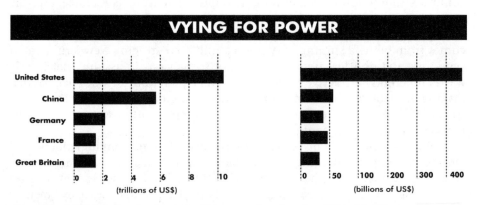

VYING FOR POWER

The graph on the left shows five selected countries with large gross domestic products (GDPs), derived from purchasing power parity calculations. The graph on the right depicts the military spending budgets of those countries. The graphs suggest that the United States is clearly the dominant economic and military power today, much like the British Empire at its height.

attraction extends for beyond of range of AOL-TimeWarner and CNN. It is so attractive that millions of foreigners want either to visit the country or to move here permanently. In 2000, for example, more than 50 million people visited the United States, making it the world's second most popular holiday destination (after France). That figure is more than double the approximately 20 million US citizens who traveled abroad on vacation. The United States also remains a popular destination for immigrants, with an annual net influx of around three people per thousand of population. Between 1974 and 1998, around 16.7 million foreigners came to live in the United States. About 26 million current US residents were born abroad, a number that vastly exceeds the four million US-born residents abroad. This is, of course, in marked contrast to the experience of Great Britain, which was a remarkable exporter of people throughout its imperial heyday. Between 1850 and 1950, nearly 18 million people left the British Isles.

But does this make the United States more or less powerful? Proponents of the "soft power" thesis argue that the very large numbers of foreign students who come to US universities act—unwittingly—as the agents of US empire when they return to their native lands, imbued with the distinctive value systems of the Harvard Business School or the Stanford Political Science Department. "The ability of the American empire to govern its domains," argues James Kurth, "will depend upon its success in producing this distinct kind of immigrant/ emigrant to serve as its distinct kind of imperial civil official." There are two reasons why this seems over-optimistic. First, a substantial proportion of the foreign students simply never return home to spread the good news about US principles and practice. The second is that a very substantial number of the leading nationalists who opposed and ultimately supplanted British rule in both Asia and Africa were themselves the beneficiaries of British university education.

The United States, then, is an empire—but a peculiar kind of empire. It is militarily and economically peerless. It has great, though not unbounded, cultural reach. Yet it has distinctive limitations. It is an empire based not on colonization, but on net immigration. There are also important limits to the way in which its wealth can be deployed. First, there is good reason to fear that, in the foreseeable future, the costs of the US welfare system—specifically, the systems of Medicare and Social Security—will begin to outstrip tax revenues. According to one recent estimate, the difference between the present value of all the federal government's future liabilities and the present value of all its future tax receipts amounts to a staggering US$44 trillion. Only steep cuts in public expenditure or increases in taxation will enable the government to avoid a grave fiscal crisis.

Secondly, the prosperity of the United States has become heavily reliant on very large inflows of foreign capital. With the current account deficit rising above five percent of GDP last year, much (not least the exchange rate of the dollar) depends on the continued willingness of foreign investors to put their savings into dollar-denominated assets. Once again, the contrast between Britain in her imperial prime is pronounced. In the British case, net foreign investment was consistently positive between the mid 1870s and World War I, rising to a peak of nine percent of GDP in 1913. Moreover, the destinations of British overseas investment were very diverse: substantial shares flowed to those relatively poor countries in which Britain had a disproportionate strategic interest. By comparison, US citizens who invest abroad favor Europe (especially Britain) and the Pacific (especially Japan, Australia, and Hong Kong). Barely one percent of US Foreign Direct Investment goes to the Middle East, and even less (0.8 percent) goes to China. This is a far cry from the "dollar diplomacy" of the 1920s, when US loans to strategically important countries in Europe and Latin America played an important role in underpinning US foreign policy. Today, foreign investors are theoretically the ones who have leverage over the United States, since fully 40 percent of the federal debt in public hands is held by foreigners.

This is not to say that those pessimists are right who predict imminent relative decline for the United States. What it does mean is that the United States is not quite the *hyperpuissance* of French nightmares. And what it also means is that, in dealing with transnational threats such as terrorism, international crime, nuclear proliferation, and infectious diseases like AIDS or SARS— to say nothing of global warming—the United States can achieve relatively little by acting unilaterally. As surely as the continuation of international free trade depends on multilateral institutions, so too does the successful prosecution of the war against terrorism.

Does this mean that the United States is not, after all, an empire? On the contrary. As that great imperial statesman Lord Salisbury well understood, there was nothing more dangerous to a great empire than what he called, with heavy irony, "splendid isolation." Then as now, the great Anglophone empire needs perforce to work in concert with the lesser—but not negligible—great powers in order to achieve its objectives.

Consider just one example. It is becoming abundantly clear following the invasions of Afghanistan and Iraq that the United States is not capable of effective peacekeeping—that is to say, policing—without some foreign assistance. Peacekeeping is not what US soldiers are trained to do, nor do they have much appetite for it. It also seems reasonable to assume that the US electorate will not tolerate US soldiers' prolonged exposure to the unglamorous hazards of "low-intensity conflict," with suicide bombers at checkpoints, snipers down alleys, and missile grenade attacks on convoys. The obvious solution is to continue the now well established practice of delegating peacekeeping to the United Nations and, under its auspices, to the US European allies. According to figures published in *Foreign Policy* magazine, the EU states contributed more than twice as much on UN peacekeeping operations as the United States in the years 2000 and 2001.

It is also noteworthy the EU states also contributed three times as much in effective aid to poor countries. Those, like Robert Kagan, who dismiss the Europeans as Kant-reading Venusians—as opposed to America's macho Martians— overlook the crucial significance of Pluto in the process of "nation building." Without hefty investment in creating the rule of law and priming the pump of economic recovery, countries like Afghanistan and Iraq will stagnate, if not disintegrate altogether. Unless the United States radically alters its attitudes toward peacekeeping and aid, it will have little option but to cooperate with the more generous Europeans. Unilateralism, like isolation, is not so splendid after all. Indeed, it is seldom a realistic option for an empire.

Dangers of Denial

The Victorian historian J. R. Seeley famously joked that the British had "conquered and peopled half the world in a fit of absence of mind." In acquiring their empire, the United States has followed this example. Few Europeans today doubt the existence of a US empire. But as the German theologian Reinhold Niebuhr noted in 1960, Americans persist in "frantically avoiding recognition of the imperialism [they] in fact exercise."

Does it matter? The answer is yes. The problem with an empire that is in denial about its own imperial nature is that it tends to make two mistakes when it chooses to intervene in the affairs of lesser states. The first is to attempt economic and political transformation in an unrealistically short timeframe. The second is to allocate insufficient resources to the project. As I write, both of these mistakes are being made in Iraq and Afghanistan. By insisting that US forces will remain in Iraq until a democratic government can be established "and not a day longer," US spokesmen unintentionally create a powerful disincentive for local people to cooperate with them. Who in Iraq today can feel confident that, if he lends support to US initiatives, he will not simply lay himself open to the charge of collaboration when the US troops depart?

Moreover, who would wish to cooperate with an occupying force that spent all its resources on itself and devoted next to nothing to aid or reconstruction? A successful empire is seldom solely based on coercion; there must be some economic dividends for the ruled as well as the rulers, if only to buy the loyalty of indigenous elites. Yet in Iraq and Afghanistan the amounts of money the United States has made available to potential local partners have been paltry.

To put it bluntly, the United States is acting like a colossus with an attention deficit disorder engaged in cut-price colonization. And that is perhaps the reason why this vastly powerful economy, with its extraordinary military capability, has had such a very disappointing record when it has sought to bring about changes of regime abroad. According to one recent study, just four out of 16 US military interventions in foreign countries have been successful in establishing US-style institutions over the past century. The worst failures—in Haiti, Vietnam, Cuba, and Cambodia—might well be attributed to this fatal combination of a truncated time horizon and inadequate resources for non-military purposes.

There is no question, as we have seen, that the United States has the raw economic resources to take on the old British role as underwriter of a globalized, liberalized economic system. Nor is there any doubt that it has the military capability to do the job. On both scores, the United States is already a far more powerful empire than Britain's ever was. Perhaps—though I am less persuaded about this—its "soft power" is also greater. Yet the unspoken American Empire suffers from serious structural weaknesses. It imports rather than exports high quality human capital. It also imports more capital than it exports—and exports virtually none to pivotal regions like the Middle East. It underestimates the need to act in partnership with allied great powers. And its efforts at nation-building are both short-term and under-funded.

Some US neo-imperialists like to quote Kipling's "White Man's Burden," written in 1899 to encourage US President William McKinley's empire-building efforts in the Philippines. But Kipling wrote another poem, two years earlier, which they would also do well to remember. Entitled "Recessional," it was a somber intimation of mortality, perfectly crafted to temper late Victorian delusions of grandeur:

> Far-called our navies melt away—
> On dune and headland sinks the fire—
> Lo, all our pomp of yesterday
> Is one with Nineveh and Tyre!
> Judge of the Nations, spare us yet,
> Lest we forget—lest we forget!

POSTSCRIPT

Must America Exercise World Leadership?

The disagreement between Robert J. Lieber and Niall Ferguson mirror the conflict between President Bush and those who fashioned the unilateralism of American foreign policy in the aftermath of 9/11 and the multilateralism that was dominant for decades after the end of the Second World War. The older policy depended upon the cooperation of leading nations allied with the United States in containing the Soviet Union and international aggression. The newer policy is premised on the view that the threat of terrorism and the potential use of weapons of mass destruction require the employment of preventive war (in anticipation of a future enemy attack) or even preemptive war (striking when an enemy attack is imminent).

Does support for the Bush doctrine require that America become the policeman of the world—or simply a prudent leader when emergency action is required? Does opposition to the Bush doctrine mean that the United States must never act in the absence of United Nations approval—or may it act to protect American interests when they are threatened? These and related questions are bound to surface in the coming years as Democrats and Republicans battle it out to win the hearts and minds of the American people.

The evolution of American international relations is related in Walter Russell Mead, *Special Providence: American Foreign Policy and How It Changed the World* (Alfred A. Knopf, 2001). Mead's more recent *Power, Terror, Peace, and War: America's Grand Strategy in a World of Risk* (Vintage, 2005) sees a major shift in the world toward a global capitalism, which, he argues, has been largely beneficial.

Preemption is supported by John Lewis Gaddis, "A Grand Strategy of Transformation" (*Foreign Policy*, November–December 2002) who rhetorically asks: "Who would not have preempted Hitler or Milosevic [the Serbian leader who precipitated war in the former Yugoslavia] or Mohammed Atta [leader of the 9/11 terrorists], if given the chance?" Obviously, though, America's aggressive world leadership has come at a cost: America is disliked by many people in the rest of the world. Why is that? Is it the fault of the United States, or can it be attributed to irrational motives of the critics, such as jealousy or displaced anger? Using extensive survey data, Andrew Kohut of the Pew Research Center and international economist Bruce Stokes attempt to answer these and related questions in *America Against the World: How We Are Different and Why We Are Disliked* (Holt Paperback, 2007).

Robert Kagan and William Kristol have defended America's "role as guarantor of national security in the Middle East," in "The Right War for the

Right Reasons," in *The Weekly Standard*, February 23, 2004. Ivo H. Daalder and James M. Lindsay, *America Unbound: The Bush Revolution in Foreign Policy* (Brookings Institution, 2003) conclude that "the fundamental premise of the Bush revolution—that America's security rested on an America unbound—was mistaken." Alan Curtis has edited a volume of essays that are highly critical of post-9/11 national policy in foreign and domestic affairs, *Patriotism, Democracy, and Common Sense: Restoring America's Promise at Home and Abroad* (The Milton S. Eisenhower Foundation and Rowman & Littlefield Publishers, 2004).

The disagreement between Robert J. Lieber and Niall Ferguson is not likely to be soon resolved. On the contrary, it is likely that a major element in the outcome of the presidential election of 2008 will be how the American electorate perceives America's future role in the world.

ISSUE 22

Should Federal Taxes Be Increased?

YES: **Aviva Aron-Dine,** from *Tax Cuts: Myths and Realities* (Center on Budget and Policy Priorities, 2008)

NO: **Brian M. Riedl,** from *Ten Myths About the Bush Tax Cuts* (The Heritage Foundation, 2007)

ISSUE SUMMARY

YES: Aviva Aron-Dine, former policy analyst at the Center on Budget and Policy Priorities, believes that the tax cuts adopted in the George W. Bush presidency have hurt the economy, have not benefited most Americans, and have increased the national debt.

NO: Brian Riedl, budget analyst at The Heritage Foundation, concludes that the tax cuts adopted in the presidency of George W. Bush have encouraged economic growth, benefited lower-income Americans most, and have increased tax revenues.

Benjamin Franklin is credited with having first said, "In this world nothing is certain but death and taxes." That does not mean that we have to look forward to either one. When the colonists confronted the collection of taxes by Great Britain, they proclaimed, "No taxation without representation," and moved toward revolution and the creation of the United States.

Resistance to national taxation continued until the Sixteenth Amendment to the U.S. Constitution was ratified in 1912 enabling the federal government to levy taxes directly on income. The following year, Congress adopted a graduated income tax, ranging from a 1 percent tax on individuals and businesses earning over $4,000 (most Americans did not earn that much) up to 6 percent on incomes over $500,000. Since then, tax rates have gone up and down, but some measure of progressivity—higher rates for higher incomes—has been retained. However, every major change in the tax code has produced new deductions, concessions, and loopholes that benefit some groups to the disadvantage of others, lengthen and complicate the law, and stimulate a major tax-filing occupation for accountants and tax lawyers.

No one likes taxes, but upon reflection, Americans are likely to agree with Supreme Court Justice Oliver Wendell Holmes, Jr. that "taxes are what we pay for civilized society." Almost all critics of high taxation, apart from anarchists who oppose all government and extreme libertarians who oppose almost all government, acknowledge that government has an essential role to play. No other way has been devised to pay for such essential services as public education, police and fire protection, roads and public transport, and the military defense of the nation. So the political question for almost all Americans is not whether or not they should be taxed but how and how much. Of course, other issues, such as trade, environmental policy, Social Security, and Medicare also raise questions as to what is the appropriate role and cost of government.

By the standards of other nations, American taxes are low. Almost every other industrial nation has higher rates of taxation. According to the Organization for Economic Cooperation and Development (OECD), all American taxes amount to approximately one-quarter (most recently, 26 percent) of the nation's gross domestic product (GDP), compared to one-half in Sweden (50 percent) and Denmark (49 percent). The average tax rate for the 30 nations in the OECD is 36 percent of GDP. High-tax countries often pay for services, such as health care, that are privately financed in the United States.

Americans appear to respond more favorably than citizens of other countries to proposals to lower taxes. When presidential candidate George H. W. Bush in 1988 said, "Read my lips. No new taxes," he enhanced his prospects for election. But when he was president and ran for reelection in 1992, his broken promise contributed to his defeat. His successor, President Bill Clinton favored higher taxes in order to eliminate a national budget deficit.

President George W. Bush secured the enactment of substantial tax cuts in 2001, 2002, and 2003. He argued that these would result in new investments that would revive a declining economy. His critics maintained that the tax cuts were of significant benefit only for the wealthiest Americans and blamed them, in part, for the nation's half-trillion dollar deficit.

Any thoughtful consideration of higher or lower taxes must broach the question of the policy's impact upon the national debt, which the Concord Coalition calculated to be nearly $10 trillion at the end of August 2008. Politicians and pundits debate which tax policies will reduce the indebtedness of the United States to foreign investors, and what the consequences of deficit financing are for a healthy American economy.

One major issue of tax policy became a central issue dividing Senators John McCain and Barack Obama, respectively, the Republican and Democratic presidential candidates in 2008. McCain favored making permanent the tax cuts of the Bush presidency and Obama favored eliminating the tax cuts for individuals earning over $250,000 a year.

Both the supporters and critics of higher taxes attack what they portray as the "myths" of their opponents. Aviva Aron-Dine, spelling out the conclusions of the Center on Budget and Policy Priorities, argues that recent tax cuts have hurt Americans who are less prosperous and have failed to improve the economy, and increased the federal deficit. Brian M. Riedl, summing up the analysis of The Heritage Foundation, maintains that lower-income Americans have benefited more than those who earn more and that the economy improved as a consequence of the tax cuts.

YES

Aviva Aron-Dine

Tax Cuts: Myths and Realities

Since 2001, the Administration and Congress have enacted a wide array of tax cuts, including reductions in individual income tax rates, repeal of the estate tax, and reductions in capital gains and dividend taxes. Nearly all of these tax cuts are scheduled to expire by the end of 2010. Making them permanent would cost about $4.4 trillion over the next decade (when the cost of additional interest on the federal debt is included).

Because important decisions about these tax policies must be made in the next few years, it is essential to understand their effects on deficits, the economy, and the distribution of income. Supporters of the tax cuts have sometimes sought to bolster their case by understating the tax cuts' costs, overstating their economic effects, or minimizing their regressivity. Here, we address some of the myths heard most frequently in recent tax-cut debates.

Tax Cuts and Deficits

Congressional Budget Office data show that the tax cuts have been the single largest contributor to the reemergence of substantial budget deficits in recent years. Legislation enacted since 2001 added about $3.0 trillion to deficits between 2001 and 2007, with nearly *half* of this deterioration in the budget due to the tax cuts (about a third was due to increases in security spending, and about a sixth to increases in domestic spending). Yet the President and some Congressional leaders decline to acknowledge the tax cuts' role in the nation's budget problems, falling back instead on the discredited nostrum that tax cuts "pay for themselves."

Myth 1: Tax cuts "pay for themselves."

> "You cut taxes and the tax revenues increase."
> —*President Bush, February 8, 2006*

> "You have to pay for these tax cuts twice under these pay-go rules if you apply them, because these tax cuts pay for themselves."
> —*Senator Judd Gregg, then Chair of the Senate Budget Committee, March 9, 2006*

Reality: A study by the President's own Treasury Department confirmed the common-sense view shared by economists across the political spectrum: cutting taxes decreases revenues.

From *Center on Budget and Policy Priorities*, May 9, 2008 update. Copyright © 2008 by Center on Budget and Policy Priorities. Reprinted by permission. http://www.cbpp.org

Proponents of tax cuts often claim that "dynamic scoring"—that is, considering tax cuts' economic effects when calculating their costs—would substantially lower the estimated cost of tax reductions, or even shrink it to zero. The argument is that tax cuts dramatically boost economic growth, which in turn boosts revenues by enough to offset the revenue loss from the tax cuts.

But when Treasury Department staff simulated the economic effects of extending the President's tax cuts, they found that, at best, the tax cuts would have modest positive effects on the economy; these economic gains would pay for *at most 10 percent* of the tax cuts' total cost. Under other assumptions, Treasury found that the tax cuts could slightly *decrease* long-run economic growth, in which case they would cost modestly *more* than otherwise expected. . . .

The claim that tax cuts pay for themselves also is contradicted by the historical record. In 1981, Congress substantially lowered marginal income-tax rates on the well off, while in 1990 and 1993, Congress raised marginal rates on the well off. The economy grew at virtually the same rate in the 1990s as in the 1980s (adjusted for inflation and population growth), but revenues grew about twice as fast in the 1990s, when tax rates were increased, as in the 1980s, when tax rates were cut. Similarly, since the 2001 tax cuts, the economy has grown at about the same pace as during the equivalent period of the 1990s business cycle, but revenues have grown far more slowly.

Some argue that, even if most tax cuts do not pay for themselves, capital gains tax cuts do. But, in reality, capital gains tax cuts cost money as well. After reviewing numerous studies of how investors respond to capital gains tax cuts, the Congressional Budget Office concluded that "the best estimates of taxpayers' response to changes in the capital gains rate do not suggest a large revenue increase from additional realizations of capital gains—and certainly not an increase large enough to offset the losses from a lower rate." That's why CBO, the Joint Committee on Taxation, and the White House Office of Management and Budget all project that making the 2003 capital gains tax cut permanent would cost about $100 billion over the next ten years.

Myth 2: Even if the tax cuts reduced revenues initially, they boosted revenues and lowered deficits in 2005 to 2007.

> "Some in Washington say we had to choose between cutting taxes and cutting the deficit . . . Today's numbers [the updated 2006 budget projections] show that that was a false choice. The economic growth fueled by tax relief has helped send our tax revenues soaring."
>
> —*President Bush, July 11, 2006*

Reality: Robust revenue growth in 2005–2007 has not made up for extraordinarily weak revenue growth over the previous few years.

When discussing revenue growth since the enactment of the tax cuts, Administration officials typically focus only on revenue growth since 2004. This provides a convenient starting point for their arguments, as it sets a very low bar. In 2001, 2002, and 2003, revenues fell in nominal terms (i.e. without adjusting for inflation) for three straight years, the first time this has occurred since before World War II. Measured as a share of the economy, revenues in

2004 were at their *lowest level since 1959*. Given this historically low starting point, it is not surprising that revenues have recovered since then. Supporters of the tax cuts selectively cite revenue growth over just the past three years to argue that the tax cuts fueled increases in revenues.

Even taking into account the growth in revenues in fiscal years 2005–2007, total revenues have just barely increased over the 2001–2007 business cycle, after adjusting for inflation and population growth. (The business cycle began in March 2001, when the 1990s business cycle hit its peak and thereby came to an end.) In contrast, six and a half years after the peak of previous post-World War II business cycles, real per-capita revenues had increased by an average of 12 percent, and in the 1990s, real per-capita revenues were up 16 percent. Revenues in 2007 were still more than $250 billion short of where they would have been had they grown at the rates typical in other recoveries.

Further, while the Administration has credited the tax cuts with the drop in the fiscal year 2007 deficit to "only" $162 billion, the 2007 budget would have been in *surplus* were it not for the tax cuts. Based on Joint Committee on Taxation estimates, the total 2007 cost of tax cuts enacted since January 2001 was $300 billion (taking into account the increased interest costs on the debt that have resulted from the deficit financing of the tax cuts). This means that even with the spending for the wars in Iraq and Afghanistan, the federal budget would have been in surplus in 2007 if the tax cuts had not been enacted, or if their costs had been offset. While supporters of these tax cuts claim that their positive economic effects have lowered their cost, the non-partisan Congressional Research Service found in a September, 2006 report that "at the current time, as the stimulus effects have faded and the effect of added debt service has grown, the 2001–2004 tax cuts are probably costing more than their estimated revenue cost."

Looking out over the next several decades, when deficits are projected to be far larger (because of the impact on the budget of the continued rise in health care costs and the retirement of the baby boomers), the tax cuts, if extended, will still be a major contributor to the nation's fiscal problems. To put the long-run cost of the tax cuts in perspective, the 75-year Social Security shortfall, about which the President and Congressional leaders have expressed grave concern, is less than *one-third* the cost of the tax cuts over the same period.

Tax Cuts and the Economy

A consistent finding in the academic literature about the effects of tax cuts on the economy is that these effects are typically modest. In the short run, well-designed tax cuts can help to boost an economy that is in a recession. In the longer run, well-designed tax cuts can have a modest positive impact if they are fully paid for. For example, the recent Treasury analysis found that if the President's tax cuts were made permanent *and* the costs of the tax cuts were paid for by reductions in programs, economic growth would increase by a few hundredths of one percentage point annually. Meanwhile, studies by economists at the Joint Committee on Taxation, the Congressional Budget Office, the Brookings Institution, and elsewhere have found that if tax cuts are not paid for with spending reductions, they are likely to have modest *negative* effects on the economy over time, because of the negative effects of the increased deficits. Tax-cut proponents often claim that the economy will be badly damaged if the tax cuts are not extended; these claims are without foundation.

Myth 3: The economy has grown strongly over the past several years because of the tax cuts.

> "The main reason for our growing economy is that we cut taxes and left more money in the hands of families and workers and small business owners."
> —*President Bush, November 4, 2006*

Reality: The 2001–2007 economic expansion was sub-par overall, and job and wage growth were anemic.

Members of the Administration routinely tout statistics regarding recent economic growth, then credit the President's tax cuts with what they portray as a stellar economic performance. But as a general rule, it is difficult or impossible to infer the effect of a given tax cut from looking at a few years of economic data, simply because so many factors other than tax policy influence the economy. What the data do show clearly is that, despite major tax cuts in 2001, 2002, 2003, 2004, and 2006, the economy's performance between 2001 and 2007 was [far] from stellar.

Growth rates of GDP, investment, and other key economic indicators during the 2001–2007 expansion were *below* the average for other post-World War II economic expansions. Growth in wages and salaries and non-residential investment was particularly slow relative to previous expansions, and, while the Administration boasts of its record on jobs, employment growth was weaker in the 2001–2007 period than in *any* previous post-World War II expansion.

Median income among working-age households, meanwhile, *fell* during the expansion. Census data show that among households headed by someone under age 65, median income in 2006, adjusted for inflation, was $1,300 *below its level during the 2001 recession.* Similarly, the poverty rate and the share of Americans lacking health insurance were higher in 2006 than during the recession.

Myth 4: Even if economic growth and the job market were weak during the early stages of the recovery, the capital gains and dividend tax cuts turned the economy around in 2003.

> "Since the tax rates on capital gains and dividends were reduced in 2003, we have seen strong steady economic growth, resulting in higher employment."
> —*Representative Bill Thomas, then Chair of the Ways and Means Committee, May 17, 2006*

Reality: The available evidence indicates that the capital gains and dividend tax cuts were not the cause of improvement in the economy in 2003.

The President and other tax-cut advocates have credited the capital gains and dividend tax cuts with the fact that the economy performed better between 2003 and 2007 than in the earlier part of the expansion. But they have produced no evidence to support their leap from correlation (the tax cuts *coincided* with improvement in the economy) to causation (the claim that the tax cuts *caused* the improvement). Furthermore, they have ignored evidence that indicates there was little or no causal connection.

Notably, informed observers such as Federal Reserve Chairman Ben Bernanke (then a Federal Reserve Board governor) were predicting improvement in the economy *before* the 2003 tax cuts were enacted. In addition, supporters of enacting these tax cuts, such as conservative economist Gary Becker, acknowledged at the time that, whatever the tax cuts' long-run effects on economic growth, they would *not* boost the economy in the short term.

Also striking is the fact that the expansion of the 1990s followed a pattern similar to the 2001–2007 expansion, especially with respect to investment growth (which the dividend and capital gains tax cuts were supposed to encourage). Investment was weak in the early 1990s and then began to improve about two years into the expansion. But in the 1990s, that improvement—which was greater than the improvement in the early 2000s—coincided with a tax *increase*. If one accepts the notion that any economic change that follows a tax change must have been *caused* by the tax change, one would have to conclude that tax increases promote stronger investment growth than tax cuts. The more reasonable conclusion, of course, is that weak recoveries eventually tend to return to historical norms.

Moreover, even growth since 2003 has been less than impressive. GDP, wage and salary, and employment growth have remained below average for a post-World War II recovery, while growth in non-residential investment has only matched the historical norm.

Myth 5: Extending the tax cuts is important for the economy's long-run health.

> "To keep this economy growing and delivering prosperity to more Americans, we need leaders in Washington who understand the importance of letting you keep more of your money, and making the tax relief we delivered permanent."
> —*President Bush, October 28, 2006*

Reality: Extending the tax cuts without paying for them would be more likely to reduce economic growth over the long run than to increase it.

Researchers at the Joint Committee on Taxation, the Congressional Budget Office, and the Brookings Institution have all found that large unpaid-for tax cuts reduce economic growth over the long run. For example, a study by Brookings Institution economist William Gale and then-Brookings economist (now CBO director) Peter Orszag concluded that making the 2001 and 2003 tax cuts permanent without offsetting their cost would be "likely to reduce, not increase, national income over the long run." Similarly, in a study in which it examined the economic effects of reductions in individual and corporate tax rates and an increase in the personal exemption, the Joint Committee on Taxation found, "Growth effects eventually become negative without offsetting fiscal policy [i.e. without offsets] for each of the proposals, because accumulating Federal government debt crowds out private investment."

The reason behind these results is that, even if tax cuts have modest positive effects on work and savings decisions, those effects are outweighed by the negative consequences of higher budget deficits. In claiming that tax cuts will boost savings, investment, and GDP growth, supporters often seem to forget that national savings has two components: private and public (i.e., government) savings. Tax cuts could positively affect private savings, although, as the Congressional Research Service has noted, studies have failed to find large effects. But when the federal government runs a deficit, it pays for the deficit by borrowing money from the private sector, which reduces national savings. By adding to deficits, unpaid-for tax cuts thus generally *reduce* national savings.

Making the tax cuts permanent would add about $4.4 trillion to deficits over the next decade, when the additional interest costs on the national debt are included. The resulting decrease in national savings would mean fewer funds available for investment, reducing the size of the capital stock (the total supply of equipment, buildings, and other productive capital in the economy). With less capital available, future workers would be less productive, and as a result, national income over the long run would be lower than it otherwise would be. (As discussed above, even if paid for, the positive effects of the tax cuts on the economy would be quite small. Moreover, paying for the tax cuts with spending cuts would require deep cuts in federal programs, as discussed below in Myth 8.)

Tax Cuts and Fairness

The tax cuts enacted in recent years have gone disproportionately to high-income Americans. In 2007, the 0.3 percent of households with incomes above $1 million received about *$120,000*, on average, from the 2001 and 2003 tax cuts, according to estimates by the Urban Institute-Brookings Institution Tax Policy Center. In contrast, households in the middle of the income spectrum received tax cuts averaging $740. The Tax Policy Center estimates also show that the tax cuts represent a larger fraction of income for high-income households than for low- or middle-income households, a clear indication of these tax cuts' regressivity.

Myth 6: The tax cuts have made the tax system more progressive.

> "The President's tax cuts have made the tax code more progressive, which also narrows the difference in take-home earnings."
> —*Council of Economic Advisers Chair Edward Lazear and Katherine Baicker, then a member of the Council of Economic Advisers, May 8, 2006*

Reality: The tax cuts have made the distribution of take-home pay more unequal—at a time when inequality in before-tax income has also increased.

A progressive tax change, like a progressive tax system, is one that reduces inequality. In Lazear and Baicker's terms, it is a tax cut that "narrows the difference in take-home earnings." Take-home earnings consist of a person's income after taxes have been paid. So a progressive tax cut would be one that raised after-tax incomes for those at the bottom of the income spectrum by a larger percentage than for those at the top, increasing their share of total take-home pay.

The President's tax policies, however, have *widened* the differences in take-home pay between high- and low- and middle-income households, according to Tax Policy Center estimates. When the tax cuts are fully in effect, households with incomes above $1 million will receive tax cuts equivalent to an increase of 7.5 percent in their after-tax income. Households in the middle of the income spectrum will receive tax cuts equal to only 2.3 percent of their income. And households in the bottom quintile will gain by less than one percent.

Put another way, households with incomes over $1 million will hold a larger fraction of total U.S. after-tax income than they would have received without the tax cuts, while households in the middle and bottom quintiles will hold a smaller share. The tax cuts thus have widened, rather than narrowed, income gaps, making them regressive.

While comparisons of percent changes in after-tax earnings measure the tax cuts' effect on the distribution of income, the dollar values of the tax cuts received by different income groups are also relevant to evaluating these tax cuts' overall fairness. For example, over the next ten years (assuming the tax cuts are extended), more than $800 billion will be spent on tax cuts for the 0.3 percent of households with incomes above $1 million, with these tax cuts averaging over $150,000 per-household annually. At issue is whether this represents an appropriate use of scarce public resources.

The skewed distribution of the tax cuts is of particular concern given that, since 2001, gaps in *before-tax* income have widened. As of 2006, the highest-income 1 percent of households held a larger share of total pre-tax income that in any year since 1928.

Myth 7: The tax cuts have made the tax system more fair to small business owners.

> "We cut the taxes on the small business owners . . . [I]t makes sense to let small businesses keep more of the money they make."
> —*President Bush, April 13, 2006*

Reality: The President's tax cuts affect small business owners much as they affect the population as a whole: they provide large gains to those with high incomes and little benefit to others.

One major benefit the President's tax cuts have supposedly offered small business owners is the reduction in the top individual income tax rate, from 39.6 percent to 35 percent. Because small business owners pay individual income tax on their business income, the Administration contends that they are disproportionate beneficiaries of the rate reduction.

But a Tax Policy Center analysis found that only 1.3 percent of filers with small business income are subject to the top income tax rate and so benefit from lowering it. Moreover, these households hardly conform to the popular image of a small business owner: they derived, on average, less than a third of their total income from a small business.

An even more muddled mythology surrounds the issue of small business owners and the estate tax. Despite oft-repeated claims that the estate tax has dire consequences for family farms and small businesses, there is in fact very little evidence that it has any significant impact on these groups. An analysis by the Congressional Budget Office found that exceedingly few farms and small businesses owe any estate tax. Indeed, the American Farm Federation acknowledged to the *New York Times* that it could not cite a single example of a farm having to be sold to pay estate taxes.

Myth 8: Even if high-income taxpayers have received the largest gains from the tax cuts, taxpayers across the income spectrum have benefited.

> "President Bush's tax relief benefits all taxpayers."
> —*White House Fact Sheet, May 11, 2006*

Reality: Taking into account the fact that their costs eventually must be paid for, most American families likely will *lose* from the tax cuts over the long run.

Claims that all taxpayers are winners from the President's tax cuts rest on the false assumption that Congress and the President can provide trillions of dollars in tax cuts without anyone ever footing the bill. As noted in Myth 1, the tax cuts so far have been financed by deficits, and most proposals to extend them include no measures to offset their costs. In the long run, however, it is widely recognized that deficit-financed tax cuts eventually must be paid for. As former Federal Reserve Chairman Alan Greenspan warned, "If you're going to lower taxes, you shouldn't be borrowing essentially the tax cut. And that over the long run is not a stable fiscal situation." Simply stated, funds that are borrowed must eventually be paid back.

When the tax cuts ultimately are paid for, the costs will be very large and the choices difficult, especially given the bleak long-term deficit outlook. Once the tax cuts are fully in effect, their annual cost will be equal, in today's terms, to the entire annual budgets of the Departments of Education, Homeland Security, Housing and Urban Development, Veterans' Affairs, State, Energy, and the Environmental Protection Agency *combined*. If the tax cuts are extended without offsets, balancing the budget in 2012 will require cutting Social Security benefits by 36 percent, cutting defense by 40 percent, cutting Medicare by 55 percent, or cutting every other program other than Social Security, defense, Medicare, and homeland security (including education, medical research, border security, environmental protection, veterans' programs, and programs to assist the poor) by an average of almost one-fourth. For most Americans, keeping the tax cuts at the cost of implementing any of the above options would be a bad bargain.

Even if the tax cuts' costs are eventually paid for through a more balanced package of spending reductions and progressive tax increases, data from the Tax Policy Center show that, on average, the bottom four-fifths of households will lose more than they gain from the combination of tax cuts and the financing for them. That is, once the need to pay for the tax cuts is taken into account, the 2001 and 2003 "tax cuts" are best seen as *net tax cuts* for the top 20 percent of households, as a group, financed by *net tax increases or benefit reductions* for the remaining 80 percent of households, as a group.

Brian M. Riedl

NO

Ten Myths About the Bush Tax Cuts

The Democratic majority in the U.S. House of Representatives must decide whether to write a budget extending, expiring, or repealing the Bush tax cuts. These tax cuts have provided a convenient scapegoat for the nation's budget and economic challenges. Despite a 42 percent spending increase in 2001, critics charge that the tax cuts have starved popular programs. Despite surging economic growth and 5 million new jobs since 2003, critics also charge that the tax cuts have not helped the economy. Finally, despite making the income tax code more progressive, critics charge that the tax cuts have widened inequality.

Nearly all of the conventional wisdom about the Bush tax cuts is wrong. In reality:

- The tax cuts have not substantially reduced current tax revenues, which were in fact not far from the 2000 pre-tax cut baseline and over the 2003 pre-tax cut baseline in 2006;
- The increased child tax credit, 10 percent tax bracket, and fix of the alternative minimum tax (AMT) reduced tax revenues much more than most of the "tax cuts for the rich";
- Economic growth rates have more than doubled since the 2003 tax cuts; and
- The tax cuts shifted even more of the income tax burden toward the rich.

Setting optimal tax policy requires governing with facts rather than popular mythology, which is why it is important to set the record straight by debunking 10 myths about the Bush tax cuts.

Myth #1: Tax revenues remain low.
Fact: Tax revenues are above the historical average, even after the tax cuts.

Tax revenues in 2006 were 18.4 percent of gross domestic product (GDP), which is actually above the 20-year, 40-year, and 60-year historical averages. The inflation-adjusted 20 percent tax revenue increase between 2004 and 2006 represents the largest two-year revenue surge since 1965–1967. Claims that Americans are undertaxed by historical standards are patently false.

From *The Heritage Foundation Backgrounder*, #2001, January 29, 2007. Copyright © 2007 by The Heritage Foundation. Reprinted by permission.

Some critics of President George W. Bush's tax policies concede that tax revenues exceed the historical average yet assert that revenues are historically low for economies in the fourth year of an expansion. Setting aside that some of these tax policies are partly responsible for that economic expansion, the numbers simply do not support this claim. Comparing tax revenues in the fourth fiscal year after the end of each of the past three recessions shows nearly equal tax revenues of:

- 18.4 percent of GDP in 1987,
- 18.5 percent of GDP in 1995, and
- 18.4 percent of GDP in 2006.

While revenues as a percentage of GDP have not fully returned to pre-recession levels (20.9 percent in 2000), it is now clear that the pre-recession level was a major historical anomaly caused by a temporary stock market bubble.

Myth #2: The Bush tax cuts substantially reduced 2006 revenues and expanded the budget deficit.
Fact: Nearly all of the 2006 budget deficit resulted from additional spending above the baseline.

Critics tirelessly contend that America's swing from budget surpluses in 1998–2001 to a $247 billion budget deficit in 2006 resulted chiefly from the "irresponsible" Bush tax cuts. This argument ignores the historic spending increases that pushed federal spending up from 18.5 percent of GDP in 2001 to 20.2 percent in 2006.

The best way to measure the swing from surplus to deficit is by comparing the pre-tax cut budget baseline of the Congressional Budget Office (CBO) with what actually happened. While the January 2000 baseline projected a 2006 budget surplus of $325 billion, the final 2006 numbers showed a $247 billion deficit—a net drop of $572 billion. This drop occurred because spending was $514 billion above projected levels, and revenues were $58 billion below (even after $188 billion in tax cuts). In other words, 90 percent of the swing from surplus to deficit resulted from higher-than-projected spending, and only 10 percent resulted from lower-than-projected revenues.

Furthermore, tax revenues in 2006 were actually above the levels projected before the 2003 tax cuts. Immediately before the 2003 tax cuts, the CBO projected a 2006 budget deficit of $57 billion, yet the final 2006 budget deficit was $247 billion. The $190 billion deficit increase resulted from federal spending that was $237 billion more than projected. Revenues were actually $47 billion *above* the projection, even after $75 billion in tax cuts enacted after the baseline was calculated. By that standard, new spending was responsible for 125 percent of the higher 2006 budget deficit, and expanding revenues actually offset 25 percent of the new spending.

The 2006 tax revenues were not substantially far from levels projected before the Bush tax cuts. Despite estimates that the tax cuts would reduce 2006 revenues by $188 billion, they came in just $58 billion below the pre-tax cut revenue level projected in January 2000.

The difference is even more dramatic with the pro-growth 2003 tax cuts. The CBO calculated that the post-March 2003 tax cuts would lower 2006 revenues by $75 billion, yet 2006 revenues came in $47 billion *above* the pre-tax cut baseline released in March 2003. This is not a coincidence. Tax cuts clearly played a significant role in the economy's performing better than expected and recovering much of the lost revenue.

Myth #3: Supply-side economics assumes that all tax cuts immediately pay for themselves.
Fact: It assumes replenishment of some but not necessarily all lost revenues.

Attempts to debunk solid theories often involve first mischaracterizing them as straw men. Critics often erroneously define supply-side economics as the belief that all tax cuts pay for themselves. They then cite tax cuts that have not fully paid for themselves as conclusive proof that supply-side economics has failed.

However, supply-side economics never contended that *all* tax cuts pay for themselves. Rather the Laffer Curve (upon which much of the supply-side theory is based) merely formalizes the common-sense observations that:

1. Tax revenues depend on the tax base as well as the tax rate;
2. Raising tax rates discourages the taxed behavior and therefore shrinks the tax base, offsetting some of the revenue gains; and
3. Lowering tax rates encourages the taxed behavior and expands the tax base, offsetting some of the revenue loss.

If policymakers intend cigarette taxes to discourage smoking, they should also expect high investment taxes to discourage investment and income taxes to discourage work. Lowering taxes encourages people to engage in the given behavior, which expands the base and replenishes some of the lost revenue. This is the "feedback effect" of a tax cut.

Whether or not a tax cut recovers 100 percent of the lost revenue depends on the tax rate's location on the Laffer Curve. Each tax has a revenue-maximizing rate at which future tax increases will reduce revenue. (This is the peak of the Laffer Curve.) Only when tax rates are above that level will reducing the tax rate actually increase revenue. Otherwise, it will replenish only a portion of the lost revenue.

How much feedback revenue a given tax cut will generate depends on the degree to which taxpayers adjust their behavior. Cutting sales and property tax rates generally induces smaller feedback effects because taxpayers do not respond by substantially expanding their purchases or home-buying. Income taxes have a higher feedback effect. Nobel Prize-winning economist Ed Prescott has shown a strong cross-national link between lower income tax rates and higher work hours. Investment taxes have the highest feedback effects because investors quickly move to avoid higher-taxed investments. Not surprisingly, history shows that higher investment taxes deeply curtail investment and consequently raise little (if any) new revenue.

Yet, using the standard set by some, even a hypothetical tax cut that provides real tax relief to millions of families and entrepreneurs and creates enough new income to recover 95 percent of the estimated revenue loss would be considered a "failure" of supply-side economics and thus merit a full repeal.

Myth #4: Capital gains tax cuts do not pay for themselves.
Fact: Capital gains tax revenues doubled following the 2003 tax cut.

As previously stated, whether a tax cut pays for itself depends on how much people alter their behavior in response to the policy. Investors have been shown to be the most sensitive to tax policy, because capital gains tax cuts encourage enough new investment to more than offset the lower tax rate.

In 2003, capital gains tax rates were reduced from 20 percent and 10 percent (depending on income) to 15 percent and 5 percent. Rather than expand by 36 percent from the current $50 billion level to $68 billion in 2006 as the CBO projected before the tax cut, capital gains revenues more than doubled to $103 billion. Past capital gains tax cuts have shown similar results.

By encouraging investment, lower capital gains taxes increase funding for the technologies, businesses, ideas, and projects that make workers and the economy more productive. Such investment is vital for long-term economic growth.

Because investors are tax-sensitive, high capital gains tax rates are not only bad economic policy, but also bad budget policy.

Myth #5: The Bush tax cuts are to blame for the projected long-term budget deficits.
Fact: Projections show that entitlement costs will dwarf the projected large revenue increases.

The unsustainability of America's long-term budget path is well known. However, a common misperception blames the massive future budget deficits on the 2001 and 2003 tax cuts. In reality, revenues will continue to increase above the historical average yet be dwarfed by historic entitlement spending increases.

For the past half-century, tax revenues have generally stayed within 1 percentage point of 18 percent of GDP. The CBO projects that, even if all 2001 and 2003 tax cuts are made permanent, revenues will still increase from 18.4 percent of GDP today to 22.8 percent by 2050, not counting any feedback revenues from their positive economic impact. It is projected that repealing the Bush tax cuts would nudge 2050 revenues up to 23.7 percent of GDP, not counting any revenue losses from the negative economic impact of the tax hikes. In effect, the Bush tax cut debate is whether revenues should increase by 4.4 percent or 5.3 percent of GDP.

Spending has remained around 20 percent of GDP for the past half-century. However, the coming retirement of the baby boomers will increase Social Security, Medicare, and Medicaid spending by a combined 10.5 percent of GDP. Assuming that this causes large budget deficits and increased net spending on interest, federal spending could surge to 38 percent of GDP and possibly much higher.

Overall, revenues are projected to increase from 18 percent of GDP to almost 23 percent. Spending is projected to increase from 20 percent of GDP to at least 38 percent. Even repealing all of the 2001 and 2003 cuts would merely shave the projected budget deficit of 15 percent of GDP by less than 1 percentage point, and that assumes no negative feedback from raising taxes. Clearly, the French-style spending increases, not tax policy, are the problem. Lawmakers should focus on getting entitlements under control.

Myth #6: Raising tax rates is the best way to raise revenue.
Fact: Tax revenues correlate with economic growth, not tax rates.

Many of those who desire additional tax revenues regularly call on Congress to raise tax rates, but tax revenues are a function of two variables: tax rates and the tax base. The tax base typically moves in the opposite direction of the tax rate, partially negating the revenue impact of tax rate changes. Accordingly, . . . little correlation [is seen] between tax rates and tax revenues. Since 1952, the highest marginal income tax rate has dropped from 92 percent to 35 percent, and tax revenues have grown in inflation-adjusted terms while remaining constant as a percent of GDP.

[A] nearly perfect correlation [is seen] between GDP and tax revenues. Despite major fluctuations in income tax rates, long-term tax revenues have grown at almost exactly the same rate as GDP, remaining between 17 percent and 20 percent of GDP for 46 of the past 50 years. [The] top marginal income tax rate topped 90 percent during the 1950s and . . . revenues averaged 17.2 percent of GDP. By the 1990s, the top marginal income tax rate averaged just 36 percent, and tax revenues averaged 18.3 percent of GDP. Regardless of the tax rate, tax revenues have almost always come in at approximately 18 percent of GDP.

Since revenues move with GDP, the common-sense way to increase tax revenues is to expand the GDP. This means that pro-growth policies such as low marginal tax rates (especially on work, savings, and investment), restrained federal spending, minimal regulation, and free trade would raise more tax revenues than would be raised by self-defeating tax increases. America cannot substantially increase tax revenue with policies that reduce national income.

Myth #7: Reversing the upper-income tax cuts would raise substantial revenues.
Fact: The low-income tax cuts reduced revenues the most.

Many critics of tax cuts nonetheless support extending the increased child tax credit, marriage penalty relief, and the 10 percent income tax bracket because these policies strongly benefit low-income tax families. They also support annually adjusting the alternative minimum tax exemption for inflation to prevent a massive broad-based tax increase. These critics assert that repealing the tax cuts for upper-income individuals and investors and bringing back the pre-2001 estate tax levels can raise substantial revenue. Once again, the numbers fail to support this claim.

In 2007, according to CBO and Joint Committee on Taxation data, the increased child tax credit, marriage penalty relief, 10 percent bracket, and

AMT fix will have a combined budgetary effect of $114 billion. These policies do not have strong supply-side effects to minimize that effect.

By comparison, the more maligned capital gains, dividends, and estate tax cuts are projected to reduce 2007 revenues by just $36 billion even before the large and positive supply-side effects are incorporated. Thus, repealing these tax cuts would raise very little revenue and could possibly even reduce federal tax revenue. Such tax increases would certainly reduce the savings and investment vital to economic growth.

The individual income tax rate reductions come to $59 billion in 2007 and are not really a tax cut for the rich. All families with taxable incomes over $62,000 (and single filers over $31,000) benefit. Repealing this tax cut would reduce work incentives and raise taxes on millions of families and small businesses, thereby harming the economy and minimizing any new revenues.

Myth #8: Tax cuts help the economy by "putting money in people's pockets." Fact: Pro-growth tax cuts support incentives for productive behavior.

Government spending does not "pump new money into the economy" because government must first tax or borrow that money out of the economy. Claims that tax cuts benefit the economy by "putting money in people's pockets" represent the flip side of the pump-priming fallacy. Instead, the right tax cuts help the economy by reducing government's influence on economic decisions and allowing people to respond more to market mechanisms, thereby encouraging more productive behavior.

The Keynesian fallacy is that government spending injects new money into the economy, but the money that government spends must come from somewhere. Government must first tax or borrow that money out of the economy, so all the new spending just redistributes existing income. Similarly, the money for tax rebates—which are also touted as a way to inject money into the economy—must also come from somewhere, with government either spending less or borrowing more. In both cases, no new spending is added to the economy. Rather, the government has just transferred it from one group (e.g., investors) in the economy to another (e.g., consumers).

Some argue that certain tax cuts, such as tax rebates, can transfer money from savers to spenders and therefore increase demand. This argument assumes that the savers have been storing their savings in their mattresses, thereby removing it from the economy. In reality, nearly all Americans either invest their savings, thereby financing businesses investment, or deposit the money in banks, which quickly lend it to others to spend or invest. Therefore, the money is spent by someone whether it is initially consumed or saved. Thus, tax rebates create no additional economic activity and cannot "prime the pump."

This does not mean tax policy cannot affect economic growth. The right tax cuts can add substantially to the economy's *supply side* of productive resources: capital and labor. Economic growth requires that businesses efficiently produce increasing amounts of goods and services, and increased production requires consistent business investment and a motivated, productive workforce. Yet high marginal tax rates—defined as the tax on the next dollar earned—serve as a disincentive to engage in such activities. Reducing marginal tax rates on businesses and workers increases the return on working, saving, and investing, thereby creating more business investment and a more productive workforce, both of which add to the economy's long-term capacity for growth.

Yet some propose demand-side tax cuts to "put money in people's pockets" and "get people to spend money." The 2001 tax rebates serve as an example: Washington borrowed billions from investors and then mailed that money to families in the form of $600 checks. Predictably, this simple transfer of existing wealth caused a temporary increase in consumer spending and a corresponding decrease in investment but led to no new economic growth. No new wealth was created because the tax rebate was unrelated to productive behavior. No one had to work, save, or invest more to receive a rebate. Simply redistributing existing wealth does not create new wealth.

In contrast, marginal tax rates were reduced throughout the 1920s, 1960s, and 1980s. In all three decades, investment increased, and higher economic growth followed. Real GDP increased by 59 percent from 1921 to 1929, by 42 percent from 1961 to 1968, and by 31 percent from 1982 to 1989. More recently, the 2003 tax cuts helped to bring about strong economic growth for the past three years.

Policies which best support work, saving, and investment are much more effective at expanding the economy's long-term capacity for growth than those that aim to put money in consumers' pockets.

Myth #9: The Bush tax cuts have not helped the economy.
Fact: The economy responded strongly to the 2003 tax cuts.

The 2003 tax cuts lowered income, capital gains, and dividend tax rates. These policies were designed to increase market incentives to work, save, and invest, thus creating jobs and increasing economic growth. An analysis of the six quarters before and after the 2003 tax cuts (a short enough time frame to exclude the 2001 recession) shows that this is exactly what happened:

- GDP grew at an annual rate of just 1.7 percent in the six quarters before the 2003 tax cuts. In the six quarters following the tax cuts, the growth rate was 4.1 percent.
- Non-residential fixed investment declined for 13 consecutive quarters before the 2003 tax cuts. Since then, it has expanded for 13 consecutive quarters.
- The S&P 500 dropped 18 percent in the six quarters before the 2003 tax cuts but increased by 32 percent over the next six quarters. Dividend payouts increased as well.
- The economy lost 267,000 jobs in the six quarters before the 2003 tax cuts. In the next six quarters, it added 307,000 jobs, followed by 5 million jobs in the next seven quarters.

Critics contend that the economy was already recovering and that this strong expansion would have occurred even without the tax cuts. While some growth was naturally occurring, critics do not explain why such a sudden and dramatic turnaround began at the exact moment that these pro-growth policies were enacted. They do not explain why business investment, the stock market, and job numbers suddenly turned around in spring 2003. It is no coincidence that the expansion was powered by strong investment growth, exactly as the tax cuts intended.

The 2003 tax cuts succeeded because of the supply-side policies that critics most oppose: cuts in marginal income tax rates and tax cuts on capital gains and dividends. The 2001 tax cuts that were based more on demand-side tax rebates and redistribution did not significantly increase economic growth.

Myth #10: The Bush tax cuts were tilted toward the rich.
Fact: The rich are now shouldering even more of the income tax burden.

Popular mythology also suggests that the 2001 and 2003 tax cuts shifted more of the tax burden toward the poor. While high-income households did save more in actual dollars than low-income households, they did so because low-income households pay so little in income taxes in the first place. The same 1 percent tax cut will save more dollars for a millionaire than it will for a middle-class worker simply because the millionaire paid more taxes before the tax cut.

In 2000, the top 60 percent of taxpayers paid 100 percent of all income taxes. The bottom 40 percent collectively paid no income taxes. Lawmakers writing the 2001 tax cuts faced quite a challenge in giving the bulk of the income tax savings to a population that was already paying no income taxes.

Rather than exclude these Americans, lawmakers used the tax code to subsidize them. (Some economists would say this made that group's collective tax burden *negative*.) First, lawmakers lowered the initial tax brackets from 15 percent to 10 percent and then expanded the refundable child tax credit, which, along with the refundable earned income tax credit (EITC), reduced the typical low-income tax burden to well below zero. As a result, the U.S. Treasury now mails tax "refunds" to a large proportion of these Americans that exceed the amounts of tax that they actually paid. All in all, the number of tax filers with zero or negative income tax liability rose from 30 million to 40 million, or about 30 percent of all tax filers. The remaining 70 percent of tax filers received lower income tax rates, lower investment taxes, and lower estate taxes from the 2001 legislation.

Consequently, from 2000 to 2004, the share of all individual income taxes paid by the bottom 40 percent dropped from zero percent to –4 percent, meaning that the average family in those quintiles received a subsidy from the IRS. By contrast, the share paid by the top quintile of households (by income) increased from 81 percent to 85 percent.

Expanding the data to include all federal taxes, the share paid by the top quintile edged up from 66.6 percent in 2000 to 67.1 percent in 2004, while the bottom 40 percent's share dipped from 5.9 percent to 5.4 percent. Clearly, the tax cuts have led to the rich shouldering more of the income tax burden and the poor shouldering less.

Conclusion

The 110th Congress will be serving when the first of 77 million baby boomers receive their first Social Security checks in 2008. The subsequent avalanche of Social Security, Medicare, and Medicaid costs for these baby boomers will be the greatest economic challenge of this era.

This should be the budgetary focus of the 110th Congress rather than repealing Bush tax cuts or allowing them to expire. Repealing the tax cuts would not significantly increase revenues. It would, however, decrease investment, reduce work incentives, stifle entrepreneurialism, and reduce economic growth. Lawmakers should remember that America cannot tax itself to prosperity.

POSTSCRIPT

Should Federal Taxes Be Increased?

Because many tax cuts adopted in the Bush presidency are due to expire at the end of 2010, national tax policy is a major issue confronting the 111th Congress that took office in January 2009. In order to adopt new regulations, Congress must review how the tax policies adopted in the Bush presidency have fared.

As the preceding essays make evident, the liberal Center on Budget and Public Policies and the conservative Heritage Foundation can look at the same statistics and charge that the other side is engaging in perpetuating myths without any empirical foundation. Mindful of the cynical cliché that figures don't lie but liars figure, Congress and the president need to closely examine the evidence of the recent past.

Some of the consequences of the tax reductions that were adopted in the Bush presidency should provide guidance for our fiscal future. Have those tax cuts increased incentives for investment and spending, thus bolstering the economy and increasing tax revenues in the long run? Or have they unfairly rewarded upper-income earners, increased federal deficits, and made it more difficult for Congress to adopt costly reforms that would benefit lower- and middle-income citizens?

Any calculation must take into account the exceptional circumstances and consequences of the cost of conducting war in Iraq and Afghanistan, the continuing movement of manufacturing out of the United States into other countries, and the escalating cost of oil and its impact upon the American economy.

Tax policy is as complex as it is controversial. Every American would like to simplify taxes, but how? Should the income tax be replaced by a flat tax, a sales tax, a consumption tax, a wealth tax, or some other method of paying for government? Should capital income (the return from saving or investment) be taxed at the same rate or less or more than income from employment? Should the Social Security tax, presently set at 12.4 percent of wages up to $94,200, be extended to all incomes? Should tax policy seek to provide economic relief for disadvantaged Americans? Should taxes reflect the income distribution before taxes?

Bush era tax cuts are defended in John Podhoretz, *Bush Country: How Dubya Became a Great President While Driving Liberals Insane* (St. Martin's Press, 2004). Those policies are attacked in David Cay Johnston, *Free Lunch: How the Wealthiest Americans Enrich Themselves at Government Expense (and Stick You with the Bill)* (Portfolio, 2007).

Joel Slemrod and Jon Bakija, *Taxing Ourselves: A Citizen's Guide to the Debate Over Taxes* (The MIT Press, fourth edition, 2008), provides an introduction to one of the most arcane areas of public policy. It succeeds in explaining opposing positions without either academic jargon or political prejudice.

C. Eugene Steuerle, *Contemporary U.S. Tax Policy* (The Urban Institute Press, 2004), seeks to provide an unbiased analysis of the evolution of national tax legislation since 1980. Alan J. Auerbach and Kevin A. Hassett, eds., *Toward Fundamental Tax Reform* (The AEI Press, 2005), offer a collection of short essays by tax policy experts who represent a variety of viewpoints. Like most examinations of present tax law, they agree that there must be a better, fairer, simpler alternative, but disagree on what that alternative is.

ISSUE 23

Does Conservatism Get the World Wrong?

YES: Robert Borosage, from "Conservatism Itself," *The American Prospect* (June 17, 2007)

NO: Alfred S. Regnery, from "Ideas Still Have Consequences," *The American Spectator* (December 2007/January 2008)

ISSUE SUMMARY

YES: Robert Borosage, codirector of the Campaign for America's Future, contends that conservative policies have failed because they make America weaker abroad and more unequal at home.

NO: Alfred Regnery, publisher of the *American Spectator* magazine, contends that conservative principles are powerfully resilient, have been woven into our laws and institutions, and may well be the most accepted political force in America.

Conservatism, derived from the verb "to conserve" is not so much a doctrine as an attitude. It has been defined as "a hostility to radical social change, particularly social change that is instituted by the force of the state and justified by an appeal to abstract rights or to some utopian aim." Edmund Burke, an eighteenth-century British Parliamentarian, is often credited as one of the founders of modern-day conservative thinking, largely on the strength of his *Reflections on the Revolution in France,* a polemical work decrying the "metaphysical" theorists who inspired the French Revolution. Burke and other European conservatives described the nation in organic terms, as a plant that grows slowly and requires careful nurture; changes can be made only incrementally and in keeping with deep-rooted traditions.

How does that general worldview apply to America? At first glance, it does not seem to fit very well. Conservatives abhor revolution, yet the United States was born in revolution. Conservatives distrust grand abstractions, yet this nation, as Abraham Lincoln observed, is "dedicated to the proposition that all men are created equal." Conservatives are wary of democracy on grounds that it encourages demagogues who trade on emotion rather than sober thought, but

Americans are proud of their democracy. American conservatives respond to these challenges by pointing out that formal documents like the Declaration of Independence constitute only one part of the American polity; the larger part consists of the customs and mores of its people—the "habits of the heart," as Alexis de Tocqueville, a French visitor in the 1830s, called them. And American habits are conservative: patriotic, religious, domestic, and moderate. Long before the Revolution of 1776, Americans had already learned these habits, and the Revolution itself (unlike the French Revolution) did not attempt to change them: it was a political revolution, not a social one, based upon sober, not utopian, expectations.

Even so, any attempt to depict American conservatism as a perfectly consistent set of Burkean principles, or even attitudes, is bound to fail. The American conservative movement, if it can be called that, is a heterogeneous array of interests united mainly by opposition to the left; during elections they pull together uneasily, usually in support of Republican candidates. There are many divisions and subdivisions within conservatism but the main groupings are three: fiscal conservatism, cultural conservatism, and neoconservatism.

Fiscal conservatism. Since the 1930s, in opposition to the Democrats' New Deal, this has been a constant feature of Republican platforms. It argues for low taxes and low government spending—indeed, for trimmed-down government everywhere, especially in Washington. The national government's role should be to maintain public order, to promote the nation's interests abroad, and to defend it against foreign enemies. Anything beyond that risks entering the slippery slope to a "nanny state."

Cultural conservatism. This appeared as a kind of backlash to changes in American mores since the 1960s, changes facilitated in part by judicial decisions. Courts have decriminalized pornography and homosexual acts, legalized abortion and single-sex marriage, and banned prayers in public schools. Cultural conservatives seek to contain, restrict, and, if possible, reverse cultural trends they regard as destructive; their proposals range from constitutional amendments reversing some of these court decisions to selecting judges pledged to "originalism," that is, reading constitutional clauses strictly according to their meaning at the time of adoption.

Neoconservatism. This emerged in the early 1970s as a designation adopted by former liberals who left the fold because of what they considered its weakness in countering communist aggression. Today, the menace of world communism is almost gone, but since Islamic jihadism seems, to many, to have taken its place, neoconservatism still has adherents. They are generally liberal on domestic issues such as social welfare and regulation of industry, but "hawkish" in foreign policy, all of which they consider to be in the spirit of Franklin Roosevelt, Harry Truman, and John F. Kennedy. This has led conservative purists to question whether "neoconservative" is in any sense conservative.

What are the merits of this three-branched movement called conservatism? In the following selections, liberal editor Robert Borosage contends that it is out of touch with today's realities, while conservative publisher Alfred Regnery thinks that conservative principles are vital and resilient.

YES

Robert Borosage

Conservatism Itself

We have to recognize that this was a defeat for Republicans, not for "conservatives," former House Speaker Newt Gingrich summarized the 2006 Republican election rout. Republicans, George Will echoed, "were punished not for pursuing but for forgetting conservatism." Conservatives now react to the debacle that is the Bush administration with two general strategies—denial and disavowal. Conservatives are cutting and running from George W. Bush, blaming him for straying from the conservative gospel, and invoking, by contrast, an iconic Ronald Reagan as exemplar of that faith.

But the spin won't cover the reality. Over the first six years of the Bush administration, conservatives largely had their way. With Bush and Karl Rove pursuing a political strategy of feeding their base, Tom DeLay ramrodding the conservative majority in the Congress, and the corporate lobby enforcing discipline, movement conservatives set the course of the country—with catastrophic results.

Each of the signature Bush follies—Iraq, Katrina, Enron, privatization of Social security, the Terri Schiavo case, trickle-down economics that didn't trickle—can be traced directly to conservative ideas and the conservative think tanks and ideologues that championed them. In every case, conservatism failed, not simply because of corruption or incompetence, but because of original conception. Sensate conservatives have, in the words Irving Kristol once applied to liberals, "been mugged by reality." Actual existing conservatism fails because it gets the world wrong. And invoking Reagan offers not salvation but confirmation of that failure, for Reagan championed many of the same ideas and inflicted similar debacles on the nation.

The war in Iraq was driven by the neoconservatives who lobbied for it long before September 11 or the Bush presidency. Infatuated with an America free to act as the lone hyperpower, they celebrated the imperial presidency and scorned the constraints that might be imposed by congressional debate, by our allies, by the UN, by arms control and international law. Steeped in the Cold War face-off, they had neither understanding of nor much interest in the stateless fanatics that would strike on 9-11. Rogue nations—the "axis of evil"—made better targets. America would spread democracy at the end of smart bombs.

The result is the worst foreign policy fiasco in American history. The war the conservatives made will squander no one knows how many lives and an estimated $2 trillion, demoralizing our military in an occupation in the midst of a civil war that alienates our allies, emboldens our enemies, and provides al-Qaeda and its offshoots with recruits across the Muslim world. The conservatives' scorn for international law led directly to the horrors of Abu Ghraib; the imperial presidency to the shame of Guantanamo.

Reagan's reign featured many of the same ideas, the same ideologues, with some of the same disastrous results. In his first term, he too championed U.S. military prowess, doubled the military budget, scorned arms control, the UN, and international law. Goaded by the neocons, he launched an illegal covert effort to overthrow Nicaragua's Sandinista government. His policies divided us from our allies. The blowback from his covert wars included bin Laden and what became al-Qaeda, which received U.S. training and aid in the covert war in Afghanistan. His imperial presidency ended in the Iran-Contra scandals, which paralyzed the last years of his second term.

Unlike Bush, however, Reagan ultimately had the sense to see beyond the neocons. When Soviet Premier Mikhail Gorbachev essentially sued for peace, neocons dismissed it as a trick, and conservatives railed at Reagan for entertaining the arms negotiations that led eventually to the end of the Cold War.

Reagan also knew when to cut his losses. When Marines he'd fecklessly dispatched into the midst of the Lebanese civil war were blown up in a terror bombing, he quickly got them out of there, distracting attention from the mess by invading hapless Grenada.

Under Bush, the corporate lobby dictates economic policies—top-end tax cuts, deregulation and privatization, corporate trade policies, the war on labor unions. The result is slow growth, Gilded Age inequality, the worst corporate wilding since the robber barons, stagnant wages for most, and growing pressures on kitchen-table basics. Bush's global trade policies have ravaged American manufacturing, while producing the largest trade imbalances and foreign indebtedness in the annals of time.

But again, Reagan offers no salvation for conservatives. He championed a similar set of policies—what George Bush Sr. tabbed as "voodoo economics,"— promising top-end tax cuts, increases in military spending, and balanced budgets. In the process he helped produce the worst recession since the Great Depression, growing inequality, and record deficits. His trade policies laid waste to American manufacturing. His assault on labor and opposition to the minimum wage contributed to a decade in which wages stagnated while CEO salaries soared. Ten million Americans lost jobs to plant closings and layoffs from 1983 to 1988, with half of those who found work forced into jobs that paid less. And the recovery had been purchased on credit: It was during Reagan's presidency that the United States was transformed from global creditor to the world's greatest debtor nation.

Under Bush, the conservative belief that markets police themselves left corporations less accountable. This led directly to Enron and WorldCom, and literally hundreds of CEOs cooking their books, backdating stock options, and running up stock prices so they could cash out and clean up.

Again, Reagan provided precedent, not exception. His ruinous regulatory policies featured the deregulation of the savings and loan industry, producing the costliest financial scandal in U.S. history, with the bailout costing taxpayers more than $130 billion.

Under Bush, the "small government" conservatives found ample opportunity to effect their scorn for government. Corporate lobbyists were appointed to disembowel the agencies tasked with policing their clients, enforcement budgets were cut, as were domestic programs aimed at the poor. What Rick Perlstein has dubbed "e. coli conservatism" led to poisonous and uninspected food; denial of catastrophic climate change; and the weakening of workplace, consumer, and environmental protections.

Katrina was their signature catastrophe. Before Bush even got to office, conservatives scorned FEMA as a bloated entitlement agency. So Bush cut its budget, booted it out of the Cabinet, and stocked it full of cronies. The professionals departed in dismay. The incompetence and cronyism personified by "Brownie, you're doing a heck of a job" was a direct expression of the conservative disdain for the government they were running.

Reagan's scorn for government also had predictable effects. As his chronicler, Lou Cannon, writes, "Reagan thought so little of government that he did not think enough about it." The Department of Housing and Urban Development led the scandals, "enveloped," as a unanimous House Government Operations Committee reported, "by influence peddling, favoritism, greed, fraud, embezzlement and theft." By the end of Reagan's terms, 138 administration officials had been convicted, indicted, or subjected to official investigations for official misconduct and/or criminal violation—more than in any prior administration.

Under Bush, social conservatives pushed to get government into our hospital rooms and out of the boardroom. Bush appealed to the fundamentalist right with a politics of polarization and pork. He cut short one of his many vacations to join the Republican Congress in intervening in Terri Schiavo's personal tragedy. He banned federal support for stem cell research and doled out billions to fundamentalist church allies in his faith-based programs. The Federalist Society insured ideologues were appointed to the bench. And of course the specter of gay marriage was used to divide the country and mobilize the faithful.

Preferring doctrine to science had untold consequence. Not only was promising research starved of funds, but other nations captured the lead in what will be the growing biogenetic industries of the future. The right-wing judicial activists are just beginning their drive to roll back citizen rights and empower markets.

Reagan set the same course. He ended Republican support for choice, campaigned against equal rights for women, and perfected race-baiting politics, elevating the mythic Cadillac-driving welfare queen into a national symbol. He, too, packed the courts with ideologues. Conservatives now deify him as a man who brought us together, but his political strategy, a more sophisticated version of Richard Nixon's, was quite purposefully designed to drive us apart.

The problem isn't incompetence or deviation from the conservative course. The problem is actual existing conservatism itself. It celebrates military prowess when the threats to our security—stateless terrorists, catastrophic climate change, proliferation of weapons of mass destruction, the growing gulf between rich and poor—have no military solution. It offers no answer to a corporate sector shredding the private social contract that guaranteed many workers healthcare, pensions, job security, and family wages. It opposes the very reforms vital for our economic future—the transition to clean energy and conservation, support of a world-class education system, and provision of affordable health care and retirement security.

After a quarter century of conservative dominance—from Reagan to Gingrich to Bush and DeLay—the verdict is in. Conservatives cannot be trusted to guide the government they scorn. Not because they are incompetent or corrupt (although incompetence and corruption abound), but because they get the world wrong. Their policies foster an America that is weaker and more isolated abroad, divided and more unequal at home. That was as true for Ronald Reagan, who helped give birth to this conservative era, as for George Bush, whose failed presidency should bury it.

Ideas Still Have Consequences

As conservatives and pundits survey the prospects facing the right in the 2008 presidential election, they invariably conclude that conservatism is over, or at best still twitching just a little. Conservatives often think they might as well find another cause or, worse, prepare to move abroad. Before they do so, however, I think it might be worthwhile to take a look at the state of affairs 40 years ago, when *The American Spectator* was founded, and to remind ourselves of just how far we have come since, of where we are, and what resources we have.

It may seem so in Washington, but the world does not revolve around politics. Politics reflects the culture and the way people think, and political success can endure only when it is preceded by a strong and sound political philosophy. Even then, in a culture such as ours, neither side has a lock on electoral politics. Elections are won and lost for all sorts of reasons other than the strength of the philosophy behind the candidates or the general political attitude of the country. There are shifts in short-term political trends and candidates who do not live up to their billing, as well as wars and other matters that override normal considerations, each of which may turn an election one way or another. A first-rate sports team may have the best players, the best coach, the best equipment, and the best training, but it still loses games. So it is with politics.

It has often been said that conservatism is a movement of ideas. John Maynard Keynes, who should know, said that "ideas are more powerful than is commonly understood. Indeed, the world is ruled by little else. . . . Sooner or later, it is ideas, not vested interests, which are dangerous for good or evil." Keynes may have been wrong about economics, but he was right about the power of ideas. In fact, his ideas about economics *did* rule much of the world, at least until the revival of free market economics replaced them, relegating Keynesianism to the ash heap of history.

Conservatism is much more than a political alternative to liberalism, and much more than a set of policies advocated by a political party or an administration. Its ideas are complex and they often conflict with each other, but they nevertheless provide conservatives with a surprisingly consistent worldview. It was ideas—the philosophy of conservatism—that the students at Indiana University set out to introduce as they decided to start publishing their little journal 40 years ago. Theirs was one of many similar journals, some

From *The American Spectator*, December 2007/January 2008, pp. 20–25. Copyright © 2008 by American Spectator, LLC. Reprinted by permission.

started by students, some by professional journalists, and others by just true believers, that emerged in the late 1960s, and which, in the aggregate, have helped to define the issues and to develop the ideas that formed the bedrock of the early conservative movement.

When he started *National Review* in 1955, Bill Buckley made no bones about what he wanted to accomplish. "This magazine," he wrote in his prospectus, "will forthrightly oppose the prevailing trend of public opinion; its purpose, indeed, is to change the nation's intellectual and political climate." Which is exactly what *National Review, The American Spectator,* and the rest of the intellectual conservative movement have been doing for the past 40 years.

<hr>

By the late 1960s, the foundation for the new American conservative movement had largely been laid, and the three-part structure that would become one of the most interesting and robust of the American experience was being built. First, there were Friedrich Hayek, Ludwig von Mises, Milton Friedman, and the rest of the economic libertarians, who were largely concerned with individualism and freedom, believing that government should not meddle in business and the economy, but should allow free markets to thrive on their own. Second, anti-Communism, which would form the backbone of much of the movement, had been articulated by the likes of Whittaker Chambers, James Burnham, and Frank Meyer, and a wide-ranging network of scholars and activists were making their voices heard from one end of the country to the other. Finally, the traditionalists—men like Richard Weaver and Russell Kirk, who were more interested in preserving what was left of Western civilization and culture—believed that political problems were, at root, religious and moral problems.

In terms of politics, there were a few conservatives, but they were largely conservative Republicans or Southern Democrats counting on their respective parties for support. Although the foundation for a movement had been laid, there was much to be done before conservatism could become a cohesive political philosophy capable of having much influence on the way the country worked. Outside right-of-center political forces, such as activist and lobbying organizations, think tanks, grassroots groups, and political action committees, were scarce. Liberalism, on the other hand, was thriving as never before. Lyndon Johnson's Great Society was going full tilt—creating new agencies, departments, social programs—and spending money with the zest of another New Deal. Democrats enjoyed their largest margins, in both Congress and the state houses, in almost three decades.

Before 1967 only three elections involving real conservatives ever received national attention, and only one of those was won by a conservative. First was the 1964 presidential election starring Barry Goldwater as the Republican candidate, and the first authentic conservative ever nominated on a major party ticket. Although Goldwater lost to Lyndon Johnson in a landslide, taking a good part of the Republican congressional delegation, such as it was, down with him, conservatism's first presidential campaign changed the political scene forever. The campaign gave tens of thousands of conservatives a taste of national politics, and while Republicans may have been left depressed by their candidate's awful showing, conservatives found a silver lining in the clouds of defeat.

"Twenty Seven Million Americans Cannot Be Wrong" became their watchword, as the newly minted young conservatives and recharged, middle-age volunteers looked around for the next enterprise. The Goldwater campaign had been like nothing they had ever experienced, and it was exhilarating. Pat Buchanan, himself a former Goldwater volunteer, wrote, "Like a first love, the Goldwater campaign was, for thousands of men and women now well into middle age, an experience that will never recede from memory, one on which we look back with pride and fond remembrance." The Goldwater campaign had several other benefits as well: It introduced conservatives to their next political hero, Ronald Reagan; it brought the conservative intellectual and political forces together for the first time; and it started the purge of the hated Rockefeller faction from the Republican Party.

The second was the sometimes comical third-party campaign launched by William F. Buckley Jr. in 1965 for mayor of New York—comical not because of the issues, but because of Buckley's attitude toward the press and toward stupid questions. Running against liberal Republican Congressman John Lindsay and liberal Democrat Abraham Beame, Buckley vowed not to suck up to any special interests, but to use the best conservative arguments he could muster. The election was particularly important because it gave Buckley a national bully pulpit from which to talk about conservative principles without worrying about whom he might offend—an echo of Goldwater's campaign a year earlier, except that Buckley knew he could not win, so it didn't matter whom he irritated. In a typical Buckley retort to a reporter who asked what he would do about a threatened water shortage, Buckley quipped, "Let them drink wine."

With his charm and wit, Buckley was able to make the case for conservative ideals and principles in a way that Barry Goldwater could not. The city's worst problems were largely due to the black and Puerto Rican underclass—issues no politician would dare confront. But Buckley did, pointing out that government-run social programs usually made things worse, citing studies by the few liberals who recognized their shortcomings—policy intellectuals like Irving Kristol, Pat Moynihan, and Daniel Bell, among others. Although he wound up getting just 13 percent of the vote, the fact that 340,000 New Yorkers voted for Bill Buckley invigorated conservatives from coast to coast. Said the *New York Times* many years later: "Buckley's bid for office was an important chapter in one of the crucial events in modern political history, the transformation of the consensus politics of the peak cold-war years of the 1950s and early '60s, its agenda set by liberals, into the more polarized politics of our era, ruled by conservatives."

Third, conservatives were heartened in November 1966 when their favorite Hollywood actor was elected governor of California, beating incumbent liberal Democrat Pat Brown by one million votes, the same margin by which

Goldwater had *lost* California two years earlier. Ronald Reagan would of course prove to be the quintessential conservative politician: one grounded in conservative ideas, one with a sunny personality and a friendly smile, and one who could appeal to voters in numbers never imagined. After he was sworn in as governor in January 1967 he immediately assumed a national status, and by 1968 he was the most charismatic Republican speaker and the party's best fundraiser, attracting enthusiastic crowds wherever he went. He told friends that it was important for him to enunciate conservative principles and pull the Republican Party in a conservative direction. Reagan's election taught conservatives that it was possible to win, and his two successful terms as governor would teach them that conservatives could govern.

Over the next four decades, conservative ideas caught on, the journals grew, books were published, think tanks and activist groups were organized, candidates were elected to office, and the movement became perhaps the most significant force in American politics.

⋅◦⦿◦⋅

So where have we come in those 40 years? It would take many more pages than the *Spectator* has available to fully answer that question (in fact I just wrote a whole book about it, and it too only touches on the subject), but let me focus on a few key areas.

First, in the ideas department, we conservatives have made enormous strides. We virtually dominate thinking on economics, government spending and taxation, legal theory, education and social policy, foreign policy, and politics itself. The economic principles explained by Hayek, von Mises, Friedman, and the rest drive public policy, and much of the world has adopted them over the past couple of decades; free market economics now has more influence on the way the world works than any political party anywhere. Liberals have no theory of taxation or government spending other than redistributing the wealth and using tax policy to buy votes. Conservatives, on the other hand, have developed a thorough body of scholarship on the issue, can count any number of economists, including no fewer than nine Nobel laureates in economics, and best of all have the satisfaction of having applied their economic and tax policy and proved that it works.

Next are the courts and the law. When Nixon ran for president in 1968, he announced that he would only appoint "strict constructionist" judges who would decide cases according to the written law, not legislate from the bench. Until that time, the federal courts, bulging with liberal judges, were moving the political landscape sharply to the left in decisions on civil rights, crime, reapportionment, prayer in schools, forced busing, obscenity, and federalism.

But Nixon had no yardstick by which to determine who would be a strict constructionist judge or not, so he did what presidents had always done—he appointed well-connected lawyers and friends from the lower courts. Out of four Nixon Supreme Court appointments, only one, William Rehnquist, was a conservative, and that was by the luck of the draw. The other three—Warren Burger, Harry Blackmun, and Lewis Powell—continued doing what Earl

Warren and William Brennan (both appointed by Dwight Eisenhower) had started years earlier.

By contrast, when two Supreme Court vacancies opened up in 2005, conservatives delivered a list of acceptable judges to the White House, put together a coalition of some 80 conservative organizations to pressure the Senate to confirm them, and raised sufficient funds to run a very substantial lobbying campaign, with the result that two of the most conservative Supreme Court picks in history were nominated—and not men the President would have named had he had his way—and confirmed by a Senate that could have otherwise easily defeated them. Today nearly half of all federal judges are conservatives, appointed by Reagan and both Bushes, under a system of careful analysis to determine what sort of judges they would be. As a result they will dominate the courts for many years to come.

In terms of legal thought, the concept of originalism—the way judges should think about and apply the Constitution—has earned an accepted place in legal theory and is the benchmark against which a Republican president appoints, or should appoint, judges. According to Robert Bork, originalism is the only approach that can make judicial review democratically legitimate, and simply means that the judge must discern from the relevant materials—debates at the Constitutional Convention, the Federalist Papers and the Anti-Federalist Papers, newspaper accounts of the time, debates in the state ratifying conventions, and the like—the principles the ratifiers understood themselves to be enacting. The remainder of the task is to apply those principles to unforeseen circumstances, a task that law performs all the time. Any philosophy that does not confine judges to the original understanding inevitably makes the Constitution the plaything of willful judges.

~◦~

In the political realm, conservatives, who in 1968 had virtually no political clout, now control one of the two major political parties (although many conservatives don't realize that) and many (but not enough!) seats in Congress, and have many competent people ready and able to serve a conservative administration. Conservative issues and principles are present everywhere, in every election, and may very well be the most accepted political force in the country, regardless of recent election returns.

After Nixon was elected on a conservative platform, he proceeded to appoint liberal Republicans to his cabinet (he would have had trouble finding more than a handful of conservatives, and certainly not enough even to begin to populate his administration), and to push through many new, big government programs. Within a year or so, conservatives were so disenchanted with Nixon and his entourage that they would have gladly thrown him over had they had anybody else to run against him or the clout to do anything about it. Today, after a successful Reagan administration and subsequent conservative takeover of the House of Representatives, a candidate's acceptability is measured not by how liberal he is, or how moderate, but how conservative. Those who are not conservative, of whom there are understandably many, fall over backward to try to convince the voters that they are, in fact, candidates of the right. The fact that no current presidential candidate is a true-blue conservative is probably the fault of the movement itself in not cultivating its own candidates willing and able to run.

When the *Spectator* was founded, in the fall of 1967, conservative voices in the media were almost inaudible. *National Review, Human Events,* and a couple of other small journals were published and had modest circulations, but the mainstream media, as it came to be called, dominated everything else. If conservative books were published, they mostly came from a small and struggling house owned and operated by my father in Chicago; New York publishers would have virtually nothing to do with them. Today, although there is no end to accusations and charges of left-wing media bias—mostly justified— conservatives in fact have a huge media presence. Most New York publishing houses have a conservative imprint; there are dozens of columnists and editorial writers; conservatives virtually own talk radio and control a large segment of websites and blogs; and although Fox News is "fair and balanced," at least it is not dominated by the left.

∗❦∗

But by no means have conservatives won the war. As with any political or philosophical movement, some things began to come undone as conservatism matured. The conservative movement suffers from middle age, and in a sense has become a victim of its own success. At first it was made up of true believers—was there any other reason to join a movement with no clout at all? But as its strength grew, as it gained stature and popularity, more people joined, often not because they believed in its principles but because it was good politics, or just because it was the thing to do. And all too often, many did not understand the principles for which the movement stood. The word "conservative" became a label, and it applied to virtually everybody who wasn't a liberal.

The problem, in a nutshell, was with the politicians. As conservatives began to be elected, winning control of the Congress as well as many state and local offices by 1994, they basked in the perks and the power. They convinced themselves that the most important thing they could do was to get re-elected, and the best way to do so was to satisfy the voters by spending the taxpayers' money. Before long Republicans, which most conservatives were, began to look indistinct from the Democrats they had replaced. As one wag put it, they got elected by calling Washington a cesspool, but after a couple of years on the job, they realized it was really a hot tub. The true conservatives, those who had elected them in the first place, assuming they would actually act like conservatives, did not like it at all.

Other politicians, who knew they needed to call themselves conservatives, wanted to fudge the idea by qualifying their conservatism. George W. Bush, who had few conservative instincts, announced during the 2000 primary season that if elected he would govern as a "compassionate conservative." Nobody ever quite knew what a compassionate conservative was, although as

Bush worked his way through his first term and into his second, it became evident that there was more compassion than conservatism in the phrase.

Today, the conservative movement has evolved from three to four branches—one heart and four heads, it has been said—the traditionalists, sometimes called paleocons, the libertarians, the neoconservatives, and the religious right. They form a sometimes unified, sometimes fractious coalition, agree on some things and disagree on more, but are unanimous in their distaste for liberalism. According to conservative historian George Nash, the movement "has proved remarkably resilient, united in part by overlapping aspirations and by a recurrent sense of mortal challenge from enemies at home and abroad." Its future will probably always be laden with difficulty, but a future, it is certain, there will be.

POSTSCRIPT

Does Conservatism Get
the World Wrong?

"The problem," in Borosage's words, "isn't incompetence or deviation from the conservative course. The problem is actually existing conservatism itself." He cites several perceived policy failures during the Bush administration, which he traces to conservative thought. Critics might reply that some of these, such as Katrina, can just as easily be traced to liberal policies at the state and local levels, while others, such as Bush's judicial appointments, would not be considered failures at all by conservative standards. Still, there is no doubt that for the near future the memory of the Bush administration will remain an embarrassment for conservatives, which is why conservative spokesmen like Newt Gingrich want to distance themselves from it.

Regnery's essay touches some of the themes covered in his latest book, *Upstream: The Ascendance of American Conservatism* (Threshold Editions, 2008). Regnery is the son of Henry Regnery, who founded the famous conservative publishing house that launched the career of William F. Buckley and other conservative luminaries in the 1950s. Regnery's book is an affectionate look back at the founding era of modern conservatism. Jerry Z. Muller's *Conservatism* (Princeton, 1997) is an anthology ranging from David Hume to Irving Kristol. *Arguing Conservatism: Four Decades of Intercollegiate Review*, edited by Mark C. Henrie (Intercollegiate Studies, 2008), reprints essays from that journal by Robert Bork, Willmore Kendall, and Robert Nisbet, among others. Mickey Edwards, *Reclaiming Conservatism: How a Great American Political Movement Got Lost—and How It Can Find Its Way Back* (Oxford, 2008) is an anguished cry from a conservative founding trustee of the Heritage Foundation, who thinks that conservatism has been hijacked by the "religious right." Russell Kirk's *The Conservative Mind* (BN Publishing 2008), first published in 1953, remains one of the classic works on conservative thought. Kirk's extension of the "conservative" label to activist-government promoters like Alexander Hamilton and John Marshall shows how hard it is to make the label fit an American context. Another older book still in print is Milton Friedman's *Capitalism and Freedom* (University of Chicago, 1962). Friedman seems to fit the profile of a fiscal conservative although he has always considered himself a "classical" liberal, a philosophical category we explored in the Introduction to this book (see pp. xviii–xix).

It may be difficult to pin down the precise meaning of American conservatism, but it seems likely that it will be around for as long as its perennial opponent, liberalism, is in the field. The two sides are perpetually at odds, which is not necessarily a bad thing as long as they fight fairly. Perhaps, the model should be late-Victorian England, where both sides observed certain civil rules of combat, prompting Gilbert and Sullivan to depict them as children with eternal but benign differences. "For every boy and every gal born into the world alive/Is either a little liberal, or a little conservative."

Contributors to This Volume

EDITORS

GEORGE McKENNA is professor emeritus and former chair of the Department of Political Science, City College of New York. He has written or edited eight books on politics and society, including his latest, *The Puritan Origins of American Patriotism* (Yale, 2007). He is currently working on a biography of Booker T. Washington.

STANLEY FEINGOLD, recently retired, held the Carl and Lily Pforzheimer Foundation Distinguished Chair for Business and Public Policy at Westchester Community College of the State University of New York. He received his bachelor's degree from the City College of New York, where he taught courses in American politics and political theory for 30 years, after completing his graduate education at Columbia University. He spent four years as visiting professor of politics at the University of Leeds in Great Britain, and he has also taught American politics at Columbia University in New York and the University of California, Los Angeles. He is a frequent contributor to the *National Law Journal* and *Congress Monthly,* among other publications.

AUTHORS

AVIVA ARON-DINE is a policy analyst with the Center on Budget and Policy Priorities, a group which promotes what it perceives as the interests of low-income Americans.

ROBERT BOROSAGE is the president of the Institute for America's Future and the codirector of the Campaign for America's Future, organizations launched to counter what their founders consider to be a rightward drift of U.S. politics.

STEPHEN G. BREYER is associate justice of the United States Supreme Court.

GEORGE W. BUSH was the 43rd president of the United States.

MICHAEL F. CAIRO has written on foreign policy formation, human rights, and national security. He has taught at Virginia Commonwealth University, Southern Illinois University at Carbondale, the University of Wisconsin at Stevens Point, and Georgetown College.

CHRISTOPHER C. DeMUTH is president of the American Enterprise Institute for Public Policy Research. He has served in several administrative capacities in the executive branch of the federal government and on the faculty of the Kennedy School of Government at Harvard University.

J. R. DUNN is the former editor of the *International Military Encyclopedia* and a frequent contributor to *The American Thinker*, for which he recently wrote several articles entitled "Prospects of Terror: An Inquiry into Jihadi Alternatives."

IVAN ELAND, former director of defense policy studies at the Cato Institute, writes on a variety of topics related to U.S. foreign and defense policies. He is the author of the book *Putting "Defense" Back into U.S. Defense Policy: Rethinking U.S. Security in the Post-War World.*

NIALL FERGUSON has been a professor of modern European history at Oxford University and financial history at New York University. He is the author of *The Pity of War,* a history of the first World War, and *The Cash Nexus: Money and Power in the Modern World.* His book, *Empire: How Britain Made the Modern World,* was adapted for a television series. His most recent work is *Colossus: The Price of America's Empire.*

F. GREGORY GAUSE III is associate professor of political science at the University of Vermont and director of its Middle Eastern program.

ROBERT P. GEORGE is the McCormick Professor of Jurisprudence and director of the James Madison Program in American Ideals and Institutions at Princeton University. Recently, he was appointed by President George W. Bush to the President's Council on Bioethics. He previously served on the U.S. Commission on Civil Rights and as a judicial fellow at the Supreme Court of the United States.

JOHN C. GOODMAN is the founder of the National Center for Policy Analysis and the author of *Economics of Public Policy.*

MARY GORDON is a novelist and short-story writer. She is the author of *Penal Discipline: Female Prisoners* (Gordon Press, 1992), *The Rest of Life: Three Novellas* (Viking Penguin, 1993), and *The Other Side* (Wheeler, 1994).

AL GORE was the Vice President of the United States, 1993–2001, and the Democratic candidate for president in 2000. He is the author of two books on environmental issues: *Earth in the Balance: Ecology and the Human Spirit* (Plume Books, 1992) and *An Inconvenient Truth* (Rodale Books, 2006), and the narrator of a documentary film based on the latter book.

DAVID GRAY ADLER is a professor at Idaho State University and the author of books and articles on foreign policy and presidential war powers.

MARK GREEN is a political activist and frequent candidate who worked and wrote with consumer advocate Ralph Nader. He is coeditor, with Eric Alterman, of *The Book on Bush: How George W. (Mis)leads America* (Viking, 2004).

LEE H. HAMILTON, who served in the U.S. House of Representatives for 34 years, was vice chairman of the 9/11 Commission and currently serves on the President's Homeland Security Advisory Council.

DAVID A. HARRIS is Balk Professor of Law and Values at University of Toledo College of Law and Soros Senior Justice Fellow. He is the author of *Profiles in Injustice: Why Racial Profiling Cannot Work* (New Press, 2002).

NAT HENTOFF writes a weekly column for *The Village Voice,* the leading New York alternative weekly. He has written novels, biographies, and books on civil liberties, including *Free Speech for Me and Not for Thee: How the American Left and Right Relentlessly Censor Each Other.* Among other publications, he has written for *The New Yorker,* the *Atlantic, New Republic, Commonweal,* and on jazz for *The Wall Street Journal.*

ROBERT JERVIS is professor of international relations at Columbia University. In addition to articles in leading international relations periodicals, he is the author of several books, including most recently *American Foreign Policy in a New Era* (Routledge, 2005).

ROBERT D. KAPLAN is a journalist and editor of *Atlantic Monthly,* whose writings have also been featured in *The Washington Post, The New York Times, The New Republic,* and *The Wall Street Journal.*

ANTHONY KENNEDY is an associate justice of the United States Supreme Court. He was appointed in 1987 by President Ronald Reagan.

EZRA KLEIN is a writing fellow for *The American Prospect* magazine.

CHARLES KRAUTHAMMER is a syndicated columnist whose articles appear in the *Washington Post, Time* magazine, and other publications.

MARK KRIKORIAN is executive director of the Center for Immigration Studies.

ROBERT J. LIEBER is professor of government and international relations at Georgetown University, and the author or editor of thirteen books on international relations and U.S. foreign policy.

GLENN C. LOURY is university professor, professor of economics, and director of the Institute on Race and Social Division at Boston University.

JEFF MADRICK, editor of *Challenge* magazine, is a visiting professor at Cooper Union in New York. He is the author of several books, including *Why Economies Grow: The Forces That Shape Prosperity and How to Get Them Working Again* (Basic Books, 2002). His articles appear in *The American Prospect* and *The New York Review of Books.*

HEATHER MacDONALD is contributing editor of *City Journal* and a fellow at the Manhattan Institute. She is the author of *The Burden of Bad Ideas: How Modern Intellectuals Misshape Our Society* and *Are Cops Racist?: How the War Against the Police Harms Black Americans.* She contributes frequently to the New York *Daily News,* the *New York Post,* and the *Weekly Standard.*

THOMAS E. MANN is a political scientist, author, columnist, and frequent guest on public affairs television programs. Based at the Brookings Institution, his specialties include the U.S. Congress and the electoral process.

ANDREW C. McCARTHY was the U.S. attorney who led the 1995 terrorism prosecution that resulted in the conviction of Islamic militants for conducting urban terrorism, including the 1993 World Trade Center bombing. His essays have been published in *The Weekly Standard, Commentary, Middle East Quarterly,* and other publications.

WILFRED M. McCLAY holds the SunTrust Chair of Humanities at the University of Tennessee at Chattanooga.

DANIEL PIPES is director of the Middle East Forum, a member of the presidentially appointed U.S. Institute for Peace, and a columnist for the *New York Sun* and the *Jerusalem Post.* His most recent book is *Miniatures: View of Islamic and Middle Eastern Politics* (Transaction Publishers, 2003).

ALFRED S. REGNERY, an attorney, is counsel of the Washington law firm of Keller and Hackman. He served as administrator of the U.S. Justice Department during most of the Reagan Administration and is now chairman of Foundation for American Studies in Washington, DC.

BRIAN M. RIEDL is the Grover M. Herman Fellow in Budgetary Affairs in the Thomas A. Roe Institute for Economic Policy Studies at the Heritage Foundation, a conservative research organization.

MARK J. ROZELL is a professor at George Mason University and the author and editor of books and articles on religion and politics, executive privilege, and southern and state politics.

JOHN SAMPLES is the director of the CATO Institute Center for Representative Government. He is a frequent contributor to *The American Spectator* and other publications.

ANTONIN SCALIA is an Associate Justice of the United States Supreme Court. He was appointed in 1986 by President Ronald Reagan.

FRANK SHARRY is executive director of the National Immigration Forum.

JOHN PAUL STEVENS is an associate justice of the United States Supreme Court.

ANDREW SULLIVAN is a journalist, blogger, and former editor of *The New Republic,* to which he frequently contributes.

WALTER E. WILLIAMS is the John M. Olin Distinguished Professor of Economics at George Mason University.

JOHN C. YOO, a professor of law at Boalt Hall, University of California, Berkeley, served as deputy assistant attorney general in the Office of Legal Counsel in the U.S. Department of Justice from 2001 to 2003. He is the author of *The Powers of War and Peace* (University of Chicago, 2005) and *War by Other Means: An Insider's Account of the War on Terrorism* (Grove/Atantic, 2006).

HOWARD ZINN, historian, playwright, and social activist, is best known for his book, *A People's History of the United States.* He has taught at Spelman College and Boston University, and has been a visiting professor at the University of Paris and the University of Bologna.